Encyclopedia of
Financial Gerontology

ENCYCLOPEDIA OF FINANCIAL GERONTOLOGY

Lois A. Vitt and
Jurg K. Siegenthaler, Editors-in-Chief

Consulting Editors
Neal E. Cutler and Stephen M. Golant

Associate Editors
Ann S. Reilly, Linda A. Siegenthaler
Charlotte H. Twombly, Thomas M. Wootten

Published under the Auspices of the Institute for Socio-Financial Studies

Greenwood Press
Westport, Connecticut • London

Library of Congress Cataloging-in-Publication Data

Encyclopedia of financial gerontology / Lois A. Vitt and Jurg K.
  Siegenthaler, editors-in-chief ; consulting editors: Neal E. Cutler
  and Stephen M. Golant ; associate editors: Ann S. Reilly . . . [et
  al.].
      p.   cm.
  ''Published under the auspices of the Institute for Socio-Financial
Studies.''
  Includes bibliographical references and index.
  ISBN 0–313–28549–7 (alk. paper)
  1. Aged—Economic conditions—Encyclopedias.   2. Financial
security—Encyclopedias.   3. Aged—Finance, Personal—Encyclopedias.
4. Aged as consumers—Encyclopedias.   5. Retirement income—Law and
legislation—United States—Encyclopedias.   I. Vitt, Lois A.
II. Siegenthaler, Jürg K.
HQ1061.E54   1996
305.26'03—dc20   95–20793

British Library Cataloguing in Publication Data is available.

Library of Congress Catalog Card Number: 95–20793
ISBN: 0–313–28549–7

First published in 1996

Greenwood Press, 88 Post Road West, Westport, CT 06881
An imprint of Greenwood Publishing Group, Inc.

Printed in the United States of America

The paper used in this book complies with the
Permanent Paper Standard issued by the National
Information Standards Organization (Z39.48–1984).

10 9 8 7 6 5 4 3 2 1

Contents

The Editors

EDITORS-IN-CHIEF

LOIS A. VITT, Ph.D., a finance sociologist, is Founder and Director of the Institute for Socio-Financial Studies (ISFS), Middleburg, Virginia. Dr. Vitt has a long track record of accomplishments in business, management, and finance, and conducts interdisciplinary sociofinancial research on issues involving aging, housing, tax, and financial literacy. Financial sociology, financial gerontology, and the social psychology of housing are teaching interests, and she has developed curricula for university courses and certificate programs on these subjects. Dr. Vitt is an adjunct faculty member of the American University, and, as a Certified Clinical Sociologist, she maintains a practice in sociofinancial counseling for mid-life and elderly clients. She was formerly a consultant to major investment banking firms; she pioneered the development of financing instruments for the capital markets and for home purchases; and she was founder and CEO of companies whose objective was to make homeownership more accessible.

JURG K. SIEGENTHALER, Ph.D., is Professor of Sociology at the American University. His research and teaching earlier—at Cornell, UCLA, and Rutgers—have encompassed the sociology of work and organizations as well as social policy analysis. Interests in work and retirement issues connected his previous specialization with social-gerontological topics. Among his studies in recent years are an international comparison of rights of the elderly, a study on time use among the elderly, a review of innovations in different social security systems in response to population aging and other social changes, and an examination of how systems of social protection provide for older single women. He has been a visiting researcher with the International Social Security Association and the U.S. Social Security Administration. A special interest of his is the relationship between aging research, policy, and professional practice as the field develops and meets the challenges of today's aging experiences.

CONSULTING EDITORS

NEAL E. CUTLER, Ph.D., is Director of the Boettner Center of Financial Gerontology at the School of Social Work, University of Pennsylvania, and in 1994 was named as the first holder of the Joseph E. Boettner/Davis W. Gregg Chair in Financial Gerontology at Widener University in Chester, Pennsylvania. The Boettner Center conducts an international program of applied research and education on the impact of population aging and individual aging on the financial well-being of individuals and families—a program directed toward establishing stronger linkages among gerontological and financial services professionals. Before coming to Boettner in 1989, Dr. Cutler spent 16 years as Professor of Gerontology and Political Science at the University of Southern California Andrus Gerontology Center. He is coeditor of *Aging, Money, and Life Satisfaction: Aspects of Financial Gerontology*, published by Springer (1992), and writes "Financial Gerontology," a bimonthly column in the *Journal of the American Society of CLU & ChFC*.

STEPHEN M. GOLANT, Ph.D., a gerontologist and geographer, is currently a Professor in the Department of Geography and Adjunct Professor in the Department of Urban and Regional Planning at the University of Florida. Before assuming these positions in 1980, he was for eight years an Assistant and Associate Professor in the Committee on Human Development (Department of Behavioral Sciences) and Department of Geography at the University of Chicago. He has been conducting research on the American elderly population for the past 23 years and has served as a consultant to numerous private and public organizations. Funded by grants from the National Institute on Aging and the National Science Foundation, his studies have variously focused on the dwelling and neighborhood conditions of older Americans, the strengths and weaknesses of their housing and long-term care alternatives, and their location and migration patterns. He has published more than 60 papers on his research interests and has authored or edited six books, including *Housing America's Elderly: Many Possibilities, Few Choices*, published by Sage. Dr. Golant is a Fellow of the Gerontological Society of America.

ASSOCIATE EDITORS

ANN S. REILLY, Ph.D., a gerontologist and sport psychologist, is codirector of the research track on Sports and Money in America at the Institute for Socio-Financial Studies (ISFS). Her current research interests include the financial well-being of aging athletes. Dr. Reilly is an educator and writer in sport psychology, whose publications include *Sport Psychology: Considerations for*

Maximizing Your Potential in Sports, and *Competitive Riding: A Sport Psychology Guide*. She was formerly on the faculty of Sweet Briar College, and taught sport psychology at the University of Virginia, from which she received her M.Ed. and Ph.D.

LINDA A. SIEGENTHALER, M.A., is a senior economist in the Center for Primary Care Research at the Agency for Health Care Policy and Research. Her analytic and policy interests focus on cost, access, and organizational issues affecting the health system, and the health and economic status of the elderly and disabled. Ms. Siegenthaler has also published studies in cross-national research on these topics. She received her M.A. degree in Economics from the University of California, Los Angeles, and completed graduate training in health and labor economics at Cornell and Rutgers Universities.

CHARLOTTE H. TWOMBLY, Ph.D., a research fellow at ISFS, is currently working on a research design for a study of financial literacy in the United States. Dr. Twombly has been a research consultant and educator in diverse areas of sociology for 25 years. She is currently an adjunct faculty member at Montgomery College and has previously been an adjunct professor at the American University, where she earned her Ph.D. Her work in family sociology, social stratification, and cross-cultural studies led her to recent research on social class, time use patterns of the elderly, and financial gerontology.

THOMAS M. WOOTTEN, Attorney at Law, a sociofinancial counselor and attorney, is a research fellow at ISFS engaged in the design of the Institute's research track on Financial Literacy in America. Formerly, Mr. Wootten, an expert on tax, pensions, and employee benefits, was a consultant for Coopers & Lybrand, Chicago, and Touche, Ross & Co., New York, for six years. He practiced law at the Chicago office of Noble, Lowndes for three years. He conducts corporate training and development seminars and is working on his MSW at Virginia Commonwealth University. Mr. Wootten is a graduate of Penn State and earned his law degree at the College of William and Mary.

The Contributors

The opinions expressed in the articles in this *Encyclopedia* are those of the author(s), and do not necessarily reflect those of the agencies or organizations with which they work or are affiliated.

Michele Adler, M.P.H., Office of Disability, Aging and Long-Term Care Policy, Department of Health and Human Services, Washington, DC

Christopher S. Alexander, M.B.A., William G. McGowan School of Business, Kings College, Wilkes-Barre, PA

James A. Anderson, Ph.D., College of Weekend Studies, Jacksonville University, Jacksonville, FL

Sia Arnason, C.S.W., Brookdale Center on Aging, Hunter College, New York, NY

Thomas D. Begley, Jr., Attorney-at-Law, Begley & Pepe, PC, Moorestown, NJ

Analee E. Beisecker, Ph.D., Department of Preventive Medicine, University of Kansas, Kansas City, KS

Thomas D. Beisecker, Ph.D., Department of Communication Studies, University of Kansas, Lawrence, KS

Robert H. Binstock, Ph.D., Department of Epidemiology & Biostatistics, School of Medicine, Case Western Reserve University, Cleveland, OH

William D. Bland, Ph.D., Department of Sociology, St. Paul's College, Lawrenceville, VA

Julia E. Bradsher, Ph.D., Institute for Health & Aging, University of California, San Francisco, CA

Kenneth A. Bretthorst, First St. Louis Securities, Inc., St. Louis, MO

Veronica M. Bukowski, M.A., Bukowski-Stanton Associates, New Hope, PA

Cathleen Burnett, Ph.D., Department of Sociology, University of Missouri, Kansas City, MO

Monica Cain, M.A., Department of Economics, Wayne State University, Detroit, MI

W. Donald Campbell, M.B.A., Consultant in Housing Finance, Falls Church, VA

Coral S. Carey, Ph.D., American Rehabilitation Association, Reston, VA

Frances M. Carp, Ph.D., San Jose, CA

Susan M. Chambré, Ph.D., Department of Sociology and Anthropology, Baruch College, New York, NY

Yung-Ping Chen, Ph.D., Frank J. Manning Eminent Scholar's Chair of Gerontology, University of Massachusetts—Boston, Boston, MA

Alfred J. Chiplin, Attorney-at-Law, National Senior Citizens Law Center, Washington, DC

David L. Christopherson, Ph.D., C.L.U., Department of Finance, Insurance & Real Estate, St. Cloud State University, St. Cloud, MN

Elizabeth Clemmer, Ph.D., Public Policy Institute, American Association of Retired Persons, Washington, DC

Christine Cody, R.N.C., M.S.N., National Hospice Organization, Arlington, VA

Mary Phillips Coker, Sociology Department, American University, Washington, DC

John Collins, Ph.D., Department of Religion, Wake Forrest University, Winston-Salem, NC

Francis P. Conner, A.C.S.W., L.M.S.W., Department of Sociology, West Georgia College, Carrollton, GA

Fay Lomax Cook, Ph.D., School of Education and Social Policy, Northwestern University, Evanston, IL

William H. Crown, Ph.D., Policy Center on Aging, Florence Heller Graduate School, Brandeis University, Waltham, MA

Neal E. Cutler, Ph.D., Boettner Center of Financial Gerontology, School of Social Work, University of Pennsylvania, Philadelphia, PA

Nancy Dailey, Department of Sociology, American University, Washington, DC

C. L. (Tim) Dimos, Attorney-at-Law, Middleburg, VA

Andrew Quang Do, Ph.D., Department of Finance, San Diego State University, San Diego, CA

Kenneth J. Doran, Attorney-at-Law, Doran Law Offices, Madison, WI

Michael E. Edleson, Ph.D., Harvard Business School, Boston, MA

Lisa J. Edwards, Department of Sociology, American University, Washington, DC

Carroll L. Estes, Ph.D., Institute for Health & Aging, University of California, San Francisco, CA

Ann E. Fade, R.N., J.D., Choice in Dying, Inc., New York, NY

Mark Fagan, Ph.D., Department of Sociology and Social Work, Jacksonville State University, Jacksonville, AL

Ronald A. Fatoullah, Attorney-at-Law, Ronald Fatoullah and Associates, Great Neck, NY

Lucy R. Fischer, Ph.D., Senior Investigator, Group Health Foundation, Minneapolis, MN

Mark S. Fischer, Ph.D., C.F.P., C.L.U., Fischer on Finance, Minneapolis, MN

Gregory S. French, Attorney-at-Law, Pro Seniors, Cincinnati, OH

Irene Glasser, Ph.D., Department of Sociology, Eastern Connecticut State University, Willimantic, CT

Stephen M. Golant, Ph.D., Department of Geography, University of Florida, Gainesville, FL

Rebecca Gronvold-Hatch, Ph.D., Kaiser Permanente, Pasadena, CA

Joan Matson Gruber, C.F.P., G.R.I., Maturity Market Consultant, Dallas, TX

Linda Havir, Ph.D., Gerontology Program, St. Cloud State University, St. Cloud, MN

Catherine Hawes, Ph.D., Program on Aging and Long-Term Care, Social and Health Policy Research Center, Research Triangle Institute, Research Triangle Park, NC

Rona S. Henry, M.B.A., M.P.H., Robert Wood Johnson Foundation, Princeton, NJ

David P. Higgins, Ph.D., Graduate School of Management, University of Dallas, Irving, TX

Barbara A. Hirshorn, Ph.D., Institute of Gerontology, Wayne State University, Detroit, MI

Karen C. Holden, Ph.D., School of Family Resources and Consumer Sciences, University of Wisconsin, Madison, WI

Andrew Holmes, Ph.D., Department of General Business and Finance, Sam Houston State University, Huntsville, TX

Harriet Howe, Ph.D., Director, Ombudsman Program, Institute of Socio-Financial Studies, Middleburg, VA

Denise T. Hoyer, Ph.D., Department of Management, Eastern Michigan University, Ypsilanti, MI

Donald A. Hunsberger, Attorney-at-Law, Brown and Streza, Orange, CA

Kennes C. Huntley, C.L.U., Department of Finance, Insurance and Real Estate, Mankato State University, Mankato, MN

Lori Janus, M.S., Central Minnesota Council on Aging, St. Cloud, MN

Gail A. Jensen, Ph.D., Institute of Gerontology, Wayne State University, Detroit, MI

David R. Johanson, Attorney-at-Law, Graham & James, San Francisco, CA

Marshall B. Kapp, J.D., M.P.H., Office of Geriatric Medicine and Gerontology, Wright State University, Dayton, OH

T. Erle Keefer, Glendan, Ltd., Flint Hill, VA

Mary Ann Keefer, B.A., M.A., Glendan, Ltd., Flint Hill, VA

James E. Konlande, D.C., Life Chiropractic College West, San Lorenzo, CA

Janet L. Kuhn, Law Offices of Janet L. Kuhn, McLean, VA

Ronald M. Landsman, Attorney at Law, Ron M. Landsman, PA, Bethesda, MD

Jeff L. Lefkovich, M.S., M.A., Jewish Home for the Aged, New Haven, CT

Charles F. Longino, Jr., Ph.D., Department of Sociology, Wake Forest University; Department of Public Health Sciences, Bowman Gray School of Medicine, Winston-Salem, NC

Robert D. Manning, Ph.D., Department of Sociology, American University, Washington, DC

Jerry J. McCoy, LL.B., Attorney-at-Law, Washington, DC

Christopher R. McDowell, 1LT, Legal Assistance Attorney, U.S. Army, Huntington, WV

Hunter McKay, M.P.P., Center on Aging, University of Maryland, College Park, MD

Mark Meiners, Ph.D., Center on Aging, University of Maryland, College Park, MD

Steven S. Miner, Steven Miner Research and Appraisal, Salem, OR

Scott A. Miskiel, M.S., Deloitte & Touche, LLP, Portland, OR

Karlyn Mitchell, Ph.D., College of Management, North Carolina State University, Raleigh, NC

Harry R. Moody, Ph.D., Brookdale Center on Aging, Hunter College, New York, NY

Steven R. Moore, R.P.H., M.P.H., Office of the Surgeon General, Rockville, MD

Robert J. Morlock, Institute of Gerontology, Wayne State University, Detroit, MI

Cyril Morong, Ph.D., Department of Economics, Lyon College, Batesville, AR

Nancy Morrow-Howell, Ph.D., George Warren Brown School of Social Work, Washington University, St. Louis, MO

Linda Murphy, M.A., University Extension, University of Missouri System, and Lincoln University, New Madrid, MO

Phyllis H. Mutschler, Ph.D., Policy Center on Aging, Brandeis University, Waltham, MA

Robert J. Myers, LL.D., International Actuarial Consultant, Silver Spring, MD

John R. Nofsinger, Department of Finance, Washington State University, Pullman, WA

Mars A. Pertl, Ph.D., Fogelman College of Business and Finance, University of Memphis, Memphis, TN

Charles D. Phillips, Ph.D., M.P.H., Program on Aging and Long-Term Care, Social and Health Policy Research Center, Research Triangle Institute, Research Triangle Park, NC

Diane S. Piktialis, Ph.D., Work/Family Directions, Boston, MA

Stephen L. Poe, Ph.D., Department of Business and Finance Administration, University of North Texas, Denton, TX

Ganas K. Rakes, Ph.D., Finance Department, Ohio University, Athens, OH

Dorothy P. Rice, Ph.D., Institute of Health and Aging, University of California, San Francisco, CA

Jihane K. Rohrbacker, National Association of Professional Geriatric Care Managers, Tuscon, AZ

Sandra Rosenbloom, Ph.D., Drachman Institute for Land and Regional Development Studies, University of Arizona, Tucson, AZ

Jeffrey I. Roth, Attorney-at-Law, Jacob D. Fuchsberg Law Center, Touro College, Huntington, NY

Linda R. Rounds, Ph.D., School of Medicine, University of Texas, Galveston, TX

N. Lee Rucker, M.S.P.H., National Council on Prescription Information and Education, Washington, DC

Cynthia Rudder, Ph.D., Nursing Homes Community Coalition of New York State, New York, NY

Debra S. Sacks, R.N., J.D., Brookdale Center on Aging, Hunter College, New York, NY

Judith A. Sangl, ScD., M.P.H., Office of Research and Demonstrations, Health Care Financing Administration, Silver Spring, MD

Kathleen K. Scholl, Ph.D., U.S. General Accounting Office, Washington, DC

Patricia Selby, M.S.W., Disability Initiative Program, American Association of Retired Persons, Washington, DC

Dennis G. Shea, Ph.D., Department of Policy and Administration, Penn State University, University Park, PA

Jurg K. Siegenthaler, Ph.D., Department of Sociology, American University, Washington, DC

Linda A. Siegenthaler, M.A., Agency for Health Care Policy and Research, Rockville, MD

Michael A. Smyer, Ph.D., Graduate School of Arts and Sciences, Boston College, Chestnut Hill, MA

Ben J. Sopranzetti, Ph.D., Department of Education and Finance, Seattle University, Seattle, WA

Richard H. Stanton, Bukowski-Stanton Associates, New Hope, PA

Norman Stein, School of Law, University of Alabama, Tuscaloosa, AL

Catherine M. Sullivan, M.P.A., The Brookings Institution, Washington, DC

Ralph B. Swisher, Ph.D., Federal Emergency Management Agency, Washington, DC

Joseph D. Teaff, Ed.D., Department of Health, Education and Recreation, Southern Illinois University, Carbondale, IL

John H. Thornton, Ph.D., C.L.U., College of Business Administration, University of Texas, Denton, TX

Paul Thrasher, C.P.A., Halt, Jackson and Thrasher, Alexandria, VA

Sandra Timmerman, Ed.D., Consultant on Gerontology, Half Moon Bay, CA

David J. Tolan, Attorney-at-Law, Tolan Schueller and Associates, Ltd., Milwaukee, WI

Katherine M. Treanor, M.S.W., Guthrie Capital Corporation, Washington, DC

Kathleen Treat, M.S.W., Center on Aging, University of Maryland, College Park, MD

Ronald Turner, Attorney-at-Law, University of Alabama, School of Law, Tuscaloosa, AL

Peter Uhlenberg, Ph.D., Department of Sociology, University of North Carolina, Chapel Hill, NC

Thomas Visgilio III, M.A., Department of Gerontology, King's College, Wilkes-Barre, PA

Lois A. Vitt, Ph.D., Institute for Socio-Financial Studies, Middleburg, VA

Anne S. Welch, M.A., Program in Human Development and Social Policy, School of Education and Social Policy, Northwestern University, Evanston, IL

Robert Whaples, Ph.D., Department of Economics, Wake Forest University, Winston-Salem, NC

Joshua M. Wiener, Ph.D., The Brookings Institution, Washington, DC

Brett Williams, Ph.D., Department of Anthropology, American University, Washington, DC

David P. Willis, M.P.H., National Institute on Aging, Bethesda, MD

Deborah G. Wooldridge, Ph.D., Southeast Missouri State University, Cape Girardeau, MO

Alma P. Yaros, Attorney-at-Law, Pro Seniors, Cincinnati, OH

Mary Jane Yarrington, Department of Research and Policy Development, National Committee to Preserve Social Security and Medicare, Washington, DC

Core Topics

Economic and Income Security

Accelerated Death Benefits

Cost-of-Living Adjustments (COLAs)

Disability Programs, Federal

Economic Hardship Measures in the Older Population

Economic Status of the Elderly

Economic Status of Elderly Women

Employee Retirement Income Security Act (ERISA)

Individual Retirement Accounts (IRAs)

Keogh Plans

Life Insurance

Medical Savings Accounts (MSAs) and Medical IRAs

Pension Fund Trends

Social Security Program of the United States

Social Security: Benefits for Disabled Individuals

Social Security: Special Minimum Benefit

Supplemental Security Income (SSI)

Veterans' Benefits

Employment, Work, and Retirement

Age Discrimination in Employment Act (ADEA)

Business Succession Planning

Health Care and Health Insurance

Leisure

Minority Elders

Nutrition Programs

Oldest Old

Religious Giving by Elders

Service Credit Programs

Transportation

Travel

Vacation Homes and Recreational Property

Volunteering

Volunteers, Older

Wealth Span

Preface

Money is the main, moving force of human life at the present stage of civilization. Our relationship to nature, to health and illness, to education, to art, to social justice, are all increasingly permeated by the money factor.

Jacob Needleman, 1991

This *Encyclopedia* was the brainchild of George Butler of Greenwood Press, who first mentioned it during the 1991 annual meetings of the American Sociological Association. The contributions compiled in this volume document what George had the foresight to know—that the array of increasingly complex financial concerns in modern society constitutes a "main, moving force of human life" for growing numbers of older persons.

Finance is a family of academic and applied fields—art and science—involving the acquisition, exchange, and management of money by individuals and organizations—private and public. Gerontologists, of course, analyze issues of individual and population aging through many different disciplinary prisms. *Financial Gerontology,* then, is the study of aging within financial contexts, or as defined by Davis W. Gregg in 1990, a field concerned with the dynamics of financial security, well-being, and the quality of life during the life cycle and across generations.

The *Encyclopedia* is intended for use by researchers, professional practitioners, educators, and students across the many applied fields and academic disciplines who focus on finance, aging, and the elderly. It will be useful as well to others, those with aging relatives, or older persons themselves who are personally or proactively interested in dealing with the array of financial concerns that confront us in our daily lives.

Throughout the *Encyclopedia*, authors address the question of resources in the course of aging. Resources may be constraining, but they also enable and facilitate what we want and need as individuals, as families, and as a society. If gerontology generates solutions to questions raised about aging, financial gerontology covers the same ground by pointing to the material means on which many of these solutions rest. The contributors to this volume have thus given new contours and greater profile to financial gerontology, building from many perspectives and upon many foundations. Gerontology has been traditionally multidisciplinary, and finance affects the quality of later life in ways difficult to generalize. Our challenge was to select a representative number of topics that would delineate the promises of our larger field of inquiry.

From the macro-level perspective of Carroll Estes's seminal *Aging Enterprise,* aging phenomena are seen as molded by the larger economic system. Observed through a prism of political economy, the institutions and policies that involve the elderly are economically and politically structured. This makes sense as we watch the markets and programs that relate to older persons constantly expand and become more complex. Financial gerontology links strongly with this view, considering the myriad policy issues faced in financing adequate retirement incomes or the health care needs of older people.

Financial planners and advisors have been absorbing gerontological research insights for some time as they, too, are reorienting themselves toward the financial needs and economic well-being of older persons and their families. Personal financial management, then, may be seen as the micro-level antecedent of financial gerontology. Through the vision and philanthropy of Joseph E. Boettner and Davis W. Gregg, and the creation of the Boettner Institute of Financial Gerontology, issues of financial security and human well-being in the older years have become synthesized. Financial security inevitably means having income in later life from public and private retirement funds, and from savings and investments. Thus these topics are linked again, full circle, to the capital markets and to the larger economic and political structure.

While recognizing earlier foundations, the *Encyclopedia* is broadly focused and not committed to a single tradition or perspective. We are excited about the countless and continuous ways in which the knowledge, ideas, programs, traditions, concerns, and positions taken by our contributors interact to form a convincing and urgent call for more research in this emerging field. In a proactive sense, we hope the expertise brought to this handbook will help enhance decision making by people themselves as consumers and citizens. This differs from views that focus solely on capturing elderly markets, or those that see only fiscal problems resulting from an aging population. It is our desire, instead, to offer insights that translate into knowledge that empowers people.

We share the larger vision of the original *Encyclopedists*—to take stock of knowledge and disseminate it for greater popular enlightenment. Of course, we do not claim the magnificence and comprehensiveness of their project, as we have just begun to address this vast subject. But we do sense that, across the many entries in this volume, something like a new overview or redefined understanding of financial gerontology has emerged that did not exist before. That understanding, we hope, will serve readers in the future as new demographic and economic realities confront them, and as financial gerontology perspectives are linked to the policy issues of the day.

Entries have been arranged to provide information at any alphabetical point. Readers are directed elsewhere by asterisks (*), which signify that another article can be found on the particular topic, or by the references to other topics that appear at the end of each article. For those readers who are interested in using the *Encyclopedia* as a textbook, a core set of articles under generic headings such as Employment; Work and Retirement; Financial Advice and Services; Housing; and other headings, appear in the *Core Topics* chapter. Readers are also directed to Appendix B, Organizations and Resources, for the addresses and telephone numbers of the organizations, or to access the resources, referred to in many entries.

Encyclopedia contributors successfully met a number of challenges, especially the time and space constraints imposed upon them by the editors' decision to include the broad and varied range of topics compiled in this introductory volume. Most impressively, they were able to present their information succinctly, giving brief exposure to their broad knowledge of complex topics in the hope that readers would be stimulated to undertake further study in greater depth.

We were greatly assisted by consulting editors Neal E. Cutler and Stephen M. Golant, who provided valuable suggestions for clarity, contributed topics, added text, or improved presentation. Associate editor, Linda A. Siegenthaler, was particularly helpful in guiding the selection and editing of the contributions on health and aging. Associate editors, Ann S. Reilly, Charlotte H. Twombly, and Thomas E. Wootten, helped substantially in the process of editorial review and in our relentless quest to stay within required space limitations. The participation of the associate editors was indispensable, and we are grateful to them, but decisions made that reduced the length (and undoubtedly the richness) of some entries are entirely the responsibility of the editors-in-chief.

Special thanks are due to Mary Phillips Coker for her good-natured and persistent efforts in recruiting authors. We are particularly grateful to production manager Karen McMahon, for her dedicated and competent administrative and technical assistance throughout our entire endeavor. Thanks are also due our excellent and tireless proofreader, Eric Bruner. Finally, we want to thank Mildred Vasan at Greenwood Press for her gracious and expert guidance and to acknowledge the financial support of the Institute for Socio-Financial Studies, without which this publication would not have been possible. We especially acknowledge and appreciate the generous contributions of Carter Eskew.

Lois A. Vitt
Jurg K. Siegenthaler

Introduction

It is a major undertaking to collect such an impressive range of topics pertaining to financial gerontology for the first time in one volume. Critics may point to sins of inclusion or omission, but this work blazes the trail for scholars, students, practitioners, and others interested in financial issues informed by several academic and practice disciplines from an aging perspective. For this pioneering multidisciplinary product, Lois Vitt and Jurg Siegenthaler deserve appreciation from those of us concerned with the economic well-being of older people.

The editors have advanced the accomplishments of the late Joseph E. Boettner and the late Davis W. Gregg, both of whom I was privileged to know well, particularly in my role as research coordinator for the study committee that proposed the Boettner Research Institute. We had numerous conversations about the relationships between the micro aspects of financial well-being of individuals and families on the one hand, and the macro dimensions of economic policies and societal economic institutions on the other. In a letter I treasure, Dave wrote on July 19, 1993: "To me you will always be a person in the vanguard insofar as financial gerontology is concerned. . . . You and I did some good thinking back in the early '80s that led to . . . how a research institute . . . can start at alpha and move steadily toward omega."

Financial gerontology was thus launched by Joe Boettner and Dave Gregg, and the steady move toward omega is being furthered by the work of Neal Cutler, president of the institute now known as the Boettner Center of Financial Gerontology. But more players are needed in the arena that concerns itself with the economic well-being of older people. I share the vision of Lois Vitt and Jurg Siegenthaler to incorporate financial gerontology in the research, teaching, and service activities of the institutes and centers of gerontology around the country.

As this area of specialization develops, I believe it is important to call attention to two points that cannot be overemphasized: a supply-and-demand view of economic security, and the overarching influence of macroeconomic policies on the economic security of the elderly.

A Supply-and-Demand View of Economic Security

Financial gerontology is concerned with the economic well-being of the elderly. Economic well-being is generally discussed in reference to several different criteria, such as income, wealth, or consumption. Over the years, the gap has narrowed between the elderly and the non-elderly insofar as income is concerned. Some conclude that the elderly have reached the same level of economic security as the non-elderly. Even if the elderly have gained income parity with the non-elderly in terms of poverty rates, one may not infer that their economic security levels are the same.

Economic security is a broader concept than income security. A person is concerned not only with the acquisition of income and assets, but also with their retention and disposal. It is well known, for example, that the elderly when compared to the non-elderly are at greater risk and must budget more income for medical and personal care services, despite Medicare and Medicaid. Potentially significant expenditures for health care, however, generally are not explicitly considered when assessing the economic status of the elderly versus the non-elderly. A more accurate assessment of economic security may be accomplished only when income, wealth, and consumption expenditures are comprehensively considered.

Income

The income status of the elderly has substantially improved in the last 25 years, but income status often is discussed by reference to the incidence of poverty. In 1966, for example, the poverty rate among the elderly was slightly more than double the poverty rate among the non-elderly. Since then, the elderly poverty rate has fallen, and the non-elderly poverty rate rose to approximately 13% in 1992. In terms of per capita income, statistics show that the elderly have reached the relative standing of the non-elderly over the last two decades.

Net Worth

Another criterion is ownership of wealth, or more precisely, net worth, which is the value of assets minus the value of liabilities. In terms of wealth, the elderly also fare well. Wealth holding by persons 65 and older is the highest among all age groups except those between 55 and 64 years old. Some conclude that the elderly are better off than the non-elderly, but a good deal of their net worth is in traditionally illiquid forms. Combining illiquid and liquid assets in order to measure economic capacity implies converting illiquid assets into readily spendable income. Home equity, for example, represents a significant part of net worth, but how meaningful is it to impute income from home equity?

Some see the increasing use of home equity lines of credit among middle-aged homeowners as a harbinger of their future comfort with reverse mortgages. But encumbered home equity in middle age is likely to reduce the equity that may be needed for retirement income. This is an important issue, because home equity can be a resource with which to finance consumption in old age. It is especially significant since home equity is increasingly seen as a viable resource to help finance future long-term care.

Consumption

The third criterion uses consumption expenditures to infer economic well-being. Neither income nor wealth is a good measure, some argue, and they propose that consumption is a superior measure of economic well-being. For example, in 1986, the ratio of income between the affluent and the poor was 16-to-1. But in terms of spending per consumer-unit, they would infer that life at the bottom of the American money-income distribution was only moderately less attractive than at the middle, and about half as attractive as at the top. In light of income, a vast difference existed between the poor and the affluent: if a poor person had \$1, the affluent person had \$16. According to per-consumer-unit spending, however, for every \$1 spent by the poor, the middle class spent \$1.29, and the affluent spent \$2.31. Seen in terms of consumption, the difference between rich and poor was much narrower than in terms of income.

On four essential consumer expenditures—food, shelter, apparel, and medical care—for every \$1 spent by the poor, the middle class spent \$1.14, and the affluent spent \$1.82. The difference between poor and rich was even smaller when considering consumer expenditures for these four basic necessities. This view must not be taken lightly.

Of the five income distribution quintiles, only the top two showed an excess of income over expenditures; they were not savers. All three lower quintiles showed expenditures over income; they were dissavers. Perhaps the humorist Artemus Ward anticipated the consumption measure when he said, ''Let us all be happy and live within our means, even if we have to borrow the money to do so.'' Consumption as a measure of economic well-being can be misleading.

How well-off are the elderly under this measure? The same data source, the Consumer Expenditure Survey for 1986, conducted by the Bureau of Labor Statistics, provided information for seven age groups. Per-person spending on the four basics by the oldest two age groups (65–74, and 75+) was higher than all five younger groups. Were the elderly enjoying a higher measure of economic welfare than the non-elderly?

Per-person spending on food, shelter, and apparel, with minor exceptions, was remarkably similar among all age groups. Health care, however, accounted for about 18% of the four basics for the 65–74 age group, and more than 25% of the four basics for the 75+ group, compared with 9% for the 45–54 age group, and less than 7% for all the younger age groups. That the elderly group spends more of its total budget on health care is not surprising. But the inference from using consumption as a measure is that if the elderly spend less on health care, their economic well-being would be lower. Conversely, young age groups can improve their economic well-being by spending more on health care. The irony is apparent.

Supply of and Demand for Resources

Income, wealth, and consumption may be viewed from the standpoint of supply and demand. In that light, income and wealth represent the supply of resources, and consumption represents demand for those resources. In order to measure economic well-being, therefore, income, wealth, and consumption should be included. Even if the elderly have achieved income and wealth levels on par with the non-elderly, it does not follow that their economic security is the same as younger groups, because older people are faced with an actual or potential higher demand on resources for health care, including long-term care.

Health care expenditures represent what could be called a *first claim on income*. When the income and assets of the elderly and non-elderly are equal, the supply of resources is the same for both groups. After the first claim is deducted from these resources, however, an obvious disparity in resources results between elderly and non-elderly groups. It is difficult to exaggerate the importance of health care to older Americans. A pre-Socratic philosopher, Heraclitus, said it well in 500 B.C.: "When health is absent, wisdom cannot reveal itself, culture cannot become manifest, strength cannot fight, wealth becomes useless, and intelligence cannot be applied."

Role of Macroeconomic Policies

Another important factor is the role of macroeconomic policies in financial gerontology. Through its influence on the overall economy, the federal government's fiscal, monetary, and regulatory policies significantly affect people's economic security. The high rates of inflation and unemployment in the late 1960s and the 1970s, particularly when inflation and unemployment coexisted, had major consequences on the financial status of the nation's Social Security program. High inflation rates increased the outflow of benefit payments, and high unemployment rates reduced the inflow of tax revenues. Massive accumulation of national debt in the 1980s has harmed old-age economic security through budget cuts for a variety of programs (though exempting Social Security). The insistence on the "revenue-neutral" criterion in deliberations leading to the Tax Reform Act of 1986 was also directly related to large budget deficits.

By its influence on money supply and interest rates, monetary policy may have a number of direct and indirect effects on the elderly's economic security. Interest rates, for example, bear directly on the earning power of savings, certificates of deposit (CDs) and other financial investments. Indirectly, interest rates also affect the feasibility of borrowing against or converting home equity. High interest rates, for example, form the basis for high discount rates, which in turn lower monthly income payments produced from home equity conversions.

Appendix A to this *Encyclopedia* lists 24 pieces of legislation enacted between 1975 and 1993 affecting employee and retirement benefits. It also refers to 17 other revenue laws, enacted from 1980 to 1993, with provisions changing the scope, types, and levels of retirement income. Efforts to curb the budget deficit have produced legislation limiting tax preferences of private pensions. The Tax Equity and Fiscal Responsibility Act of 1982 and the Tax Reform Act of 1986 reduced the funding and contribution limits for both defined benefit and defined contribution plans. Most significantly, the Omnibus Budget Reconciliation Act of 1987 reduced the full funding limits for defined benefit plans from 100% of ongoing plan liability to 150% of benefits accrued to date.

A productive and growing economy is the foundation of economic security for young and old alike. Providing such security in old age requires more than designing, monitoring, and revising financial mechanisms. Social Security, pensions, savings, employment, public assistance, Medicare, Medicaid and other health provisions—topics covered in some depth in this *Encyclopedia*—are, of course, essential considerations. Concerns for old-age economic security, however, must also include macroeconomic policy. How the government uses its fiscal, monetary, and regulatory authority provides the framework for creating and maintaining sound financial mechanisms and lies at the center of financial gerontology itself.

Yung-Ping Chen, Ph.D.

A

ACCELERATED DEATH BENEFITS, payment by an insurance company of part, or all, of a life insurance policy's death benefits* in advance of the policyholder's death if certain qualifying events occur. An understanding of accelerated death benefits may help people who are facing death, life-threatening medical events, or confinement to a nursing home or extended care facility access funds that are available under accelerated death benefit (ADB) options in life insurance policies. Familiarity with life insurance* basics, life insurance regulation, and some fundamental tax issues aids understanding of accelerated death benefits.

Life Insurance Policy Premises

An insurance company will pay the face amount of a life insurance policy to the beneficiary or estate upon the death of the insured. This is true of term, endowment, or whole life policies. A promise to pay upon death is the only promise made in term life policies. An endowment policy matures if the insured survives the policy's term. A whole life policy pays whenever the insured dies, or upon the insured's survival to age 100.

Endowment and whole life insurance policies also accumulate savings, or cash value, which is expected to equal the face amount (death benefit) of the policy at the end of the policy term. The policyowner can borrow from this cash value, creating a lien against the policy's death benefit for the loan amount plus interest. A policyowner who borrows against the cash value may use the money for any purpose, including costs associated with poor health. An insured's access to cash values is a ''living benefit'' available to the borrower without tax liability.

Other Living Benefits

Although funds provided under a life insurance policy's accelerated death benefit option are sometimes called living benefits, this term is sometimes used to describe payments made by viatical settlement firms, a very different practice. A viatical settlement firm provides cash to terminally ill policyowners by purchasing their life insurance policies. The firm then names itself as beneficiary, continues paying the policy premiums, and collects the policy proceeds upon the death of the insured. The viatical settlement firm is subject to income tax on the difference between its cost basis in the policy and the benefits it receives, so the amount paid by the firm for the policy is far less than its face value.

During the late 1980s, Canadian life insurers introduced accelerated death benefit options to help terminally ill AIDS patients, and they have become an increasingly popular product of U.S. life insurers. Though the original intent was to help AIDS victims, the ADB option can be an important living benefit to anyone facing the costs associated with a terminal illness or other life-threatening medical condition.

The Accelerated Death Benefit Option

The ADB option permits the policyowner to receive a percentage of a policy's death benefit upon the occurrence of a qualifying event: diagnosis of a terminal illness where the remaining life expectancy is a year or less; permanent confinement to a nursing care facility; or onset of a dread disease, such as cancer, even though the insured's life is not immediately endangered. When exercised due to terminal illness, the ADB payment typically is determined by discounting some or all of the death benefit. In most policies, some type of medical certification that a qualifying event has occurred must be provided to the insurer before the option may be exercised.

The ADB option is becoming an increasingly popular feature of traditional life insurance. According to a 1994 survey by the American Council of Life Insurance and the Life Insurance Marketing and Research Association, the number of ADB option policies increased from about 1.13 million to 18 million from 1991 to 1994, and the number of insurers offering this feature increased from 113 to 215 during this same time period (Armstrong 1994; Brostoff 1994). More employers include the ADB option as part of group life plans, given the low cost of providing this popular benefit to employees.

Terms of ADB options vary from insurer to insurer, and can be offered as a feature of a new policy or a rider to an existing one. Depending on policy terms and state laws, the maximum amount that can be accelerated ranges from 25 to 100% of a policy's face value. The policyowner may receive an ADB payment as a lump sum or in monthly installments, and no restriction is made on the use of such funds. In some policies, the ADB payment becomes a lien against the policy's death benefit, in which event access to the policy's cash value may be restricted by the amount of the lien.

Costs of ADB options also vary. Although some insurers charge an additional premium for the ADB option, many ADB policies do not carry an additional charge unless the option is exercised. Some insurers charge no additional premium for this feature. When the option is exercised, the insurer may charge a percentage of the policy's face value, an administrative fee, or both. Typically, the fee charged offsets interest lost by the insurer in paying the death benefit earlier than actuarially anticipated.

Prudential Insurance Company of America, in 1990, was the first major U.S. insurer to offer the ADB option and is among the top insurers in the nation in terms of ADB claims paid. From 1990 to 1994, Prudential paid more than $55 million on 680 claims for ADB payments, an average payment of more than $80,000 per claim (Armstrong 1994). About one-half of these payments went to cancer patients, about 27% went to AIDS victims, about 12% went to heart patients, and the remainder went to those diagnosed with other terminal illnesses. Under the Prudential ADB policy, insureds may accelerate up to 90% of the policy's face value if they are diagnosed with a terminal illness, and up to 70 or 80% of the policy's face value if they are confined to a nursing home*.

Limitations on Life Insurance Policies Offering ADB

ADB options often may not be exercised when life expectancy is greater than one year, or when the insured illness is not considered a qualifying event. Many ADB policies limit the amount of the death benefit that can be accelerated, and ADB options and payments may cause the policyowner to be ineligible for Medicaid or other government benefits provided under public assistance programs.

ADB policies have been criticized on the ground that this feature defeats the purpose of life insurance, and usurps funds necessary to provide for family members after the insured's death (Clark 1994). Unrestricted access to these funds, it can be argued, may save or prolong the life of the insured, which may not be in the best interests of the insured's dependents. As a result, many state laws limit the amount of the death benefit that may be accelerated and paid to the insured. Conversely, acceleration of the entire death benefit permits more of the insured's medical bills and other expenses to be paid prior to death, leaving more of the insured's other assets available to meet the needs of family and dependents.

Currently, the primary limitation of ADB policies is uncertainty surrounding how accelerated benefit payments should be treated for income tax purposes. Although life insurance proceeds usually are not taxable to the beneficiary, it is unclear whether receipt of an accelerated payment of the death benefit to the policyowner would be taxed. Current law indicates that payments received under a life insurance contract prior to death are taxable to the extent the amount exceeds premiums paid, but the Internal Revenue Service (IRS) has not made a final determination about how accelerated death benefits should be taxed.

In 1992, the IRS proposed regulations providing that payments of "qualified"

ADBs be treated as insurance paid at the death of the insured, thus exempt from federal tax. The insured must be reasonably expected to die within 12 months of the time the ADB payment is made, and the insurer must have followed certain discounting procedures in calculating the amount of the ADB. The IRS, however, did not formally adopt these proposed regulations nor indicate when the regulations may be finalized. Tax proposals are being discussed in Congress about both ADBs and viatical settlements. Any policyowner who wishes to exercise the ADB option should consult a tax attorney* or financial advisor* prior to doing so.

Life insurance policies with the accelerated death benefits option offer a feasible, compassionate response to financial problems brought about by the onset of terminal illness. There is still a need for clarifying federal legislative or regulatory action to enable life insurers to offer ADB policies in an environment free of tax uncertainty. (See also DEATH BENEFITS, LIFE INSURANCE, and LONG-TERM CARE INSURANCE: PRIVATE.)

Organization

American Council of Life Insurance

Suggested Reading

American Council of Life Insurance. 1994. *What You Should Know About Accelerated Benefits.* Washington, DC: Author.

References

Armstrong, Sean. 1994. "AIDS and the Trusted Adviser: Accelerated Life Insurance Benefits for Terminally Ill Patients." *Best's Review—Life-Health Insurance Edition.*

Brostoff, Steven. 1994. "Big Rise In Living Benefits' Availability." *National Underwriter—Life & Health/Financial Services Edition.*

Clark, Jane Bennett. 1994. "Life Insurance for the Living." *Kiplinger's Personal Finance Magazine.* June: 120.

Stephen L. Poe, John H. Thornton, and Kennes C. Huntley

ACCIDENT INSURANCE, a form of indemnity insurance that covers medical expenses, disability, death, or expenses sustained as the result of an accident. While the inclusion of accidental loss clauses in disability* and Medicare Supplemental Insurance* policies is important, the value of policies that only cover accidents is questionable.

As with any type of insurance, insurance premiums spent should provide a needed benefit when loss occurs. Most experts question the value of accident insurance, especially if decisions to purchase such coverage are driven, as people age, by fear of increased vulnerability to accidents. A careful distinction must be made between an "accident" as a cause of loss and "Accident Insurance" as a type of protection. Most indemnity insurance covers accidents, but "Accident Insurance" covers only accidental death and dismemberment.

Accidents Only

An accident-only policy pays a stated amount per day (e.g., $100/day) when an individual is hospitalized for an injury caused by an accident. One appeal of accident insurance policies is the method of payment, which typically is made directly to the policyholder rather than to the hospital. While some may argue that the proceeds can be used to offset non-medical expenses, accident policies pay only in the event of an accident, and most hospitalization occurs because of illness.

Accidental Death and Dismemberment (AD&D)

This type of policy, or endorsement to life insurance* or disability insurance, pays a benefit upon accidental death or loss of a limb, hearing, or eyesight because of an accident. For example, the accidental death benefit may be a specified amount in the event of death by accident (e.g., $10,000). The dismemberment feature will also pay a specified amount upon loss of two limbs (e.g., $10,000) or a lesser amount in the event of the loss of one limb (e.g., $5,000).

The value of this policy, or endorsement, must be assessed relative to the need for such coverage. As people age, it is likely that some wealth has been accumulated, and the AD&D benefit may be a ''windfall'' and not needed. If one has not accumulated wealth, then the advisability of spending money for the premium should be closely examined. Further, some AD&D policies provide coverage only until a specified age.

Travel Accident

These policies pay a specified benefit if death occurs while traveling. They are offered through credit cards*, are specially purchased for annual travel, or are bought as trip insurance at an airport or with a travel ticket. Travel accident insurance, when provided through a credit card, is generally sufficient to cover any need.

Accident insurance by itself seldom is of substantial value. While accident as a cause of loss is important in health insurance, it should be coupled with sickness as a cause of loss. When considering accident insurance alone, older persons should seriously consider the need for, and thus the value of, such coverage. (See also LIABILITY INSURANCE, LIFE INSURANCE, and TRAVEL.)

References

Bailard, Thomas E., David L. Biehl, and Ronald W. Kaiser. 1989. *How to Buy the Right Insurance at the Right Price.* Homewood, IL: Dow Jones-Irwin.

Dorfman, Mark S. 1994. *Risk Management and Insurance,* Fifth Edition, Englewood Cliffs, NJ: Prentice-Hall.

Household Financial Services, Money Management Institute. 1988. *Your Insurance Dollar.* Prospect Heights, IL: Household Financial Services.

Rejda, George E. 1992. *Principles of Risk Management and Insurance,* Fourth Edition. New York: Harper-Collins.

Mars A. Pertl

ACCOUNTANTS, professionals who are trained for and work in the field of accounting. Accountants generally have extensive academic experience in accounting, but their degrees, including advanced degrees, may be in business administration, finance, or economics. Some accountants choose to work for organizations as employees, while others choose to provide accounting services to clients for a fee. An accountant who provides such services, in most states, must be registered and licensed as a "Public Accountant." Public accountants are entitled to call themselves Certified Public Accountants (CPAs) when they have passed a rigorous examination, known as the Uniform Certified Public Accountant Examination, administered by the American Institute of Certified Public Accountants (AICPA).

CPAs and other public accountants practice as sole practitioners or affiliate into accounting firms, which range in size from small, to large local and regional, to national or international. Most organizations require accountants to be qualified as CPAs. Individuals, including seniors, usually are best served by sole practitioners or smaller firms where accountants specialize in providing personal service. Services usually fall into three areas: (1) accounting and audit; (2) tax planning and preparation of tax documents; and (3) management consulting.

Accounting and auditing services are more commonly provided to businesses than to individuals, although business financial statements and reports are often utilized by business owners in their personal financial affairs. Services include reviewing books of account, assisting with the recording of transactions, and the "attest" function of the CPA, whereby a CPA examines a financial statement and underlying books of account. He or she renders an independent opinion that the financial statement is materially complete and accurate and presented in conformity with professional standards (referred to as Generally Accepted Accounting Principles, or GAAP). Such statements show the financial condition of particular organizations or persons and are used to aid in financial decision making.

Tax planning and preparing federal and state tax forms prompt most individuals to seek an accountant. Accountants are also usually well equipped to assist their clients in the event of a federal or state income tax audit. Some accountants are experienced in estate planning*, including charitable contribution strategies, estate valuation services, preparation of wills*, and business succession planning*. These services are often provided in tandem with related legal services, and many accountants can recommend attorneys* in these areas, if necessary.

Management consulting services include the design of automated accounting systems, payroll, and employee compensation plans. Services of interest to older persons might include business valuation services (when valuing an estate) or litigation support.

Some qualities to look for in the selection of an accountant are reputation, professional accreditation (academic degrees, certification), and professional affiliations (membership in the AICPA or relevant state societies). Experience is of paramount importance. The body of accounting information is immense; the accountant chosen should have a specialty in the client's area of interest, or should be a member of an accounting firm large enough to embody several areas of specialization.

Personal chemistry is most important in establishing a relationship with an accountant where personal finances are discussed. A good rule of thumb is to interview three different accountants before choosing one, and a list of candidates can be developed by asking friends and relatives for suggestions. A personal banker or lawyer may also have suggestions. The local state society of CPAs will provide a list of CPAs in a specific state. (See also ASSETS ALLOCATION AFTER RETIREMENT, ATTORNEYS, BUSINESS SUCCESSION PLANNING, CHARITABLE CONTRIBUTIONS, ESTATE PLANNING, FINANCIAL ADVISORS, FINANCIAL COUNSELING.)

Organizations

American Institute of CPAs
National Society of Public Accountants

References

Accounting Principles Board. October 1970. *Basic Concepts and Accounting Principles Underlying Financial Statements of Business Enterprises.* New York: AICPA.
Needles, Belverd E., Jr. 1989. *Financial Accounting,* Third Edition. Boston: Houghton Mifflin.
Needles, Belverd E., Jr., Henry R. Anderson, and James C. Caldwell. 1990. *Principles of Accounting,* Fourth Edition. Boston: Houghton Mifflin.
National Association of Accountants. 1983. *Standards of Ethical Conduct for Management Accountants.* Statement Number 1C. Montvale, NJ: Author.

Paul Thrasher

ADULT DAY CARE. See Day Programs For Adults.

ADVANCE CARE PLANNING. See Accelerated Death Benefits; Advance Directives; Durable Power of Attorney; Living Will; Long-Term Care Insurance.

ADVANCE DIRECTIVES, legal documents used to provide instructions about future medical care in the event of serious illness or incapacity. Advance directives enable a person to maintain control as death approaches, and they relieve family members and loved ones of the burden of having to make difficult medical decisions.

End-of-life medical treatment can be very costly. Approximately 28% of all Medicare* expenditures occur in the last year of life (Lubitz and Riley 1993), and many fear that assets accumulated over a lifetime could quickly dissipate in unwanted medical treatment. While there is yet no evidence that using advance directives lowers health care costs, they can and do save individuals from receiving unwanted medical treatment and indirectly save medical expenses.

Types of Advance Directives

There are two types of advance directives: the living will* and the durable power of attorney* for health care. Both enable individuals to plan for future medical treatment, but they accomplish this in different ways. In living wills, individuals specify their treatment wishes in writing. Subject to certain legal limitations, instructions are given concerning the use or withdrawal of artificial life-support in end-of-life situations. Living will laws often require the attending physician, and sometimes an additional physician, to certify that the patient's condition is not expected to improve before the advance directive can be given effect. Every state except Massachusetts, Michigan, and New York has passed legislation regulating the use of living wills (Choice In Dying 1994). Living wills are legally valid in all states, as long as they clearly express the person's wishes.

A durable power of attorney is a document used to appoint an agent to handle matters of personal finance and property during periods of incapacity. As acceptance grew for the idea of planning in advance for health care, durable powers of attorney were adapted and used to appoint agents who can make medical treatment decisions. Currently, 48 states and the District of Columbia have enacted legislation authorizing the appointment of agents to make health care decisions (Choice In Dying 1994). Alaska and Alabama are the two states without such laws. The majority of these statutes require the agent to make health care decisions according to the patient's wishes, if known, or in the patient's best interests. The scope of an agent's authority is generally broader than the provisions contained in a living will. An agent is typically not limited to decisions about ending life support. These documents also address matters of health care management, and grant the power to procure health care services and personnel. Medical power of attorney laws often set restrictions on who can serve as an agent. Frequently, health care providers and health care institutions are not permitted to act as agents for patients in their care.

Historical Development

Advance directives were developed in response to the technological advances of modern medicine. The first living will was drafted at a 1967 meeting of the Society for the Right to Die, but nine years passed before the first living will law was enacted. In 1976, California became the first state to pass legislation that directly addressed the issue of end-of-life decision making. Also in 1976, the *Quinlan* case in New Jersey became the first right-to-die case to reach a state supreme court. Karen Ann Quinlan, a 21-year old woman, was in a persistent vegetative state as a result of respiratory arrest. Her father sought court approval to remove her from the ventilator that was breathing for her. The court ruled that individuals have a constitutional right to refuse medical treatment and ordered the treatment stopped.

In 1990, the United States Supreme Court issued its landmark decision in the

Cruzan case. In *Cruzan,* the court recognized that every competent individual has a constitutional interest in being free from unwanted medical treatment. The case involved a young woman who was permanently unconscious after a car accident, and whose life was being sustained by artificial tube feedings. The Missouri Supreme Court had ruled that tube feeding could not be stopped unless clear and convincing evidence of Ms. Cruzan's wish to refuse such treatment could be provided. Although the United States Supreme Court found a constitutional basis for the right to refuse medical treatment, the Court ruled that Missouri's clear and convincing evidence requirement was constitutionally permissible. Left unanswered was the extent to which states could act for incompetent patients.

The *Cruzan* decision also addressed the question of one's right to refuse artificial nutrition and hydration. Early right-to-die legislation frequently required that tube feeding be provided even when other types of life-sustaining treatment could be terminated. In the *Cruzan* decision, the United States Supreme Court explicitly rejected the idea that tube feeding is different from other forms of life support. While some older advance directive laws still limit a person's right to refuse tube feeding, such distinctions are constitutionally suspect. Newer statutes generally recognize that nutrition and hydration may be refused, but require that instructions for such refusal be explicitly set forth in the advance directive.

In 1991, Congress passed the Patient Self Determination Act (PSDA), which requires federally funded health care institutions to provide patients with information about their rights to make advance directives. Health care facilities must also provide staff and community education on the use of advance directives, although there has been no federal oversight on how well facilities have met such obligations. The PSDA leaves the substance of laws regarding advance directives to states and it is too early to judge the impact PSDA will have on the use of advance directives. It is clear, however, that the public is interested in more information about them. A 1991 Gallup poll found that 84% of the public would wish to terminate life support if there was no hope for recovery, while only 9% would wish to continue life support. In the same survey, 75% of respondents said they wanted a written living will at some future time, while only 17% said they would not want one.

Religion and Refusal of Treatment

Most religions do not specifically address the use of advance directives. Instead, they focus on two related issues: when it becomes appropriate to withhold or withdraw medical treatment, and how treatment termination is distinguishable from suicide and assisted suicide. In general, major religious traditions permit limits on medical treatment provided at the end of life.

Roman Catholic doctrine generally permits patients to refuse life-sustaining treatments. In the Church's statement on refusal of life-sustaining treatment, the

Declaration on Euthanasia (1980), Pope John Paul II announced that medical treatments may be withdrawn if they impose on the patient:

strain or suffering out of proportion with the benefits which he or she may gain from such techniques. . . . [W]hen inevitable death is imminent in spite of the means used, it is permitted in conscience to take the decision to refuse forms of treatment that would only secure a precarious and burdensome prolongation of life, so long as the normal care due to the sick person in similar cases is not interrupted.

This position of the Roman Catholic Church has been interpreted differently among individuals, groups, and clergy. The greatest disagreement centers on whether artificially administered nutrition and hydration may be withheld or withdrawn under the *Declaration.*

Most mainline Protestant churches have taken positions that are generally consonant with those articulated by the Roman Catholic Church. In the Protestant religious tradition, there is no absolute authority or specific formula to guide end-of-life medical treatment. There is a rich tradition affirming the values of individual autonomy and responsibility toward others, however, which would argue in favor of a person's right to refuse unwanted medical treatment (Hill and Shirley 1992).

Reformed and Conservative Judaism do not oppose withholding or withdrawing treatments that prolong the dying process, although there is disagreement among Conservative rabbis about whether artificial nutrition and hydration may be withheld or withdrawn. In Orthodox Judaism, all life-prolonging measures are required to be provided unless a person cannot be kept alive for more than three days.

Limitations on the Right to Refuse Medical Treatment

The portability of advance directives may be the greatest limitation on their use. It is unclear whether an advance directive written in one state must be honored in another. Increasingly, states guarantee reciprocity if out-of-state documents have been executed properly under either state's law, but many states still lack such reciprocity. Moreover, hospitals and nursing homes* are risk-averse and may be unwilling to honor an out-of-state advance directive even with the legislative authorization to do so.

Another limitation on the right to refuse unwanted treatment consists of ''conscience exclusions,'' which allow a health care facility to reject advance directive provisions on principle, if honoring them would violate a religious or moral belief. Although facilities are required to give written notice of such a policy at the time of admission, many patients and families fail to read them thoroughly, or to understand the importance of the materials they are given. Facilities that will not stop treatment must transfer a patient to one that will. In practice it is difficult, however, to find facilities willing to admit patients solely for the purpose of terminating treatment so that death can occur. Even where the law is clear that a competent adult may refuse medical treatment through an advance directive, many health care facilities remain reluctant to stop treatment. Reasons include misunderstanding of the law; conviction that what is medically appropriate is not consistent with personal, moral, or religious beliefs; and concern about potential liability.

Trends and Alternative Directives

Two new types of law permit end-of-life medical treatment decisions by others in the event of incapacity. The first involves surrogate decision making and provides that individuals, usually in order of priority, are empowered to make decisions for an incompetent patient who has no living will or durable power of attorney for health care. While this simply codifies health care decisions traditionally made for incompetent patients, increasing medical regulation and oversight and fears of liability have made doctors reluctant to rely any longer on informal decision making without explicit legislative authorization. Commonly, the surrogate (typically a family member or close friend) is required to consider the patient's personal, moral, or religious beliefs when making decisions. Surrogate decision making is often included as a provision within a living will statute. Twenty-three states and the District of Columbia currently provide for surrogate decision making (Choice in Dying 1994).

The second type of law is a nonhospital do-not-resuscitate (DNR) order. Emergency medical technicians, feeling trapped by laws that require aggressive treatment for individuals obviously near the end of life, have joined state medical associations and other organizations to develop and lobby for nonhospital do-not-resuscitate orders. DNR orders allow individuals to refuse emergency resuscitation in advance of an emergency. Usually a DNR order must be completed by an individual and his or her doctor. Some nonhospital DNR legislation provides for wallet-size versions of the official form or for identification bracelets or necklaces to indicate that the individual should not be resuscitated. In order to be effective, the individual must keep the form or other official notification on hand at all times so that it is available to emergency personnel. So far, 19 states have statutes authorizing nonhospital DNR orders, but more are likely to be passed (Choice in Dying 1994). Because both DNR laws and local policies are new, the public and many health care professionals remain unaware of them.

Beyond these legal developments, discussion and research focuses on the larger process of communication among patients, their health care providers, families, and others regarding appropriate care when a patient cannot make decisions. The goal of such advance care planning is to shape future clinical care to fit people's preferences and values (Teno et al. 1994). (See also ACCELERATED DEATH BENEFITS, DURABLE POWER OF ATTORNEY, LIVING WILL, MEDICARE, NURSING HOMES.)

Organization
Choice in Dying, Inc.

Suggested Readings

Health Care Financing Administration. 1994. *Medicare and Advance Directives*. Washington, D.C.: Author.
National Eldercare Institute on Health Promotion. 1994. "Advance Directives: An Important Aspect of Self-Care." *Perspectives in Health Promotion and Aging*, 9 (2).

References

Choice In Dying. 1994. *Right-to-Die Law Digest*. New York.
Cruzan v. Director, Missouri Department of Health (1990) 110 S Ct 2841.
Declaration on Euthanasia, adopted by the Sacred Congregation for the Doctrine of the Faith, approved by Pope John Paul II, released to the public June 26, 1980.
Gallup, G., and F. Newport. 1991. "Mirror of America; Fear of Dying." *The Gallup Newservice* 55: 33.
Hill, T. Patrick, and David Shirley. 1992. *A Good Death*. New York: Addison-Wesley.
Lubitz, James, D., and Gerald F. Riley. 1993. "Trends in Medicare Payments in the Last Year of Life." *New England Journal of Medicine* 328: 1092–96.
In Re Quinlan (1976) 70 NJ10.
Schneiderman, Lawrence J., J. Kronick, R. Kaplan, J. Anderson, and R. Langer. 1992. "Effects of Offering Advance Directives on Medical Treatments and Costs." *Annals of Internal Medicine* 117: 599–606.
Teno, Joan M., Hilde Lindemann Nelson, and Joanne Lynn. 1994. "Advance Care Planning: Priorities for Ethical and Empirical Research." *Hastings Center Report,* Special Supplement (November-December).

Ann E. Fade

AGE DISCRIMINATION IN EMPLOYMENT ACT (ADEA),

statute promoting employment of older persons based on ability rather than age and prohibiting arbitrary age discrimination in employment. The ADEA protects working men and women at least 40 years of age and renders unlawful an employer's failure or refusal to hire, discharge, or otherwise "discriminate against any individual with respect to his compensation, terms, conditions, or privileges of employment, because of such individual's age." Also prohibited is age discrimination by employment agencies or labor organizations.

The ADEA has been subject to constant legislative amendment and to changing judicial attitudes. Initially, judicial interpretation of the ADEA was expansive. Beginning in the late 1980s, however, the Supreme Court decided a number of cases in ways that contracted the scope of ADEA protections, the most significant of which was the elevation of "intent to discriminate" in ADEA litigation.

Enactment of ADEA

Title VII of the Civil Rights Act of 1964 prohibits employment practices that discriminate on the basis of "race, color, religion, sex, or national origin." Congress considered, but rejected, amendments to add age to Title VII's list of prohibited categories, but Title VII did require the secretary of labor to prepare a study of age discrimination in employment that would detail the effects on both individuals and the economy. The report, "The Older American Worker: Age Discrimination in Employment," revealed that many employers did practice age discrimination based on stereotypes about older persons. Age discrimination was found to harm the economy by depriving it of productive workers, federal revenues by increasing costs of government benefits, and individuals by inflicting economic and psychological injury.

In 1967, President Lyndon B. Johnson submitted a draft age discrimination bill to Congress with this message on age discrimination:

In economic terms, age discrimination is a serious—and senseless—loss to a nation on the move. But the greater loss is the cruel sacrifice in happiness and well-being, which joblessness imposes on these citizens and their families. Opportunities must be opened up to the many [older] Americans who are qualified and willing to work. We must end arbitrary age limits on hiring.

Initially, ADEA prohibited age discrimination only in the private sector, and then only against employees between ages 40 and 65. Congress subsequently extended protection to most federal and state employees and expanded the class of protected employees, in 1978, first to include employees through age 70 and later to lift the age ceiling altogether. Thus, the ADEA today covers most private-sector and public employees who are 40 years of age or older. It exempts, however, small employers with fewer than 20 employees.

Most states have age discrimination legislation, and some are more expansive than the ADEA. The important distinction between the ADEA and some state laws is that action can be brought against an employer of fewer than 20 employees. ADEA does not preempt state law.

Proving Violations of ADEA

Two categories of claims are brought under ADEA: disparate treatment claims and disparate impact claims. Disparate treatment claims are those in which an individual (or class of individuals) contends that an employer refused employment, refused a salary or promotion, or terminated employment because of age. Disparate impact claims arise when an employee challenges an age-neutral employment practice that has a disproportionate statistical impact on older employees. Modes of proof of disparate treatment and disparate impact cases are somewhat different.

An individual may present disparate treatment through direct proof that an employer refused to promote the individual because he or she was too old for the job. Most employers, however, are sufficiently sophisticated to avoid direct discriminatory action, and when such proof is lacking, employees must prove an ADEA violation through inferential rather than direct evidence.

Courts have developed a procedure of shifting burdens in ADEA cases in which direct evidence is not available. Sometimes referred to as the *McDonnell Douglas* procedure, it is named after a Supreme Court decision outlining the procedure in a Title VII case. An aggrieved individual initially must prove a prima facie case of age discrimination, which will generally be established if employees prove: (1) they are in the protected class of employees (i.e., they were over 40 at the time of the alleged discriminatory act); (2) they were seeking a job or were an employee; (3) as a job seeker they were qualified for the job; and (4) as an employee they were qualified for promotion, job retention, salary increase, or other employment benefit, and the employer failed to hire, retain, promote, or reward the individual.

If the individual proves a prima facie case, the employer must produce evidence rebutting the inference created by the prima facie case. The employer meets this burden by articulating a legitimate, nondiscriminatory reason for its actions. The burden of proof then shifts to the plaintiff who must prove that age discrimination was the more likely reason for the employer's actions.

Disparate impact cases are proved in a similar manner. The plaintiff must begin the case by presenting a prima facie case of disparate impact and show, generally with statistical data, that an employer's practices have a significant adverse effect on older employees. The employer must then produce evidence showing that the practice was job-related or had a "manifest relationship" to the employer's business. The plaintiff can rebut the employer's explanation by demonstrating either that the employer could have satisfied its legitimate business purposes in a less discriminatory manner, or that the employer was using the practice as a pretext for discrimination.

In a 1993 Supreme Court case, *Hazen Paper Co. v. Biggins,* three justices questioned whether the ADEA offers relief for disparate impact alone. It is part of a clear trend in the federal judiciary to insist on clearer proof of actual discriminatory motivation before awarding relief in civil rights cases generally, and in ADEA cases particularly.

Employer Defenses to ADEA Claims

The ADEA arms employers with affirmative defenses against claims of age discrimination. The most important of these defenses is that "age is a bona fide occupational qualification reasonably necessary to the normal operation of the particular business." For example, courts have permitted mandatory retirement ages for certain law enforcement officials. But one court struck down an airline policy of refusing entry-level employment to pilots over 35 years of age, while another court approved a bus company's policy of refusing entry-level employment to drivers over 40 years old. The ADEA also provides defenses for employers who can demonstrate that an employment decision was based on: (1) "reasonable factors other than age," (2) "good cause," (3) a "bona fide seniority system," (4) "corporate reorganization," or (5) a "bona fide employee benefit plan." There is sometimes a close correlation between these defenses and the employer's burden.

It is noteworthy that an employer may not adopt a policy of discharging employees over age 40 involuntarily in a corporate reorganization, nor adopt a seniority system that retires an employee over age 40 involuntarily. The Equal Employment Opportunity Commission, and virtually all federal courts that have considered the question, took the position that older employees could be treated differently in an employee benefit plan only if the employer could demonstrate a cost justification for the disparate treatment. In a surprising decision, *Public Employees Retirement System v. Betts* ([1989] 109 5 Ct 2854), the Supreme Court rejected the "cost justification" approach, and held that an employer could discriminate on the basis of age in employee benefit plans unless the employee could show that the plan was actually intended to discriminate "in some non-fringe benefit aspect of the employment relationship." Congress reacted to the *Betts* decision with the Older Workers Benefit Protection Act of 1990 (OWBPA), which expressly overruled *Betts*. Under the statute, an employee benefit plan is "bona fide" only "where, for each benefit or benefit package, the actual amount of payment made or cost incurred on behalf of an older worker is no less than that made or incurred on behalf of a younger worker." An employer can defend age discrimination by showing that the employee waived his or her ADEA rights, but unless a waiver meets minimum statutory standards—enacted by Congress in the OWBPA—the waiver is not valid.

Courts also have allowed employers to defeat ADEA claims if they can demonstrate that the adverse employment action involved no age-discriminatory motive. An open question is whether an employer is limited by the facts known at the time of discharge. Assume, for example, that a 45-year-old employee is discharged because of age, and that after an action is initiated under ADEA, a misrepresentation is found on the employee's job application. Whether the employer can defend the discriminatory charges based upon this newly discovered information has not yet been decided by the courts.

Criticism of the ADEA

Some in the business and academic communities have argued that the ADEA is unwise, inefficient legislation. In a controversial book, *Forbidden Grounds: The Case Against Employment Discrimination Laws,* published in 1992, University of Chicago law professor Richard Epstein argues that discrimination statutes serve no legitimate purpose. In the marketplace for labor, employers and employees will agree to contract, one for the services of the other, if such contracts offer gains to each. Barring structural failure in the marketplace, labor can be expected to "move to jobs where it is most highly valued." Epstein writes that "the right policy" in the employment market "is to keep all barriers as low as possible." But the ADEA has "precisely the opposite effect, since it raises barriers to entry."

Epstein suggests that discriminatory employment policies are generally "business decisions . . . made for reasons that reduce the internal costs of production." A firm that "passes over superior older workers in favor of inferior younger ones will find itself at a cost disadvantage that it cannot recoup in the market.'' Epstein argues that no market imperfection justifies ADEA.

Epstein is criticized for ignoring the psychological harm imposed by discriminatory employment practices. Although costs of discrimination may be difficult to quantify, they are real and merit reflection. If widespread market failure did exist in 1967, and if the ADEA helped correct it, the ADEA may have actually increased societal net wealth rather than decreased it, as Epstein believes.

The Future of the ADEA

Judicial trends have narrowed the scope of ADEA and other civil rights legislation. Increasingly, courts are calling on plaintiffs in employment discrimination cases to prove motive, a difficult burden. Cases such as *Betts* suggest that the Supreme Court is reversing what seemed to be settled and accepted law. Congress, which in the past amended the ADEA to make it more hospitable for employees (including amendments to reverse narrowing Supreme Court decisions), is less inclined to expand the reach of the civil rights laws. As a result, plaintiffs increasingly may seek redress in state law when available.

These judicial and legislative trends come at an unusual time in the demographic life of the ADEA: members of the baby boom generation are now moving into protected status under the ADEA and a majority of the workforce will soon have ADEA protection. If the majority will benefit from ADEA protection, strong political pressures may develop to maintain or even expand protections. Equally potent resentment by unprotected workers who contend that the statute blocks employment opportunities for workers under 40 may counteract such pressures, however. It is difficult to predict what this will mean in terms of age discrimination and the political forces that strengthen or weaken legal protections for older workers. (See also EMPLOYMENT OF OLDER AMERICANS and WORKING RETIREES.)

References

Hazen Paper Company v. Biggins (1993) 113 S Ct 1701.
Public Employees Retirement System v. Betts (1989) 109 S Ct 2854.
Rosen, Benson, and Thomas H. Jerdee. 1976a. ''The Influence of Age Stereotypes on Managerial Decisions.'' *Journal of Applied Psychology.* 61: 428–32.
Rosen, Benson, and Thomas H. Jerdee. 1976b. ''The Nature of Job-Related Stereotypes.'' *Journal of Applied Psychology* 61: 180–83.
Rosen, Benson, and Thomas H. Jerdee. 1985. *Older Employees: New Roles for Valued Resources.* Homewood, IL: Dow Jones-Irwin.
Doering, Mildred, Susan R. Rhodes, and Michael Schuster. 1983. *The Aging Worker: Research and Recommendations.* Beverly Hills, CA: Sage.

Norman Stein and Ronald Turner

AGENTS AND BROKERS, persons authorized to represent others or to negotiate on their behalf, usually for compensation. Health and financial concerns of older people and their families bring them into contact with an array of professional agents and others who operate under the laws of agency: accountants*; attorneys*; financial advisors*; attorneys-in-fact; real estate and insurance agents; trustees; and persons who have been authorized to make medical decisions under advance directives*. There is very little literature that distinguishes between agency and brokerage, and much confusion surrounds the practices and ethics of those who are engaged to act on the older person's behalf, especially those in fiduciary relationships.

An agent is a person or entity authorized by another (the "principal") to represent and to act on the principal's behalf. The agreement of agent and principal constitutes an agency relationship. The agent acts only with the principal's consent and is subject to his or her direction and control. When acting under an agency arrangement, the agent's chief obligations are: (1) loyalty to the principal, (2) obedience to the principal's instructions, (3) diligence in the performance of duties, (4) accountability for the principal's funds or property, and (5) full disclosure to the principal of all material facts. Actions taken under an agency relationship bind the principal in third-party transactions. Thus, third parties dealing with agents must bear in mind that the first loyalty of the agent, by law, is owed to the principal. There are many types of agency appointments, but most fall under two broad categories of agency: general and special.

A broker is an agent employed to make bargains and contracts for compensation, according to *Black's Law Dictionary*. When a broker enters into a transaction as a middle person or negotiator to bring buyer and seller together, he or she is acting as a "dual agent." There are many different types of brokers, and the term extends to almost every area of business. The term *broker* is often misused and misunderstood by consumers when referring to real estate, insurance, and other types of persons who actually work in agency relationships under most state laws. Certain industries are often closely regulated—the real estate and legal industries for example—and their members are required to disclose agency relationships, obligations, and fee arrangements, and to avoid conflicts of interest. In other industries—such as insurance and securities, and commission-based financial planning—advisors* and counselors do not supervise closely the agency and disclosure practices of their representatives. As a result, securities brokers—even those who are well-intentioned—often call themselves financial advisors* or financial service representatives. The effect of this is to elevate their profession and obscure how they are compensated.

General and Special Agents

General Agents have been delegated authority by a principal to handle all matters connected with a particular (personal or business-related) situation, trade, or employment. They may exercise extremely broad authority, without restriction or qualification, for a principal: enter into several types of contracts; make decisions; buy and sell property, goods, and services; and enter into short- or long-term obligations, contracts, and commitments. A *managing agent* may be vested with exclusive and general power to exercise complete judgment and discretion in all management matters for his or her principal (person or organization).

Special Agents are appointed to act on behalf of their principals in a limited capacity, usually in a single transaction or a series of acts not involving a continuity of service. An example of special agency is a literary agent appointed to enter into publishing negotiations and contracting arrangements on an author's behalf. A purchasing agent is typically a special agent as well, authorized to act on behalf of a company concerning matters of purchasing special materials such as supplies or inventory. A purchasing or literary agent would not be authorized to bind his or her principal in any matter other than the transaction or series of acts explicitly specified in an agency agreement.

Whether dealing with a special or general agent, third parties who have contact with agents should determine the exact scope of authority and range of actual power that have been delegated by the principal to the agent. It is important for anyone who deals with an agent to know directly from the principal, in as clear a manner as possible, what the scope of authority is in order to make informed judgments as to the appropriateness of the transaction under consideration. Without this knowledge, the third party dealing with an agent runs the risk of entering into agreements that go beyond the scope of the agent's authority. When compensation is involved, it is important to become aware of the fees charged or commissions customarily paid in the particular agency arrangement.

Common Agency Arrangements

Insurance agents are agents of insurance companies who have been hired as: (1) general agents to manage sales operations on either a local or a regional basis; or (2) special agents authorized only to sell insurance. An insurance general agent is authorized to act on behalf of a specific insurance company with respect to nearly every business matter concerning sales operations. They may not make underwriting or premium determinations. Insurance special agents are authorized only to sell insurance and do not have the authority to modify any terms of existing insurance agreements. Insurance agents, who earn commissions based on the insurance they sell, may represent one or many different companies. Since the cost of insurance varies greatly from company to company, it is important to shop for comparable coverage and service. Not surprisingly, high cost policies usually pay high commissions to agents.

Real estate agents usually represent the seller of real estate. If an agent acts as a buyer's agent they are still compensated from the sales commission paid by the seller unless specific alternative compensation arrangements have been made. The loyalties of real estate agents may seem especially confusing to buyers, since they can be genuinely motivated to bring buyers and sellers into harmonious and satisfactory transactions. Under real estate agency agreements (listings), however, agents are hired to sell real estate, and it is the seller who is the principal in this agency relationship.

Financial advisors or *managers,* employed as agents to manage assets or purchase investments on behalf of principals, are often acting instead as dual agents or brokers, and compensated by commissions based on sales of the financial products sold or fees based on a percentage of assets managed. Some financial advisors charge a fee only for the time spent on a client's behalf. It is always important to understand the exact relationship one has with a financial services professional, his or her motivation for recommending an investment, and the manner in which the representative is compensated.

Many uncompensated agency relationships can exist in the lives of older persons as well, but all agency agreements require great care and planning before entering into them. Among the more serious types of agency created are those in which persons are delegated authority under powers of attorney, durable powers of attorney, and advance directives for health care in the event of incapacity. (See also ACCOUNTANTS, ADVANCE DIRECTIVES, DURABLE POWER OF ATTORNEY, FINANCIAL ADVISORS, and LIVING WILL.)

Organizations

National Association of Personal Financial Advisors
International Association of Financial Planning
Institute of Certified Financial Planners
International Board of Standards and Practices for Certified Financial Planners, Inc.
Insurance Company Safety Ratings
Standard & Poor's
Moody's
Duff & Phelps

References

Conard, Alfred F., Robert L. Knauss, and Stanley Siegel. 1977. *Agency: Cases, Statutes and Analysis.* Mineola, NY: Foundation Press.
Howell, Rate A., John R. Allison, and Robert A. Prentice. 1988. *Business Law Text and Cases.* Chicago: Dryden Press.
O'Donnell, Jeff. 1991. *Insurance Smart.* New York: John Wiley & Sons.
Ross, Richard D. 1994. *The Handbook of Stock Brokerage Accounting.* New York: New York Institute of Finance.
Savage, Terry. 1994. *New Money Strategies for the '90s.* New York: Harper Collins.

Donald A. Hunsberger

ANNUITIES, yearly payments fixed by contract from one party, the payor, to a second party, the annuitant. Annuities are one of the most popular investments available in the financial marketplace. They are used for funding pension programs, deferred compensation agreements between businesses and executives, private investment programs, and charitable programs such as charitable remainder annuity trusts and outright gifts of annuities to charities. They are also used to settle lawsuits.

Commercial Annuities

Commercial annuities are the most common forms of annuities and represent a contract between the purchaser of the annuity and an insurance company. They are classified primarily on the basis of: (1) the time when payments will be made by the insurance company; (2) the way in which the interest rates are calculated; and (3) the number of years for which the insurance company is bound to make payments to the annuitant. Each of these categories is considered below.

Time for Payout

Insurance companies market two types of annuities—those that make immediate payments to the payee, and those that provide for payments at a later date. The first type of annuity is called an immediate annuity, and the second is a deferred annuity. Individuals who purchase immediate annuities are seeking to convert funds into a long-term stream of income that commences from the date of purchase. The advantages of an immediate annuity are the tax treatment of the annuity payments, and guarantees by the insurance company concerning interest rates or pay-out.

A deferred annuity provides the features of an immediate annuity, and postpones taxation on the growth of the principal until the time when annuity payments are actually made to the annuitant.

Interest Rate Calculations

Interest commitments that insurance companies enter into call for either fixed interest payments or variable interest payments. Under fixed interest payment commitments, insurance companies commit set interest payments for the life of the annuity agreement. Thus, the risk concerning interest rates is shared by the insurance company and the annuitant. If market interest rates increase, the insurance company earns a profit on the annuity; conversely, if market interest rates decrease, the insurance company loses money on the annuity obligation.

A variable annuity contract places the risk on the annuitant. If market interest rates go up, those increases in interest rates are passed directly to the annuity owner in the form of higher annuity payments. Conversely, if interest rates go down, the periodic payments will be decreased.

Length of Term

The following classifications are the most common terms guaranteed under annuity payment obligations:

Term Certain, also known as years certain, involves the promise of the insurance company to make payments for a specified number of years regardless of the number of years the annuitant survives. For example, with a 20-year certain term, the insurance company commits to payments for 20 years, even if the annuitant dies prior to the end of the 20-year term. It should be noted that the longer the term certain, the lower the amount of money the insurance company is willing to promise to pay for the period involved.

Life terms are commitments by the insurance company to make payments until the annuitant dies. The risk for payment is shared by both the owner of the annuity and the insurance company. If the annuitant lives only one year after paying the funds to the insurance company, the insurance company enjoys a significant profit on the transaction. If the annuitant lives 60 years beyond making the payment to the insurance, then the annuitant is the winner.

Life-only annuities refer to annuities that are written with one spouse as the annuitant, without reference to the life of the other spouse. These contracts are contrasted with joint annuities.

Joint and survivor refers to an annuity whose payments are based on the life expectancies of two or more individuals, most commonly the lives of a husband and wife. Under the terms of a joint and survivor annuity, the pay-out period is calculated based on the combined life expectancies of the husband and wife. The death of one spouse does not end the obligation of the insurance company to continue paying benefits to the surviving spouse. In fact, the entire basis of a joint and survivor annuity rests on the principal that payments will continue to be made regardless of which spouse survives the other. Again, payments under a joint and survivor annuity are significantly lower than payments based on the life of one spouse alone.

Private Annuities

By contrast to commercial annuities, private annuities are not paid by insurance companies, but are paid by individuals in exchange for the transfer of property to the payor. Private annuities are frequently established where the property that is being exchanged is of importance, or particular significance to the parties involved with the transaction (usually a parent and a child), and there is a desire to maintain control over the property being transferred at the same time that the property is being removed from the estate of the transferor. In other words, private annuities are often established where a parent wishes to remove a piece of property from his or her estate and passes the property to a child in exchange for a promise to make periodic payments of an agreed amount to the parent.

Tax Treatment of Annuities

Every payment under an annuity agreement is broken down into two parts: (1) A return of principal, which is a withdrawal of a portion of the money originally paid into the annuity; and (2) the payment of interest. The first part, the return of principal, is not taxable to the payee, while the second part, the interest, is treated as taxable income.

In order to determine the amount of each annuity payment that is taxable, the Internal Revenue Code, under Section 72, provides a calculation, termed the *exclusion ratio,* for specifying what portion of the payment is interest, and what portion is a return of principal. Section 72 provides a formula for taxing annuity payments:

$$\frac{\text{Total Annuity Contribution}}{\text{Total Expected Payments}} \times \text{Payment Amount} = \text{Tax due from each annuity payment}$$

By calculating this formula, the annuitant can determine the tax status of each payment, or the total tax liability for any given year. The tax treatment of annuities (which permits the tax liability to be spread out over a period of years) is its chief advantage as an investment vehicle. In order to calculate the exclusion ratio, an assumption has to be made concerning the life expectancy of the annuitant. To do so, the parties must look to an actuarial table and base the exclusion ratio on the life expectancy of the annuitant. If the annuitant outlives his or her life expectancy, the entire payment may become taxable. (See also CHARITABLE CONTRIBUTIONS, LIFE INSURANCE, and PENSION FUND TRENDS.)

References

Advanced Underwriters Service, Updated Monthly. Chicago: Dearborn R&R.

Black, Kenneth, Jr., and Harold D. Skipper, Jr. 1994. *Life Insurance.* Englewood Cliffs, NJ: Prentice-Hall.

U.S. Congress, Senate Committee on Labor and Human Resources, Subcommittee on Labor. 1994. *Recent Court Decisions Affecting ERISA and Executive Life Annuities: Hearing Before the Subcommittee on Labor of the Committee on Labor and Human Resources.* Washington, D.C.: U.S. Government Printing Office.

Williamson, Gordon K. 1993. *All About Annuities: Safe Investment Havens for High-Profit Returns.* New York: John Wiley & Sons.

Donald A. Hunsberger

AREA AGENCIES ON AGING. See Older Americans Act (OAA).

ASSET PROTECTION. See Assets Allocation After Retirement; Cash Flow Planning for Retirees; Estate Planning; Financial Advisors; Financial Counseling; Medicaid Planning; Trusts; Wills.

ASSETS ALLOCATION AFTER RETIREMENT, an approach to investment decision making under age-specific circumstances. During working years, when assets are most likely to be acquired, asset allocation is relatively simple. After some provision for liquidity (usually three to nine months' income), other financial assets can be considered long-term, permitting the saver to be somewhat aggressive in how they are invested. Most financial advisors* agree that people in their 20s or 30s should keep most retirement savings in variable-return securities, financial assets that rise and fall in value with the market, such as common stock. Securities not having a guaranteed return have a higher expected yield, and historically have out-performed fixed-return assets (e.g., bonds*) by more than 5% per year. In some years variable-return investments earn several times the returns of fixed-return assets, and in other years they have negative returns. But over a reasonably long period (e.g., five years), variable-return securities almost always out-perform fixed-return assets.

It is generally worth the risk of uncertain return to earn an additional 5%. Consider a 25-year-old saver deciding between a fixed account with a 7% return and a variable account expected to earn 12%. If this saver invests $100 per month until age 65, the fixed account will be worth $262,481. If the variable return account had been chosen, however, the account would have grown to $1,176,477—a difference of $913,996. Since year-to-year variations in the market historically average a higher return, it is easy to see why young savers are directed into variable-return investments and why they are advised to buy and hold them for the longer term.

As investors age, however, their ability to take advantage of the benefits of variable return securities diminishes. The nature of retirement requires liquidation of assets to provide current income, and when assets are sold, a commensurate decline in income based on a decreasing capital account also occurs.

Fear of reduced income prompts many retirees to invest in more predictable fixed-return assets, but this investment strategy risks possible loss from inflation. Sixty-five-year-olds, on average, have 17.3 years left to live (15.2 years for men and 19.0 years for women). This means that 65-year-old retirees must plan for at least 20 years of retirement. If they invest only in fixed-return assets, they will achieve little real portfolio growth, due to inflation. A $250,000 retirement nest egg, for example, invested in fixed accounts earning 7%, will provide an income of approximately $2,000 per month for 20 years. While this may be adequate today, inflation may reduce the purchasing power of this income over time. By the 20th year, assuming an inflation rate of 3%, the purchasing power of $2,000 will be $1,107. At 5% inflation, this monthly income would be worth only $754. Many retirees face this potential dilemma as they try to allocate their financial assets. Investment only in stocks yields no current income, but investment in fixed income securities may fail to meet their needs for growth to offset the effects of inflation.

Mixed Allocations of Assets

A mixed allocation approach is called for, with some investments in fixed-return assets and some portion invested in variable-return assets. The question is how much should be allocated to each type of investment, and how should this change as retirees grow older? Most retirees tend to worry more about market risk than inflation risk, and tend to buy portfolios dominated by fixed-return assets. Inflation effects must be considered, however, when the planning horizon is greater than five years. As a retiree ages, inflation risk becomes less important. Proper allocation, then, requires consideration of how time affects both market risk and inflation risk.

One guideline to follow in this situation is to invest a percentage equal to 100 minus the retiree's age in variable-return assets: for a 62-year-old, 38% (100 minus 62) of assets; the balance in fixed-return assets. By the time one reaches age 75, this percentage will be down to 25%. As individuals grow older, their expected planning horizon becomes shorter. This reduces the significance of inflation risk, making a more conservative approach appropriate. It should be noted that this is a conservative guideline. Healthy 60-year-olds may be justified in keeping more than 40% of their portfolios in variable return assets.

The basic principle underlying all retirement planning strategies regardless of the age of the planner is diversification. Individuals who have decided that they want to put 40% of their portfolio in variable-return assets and 60% in fixed-return assets still must decide how to invest within these categories. The overwhelming majority of people should invest through some type of mutual fund rather than trying to purchase individual securities. Mutual funds provide two essential elements not readily available to the purchasers of individual assets: diversification and low transaction cost. Mutual funds offer professional management, which eliminates the need for constant analysis by savers. Mutual funds, which do charge a management fee, are generally a bargain for small investors.

With more than 2,000 different funds from which to choose, this can be complex. There are two approaches to this problem. First, savers can narrow the funds down independently. *Fortune* and *Forbes* magazines rank the performance history of many of the top funds on a yearly basis. The rankings are done by category. As a place to start, look at investment-grade bond funds for the fixed assets and the ''growth and income'' common stock funds for the variable assets. These rankings are complete with phone numbers that can be called to obtain additional information. A second approach would be to work with a professional financial planner who will do the leg work for you.

Both of these approaches have pitfalls. By doing it alone investors may miss valuable guidance and tax information. On the other hand, when professional financial advisors are contacted, advice may be motivated by self-interest, rather than what is best for the retiree. In either case, it should be remembered that financial planning decisions rarely must be made in haste. One may simply put the money in a money market fund or Certificate of Deposit for a few weeks or even months during the decision-making period. Take time and gather information from several sources before funds are invested. If professional help is desired, talk with at least three advisors.

After the initial set-up of the portfolio, changes will need to be made periodically in order to adjust for changes in the expected planning horizon. A valuable guideline is to consider making changes at least once a year but not more than twice a year. The annual review is a time to consider changes. It is not necessary to change every year. Again, financial decisions rarely need to be made in a hurry. Any changes should be contemplated over a period of at least two weeks.

Financial planning becomes more complicated prior to and during retirement. The need for current income invalidates the typical assumptions that long-range planners use. In order to balance the market risk and inflation risk associated with postretirement planning, a mixed approach must be employed. Assets must be allocated over both fixed-return assets such as bonds and variable-return assets such as common stock. As a retiree grows older, the balance of these two types of assets can change. However, these problems are not insurmountable. The guidelines suggested above provide a framework that will balance portfolios to provide for current income and allow for growth to overcome problems with inflation. (See also BONDS, COMMODITIES, DERIVATIVES, EQUITY SE-CURITIES, ESTATE PLANNING, FINANCIAL ADVISORS, MUTUAL FUNDS, and SAVINGS INVESTMENTS.)

References

Breitbard, Stanley H., and Donna Sammons Carpenter. 1988. *The Price Waterhouse Book of Personal Financial Planning.* New York: Henry Holt.

Malkiel, Burton G. 1985. *A Random Walk Down Wall Street.* New York: Norton and Company.

Peterson, Raymond H. 1994. *Accounting for Fixed Assets.* New York: John Wiley & Sons.

Andrew Holmes

ASSISTED LIVING, living arrangements promoting the philosophy of personal control and responsibility for frail older persons within home-like group residences. Assisted living arrangements generally include:

• Group or congregate living situations that provide room and board as well as social and recreational opportunities

• Assistance to residents who need help with personal care needs and medications

• Protective oversight or monitoring

• Help around-the-clock and on an unscheduled basis (Kane and Wilson 1993).

Various studies estimate that 1.2 million residents live in 40,000 to 65,000 assisted living facilities in the U.S. (Dewey 1994). In the assisted living setting, residents remain in charge of their own lives. They exert as much responsibility as their physical and mental capacities permit, including their right to make decisions about their care and safety.

Many facilities and states that do not use the term "assisted living" have programs that meet this definition. Conversely, facilities that offer little personal care assistance or nursing homes* that offer institutional care are not included in the definition, even if they describe themselves as offering assisted living. Usually, residential facilities using the term *assisted living* espouse a philosophy of resident autonomy, but the degree to which their management practices reflect the philosophy may vary.

Background

Until recently, much of the discussion about reforming long-term care has focused on institutional care and has centered on nursing home financing and access—how to provide nursing home care to people without impoverishing them or depleting the public treasury. Over the last decade, however, private developers and administrators of state programs, led by Oregon, have offered assisted living as a way of providing support services to significantly impaired people in a group residential environment. Assisted living offers many frail older persons appropriate care while preserving their dignity and autonomy and, in many situations, it can do so at a lower cost than nursing homes or home care. Frail older persons, fearing the institutional character and loss of independence associated with life in a nursing home, have embraced the arrangements and philosophy of assisted living.

The aim of assisted living is to enable frail older persons to live as independently as possible in a home-like atmosphere. This is accomplished through building design and care practices that facilitate independent functioning and reinforce residents' autonomy, dignity, privacy, and right to make choices. The philosophy of resident independence encompasses the concept of "the dignity of risk," also advocated by members of the disability community. It asserts the rights of residents to make decisions about their care and safety that others may consider risky. It is based on the notion that psychological health and well-being should be considered along with physical safety.

Living Arrangements and Assistance

In better facilities, the design of the building reflects the philosophy of promoting independence (Regnier 1994). Residents usually live either in private rooms with baths, individual temperature controls, and doors that lock, or in small apartments with kitchenettes. They often bring their own furniture. The decor and scale are home-like throughout the building, often with one or more small sitting rooms that encourage residents to visit with each other and entertain guests. Many assisted living facilities explicitly avoid fluorescent lighting, long corridors, tile floors, and the nursing stations that are associated with nursing homes. The facilities, however, typically provide handrails, wide hallways, some type of emergency call system, and grab bars and other features in bathrooms, all of which help assure physical security and promote independence. The buildings also include a laundry, central kitchen, and other areas to support the delivery of services.

Assisted living buildings vary in size and type. They may be freestanding structures expressly designed to enhance the independence of frail older persons. Many continuing care retirement communities* have a campus that includes three levels of housing and services: independent housing with some social and recreational services and perhaps one communal meal, an assisted living building to which residents move when they need personal care assistance or monitoring, and a separate building for nursing care. Other structures, including large private homes, schools, hotels, and nursing homes, have been remodeled to accommodate assisted living programs. The size of the buildings ranges from those in which 15 or fewer residents live (often in remodeled homes) to those with 100 or more residents. In building new structures, many developers choose to accommodate about 30 to 70 residents, which they believe is few enough to retain some residential character but large enough to allow economies of scale in providing services.

The typical program of assistance offers help with at least some activities of daily living (ADLs)—dressing, bathing, using the toilet, transferring to and from a chair, or eating—as well as supervision of medication and protective oversight. Before moving in, the resident or a family member describes the resident's needs and works with the staff to decide what help will be provided, how, and when. Most facilities offer a standard package of services, but they differ in what they "bundle" into these packages. They may also provide additional services "in-house," if needed, but at a higher fee, or help arrange for such services, including nursing care, from a third-party provider. Residents can also obtain assistance around the clock. Other services usually available include help with arranging doctor appointments, transportation for shopping and other excursions, social and recreational activities, housekeeping, nutrition counseling, and provision for special diets. Residents' preferences are taken into account in the scheduling of services, such as help with a bath. Residents often have the option of doing their own laundry, making their beds, cleaning their apartments, and fixing tea and coffee or light meals. Relatives are also encouraged to visit and join in these tasks.

Assisted Living Compared to Other Living Arrangements

While assisted living is similar to home care, congregate housing, board and care homes, and nursing homes, it differs from those programs in significant ways.

Home Care. The minimum time block for which home care usually can be scheduled is two hours. While this is ideal for help with dressing, bathing, housekeeping, and meal preparation, two-hour time blocks are inappropriate when assistance needs to be available throughout the day and evening. Assisted living can take advantage of economies of scale by using a core staff to offer both brief periods of assistance and general oversight to a much larger group of people than can home care. For this reason, assisted living is particularly appropriate for persons without friends or relatives to supplement assistance purchased from home health agencies.

Congregate Housing. Congregate housing programs usually offer support services such as a meal a day, transportation, and housekeeping to residents living in private apartment units. Although residents may be able to obtain assistance with some ADLs, even otherwise excellent congregate housing programs may not offer protective oversight and 24-hour assistance.

In those states that prohibit assisted living facilities from providing extensive help with ADLs, such as North Carolina, assisted living facilities offer meals and other services similar to congregate housing, and ADL assistance is provided by home health agencies on a contractual basis. This third-party arrangement allows services tailored to each resident's needs but may cost more, since residents pay the home health agency for care in 15-minute segments, even if they need only a few minutes of assistance with a given task.

Board and Care Homes*. Most board and care homes offer the protective oversight, home-like atmosphere, and some of the ADL assistance available in assisted living. The board and care industry, however, has been plagued with allegations of abuse and low quality (GAO 1990). Meager levels of public assistance available for the low-income residents who comprise about one-half of the population in board and care homes across the country exacerbate these problems (Hawes et al. 1993). In contrast, developers of assisted living have aimed their programs at moderate-and upper-income groups. In Oregon, where assisted living is available to low-income persons, public funding has been adequate for quality programs. To date, assisted living has avoided the quality-of-care problems that have afflicted board and care, as the market-driven nature of assisted living has helped to promote good quality.

Nursing Homes. Nursing homes usually care for persons with complex or unstable medical conditions who need continuing nursing supervision. Standardization of services in nursing homes and the assignment of two or more residents to a room, while encouraging quality care and cost control, have also contributed to nursing homes' institutional and regimented atmosphere. The requirement that a nurse always be on duty enables nursing homes to serve residents with various medical needs, but adds a medical orientation to nursing home life and raises costs.

In the absence of studies controlling for levels of frailty or intensity of services, estimates of cost savings in assisted living must be made cautiously. Cost data from Oregon, the only state to mandate assisted living to serve nursing home-eligible residents, do indicate some potential for savings. Rates for Oregon's assisted living residents who receive Medicaid, all of whom are nursing home-eligible, are about two-thirds as much as Medicaid rates for Oregon's nursing home residents (Hawes et al. 1993). That assisted living is serving persons with somewhat lower levels of service needs is illustrated by the fact that 20% of Oregon's assisted living residents eventually move to nursing homes. That 80% do not need to move to nursing homes, when many are nursing home-eligible, indicates the potential savings to both Medicaid programs and private-pay residents.

Private Sector Fees and Public Assistance Programs

Developers have built and marketed assisted living primarily for affluent older persons, those able to pay $1,000 a month or more, a cost prohibitive for most older persons. According to a survey of 63 assisted living facilities in 1992, only seven facilities charged a single rate. The other 56 facilities charged varying rates, depending upon room sizes or apartments, or for assistance beyond the facility's standard package of services. The lowest median rate for shelter, food, and standard services was $995 per month ($33 per day), and the median highest rate was $1,639 ($55 per day) (Kane and Wilson 1993).

About one-half the 63 programs surveyed by Kane and Wilson (1993) had residents receiving any public assistance either for shelter or for services, and most of these programs had only a few such residents.

Public assistance for low-income persons is almost always inadequate to cover charges in typical assisted living programs. The federal government provides Supplemental Security Income (SSI)* payments to impoverished elderly and disabled persons, but the maximum was $442 a month in 1994. Although most states and some counties provide an additional amount, the total is far short of the typical base cost of $1,000 for assisted living arrangements.

Since it began in 1965, however, the federal Medicaid program has subsidized care in nursing homes. States pay varying proportions of the Medicaid rate, from 21% to 50%, depending on the cost of nursing home care in the state and the per capita income in the state. States have begun recognizing that assisted living can postpone or substitute for some nursing home admissions, offering states the potential to reduce their Medicaid expenditures. In an AARP survey in 1994, Donna Folkemer found that of the 45 states (and the District of Columbia) responding to the survey questionnaire, 25 report using at least one Medicaid-sponsored program to fund services for persons in a residential care setting (including assisted living, board and care, and adult foster care homes).

Often, these programs serve relatively few people or are otherwise limited in scope, but there are a few exceptions. Texas, for example, has just been granted a Medicaid waiver than can cover up to 22,000 persons in a range of settings, including assisted living. Oregon is able to cover the entire cost of care for very low-income residents by using its Medicaid waiver to cover the costs of all services, and residents' SSI payments to cover room and board.

Financing Assisted Living Construction

Developers indicate that obtaining financing for construction of assisted living facilities is their greatest concern (Redfoot 1994). The 1992 Housing Act extended Section 232 of the Federal Housing Administration's (FHA) mortgage insurance program to include assisted living facilities. (Section 232 already covered nursing homes and board and care homes.) The availability of mortgage insurance for assisted living should make financing easier to obtain, thereby reducing financing costs. The resulting savings may enable developers to make assisted living more available to persons with lower incomes. Section 232 could also enable linkages among FHA, state housing finance agencies, and government-sponsored enterprises (GSEs) for risk-sharing demonstration projects (Redfoot 1994).

Changes around the Corner

To date, assisted living has been primarily a private market phenomenon. Most residents pay privately, and most facilities have been developed and managed with no funding or regulation at the federal level, almost no funding from states, and varying degrees of state regulatory oversight. This could change since the federal government and many states now recognize that assisted living offers the possibility of less costly care to many persons who might otherwise enter nursing homes. The federal government is slowly permitting states to obtain Medicaid funds for assisted living facilities as an alternative to nursing home admission. States are actively examining how much regulation is suitable and what levels of resident frailty they believe appropriate for assisted living facilities in their state.

Ongoing discussions among policymakers, regulators, providers, and consumers and their advocates, may eventually resolve the issues of frailty level (how much ''aging in place'' is appropriate for assisted living before a very frail resident needs to move to a nursing home?); living arrangements (should private rooms with baths be mandatory?); risk and autonomy (to what extent can the resident make decisions about lifestyle and care, even if the decision increases the resident's risk of health or safety problems?); flexibility of regulations (how much leeway should providers have to determine procedures in their facility?); and financing (how to make the advantages of assisted living available to persons with low income). (See also BOARD AND CARE HOMES, CONTINUING CARE RETIREMENT COMMUNITIES, HOME CARE SERVICES FOR THE ELDERLY, NURSING HOMES, and SUPPLEMENTAL SECURITY INCOME.)

Organizations

American Association of Retired Persons
Assisted Living Facilities Association of America (ALFAA)

Suggested Reading

Mollica, Robert L., et al. 1992. *Building Assisted Living for the Elderly into Public Long Term Care Policy: A Guide for States.* Waltham, MA: Institute for Health Policy.

References

Dewey, Jeanne. 1994. ''The Shaping of an Industry: Will the Assisted Living Boom Lead to New Regulation?'' *Provider* (November).

Folkemer, Donna. 1994. *State Use of Home and Community-Based Services for the Aged under Medicaid: Waiver Programs, Personal Care, Frail Elderly Services and Home Health Services.* Washington, DC: AARP.

General Accounting Office. 1990. *Board and Care: Insufficient Assurances That Residents' Needs Are Identified and Met.* Washington, DC: Author.

Hawes, Catherine, Judith Wildfire, and Linda Lux. 1993. *The Regulation of Board and Care Homes: Results of a Survey in the 50 States and the District of Columbia. National Summary; State Summaries.* Washington, DC: AARP.

Kane, Rosalie A., and Karen Brown Wilson. 1993. *Assisted Living in the United States: A New Paradigm for Residential Care for Frail Older Persons?* Washington, DC: AARP.

Redfoot, Donald L. 1994. "Long Term Care Reform and the Role of Housing Finance." *Housing Policy Debate*, 4:23–25.

Regnier, Victor A. 1994. *Assisted Living Housing for the Elderly: Design Innovations from the United States and Europe.* New York: Van Nostrand Reinhold.

Elizabeth Clemmer

ATTORNEYS, individuals who advocate on behalf of, or counsel others, or are employed to prepare for trials in courts of law. While Elder Law Practice* is growing more important as the population ages, there are many areas or specialties within the practice of law. A specialty involves additional study, training, or experience. A patent attorney, for example, frequently has additional training as an engineer in order to perform within the specialty area of patent law. In seeking an attorney, a client should inquire about the attorney's background to determine the level of his or her expertise in the area of specialized need. Local bar associations can also refer attorneys by specialization.

Areas of Specialization

Appellate Law. Attorneys handling litigation matters that have progressed beyond the trial level are appellate attorneys. Courts of appeal include both state and federal courts, as well as the supreme courts of the states and the federal government. Generally, the party who has lost a trial is the person who appeals, although either party may need to seek an attorney who specializes in the appeals process and has taken cases before courts of appeal in the past.

Business and Corporate Law. Attorneys who specialize in the area of business and corporate law practice in a wide range of areas. They typically review contracts; incorporate businesses; review leases, contracts, and promissory notes; consider matters of securities law; and in general, advise business owners and managers. Because of the broad area of practice within this specialty, practitioners of business law frequently have additional training or education such as a CPA or an MBA. Business and corporate attorneys need knowledge and familiarity in the areas of banking, finance, securities law, corporate law, and general management in order to serve the interests of their business and corporate clients. They usually do not go to trial and more frequently are transactional lawyers.

Business Litigation. Attorneys specializing in business and corporate litigation are trial lawyers rather than transactional attorneys in most cases. In this specialization, as with most areas of litigation, the most important asset of a business litigator is his or her litigation experience, rather than knowledge of business and corporate law. Business litigators generally sue over matters such as collections, contract law, copyright or trademark infringement, unfair business practices, or other business matters.

Bankruptcy Law. Bankruptcy law involves dealing with the federal bankruptcy statutes, which allow individuals to reorganize and/or terminate indebtedness by declaring bankruptcy. Under this law, the rights of the bankrupt and the creditors (entities owed money by the bankrupt) must be protected. In bankruptcy law, attorneys usually specialize in representing either the bankrupt or the creditors. It is not common practice in most larger jurisdictions for attorneys to represent both creditors and bankrupt individuals, although it does happen on occasion. A person seeking a bankruptcy attorney should make an effort to find an attorney who customarily represents individuals in similar situations. When seeking protection against a bankruptcy proceeding by a debtor, one should seek a creditor's bankruptcy attorney.

Construction Law. Certain lawyers specialize in the area of law related to constructing and/or demolishing buildings. Lawyers practicing in the area of construction law must be familiar with municipal regulations, building codes, civil engineering, soil engineering, zoning, construction financing, and local building practices. As with many areas of the law, lawyers who practice in this field are important to seek out not just for their knowledge in the legal area, but also for their knowledge of how construction practices work in their geographic regions. The problem of working with a general practitioner in matters of construction law arise from the fact that frequently attorneys not familiar with construction practice are similarly unfamiliar with practical problems of dealing with local governments and other bureaucracies in matters of seeking permits, gaining approval of plans, or obtaining other required clearances.

Copyright Law. Individuals who seek to publish magazine articles, books, music, poetry, or computer software programs should work with a copyright lawyer. Copyright lawyers protect the rights of their clients who have created any form of written or performed work. Copyright lawyers often also practice trademark and patent law (see below). Copyright law, like patent law, is highly specialized and requires detailed familiarity with pertinent federal statutes.

Criminal Law. Attorneys who practice criminal law work either as prosecutors on behalf of a government body, or as defense counsel on behalf of individuals accused of criminal acts. When seeking the services of a criminal attorney, it is advisable to find someone who has dealt specifically with the alleged crime. An individual accused of violating a criminal statute against drunk driving, for example, should seek an attorney who regularly defends against drunk driving charges. Lawyers who defend against particular crimes are more familiar with jury responses, and more knowledgeable about the particular criminal statute that may have been violated. Criminal lawyers are trial lawyers who should be able to demonstrate prior experience before the courts in question, whether municipal, state, or federal. A lawyer who has not had criminal trial experience in the past is not a good candidate to defend in a criminal law trial.

Elder Law. Attorneys who are engaged in elder law practice* are experienced in working with state and federal statutes related to Medicaid and Medicare, state and federal social services programs, estate, probate, and trust law, as well as matters related to conservatorship and retirement law. Attorneys who practice in the area of elder law are not necessarily prepared to practice in every area of law in which an older person may require assistance. Rather, this area is specialized in the specific matters referenced above.

Estate, Probate, and Trust Practice. Estate planning lawyers (often elder law practitioners) must be experienced in matters of taxation, property law, and to some extent, family law. They assist their clients in drafting wills and trusts, and in other matters related to the ownership of property, in a fashion that will minimize the cost of probate and estate taxes and fees. Attorneys who are not experienced in estate planning should not be called upon to draft complicated testamentary documents, since the area is highly specialized and an inexperienced lawyer in this field can cause unexpected transfer fees to result at the time of death.

Family Law. Family attorneys handle adoptions, separations, and divorces, and help alter or amend family status. Lawyers who have never tried a divorce case should advise prospective clients that they are unfamiliar with this area of the law. A client who is sued for divorce or who intends to sue for divorce should seek the advice and counsel of a family law attorney. Of all the areas of legal practice, few are more prone to misinformation than the area of family law practice. It is best to seek out the services of a family law attorney as soon as one is needed, rather than relying on the advice of friends. Family law attorneys must also be familiar with the effects of tax law as a result of divorce.

Immigration Law. Immigration attorneys assist clients in seeking visas to foreign countries and in seeking "Green Cards" that permit foreigners to reside in the United States. They also help clients from foreign nations obtain citizenship in the United States. Immigration law is largely federal, and it is highly important that an individual wishing to assist friends or family members in obtaining work permits or temporary visas in the United States seek an immigration law attorney. Since violations of immigration law are federal offenses that carry serious penalties, the assistance of an immigration attorney is crucial to assure smooth transition for individuals needing help in these matters.

Insurance Law. Lawyers who practice in the area of insurance law specialize in a subspecialty of business and corporate law. They represent two types of clients: insurance companies who wish to protect their interests from claimants, and individuals who seek to enforce claims against their own insurance companies or those of individuals who caused them to suffer some loss. In both cases, insurance attorneys usually have a background in both business law and trial law, with the trial experience being the more important of the two areas.

International Law. Individuals who wish to conduct business outside the United States, or who seek to transact even a single matter in a foreign country, should seek the services of an international law practitioner. These attorneys, besides having experience in international law, should have experience with the particular foreign nation. International attorneys should be familiar with the legal aspects of international law, as well as cultural and social customs of the particular nations in which business is to be conducted.

Labor Law. Labor lawyers practice in two specific areas: they represent employers, and they represent employees. As with bankruptcy law, lawyers seldom practice on both sides of labor law. Someone seeking the services of a labor attorney, therefore, should determine whether the attorney has historically represented employers or employees, and be guided accordingly to the type of representation needed. Labor lawyers work both as trial lawyers and as negotiators for their clients. Some labor lawyers also work with employers to create documents such as employee handbooks and employment contracts designed to protect the employer from lawsuits by employees. Labor law involves federal statutes, including the Americans with Disabilities Act (ADA), the Employee Retirement Income Security Act (ERISA*), the National Labor Relations Act (NLRA), and state laws related to workers' compensation and unemployment insurance. Labor lawyers should also be familiar with such matters as sexual harassment, age discrimination, and wrongful termination.

Patent and Trademark Law. Lawyers who practice in the area of patent and trademark law strive to protect the property rights of their clients regarding new inventions and the business symbols that their clients may develop. Patent and trademark attorneys, like copyright attorneys, frequently conduct searches to determine whether inventions or trademarks have been previously claimed or discovered by other parties. Patent and trademark attorneys may be trained as engineers prior to becoming attorneys, as they are often required to examine blueprints or product designs. An individual who seeks to obtain a patent or trademark should deal only with a specialist in this area.

Personal Injury/Medical Malpractice. Attorneys who represent clients in lawsuits concerning accidental injuries or other physical harm, including medical malpractice claims, are referred to as personal injury attorneys. Attorneys defending against personal injury lawsuits are usually defense attorneys or insurance attorneys. Most personal injury attorneys enter into contingent fee agreements, where clients agree to pay a percentage of any judgment awarded in lieu of hourly fees. Lawyers who represent injured parties usually do not work as defense attorneys or insurance attorneys. In medical malpractice litigation, the plaintiff must establish (1) that a physician-patient relationship existed, (2) the applicable standard of care (a national standard), (3) violation of the standard of care, (4) that the injury is compensable, and (5) a causal connection exists between the violation of care and the harm. The plaintiff must produce appropriate expert witnesses to substantiate the claim. Medical malpractice lawyers' charges vary widely. A contingency fee may be based upon an increasing percentage should a case extend over a long period of time, typically from one-fourth to two-thirds of the award, although some states regulate the amount of this percentage.

Real Estate Law. People who buy or sell property may do so without the assistance of an attorney, choosing instead to work with real estate agents and brokers until settlement, which usually involves lawyers skilled in the practice of real estate law. The cost of using an agent or broker*, however, ranges from 3–to–6% of the total transaction cost and is primarily justified when the agent or broker finds a buyer for the property. When a buyer is already known to the seller, however, it is generally less expensive to obtain the services of a real estate attorney, who will typically charge by the hour, rather than a percentage of the transaction. People buying property, on the other hand, are well advised to use real estate attorneys who can assist them with both the legal and transactional complexities of contracting, title work, financing, and settlement.

Tax Law. One of the most highly specialized areas of legal practice is tax law. Many lawyers in this area have additional training beyond their law degrees, evident by such degrees or designations as CPA, MBA, or LLM. Few lawyers are able to practice in the area of tax law while working in other fields because the tax law is quite complex. Tax attorneys assist clients in matters of personal income tax, estate tax, corporate tax, and real estate tax. Within these and other tax areas, lawyers are more particularly trained and highly specialized in civil or criminal tax court matters.

There are many other areas of specialization in the law besides those listed in this article. Any person seeking the services of an attorney should ask for a referral to an attorney who has performed these services in the past. (See also AGENTS AND BROKERS, BANKRUPTCY, BUSINESS SUCCESSION PLANNING, ELDER LAW PRACTICE, ESTATE PLANNING, TRUSTS, and WILLS.)

References

Bonsignore, John J., et al. 1989. *Before the Law: An Introduction to the Legal Process.* Boston: Houghton-Mifflin.

Cohen, Morris R. 1994. *Law and the Social Order: Essays in Legal Philosophy.* Holmes Beach, FL: Wm. W. Gaunt.

Jones, Vivian C. 1994. *Legal Research for Non-Lawyers: A Self-Study Manual.* Washington, DC: Special Libraries Association.

Roth, Bette J., Randall W. Wulff, and Charles A. Cooper. 1993. *The Alternative Dispute Resolution Practice Guide.* New York: Lawyers Cooperative Publishing.

Donald A. Hunsberger

B

BANK ACCOUNTS. See Banking Services for the Mature Market; Individual Retirement Accounts (IRAs); Medical Savings Accounts and Medical IRAs; Savings Account Trusts; Savings Investments; Wealth Span.

BANKING SERVICES FOR THE MATURE MARKET, services and products offered through banks that are of interest to mature adults, including checking and savings accounts, trusts*, annuities*, savings certificates, reverse mortgages*, safety deposit boxes, money orders, traveler's checks, account information, direct deposit, automated teller machines, check balancing, and bill payment, along with education on estate planning*, probate*, and financial management. Only 5% of the 65-and-older population reside in institutions, and most older people live independently in the community. This older population regularly conducts banking activities. In fact, customers who are 50 years old and older use four times as many retail banking services as younger patrons (Sullivan 1990).

Customers over the age of 50 account for 60% of retail bank deposits (Allen 1991), and the average older customer has more than $60,000 in deposits spread across 3.7 institutions (Massie 1989; 1990). Persons 60 and older maintain an average of $6,000 in their savings accounts, while 52% maintain more than $10,000 in savings accounts (*American Demographics* 1983). Most older people have an average of $3,000 more in their checking accounts than other age groups (Sullivan 1990). Checking account customers visit banks about three times a month, while savings account customers visit only three times a year (Massie 1990). Those 50 years old and older own 80% of the money in savings and loans institutions (Champ 1991); 21% of older persons hold certificates of deposit averaging $10,000, and 18% of money market accounts with a median value of $11,000 are held by older customers (England 1987). Major exceptions to this include minority group members, women, and the oldest old (those 85 and older), who often have few assets, little savings, and low security benefits. The needs, preferences, values, and expectations about banking services differ for 60-year-olds and 85-year-olds (Little 1987).

Banking Practices

Older persons, historically, have definite banking preferences and practices. Many experienced the Great Depression and the stock market crash in 1929, followed by bank failures in the 1930s. The majority of people 50 years old or older use multiple banks, as they do not trust all of their financial resources, activities, and outcomes to one bank (Masie 1990).

Skepticism about future financial security is evident in the purchasing behavior of older people. They are more likely to pay in cash, make deposits rather than withdrawals, and look for low-risk and relatively liquid investments. Expectations reflect an era when business transactions were conducted on a personal basis after trust had been established through personal interaction.

One Study on Banking Service Needs and Preferences

A series of focus group discussions, telephone interviews, and personal interviews was conducted in 1992 to explore specific banking service needs of older customers and strategies for providing banking services. A total of 41 persons 50 years old and older and 37 care providers were interviewed in a community of 70,000 people in the upper midwest. Participants were physically and financially independent, well informed, well educated, and middle class. The majority of the older participants in this study were female, widowed, aged 80–89, and had monthly incomes of $967 or less. The care providers were primarily female, married, under 59 years old, and had monthly incomes between $2,168 and $2,767.

Two major fears of older people surfaced: (1) that they will outlive their finances, and (2) that their health will deteriorate and result in their dependence on someone else for care (Sherden 1990). These fears, and sensitivity to discussing financial matters, made it difficult to recruit older participants for the study. They were also reluctant to discuss these private matters in a group setting.

This research showed that about 85% of the older people surveyed received some form of banking assistance, the two most frequent being transportation (55%) and help with banking transactions (51%). Only 3% of those surveyed reported receiving no assistance. The majority of assistance was provided by family members (57%) with whom they were in contact one or more times each week (65%).

Transportation, the number one item of assistance required, was reported as being adequately met. A majority use direct deposit (88%), make few withdrawals each month, and live within five miles of their banks (83%). These banking practices limit the need for visits to the bank. While 74% of the older participants were widowed, they accounted for 100% of the respondents who reported need for assistance with recording bank transactions, balancing check-books, opening an account, applying for a loan (to establish credit), obtaining access to safe-deposit boxes, and writing checks.

Differences were noted between care providers' responses and older partici-pants' responses. Care providers stated that 84% of older persons need assistance with recording transactions, but only 18% of older participants in the study stated this need in the questionnaire. Focus group discussions revealed that older people currently in control of their own financial matters typically were not recording their transactions or balancing their checkbooks, but stated no assis-tance was needed with these tasks. Some participants said a family member did banking for them, yet they also replied in the questionnaire that they did their own banking. This finding suggests that older people feel in control of their finances even when they receive assistance.

Two major themes were identified during focus group discussions and inter-views: (1) bank patronage decisions and pricing; and (2) perceptions of bank personnel, programs, products, and services. The majority of those surveyed were longtime customers of their banks. When accounts were transferred, cus-tomers did so for higher interest returns on investments and accounts, more convenient bank locations or branches, problems that were not satisfactorily resolved, or lack of investment advice. A commonly expressed sentiment was that quality of bank service is falling while fees, charges, and interest rates on loans are rising.

Although older participants in the study generally perceive tellers as friendly, banks consistently were criticized for lacking knowledgeable tellers. There is a general sense of distrust of the information supplied by tellers, as they are per-ceived as minimum wage earners with high turnover rates and a lack of formal banking education and banking experience, and as having difficulty identifying with older customers and their needs.

Older participants do not feel comfortable asking tellers for assistance. They believe their financial information will be held in confidence only by bank of-ficers, but bank officers are perceived as cold and unfriendly. Widows, in par-ticular, are intimidated and afraid to ask for help from bank officers since they often have limited, if any, past contact with them. Older customers expect to be acknowledged by name, and they are offended when asked for identification to make a withdrawal or to cash a check.

Participants were asked to recommend programs, products, and services that, if offered by a new bank in town, would motivate them to open a new account. Participants preferred free checking, premium interest on both checking and savings accounts with no minimum balance, free safe-deposit boxes, larger check blanks, no charge for duplicate checks, financial management advice, and long-term health care insurance. They also wanted help with daily financial concerns such as reading monthly statements, balancing checkbooks, and calculating interest. Seminars on trusts, estate planning, probate, and living wills*, as well as free advice on financial management and on investments with low risk were requested. Large print on monthly statements, no-charge postage for banking by mail, free telephone transfers, tax advice, free travelers checks, no-charge account information, a copy of monthly bank statements for financial managers other than the account holder, and temporary financial management while a caregiver is on vacation were also desired. Automatic teller machines or mobile bank branches that serve the homebound, nursing homes, senior high rises, and senior centers would make banking more convenient for older customers and care providers.

Failure to record and balance checkbooks was generally due to limited recording space and/or memory loss. This laxity in recording and balancing does not seem to be a problem resulting in overdrafts, since older customers write few checks and maintain a high balance. Balancing their accounts tests their memory and serves as a reminder that their memory may be failing. What appears to be forgetfulness may actually be caused by arthritis, failing vision, or hearing difficulties. When information is not heard or seen, it will not be remembered. Duplicate checks can compensate for memory and sensory losses and could also assist care providers. However, for many older people, duplicate checks may be of little value, since the carbon copy is difficult to read and the majority do not record transactions or balance their checkbooks. Care providers favored duplicate checks, as there is a bank charge each month to balance their client's accounts when checks are not recorded.

Large print on monthly statements with bold lettering on the balance figure was recommended. A frequent complaint was that the balance number is in small print, making it difficult to read. Participants who do balance their checkbooks rely on the balance figure provided on their monthly statement. Care providers believed that larger check blanks would enable older people to maintain control over writing their own checks longer, thus providing them with a sense of independence.

Participants did not want to be charged for account information from a bank employee. They definitely preferred information from bank employees over the phone rather than from a telephone computer system. They tolerated computer information only until they had an opportunity to talk with a bank employee to confirm the computer's answers. They felt they deserved special discounts or rates on services and products, especially when the services were perceived as of little or no cost for banks to offer. For example, participants said they generally maintain high balances in their checking accounts so the idea of premium interest without having to maintain a minimum balance was appealing.

Six of the participants used ATMs and a seventh had used them until the fee increased to $2 per transaction. For all ATM users, a family member had demonstrated the use of the machine for deposits and withdrawals. In general, older participants distrusted ATMs because they did not understand the computer system connecting various banking sites, preferred the social experience of banking in person, feared being mugged while using ATMs in remote or outside areas, and sometimes had difficulty with the small buttons on the machines. These findings are similar to those of Sherden (1990), who found that ATMs were most often used by men 55 to 64 years old (55%) and least used by women 65 to 75 years old (28%). Overall, 29% of the Sherden sample used ATMs. However, when the participants were provided with ATM cards and instructions along with a free three-month trial period, 100% said they would continue to use their ATM card.

What Banks Can Do for Their Mature Patrons

Although there are data available on the financial status of mature adults, not much is known about why older customers patronize or change banks, and there is a lack of information about the needs and preferences of older customers in regard to banking personnel, products, and services. Not much thought has been put into making the physical and social banking environment and communication techniques appropriate for mature customers.

A common banking service problem identified in the interviews was poor access to information. Older participants were also found to value a bank that can offer convenience, reliability, security, and a sense of independence. The three services older participants wanted most from their banks were higher interest returns, free services, and personal attention.

It is clear that banking institutions must give attention to customer service, pricing, and marketing strategies, along with new or modified programs, products, and services. Customer services to mature adults can be improved by providing suitable physical and social banking environments. A reduced ability to communicate resulting from visual problems, hearing deterioration, and/or loss of strength does not mean that the older person's mental ability has deteriorated. Such changes should not impede anyone's banking activities.

Furthermore, there is a need to recognize not only that the mature banking customer in the future will be different from today's customer, but also that there will be increasing diversity within the older population. (See also ANNUITIES, ESTATE PLANNING, LIVING WILLS, PROBATE, REVERSE MORTGAGES, SAVINGS ACCOUNT TRUSTS, and SAVINGS INVESTMENTS.)

References

Allen, Pat. 1991. "Do Your Seniors Get the Royal Treatment?" *Savings Institutions* (April), 18–23.

"Discretionary Income." 1983. *American Demographics* (December), 12–13.

Champ, Rita. 1991. "Myths of the Mature Market." *Bank Management* (September), 47–49.

England, Robert. 1987. "Greener Era for Gray America." *Insight* (March), 8–11.

Little, Michael. 1987. "Assessing Lifeline Banking Services." *Journal of Retail Banking* (Summer), 41–49.

Massie, Marcy. 1989. "Don't Take Seniors for Granted." *Bank Marketing* (November).

Massie, Marcy. 1990. "Package Deal for the Mature Market." *Bottomline* (March), 79–
    83.
Sherden, William. 1990. "The Mature Market Starts to Grow Up." *Bankers Magazine*
    (July-August), 36–41.
Sullivan, Michael. 1990. "Senior—Today's Hottest Market." *U.S. Banker* (June), 16–
    22.

Lori Janus and Linda Havir

BANKRUPTCY, a set of legal procedures for dealing with severe debt problems. Nearly one million Americans each year file bankruptcy cases to seek relief from debts. Older persons are underrepresented in bankruptcy filings, as they tend to be financially better established and less likely to be involved in aggressive or risky activities. Nevertheless, elderly bankruptcy filers each year total at least in the tens of thousands.

Debt problems can coincide with poverty, but they are not the same thing. A person having substantial assets and income and a comfortable lifestyle can become financially overextended from either a precipitous drop in income or surge in debt, while someone with extremely limited means may be financially stable with few or no debts. If necessary, bankruptcy can eliminate or modify debts sufficiently to give the petitioning debtor a financial fresh start.

There are two types of bankruptcy cases ordinarily applicable to individuals: (1) Chapter 7 Bankruptcy, and (2) Chapter 13 Bankruptcy, named for the sections of the law that provide for them. A Chapter 7 case is sometimes referred to as "straight bankruptcy," and formally is called a "liquidation" case, referring to the potential sale of the petitioning debtor's property for cash to pay debts. In most cases, however, little or no property is actually sold. The primary effect of a Chapter 7 case is usually the discharge or cancellation of some or all debts. The personal bankruptcy alternative is a Chapter 13 debt adjustment plan, under which the petitioner makes at least partial payment on debts through the court, usually over three to five years. Individuals are also eligible, under certain conditions, to file a Chapter 11 Bankruptcy Proceeding, a reorganization option designed primarily for corporations and other businesses.

Bankruptcy cases are governed by federal law (Title 11, U.S. Code) and are handled in a special branch of federal court. Each state has one or more federal court districts, depending on population, and some districts have offices in more than one city or conduct some court hearings in cities other than where the court offices are located.

The Bankruptcy Process

A bankruptcy case is initiated with the filing of a petition (a short formal invocation of the law) and a prescribed group of disclosure forms with an office of the bankruptcy court. The disclosure forms include lists of debts and assets, statements of income and expenses, and certain other financial information. In a Chapter 13 case, the petitioner also files a specific plan for making payments through the court. A husband and wife can file a joint petition under either chapter.

The filing triggers a sweeping court order that prohibits further debt collection efforts by creditors against the petitioning debtor while the bankruptcy case is pending. This prohibition, known as an "automatic stay," halts legal proceedings such as lawsuits, federal and state tax collections, wage garnishments, and foreclosures, and it also stops collection letters and telephone calls. With regard to many creditors, this prohibition is destined to become permanent through a later "discharge of debts" court order. Even creditors who are not subject to the permanent discharge are temporarily restrained by the automatic stay from attempting to collect.

There is a mandatory court appearance about one month or longer after the filing, depending upon the jurisdiction. The hearing is formally called a meeting of creditors, although creditors need not attend and rarely do. At the hearing, a trustee who has been appointed by the court to review the case requests the debtor to verify under oath that the information in the filing is accurate, and requests additional information as necessary. A routine Chapter 7 case may be essentially complete at that point. If no creditor objects and the trustee does not seek to sell any of the debtor's property, the court will issue the order discharging debts and close the case within as few as four months from the filing.

In a Chapter 13 case, the debt repayment plan is submitted after the meeting of creditors for approval or confirmation by the judge. The trustee makes a recommendation for or against confirmation based on his or her analysis of the legality and financial feasibility of the plan. Creditors may also object, and a hearing is held by the judge if necessary. If the plan is confirmed, payments through the trustee proceed, and if denied, the petitioner usually has three choices: amend the plan and try again, switch to a Chapter 7, or dismiss the case and deal with the debts outside of bankruptcy law.

Dischargeable and Non-Dischargeable Debts

Many types of debts may be discharged in a bankruptcy case, assuming that the debtor meets the tests and requirements of the law. There are two groups of exceptions: bankruptcy law classifies certain types of debts as non-dischargeable; and most liens, including real estate mortgages and automobile purchase loans, remain valid after a bankruptcy.

More specifically, most taxes are non-dischargeable, although income taxes that have been due for at least three years are usually dischargeable if no fraud exists. Alimony and child support payments (past or future) owed by the debtor are non-dischargeable. A debt owed by one spouse to another to balance a divorce property settlement, however, may be discharged. Some student loans are not dischargeable, unless seven years have passed from the date payments began. This rule is usually interpreted also to apply to parents or others who have co-signed a student loan.

A debt resulting from the use of a false financial statement by the debtor or from actual fraud is not covered by a discharge. A debt arising from embezzlement, larceny, or deliberate injury to property is non-dischargeable. Criminal fines and restitution are non-dischargeable. Claims or court awards for death or personal injury from an auto accident in which the debtor was driving while impaired by alcohol or other drugs is non-dischargeable. Other auto accident claims involving property damage only, or based only on ordinary negligence, are dischargeable.

Mechanisms for creditors claiming an exception to discharge varies. An adversary action may be filed by a creditor opposing discharge of a debt, fraud, embezzlement, larceny, and injury to property exceptions are subject to a filing deadline in the bankruptcy court, and other exceptions require no particular steps by the creditor since by their nature they are non-dischargeable. Unless a specific exception applies, virtually any debt or financial obligation can be discharged in bankruptcy.

Mortgages and Liens

Real estate mortgages, automobile liens, and other liens against property of the debtor usually are unaffected by a bankruptcy filing. Most creditors retain the right to go after the property for at least partial payment of the debt. Liens on household goods or similar personal property, however, that have declined in value from the original purchase price of the collateral usually are cancelled outright in the bankruptcy, as are liens arising from many lawsuits and court judgments.

When a lien does survive a bankruptcy, the debtor generally has three choices for dealing with the situation afterward: (1) the debtor can keep the collateral and keep paying the loan (home mortgages and car loans are often handled in this way); (2) the debtor can surrender the collateral and discharge the debt; or (3) the debtor can negotiate new payments based on the value of the collateral. Where the amount of the debt exceeds the value of the collateral, creditors are often willing to negotiate a new deal.

Bankruptcy Effects on Property

To obtain a discharge of debts under Chapter 7, the petitioning debtor must submit his or her property for possible sale to retire debts, as far as it will go. In fact, however, little or no property usually is sold this way. There are two classes of property not subject to sale, and these exceptions often cover all of the debtor's property. The first exception is for property subject to a lien or mortgage. For example, a debtor owning a $100,000 home free of debt would, in most states, be forced to accept a sale of the house, with some or all of the proceeds going to creditors. If the home were subject to a $100,000 mortgage, however, the home and mortgage would ordinarily pass through the bankruptcy case unaffected. This principle usually applies as well to automobiles and other collateralized property. The second exception involves ''exempt property.''

Actual exempt property rules vary greatly from state to state, and where federal exemptions apply, the debtor may keep specific property even while unpaid debts are permanently discharged. All values are based on net value or "equity" above the amount of any liens and are doubled for a joint husband and wife filing. Property values in federal exemptions are $3,750 in homestead equity; $1,200 in a motor vehicle; $4,000 in household furnishings and personal apparel; $4,000 in life insurance cash value; all social security benefits and nearly all pension accounts; certain other small amounts or specialized items; and $4,150 in the debtor's choice of any property, including additional amounts of the specific categories just listed. Exempt property laws in some states are more generous, including homestead exemptions that range up to $100,000 and, in a few states, such exemptions for homes with no dollar limit at all. Some states, however, have property exemptions that are more limited than the federal exemptions.

Causes of Bankruptcy

Every case is different, but a few basic themes occur in nearly all bankruptcies. The most frequent cause is unemployment, and illness or injury is often a factor. A sudden drop in income is the simplest way of turning a reasonable debt load into an unmanageable one. A significant minority of the population is vulnerable to incurring medical expenses beyond insurance benefits and/or their ability to pay directly. For a person in the work force, medical problems can also interfere with income. Divorce or separation usually increases expenses without increasing resources. Business failures often leave an owner with substantial debts. Poor planning and irresponsible use of credit are less pervasive causes of bankruptcy than is widely assumed, but they do occur.

Regardless of the origin of debt problems, some individuals endure years of collection calls and letters, and even legal proceedings, without filing or even considering bankruptcy. Others realize they are headed for serious trouble, and begin to take steps toward filing bankruptcy before they actually miss a payment.

Chapter 13 Repayment Plan

Many more Chapter 7 bankruptcy cases are filed each year than Chapter 13 debt repayment cases. This is not surprising, as a Chapter 7 bankruptcy produces a prompt discharge of debts, while a Chapter 13 requires a lengthy series of payments through the court, usually over three years. There are several reasons, however, why a few choose Chapter 13.

A debtor having property that is unprotected by exemption laws or liens, which would be lost in a Chapter 7, may be able to keep his or her property by filing under Chapter 13. Chapter 13 rules allow a debtor to catch up on and reinstate a home mortgage, even after the lender initiates foreclosure and refuses to negotiate. To make this process work, the debtor must continue to make both the required original payments plus catch-up payments. A Chapter 13 filing may be used by a debtor with a recent Chapter 7 discharge, since while the same debtor cannot receive another Chapter 7 discharge for a prescribed number of years, it is possible to file again under Chapter 13. Sequential filings often indicate than an individual has serious underlying problems and may be in need of financial or other counseling.

A few kinds of debts that are classified as non-dischargeable in a Chapter 7 bankruptcy, including some accident and injury claims, can be discharged in a Chapter 13 even if only a small percentage is paid through the court. Additionally, a debtor can sometimes use Chapter 13 to pay a debt while preventing the creditor from going after a co-signer. In practice, however, the same result can usually be achieved with voluntary payments after a Chapter 7 filing.

Bankruptcy and Credit Ratings

Most people considering bankruptcy are concerned about their credit rating, but this should not be a substantial factor in the decision-making process. If debt problems are serious enough to consider bankruptcy, resolving existing debts must be the overriding concern. A bankruptcy filing may actually improve access to credit. It removes most current debt, always a key factor in new credit decisions, and assures there will be no further Chapter 7 filings for many years. Where overextended credit is the cause of bankruptcy, taking steps toward future borrowing may be unwise. While some assume that a Chapter 13 repayment filing is preferable from a future-credit perspective, there is no foundation for this belief.

Hiring a Bankruptcy Lawyer

Bankruptcy is a specialized area of law. Persons with debt problems should take care to locate attorneys* who are experienced in bankruptcy law. Unless the matter is urgent, comparison shopping for a lawyer is highly recommended. While it is legally possible to file without the assistance of a lawyer, the law is complex enough to make this a risky course. If the debtor does not have enough property or income at stake to justify the attorney's fees, the stakes probably do not justify bankruptcy either. (See also ATTORNEYS, CREDIT CARDS, ELDER LAW PRACTICE, HOMEOWNERSHIP, and LIFE INSURANCE.)

References

American Institute of Certified Public Accountants, Tax Division. 1992. *Bankruptcy Tax Practice Reference Guide*. Washington, DC: AICPA.

Cowans, Daniel R. 1994. *Cowans Bankruptcy Law and Practice*. St. Paul, MN: West Publishers.

Doran, K. 1991. *Personal Bankruptcy and Debt Adjustment*. New York: Random House.

Haman, Edward A. 1994. *How to File Your Own Bankruptcy (Or How To Avoid It): With Forms*. Clearwater, FL: Sphinx Publishers.

Sullivan, J., E. Warren, and J. Westbrook. 1989. *As We Forgive Our Debtors*. Oxford: Oxford University Press.

U.S. Congress, House Committee on the Judiciary. 1994a. *Bankruptcy Amendments of 1994*. Washington, DC: U.S. Government Printing Office.

U.S. Congress, House Committee on the Judiciary. 1994b. *Bankruptcy Reform.* Washington, DC: U.S. Government Printing Office.

Kenneth J. Doran

BOARD AND CARE HOMES, residential settings that provide more support services than boarding or rooming houses and most congregate apartments, but usually not the level of care that persons receive in a nursing home. They are usually defined as non-medical, community-based residential settings that house two or more unrelated adults and provide room, meals, protective oversight or supervision, and some type of assistance or personal care, such as medication supervision or reminders, help with bathing, dressing, and other daily activities, organized activities, and transportation to medical appointments. Board and care homes are typically thought of as being small and providing residential care in a more home-like environment than nursing homes.

Both policymakers and the elderly and their families have sought to expand the range of alternatives by which persons who have chronic illnesses or disabilities, or need assistance with basic activities of daily living, can receive care. Families are the major source of such care and assistance to the elderly, providing more than 75% of long-term care. But other arrangements support the efforts of families when more care than the family can provide is needed, or no family members are available. These include nursing homes, adult day care programs, home health care, and a variety of residential settings with support services, including congregate apartments and board and care homes.

Characteristics of Board and Care

There is considerable variation across the country in what board and care homes look like, whom they serve, their cost, and regulation. They are known by more than thirty different names, including personal care homes, rest homes, domiciliary care homes, residential care homes, adult congregate living facilities, homes for the aged, adult foster care homes, and assisted living facilities. Estimates of the number of homes vary across studies, but a recent comprehensive survey of the 50 states and the District of Columbia, conducted for the American Association of Retired Persons (AARP), found approximately 32,000 board and care homes that serve an elderly population and also include some younger persons with disabilities (Hawes et al. 1993). Between 34,000 and 36,000 facilities, including board and care homes and group homes, are specifically licensed to serve only a special population, such as persons with chronic mental illness or developmental disabilities (Clark et al. 1994). There are approximately 600,000 beds in licensed board and care homes of various types, mostly serving the elderly population.

There are an unknown number of unlicensed homes, including small homes and assisted living facilities that, in some states, are not required to be licensed. Some homes have avoided licensing and operate illegally (Hawes et al. 1993). While no definitive number is available, estimates are between 20,000 and

30,000 (U.S. House of Representatives 1989). These unlicensed facilities also vary greatly and include personal residences, larger multiunit retirement facilities, and assisted living facilities.

Board and care homes vary from two beds in private homes to more than 1,400 beds in highrise buildings. While most homes are small, with between two and 10 beds, most residents of board and care homes live in larger facilities. A recent study funded by the U.S. Department of Health and Human Services (DHHS), conducted by the Research Triangle Institute (RTI), found that while 67% of licensed homes have 10 or fewer beds, nearly two-thirds of residents are in homes with 11 or more beds (Hawes et al. 1994). One-third reside in facilities with 51 or more beds. More than half reside in unlicensed homes with more than 51 beds. These larger unlicensed homes include assisted living facilities and retirement communities that provide meals, protective oversight, and some services. More than 80% of licensed homes are for-profit facilities. Eighty percent of unlicensed homes are for-profit facilities and 40% are nonprofit.

In addition to size, board and care homes vary in terms of the physical environment, monthly charges, services, and mix of residents. They vary from three to four residents to a room in modest surroundings to private apartments with plush settings. Most have common areas with community or living rooms and outside sitting areas, although only about half allow residents access to a kitchen to fix a snack. Homes also vary in homelike or institutional environment and in whether residents may bring furniture or only a few possessions.

Homes also vary in mix of residents. Some homes have a mainly elderly mix of residents. Data from the 10-state RTI study found that more than 60% of the 3,200 residents were 75 or older; more than 30% were 85 or older. Other homes, though not specifically licensed as such, house mainly persons with persistent mental illness or developmental disabilities. In states where the use of psychiatric hospitals has been reduced, board and care homes are an important alternative for the mentally ill. Other homes include: frail elderly; persons with cognitive impairment; dementia, such as Alzheimer's Disease; mental illness; and developmental disabilities. Moreover, board and care homes are also coping with more complex problems. Forty-three percent of homes report having residents with alcohol abuse problems, and 14% report drug abuse problems. Some states are also finding that board and care homes are increasingly being used to provide shelter for persons who have been homeless (Hawes et al. 1994).

To meet the needs of this amazing mix of residents, board and care homes offer a wide range of services. More than 90% of licensed homes report providing three meals a day, laundry, some personal care such as bathing and dressing, storage, and supervision and assistance with administration of medications. More than 80% of the licensed homes report providing organized activities, recreational trips, and transportation to medical appointments. Only 25% report providing nursing care by a licensed nurse, but half report that outside agencies provide nursing care. Homes vary on whether residents who need nursing care may stay in the home. Some states, such as Florida and Oregon, allow daily nursing care to be provided in some classes of board and care homes, while others limit the services such homes may provide.

Payment and Regulation

Regulation of board and care homes is largely a state responsibility, and each state sets its own standards. Unlike nursing homes, no federal quality of care and life or safety standards exist for board and care homes, nor is there any federal policy on payment. As a result, in most states, the care of residents is paid by residents or their families, or the federal Supplemental Security Income* program. SSI, available to persons who are poor and aged, blind, or disabled, is the main source of public funds for board and care, although some states also use Medicaid* funds to pay for some services to residents, usually through waiver programs that are available to only a limited number of persons. In addition, in all but 10 states (as of 1991), the state will supplement the federal SSI payment with a state assistance payment. The AARP study, conducted by RTI, found that state supplemental payments for SSI recipients range from a few dollars per month to more than $600 per month. In 1990, the total public payments available from SSI and State Supplemental Payments (SSP) ranged from $383 per month per resident in the 10 states that did not supplement all SSI residents, to more than $1,000; however, in 38 states and the District of Columbia in 1990, the total monthly payment (SSI plus SSP) per resident was less than $685 per month (Hawes et al. 1993). The RTI study for DHHS found that, in 1993, 81% of the SSI rates with state supplements ranged from $400 per month to $700 per month. These monthly rates generally cover room, board, personal laundry, special diets, and assistance with eating, dressing, and toileting. However, in about one-fifth of the licensed homes, there is an additional charge if the resident needs a special diet or personal assistance with eating, dressing and toileting, and three-fourths of the homes charge extra for incontinence supplies. Among unlicensed homes, almost half charged extra for special diets, 35% added charges for personal laundry, and 30% charged extra if the resident needed help with personal care. Private pay rates ranged from $600 per month up to $4,200 per month; 74% of the rates were between $800 and $4,200 per month (Hawes et al. 1994).

Just as there is tremendous variability across homes and across states in terms of payment policies, considerable variation is found across the states in the nature of the regulatory system established to ensure resident safety, quality of care, and quality of life. Studies have noted these variations and raised questions about the effectiveness of state regulation in ensuring adequate quality of care and life, as well as safety, in board and care homes (U.S. Department of Health and Human Services 1990; General Accounting Office 1989; U.S. House of Representatives 1989). The study by RTI for AARP found that there are more than 62 agencies in the 50 states and District of Columbia that license board and care homes (under different names), ranging from departments of health to offices on aging. Inspection of homes ranges from monthly in one state to every

18–24 months in another, although a majority of states inspect homes once a year. Some notify homes in advance of inspection, while others conduct unannounced inspections. Some use nurses or social workers to inspect homes, while others rely on generalists or sanitarians. Fire departments inspect all licensed homes in all states. States also vary in terms of how they deal with homes that fail to comply with the minimum standards set for health and safety (Hawes at al. 1993).

Information for Consumers

The variability across homes and states offers many positive possibilities to consumers, but also makes gathering and evaluating information prior to selecting a board and care home absolutely essential. Consumers can choose small homes with a more personal environment, large facilities offering a wide range of services, a shared room, or a private apartment. They can seek homes with a relatively homogenous set of residents or homes with a mix of younger and older persons having a range of conditions and needs. They can select homes that provide minimal assistance or a wide range of services that will vary as the resident's needs change. Choices include homes with protective and specialized environments, and homes that offer a less structured environment and greater autonomy.

Consumers and their families should consider what aspects of the environment—physical setting and amenities, services provided, and philosophy about care—are most important. They should consider how the home will address changing needs over time and what will happen if private funds are exhausted and help from public programs, such as SSI or Medicaid, is needed to pay for care. Thus, the consumer and his or her family may wish to know in advance:

- What range of services does the home offer?

- What activities are available? Does the home arrange transportation to senior centers, shopping, entertainment, and medical appointments?

- What autonomy and choices are available? Do residents decide about bedtime? Can they fix a meal or eat a snack? Can residents close their door for privacy? Do staff knock on the door before entering the room? Is there assigned seating at meals? Must residents get permission to leave the facility for the day? What are the policies on visiting hours?

- Is there a residents' council that participates in setting policies and addressing problems or complaints? Is there a residents' bill of rights?

- How will a temporary illness or change in condition requiring more assistance or nursing care be handled?

- Does the home have an existing arrangement with a home health agency or temporary nursing service, and if so, what is the reputation of that agency?

- Will the home allow hospice care if the resident has a terminal illness and wishes to remain in the home until death?

- What is the home's policy and practice on the use of physical restraints?
- If the resident needs help taking medications, who in the home provides such assistance or supervision, and what are their qualifications?
- What does the home do to help residents maintain their maximum physical, social, and cognitive functioning?
- What is the resident mix?
- What is the monthly rate? What does it cover? What is extra? What happens if the resident changes from private pay to SSI or some other public payment?
- What is the home's policy on discharging residents?
- Who licenses or regulates the home? Who acts on complaints or helps resolve problems that may arise?

Several agencies or groups help consumers and their families evaluate homes and make choices, and they often have local chapters and guides. Long-term care ombudsmen*, well-known for their important and positive role in nursing homes, can be accessed through local or area agencies on aging, and visit residents in board and care homes to help resolve problems or complaints. The National Citizens' Coalition for Nursing Home Reform (NCCNHR) has become increasingly active in helping consumers and their families with issues related to board and care. Finally, state licensing agencies and national and state-level associations representing board and care homes can provide information and address complaints filed or problems brought before them. (See also HOME CARE SERVICES FOR THE ELDERLY, MEDICAID, NURSING HOMES, OMBUDSMAN, and SUPPLEMENTAL SECURITY INCOME.)

Organizations

Alzheimer's Association
American Association of Retired Persons
American Association of Services and Homes for the Aging
American Health Care Association
Assisted Living Facilities Association of America
National Association of State Long-Term Care Ombudsman Programs
National Citizens' Coalition for Nursing Home Reform
Older Women's League

References

Clark, R. F., J. Turek-Brezina, C. Chu, and C. Hawes. 1994. "Licensed Board and Care Homes: Findings from the 1991 National Health Provider Inventory." Paper presented at the Annual Meeting of the Gerontological Society of America, Atlanta.

General Accounting Office. 1989. *Board and Care: Insufficient Assurances That Resident Needs Are Identified and Met.* Washington, DC: Author.

Hawes, C., V. Mor, and F. Brown. 1994. "The Effect of Regulation on Quality of Care in Board and Care Homes: Results From a 10-State Study." Paper presented at the Annual Meeting of the Gerontological Society of America, Atlanta.

Hawes, C., J. Wildfire, and L. Lux. 1993. *The Regulation of Board and Care Homes:*

Results of a Survey in the 50 States and the District of Columbia: National Summary. Washington, DC: AARP.

U.S. Department of Health and Human Services, Office of the Inspector General. 1990. *Board and Care.* Washington, DC: US DHHS.

U.S. House of Representatives, Select Committee on Aging. 1989. *Board and Care Homes in America: A National Tragedy.* Washington, DC: GPO.

Catherine Hawes

BOETTNER CENTER OF FINANCIAL GERONTOLOGY. The applied research agenda of the Boettner Center of Financial Gerontology at the School of Social Work of the University of Pennsylvania embraces both population aging and individual aging, and focuses on the multiple relationships among demographic trends, individual attitudes, financial security, and life satisfaction during the life cycle and across generations. The center pays particular attention to the economic and demographic characteristics of the baby boom, and how its middle-aging shapes the financial perceptions, fears, and expectations of the United States in the 1990s and in the first decades of the twenty-first century.

The First Generation: The Origins of Financial Gerontology and the Boettner Institute

The origins of the Boettner Institute are rooted in the vision of two far-sighted, charitable men, Joseph E. Boettner and Davis W. Gregg, a successful businessman and a successful educator, respectively. Born in 1903, Joseph Emery Boettner entered the insurance business almost accidentally. A star high school athlete, he was recruited to play in the semi-pro intramural teams of Philadelphia's booming insurance industry. A few years later he and a few friends purchased the failing Philadelphia Life Insurance Company for $1 per share and built it into a successful company. His post–high school education came from the American College of Life Underwriters, the professional training division of the University of Pennsylvania Wharton School's academically oriented insurance curriculum. The college became independent of the university in 1927, and Mr. Boettner earned his Chartered Life Underwriter (CLU) designation in 1934.

Born in 1918, Davis Weinert Gregg graduated from the University of Texas and earned his doctorate in economics from the University of Pennsylvania in 1947, where he studied under the legendary Wharton professor of insurance Solomon S. Huebner, founder of the American College of Life Underwriters. Dr. Gregg was on the faculty of Stanford University when Professor Huebner asked him to come back to the insurance college for a short time. Dr. Gregg's "short time" spanned four decades, and he served as president of the college for twenty-eight years.

During these years, the high school athlete from West Philadelphia and the Wharton Ph.D. from Texas developed a life-long relationship that evolved into brotherly love. Mr. Boettner began using his wealth to support higher education, endowing chairs at Penn State University, Temple University, and The American College. Although the academic focus of these gifts was insurance research and education, personal experience and changing business perspectives, as he grew older, expanded his opinions about the educational needs of the life insurance industry. He came to realize that he was outliving his accountant, his lawyer, his dentist, his doctor, and other important professionals in his life. While his own financial resources allowed him to deal with these changes successfully, he thought about the average older person facing similar challenges and setbacks, and how appropriate education could be channeled to meet such challenges.

Davis Gregg's intellectual and administrative leadership transformed the nature of The American College of Life Underwriters. Its original professional designation, the Chartered Life Underwriter focused on life insurance. However, elaborate insurance products such as whole life and universal life insurance now serves a combined insurance and investment function. Dr. Gregg also expanded the educational offerings of his college and created a second professional designation, the Chartered Financial Consultant (ChFC) in recognition of the societal need for a corps of financial advisors.

By the 1980s, Mr. Boettner's concerns about old age and citizen education began to merge with Mr. Gregg's insights about the need for more comprehensive professional education in life insurance and financial services. From these joint concerns came the idea of a new research institute that would focus on the interconnections between personal finance and insurance and social gerontology. Gerontology was a growing academic field, but questions remained: Was there a need for such a focused education and research organization, and if the need did exist, was the highly specialized American College the appropriate site for such an institute?

With a small gift from Mr. Boettner, Dr. Gregg established a Study Committee of nationally known gerontologists to explore these two questions. It met over a two-year period and agreed on four organizing principles: (1) that there was indeed a need for specialized research that combined gerontology with financial planning; (2) that a social gerontology research center could succeed at a small specialized business school; (3) that the permanent director of the institute should be an experienced gerontologist because the resources for insurance research and education would be provided by the college's faculty; and (4) that the new institute should be communicating gerontological concerns to insurance and financial professionals, and simultaneously, finance issues to gerontologists.

The Second Generation: A National Program of Applied Financial Gerontology Research

On July 4, 1986, The American College officially established the Boettner Research Institute, soon renamed to reflect its financial gerontology content and focus, and recruited Dr. Neal E. Cutler as the new, permanent director.

From 1989 to 1991 Gregg, Boettner, and Cutler, with the assistance of a national Research Advisory Committee of gerontology, insurance, and finance academics and practitioners, developed a framework for applied research in financial gerontology. The initial professional and public recognition of the importance of financial gerontology exceeded the expectations of the institute's founders. A broader set of academic skills and interests than originally envisioned were necessary to meet the challenge of this new field. So in 1992, the Boettner Institute became chartered as a nonprofit charitable educational corporation, with an independently appointed board of trustees of prominent business and gerontology academics and practitioners. The trustees voted to move the Boettner Institute from The American College and accept an invitation to become affiliated with the University of Pennsylvania in Philadelphia.

The Boettner Lectures. The keynote lecture given in 1987 by Dr. George Maddox of Duke University, at a research symposium convened to celebrate the launching of the Boettner Institute, defined the beginning of an annual series of national lectures alternating between gerontology and finance specialists. The lecture is regularly scheduled to be given in October in the Gregg Educational Conference Center on the campus of The American College. The Boettner Lectures have included:

George L. Maddox (1987), *Age and Well-Being.*

William C. Greenough (1989), *Critical Policy Issues for Pensions.*

Matilda White Riley (1990), *Aging in the Twenty-First Century.*

Davis W. Gregg (1992), *The Human Wealth Span: A Life Span View of Financial Well-Being.*

Linda K. George (1993), *Financial Security in Later Life: The Subjective Side.*

James E. Birren (1994), *Age, Information, and Consumer Decisions-Making: Maintaining Resources and Independence.*

Dallas L. Salisbury (1995), *Recent Trends in Pensions, Benefits, and Retirement: In-House Research.*

Early research analyzed the impact of trends in middle-aging versus older-aging on savings, retirement, health care, and long-term care. Although the consequences of increasing longevity for Social Security and Medicare are widely recognized, less well-known is the impact of longevity on family structure. Such demographic and social changes define a fundamental proposition of the Boettner Institute's research and education activities: that financial decisions are family decisions. Because a rapidly aging population is found in virtually all economically advanced countries, in the next 25 years Boettner Institute research will have an international as well as national focus.

Extramural Research Grants. A national program of small grants to researchers at academic institutions, including doctoral dissertation fellowships, is directed to expanding the pool of ideas, issues, data sources, and researchers contributing to the development of financial gerontology. Projects funded by the Institute have examined, for example, the profile of net worth among older households; the financial and social characteristics of "DIPPIES"—dual-earner couples who have double income (DI) while working and Plural Pensions (PP) in retirement; age and cohort patterns in consumer expenditures; trends in long-term care insurance* as an employee benefit; and financial characteristics of early retirees. Boettner Dissertation Fellows have studied such varied topics as methodological problems in the measurement of age in the U.S. census, the nature of economic competition in the nursing home industry, demographic trends in the purchase of life insurance, and the role of family members in providing home care to older relatives.

Financial Journalism: The Bimonthly Financial Gerontology Column. One of Joseph Boettner's central goals in endowing the institute was to facilitate communication of gerontological insights and research findings to the insurance and financial services profession. The American Society of CLU & ChFC is the professional association of men and women who received their CLU and ChFC designations from The American College (of Life Underwriters) in Bryn Mawr, Pennsylvania. The bimonthly *Journal of the American Society of CLU & ChFC*, received by 35,000 members of the society, regularly includes a series of professional practice columns with each issue's research articles. In 1990, the American Society invited Dr. Cutler to add a new Financial Gerontology column to the *Journal*'s regular offerings. More than 25 columns written since then have covered a broad range of topics, some with business and marketing orientations, others emphasizing aging concerns and the linkages between gerontological research and insurance and financial services.

The Future

Within one year to the day, the two founders of the Boettner Institute of Financial Gerontology passed away: Davis Weinert Gregg on October 27, 1993, and Joseph Emery Boettner on October 27, 1994. But the fundamental mission of their institute—to respond to the financial needs of an aging society through development of academically robust linkages between financial and gerontological educators, professionals, and service providers—continues to develop on the foundation they established. Substantively, the institute maintains its interest in the patterns and impact of middle-aging on retirement, families, health, and financial planning in the United States and other countries and new research themes begun in mid-1994 will be developed over the next several years.

Two organizational developments give the Boettner Institute staff and trustees new resources to more fully realize the mission of creating stronger linkages among financial and gerontological practitioners. The institute's activities at the University of Pennsylvania have expanded to include collaboration with the School of Social Work, where it has been relocated, and it is now known as the Boettner Center of Financial Gerontology. Because of social work's practitioner degree programs and clinical research agenda, the Boettner Center will be involved with faculty and students whose interests focus on the development of knowledge and skills relevant to financial and gerontological professionals and service providers.

In the months following Dr. Gregg's unexpected death, Mr. Boettner developed and implemented plans for a permanent educational memorial to his friend: He endowed the Joseph Boettner/Davis Gregg Chair in Financial Gerontology at Widener University in Chester, Pennsylvania, near Philadelphia. While the Boettner Center at the School of Social Work, University of Pennsylvania, will continue to emphasize applied research, the Boettner/Gregg Chair in Financial Gerontology at Widener University will emphasize professional education in such applied human service fields as business, health administration, social work, legal studies, nursing, and clinical psychology, as these and other departments at Widener incorporate financial gerontology into their curricula and degree programs. Mr. Boettner further specified that the activities of the new Chair at Widener be developed in close coordination with the Boettner Center. Toward that end, and in keeping with Mr. Boettner's wishes, Widener University announced in 1994 that Dr. Cutler would be the first holder of the Boettner/ Gregg Chair. Thus, the vision of applied research and education in financial gerontology of two life-long friends, a businessman and an academic, comes full circle in an institute and a chair that link their names and their insights. (See also SOCIAL WORK, GERONTOLOGICAL; HEALTH AND LONGEVITY; and WEALTH SPAN.)

References

Cutler, N. E. 1994. ''Understanding the Senior Market in 1995: Three Principles of Financial Gerontology.'' *Broker World* (May), 30–35.

Cutler, N. E., D. W. Gregg, and M. P. Lawton. 1992. *Aging, Money, and Life Satisfaction Aspects of Financial Gerontology.* New York: Springer.

Doyle, R. J., K. B. Tacchino, T. Kurlowicz, N. E. Cutler, and J. A. Schnepper. 1992. *Can You Afford to Retire?* Chicago: Probus.

Gregg, D. W. 1990. ''Introduction to Financial Gerontology.'' *Journal of the American Society of CLU & ChFC* (November), 9.

Gregg, D. W. and N. E. Cutler. 1990. *Financial Gerontology and the Middle-Aging of People and Populations: Implications for Future Planning in Insurance World-Wide.* Paris: Proceedings of the International Insurance Society.

Neal E. Cutler

BONDS, financial contracts between lenders and borrowers in which a borrower agrees to repay a loan with interest according to a prearranged timetable. Most bonds have terms of 7–30 years, and differ from other types of loan contracts by being brought to market by an investment bank for a borrower (the issuer), and then traded in financial markets. Bonds are well suited to retired investors wanting a steady cash income stream over long periods of time.

Until the 1970s, bond investing was uncomplicated, with most investors pursuing simple buy-and-hold strategies. Investors needing to sell their bonds benefited from stable bond prices. Defaults were rare because borrowers were of high-quality credit, and these factors combined to make bonds fairly safe investments. Since the 1970s, however, investing in bonds has become more complex due to greater price volatility, a decline in the credit quality of borrowers, and a spate of bond market innovations. While bonds can still be safe investments, greater care is needed in selecting them.

The Basic Bond Contract

The most common type of bond is a promise by the issuer to make payments of interest over the term of the bond, and to repay the principal (face amount) of the bond when it is due. If the bond is purchased at a price below the face value, the yield to maturity (return on investment) is greater than the stated interest rate. If the bond is purchased at a price above the face value, the yield to maturity is less than the stated interest rate.

Additional bond features are provided in the bond indenture, the loan agreement between the issuer and those who buy the bonds. One feature is that a bond issue is secured by specific assets, or that it is unsecured and backed only by the earning power of the borrower. Another feature is seniority, that is, how far up in the queue of claimants the bondholder stands in the event of default. The borrower may have the right to pay off the bond before its maturity date, known as the call feature, or be obliged to repay the bond gradually, according to a timetable, rather than on the maturity date. In addition to these features, the indenture may include any number of protective covenants, which are detailed promises designed to protect lenders. Compliance with all terms of the indenture is monitored by the trustee, usually a bank.

Certain bond features do not typically appear in the indenture: tax treatment, credit quality, and marketability. Tax treatment depends on characteristics of both the borrower and lender, making generalizations difficult. Interest income is usually taxed as ordinary income in the period received, although interest from bonds issued by some government units may be exempt from taxes. Capital gains are taxed only if realized.

Higher rates of return are required from less creditworthy borrowers as compensation for bearing the risk of default. To aid investors in credit quality judgments, borrowers pay a bond-rating agency to assess the likelihood of default. The leading bond rating agencies, Moody's and Standard and Poor's (S&P), use similar standards and rating schemes. Both agencies categorize bonds as either "investment grade" or "speculative grade," also known as junk bonds. Default is unlikely on the former, whereas default is more likely, or has already occurred, on the latter. Within these broad categories the agencies assign finer ratings. The agencies continually monitor borrowers for changes in credit quality, and may upgrade or downgrade bonds as situations change.

A final bond feature not covered in the indenture is marketability. Although a few bond issues are traded on exchanges such as the New York Stock Exchange, most are traded in over-the-counter markets by bond dealers. A bond dealer stands ready to buy bonds at a price called the "bid price" and to sell bonds at a higher price called the "ask price." The difference, the "bid-ask spread," is the transaction cost a bondholder pays when buying or selling bonds. Whether a bond can be sold quickly at a fair price depends mainly upon the average daily trading volume in the bond issue. Trading volumes range from heavy to thin.

Bond Prices, Returns, and Risks

An investor who wants to sell a bond prior to maturity must be concerned with bond prices and how they relate to bond returns. Although the price, return, and risk properties of bonds cannot be fully detailed without the use of mathematics, the basics are easily described.

Bonds earn their returns in two ways: interest (the income yield) and value changes (the capital gains yield). Since interest payments are fixed, fluctuations are reflected in the current price an investor is willing to pay for the bond. A simplified illustration is useful. Suppose an investor buys a 10-year, $1,000 par-value bond with a 6% interest rate (coupon). If the market interest has increased from 6% to 8% since the bond was purchased, the bond's value (price) will decrease from $1,000 to $864.10. A decrease in market interest, for example to 5%, will have the opposite effect. The $1,000 bond will become more valuable and increase to $1,135.90.

To use another example, if the market return of a 20-year, $1,000 bond with a 10% coupon declines from 10% to 8%, the bond's value (price) will rise from $1,000 to $1,197.93. The longer the term of a bond, as the example shows, the more sensitive is its price to changes in required return. Hence, a 2% change in required return produces a larger price change in the 20-year bond than the 10-year bond ($197.93 versus $135.90).

There are several risks of investment in bonds. Interest rate risk is the uncertainty in a bond's return due to uncertainty about future required market returns. An investor who buys a bond knows the interest income from the bond but faces the risk that future market increases could reduce the value of the bond. This is a problem if the investor needs to sell the bond unexpectedly. This form of interest rate risk is called price risk, which increases with a bond's term to maturity (duration). Although an investor can minimize exposure to price risk by investing in bonds with short durations, this strategy exposes the investor to another form of interest rate risk, reinvestment risk.

An investor in short-term bonds must find new bonds when old ones mature. Market changes may force the investor to accept new bonds with lower rates of interest. Unfortunately, an investor can minimize exposure to reinvestment risk only by investing in longer-term bonds and, thereby, increasing exposure to price risk.

Additionally, bonds are prone to inflation risk. Returns earned by bonds with given terms to maturity reflect a consensus forecast of the average annual rate of inflation expected during that term. Actual inflation rates may differ substantially from expectations, however. An unexpected increase in the inflation rate reduces the purchasing power of bond income and, hence, the effective (or real) return from a bond.

Default risk, that is, the risk that the borrower will fail to make a payment of interest or principal, is another type of risk. Borrowers more prone to default must offer bonds with higher coupons. Subsequent changes in the financial condition of the issuer, as tracked by bond rating agencies, may affect the return investors require to hold the bonds and, hence, their market price.

Most bonds are also subject to prepayment risk, the risk that the borrower will repay the loan early. Prepayments occur most often in the wake of a general decline in interest rates, when borrowers can obtain new loans at lower rates. Prepayments force bond investors to seek new investments at a time when bond returns are less favorable. A final form of risk is liquidity risk, the risk that an investor will be unable to sell a bond quickly at a fair price. Liquidity risk is inversely related to the volume of daily trading in the bonds, and varies considerably by bond type and by issuer.

Major Bond Issuers

Major issuers of bonds held by private individuals include the U.S. Treasury, corporations, municipal governments, and specialized mortgage lenders. Bonds of these issuers differ mainly in their credit quality, tax treatment, and marketability.

The U.S. Treasury sells both marketable and nonmarketable bonds. Treasury bonds with terms of between two and 10 years are called Treasury notes. The minimum denomination for marketable Treasury bonds is $1,000. Backed by the taxing power of the U.S. government, Treasury bonds are virtually free of default risk. Interest income is subject to federal income tax but not state and local income tax. Marketable Treasury bonds are actively traded in "thick" markets.

Like the U.S. Treasury, corporations sell both marketable and nonmarketable bonds. (Mortgage bonds, debentures, subordinated debentures, and convertible bonds are special types of corporate bonds.) In contrast to stockholders, bondholders are not owners, have no voice in corporate governance, and have no claim on corporate income beyond the interest and principal payments stipulated in the bond indenture. Most corporate bonds have $1,000 par values and their interest is subject to income tax. Most marketable corporate bonds trade relatively infrequently, making them less liquid than Treasury bonds.

Until the late 1970s, only large corporations with unblemished credit records could sell bonds, with the result that most corporate bonds were of investment grade. During the 1980s, however, bond investors became willing to accept greater default risk in return for higher coupons. This change in investor sentiment led to bond selling by corporations whose creditworthiness warranted speculative bond grades. The evolution of the so-called junk bond market was arguably the most important bond market innovation of the 1980s. Until the October 1987 stock market crash, investors holding well-diversified junk bond portfolios enjoyed returns that more than compensated for the default risk of the bonds. Since then, returns have been substantially lower.

Municipal bonds are bonds sold by state and local governments to finance such projects as road building and school construction. Municipal bonds fall into two broad categories: general obligation bonds backed by the taxing powers of the issuing government, and revenue bonds backed by the projects financed. Municipal bonds sell in minimum denominations of $5,000. Interest income is exempt from federal income tax, and is usually exempt from state income tax when the bondholder resides in the state of the issue. Municipal bonds are prone to default risk; consequently, municipalities pay to have their bonds rated. Daily trading volumes range from moderately high for recent, large offerings to low for older and smaller offerings.

Bonds backed by mortgages have become increasingly popular since their development in the 1970s. Pass-throughs and collateralized mortgage obligations or CMOs are special types of mortgage-backed bonds. Most mortgage-backed bonds are issued by one of three federal agencies: the Government National Mortgage Association, the Federal National Mortgage Association, and the Federal Home Loan Mortgage Corporation. These agencies buy mortgages and sell bonds whose payments are based on the mortgage payments. Thus, mortgage-backed bonds are much like shares in a mutual fund. Minimum denominations are $25,000. Interest income from mortgage-backed bonds is taxed as ordinary income. Because these three federal agencies have the implicit guarantee of the U.S. federal government, mortgage-backed bonds issued by them are virtually free of default risk. Mortgage-backed bonds issued by these agencies are actively traded.

Investment Strategies

The choice of an investment strategy hinges on the investor's investment objective. Three common investment objectives are income generation, total return maximization, and capital protection. Different objectives involve different trade-offs between the two components of bond return and the five types of risk.

Investors seeking stable incomes are more concerned with the income component of bond returns than with the capital gains component. Investors with this objective should probably favor a buy-and-hold strategy, buying and holding bonds with high coupons, low default risk, and low prepayment risk. In practical terms this means gravitating toward longer-term, high-grade Treasury, corporate, municipal, and mortgage-backed bonds.

Investors seeking maximum total return give equal weight to the income and capital gains components of bond return. Total return maximization requires the assumption of substantial risks. Maximizing income return probably requires a willingness to consider high-coupon, speculative-grade corporate and municipal bonds, which subject the investor to default risk. Maximizing capital gains return probably requires a willingness to realize capital gains and cut capital losses by selling "winners" and "losers" at appropriate times, transactions that subject the investor to liquidity risk and reinvestment risk. Capital gains returns can sometimes be enhanced by altering the duration of a portfolio to take advantage of changes in investors' required returns on bonds. However, in light of the relatively low historical return on bond portfolios generally, especially in inflation-adjusted terms, investors seeking to maximize total return would do well to consider investing in common stocks instead of bonds.

Investors striving to protect the value of their portfolios are more concerned with the possibility of capital losses than with generating income. Investors with this objective should probably focus on high-quality, shorter-term bonds, thereby minimizing possible losses from default risk and the price component of interest rate risk. In practical terms this probably means selecting shorter-term Treasury, corporate, municipal, and mortgage-backed bonds.

A relatively recent bond market development is the growth of bond mutual funds. Similar to equity mutual funds, bond mutual funds purchase bonds and sell shares representing proportional ownership in the underlying bonds. Bond funds tend to specialize in a particular type of bond (Treasury, corporate, municipal, or mortgage-backed) and a particular term-to-maturity (short-term, intermediate-term, or long-term). Bond funds aid in the construction of diversified bond portfolios, since shares in bond funds can be purchased for amounts far smaller than the minimum denominations of most types of bonds. Greater diversity also potentially reduces exposure to interest rate risk, default risk, and prepayment risk. Bond funds also tend to reduce liquidity risk, since shares of bond funds trade more actively than do the underlying bonds. Although bond funds offer investors new opportunities to reduce risk, these funds are by no means free of risk. Investors should select bond funds with investment objectives compatible with their own. (See also ASSETS ALLOCATION AFTER RETIREMENT, MUTUAL FUNDS, and WEALTH SPAN.)

References

Fabozzi, Frank J., ed. 1991. *The Handbook of Fixed Income Securities*, Third Edition. Homewood, IL: Dow Jones-Irwin.
Logue, Dennis E., ed. 1995. *The WG&L Handbook of Financial Markets*. Cincinnati, OH: South-Western Publishing.
Thau, Annette. 1995. *The Bond Book*. Chicago: Probus Publishing.

Karlyn Mitchell

BROKERS. See Agents and Brokers.

BUDGET TECHNIQUES. See Cash Flow Planning for Retirees; Financial Counseling.

BUSINESS OWNERSHIP. See Age Discrimination in Employment Act (ADEA); Business Succession Planning; Employee Stock Ownership Plans (ESOPs); Employment of Older Americans; Entrepreneurship.

BUSINESS SUCCESSION PLANNING, a process by which management and ownership of a business entity is transferred from one person or group to another, thus allowing the business to continue. The process may become complicated when transferors and transferees are members of the same family. Factors such as equality and fairness may prevail over business factors such as experience, technical ability, and accountability. Business succession has a gerontological component since a high percentage of businesses are transferred because the owner would like to retire, is concerned about obtaining funds for retirement, or wishes to transfer the responsibility to the next generation.

Only recently has the emotional aspect of business succession planning been recognized by practitioners. Since many problems in the construction of a successful business plan are legal and financial, successful technicians in this field tend to be attorneys* and financial advisors*. A client, especially the founder of the enterprise, tends to identify with the company. This strong identification may account for both the reluctance of entrepreneurs to retire and the observed, shortened life expectancy of those who do.

The business succession planning process involves two areas, which should be considered separately: family and ownership, and issues concerning business management. If ownership of the business will be transferred within the family, issues include stock distribution to children, equal stock rights, selling rights, and rights to employment. None of these, however, relates solely to the efficient, profitable operation of the enterprise. They concern continuation of a successful family relationship, but if not addressed as an integral part of the planning, the successful continuation of the business may be impossible.

Ownership succession raises other issues, including control, the protection of nonvoting or minority shareholders, company philosophy regarding income distribution, compensation, and prerequisites for those active in the business versus inactive shareholders demanding high dividends. Transfer of ownership may require significant amounts of cash and sophisticated tax planning and other technical assistance. Within a family situation, the problem is complicated by the parties seeking to justify a low value for tax purposes but ''fair market value'' for interfamily transfers. Tax law is designed to frustrate efforts by entrepreneurs selling their businesses to family members for less than fair market value. If the business is to be sold to other than a family member, fair market value is, of course, the appropriate price. In either case, the source of cash and method of payment is critical to the success of a succession plan.

Another consideration in an ownership succession plan is time. Business owners frequently believe they have completed a succession plan when they have instead executed a ''buy/sell'' agreement. These agreements deal with ownership but, in most cases, do not address problems incident to the family or ownership systems. Most important, buy/sell agreements are contingency plans, and they provide for the evolution of stock interests when some event (e.g., death, disability, or retirement) occurs. They do not address the more complex problems of transition necessary for a successful succession plan.

Management succession issues may conflict with family ownership arrangements. Successful management depends on accountability. Few family businesses establish job descriptions for family members or conduct performance evaluations or reviews. In today's competitive environment, management must have the power to establish performance criteria and to enforce these standards. In family businesses, questions arise regarding power to establish criteria and enforce standards. Compensation strategies for successful businesses will be based on accomplishments, rather than on family ties.

Retirement Planning

A critical element in the decision by a business owner to devise a succession plan may be whether he or she has adequate sources of retirement income, independent of the enterprise. The retirement decision carries psychological and economic factors. For many entrepreneurs, their businesses are central to their lives; the mortality component associated with retirement planning may prevent effective business succession planning. Therefore, if the succession plan is designed to become effective when the business owner retires, instead of during working years when the business owner can plan to use the proceeds to acquire a new business or to diversify investments, the development of a retirement strategy may be essential for the succession plan itself.

The psychological component of this strategy must take into account the identification problem through a period of mentoring and task transferral. The time for actual transfer of management responsibilities (not necessarily simultaneous with the transfer of control) should be fixed, and the entrepreneur/founder should thereafter act only as counselor.

When the retiring party fails to create a new focus for the energies that have brought business success, internal conflict and crisis may result. It is recommended that retirees phase into retirement using volunteer work, politics, travel, sports, or education as replacement activities for work. The key is to avoid the shock of a sudden retirement.

Financial Aspects of Business Succession Plans

If the business is to be sold, a cash purchase presents fewest problems for the entrepreneur when the sum is sufficient to create adequate retirement cash flows. When ownership transfer is to be accomplished through gifts, installment payments, or sophisticated transfer arrangements, certain issues must be addressed. They include the cash flow needs of the entrepreneur, future inflation, and the extent to which other assets, income potential, and qualified plan investments exist.

A strategic plan for business succession overarches considerations of retirement security and psychological adjustment. Here, considerations of wealth transfer, family equity, management ability, accountability, and tax efficiency must be harmonized. The technical assistance of experienced tax and legal advisors is valuable. Where there are competing interests within a family, it may also be prudent to retain the services of a business psychologist to help the parties understand how they may best contribute to the success of the family enterprise.

In summary, addressing tax and technical legal issues is essential to the success of a business succession plan, but the parties must also recognize the emotional component that is frequently present in these transactions. Matters of control, asset balancing, retirement security, and personal identification can become threshold considerations that must be addressed before the process can begin. Beginning the process as early as possible can minimize the emotional concerns and allow development of the planning in a deliberative fashion. (See also ATTORNEYS; FINANCIAL ADVISORS; RETIREMENT, HISTORY OF; EMPLOYMENT OF OLDER AMERICANS, and WORKING RETIREES.)

References

Alcorn, P. 1982. *Success and Survival in the Family-Owned Business.* New York: McGraw-Hill.

Chasman, Herbert D. 1983. *Who Gets the Business?* Rockville Center, NY: Farnsworth Publishing.

Cohn, Mike. 1992. *Passing the Torch.* New York: McGraw-Hill.

Danco, L. 1975. *Beyond Survival.* Cleveland, OH: Center for Family Business.

Drucker, P. F. 1985. *Innovation and Entrepreneurship.* New York: Harper & Row.

Hollander, B. S. 1983. ''Family-Owned Business as a System: A Case Study of the Interaction of Family, Task, and Marketplace Components.'' Unpublished doctoral dissertation, School of Education, University of Pittsburgh.

Lansberg, I. 1985. ''The Succession Conspiracy: Mapping Resistances to Succession Planning in First-Generation Family Firms.'' Unpublished paper, Yale University.

Rosenblatt, P. C., L. de Mik, R. M. Anderson, and P. A. Johnson. 1985. *The Family in Business: Understanding and Dealing with the Challenges Entrepreneurial Families Face.* San Francisco: Jossey-Bass.

Ward, John L. 1987. *Keeping the Family Business Healthy.* San Francisco: Jossey-Bass.

David J. Tolan

C

CAPITAL GAIN, profits that occur from the sale or exchange of capital assets, typically investments in equity securities*, bonds*, or real estate. While the value of these assets or investments may increase during the period of ownership, taxes are deferred until the item is sold and the owner receives income or profits in excess of the purchase price plus costs. Capital gains are defined by the Internal Revenue Service (IRS) as short-term if an asset is held for less than one year and long-term if held for longer than one year. Most older persons, and their financial advisors*, must be familiar with and carefully consider the current tax consequences within their overall financial picture when deciding to sell or exchange assets. Capital gain taxation policy is the subject of ongoing discussion in Congress and may change in future legislation.

Current Tax Treatment

The current federal tax on net long-term capital gains is limited to a maximum rate of 28%. All capital gains, whether short-term or long-term, are treated as ordinary income and do not provide tax benefits unless the taxpayer's marginal tax bracket exceeds the 28% level. The IRS requires a taxable income of $53,500 for a single taxpayer or $89,150 for a married taxpayer filing jointly under current tax rules to exceed the 28% tax bracket. Net short-term and long-term losses are deductible dollar for dollar against ordinary income up to $3,000, with unlimited carryover for excess loss deductions. Prior to 1987, 60% of long-term capital gains were excluded from taxable income, to encourage investment and stimulate economic growth.

Most Frequent Usage

For many people, the largest single capital gains transaction is usually the sale of a residence. This occurs when the home is sold for more than the original purchase price plus the costs of any improvements. In this situation, the capital gains tax will be deferred if the taxpayer involved purchases a replacement residence for the same or higher price within 24 months. Individuals over 55 are allowed a one-time capital gains exclusion of $125,000 when selling a residence. The specifics of the tax code and the interpretations can and do change from year to year. Individuals should consult professional tax experts who are fully up to date on the tax code. (See also ELDER TAXPAYER ISSUES, EQUITY SECURITIES, ESTATE PLANNING, and FINANCIAL ADVISORS.)

References

Hoerner, J. Andrew. 1992. *The Capital Gains Controversy: A Tax Analysis Reader.* Arlington, VA: Tax Analysts.
Lasser, J. K. Annual. *Your Income Tax.* New York: Simon Schuster.
Rosefsky, Robert S. 1993. *Personal Finance.* U.S. Tax Code. New York: John Wiley & Sons.
Rothman, Howard J., and William A. Friedlander. 1994. *Capital Assets.* Washington, DC: Tax Management.

Ganas K. Rakes

CAREGIVING FOR THE ELDERLY, providing financial, instrumental, emotional, and other types of long-term support for elderly parents, spouses, or friends who become chronically ill or disabled. A long-term, perhaps permanent, unbalanced flow of assistance distinguishes caregiving from other close relationships. As more adults survive to old age, caregiving needs and the corresponding financial costs of caregiving will accelerate for large numbers of people.

Demographic and Health Characteristics

The average life expectancy of Americans is 75 years. However, there is a seven-year sex gap, with women surviving to age 78 on average and men only 71 years (Harris 1990). This disparity significantly affects the social structure—marital status, living arrangements, and income—and hence the caregiving needs of the older population. At age 75 and older, more than two-thirds of women are widows. Older women are more likely to rely on family members to provide for their caregiving needs. While most have adult children with whom they maintain contact, few older adults live with their children. Most prefer to live nearby, but in separate households.

Health technology and living standards have extended Americans' longevity and increased their prospects of surviving bouts with degenerative diseases such as heart disease, cancer, or stroke. Due to the chronic nature of these illnesses, multiple hospitalizations are likely to occur in later life (Harris 1990), but it is not until ages 85 and older that about half of this population report the inability to perform major activities due to chronic illness.

Caregivers for the Elderly

There are approximately 18 million caregivers in the United States providing assistance to chronically ill or disabled persons. Family caregivers provide two-thirds of all home care services for the elderly*, which have an estimated market value of more than $190 billion a year (National Family Caregivers Association [NFCA] 1994). With regard to the elderly, it is estimated that about 13 million Americans are prospective caregivers of disabled spouses or parents age 65 or older; a subset of 4.2 million spouses and adult children actually provide hands-on or supervisory assistance to impaired elders living in the community (Stone 1991). In a recent survey of caregivers, it was found that 81% are women; 79% are married; 75% are ages 40–59; 50% have provided care for 1–5 years; and 50% have provided care for six years or longer (NFCA 1994). Of women care-givers, 37% concurrently hold paid jobs. In addition to paid work averaging 31 hours, they provide caregiving labor averaging over 20 hours per week (U.S. House of Representatives 1988).

Primary caregivers for elderly men are generally their wives, whereas primary caregivers for elderly women are most often adult children (Harris 1990). Caring for chronically ill or aging parents constitutes a normative response of adult children, mostly daughters, although sons and daughters-in-law provide some of the help needed. Proximity and closeness to a parent, however, may determine who becomes the actual primary caregiver.

With a growing aged population, more adult children are likely to provide some sort of parent caregiving, involving financial help, routine daily support, back-up care, or only occasional care. Such support may include assistance with daily personal activities, shopping, cooking, house cleaning, laundry, transportation, home maintenance, and financial management. In more severe circumstances, caregivers help with tasks such as bathing and dressing (Cantor 1991). Beyond these household and personal care tasks, 88% of respondents to the NFCA (1994) survey reported that providing emotional support was their primary caregiving responsibility, and 63% noted that guardianship* was a major responsibility.

The involvement of adult children in caregiving is often precipitated by a health crisis or death of one parent. Or, the adult children gradually become aware that an aging parent is having difficulty managing aspects of daily living and needs assistance. They begin by assisting with periodic, routine tasks such as shopping or cleaning, and progressively become involved in daily tasks and activities. A goal in caregiving is to help an older person remain independent for as long as possible by providing instrumental support (i.e., running errands, providing household assistance, managing financial affairs) without overfunctioning for him or her. Emotional support fulfills older persons' needs to feel loved, cared about, esteemed, and valued.

Caregiver Demands and Stress

Increased employment opportunities for women and the return of middle-aged women to the labor force has made caring for older parents more difficult. As more women work outside the home, there is less time available to care directly for aging parents. Daughters who work full-time provide about the same amount of physical care as homemaker daughters, but they are more likely to pay helpers for some care. Sons of dependent older parents are more involved in managing finances and typically hire others to provide personal care.

The caregiver relationship between adult children and older parents is significantly influenced by the quality of past relationships. While many caregivers experience satisfaction from the love they give and receive from an aging parent, hostile past relationships often lead to conflicts exacerbated by resentment over the increasing dependency of an older parent. Even when elder care is provided with love and affection, the burden of caring for a dependent parent may be stressful for the caregiver. An adult child often must balance a parent's needs with those of spouse and children. Debilitating health problems increase demands on time, and an especially demanding example that requires intense caregiving is Alzheimer's Disease. Caregivers themselves may be at increased health risk, particularly as they age themselves. They generally experience a degree of loss of self and family, have a tendency toward depression, and often feel frustrated and sad. The following multiple burdens of caregiving—thus sources of stress—are most often noted: loss of leisure time (47%); role reversals and changed family dynamics (41%); and a sense of isolation and lack of understanding from others (40%) (NFCA 1994). Caring for an impaired elderly parent can be so demanding that even the most loving adult children may experience resentment and guilt. They may desire more freedom, and simultaneously feel guilt over not doing enough.

The placement of an elderly person in a nursing home* may become both a consequence and a cause of excessive caregiver stress. If and when nursing home placement is considered, a well-informed, well-discussed choice is more likely to lead to a satisfactory solution. Even after institutionalization, however, caregiving burden may persist, especially for spouses whose partner must make the transition to nursing home care (Novak and Guest 1992). Stress levels experienced by partners and by adult children caregivers also depend on the closeness of the relationship, the severity of impairment, and the financial ability to pay for outside help (Walker et al. 1990). While caregivers must often reshape their lives to meet the requirements of those receiving care, they must also maintain their own well-being. They are well advised to stay actively involved in outside relationships and activities to avoid burnout.

Financial and Other Support for Caregivers

Ranked highest by caregivers to help ease burdens is affordable respite care and household help. Both the public and private sectors are beginning to provide respite programs, adult day care centers, and support groups that offer temporary relief for families providing care, but experts and families find they fall far short of the growing need. Most must turn instead to other family members and friends when seeking support regarding caregiving problems, but a large majority report they receive no help from family members (NFCA 1994).

At the federal level, health-related assistance has been part of Medicare* and Medicaid,* but it is only through programs made possible by the Older Americans Act* of 1965 that caregivers (rather than the beneficiary) can be involved and may obtain relief. Concretely, the local area agency on aging can provide basic information and assistance with regard to home health care and homemaker services. Adult day care centers also offer respite care services, which allow the primary caregiver (usually a spouse or adult child) to take some time off from his or her responsibility. The amount of respite time ranges from a few hours to a weekend, or longer vacations.

Support programs such as homemaking services and respite care alleviate some of the primary caregiver's workload, allowing more time for personal needs. Given proper coordination of available services, made possible through case management, the numbers of caregivers who have access to respite, counseling, training, and information on newly available programs can substantially increase. Some research has explored the consequences of payment for caregiving, although much more work on the financial aspects of caregiving is needed. One study of caregivers receiving government financial assistance for informal in-home care to disabled veterans found such assistance to be a workable component of an integrated service delivery system (Adamek 1992). While tax relief is also available for adult children providing financial support for dependent elderly parents, the financial burdens of caregiving should be anticipated and planned for before the need arises, wherever possible.

The Future

The problems of caring for dependent aging parents are likely to be more severe in the future for at least two reasons. First, the fastest growing segment of the population are persons age 85 and older. Major sociofinancial changes must occur to deal with this increasing age group that require greater awareness and caregiving support than is available presently from either families or public support systems. Secondly, baby boomers born between 1946 and 1964 will strongly affect population aging during 2010–2030. The lower fertility rates of baby boomers means there will be fewer adult children to care ultimately for aging parents.

The more immediate situation, however, is less predictable. For some time into the new century, more middle-aged persons will be available to provide caregiving for the elderly. Whether they will be able to offer support will depend on their labor force participation, geographical dispersion, marital disruption, and other factors including the financial burdens of caregiving, all of which have been increasing. Yet even as these trends increase, adult children continue to provide parental care; the rate of institutionalization for elderly persons has not increased over the last two decades. Measured optimism is thus in order (Himes 1992).

As the baby boom generation fully moves into old age, there will be an enormous burden on every social institution in society to meet its caregiving needs. Although the family undoubtedly will continue to provide primary caregiving for the elderly, there must also be a shift of some of this responsibility to public and private sources of subsidiary, professional care to offset diminishing numbers in the prospective caregiving population.

Alternatives to traditional family caregiving include quasi-family living arrangements and elder foster care. In the quasi-family situation, older persons live together, sharing household expenses and hiring their own professional staff to provide housekeeping and personal services. The quasi-family functions as a mutual self-help group for the elderly. Another approach is a foster home setting for the elderly. Elder foster care would fill the gap when the elderly either do not have children or when adult children are unable or unwilling to help with caregiving. Some states have instituted elder foster care for older persons receiving Medicaid assistance.

A range of alternatives has been offered by the rapid growth of assisted living arrangements for the elderly. Since a number of these new solutions are more cost-effective than nursing home placement or other institutional care, existing caregiving programs could be enhanced and expanded in the next decade, and the cost shared between individuals or families and the public. (See also ASSISTED LIVING, NURSING HOMES, LONG-TERM CARE INSURANCE, MEDICAID, MEDICAID PLANNING, OLDER AMERICANS ACT, SOCIAL WORK, GERONTOLOGICAL, and WEALTH SPAN.)

Organizations

Children of Aging Parents
Eldercare Locator
National Family Caregivers Association (NFCA)
National Institute on Aging Alzheimer's Disease Education and Referral Center (ADEAR)

Suggested Reading

American Association of Retired Persons. 1994. *Caregiver Resource Kit.* Washington, DC: AARP.
Sherman, J. 1994. *Preventing Caregiver Burnout.* Golden Valley, MN: Pathway Books.
Susik, Helen. 1995. *Hiring Home Caregivers: The Family Guide to In-Home Eldercare.* San Luis Obispo, CA: Impact Publications.
Walker, Susan C. 1994. *Keeping Active: A Caregiver's Guide to Activities with the Elderly.* Lakewood, CO: American Sourcebooks.

References

Adamek, Margaret E. 1992. ''Should the Government Pay? Caregiver Views of Government Responsibility and Feelings of Stigma about Financial Support.'' *Journal of Applied Gerontology* 11: 283–97.

Cantor, Marjorie H. 1991. "Family and Community: Changing Roles in an Aging Society." *Gerontologist* 31: 337–46.

Harris, Diana K. 1990. *Sociology of Aging,* Second Edition. New York: Harper & Row.

Himes, Christine L. 1992. "Future Caregivers: Projected Family Structures of Older Persons." *Journal of Gerontology: Social Sciences* 47: S17–26.

National Family Caregivers Association. 1994. *Caregiver Member Survey Report.* Kensington, MD: Author.

Novak, Mark, and Carol Guest. 1992. "A Comparison of the Impact of Institutionalization on Spouse and Nonspouse Caregivers." *Journal of Applied Gerontology* 11: 379–94.

Stone, Robyn. 1991. "Defining Family Caregivers of the Elderly: Implications for Research and Public Policy." *Gerontologist* 31: 724–25.

U.S. House of Representatives, Select Committee on Aging. 1988. *Exploding the Myths: Caregiving in America.* Washington, DC: GPO.

Walker, Alexis J., Hwa-Yong Shin, and David N. Bird. 1990. "Perceptions of Relationship Change and Caregiver Satisfaction." *Family Relations* 39: 147–52.

William D. Bland

CASH FLOW PLANNING FOR RETIREES, the preparation of a set of financial calculations that project the sources of funds after retirement and the variety of uses to which they will be allocated. A capital account encompasses the total value of all income-producing assets other than annuities*, qualified retirement plans, and non-qualified retirement plans such as Individual Retirement Accounts (IRAs)*. Projections show the intended use of funds, which are then subtracted from the total sources of funds from year to year. Positive or negative annual cash flow is added to, or subtracted from, the capital account balance at the beginning of each year, projected into the future. The cash flow projection illustrates whether the capital account value will increase or decrease over time.

These projections are usually prepared by financial professionals as part of an overall financial plan, and are reviewed and updated periodically. This is not a budgeting process, but a process designed to indicate prospective wealth accumulation or capital depletion. The number of years addressed in the projection is discretionary, but ideally it will extend beyond the actuarial life expectancy for the retiree. The annual cash flow calculation originated in the business environment, but has come into use in the area of personal finance with the advent of personal financial planning performed by professionals. A comprehensive personal financial planning process addresses the following major areas: cash flow and debt management, risk management, investments; income tax, estate planning, and retirement planning. The annual postretirement cash flow calculation illustrates the expected performance of each of the areas addressed in the comprehensive personal financial plan.

The trend in recent years has been away from comprehensive financial planning in favor of modular planning, where only the issues of immediate concern to the client are addressed. However, for the retiree, the annual cash flow projection is still one of the most important calculations. Skillful management of income and income-producing assets is as important to the retiree as career management is to the individual whose financial well-being depends on current earnings from employment.

The purpose of the postretirement annual cash flow calculation is to provide a broad overview of the retiree's financial future given his current position. Potential problem areas become evident. If these areas are adequately addressed, it is possible to avoid financial dependence or unnecessary income, gift, and estate taxes. Typically the calculation is performed utilizing the retiree's current set of circumstances. In subsequent annual cash flow projections, variables are introduced to test the impact of proposed changes in the retiree's financial situation, and the effect of changes in circumstances that might occur.

Careful management of income-producing assets, sources of funds (including income) and uses of funds (including expenses) is of utmost importance to assure a positive annual cash flow since, in most cases, the retiree no longer has earned income. It is also necessary to determine if: (1) estate reduction strategies are indicated due to an increasing capital account; (2) the capital account will diminish over time, resulting in a reduction in the future standard of living; and (3) the capital account will diminish to the extent that the retiree will become financially dependent on family, community, or government resources.

Sources of funds for the retiree can include the following:

- Social Security benefits
- Defined benefit pension plan distributions
- Defined contribution (profit sharing, money purchase, 401K, etc.) plan distributions
- Individual Retirement Account (IRA) distributions
- Keogh (HR-10) plan distributions
- Annuity contract (qualified and non-qualified) benefits
- Earned income
- Trust beneficiary income
- Invested inheritance or insurance proceeds
- Investment portfolio income
- Medicare benefits
- Medicaid benefits
- Long-term care insurance benefits
- Disability income insurance benefits
- Gifts or subsidies from family or community resources
- Casualty or liability loss awards or settlements
- Charitable remainder trust income

Uses of funds for the retiree can include:

- Annual fixed living expenses
- Annual variable living expenses
- Federal income tax
- State income tax
- Estate settlement expenses (including estate tax)
- Inheritance tax
- State death tax
- Gifts
- Unusual travel expenses
- Home modifications or improvements
- Adaptation of home for in-home care
- Domestic services when retiree is incapacitated
- In-home care
- Institutional care
- Unusual medical care and prescriptions not paid for by insurance, Medicare, or Medicaid
- Costs associated with unlaunched children
- Costs associated with care of single relatives, elderly parents, grandchildren, incapacitated adult children
- Legal expenses associated with estate planning
- Moving expenses
- Expenses related to purchase or sale of residence or other property
- Cash purchase of automobile
- Lump sum retirement of debt
- Charitable gifts

Developing an annual cash flow projection requires that the preparer understand all areas of the retiree's financial affairs, including when his circumstances could or will change. Sources of funds could either diminish or become unavailable. Failure of income-producing entities such as banks and insurance companies, retirement of mortgages held by the retiree, and death of a spouse receiving life-only pension benefits are a few examples of how a source of funds could be reduced or extinguished. The preparer needs to include expenses when it is anticipated that they will occur. The premium for Medicare Part B should begin in the month that the retiree turns age 65, for instance. If the projection will include possible institutional expenses, then the preparer needs to consider reducing the variable community living expenses to reflect that they will be included in the institutional expense. These are just a few examples of how possible changes in sources and uses of funds are dealt with.

The annual cash flow calculation is dynamic, unlike a monthly cash flow calculation. Since annual cash flow illustrates use of money over time, certain assumptions about the future should be included in the calculation: the life expectancy of the retiree and spouse; the future health of the retiree and spouse and the potential need for in-home or institutional care; the viability of entitlements such as Medicare, Medicaid, and Social Security; changes in the Internal Revenue Code that will affect income tax liability; inflation rates for various time periods for variable living expenses, medical care, and in-home and institutional care; and rates of return on the personal investment portfolio, Individual Retirement Accounts, variable annuities, and variable life insurance.

The preparer will need to review the calculations periodically (quarterly, semi-annually, or annually), and when major changes are occurring in the financial situation of the retiree. (See also ASSETS ALLOCATION AFTER RETIREMENT, ANNUITIES, CHARITABLE CONTRIBUTIONS, FINANCIAL ADVISORS, FINANCIAL COUNSELING, INDIVIDUAL RETIREMENT ACCOUNTS, KEOGH PLANS.)

References

Cavill, Ronald W. and Patricia Houlihan. 1995. *Finances After 50: Financial Planning for the Next 50 Years.* Washington, DC: United Seniors Health Cooperative.

Gordon, Harley. 1991. *How to Protect Your Life's Savings from Catastrophic Illness and Nursing Homes.* Boston: Financial Planning Institute, Inc.

Hallman, G. Victor, and Jerry S. Rosenbloom. 1993. *Personal Financial Planning.* New York: McGraw-Hill.

White-Means, Shelley I., and Joni Hersch. 1993. "Economic Viability among Post-Retirement Aged Women." *Journal of Aging & Women* 4: 19–36.

Joan Matson Gruber

CHARITABLE CONTRIBUTIONS, gifts made to eligible organizations consistent with existing laws, and designed to benefit society from an educational, religious, moral, physical, or social standpoint.

One characteristic of American society is its array of nonprofit institutions. Writing nearly 200 years ago in *Democracy in America*, Alexis de Tocqueville observed upon visiting the United States:

Americans of all ages, all stations in life, and all types of disposition are forever forming associations. . . . [They] combine to give fetes, found seminaries, build churches, distribute books, and send missionaries to the antipodes. Hospitals, prisons, and schools take shape in that way. . . . In every case, at the head of any new undertaking, where in France you would find the government or in England some territorial magistrate, in the United States you are sure to find an association.

Today, U.S. colleges and universities, hospitals, schools, zoos, museums, and other institutions are admired worldwide. One factor that makes these institutions unique is that so many of them are supported primarily by the voluntary contributions of cash and property from private citizens. This system of voluntary support for nonprofit institutions is sometimes characterized as a parallel to the private enterprise economic system.

Why We Give

Contributions are encouraged by such widely varied motivations as the affection one feels for his or her college, the gratitude of a patient treated in a nonprofit hospital, the compassion of a person whose loved one has been lost to a dreaded disease for which a cure is being sought, or the deep feelings a church-goer holds for his or her congregation. While individual motivations differ, an incentive encouraging charitable giving is the tax treatment of charitable contributions in the United States.

The most fundamental tax incentive is the income tax charitable deduction. Amounts given to qualified charitable organizations can be deducted from the donor's income in computing his or her income tax. There are a number of detailed limitations, but for most donors who itemize their deductions, amounts given to charity are deductible up to one-half of their income. Any excess over the amount deductible in a given year may be carried over and deducted in each of the five subsequent taxable years.

Contributors Must Have Receipts

All tax deductions must be proven, since the Internal Revenue Service is understandably skeptical of the taxpayer who has no evidence to support a claimed deduction. Charitable contributions, however, are subject to even more stringent rules in this regard.

Beginning in 1994, donors' deductions for contributions of $250 or more may be disallowed unless they have timely receipts from their donees stating the amount contributed (or, in the case of property contributions, a description of the contributed property), plus a description and the estimated value of any goods or services provided to the donee in consideration of his or her contribution. If no goods or services are given to the donor, the receipt must state that fact. This latter rule is designed to prevent donors from claiming deductions for amounts that are really purchases rather than contributions. An example would be a payment of $1,000 to a symphony orchestra organization for a fundraising event, where the donor received the right to attend a concert and a postconcert dinner; if the value of the concert and dinner totals $250, the donor's deduction is limited to $750 and the receipt must tell him so.

Many individuals give freely of their time, talents, and money. These contributions of services and other volunteer time are not deductible, although volunteers may deduct any out-of-pocket expenses incurred in rendering services to a charitable organization. Blood donors likewise receive no tax benefits.

Planned Giving: More for the Money

In addition to a straightforward gift of cash or property, there are other ways to structure charitable contributions so as to provide substantial benefits to the donor and the recipient. This approach, often referred to as planned giving, generally involves contributions that produce an income stream to the donor, followed by an eventual transfer to a charitable beneficiary. The term *planned giving* refers to gifts other than simple cash donations and is subject to a number of sophisticated rules. Planned giving transfers can offer particularly attractive benefits to persons who are either retired or planning for their retirement. Several planned giving vehicles are designed specifically for donors who, like retirees or prospective retirees, want to make a charitable gift but are also concerned about their income.

Charitable Remainder Trusts (CRTs)

These are trusts that make distributions to the donor or another beneficiary for life, or for a term of up to twenty years, then turn the remaining trust property to a charitable beneficiary. There are two types of CRTs. The charitable remainder unitrust pays a stated percentage (at least 5%) of the trust corpus to the donor or other beneficiary each year. Thus, if the value of the trust assets doubles, the current payout will also double, and if the value of the trust declines, the distributions likewise go down. The other type, the charitable remainder annuity trust, pays out a fixed amount to its current beneficiaries each year for as long as the trust continues. Some donors like the certainty of a fixed payout, while others prefer the potentially increasing income provided by the unitrust alternative.

Upon creating a CRT, the donor receives a current income deduction equal to the actuarial value of the charitable remainder interest in the trust. If the trust is funded with appreciated property (i.e., property that would produce a capital gain, and hence a capital gains tax if the donor sold it instead of contributing it), an additional benefit is available. Because the CRT is exempt from income tax, this capital gains tax will be avoided if the property is transferred to the trust and then sold by the trustee.

Pooled Income Funds

The CRT can produce dramatic results, but may be impractical for smaller gifts, since donors must create and maintain a trust with the help of attorneys* knowledgeable in this area. There is annual upkeep as well, for the trust must file annual income tax returns, and perhaps pay trustee's fees and other expenses as well. These expenses may be justified if the donor is contemplating a fairly large gift of $50,000 or more, since the donor can customize the trust to fit his or her plans.

This expense is avoided when a donor uses a pooled income fund operated by a charity in lieu of creating a trust. The fund pools together the contributions of many donors into a single investment fund that pays income to the donors for life, and at the donor's death distributes the donor's share to the charity that maintains it. As with the CRT, the donor receives a charitable tax deduction for the actuarial value of the charity's interest in the donor's contribution.

The expense of creating and maintaining a pooled income fund is borne by the fund's sponsoring charity. The donor signs a one-page instrument of transfer and sends it back to the charity with a contribution. Most funds have a minimum contribution, usually $5,000. The fund is usually managed by a skilled investment manager at no cost to the donor.

While the pooled income fund resembles a mutual fund, it is actually very different. Many planned giving vehicles resemble investments, but they are not investments, and this is important to remember. All of the tax benefits flow from the pooled fund or trust because the property contributed has been to a charitable organization. This is the opposite of an investment, which the purchaser owns and can sell or leave to children or other private beneficiaries.

Charitable Gift Annuities

The charitable gift annuity is a different arrangement that produces a result much like the CRT or the pooled income fund. Instead of a trust or fund, the charity and the donor enter into a private annuity arrangement. The donor gives the charity cash or property and receives in exchange the charity's promise to pay to the donor (and/or another beneficiary) a stated amount for life. The actuarial value of the annuity stream is less than the value of the cash or property given to the charity, and the difference is the amount of the donor's income tax charitable deduction.

Planning for Retirement—A Practical Example

Norris and Martha have some stock they bought 10 years ago for $12,000. This stock is now worth $75,000, but pays them only $1,000 per year in dividends. If they sell the stock to reinvest in higher-income investments, they will have only about $52,000 left after capital gains taxes. At a 5% return, that would produce income of $2,600 per year. They would like to provide an eventual bequest to their church, but feel they will need their nest egg for retirement.

If Norris and Martha transfer the stock to a CRT, the trustee can sell the stock and have virtually the entire $75,000 available to reinvest; at 5%, that would produce annual income of $3,750, an increase of more than 40%. The trust will provide Norris and Martha with an income stream that will continue for as long as either is alive, and upon the death of the last, the remaining trust property will pass to their church. If they want even more income, they can have their trust drafted with a higher payout, 7% or 8%, for example.

Additionally, Norris and Martha will be entitled to an income tax deduction in the year they create the trust. The amount of that deduction depends upon several variables—their ages, the terms of the trust (primarily its pay-out rate), and the IRS actuarial interest rate for the month in which they create the trust.

Although this example involved a CRT, Norris and Martha may receive similar benefits using a pooled income fund or a charitable gift annuity. Selecting the best vehicle may require the help of an experienced charitable gift planner.

Other Charitable Arrangements

There are other ways to structure charitable contributions to cover particular financial circumstances. For example, a person might use a charitable lead trust to generate large estate and gift tax savings on large transfers. Such a trust operates much like the CRT, except the positions of the parties are reversed. The charitable lead trust makes distributions to charity for a stipulated number of years, after which the remaining trust property is turned over to the donor's family. Such trusts are often established by means of a decedent's will*. Newspaper accounts described the use of such an arrangement under Jacqueline Kennedy Onassis's will to virtually eliminate estate taxes on her large estate.

A bargain sale arrangement may be used to transfer property to charity by means of a sale, but the price is less than the full value of the property. For example, a school may want to acquire land adjacent to its campus; the owner is willing to sell it to the school for $40,000 even though it is worth $100,000. Thus, the "seller" is really a donor, and has made a $60,000 charitable contribution. He or she has also made a sale, and may have a capital gains tax to pay. On these facts, since the property was sold for only 40% of its full value, only 40% of the tax basis would be used in computing capital gain.

Finally, some donors are reluctant to make a contemplated charitable contribution because they do not want to deny their children or other beneficiaries the property they would be contributing to charity. For this situation, the donor might want to consider a wealth replacement trust. Although not an actual charitable device, such a trust is often used in conjunction with a sizeable charitable transfer. For example, if a donor is considering making a contribution of $100,000 to a CRT, some of the distributions from the trust could be used to buy a $100,000 life insurance policy through an irrevocable life insurance trust. Such a trust is called a wealth replacement trust because it allows the donor to replace the wealth being given to charity. The CRT will provide the donor with an income stream for life, and upon the donor's death, the charity receives the property remaining in the CRT and family beneficiaries receive the policy proceeds, with no estate tax payable on either amount.

A wealth replacement trust requires caution. If a donor has reservations about the amount of a proposed charitable contribution, the proposed contribution may be too large. No responsible charity, under normal circumstances, would encourage a donor to give away a major portion of the donor's estate while he or she was still alive and potentially needed the funds. Moreover, the purchase of insurance is entirely separate from the proposed charitable contribution, and the donor must decide whether such insurance is necessary or desirable. (See ATTORNEYS, ELDER LAW PRACTICE, ELDER TAXPAYER ISSUES, ESTATE PLANNING, LIFE INSURANCE, PENSION FUND TRENDS, TRUSTS, and WILLS.)

References

Arthur Andersen and Co. (Updated periodically) *The Tax Economics of Charitable Giving*. Chicago: Author. (Contact the Arthur Andersen office nearest you for publishing and price data.)

Bowen, William G. 1994. *The Charitable Nonprofits: An Analysis of Institutional Dynamics and Characteristics*. San Francisco: Josey-Bass.

Colliton, James W. 1993. *Charitable Gifts*. Colorado Springs, CO: Shepard's/McGraw Hill.

Internal Revenue Code (Title 26, U.S. Code), Section 170.

Nagai, Althea K., Robert Lerner, and Stanley Rothman. 1994. *Giving for Social Change: Foundations, Public Policy, and the American Political Agenda*. Westport, CT: Praeger.

U.S. Congress, Senate Committee on Commerce, Science, and Transportation, Subcommittee on the Consumer. 1994. *Charitable Solicitation Fraud: Hearing before the Subcommittee on Consumer of the Committee on Commerce, Science, and Transportation*. Washington, D.C.: U.S. Government Printing Office.

Jerry J. McCoy

COHABITATION, heterosexual couples living together without legally being married. Although infrequent, cohabitation does occur among couples older than 65. As with marriage* after age 65, availability of a partner plays a significant role in cohabitation trends. Since most men ages 65 and older are married, there is a shortage of men 65 and older for cohabitation. More women than men survive to older ages, but even so, older men cohabit at rates two to three times the rates for older women. The U.S. Census Bureau estimates that among the unmarried population in 1990, 4% of men ages 65 and older and 1% of women ages 65 and older were cohabiting. This percentage varies with race/ethnicity and five-year age groupings.

For many older people to consider cohabitation as an alternative to other living arrangements, they must have strong reasons that transcend their natural unwillingness to go against societal and familial customs. Economic factors may constitute the most important reason seniors have to consider cohabitation. The adage, "Two can live cheaper than one" is not without some truth, and economic incentives to cohabit may parallel economic theories of marriage. If both partners have resources to contribute to the household, there may be economic gains to cohabitation in retirement. Constraints to marriage for seniors may come in the form of federal taxes and Social Security* or death benefits*.

A marriage penalty or tax on marriage originates from the "breadwinner system," under which men earned income and women had no market earnings. One-earner couples in this system are equated with two-earner couples. Despite today's workplace realities, the marriage penalty still exists, and the retired elderly are not necessarily exempt. Elevated Social Security income is now taxable and other sources of income in retirement have always been taxable. In addition to potential loss of survivor's benefits under Social Security upon remarriage, the maximum allowable earned benefits for a two-earner couple is less than it would be if each were collecting benefits as individuals. Private pensions can be at risk upon remarriage as well. Eligibility for Medicaid* benefits is another important economic consideration for those elderly who might wish to remarry. When an eligible person marries, Medicaid regulations require that the savings of the new partner must be exhausted before eligibility is reinstated.

Intergenerational inheritance* transfers may also be a factor in decisions either to remarry or cohabit. Research indicates that adult children cite inheritance as the biggest concern in their opposition to remarriage of parents. Courts, however, are moving toward recognition of cohabitational relationships, and pre-cohabitation contracts may become necessary to ensure that inheritance will pass directly to children. In addition, trends indicate an increase in bequests to non-family members, including cohabitants, which may spur adult children to contest wills that contain such bequests.

In research that focuses on the portion of the population that is 45 years old and older, several economic factors—job income, Social Security* and Supplemental Security Income*, investment income, and homeownership—have been found to increase the likelihood that an older person will cohabit. The lower the income at advanced ages, the higher the proportion of those who cohabit. Seniors tend to cohabit if they no longer can work for health reasons or when they are eligible for entitlement income. The effects on cohabitation are not as clear for homeownership. Cohabitors are more likely to be renters than their married counterparts. However, cohabitors are more likely to be homeowners than older single persons who are not cohabiting.

At the present time, most general knowledge about cohabitation is based on data collected about the younger population (35 years old and younger). In 1990, the U.S. Bureau of the Census added ''unmarried partner'' as a relationship category for the first time, and the availability of self-reported cohabitational status in large public samples will undoubtedly encourage more studies of older cohabitants. There may remain a reluctance by seniors to report nontraditional consensual unions. The elderly often are uncomfortable with cohabitation and may be reluctant to disclose their status as cohabitors. The ageism that persists in society, especially as it relates to sexuality in later years, is reflected in the behavior of the elderly. While older people may accept children who cohabit, they may avoid cohabitation themselves due to concerns about what peers might say or think.

There are several reasons to expect an increase in cohabitation among those 65 and older. First, decreased mortality rates will increase the population aged 65 and older who are available to cohabit. Second, because divorced persons are more likely to cohabit, an increase in divorce is likely to bring about a corresponding increase in cohabitation. Third, the population aged 45 to 64 has a higher propensity to cohabit than those aged 65 and older, and it is likely that as these persons age, they will continue to have higher proportions of persons cohabiting. Finally, those who came of age during the 1960s and later have embraced cohabitation as an acceptable alternative to marriage. They undoubtedly will reflect this acceptance in their own lives as they age into the twenty-first century. (See also DEATH BENEFITS, DIVORCE AND THE ELDERLY, INHERITANCE, MARRIAGE AND THE ELDERLY, MEDICAID, SOCIAL SECURITY PROGRAM OF THE UNITED STATES, and SUPPLEMENTAL SECURITY INCOME.)

References

Eekelaar, John J., and Sanford N. Katz, eds. 1980. *Marriage and Cohabitation in Contemporary Societies: Areas of Legal, Social and Ethical Change.* Toronto: Butterworths.

Gronvold-Hatch, Rebecca. In press. *Aging and Cohabitation.* New York: Garland Publishing.

Spanier, Graham B. 1985. "Cohabitation in the 1980s: Recent Changes in the United States." In *Contemporary Marriages: Comparative Perspectives on a Changing Institution,* ed. Kingsley Davis, with A. Grossbard-Schectman. New York: Russell Sage Foundation, 91–111.

Rebecca Gronvold-Hatch

COMMODITIES, goods, produce, wares, and, in general, all items that are bought and sold in commerce. Out of this large group, only certain items are traded as commodity future contracts, mainly due to their universal acceptance and marketability throughout the world. These include, but are not limited to, raw goods in the agricultural area, such as corn, wheat, soybeans, sugar, coffee, cocoa, and orange juice. Additional examples include the meat markets of cattle, pork bellies, and other food products; the energy complex of crude oil, heating oil, and unleaded gas; and the precious metals, such as gold and silver. Newer financial instruments traded as commodities are Treasury Bonds and Treasury Bills, Eurodollars, international currencies (the British Pound, the Japanese Yen, the Swiss Franc), and more recently, stock index futures. Futures are contracts standardized in quantity and quality, for the purchase or sale of a commodity at a specified future time and place. All transactions are placed through a commodity exchange by a member of the exchange.

Commodities investment is often considered the high-wire act of the investment arena. Substantial risk is the first key term associated with commodity trading. In the hands of knowledgeable and sophisticated professionals, commodities can be an investment that provides substantial gain. As a means of enhancing financial security for one's older years, the first rule for the individual investor is to understand thoroughly the investment tool and the risk of capital; the saying that 95% of commodity players lose contains some truth. Once thoroughly understood, however, commodities trading can enhance a diversified portfolio when sufficient risk capital exists to permit it.

Buyers or sellers must post collateral, or margin, when trades are made in order to show good faith in fulfilling their future obligations. The value of contracts is determined by the price of entry, or cost per unit, multiplied by the quantity. The transactions are contractual obligations to be satisfied prior to the designated date of delivery, either by taking or making physical delivery of the approved grade and quantity of the commodity.

The majority of commodities transactions are closed out prior to delivery by offsetting sales or purchases of the same commodity on the exchange for an equivalent quantity and delivery date. Contractual obligations of certain futures contracts, for example a stock index future, are satisfied by offsetting sales or purchases or by cash settlements of the amount on the expiration date of the contract. The investor's profit or loss is the difference between the price at which he or she acquired the futures contract and its value on the offsetting trade or, if held until expiration, its value on the expiration/settlement date.

Futures markets are organized by commodity futures exchanges. The exchanges standardize the terms of all contracts, oversee trading, and coordinate all payments. Only members of an exchange are permitted to trade. Future orders received by member firms are transmitted to the exchange floor for execution. This is achieved by an open outcry system where bids and offers are presented to all members of the pit or ring present at the time.

With the advent of screen-trading computer networks, buyers and sellers are matched electronically. The two largest exchanges in the U.S. are the Chicago Board of Trade (CBOT) and the Chicago Mercantile Exchange (CME). Other exchanges include the New York Mercantile Exchange (NYMEX), the Commodity Exchange (COMEX), and the Kansas City Board of Trade (KCBOT). Foreign commodity exchanges include the London International Futures Exchange (LIFE), and the Singapore International Financial Futures Exchange (SIMEX).

In the United States, legislation by Congress was enacted to regulate trading, the exchanges, the brokers, brokerage houses, advisors, and pool operators. The controlling legislation, known as the Commodity Exchange Act (1974), is designed to promote the orderly and systematic marketing of commodities and commodity futures contracts, while preventing fraud, speculative excess, and price manipulations. The act is implemented by the rules and regulations set by the Commodity Futures Trading Commission (CFTC). The CFTC is the government agency responsible for regulating domestic commodity exchanges and commodity futures trading. The National Futures Association (NFA) is the self-regulatory body of commodity professionals. Any violations of the Commodity Exchange Act are subject to punishment including revocation of registration, civil fines, and imprisonment.

The two basic groups of participants in futures trading are "hedgers" and "speculators." Those individuals or companies directly involved with the production, marketing, or processing of certain commodities (the cash commodity or actuals market), such as farmers or mining companies, utilize futures markets primarily for hedging, a strategy designed to minimize losses from price fluctuations over a period of time. This generally covers the time between which merchandisers or processors contract to sell their raw or processed commodities and the time they must deliver. The objective of hedgers in the futures market is to protect the profit they expect to earn from their farming, merchandizing, or processing operations. Many hedge strategies share the basic concept of minimizing risk exposure to interim price fluctuations. Other examples of hedging include U.S. companies that rely on imported goods or parts for manufacturing. If the company requires five million Swiss Francs in three months to pay for parts, the company can lock in the exchange rate by using the currency futures market to offset devaluation over that period of time.

Unlike hedgers, speculators generally do not expect either to deliver or receive physical commodities, or to hedge against price volatility, but rather to profit from price fluctuations in the value of commodity futures contracts. Speculators, often derided as gamblers, provide an essential element in futures trading—liquidity. Hedgers tend to be all buyers or all sellers at a given time. Without speculators to sell to or buy from or, in other words, to take the opposite side of the risk, futures markets could not function. The efficiency of any free-market operation requires a fairly equal number of buyers and sellers, and imbalance of the buyer/seller ratio is similar to an imbalance in demand and supply of a given commodity. When corn crops are destroyed by natural forces, for example, the price of corn rises drastically because demand is greater than supply, not because of speculators in the futures market. Inflation worries may cause a rise in gold prices, not due to lack of the supply of gold, but rather to individual beliefs (correct or incorrect) that gold is a safer investment when inflation rises. Speculations in the commodity markets are essential to hedging, and help achieve a stabilization of price.

Most trading for individual investors is through brokerage houses, whether individuals are making decisions or are part of pools or funds where managers handle trading strategies. Brokerage houses charge commissions for each trade enacted, and all trading transactions are made through members of a commodity exchange. Margin accounts are set up for the trading activities, and margin requirements (basically down payments) range roughly from 5 to 20% of contract values.

In stock investments, investors are required to place a margin (down payment) of 50% or more of the stock price, with the remainder amount loaned at a broker loan rate to fulfill 100% of the purchase obligation. Commodity margins are based on fixed minimums per unit or per contract, ranging from 5 to 20% of the actual cost of the futures contracts, and are good faith performance bonds. There are no loans made to cover the additional costs of the contracts. This creates opportunities to leverage larger positions in commodities than in stocks, but price movements in commodities, relative to margin requirements, can create very large losses or profits, and it is in this area that investors must thoroughly familiarize themselves to fully comprehend the risk. Profits and losses are treated similarly to stocks in tax rules, both being capital items. However, there are no state or federal taxes involved in the purchase or sale of commodity positions.

The leap in volume of commodity trading during the last 20 years has been dramatic. Commodity trading is now global in nature, particularly in financial and currency futures trading. The different levels of income-producing investments, whether personal or corporate, domestic or international, along with the shifting coalition of interest groups, keeps the financial structure in a constant state of change. Desires to preserve and increase capital motivates financial innovations around tax and regulatory restrictions imposed by government, and reactions can be transitory or lasting. The Eurodollar bond market, for example, was created by reaction to U.S. ceilings on the rate of interest commercial banks could offer on time deposits. With the volatility of interest rates in the 1960s and 1970s, U.S. commercial banks were aware that this restriction did not apply to dollar-denominated time deposits in their overseas branches, particularly in Western Europe. Eurodollar financial futures were created and are still traded in the futures market despite subsequent regulation changes and interest rate retraction.

Currency contracts, Eurodollar bonds, and financial futures are all part of a complex and creative international investment market so intertwined it appears incomprehensible to the average investor. These complex instruments can be daunting to the uninitiated, but like the complexities of modern medical and tax forms and procedures, choices to further financial gain through commodities can be sorted through with the assistance of specialists and a thorough understanding of risk for investors, whether they are in their middle years planning for retirement or have already retired. (See also AGENTS AND BROKERS, ASSETS ALLOCATION AFTER RETIREMENT, EQUITY SECURITIES, FINANCIAL ADVISORS, and FINANCIAL COUNSELING.)

References

Bernstein, Jacob. 1993. *The Investor's Quotient: The Psychology of Successful Investing in Commodities and Stocks.* New York: John Wiley & Sons.

Miller, Merton H. 1991. *Financial Innovations and Market Volatility.* New York: Blackwell.

Schwager, Jack D. 1984. *A Complete Guide to the Futures Markets.* New York: John Wiley & Sons.

Mary Anne Keefer

CONDOMINIUMS, a form of real estate ownership, in which owners have ownership rights to individual units consisting of all airspace found within the interior surfaces of walls, ceiling, and floors, and an undivided interest in the common property of the complex. The common areas include the land under the unit, exterior walls, roof, lobbies, hallways, meeting rooms, elevators, and the surrounding areas such as parks, pools, tennis courts, and parking areas. Many of these units are located in popular retirement areas, such as California, Arizona, and Florida, appealing to retirees and elderly persons seeking warm weather.

Buyers of condominium units inevitably become members of the condominium owner's association, which governs the management of the property and its common areas. The association is run by a board of directors elected by the owners, and the board usually hires a manager and related staff to administer the complex. A condominium association is responsible for various tasks, including interior and exterior building maintenance and repairs, safety, financial and budgetary topics, rules and regulations, and social functions. It also oversees insurance and tax matters and sets forth policies concerning delinquent fees or assessments from individual owners. Subcommittees comprised of residents are often charged with specific administrative responsibilities.

Most of the monthly condominium association fees paid by owners fund routine maintenance of the condominium complex. Smaller portions fund needed interior maintenance such as plumbing or electrical work, and exterior maintenance such as roofing or landscaping. The association may also collect assessments to pay the property taxes for the common areas. Some portion of the fee is set aside in a building reserve fund in the event of large unexpected future maintenance expenses. Residents may still be charged one-time assessments to cover larger maintenance demands (e.g., new roof, plumbing) when the condominium association reserve funds are insufficient. Most importantly, the condominium association has the responsibility of enforcing rules and regulations established for the complex. Responsibilities can range from handling a complaint from a disgruntled owner to having a lien put on a unit because an individual owner has not paid the required fees or assessments.

Condominium ownership offers the elderly a host of benefits, including a maintenance-free lifestyle, a relatively low-cost form of housing, and the use of common area facilities for social functions—typically holiday parties, swimming, tennis, or golf. Some condominium complexes have gates or employ full-time security guards for added safety. Also, since most neighbors live close together, theft is discouraged and aid is available in medical and other emergencies. The satisfaction of a condominium's occupants will often depend on the regulations established for the complex and how well the management performs. Owners can voice opinions at association meetings, which are held at regular intervals, and can cover such topics as association dues or necessary changes in current rules or regulations.

Noticeable disadvantages associated with condominium unit ownership may include overcrowding, an overbearing condominium association, and limitations on financing the unit. Older persons with pets should determine whether their pets are permitted by the condominium association's regulations.

Mortgage payments on a condominium unit are typically comparable to rents paid for apartments, yet condominium ownership offers tax benefits, owner equity, and the possibility of future appreciation in value. Owners are also free to decorate the interior of the unit as they wish, unlike an apartment rental, and ownership of a condominium unit can eliminate anxieties associated with apartment living, such as fear of eviction, distaste for negotiating lease terms, or future rent increases. Since the management is often better for condominiums than for rental apartments, elderly buyers are more likely to find quieter, more mature, and more compatible neighbors.

With the high land costs associated with today's real estate markets, many developers are being forced to maximize the density of units in condominium complexes to achieve a worthwhile profit. Noises from neighbors can become a burden, especially for elderly newcomers who may have lived in single-family detached residences, and denser developments can limit the amount of privacy enjoyed by owners. Some complexes lack adequate visitor parking spaces to host guests.

Some complexes may handle requests for needed maintenance slowly, and this can be a burden for an elderly person who needs expeditious repairs. An interested buyer should become aware of all rules and regulations concerning the complex and also seek out the opinions of residents on the efficiency and consideration of management. If there is disagreement between management and owners or among owners on how situations should be implemented or handled, tension may result. Improper or inefficient management, poor market conditions, or poor construction can cause condominium association fee increases.

Financing and future refinancing should also be considered by prospective owners. Most lenders follow a set of strict guidelines when considering loans on a condominium unit. For example, if the percentage of owner-absentee (rented) units in the complex reaches a certain percentage (typically 30–50%), it will be difficult for a potential buyer to receive financing. Problems can also arise when the owner of a condominium unit wishes to obtain secondary financing, as certain lenders may refuse to make home equity loans on condominium units. Further, most lenders prefer to diversify their mortgage portfolios and will usually only make a certain number on the units in any given complex. (See also CONTINUING CARE RETIREMENT COMMUNITIES, COOPERATIVE OWNERSHIP IN HOUSING, HOMEOWNERSHIP, HOUSING, MORTGAGE INSTRUMENTS, and REVERSE MORTGAGES.)

References

Freedman, Warren. 1992. *The Law of Condominia and Property Owners' Associations.* New York: Quorum Books.

Golant, Stephen M. 1992. *Housing America's Elderly: Many Possibilities/Few Choices.* Newbury Park, CA: Sage Publications.

Miller, Joel E. 1991. *Cooperative and Condominium Apartments.* Washington, DC: Tax Management, Inc.

Wiedemer, John P. 1990. *Real Estate Finance*, Sixth Edition. Englewood Cliffs, NJ: Prentice Hall.

Andrew Quang Do

CONSERVATORSHIP. See Attorneys; Durable Power of Attorney; Elder Law Practice; Guardianship.

CONSUMER CREDIT. See Banking Services for the Mature Market; Bankruptcy; Consumer Protection for the Elderly; Credit Cards; Mortgage Instruments.

CONSUMER PROTECTION FOR THE ELDERLY, federal, state, and local statutes enacted to protect older consumers. Significant legislation that protects older consumers includes the unfair and deceptive acts and practices statutes, the home solicitation sales acts, the Truth in Lending Act, the Fair Credit Reporting Act, and the Fair Debt Collection Practices Act. Financial exploitation of the elderly can take many forms, ranging from inappropriate use of powers of attorney, where older persons lose control of their finances, to overreaching by relatives that deprives older people of limited resources. There is no area, however, that has more potential for financial abuse than the consumer area.

Unfair and deceptive acts and practices statutes, commonly known as UDAP statutes, exist in all 50 states and the District of Columbia. These statutes prohibit unfair, false, misleading, and deceptive acts or practices committed by sellers, not only in the sale of goods and services, but also in advertising or soliciting the sale of goods or services. While numerous unfair and deceptive acts or practices have been declared unlawful, several are particularly prevalent in transactions involving elderly consumers. These include: (1) representing that the subject of a consumer transaction has sponsorship, approval, performance characteristics, accessories, uses, or benefits it does not have; (2) representing that a specific price advantage exists when it does not; (3) knowingly making false or misleading statements upon which a consumer may rely to his or her detriment; and (4) using the word "free" without clearly and conspicuously setting forth all terms, conditions, and obligations upon which the "free" goods or services are contingent.

All UDAP statutes provide remedies to consumers; however, remedies and enforcement vary from state to state. In some states, consumers may sue sellers to rescind a transaction and may receive up to three times the amount of actual damages. Many state UDAP statutes also provide for the award of legal fees. Some states do not permit consumers to go to court under a consumer protection statute, but permit only the state attorney general's office to seek an order stopping the unfair or deceptive act or practice. Since remedies and enforcement vary from state to state, consumers and consumer advocates are encouraged to check their own state consumer laws.

Marketing to the elderly of durable medical equipment, such as walkers, wheelchairs, and seat lifts often involves misrepresentations in price, benefits, uses, and characteristics. Elder consumer abuse also occurs in the advertising and sale of hearing aids. A typical advertising lure is to proclaim that a hearing aid has the ability to distinguish between background noise and speech. A hearing aid, however, only amplifies sound and cannot eliminate background noise. A hearing aid cannot restore hearing loss, despite claims to the contrary. Furthermore, a supplier may advise an elderly consumer that Medicare* will pay the cost of the hearing equipment. Medicare, however, does not cover hearing aids, and pays for hearing tests only when necessary to diagnose a medical problem. The Federal Trade Commission (FTC) and the Federal Drug Administration (FDA), both of which regulate hearing aids, have obtained consent orders against manufacturers to stop false advertising and misrepresentations regarding their products.

Home Sales

Mail order, telephone, and door-to-door sales present opportunities to defraud older persons whose mobility or ability to comparison-shop is limited by money, disability, or health. The first rule is called the "FTC Door-to-Door Sales Rule." Under this rule, if a consumer is solicited in person, by telephone, or by mail at home, or if an agreement to purchase is made at a place other than the seller's place of business, the seller must give the buyer a three-day right to cancel the purchase.

Sellers must inform consumers in writing that they have this right and that, if they wish to cancel the purchase, they must sign, date, and send or deliver a cancellation form to the seller within three business days of the purchase. This rule applies to all sales, leases, or rentals of consumer goods or services with a purchase price of $25 or more. Certain home sales, such as insurance, securities, and real estate, are exempt from the rule. Also, the FTC Door-to-Door Sales Rule does not cover transactions conducted entirely by mail or telephone or arising from an immediate bona fide personal emergency.

Because of the FTC rule, every state has passed home solicitation sales acts that provide three-day rights of cancellation for home solicitation sales. Some states provide greater rights than provided under the FTC rule. In Ohio, for example, transactions made entirely by telephone or mail are covered under Ohio's Home Solicitation Sales Act if the seller initiates the contact. All state home solicitation sales statutes require sellers to notify the buyers of their right to cancel the purchase. In many states, including Ohio, if this required notice fails to comply with a state's home solicitation sales act, the three-day period of cancellation does not begin to run until the seller complies with the required notice provisions. Failure to comply with the state home solicitation sales act is itself a deceptive act or practice in violation of the state's Unfair and Deceptive Acts and Practices provisions.

The second FTC rule useful for elderly consumers is the "Mail Order Rule." This rule requires mail order sellers to have procedures that reasonably assure delivery within 30 days of receipt of the order, unless the solicitation conspicuously states otherwise. This rule also requires sellers to inform buyers of expected revised shipping dates and the reasons for delay. Buyers must be given the option to cancel when delays occur, and sellers must make prompt refunds to buyers who cancel delayed or unfilled orders. Violations of the FTC Mail Order Rule constitute unfair and deceptive acts and practices.

Credit Reporting

Consumer protection statutes exist to protect not only buyers of goods and services but also consumers who apply for and obtain credit. Two important federal statutes govern credit transactions. The first is the Truth in Lending Act (TILA), a disclosure statute intended to prevent consumers from being misled about the cost of financing a consumer transaction. The act requires disclosure by creditors of all terms of credit, so that consumers can compare the cost of credit with other prospective lenders.

Creditors must disclose the amount financed, the finance charge (expressed as an annual percentage rate), and the sum of the amount financed. They must also disclose the number, amount, and due dates of all payments and, when a debt has been collateralized, they must provide evidence that a security interest has been taken in the property. Creditors must make these credit disclosures in a clear and conspicuous manner, in writing on a form the consumer may keep.

The Truth in Lending Act also provides consumers the right to rescind within three business days any consumer credit transaction in which a security interest is or will be taken in the consumer's residence. This three-day right to cancel does not apply to mortgages used to purchase property. If a creditor refuses to rescind a transaction, the consumer may sue to rescind the transaction. Consumers may sue creditors who violate TILA to recover actual damages or statutory damages equal to twice the amount of any finance charge up to $1,000 and reasonable attorney fees.

The second statute that affects consumer credit transactions is the Fair Credit Reporting Act (FCRA). This statute regulates consumer credit reporting agencies, including credit bureaus. Since credit reports and credit histories are relied on by prospective lenders, the act requires credit reporting agencies to maintain, keep, and provide accurate and confidential credit information about consumers. Under FCRA, if a consumer is denied credit on the basis of adverse information contained in a credit history, the prospective lender must notify the consumer and supply the name and address of the credit reporting agency making the credit report. Consumers are entitled to receive copies of their credit histories without charge, if they make a request within 30 days after notification of denial of credit by a lender. Otherwise, consumers may be required to pay a charge.

Consumers may dispute the completeness or accuracy of any information contained in a credit history, and the agency must investigate the dispute within a reasonable period of time. If the investigation shows the disputed information is inaccurate or unverifiable, the information must be deleted from the credit history. If the dispute is not resolved by an investigation, consumers may prepare a brief statement explaining their side of the dispute, which must be noted in all subsequent credit reports.

A consumer may request the credit reporting agency to provide notice of a deletion of information or a copy of a borrower's explanatory statement to any lender who received a credit report within the previous six months. Consumer credit reporting agencies may not charge consumers for the cost of notifying creditors of information deletions. Credit agencies must also delete information that is more than seven years old, except in the case of a bankruptcy, which can remain on credit histories for 10 years. Violation of the FCRA by credit reporting agencies subjects them to actual damages, punitive damages for willful violations, and, if consumers are successful, court costs and reasonable attorney fees.

Debt Collection

Consumers of all ages have the right to be free from harassing or threatening action from bill collectors. Most state UDAP statutes apply to bill collectors if they commit deceptive acts. The Fair Debt Collection Practices Act (FDCPA) applies to bill collectors who collect amounts owed to third parties, but does not apply if the collector is an employee of the creditor. Under the FDCPA, debt collectors cannot make false threats to file reports with local credit reporting agencies or to institute legal action. They may not tell consumers that a garnishment of wages or a levy on the debtor's assets will be obtained; they must state instead that neither of these can happen until a court has entered a judgment against the debtor. Debt collectors may not misidentify themselves, impersonate attorneys or government officials, or send a notice which resembles a lawsuit. They are also prohibited from calling at odd times or engaging in abusive behavior.

The FDCPA requires debt collectors to inform consumers they are attempting to collect a debt and that they have 30 days from the date they receive written notice to dispute the validity of a debt. If a consumer writes within 30 days to dispute the debt, collectors must obtain and mail verification of the debt to the consumer. Violations of the FDCPA by a debt collector may result in liability for actual damages, additional damages not exceeding $1,000, court costs, and reasonable attorney fees. (See also BANKRUPTCY, CREDIT CARDS, CRIME PROTECTION, FINANCIAL ELDER ABUSE, MARKETING TO ELDERS, and MASS MEDIA AND THE ELDERLY.)

References

American Association of Retired Persons. 1993. *A Report on Hearing Aids—User Perspectives and Concerns.* Washington, DC: AARP.

Maney, Ardith, and Loree Gerdes. 1994. *Consumer Politics: Protecting Public Interests on Capitol Hill.* Westport, CT: Greenwood Press.

National Consumer Law Center. 1991. *Unfair & Deceptive Acts & Practices,* Third Edition and Supplement. Washington, DC: NCLC.

U.S. Congress, House Committee on Agriculture. 1994. *Rural Consumer Protection Act of 1994.* Washington, DC: U.S. Government Printing Office.

U.S. Congress, Senate Special Committee on Aging. 1993. *Consumer Fraud and the Elderly: Easy Prey? Hearing Before the Special Committee on Aging.* Washington, DC: U.S. Government Printing Office.

Alma P. Yaros and Gregory S. French

CONTINUING CARE RETIREMENT COMMUNITIES (CCRCs), facilities offering an array of housing, services, and health care choices, usually through a contract to which the resident agrees at the time of entry. The continuum of care refers to the notion that an elderly person may enter the community as an independent person (or member of a couple) and live in an apartment or small cottage, then move to a personal care (or assisted living) unit, and then to a skilled nursing care unit. In most CCRCs the residents take their meals in a central dining room. The contract governs the economic and care relationship between the resident and the facility, and usually provides for lifetime care of the resident. CCRC contracts take a variety of forms, from a large up-front, nonrefundable payment to pay-as-you-go arrangements. The purpose of all contracts is to provide the resident with the peace of mind that derives from the continuum of care guarantee.

Knowledge of CCRC options and how they are financed will be helpful to prospective residents, those with primary responsibility for the well-being of an older person, those who provide them with legal and financial advice, and professionals who assist clients of all ages with retirement planning.

Housing and Living Arrangements

Independent living units are much like a home, whether detached units or apartments. Residents normally transfer their furniture to the CCRC unit, which typically has one or two bedrooms, a living room, kitchen, and bath. They may retain use of their automobile, and generally experience no restriction on their activities except specified meal times if they wish to use the congregate dining room. Persons who occupy independent living units are expected to care for themselves, that is, to perform all activities of daily living (ADLs), such as bathing, dressing, eating, toileting, transferring (as from a bed to a chair), walking, and getting out of the house on one's own. They should also be able to perform most instrumental activities of daily living (IADLs), which go beyond physical activities to incorporate aspects of cognitive reasoning and social functioning. IADLs include walking outside of the home, shopping, food preparation, managing money, house cleaning, using the telephone effectively, and taking medications per instructions.

When a resident loses the ability to perform one or two ADLs or has a combination of ADL and IADL losses, the resident moves to a personal care unit, where assistance with such activities is provided by the community. These units are often one room with a bath, similar to an apartment. Residents take their meals in the congregate dining room unless they are unable to do so. Depending upon the provisions of the contract with the CCRC, personal assistance is either provided by the CCRC or may be obtained on a fee-for-service basis. In some communities, assisted living services may be provided in the independent living unit, especially if an independent spouse also resides in the unit. If there is a loss of additional ADLs and/or the CCRC resident experiences a deterioration in a chronic condition, it may be advisable for the resident to move to a skilled nursing unit. Skilled care units are usually a separate but contiguous part of the community, and are essentially attached nursing homes*. The CCRC option may be attractive to a healthy retired couple because as one spouse needs a higher level of care, they may each reside in a separate section of the community, but with ease of access to one another.

Some CCRCs provide community services for nonresidents, employees, and people on their waiting list. Adult day care, hospice, respite nursing care, delivered meals, and support groups for those who care for relatives with Alzheimer's or Parkinson's diseases are examples (American Association of Homes for the Aging 1990).

Services and Amenities

Since the CCRC is a self-contained living environment for elderly people, communities offer a variety of services to residents. These include meals, grounds maintenance, building maintenance, light and/or heavy housekeeping, activity and recreational programs, prescribed diets, transportation, laundering, emergency call and security systems, social services, and utilities. Some communities even include speech and physical therapy, podiatry, and recreational therapy. Amenities provided by many communities are activities directors, an auditorium, barber and beauty shops, carports or garages, cable television, a chaplain and chapel, a craft program, an exercise room and exercise programs, a game room, garden plots, walking trails, and even guest accommodations. Larger communities may have banks, coffee shops, golf courses, putting greens, pharmacies, saunas, swimming pools, and even physician and dentist offices on site (American Association of Homes for the Aging 1990).

CCRC Contracts and Payment Methods

Financing residency in a CCRC tends to take one of two general approaches. Under the endowment or advance fee plan, the resident makes a large up-front payment, which is then followed by more modest monthly payments during the tenure in residence. The endowment may or may not be refundable. In general, the larger the portion that is refundable, the larger the size of the endowment. In most arrangements, the portion that is refundable declines through time. Liberal refund provisions, or communities that require no endowment, compensate by charging larger monthly residence fees. Large endowments and/or stringent refund provisions tend to characterize CCRCs that provide strong guarantees of life care combined with limitations in how much monthly fees may be increased during a resident's stay in the community. Small endowments, liberal refund provisions, or communities with no entrance fee are more likely to have weaker life care guarantees.

The American Association of Homes and Services for the Aging categorizes three types of CCRC contracts. An *all-inclusive* contract provides for housing, services, amenities, and an unlimited amount of nursing care for the life of the resident. It provides for complete life care with little or no significant increase in monthly fees. This arrangement typifies the pure life care community because the contract combines a large health care insurance element with the residential living cost element. In effect, the residents share the cost of long-term nursing and catastrophic health care. A *modified* care contract includes provision for residential living services, but restricts the amount of long-term nursing care available without additional cost. For example, the contract may specify that 60 or 90 days per year of nursing care will be provided at little or no increase in the monthly fee, after which a per diem rate applicable for nursing care in the area will be charged. A modified care contract may also specify the types of nursing care that will be provided during the period of contractual coverage, with additional payment required for care not covered. In general, the modified care contract will carry lower entrance and monthly fees than the extensive contract because less nursing care is guaranteed. *Fee-for-service* contracts include residence and a limited amount of emergency nursing care. In most cases, residents are guaranteed access to the nursing facility, but pay the full cost of care on a per diem basis at prevailing market prices. Meals and all other services are acquired on a pay-as-you-go basis. Advance and monthly fees tend to be the lowest in this type of CCRC, and many fee-for-service communities require either no advance fee or a very small one (American Association of Homes for the Aging 1990). As reported in 1992, all-inclusive care contracts constituted 36% of all CCRC contracts issued, modified care contracts constituted 26%, and fee-for-service contracts 38% (Cutler 1993).

Contract Concerns

The CCRC contract combines charges for occupying a living unit, certain services and amenities, and nursing care. As such, it combines purposes and commingles funds deemed necessary for specific needs. Actuarial assessment of an advance fee requires estimation of the costs of operating the residential community over time, including the costs of food and food service and the cost of nursing care in the future. Utilization rates depend upon estimated life expectancies, when nursing care will be needed, and for what duration. In essence, the contract combines an occupancy right with a nursing care insurance policy. Occupancy costs may relate to operating expenses, amortization of construction debt, maintenance and refurbishment costs, and a reserve to repay the advance fees of residents who leave the community, when applicable. Under contracts where life care is guaranteed, nursing costs include a reserve for skilled care for residents who can no longer pay their monthly fees. At the same time, the contract never provides ownership of a living unit, nor does it provide an undivided interest in real property. Life care contracts are not forms of securities and they do not establish typical landlord-tenant relationships. They are legal oddities that have been banned in some states and severely restricted in others (Higgins 1992). Some CCRCs have failed because the sponsoring organization has underestimated life expectancy and the extent of nursing care that had to be provided. In fact, the actuarial establishment of an advance fee is very difficult, and has led to a movement away from endowment arrangements. Sponsors have exhibited a desire to shift the risk of care to residents, and residents have seen it to be in their interest to accept this risk. Smaller advance fees or pure fee-for-service contracts allow the CCRC resident access to the services of the community without bearing the risk of catastrophic financial loss, even though the monthly fees are higher (Higgins 1992).

CCRC Accreditation

CCRCs are accredited by the American Association of Homes and Services for the Aging. Standards apply to the clarity of the CCRC contract, the community's ability to render quality physical, social, and psychological services and care to its residents, and the community's financial disclosure practices. A list of accredited communities may be obtained by contacting the Continuing Care Accreditation Commission.

Deciding to Enter a CCRC

Deciding to enter into an endowment contract can be a permanent decision. Lifestyle preferences should be examined carefully. Many seniors do not wish to live in an age-segregated environment. They may prefer to be closer to family, friends, shopping, and recreational sites. Some of the benefits of a life care community can be attained with fewer restrictions and less cost. Increasingly, home care agencies are able to accomodate the loss of an ADL or IADLs through delivery of care and/or meals at home, so elderly people are able to remain in a home that contains many fond memories. It is also possible to reside in an adult community geared to active, independent retirees, and combine this option with a long-term care insurance policy to guard against the cost of nursing care while preserving the equity of one's estate. Finally, many older people wish to bequeath their estate to their children or a favorite benevolent cause. This option may be materially diminished if a large advance fee is surrendered upon entry. The decision to enter a CCRC is often difficult to undo without incurring a material economic penalty. With these cautions in mind, the CCRC lifestyle and peace of mind the life care contract may convey will continue to make the CCRC an attractive option for many elderly people.

Before committing, however, the prospective resident should be certain to ascertain the sponsorship of the community, its financial condition, and who manages the community. It is generally better if the community is managed by the sponsor rather than a third party, so there is little chance for ambiguity should it be necessary to make a claim for failure to perform under the contract. It is also important to know whether and how long-term care insurance can be considered in conjunction with the contract, and how decisions are made when it is necessary to transfer a resident from one level of care to another. (See also BOARD AND CARE HOMES, CONDOMINIUMS, COOPERATIVE OWNERSHIP IN HOUSING, HOMEOWNERSHIP, HOSPICE CARE, HOUSING,

LONG-TERM CARE INSURANCE: A CONSUMER'S GUIDE, and NURS-ING HOMES.)

Organizations

American Association of Homes and Services for the Aging
American Association of Retired Persons
Continuing Care Accreditation Commission
National Association of Senior Living Industries

References

American Association of Homes and Services for the Aging. 1990. *The Continuing Care Retirement Community: A Guidebook for Consumers.* Washington, DC: Author.
Brecht, Susan B. 1994. "Continuing Care Retirement Communities." In *Housing the Aging Population: Options for the New Century,* ed. W. Edward Folts and Dale E. Yeatts. New York: Garland, Ch. 7.
Cutler, Neal E. 1993. "The Continuing Care Retirement Community as a Consumer Information Issue." *Journal of the American Society of CLU and ChFC* 47: 32–35.
Higgins, David P. 1992. "Continuum of Care Retirement Facilities: Perspectives on Advance Fee Arrangements." *Journal of Housing for the Elderly* 10: 77–92.

David P. Higgins

COOPERATIVE OWNERSHIP IN HOUSING, a form of ownership of multi-unit housing in which a corporation holds title to the property and grants occupancy rights for specific dwelling units under proprietary leases to shareholders. When a cooperative apartment is acquired, the buyer does not purchase a unit or apartment (dwelling unit), but buys shares in the cooperative housing corporation. The cooperative buyer becomes a shareholder in the corporation and enters into a proprietary lease for a particular dwelling unit. Cooperative owners thus have leasehold rights to their housing units and ownership rights in the cooperative housing corporation. The lease payment covers a pro rata share of the amounts needed to cover operating expenses, taxes, and the mortgage debt of the whole complex. Owners of cooperative housing are eligible for income tax deductions for their shares of the mortgage interest and property taxes paid by the cooperative corporation. This is in contrast to the owners of condominiums*, who have ownership of their occupied units plus an ownership interest with all other owners in the common area. Owning a cooperative apartment can be significantly less expensive than renting an apartment because landlord profits are not found in cooperative housing.

Most of the advantages and disadvantages of condominium occupancy also apply to cooperative housing. An important distinction is that individual households with corporate stock ownership in the cooperative housing project assume the additional financial responsibility of keeping the cooperative corporation solvent. A default by a cooperative unit owner means the remaining shareowners are responsible for paying the defaulted portion of the mortgage payments, real estate taxes, and operating expenses. If there are large enough numbers of defaulted shareowners, the financial burden may have a snowball effect, causing other shareowners in the cooperative housing complex to default. This snowball phenomenon is less likely to occur in the case of condominiums, since owners are only responsible for their own mortgage payments and real estate taxes.

Obtaining financing or refinancing for a cooperative unit loan is usually more difficult, since mortgage lenders cannot take the dwelling unit itself as collateral, and many do not wish to make long-term loans that are collateralized by the shares in the cooperative corporation. (An exception occurs where cooperatives are a common form of homeownership*. In New York, for example, lenders readily make loans to purchasers of cooperatives.) This may be an important factor for prospective owners to consider, especially should the market sour and shareholders become unable to sell their units. Then the only option is to sublet temporarily, but almost all cooperative apartment projects impose subleasing restrictions on the owner. Additionally, the managing board of the cooperative can reject a prospective buyer, making the selling of one's cooperative share take longer.

As the demographic profile in the United States changes to reflect an increasingly larger elderly population, the popularity of easy-to-maintain homeownership options such as cooperatives and condominiums is likely to increase. This trend will be encouraged by the current high costs associated with purchasing raw land and building materials, compelling developers to build projects with more units per acre than before. The condominium and cooperative forms of ownership offer more affordable options to prospective elderly buyers, as well as an assortment of exterior amenities and opportunities for increased social activities. Efficiently managed cooperative and condominium projects may thus constitute excellent housing options for U.S. elders. (See also CONDOMINIUMS, HOMEOWNERSHIP, and HOUSING.)

References

Golant, Stephen M. 1992. *Housing America's Elderly: Many Possibilities/Few Choices.* Newbury Park, CA: Sage Publications.

Miller, Joel E. 1991. *Cooperative and Condominium Apartments.* Washington, DC: Tax Management, Inc.

Taishoff, Lewis C. 1981. *Cooperative Housing Conversions.* New York: Praeger.

Andrew Quang Do

CORPORATE ELDER CARE PROGRAMS, a form of employee assistance for the benefit of the employees' older relatives. Human resource professionals in U.S. companies are extending the meaning of elder care to include a variety of innovative programs designed to help employees who care for an older member of the family. Elder care has been called the pioneering employee benefit of the 1990s (Friedman 1986).

Several rapidly converging factors have contributed to the growing interest in corporate elder care programs: the aging of America, changes in family structure that have eroded traditional caregiving at home, increased employment of women outside the home, and changing societal values about the balance between work and family life. Because of the demands it places on the employed caregiver, elder care has emerged as a bottom-line issue for leading companies. Caregiving can take a personal toll on a company's employees and impair their productivity on the job.

Benefits of corporate elder care programs accrue to several constituencies: employed caregivers, their companies, and older persons who are the indirect beneficiaries of the assistance their younger relatives receive by way of information and resources to help older persons with their current needs.

Types of Corporate Elder Care Programs

Company elder care programs vary widely. Some companies have recast existing benefits—flextime programs, leave benefits, work schedule adjustments, and financial benefits—to encourage their use for the dependent care needs of employees, including care of children, adolescents, and the elderly. Others offer initiatives designed specifically for elder care. A recent survey found that medium and large companies who employ a combined 23 million workers offer at least flexible scheduling options that could be identified and actively supported as usable for elder care. Of the total, nine million people work for corporations that also provide assistance specifically designed for elder care, such as information about long-term care services and support groups for caregivers. More than eight million people work for companies planning to expand existing elder care options or to offer new ones (General Accounting Office 1994).

Publications

Substantial numbers of companies have published or distributed elder care information to their work force. These have ranged from comprehensive handbooks about the issues associated with aging and the service system to information about specific topics such as Alzheimer's Disease. Other firms have developed work and family resource libraries that include books, videos, and audio cassettes on popular elder care issues.

Fairs and Support Groups

Many companies have supplemented informational materials with workshops, seminars, and support groups for employees who are currently caring for an older relative. Numerous corporations employ outside experts or services to conduct these seminars. Topics can include financial concerns such as estate planning*, paying for nursing home* care, and understanding the insurance needs of older persons.

Financial Assistance

Few companies provide direct financial assistance to employees or their relatives, but many offer dependent care assistance plans (DCAPs) under the Internal Revenue Code to employees. This benefit, however, can help only a small proportion of employed caregivers, because DCAPs are limited to elders who are legal dependents of the employee. Several companies have offered long-term care insurance* to their employees, and the employee can usually purchase a policy for a parent. In most cases, employees pay the full premium for coverage of a portion of nursing or home care costs for themselves or their older relatives, should long-term care be needed in the future.

Consultation and Referral Services

One common response by large employers has been to take a broad approach to the range of elder care problems employees face by offering them consultation and referral services. These services have been viewed as critical, since employees cannot come to work unless they have care arrangements for their older relatives (Rodgers and Rodgers 1989). Consultation and referral services have been designed to address specific issues employees said they needed: information, referrals to care providers, and individual counseling (Neal et al. 1988).

Elder care consultation and referral services, when comprehensively delivered, include access to an elder care professional with knowledge of the community where an older relative lives. This professional provides expert counseling and helps the employee identify concerns and reach informed decisions, based on detailed knowledge of local community resources. The services also provide education through counseling and written materials that help employees select appropriate care. They can refer to providers as diverse as home health and transportation programs, elder law attorneys, and bill-paying services. Employees and their families remain responsible for selecting and paying for any services they choose.

Development of Services

Several companies have gone beyond consultation and referral programs to increase the supply and quality of elder care (and child care) services in communities where employees, retirees, or older relatives live. IBM, in 1989, earmarked a portion of its Fund for Dependent Care Initiatives for elder care projects such as respite care development and recruitment and training of in-home health and social service workers. Later, the American Business Collaboration, which used IBM funds to leverage investment by other companies with similar needs, continued some investment in the elder care infrastructure. AT&T also announced, in 1989, a significant Family Care Development Fund of $10 million, jointly funded by its unions and management. This fund provided seed money to encourage the development and improve the quality of child and elder care programs.

Decision Making

There is no best way to select an elder care program. Many companies, however, go through a series of steps in examining elder care options. These include examining existing benefit programs, assessing employees' elder care responsibilities and needs, examining costs, and selecting an approach to meet the needs of the broadest group of employees.

Improving employee morale and productivity and responding to employee requests are the primary reasons corporations offer elder care plans. Reasons given by companies not planning to introduce or expand elder care benefits include concerns about costs, lack of a needs assessment, or unawareness of the issue (General Accounting Office 1994).

But the needs of employees with elder care responsibilities are becoming clearer, as are the impact of lost productivity in American corporations, retention of top performers, absenteeism, and tardiness. While corporate elder care is still in its infancy, innovative programs already in place help companies achieve their business objectives and increase employee productivity, and older persons receive the information and care they need. As the numbers of aging Americans increases even more rapidly in the decades ahead, demand for corporate elder care programs is likely to increase and even more innovative programs are likely to be developed. (See also CAREGIVING FOR THE ELDERLY, ESTATE PLANNING, LONG-TERM CARE INSURANCE, NURSING HOMES, and POSTRETIREMENT HEALTH INSURANCE: PRIVATE.)

Organizations

The Conference Board
The Bureau of National Affairs

References

Friedman, Dana. 1986. "Eldercare: The Employee Benefit of the 1990s." *Across the Board* (June).

General Accounting Office. 1994. *Long-Term Care: Private Sector Elder Care Could Yield Multiple Benefits.* Washington, DC: GAO.

Neal, Margaret, Neal Chapman, and Berit Ingersoll-Dayton. 1988. *Eldercare, Employees and the Workplace: Findings from a Survey of Employees.* Portland, OR: Research Institute on Aging, Portland State University.

Rodgers, Francene, and Charles Rodgers. 1989. "Business and the Facts of Family Life." *Harvard Business Review* (November-December).

Diane S. Piktialis

COST-OF-LIVING ADJUSTMENTS (COLAs), periodic additions to income payments that enable recipients to purchase the same amount and quality of goods and services over time. As experienced by older Americans, however, COLAs are annual increases to Social Security* benefits and a few other income payments that reflect the previous year's inflation rate in urban areas. Although a common perception is that older persons dependent on Social Security are protected from losing purchasing power, in actuality, after a few years they often cannot maintain the level of living they had upon retirement and experience increases in their cost of living greater than increases in their retirement income.

Understanding the reasons why COLAs fail to keep up with inflation as experienced by older Americans can be beneficial for planning a secure retirement. Financial advisors* often advise their older clients to earn a return on retirement investments that is greater than the inflation rate, but their clients are often satisfied with conservative investments instead that earn the current rate of inflation. The following provides information that financial advisors can use to explain to their clients why they are jeopardizing their financial future by being content with rates of return that only meet the current rate of inflation.

Why Do COLAs Fail to Keep Up?

Key points about COLAs that affect older Americans are: (1) COLAs do not adjust for cost of living, (2) COLAs are introduced with a time lag and always reflect what happened in the previous year—not what is currently happening in the U.S. economy, (3) not all sources of retirement income have COLAs, and (4) COLAs are based on an inflation rate that older Americans do not necessarily experience.

First, COLAs are calculated with a measure that does not reflect the cost of living. The Consumer Price Index (CPI) is used to determine COLAs, but this index measures changes in prices only and does not incorporate other changes that may occur as a result of price changes. Beef prices, for example, may increase more rapidly than other meat prices, and older persons may change their shopping patterns to substitute poultry for beef. Behavior changes that alter the cost of living are not reflected in the CPI and cause the CPI to overstate inflation as experienced by those who purchase lower-priced substitutions. The CPI is based on expenditures rather than income, and does not include taxes such as income and Social Security tax contributions. Therefore, changes in tax rates are not reflected in the CPI.

Second, by the nature of how the calculations are made, COLAs reflect inflation from the previous year. When rapidly rising inflation is experienced, COLAs do not compensate for the large price increases that retired persons see currently when they shop. The reverse is true when inflation occurs at a slower pace than the previous year and the COLA is greater than the rate of change in prices older persons are currently paying.

Third, not all retirement income has COLAs. Even benefits with COLAs, such as Social Security and federal Civil Service Retirement, have experienced COLA freezes, cuts, and delays.

Fourth, the CPI used to calculate COLAs for older Americans does not necessarily reflect the changes in prices for goods and services they buy. COLAs are determined by changes in the Consumer Price Index for Urban Wage Earners and Clerical Workers (CPI-W), an inflation index based on the spending patterns of households in which more than one-half of the income comes from clerical or wage occupations. The CPI-W represents about 32% of the total U.S. population and it excludes retired persons. Another index, the Consumer Price Index for All Urban Consumers (CPI-U) is based on the expenditures reported by almost all urban residents. The CPI-U includes retired persons, professional employees, the self-employed, the poor, the unemployed, and wage earners and clerical workers (who are also in the CPI-W). It represents about 80% of the U.S. population. The CPI-W registered a lower rate of inflation in seven of the last nine years (1985–1993). Older Americans who are dependent on Social Security can lose the ability to maintain their level of living when their COLAs are based on the CPI-W.

Older Americans are thought to experience lower rates of inflation than the younger population, since older people buy fewer goods and services. This difference is important when the items purchased have different rates of price change. It has been suggested also that the broad use of senior citizen discounts lowers the cost of living for the elderly.

Consumer Price Index for the Elderly

In the late 1980s, the U.S. Department of Labor's Bureau of Labor Statistics (BLS), the government agency that calculates the CPI, was directed by Congress to calculate an experimental Consumer Price Index for the Elderly (CPI-E). This experimental index for Americans 62 years old and older was based on existing data, reweighted to reflect expenditure patterns in the elderly population. A comparison with published CPIs found that the elderly experienced a higher rate of inflation from 1983 through 1987 than the rates reported for either the CPI-W or the CPI-U. However, it is important to remember that the CPI-E was an experimental index calculated for a brief time period and is not regularly published by the BLS.

In order to calculate a Consumer Price Index for the Elderly that could be used to determine COLAs, the measure must be designed to reflect the purchase behaviors of the elderly. The item and outlet samples surveyed for the index must represent the elderly population as well. Specifically, BLS must identify what should be tracked every month and where to gather prices for these items. The Consumer Expenditure Survey, used to determine the ''market basket'' of goods and services that consumers buy for the CPI-W and the CPI-U, does not include enough older persons to determine a CPI-E market basket. The Point-of-Purchase Survey is used to learn where consumers shop, but does not include enough elderly buyers to determine which outlets should be surveyed each month.

Broadening the surveys to include a larger elderly household population would take years and would be costly, and is unlikely under current budgetary constraints. Nonetheless, since a 1% overstatement of the inflation rate costs more than $4 billion each year in Social Security, federal retirement, and military COLAs, the cost of developing a new index may be a good investment. If, however, a CPI-E demonstrates that COLAs understate inflation and Social Security COLAs increase, obviously more federal funds would be paid out in benefits.

In the meantime, planning for a solvent retirement becomes a more difficult task. To keep up with the cost of living, retirement funds need to be placed in investments where they increase in value. Doing so, however, is likely to place the funds at a greater risk of loss.

Upcoming Changes for the CPI

In January 1994, BLS Commissioner Katharine G. Abraham announced the CPI may be changed. One change would reweight nearly 400 items in the CPI market basket. Approximately every 10 years the index is adjusted for changes in the mix of items that consumers purchase. Weights (the amount of influence or importance of specific prices) of items are adjusted for the changes in how consumers allocate their expenditures. For example, preliminary data indicate that since 1982–1984, the base period for the last revision, consumers are spending less on food and beverages and more on medical care (Schmidt 1993). In the next revision, a change in the price of food will probably have less influence on inflation than it does on the current CPI and a change in the price of medical care will probably have a greater impact. Over time, the weights begin to overstate the rate of inflation. There is concern that the COLAs are too high because it has been seven years since the last revision, and the BLS would like to begin efforts to reweight the CPI in 1995. This process will take several years.

Commissioner Abraham also stated that BLS will begin to publish experimental CPI indexes to address known problems, such as calculating changes in quality of items in the CPI. These experimental indexes will not include a CPI-E, but will include several alternative ways of calculating a CPI. Since BLS prefers to publish an experimental index for a period of several years before adopting a new methodology, none of these changes is likely to be implemented in the official index in the near future. (See also CASH FLOW PLANNING FOR RETIREES, FINANCIAL ADVISORS, FINANCIAL COUNSELING, FINANCIAL PLANNING, and SOCIAL SECURITY.)

References

Amble, Nathan, and Ken Steward. 1994. "Experimental Price Index for Elderly Consumers." *Monthly Labor Review* (May).
Bureau of Labor Statistics. 1988. "An Analysis of the Rates of Inflation Affecting Older Americans Based on an Experimental Reweighted Consumer Price Index." A study prepared for the Senate Select Subcommittee on Aging. Washington, DC: U.S. Department of Labor.
Bureau of Labor Statistics. 1992a. "Consumer Price Index." *BLS Handbook of Methods.* Bulletin 2414: 176–235.
Bureau of Labor Statistics. 1992b. "How BLS Measures Changes in Consumer Prices." *U.S. Department of Labor Program Highlights.* Fact Sheet No. BLS 92–3. Washington, DC: U.S. Department of Labor.
Bureau of Labor Statistics. 1993. *Understanding the Consumer Price Index: Answers to Some Questions.* Washington, DC: U.S. Department of Labor.
Schmidt, Mary Lynn. 1993. "Effects of Updating the CPI Market Basket." *Monthly Labor Review* 116: 59–62.

U.S. Senate, Special Committee on Aging. 1987. *Developing A Consumer Price Index for the Elderly.* Washington, DC: U.S. Government Printing Office.

Kathleen K. Scholl

CREDIT CARDS, flexible instruments for purchasing goods and services on installment credit. Consumer credit buying has a long-standing tradition in American society, especially for costly purchases such as houses, automobiles, and appliances. Drastic change, however, is evident in the increasing importance of all-purpose personal credit cards (e.g., VISA, Mastercard, American Express, Discover) as banks and other financial institutions successfully lured consumers away from proprietary gasoline and department store credit arrangements. Personal credit cards now enable consumers to make purchases or other financial transactions anywhere they want through a bank loan that can be paid off at the end of the month without incurring finance charges (within the specified "grace period"), or over time at specified fixed or variable interest rates (7–24%).

Only 20 years ago, today's widespread credit card use might have seemed fantastic, but several factors combined to make credit card debt a crucial economic arena for banks and other financial institutions. Among them are banking deregulation, a decline in U.S. real estate values, an increase in personal and commercial bankruptcies*, cheaper and more efficient computer information technologies, and the collapse of the risky corporate junk bond market. At the same time, declining purchasing power (real income fell 12.4% between 1972 and 1988) made Americans more dependent on credit to cushion their deteriorating standard of living. The growth of household debt accelerated during the 1982–1983 recession, and for the affluent, credit cards became a useful convenience. They provide a detailed record of transactions, free purchase protection and insurance, instant access to cash as well as an immediate line of credit for speculative purposes (e.g., a down payment on a rental property), and other transactions (from federal taxes to city parking tickets). Some "sponsored" credit cards enable frequent users to accumulate points for a variety of consumer gifts as well as free or discounted air travel, gasoline, long-distance telephone calls, and even the down payment on an automobile.

During the 1980s, banks expanded their credit card portfolios, shifting marketing strategies from affluent "convenience" users to people of more marginal economic means. Most recently, banks have aggressively recruited out-of-work younger and older consumers, such as college students and retirees. In the process, they enormously expanded the numbers of credit card users and broadened the range of uses from travel, restaurant, and entertainment to virtually the entire realm of consumer needs: college tuition, medical care, car repairs, postal services, catalog and television (cable) "home" shopping, and most recently, groceries. As Americans have struggled with growing economic difficulties in the 1980s and 1990s, credit cards have been used to launch new households, cushion domestic crises, survive periods of unemployment, finance medical emergencies, and even to pay burial costs. With the addition of cash advances and credit card checks or vouchers, consumer credit is now available to buy or pay for anything.

Economic and Demographic Background

Over the last decade, total installment credit has escalated drastically—from about $300 billion in 1980 to nearly $800 billion in 1993. The fastest-growing component of consumer debt has been revolving credit, which is primarily composed of outstanding balances on credit cards. Credit card debt rose from $3.9 billion in 1972 to $182 billion in 1992. It grew from 27% of total installment credit in 1988 to 37% in 1993. This reflects a substantial increase in the average debt of American households and has contributed to the subsequent rise in personal bankruptcies, to an all-time high of more than one million in 1991.

Debts of Older Americans

Significantly, the most rapid growth of consumer debt has been incurred by Americans least able to pay it off in the future: older workers and retirees. For example, between 1977 and 1986, the debt/income ratio rose only modestly for the 35–44 (81.4% to 81.5%) and 45–54 (58.4% to 62.0%) age brackets, but climbed dramatically for the older 55–64 (35.7% to 51.8%) and 65–74 (19.4% to 41.2%) age groups. This trend is ominous, as the relative financial prosperity of today's retirement population becomes comprised of the more financially insecure segments of the baby boom generation.

Two important trends, economic and demographic, will profoundly increase the dependence of older Americans on consumer credit. First, the post–World War II period featured an enormous increase in the U.S. standard of living. Favorable economic conditions contributed to high personal savings rates as well as considerable appreciation of residential dwellings; in 1989, housing assets accounted for 56% of total wealth among homeowning households ages 65–74 and had reached 70% for those aged 55–64. The second key trend is the aging of the American population. The early baby boomers (born between 1946 and 1954), who will begin retiring at the end of the decade, will have benefited from the economic prosperity of the Pax Americana and will initially tend to mirror the favorable financial profile of their parents' generation. This profile includes home ownership, moderate personal savings, substantial housing price appreciation, private pensions, and the experience of dual-income households arising from the greater participation of women in the postwar work force—especially among white-collar professionals beginning in the late 1960s.

For late baby boomers (born between 1955 and 1964), the situation will be less favorable because of lower home ownership rates and modest home price appreciation in the next two decades; the collapse of the U.S. real estate market is most often seen as having been associated with the recession of 1989.

The latter demographic trend is a critical factor in explaining a future pattern of intergenerational inequality. In fact, home ownership and the related capital gains allowance for sellers 55 and older (up to $125,000) are the most important determinants of net household wealth among older Americans; 75% of those older than 64 are homeowners and 84% have paid off their mortgages. Also, home equity loans have become the most popular and prudent form of colla- teralized credit for the U.S. middle class. But many of those who missed the great real estate appreciation gift of the 1980s will become increasingly de- pendent on more costly consumer credit in the long run. Thus, personal credit cards will tend to become part of the social safety net of the struggling middle class and working poor.

Credit Card Use among the Elderly

The most striking differences in consumer credit card use among older Amer- icans are associated with age and gender. Seniors in the United States are not a homogenous population, a fact that is reflected in their social activities and consumption patterns. The lifestyle of Americans ages 55 to 70 is clearly distinct from that of senior retirees older than 70–75. The younger group is much more active, and its middle-class members are more likely to take advantage of their leisure time and discretionary income by engaging in leisure* and recreation activities, travel*, entertainment, education*, and cultural events. According to the American Association for Retired Persons, two-thirds of its VISA card hold- ers are between 50 and 65 years old, and most of their purchases fall into categories such as travel reservations, hotel accommodations, plane tickets, res- taurant meals, and consumer catalog products. In 1990, the AARP offered its first fixed-rate VISA and by 1994 it added four "Classic" VISAs and a Gold Card. Middle-class seniors are of course more familiar with consumer credit and more likely to have continued their credit card use after retirement.

Credit card use by older seniors is not only more complex but is also influ- enced by gender-based relations. This group is less active and tends to be af- fected by emotional strains of changing professional and familial roles, and the loss of a spouse. It is comprised of more single women (especially widows) having less experience with economic responsibilities and employment outside of the household. Women older than 65 are more likely to be primarily de- pendent on the retirement and Social Security benefits of their husbands. Elderly women are least likely to have credit cards, due to a lack of established credit history, and many lose them following the loss (divorce, death, institutionali- zation) of authorizing spouses.

Two countervailing factors characterize credit card usage patterns of the oldest members of the senior group. First, those older than 70 are more likely to be culturally averse to using consumer credit due to harsh memories of the Great Depression; fewer than one-third (about 30%) of AARP credit card holders are older than 64. Older retirees tend to pay for purchases with cash or checks. Lack of experience with consumer credit causes many elderly seniors to be skeptical of "amazing" credit card offers or fearful that the banks will charge exorbitant interest rates. (Occasionally, AARP receives queries over whether credit cards are free "gifts.") Secondly, many older seniors are lonely and may welcome the excitement, entertainment, or companionship of discussing orders with catalog or Home Shopping Network salespeople. AARP records indicate a high purchase-return cycle among their most elderly card holders after they realize that credit card purchases are returnable and refundable.

Older Americans of moderate means were not aggressively targeted by banks for consumer credit cards until the late 1980s. Although respected by banks because of their accumulated assets and extensive histories of creditworthiness, they generated little profit for credit card divisions. Those seniors who initially obtained credit cards tended to use them sparingly and paid off balances monthly. Furthermore, they were less likely to purchase big-ticket items (furniture, appliances, stereos) and were stereotyped erroneously as having inactive and frugal lifestyles. This changed as more economically marginal seniors received credit cards in the early 1990s and swiftly accumulated high-interest debt.

As U.S. lifespans lengthen and health care costs soar, many older Americans face outliving their available financial resources. Personal expenses are growing rapidly, and, increasingly, people are purchasing medicines and even groceries on credit. Many who had counted on living in a mortgage-free home are finding that escalating property values, rising tax assessments, and other home-related costs claim a growing portion of their fixed incomes. At the same time, difficult economic times and life-cycle crises prompt adult children and grandchildren to seek help with living costs or even to return to parents' homes. Retirees on fixed incomes may make greater use of credit cards to help their families, even when they find it burdensome to do so. Also, marketing credit cards to low-income retirees who have little experience with consumer credit often leads to frequent purchases of discretionary products.

Research and Consumer Issues

Relatively little research has explored the social dimensions of credit card debt for other than marketing or macroeconomic purposes. New research, however, is combating popular stereotypes of the indolent consumer by arguing that consumer credit trends are inextricably linked to the changing economy, falling wages and household incomes, rising consumer prices, and the increasingly prominent risk of debt in the public and corporate arenas.

Many causes and consequences of credit card debt are beyond the control of individual consumers. However, practical knowledge about credit cards can help ease some of the anxieties and burdens of credit card debt. First, the Equal Credit Opportunity Act (ECOA) of 1975 forbids discrimination in granting access to credit on the basis of race, color, religion, national origin, sex, marital status, or age. Of course, minimum financial standards must be satisfied for credit approval, but industry practices still exist that effectively evade antidiscrimination statutes, such as "scoring" procedures that approve or deny credit applications based on the age, race, or gender of the applicant.

Creditors cannot discriminate against persons receiving income from social security or public assistance and must establish clear criteria for their credit-scoring systems that evaluate income deriving from annuities and pensions. Even so, creditworthiness standards can include age as a factor as long as the evaluation procedures are statistically sound. While these vague rules have yet to be legally challenged, various forms of social discrimination are widespread but difficult to detect in the consumer credit industry. The reasons for this difficulty are that banks tend to initiate the credit card application process, many actors are involved in the final approval, and a variety of formulas are used, based on different interpretations of personal credit histories and more subjective factors.

Although the ECOA guarantees fair access to consumer credit, its purview does not include many other sources of discrimination such as different credit limits, interest rates, and financial penalties. Other laws such as the Truth in Lending Act and the Fair Credit Reporting Act are concerned with the obligation of credit card companies to disclose the financial terms of their lending agreements. Prudent consumers may take advantage of the growing competition in the industry by choosing credit cards with low or no annual fees, selecting the lowest fixed-rate card available (interest rates range from 7 to 24%), understanding the complexities of adjustable percentage rate (APR) cards, assessing the benefits of introductory "tiered" offers such as transferring credit card balances at a lower interest rate, and even shifting to sponsored cards in order to accumulate credits for free consumer gifts, leisure services, and travel.

The 1986 federal tax law reform progressively phased out the deductibility of interest charges on consumer debt such as credit cards. As a result, one of the few options for reducing the effective cost of consumer credit is to convert credit card debt into home equity loans with fully deductible interest. Also, it is important to understand that heirs cannot "inherit" personal debts, unless they have been authorized to use an account and their name appears on credit cards. Of course, creditors do have the legal right to make the first claims on the financial assets of the estate.

Consumers must be vigilant in examining their statements for clerical errors and challenge these mistakes and the procedures that calculate individual creditworthiness. Consumers have the legal right to request copies of their credit report, contest their accuracy, and insist that they be reevaluated. More troubling is the complex issue of personal privacy, as all purchases are recorded and used in assessing creditworthiness. Financial institutions consider not only how reliable someone is in making monthly payments, but also what a person is buying and where products are purchased. Thus, creditors and mass marketers know much more about consumption and living patterns than could have been imagined a couple of decades ago.

Lastly, many families have developed mutual aid strategies to help relatives who have found themselves overwhelmed with consumer debt. Some cut up credit cards. Popular psychologists suggest special care during the holidays and other meaningful social events when many people tend to overuse their credit cards. Professional remedies range from keeping a Christmas fund jar throughout the year, recording a running balance by clipping half an index card to the back of all cards, to limiting the number and/or total cost of gifts.

Clearly, such suggested changes in personal behavior may not offer much help to the growing number of people who rely on their credit cards for necessities, although they may provide guidance for those who use them for discretionary purchases. The latter is important to those baby boomers who will soon be confronting their golden years with a much smaller nest egg and much greater personal indebtedness than their parents. While today's older Americans so far have been relatively successful in resisting credit card debt, tomorrow's senior citizens may find it an unwelcome but perhaps necessary encumbrance. (See also BANKING SERVICES FOR THE MATURE MARKET, BANKRUPTCY, EDUCATION OF OLDER AMERICANS, LEISURE, MARKETING TO ELDERS, and TRAVEL.)

Organizations
Consumer Credit Card Rating Service
Consumer Credit Counseling Services
Debtors' Anonymous Association (DAA)
National Center for Financial Education
National Foundation for Consumer Credit

Suggested Readings
Corrigan, Arnold, and Phyllis Kaufman. 1987. *How to Use Credit and Credit Cards.* Stamford, CT: Longmeadow Press.
Matthews, Arlene Modica. 1993. *Your Money, Your Self: Understanding Your Relationship to Cash and Credit.* New York: Simon & Schuster.

References
Congressional Budget Office. 1993. *Baby Boomers in Retirement: An Early Perspective.* Washington, DC: CBO.
Mandell, Lewis. 1989. *The Credit Card Industry: A History.* Boston: Twayne Publishers.
Manning, Robert D., and Brett Williams. 1996. *What's Debt Got to Do With It?* New York: Basic Books.
Pollin, Robert. 1990. *Deeper in Debt: The Changing Financial Conditions of U.S. Households.* Washington, DC: Economic Policy Institute.
Ritzer, George. 1995. *Expressing America: A Critique of the Global Credit Card Society.* Thousand Oaks, CA: Pine Forge Press.
Zelizer, Viviana A. 1994. *The Social Meaning of Money.* New York: Basic Books.

Robert D. Manning and Brett Williams

CRIME PROTECTION, recognition of factors that increase vulnerability to crime and measurements and strategies to reduce possible victimization. According to the Bureau of Justice Statistics (1994), persons 65 years old or older are the least likely of all age groups in the United States to become victims of crime. In fact, crime victimization rates among the elderly have generally been declining for more than 20 years. Personal safety, however, is a growing concern for older Americans, who as a group express a high fear of crime.

The elderly, like the general population, are more likely to experience household crimes such as larceny, burglary, and motor vehicle theft, and least likely to be victimized by violent crimes such as murder, rape, and robbery (Bureau of Justice Statistics 1994). Although the elderly generally experience the lowest property victimization rates, those who live in the inner city share higher rates of all crime in common with other city dwellers.

Alston (1986) describes who is likely to become a victim of crime by three characteristics: attractiveness, exposure, and guardianship. Attractiveness is related to "benefit," as some potential victims represent greater opportunity for gain than others. Wearing jewelry or carrying a purse usually can influence attractiveness. Exposure has to do with visibility and proximity. Visibility is a factor when persons are outside on the streets, and proximity suggests that it may be easier to victimize someone close by than having to travel to some distant suburb. Guardianship refers to forms of physical or social protection. Physical protection might involve staying home after dark, whereas social protection would include walking or living with a companion.

Purse-snatching, like pocket-picking, happens on public streets, where exposure and attractiveness combine with lack of guardianship to identify certain individuals as targets. It happens to persons who appear unstable and off guard. Purse-snatching and pocket-picking are exceptions to the negative relationship between age and victimization, as persons 65 years old and older are about as likely as those younger than 65 to be victims of personal larceny with contact.

Home burglary most often victimizes older persons. In burglary, proximity, opportunity, and physical protection are key to selecting targets. Most burglars do not want to meet their victims and usually enter when no one is home. A Kansas City study of older Americans reported that most burglary victims had no outside lights burning, thus lowering their guardianship factor.

Attractiveness, exposure, and lack of guardianship are the characteristics of older persons most likely to become victims. Since older men are more likely to be out, they are more likely to become victims. Blacks are more likely than whites to be victims, due to their greater likelihood to reside in inner city areas where crime is generally higher (exposure). Marriage provides guardianship, and married people enjoy the lowest victimization rates. Despite these patterns, there is no convincing evidence that older people are particularly sought out as targets for serious crimes.

Fear of Crime

Fear of victimization may be unrelated to actual crime rates, and extreme fear can be explained partially by media exaggeration of all violent crimes. A survey of Chicago residents, however, shows that fear of crime is positively correlated to victimization rates once rates are adjusted for exposure to risk. Thus, fear of crime should not be interpreted as irrational or unjustified, and fear, in fact, can be reduced by lowering victimization rates (Stafford and Galle 1984).

Fear among older persons is greatest when they lack social integration in the neighborhood and when they see neighborhood compositions changing, abandoned buildings becoming more widespread, and unsupervised teens loitering in their proximity. These community attributes add to a sense of loss of control, a characteristic strongly related to fear of crime (Donnelly 1989).

Costs of Crime

Personal contact with offenders during the crime is likely to produce greater fear, anxiety, and feelings of vulnerability as a result of the encounter. Those who already feel powerless and alienated find these feelings reinforced. Psychological costs to older victims, however, are not uniform and do not appear to differ from those of younger victims. Although burglary is a property crime, for example, it is perceived by young and old as a personal threat because it violates the idea of home as a safe place. Financially, older persons do not, in an absolute sense, lose more than younger persons, but if they are in a marginal economic position those losses they do incur pose a greater source of hardship. Further, older persons are more likely to be injured when they are physically attacked. Ultimately, all costs of crime depend on the social, economic, and physical resources older persons possess; those of lesser means are more vulnerable to the consequences of criminal acts.

Reducing Risks of Victimization

Older persons can reduce risks by being alert and by keeping the three characteristics of victims in mind. Staying home, thus avoiding outside activities, tends to increase isolation and may increase suspicion and fear as well. A more effective strategy is to improve individual and community awareness of the risk factors.

In terms of attractiveness, older persons should look more alert, and carry a purse tightly, if at all. With regard to exposure, traveling with companions helps substantially. Guardianship support includes locked doors, bright lights, and stronger window frames. Having adequate homeowners' or renters' insurance is important. Resources available in most communities assist individuals in victimization prevention programs. The American Association of Retired Persons has a wide range of pamphlets and brochures that outline practical strategies for personal safety.

Crime prevention also requires involvement at the community level. Rather than retreating into the home and becoming prisoners of fear, older persons must become involved in neighborhood and community activities. Knowing neighbors and participating in community programs are ways of staying connected. Safety programs include school safety programs, Safe House programs, escort services, Neighborhood Watch, and local dispute resolution. Being involved reintegrates citizens into a changing community and increases commitment to the physical and social environment. Seniors, having time and experience to offer, are invaluable to these efforts. (See also CONSUMER PROTECTION FOR THE ELDERLY, ETHICS IN FINANCIAL PLANNING, FINANCIAL ELDER ABUSE, and GUARDIANSHIP.)

References

Alston, Letitia. 1986. *Crime and Older Americans.* Springfield, IL: Charles C. Thomas.

Bureau of Justice Statistics. 1994. "Elderly Crime Victims." Washington, DC: U.S. Department of Justice.

Donnelly, Patrick. 1989. "Individual and Neighborhood Influences on Fear of Crime." *Sociological Focus* 22: 69–85.

Stafford, Mark, and Omer Galle. 1984. "Victimization Rates, Exposure to Risk and Fear of Crime." *Criminology* 22: 173–85.

Cathleen Burnett

D

DAY PROGRAMS FOR ADULTS, (also known as adult day care), community-based, nonresidential group programs that serve functionally and/or mentally impaired adults. Day programs are structured to offer a variety of health, social, and related support services in a protective setting during any part of a day, but usually for less than 24 hours (National Institute on Adult Daycare [NIAD] 1994). Adult day programs serve a variety of needs and participants, ranging from the physically frail elderly to those with dementia, chronic mental illness and mental retardation, and developmental disability.

The goals of adult day programs are to: (1) promote the individual's maximum level of independence; (2) maintain or improve the individual's current level of functioning and delay deterioration; (3) foster socialization, peer interaction, and self esteem; and (4) provide support, respite, and education to families and other caregivers (NIAD 1991).

Services offered by day centers include the following: basic supervision, therapeutic activities, health monitoring, nursing care, assistance with activities of daily living (e.g., walking, eating, toileting, etc.), personal care (e.g., bathing, hair care, nail care), meals and snacks, exercise programs, rehabilitative therapies (e.g., physical therapy, speech therapy, occupational therapy), counseling, transportation, caregiver education and support, case management, and information and referrals. Day centers are normally open on weekdays during business hours. Some day centers offer extended hours of service, often accommodating the overnight or weekend needs of caregivers.

Day program participants include those who are physically impaired, socially isolated, in need of assistance with personal care, cognitively impaired (e.g., have memory loss), or limited in their ability to function independently. The average participant is 76 years old, and two-thirds of participants are women

(NIAD 1994). About one-half of participants are likely to be categorized as needing personal care assistance or support because of memory loss.

Adult day programs are of increasing importance in the continuum of community-based health and long-term care services for disabled elderly. They are often connected to nursing homes, senior programs, and hospitals. Day centers offer an alternative to nursing home placement. They can delay nursing home placement and provide respite for caregivers while allowing the elderly to remain in their homes longer.

Background

The model for adult day programs in the U.S. was the psychiatric day hospital started in the Soviet Union in the 1940s. Similar programs began in the 1950s in England. Experience showed that these programs reduced the need for in-patient beds. The first day program in the United States opened in the 1960s at Cherry Hill State Hospital in Goldsboro, North Carolina. Adult day programs subsequently expanded from medical services, transportation, and meals to offer supportive health and social services for marginally impaired and/or socially isolated individuals residing in the community. In 1976, adult day health care became a Medicaid benefit in California, New Jersey, Massachusetts, and Maryland.

Between 1969 and 1973, fewer than 15 adult day centers were in existence in the United States (Webb 1989). The number of programs increased from 300 in 1978 to more than 3,000 at present. More than one-half of all centers opened in the 1980s. Three-quarters of the programs are located east of the Mississippi River; Western states (with the exception of California) have fewer centers (Zawadski and Stuart 1990).

It is estimated that at least 10,000 day centers will be needed in the United States by the year 2000. This is based on the ability of a community with a population of 20,000 to support an adult day center, and at least 1%, or about 200 people, being candidates for the center's 20 to 30 daily slots (Conn 1991). Generally, two to three participants must be enrolled to support one daily slot, since many participants use day center services on a part-time basis.

There are no federal regulations for adult day programs. A majority of states have funding or other standards; 30 states have regulations on licensing and 44 have regulations on certification. The type of state agency overseeing adult day programs varies widely. Centers have been categorized as following either a social model or a medical model, with the major difference being whether medical services or social services are provided. Since centers usually offer a combination of services, the distinction is not necessarily clear, but public funding sources often look for the distinction nevertheless. Medicaid* is a large funder of adult day programs, but its focus is primarily on health services. Additionally, Medicaid eligibility varies by state and limits participation to those meeting income criteria.

Adult day center revenue, according to the 1989 adult day center census, is from: service fees—23%; Medicaid—29%; other state funds—10%; Title XX (Social Service Funds)—7%; Title III (Older American Act funds)—5%; other public funds—12%; philanthropy—9%; and other—4% (Zawadski et al. 1991). Nearly 90% of day centers are nonprofit organizations or public agencies.

Private long-term care insurance* has played only a small role in financing adult day centers, but there is an increasing trend for insurance companies to provide reimbursement for adult day programs in long-term care policies. Reimbursement for adult day programs by insurance companies is usually one-half the amount of nursing home reimbursement, with day center rates ranging from $30 to $50 per day.

The 1989 census of adult day centers reported that operating expenses average $150,000 per year, exclusive of in-kind contributions of $19,000, but 83% of adult centers rely on in-kind contributions (free or below-cost goods and services) to support their programs (Zawadski et al. 1991).

The average cost of providing service in 1989 was $34 per day and ranged from a few dollars to $150 per day, with one-half of the centers charging daily fees between $20 and $40. Daily fees varied by region and depended on the range of services offered. Most centers had sliding fee scales and offered discounts based on income. More than 50% of all centers responding to the 1989 census reported operating at a deficit for a large portion of their fiscal year (Zawadski et al. 1991).

New Initiative

The financial viability of adult day centers was of primary interest to the Robert Wood Johnson Foundation when, in 1987, it announced a four-year national program for adult day centers. The Dementia Care and Respite Services Program was cofunded by the Alzheimer's Association and the Administration on Aging. It sought to demonstrate that adult day centers could serve people with dementia, and that they could do so in a financially viable manner. A particular emphasis was put on fee-for-service payments, as opposed to philanthropy. The success of this program led to another foundation initiative, Partners in Caregiving: The Dementia Services Program, which will work with 50 project sites between 1992 and 1996.

Findings from the fourth year of the Dementia Care and Respite Services Program indicate that day centers can be financially self-sufficient. Four factors proved to be statistically significant predictors of better financial performance (percentage of total expenses covered by net operating revenue): a higher ratio of daily fees to unit cost; staying open a full day (i.e., 7:30 A.M. to 6:00 P.M.); receiving government fee-for-service reimbursement in addition to private pay; and a higher average daily census (Reifler et al. 1992). Overall, project sites were able to meet 63% of their total expenses with net operating revenues.

A higher ratio of daily fees to unit cost means giving consumers and funding sources the opportunity to pay the full cost of service. Because of their nonprofit status, and their mission to serve everyone who needs service, day center boards and staff are often reluctant to charge full costs for fear high fees will prevent people from using the service. One way to balance the tension between pursuing their mission while operating in a fiscally sound manner is for day centers to charge full cost but offer discounts on a case-by-case basis depending upon need. Philanthropy can then be used to fund the discounts.

Increasing the number of people served per day results in economies of scale and lowers unit cost, since some large expenses (e.g., rent, administration) remain fixed regardless of the number of people served. Pursuing government reimbursement gives day centers a way to serve people who might not otherwise be able to afford services and provides another funding stream to help cover operating expenses. Being open a full day allows day centers to serve a wider range of participants, including those whose caregivers work. More than one-third of the participants in the Dementia Care and Respite Services Program had caregivers who worked. Being open a longer day also gives non-working caregivers more choice in how they use the service.

From a marketing perspective, customers' needs should be taken into consideration, which will help make centers more competitive and thus more financially viable. From the participant's and caregiver's perspective, the quality of a program can further be judged by availability of transportation, choices in activities, links with other community services, ongoing training for staff, support services for caregivers, and a well-functioning board of directors. With widespread needs existing in the community and the profile of services and financial support becoming solidified, adult day programs' link in the continuum of care will continue to grow in importance and strength. (See also CONTINUING CARE RETIREMENT COMMUNITIES, LONG-TERM CARE INSURANCE: A CONSUMER'S GUIDE, MARKETING TO ELDERS, MENTAL HEALTH AMONG THE ELDERLY, MEDICAID, and NURSING HOMES.)

Organizations

Alzheimer's Association
Brookdale National Group Respite Program
National Council on the Aging—National Institute on Adult Daycare
Partners in Caregiving: The Dementia Services Program

References

Conn, Robert. 1991. "How Many Centers Are Needed in U.S.?" *Respite Report* 3: 8.
National Institute on Adult Daycare. 1991. *Why Adult Day Care?* Washington, DC: NIAD
National Institute on Adult Daycare. 1994. *Adult Day Care Fact Sheet.* Washington, DC: NIAD
Reifler, Burton V., Rona S. Henry, Kimberley A. Sherrill, Carolyn H. Asbury, and Janice S. Bodford. 1992. "A National Demonstration Program on Dementia Day Centers and Respite Services: An Interim Report." *Behavior, Health, and Aging* 2: 199–205.
"Ten Essentials for a Premier Program." 1994. *Respite Report,* Special Issue (Winter): 12.

Webb, Linda C. 1989. *Planning and Managing Adult Day Care: Pathways to Success.* Owings Mills, MD: National Health Publishing.

Zawadski, Rick, Mary A. Outwater, and Margi Stuart. 1991. "Financing Adult Day Care: Services Vary Widely across Nation." *NCOA Networks* (April 19), 7.

Zawadski, Rick, and Margi Stuart. 1990. "ADC Growth Uneven, But Impressive." *NCOA Networks* (August 17), 9.

Rona S. Henry

DEATH BENEFITS, (also called survivor's benefits), money and/or in-kind benefits paid to the survivors of the deceased. Survivor benefits are usually provided to eligible survivors of the deceased on receipt of proof of death, such as a copy of the death certificate. They may be paid in one lump sum, as in life insurance policies and the Social Security* lump-sum burial expense payment, or they may be paid over time, as in Social Security survivors' benefits.

Historically, death benefits go back at least to Biblical times, when a person who killed or injured someone was required by law to pay an indemnity to the injured or deceased's kin, and the person who killed or disabled a slave was required to reimburse the master. The practice of paying an indemnity in the case of wrongful death expanded over the years to include workers killed on the job and soldiers killed during war. In 1935, the Social Security Act established the practice in America of paying government benefits to dependent survivors of workers who died.

Public Death Benefits

Publicly paid death benefits come primarily from three programs: Social Security, the Veterans Administration, and Workers' Compensation. Of these, the most common is survivor's insurance under Old-Age, Survivors, and Disability Insurance (OASDI), paid to eligible dependents of deceased workers by the Social Security Administration. Eligible dependents include widows 60 years old or older, younger widows caring for children younger than 18 years old or disabled children, unmarried children younger than 18 years old (22 if still in school), or dependent parents 62 years old or older. Survivors' benefits under OASDI consist primarily of monthly payments based on earnings of the deceased if he or she was still working when death occurred. If the deceased had already retired or was receiving Social Security Disability payments at the time of death, survivors' benefits are tied to the deceased's monthly payments. Under OASDI, survivors—a spouse living with the worker at the time of death, or dependent children—are also eligible for a lump-sum payment toward funeral expenses of $255.00.

The Veterans Administration pays two types of survivors' benefits: (1) dependency and indemnity compensation (DIC) for dependent survivors of servicemen who die of a service-connected injury or illness while on active duty; and (2) death pensions for spouses and children of veterans who died of non-service-connected illness or injury. Eligibility for death pensions may depend on the income of the dependents.

Dependent survivors of all honorably discharged wartime veterans are eligible for survivors' benefits whether the death was service connected or not, while survivors of peacetime veterans are only eligible if death was service connected. "Wartime service" applies to all declared and undeclared wars such as the Korean and Vietnam conflicts.

Burial allowances (up to $300 plus $150 for burial plot) are available for veterans separated from wartime service and for peacetime veterans whose deaths are service connected. When death is service connected, moreover, survivors may apply for a $1,100 lump-sum payment in lieu of the smaller allowance when they have surviving dependents.

Veterans who are honorably discharged are eligible for burial flags and interment in national cemeteries. Spouses and minor children may also be eligible for burial in national cemeteries. Information is available from funeral directors and local veterans affairs offices.

Each state and territory pays benefits under Workers' Compensation laws to survivors of workers killed or fatally injured on the job. While the laws in each state are similar, each state controls the manner of determining eligibility, amount of benefits, and length of time survivors receive payments. Under Workers' Compensation, spouses are eligible until remarriage and dependent children are eligible until a specified age. Most states have Workers' Compensation boards or commissions that hear cases and award compensation; some states allow the court system to make these determinations. Burial allowances vary under Workers' Compensation and range from $600 in the territory of Guam to $3,000 in Louisiana.

Private Benefits

Survivors' benefits are paid under life insurance policies and through pension plans offered by employers as part of employees' benefits. Life insurance pays a predetermined sum directly to beneficiary(ies) named in the policy or to the estate of the deceased, if so designated. While benefits are usually lump-sum payments, other options are available, such as lifetime income for the spouse or periodic payments for a specific length of time. Benefits may increase in cases of accidental death and may be denied in cases of suicide.

Life insurance held by a creditor to secure payment of a debt is paid directly to the mortgage or lien holder when death of the insured occurs. Most lending institutions require such credit insurance if a loan amount is substantial, and while this requirement protects the bank, it reduces survivors' financial burden as well.

Survivors' benefits from pension plans are available under certain circumstances. If an employed spouse is vested in a pension plan but dies before retirement, a death benefit tied to the amount of retirement proceeds may be payable to the widowed spouse. When someone elects to continue payments to a spouse after death, a reduction in pension payments during lifetime is usually required. Death benefits under employee pension plans may be paid as a percentage of the employee's average pay, expected pension, or accrued pension.

Other death benefits are paid through fraternal organizations and through special life insurance plans for employees of the federal government. More specific information may be obtained from a local Social Security Administration office, VA office, Employment Security office (Workers' Compensation), and from the financial office of an employer. (See also LIFE INSURANCE, PENSIONS, SOCIAL SECURITY, and VETERANS' BENEFITS.)

References

Fruehling, James. A., ed. 1982. *Sourcebook on Death and Dying*. Chicago: Marquis-Professional Publications.

Maddox, George L., ed. 1987. *The Encyclopedia of Aging*. New York: Springer.

Quadagno, Jill. 1988. *The Transformation of Old Age Security*. Chicago: University of Chicago Press.

Francis P. Conner

DERIVATIVES, contracts written between two parties having a value that is derived from the value of underlying equity securities*, bonds*, commodities*, or other assets. Options and futures traded on exchanges are derivatives contracts, as are over-the-counter options and forwards sold by dealers and bought by investors.

As synthetic investment instruments, derivatives fashioned from currencies, stocks, bonds, commodities, and other underlying assets are designed to reduce the risks of doing business, conserve capital, and enhance earnings. They also provide a source of investment and speculation. Most age groups, including older persons, indirectly experience the effects of derivatives trading. Pension funds utilize them and many companies in which older investors hold stocks, bonds, or mutual fund* shares use them as well. There are derivatives for interest rate risks, currency risks, commodity risks, credit risks, insurance risks, and many other purposes.

Corporate stock options are a type of derivative that allow employees to profit from a change in the firm's stock price without owning the underlying shares. When homeowners apply for a mortgage and lock in an interest rate for a future settlement date, typically 60 days, they have secured a privately traded forward derivative contract (commitment) from the mortgage lender. Some money market accounts allocate part of their funds using interest rate derivatives as yield stabilizers and enhancers.

For the large majority of individual investors, derivatives are neither a common nor appropriate direct investment vehicle. Only those who are fully acquainted with derivative instruments and investment risks should consider them. Most derivatives require highly technical mathematical software to build, value, and keep fluctuating risk profiles updated. On Wall Street, the design of exotic derivatives has taken on a "rocket science" aura that requires personnel with high-level math skills and access to sophisticated computer technology. Large losses due to derivatives trading and investment have been widely publicized, and derivatives are increasingly becoming a highly controversial family of instruments.

Older persons and their financial advisors* should be familiar with the concept of derivatives, because these investments will continue as key financial tools for corporations, government bodies, pension funds, mutual funds, banks, and other institutional investors in the future. Any inducements given older individuals to use derivatives as a speculative investment, however, should be thoroughly investigated and understood, and at least one second opinion should be obtained before any such investment is made.

Types of Derivatives

Derivatives come in two basic forms: option-type and forward-type. Both types may be traded on an exchange, such as commodity futures and stock options. They may also be traded privately by an arrangement between interested parties over the counter (OTC.) Option-type derivatives give buyers the right, but not the obligation, to buy or sell an asset at a specific price over defined periods of time. The price for this right is usually a small percentage of the underlying asset value. Forward-type contracts commit buyers and sellers to trade assets at a set price on a set future date. Forward types include futures, forwards, and swaps. Normally, no money exchanges hands until the delivery date, when the contracts are often settled in cash rather than by exchanging assets. Like options, a relatively small performance margin deposit is required, which ranges from 1 to 20% of the value of the underlying assets covered by the contract. This is the *leverage effect* in the debate about derivatives.

Market Size and Leverage

The global derivatives market is estimated to be over $23 trillion, an amount greater than four times the gross domestic product (GDP) of the U.S. The estimated market size is a notional value reflecting the full value of the underlying assets, but this overstates the economic value of derivative transactions. Industry estimates indicate that the replacement cost of most derivatives that would be lost upon default by the counterparty to the transaction ranges from 3 to 6% of the notional value. To place notional value in perspective, consider an insurance policy as a form of derivative. For $750 of insurance, the car owner covers the loss of a $25,000 car. The $25,000 car represents the notional value. It would cost $750, not $25,000, to obtain a replacement policy.

The great power of derivative instruments, and most of the controversy, results from this leverage. A $10,000 performance margin deposit might control, for example, $10 million in underlying bonds, and there is real concern that during chaotic trading or a financial crisis, such leverage could trigger or accelerate a financial domino effect. Critics worry about a set of outcomes where too many participants could be over leveraged, and unable to meet margin and loss calls, which would precipitate mass liquidations of portfolios with few, or no, buyers to cushion the liquidations. The result could trigger financial and stock market collapses.

On the other hand, there are significant members of the global financial community, including central bankers, who believe that the interlocking web of derivatives will act ultimately as a smoothing effect to forestall a domino effect. They believe derivatives can dampen the impact of a financial crisis. Derivatives could allow various entities to hedge in such a manner as to forestall mass liquidations and thereby ride out intermittent financial storms that might randomly erupt. Without derivatives, they would be forced to liquidate and might accelerate financial collapse instead.

Two Types of Investors

Two classes of derivative users are *hedgers* and *speculators*. Commercial interests are the primary hedgers, because hedging is designed to lock in a price and to minimize losses that can result from price fluctuations between the time contractual obligations are made and the time they are delivered. Business, for example, contracts to deliver a raw or processed material, financing, or a financial instrument at some future time. A firm will hedge by using derivatives to protect its anticipated profit against adverse price fluctuation over the time period from order receipt to final delivery and customer payment, thereby reducing uncertainty. Unlike the hedger, the speculator primarily seeks to profit from price fluctuations in the underlying securities or assets and assumes the risks associated with such fluctuations. For the hedger, the minimum deposit represents a low-cost avenue to insure against the risk of price movement over time. For the speculator, the power of leverage represents an opportunity to multiply a relatively small initial investment into a large profit. For both types of investors, derivatives represent the potential for large losses as well.

Such leverage is at the center of debates about the appropriateness of derivatives use by certain participants. Regulation is under consideration for certain industries, such as banking and pension funds, to prohibit certain types of derivatives as not appropriate while allowing other types of derivatives that are. The challenge facing legislative and regulatory agencies worldwide is to create an environment that would allow the positive effects of derivatives to continue without excessive regulation. To this end, steps are being taken to better display, explain, and account for these complex instruments. In the immediate future, more companies and financial institutions will disclose in annual reports, mutual fund offerings, and other information sources, their use and degree of involvement in derivatives. This will better inform older investors, and their advisors, about the holdings and levels of risk within the investment portfolios of the corporations, banks, insurance companies, mutual funds, and other organizations in which they invest.

Why Derivatives Evolved

During the past 20 years, the global financial markets have witnessed an increasing demand for cost-efficient protection against the risks of large and volatile foreign exchange and interest rate movements. Without better protection against future unpredictability, companies could not function, plan, compete, and grow efficiently in global markets. When a U.S. company receives an order from Germany or Japan to be delivered in three months, it needs to hedge in a cost-effective manner against fluctuations in currency exchange rates that could wipe out its profit when paid in Deutschmarks or Yen.

Derivatives have provided the ability to "unbundle" and transfer certain risks from entities not willing, or unable, to manage the risks to those who desire to do so. U.S. companies, for example, not wanting to bear the risk of foreign exchange are now able to hedge their exposure by purchasing an option that guarantees the future exchange rate price and amount. The counterparty, the seller of the option, is willing to take on the exchange rate risk for a price called the *premium paid.*

The financial shocks in the 1980s, such as the 1987 stock market crash, the failures of major banks, insurance companies, and securities firms, and the savings and loan crisis, have continued to reinforce the need for better financial tools to anticipate and prevent future crises. As a result of major advances in finance, information processing, and communications technology, the evolution of derivatives has accelerated. Derivatives have allowed the traditional financial risks—market, credit, legal, and operational—to be managed in new, innovative, low-cost ways. In the financial, regulatory, and media arenas of the 1990s, however, negative impressions of derivatives trading is growing. But a different viewpoint suggests that derivatives are necessary financial tools to control future price and market volatility for the benefit of all consumers. Mediating these opposite viewpoints and making the disclosure, measurement, control, and use of derivatives more orderly and understandable are the challenges that face the global markets for these exotic investments. (See also BONDS, COMMODITIES, EQUITY SECURITIES, ETHICS IN FINANCIAL PLANNING, FINANCIAL ADVISORS, FINANCIAL COUNSELING, MUTUAL FUNDS, and PENSION FUND TRENDS.)

References

General Accounting Office. 1994. *Financial Derivatives.* Washington, DC: GAO.

Global Derivatives Study Group. 1993. *Derivatives: Practices and Principles.* Washington DC: Group of Thirty.

Hull, John C. 1993. *Options, Futures, and Other Derivative Securities.* Englewood Cliffs, NJ: Prentice Hall.

Marshall, John F. 1992. *Financial Engineering: A Complete Guide to Financial Innovation.* New York: New York Institute of Finance.

Smithson, Charles W. 1990. *Handbook of Financial Engineering.* New York: Harper & Row.

T. Erle Keefer

DISABILITY INITIATIVE, efforts to raise awareness about the needs of mid-life and older persons with disabilities. The Americans with Disabilities Act (ADA), by guaranteeing protection from discrimination and the provision of reasonable accommodation, provides older persons with disabilities more opportunities in everyday life. The ADA has had a significant effect on the lives of older Americans with disabilities.

The ADA defines a person with a disability as: (1) having a physical or mental impairment that substantially limits that person in some major life activity; (2) having a record of such an impairment that causes discrimination based upon past disability; or (3) being regarded as having an impairment because of physical appearance or disfigurement that causes discrimination. However, many older persons may not consider themselves disabled simply because they have experienced vision or hearing loss as part of the aging process. Thus, it is important to consider the many degrees of disability that exist, and the contexts in which the term is used. Although an older person with severe hearing loss may not consider himself disabled, he may recognize that he has some degree of impairment.

The ADA consists of five Titles, which address the areas of employment, public services, public accommodations, and telecommunications. It requires that reasonable accommodations be made in the areas of employment, access, and service provision. Reasonable accommodations are considered any changes or adjustments to the environment that permit persons with disabilities to participate more fully in, and to enjoy the benefits of, work, recreation, and public services. Such accommodations include modifications to the environment, including the physical surroundings, policies, and procedures of the workplace or business. The various governmental agencies responsible for enforcement, such as the Equal Employment Opportunity Commission (EEOC), the Department of Justice (DOJ), and the Architectural and Transportation Compliance Board, have set forth definitions and guidelines to better clarify the meaning and provisions of the ADA.

AARP and the ADA

In 1991, the American Association of Retired Persons developed the Disability Initiative as a response to the growing needs and concerns of persons with disabilities and the Americans with Disabilities Act. The Disability Initiative seeks to ensure that AARP's programs and services are accessible to staff, volunteers, and members with disabilities by acting as a catalyst for change.

The initiative serves as a central focus for AARP on all issues pertaining to persons with disabilities. Its goals include improving the quality of life for older persons; increasing the level of participation by persons with disabilities in all of AARP's programs and activities; working with other organizations on behalf of persons with disabilities; and to serve as a resource to AARP staff, volunteers, and members. In order to meet these goals, the Disability Initiative works to educate in all areas of disability, including accessibility, sensitivity, and the implications of the Americans with Disabilities Act.

Unfortunately, aging is often associated with disability, and the misconceptions and public attitudes about disability are often the biggest barriers faced by people with disabilities. There are more than 40 million Americans with disabilities, and for millions of older persons the effects of chronic illness and the loss of mobility, hearing, and vision associated with aging can be difficult and stigmatizing. For example, myths such as assuming that disability is synonymous with inability, that people who are deaf are not allowed to drive a car, that mental illness and mental retardation are the same, or that other senses become sensitive when sight or hearing are lost, are common stereotypes, especially when people have had little contact with persons with disabilities. Further, older persons may subscribe to these misconceptions, and experience feelings of self-doubt and a lack of self-esteem. However, many older persons do not consider themselves disabled, and have successfully adapted to loss of hearing, vision, or mobility.

The Disability Initiative's publications, programs, and activities strive to break down the negative attitudes and myths that persist and deeply affect the way we feel and act toward persons with disabilities. Efforts to educate AARP staff volunteers and members on the realities and needs of persons with disabilities have contributed to the creation of fact sheets, resource manuals, and articles by Disability Initiative staff members. They have also promoted staff programs, such as Deaf Awareness Week and Injury Prevention, to increase the awareness of disabilities and how they can affect everyone.

Many of the Initiative's publications and activities have focused on specific disabilities, primarily hearing, vision, and mobility loss, the disabilities most commonly associated with aging. Fact sheets, such as "Facts about Vision Loss" and "Facts about Hearing Loss," provide straightforward information on extent, causes, resources, and support for persons with vision and hearing loss.

Along with publications, the Disability Initiative has engaged in activities and programs that foster the understanding of disabilities and sensitivity to persons with disabilities. Extensive training has been done on the ADA, specifically targeting employment and public accommodations. The Disability Initiative assisted AARP's Human Resources Department and Office of General Counsel to develop a training program on Title I (Employment) of the ADA for AARP's hiring managers. This program focused on issues such as interviewing job applicants with disabilities, accommodations, and dealing with applicants with disabilities in the hiring process. The Disability Initiative also participates in regional training sessions on Title III (Public Accommodations) of the ADA. In conjunction with AARP's Consumer Affairs Department and the Legal Counsel for the Elderly, the Disability Initiative will provide support for a grant awarded to AARP by the Department of Justice, the purpose of which is to educate older persons and aging services providers about the ADA.

As the aging population expands, the needs and concerns of older persons with disabilities will continually be pushed to the forefront of interest for AARP members and the general public. Disability extends into most segments of life, including employment, recreation, service provision, transportation, and communication. The ADA is a starting point for the inclusion and integration of people with disabilities into the activities of daily life. (See also DISABILITY PROGRAMS, FEDERAL; HOME MODIFICATIONS FINANCING; HOUSING; and MENTAL HEALTH AMONG THE ELDERLY.)

References

American Association of Retired Persons. 1993a. *The Americans with Disabilities Act (ADA).* Public Policy Fact Sheets. Washington, DC: AARP.

American Association of Retired Persons. 1993b. *Facts about Hearing Loss.* Disability Initiative Fact Sheets. Washington, DC: AARP.

American Association of Retired Persons. 1993c. *Facts about People with Disabilities.* Disability Initiative Fact Sheets. Washington, DC: AARP.

American Association of Retired Persons. 1993d. *Facts about Vision Loss.* Disability Initiative Fact Sheets. Washington, DC: AARP.

Patricia Selby and Katherine M. Treanor

DISABILITY PROGRAMS, FEDERAL, programs that provide cash support, health care coverage, and direct supportive services to eligible people with disabilities. The Americans with Disabilities Act and nine federal programs serve sizeable proportions of the disabled population aged 50 or over. These programs are typically limited to people under the age of 65.

Background

Federal disability programs serve people of all ages, but most disability programs either target children or adults in their working years, typically defined as ages 18 through 64. Since the risk of becoming disabled increases with age, many programs include large numbers of people aged 50 through 64 in their later working years. In fiscal year 1989, $85 billion, or 8% of all federal outlays, were spent on these programs (Burwell et al. 1990.) They are: (1) Social Security Disability Insurance (SSDI); (2) Supplemental Security Income (SSI)*; (3) Medicare*; (4) Medicaid*; (5) Workers' Compensation; (6) Black Lung Program; (7) the Veterans Administration Disability Compensation Program; (8) the Veterans Administration Pension Program and (9) the Veterans Administration Health Services Program.

People may receive benefits from more than one program if they meet eligibility requirements. Specific eligibility requirements vary, depending on the program purpose, and requirements may change over time as the result of amendments to law, new regulations, or court decisions. Eligibility is determined by factors related to disability as well as age, income, veteran status, or work experience. Federal offices administering specific disability programs should be contacted directly for the current eligibility requirements.

The concept of disability in recent years has generally shifted from diseases, conditions, and impairments to a focus on functional deficits caused by these factors. Disability measures used in clinical settings or research often underlie or are incorporated into program eligibility. Disability is defined in research as significant difficulty with or the inability to perform certain daily functions, because of a health condition or impairment. For adults aged 18 through 64, these functions usually involve working or keeping house.

Some commonly used factors in assessing disability are:

- *Sensory Impairments*—Difficulty with or the inability to see, hear, or speak
- *Cognitive/Mental Impairments*—The presence of or resulting disabilities from cognitive/mental impairments (e.g., Alzheimer's Disease, mental illness, mental retardation)
- *Functioning of Specific Body Systems*—Capacity of specific body systems (e.g., climbing stairs, walking three blocks, lifting 10 pounds)
- *ADLs/IADLs*—Difficulty with or the inability to perform the Activities of Daily Living without assistance, typically including bathing, dressing, eating, toileting, getting in or out of a bed or chair, and walking; and/or the Instrumental Activities of Daily Living, which generally include using the telephone, shopping, preparing meals, cleaning house, doing laundry, doing yard work, managing personal finances, and managing medications.
- *Working*—Inability to work, limitations in the amount or kind of work, and/or ability to work only occasionally, irregularly, or part-time.

The Americans with Disabilities Act

The intent of the Americans with Disabilities Act of 1990 is to protect the civil rights of persons with disabilities. Equal opportunity provisions pertain to employment, public accommodation, transportation, state and local government services, and telecommunications.

For purposes of the ADA, disability is present if an individual meets one of the following three tests: (1) there is a physical or mental impairment that substantially limits one or more major life activities; (2) there is a record of such an impairment; or (3) the individual is regarded as having an impairment. The ADA definition is identical to the one used in Section 504 of the Rehabilitation Act of 1973 and in the Fair Housing Amendments of 1988 (Adler 1991).

Major Federal Disability Programs

Social Security Disability Insurance

Social Security Disability Insurance is the primary social insurance program that protects workers from loss of income due to disability. SSDI provides monthly cash benefits to disabled workers under age 65 and to certain dependents. SSDI is intended for workers who retire early (before age 65) because of a disability (Committee on Ways and Means 1993).

History. The 1935 Social Security Act established the federal social security system to provide old-age benefits for retired workers. The SSDI program was enacted in 1956 to provide benefits to workers aged 50 through 64 years who retired early because of a disability. Subsequent amendments widened SSDI coverage to include certain dependents and workers younger than age 50 (Social Security Administration [SSA] 1993).

Administration. SSDI is federally administered by the Social Security Administration.

Scope. In November 1993, 4.5 million disabled Americans received SSDI benefits: 3.7 million disabled workers under age 65, 143,000 disabled widows/widowers aged 50 to 59, and 655,000 adults under age 65 who were disabled in childhood. One-half of disabled workers were between the ages of 50 and 64. In November 1993, the average monthly benefit was $625 for disabled workers, $423 for disabled widows/widowers, and $397 for adults disabled in childhood. SSDI benefits end at age 65, when workers who retire early due to disability are converted to regular retirement benefits (SSA 1993.)

Funding. Funding is provided through the Disability Insurance portion of the Social Security payroll tax on earnings. The payroll tax is 7.65% of earnings, of which 5.6% is for the Old-Age and Survivors Insurance (OASI) portion of Social Security, 0.6% for the SSDI portion, and 1.45% for the Hospital Insurance (HI) portion of Medicare. A matching 7.65% tax is borne by employers. As of 1994, the OASI and DI parts of the payroll tax are collected only for the first $60,000 of earnings, but there is no earnings limit for the HI payroll tax.

Eligibility. In order to become eligible for SSDI, an individual must first have worked the required number of Social Security–covered work quarters, and secondly, have a severe impairment that makes him or her unable to perform his or her previous work or any other kind of substantial gainful activity. There is no means test.

Insured work quarters are credited annually for those years during which an individual works, is covered by Social Security, and earns a specified amount, which is adjusted upward each year. Only four quarters can be credited each year. In 1994, one quarter of coverage was credited for $620 of earnings.

Workers must be fully insured and persons younger than age 31 or blind must have at least 20 quarters of coverage during the 40-quarter period up to time of disability to receive SSDI. Persons who are fully insured under Social Security must have at least one quarter of coverage for every four quarters up to the time of disability. Those who have 40 quarters are fully insured for life. Workers younger than age 31 and blind individuals need a minimum of six quarters.

Disability, for SSDI, is defined as the inability to pursue any substantial gainful activity (earn more than $500 per month for disabled and $810 for blind persons) by reason of any medically determinable physical or mental impairment that can be expected to result in death or that has lasted or can be expected to last for a continuous period of not less than 12 months (Adler 1991).

After an applicant is financially qualified, a State Disability Determination unit examines medical evidence to determine if the applicant's mental or physical impairment is severe enough to have more than a minimal effect on the applicant's ability to work. If so, the applicant's medical condition is compared to the SSA listing of over 100 impairments (Public Health Service [PHS] 1991).

Applicants whose medical conditions are at least as severe as those in the listing are considered disabled. Applicants who are not found disabled are evaluated at two additional steps. A determination is made regarding whether the applicant could perform their past work, based on assessments of their physical and/or mental abilities.

For applicants who cannot perform past work, an assessment is made to ascertain their ability to perform other work that exists in the national economy. This assessment is based on the individual's functional capacity, age, education, and work experience. Generally, persons under age 50 are considered able to adapt to new work situations. Jobs are said to exist in the national economy if there are significant numbers with requirements that are within the functional abilities and vocational qualifications of applicants (SSA 1994).

Dependent coverage and survivor benefits are offered through SSDI. Disabled individuals can receive SSDI in three ways: on their own as disabled workers (described above), as widows or widowers (who are aged 50–59) of insured individuals, and as adults aged 18–64 who became disabled in childhood, whose parent(s) either receive SSDI, are Social Security retirees, or are deceased (but had been insured under Social Security).

Disability determination criteria for disabled widows/widowers is identical to those used for disabled workers and adults disabled in childhood. Dependent coverage is also provided to nondisabled family members (spouses who are either aged 60 or older or who care for one or more entitled children younger than 16). Survivor benefits are paid to the widowed aged 60 or older, to widowed of any age if they are caring for a dependent child who is either younger than 16 or disabled, to unmarried children younger than 18 (or 19 if in elementary or secondary school), or to dependent parents aged 62 or more.

Supplemental Security Income

The Supplemental Security Income (SSI) program provides monthly cash payments to low-income aged, blind, and disabled persons.

History. The SSI program was established by the 1972 amendments to the Social Security Act, which replaced earlier federal grants to the states for old-age assistance and aid to the blind and to the permanently disabled.

Administration. The SSI program is administered by the Social Security Administration.

Scope. In November 1993, 4.5 million blind or disabled persons received SSI, with monthly payments averaging about $390. Approximately 39% of those receiving SSI because of blindness or disability are aged 50 or over (SSA 1993).

Funding. Funding comes from federal general revenues. Many states have chosen the option to supplement federal SSI payments with their own funds.

Eligibility. Unlike SSDI, people receiving SSI because of blindness or disability have no work requirements, but must meet a financial means test. Persons under age 65 must meet disability and financial criteria, whereas those aged 65 or over need only meet the financial means test.

SSI payments can be received by individuals or couples. Both members of a couple must be aged, blind, or disabled and must meet the financial means test in order to collect payments. There are no dependent or survivor benefits under SSI (Adler 1991).

Disability determination for adults is the same as in the SSDI program. For children under age 18, the determination of disability is based on a standard of comparable severity.

Medicare

Medicare*, enacted in 1965, provides health insurance coverage to aged (65 or older) and disabled persons insured under Social Security. Medicare coverage has two parts. Part A, or Hospital Insurance (HI), is subject to deductibles and limits, covers inpatient hospital care, provides skilled nursing and/or rehabilitative posthospital care in a skilled nursing facility, home health care, and hospice care. Part B, or Supplementary Medical Insurance (SMI), which has monthly premiums and deductibles, covers physician services, outpatient services from certain other medical providers, approved medical equipment and supplies, and drugs that cannot be self-administered. Because HI is financed through the Social Security payroll tax, HI is automatically extended to eligible individuals. SMI is a voluntary program available only by paying monthly premiums (Burwell et al. 1990; Committee on Ways and Means 1993).

History. Medicare and Medicaid were established by the Social Security amendments of 1965. As part of the 1972 amendments to the Social Security Act, Medicare was extended, under certain circumstances, to persons receiving SSDI and to those with kidney disease (SSA 1993).

Administration. The Medicare program is administered by the Health Care Financing Administration in the Department of Health and Human Services.

Scope. In 1991, 31.5 million aged, 3.4 million disabled persons under age 65, and 72,000 persons with End-Stage Renal Disease (ESRD) were eligible for Medicare. There were $110.9 billion in Medicare payments in 1991, of which $12.5 billion were for those under 65 receiving SSDI (SSA 1993). In July 1993, approximately 2.5 million disabled individuals between the ages of 45 and 64 were enrolled in Medicare (Lazenby 1993).

Funding. Funding for the HI portion of Medicare comes from the Hospital Insurance portion of the Social Security payroll tax and is automatically deposited in the Medicare Trust Fund. In 1994, the HI payroll tax was 1.45% of earnings for employees and 1.45% for employers. Self-employed persons are taxed 2.9% of earnings for HI. The SMI part of Medicare is financed by a combination of monthly premiums, which cover about 25% of program expenditures, and federal general revenues, which cover the remaining 75%. In 1994, the monthly SMI premium was $41.10 (Committee on Ways and Means 1993).

Eligibility. Persons aged 65 or over who are entitled to Social Security are also enrolled in Medicare. There are two ways that persons under age 65 can be eligible for Medicare: (1) SSDI beneficiaries are enrolled in Medicare 24 months after receiving SSDI benefits and (2) persons in the End-Stage Renal Disease program are enrolled in Medicare after three months. Medicare recipients who are eligible because of SSDI are aged 20 to 64. Ages of recipients who are ESRD patients range from infancy to 64 years (Adler 1991).

Medicaid

Medicaid is a joint federal and state program that pays for the health care of low-income and medically indigent individuals.

History. Medicaid was established, along with Medicare, by the Social Security amendments of 1965. Medicaid replaced earlier programs that provided medical payments for needy individuals (SSA 1993).

Administration. Medicaid is jointly administered by the states and territories and the federal Health Care Financing Administration of the Department of Health and Human Services (Burwell et al. 1990).

Scope. During fiscal year 1992, $91.3 billion in Medicaid payments were made for 30.2 million persons. Nearly 15% of Medicaid recipients who were blind or disabled accounted for 37% of payments. Approximately 3.3 million of the 4.4 million persons received SSI and 500,000 did not. They accounted for $20.2 billion and $13.8 billion in Medicaid payments, respectively. Payments for nursing homes totaled $21.7 billion, or 24% of all Medicaid payments, although only 1.4 million persons received these services (Burwell 1994).

Funding. Medicaid is funded by the federal and state governments. Federal dollars come from general revenues. The federal to state match rate is derived annually by comparing the states's average per capita income to national figures. The federal share of total Medicaid spending was 57.4% in 1992. By law, this share can range from 50% to 83%. During 1992, the federal match rate was 50% for 12 states and the District of Columbia. Mississippi had the highest federal match rate at 79.99% (Congressional Research Service 1993; SSA 1993).

Services. Medicaid covers required and optional services. Required services include inpatient hospital services and physician services. Optional services include intermediate care facilities for the mentally retarded, prescription drugs* and personal care. Additional services provided under the home and community-based care waivers may include personal care services, chore services, respite care services, and adult day care*. Three Medicaid services that are important for people with disabilities are: (1) nursing facilities, (2) home health services, and (3) personal care services. Nursing facilities are mandatory for people aged

21 or over who receive cash payments from SSI or Aid to Families with Dependent Children (AFDC), but are optional services for others. Home health services are mandatory for the same Medicaid recipients for whom nursing facility services are provided. Personal care services are provided in a person's home by a qualified person under the guidance of a registered nurse (Congressional Research Service 1993).

Eligibility. Medicaid coverage is automatically extended to persons receiving cash assistance under the AFDC and generally to those who receive SSI. Medicaid coverage is also mandatory for many pregnant women and children near the poverty level. Many of the disabled who are eligible for Medicaid also receive SSI cash assistance. However, there are a number of optional state programs through which ill or disabled persons who do not receive SSI can receive Medicaid (Burwell et al. 1990; Congressional Research Service 1993).

Eligibility for Medicaid is complex and varies from state to state. People with comparable illnesses, disabilities, and incomes may be eligible for Medicaid in one state, but not in another.

Receipt of SSI guarantees eligibility for Medicaid in most states (Burwell et al. 1990). As of December 1992, 12 states had exercised their authority to impose more restrictive eligibility criteria for Medicaid than SSI uses: Connecticut, Hawaii, Illinois, Indiana, Minnesota, Missouri, New Hampshire, North Carolina, North Dakota, Ohio, Oklahoma, and Virginia. These states permit individuals to deduct their medical expenses from their incomes when determining eligibility. Under this system, known as "spend down," if an otherwise eligible applicant's income exceeded the state's income standard for Medicaid eligibility, applicants would become eligible after incurring sufficient medical expenses to reduce their income below the standard. States must extend Medicaid eligibility to certain groups of disabled people who may not receive SSI, but who are deemed to meet SSI income and resource standards.

States have other means by which to extend Medicaid to disabled persons who do not receive SSI. First, states can provide Medicaid coverage to poor disabled persons. As of January 1992, eight states (Florida, Hawaii, Maine, Massachusetts, Nebraska, New Jersey, Pennsylvania, and South Carolina) and the District of Columbia began providing Medicaid coverage to elderly or disabled poor individuals whose incomes are below the federal poverty standard and whose resources are below the SSI standard.

Second, among other options, states can elect to establish a medically needy program, under which disabled individuals whose income exceeds SSI standards but who need assistance with medical expenses can obtain eligibility by spending down. By April 1992, the medically needy option was exercised by almost all states.

Additionally, the home and community-based care waiver program, elected in every state except Arizona, and where the entire Medicaid program operates under a demonstration waiver, will aid in keeping disabled persons in the community rather than in institutions (Congressional Research Service 1993).

Workers' Compensation

Workers' Compensation provides cash payments and medical and rehabilitation services to workers (or their survivors) who have disabilities or who have died because of accidents on the job or occupational diseases (Public Health Service [PHS] 1991).

History. The first Workers' Compensation law was enacted in 1908. Most workers' compensation programs began in 1920. By 1949, all states had workers' compensation programs (SSA 1993).

Administration. There are 53 separate Workers' Compensation programs administered by the states, the District of Columbia, the Virgin Islands, and Puerto Rico. The Department of Labor within each state administers Workers' Compensation. Additionally, the Department of Labor administers Workers' Compensation programs for federal civil servants, longshore and harbor workers, and the Black Lung program.

Scope. In 1991, $42.2 billion in benefits were paid. Approximately 60% of benefits provided cash payments and 40% of benefits paid for medical and rehabilitation services. Weekly cash payments for workers vary by state, but are typically limited to no more than two-thirds of a state's average weekly wage. There are no national figures on the number of people receiving Workers' Compensation benefits.

Funding. Employers' premiums account for most Workers' Compensation funds, and average about 2% of payroll. Many employers have private insurance, some large employers are self-insured, and others operate in states that have state funds allotted for Workers' Compensation. Sometimes, modest amounts are paid by employees for medical benefits. Workers' Compensation coverage for most jobs in private industry is compulsory. Nationwide, about 88% of the labor force is covered by Workers' Compensation.

Eligibility. Disabilities or death can be caused by work-related injuries or occupational diseases, though the impact of the latter is often difficult to establish. Employer negligence is not an issue. Generally, Workers' Compensation benefits are not paid if the cause of the injury was intoxication of the worker, willful misconduct, or gross negligence.

Unlike the SSDI and SSI programs, where eligibility is limited to those with permanent total disabilities, Workers' Compensation can provide for three types of disability: permanent total disability, temporary total disability, and permanent partial disability. Temporary total disabilities are those in which a worker is unable to work, but is expected to fully recover. Most cases involve temporary total disability.

Benefits in these instances are typically paid until the person has recovered, but there are limits in some states. Usually, permanent partial disabilities are limited to injuries in which disabilities are created by the loss of a body part or damage to a generalized part of the body (e.g., head, back, nervous system) (PHS 1991; SSA 1993).

Black Lung

Black Lung benefits are paid to coal miners who are totally disabled as a result of pneumoconiosis (a disease of the lungs caused by the habitual inhalation of irritant mineral or metallic particles), to widows of miners who died from Black Lung Disease, and to their dependents (Burwell et al. 1990).

History. The Black Lung program was established by the Federal Coal Mine Health Safety Act of 1969 (SSA 1993).

Administration. The Black Lung program is administered by the Department of Labor.

Scope. About 182,000 persons were paid Black Lung benefits in December 1992. Only 36,000 were coal miners; the remainder were widows (109,000) or dependents (37,000). More than 99% of people receiving Black Lung benefits are aged 45 or over.

Funding. The Black Lung program is funded by an excise tax on coal, which is the lesser of $1 per ton of coal from underground mines (50 cents from surface mines) or 4% of the coal's selling price.

Eligibility. A miner must meet three general conditions: (1) have (or, if deceased, have had) pneumoconiosis; (2) be totally disabled by the disease (or have been totally disabled at the time of death); and (3) the pneumoconiosis must have been caused by coal mine employment.

VA Disability Compensation Program

The VA (Veteran's Affairs) Disability Compensation program provides cash assistance to veterans with service-connected disabilities, that is, illness or injury incurred while in military service. Employment is not a factor; veterans can be employed and still receive benefits (PHS 1991).

History. Veterans' health, disability, and pension programs have grown out of a long history of benefits provided to veterans. Disability pensions were provided to veterans of the Revolutionary War by the Continental Congress. In 1789, Congress enacted a veterans' pension program (SSA 1993).

Administration. The VA Disability Compensation program is administered by the Department of Veterans' Affairs (DVA).

Scope. In fiscal year 1992, 2.2 million veterans with service-connected disabilities and survivors of 314,000 deceased veterans received $12.6 billion through this program. The largest share of veterans receiving benefits for service-connected disabilities served in World War II (36.9%). Another 30.8% served during the Vietnam era. Altogether, approximately 43% of veterans with a service-connected disability were aged 65 or over in fiscal year 1992 (SSA 1993).

Funding. Funding is provided from federal general revenues.

Eligibility. An individual must have a partial or total impairment by injury or disease incurred or aggravated during military service. A VA Rating Board employs criteria developed by the DVA to rate the extent of a disability, and the illness, injury, or disease manifestations must have arisen during service. Dishonorably discharged veterans are not eligible. While the SSDI, SSI, and Black Lung programs have an "all or nothing" disability determination process, wherein a person either is or is not determined to be eligible to receive benefits, a range or band of eligibility exists in the VA Disability Compensation program. This range is contained in the disability ratings system, from 0% to 100%, and is based on the presumed reduction in income caused by the disability. Dependent allowances and survivor benefits are paid under certain circumstances.

VA Disability Pension Program

The VA Disability Pension program pays cash benefits to elderly low-income war veterans who have become permanently and totally disabled from non-service-connected causes. This program is similar to SSDI because there are employability standards (PHS 1991).

Administration. The VA Disability Compensation program is administered by the Department of Veterans' Affairs.

Scope. In fiscal year 1989, this program served 1.1 million living and deceased veterans (with survivors) at a cost of $3.9 billion. About 72% of veterans in this program were aged 65 or over in 1992.

Funding. Funding is provided from federal general revenues.

Eligibility. An individual must have an injury or disease sustained outside of military service rendering a veteran permanently and totally impaired. Impairment is determined based on the veteran's ability to function at work and at home. Persons with dishonorable discharges are not eligible. Low-income criteria are based on income and family size. During December 1991, income limits were $7,397 for a veteran living alone and $9,689 for a veteran living with one other person. Benefits are paid to surviving spouses and children if the veteran served in specified wartime periods. Survivors must meet the same conditions as for the DVA Disability Compensation program.

Veterans' Health Services

The Veterans' Health Services program, administered by the DVA, consists of a nationwide health care network that provides medical care to eligible veterans. Services must be provided to veterans with a service-connected disability, former prisoners of war, and those with low incomes. Other veterans are served on a space-available basis. Services provided include hospital care, nursing home care, and outpatient care, including rehabilitation. Care is provided through DVA facilities. However, nursing home care can be provided for a limited time in a non-DVA facility under certain circumstances (SSA 1993).

Administration. The Veterans' Health Services programs are administered federally by the Department of Veterans' Affairs.

Scope. During fiscal year 1993, net outlays for the entire Veterans' Health Services program was $14.8 billion. Approximately 910,000 patients were discharged from DVA hospitals, of whom 31% were under age 50, 27% were between 50 and 64 years of age, and the remaining 42% were aged 65 or older.

Funding. Funding is provided from federal general revenues.

Eligibility. The VA must provide hospital care and may offer nursing home care to veterans in the mandatory category. It may serve discretionary groups as space is available. The mandatory groups served include veterans: (1) with disabilities rated as "service-connected"; (2) retired from active duty for a disability incurred or aggravated while in military service; (3) receiving a VA pension; (4) eligible for Medicaid; (5) who were former prisoners of war; (6) who need care for a condition possibly related to exposure to dioxin or other toxic substances, or radiation from nuclear tests or in the American occupation of Japan; or (7) who are veterans of the Spanish-American War, the Mexican Border Period, or World War I. Care on a space-available basis is provided to low-income veterans whose disabilities are not service-connected. Outpatient care for any condition is available to veterans who have a service-connected disability rating of 50% or more, former prisoners of war, or veterans of World War I. Such care is also available for the treatment of service-connected disabilities or for care that would prevent a hospital stay (PHS 1991; SSA 1993). (See also DAY PROGRAMS FOR ADULTS, DRUGS AND THE ELDERLY, HOME CARE SERVICES FOR THE ELDERLY, MEDICAID, MEDICARE, NURSING HOMES, SOCIAL SECURITY, and SUPPLEMENTAL SECURITY INCOME.)

References

Adler, Michele. 1991. "Programmatic Definitions of Disability: Policy Implications." *1991 Proceedings of the American Statistical Association.* Government Statistics Section. Alexandria, VA: ASA.

Burwell, Brian. 1994. Unpublished Medicaid tabulations.

Burwell, Brian, Bonnie Preston, and Sarah Bailey. 1990. *Task II: Federal Programs for Persons with Disabilities.* Washington, DC: U.S. Government Printing Office.

U.S. House of Representatives Committee on Ways and Means. 1993. *Overview of Entitlement Programs.* 1993 Green Book. Washington, DC: U.S. Government Printing Office.

Congressional Research Service. 1993. *Medicaid Source Book: Background Data and Analysis (A 1993 Update).* Washington DC: U.S. Government Printing Office.

Health Care Financing Administration. 1993. *State Profile Data System, Part 1.* Baltimore, MD: HCFA.

Lazenby, Helen. 1993. Unpublished Data from the Medicare Enrollment Files.

Public Health Service. 1991. *Task Force on Determination of Disability.* Presentations on Workmen's Compensation, SSA Eligibility Process, and Veterans. Rockville, MD: Public Health Service.

Social Security Administration. 1993. "Social Security Programs in the U.S., 1993" and "Current Operating Statistics." *Social Security Bulletin* 56 (4).

Social Security Administration. 1995. *Disability Evaluation under Social Security.* Baltimore, MD: Social Security Administration.

Michele Adler

DISASTER ASSISTANCE AND THE ELDERLY, financial assistance and social services provided for the elderly at the time of and during recovery from a widespread disaster. Typical disasters are earthquakes, hurricanes, riverine floods, flash floods, tornadoes, wildfires that damage or destroy homes, and large-scale industrial accidents, such as fires or explosions.

Preparedness

Federal disaster relief is provided when an area is formally declared a disaster by the president of the United States. The declaration specifies the affected area and those eligible for disaster assistance. Federal disaster relief is managed by the Federal Emergency Management Agency (FEMA). This agency initiates and evaluates applications for disaster relief and refers applicants to national, state, or local sources for the type of emergency disaster assistance that is requested. FEMA refers elderly applicants to the appropriate state or local board on aging and to nongovernmental agencies that provide emergency services, shelter, food, clothing, and limited financial aid, such as the American Red Cross, Salvation Army, and Catholic Charities. These and other local charitable groups establish mass shelters and coordinate with other agencies that provide needed services. The federal government also maintains the Disaster Relief Fund for emergency agricultural assistance. It aids in repairing, rebuilding, replacing, or covering losses from damaged homes, businesses, crops, livestock, and farm structures.

Disaster assistance is involved in the mitigation of disasters: taking measures in advance of or during recovery from disasters that are designed to avoid or reduce the possible impact of future disasters. These include relocating out of floodplains, elevating structures or flood-vulnerable utilities within structures, building to seismic construction standards, or retrofitting existing structures to strengthen them against earthquakes.

Preparedness steps for the elderly include providing information about what to expect in the event of a disaster. Educational efforts and planning focus on disasters that are most likely to occur in their community. Elderly individuals who live independently should know where to go if evacuation is necessary. Planning may include making transportation arrangements in advance to a safe shelter, and arranging home evacuation assistance, including immediate evacuation help in case of fire. Service agencies providing evacuation assistance should know how to relocate individuals needing help.

The likelihood of disability increases with age and the need for awareness of the special needs of disabled elderly people in disaster situations is critical. For example, people with impaired mobility should know in advance what help is needed if evacuation should become necessary. Making necessary arrangements provides assurance that assistance will arrive promptly when needed.

Disaster Assistance and Long-Term Care Facilities

When considering long-term care facilities, such as nursing homes*, independent-living or assisted-living* facilities for the elderly, it is wise to inquire about the type of disaster insurance they carry and the type of disaster arrangements they will provide for the safety of their residents in the event of an actual disaster. The situation of the elderly in such settings, both before and after the trauma of disaster, is characterized by general potential vulnerability. Once the basics of shelter and food are provided, it is more difficult for older people to recover. Since recovery depends on having available financial resources for support and care, and because of the exceptional costs incurred when major disasters do occur, the quality of life for the elderly—and life itself—may be threatened substantially. Institutions must be in a position to evacuate residents to another facility and care for them adequately should a disaster occur.

Disaster relief programs are designed to help people get back on their feet and to make recovery possible. They do not restore all losses and are only available in areas formally declared disasters. Disaster relief, in the form of low-interest loans, is usually available from the government to homeowners for repairing, restoring, or replacing structures and other eligible physical property; to renters for loss and damage to home furnishings and contents; and to farmers and ranchers for damage to crops, livestock, farm structures, soil conservation measures, and other such losses. Other provisions cover unemployment due to a disaster and tax refund advances for deductible losses due to disaster. Individual assistance grants, which are limited in total amount, are available to those who cannot qualify for loans. Most state and local governments provide assistance, generally supplementary to federal assistance.

Federal disaster assistance for recovery is arranged by a visit to one of the Disaster Application Centers (DACs) in a disaster area or by telephone to a teleregistration center. An 800-number is also established to take telephone applications from victims who have telephone service. DAC locations and phone numbers are advertised through TV, radio, and newspaper ads as soon as they are established. Locations and phone numbers may also be obtained by calling FEMA. These centers do not provide for the immediate emergency food, shelter, or financial assistance described earlier.

Serious financial implications for the elderly may derive from disruption of normal living patterns, especially for those who are unprepared. While high-quality social services may help reduce the financial drain on older people's resources, individual financial preparedness is required as well.

Personal financial planning should provide for any emergency in the recognition that most governmental disaster assistance is for declared major disasters only. Preparedness measures should include available cash resources, protection of valuable papers, and access to important supplies, such as food, medications, and prescriptions. General disaster insurance for individuals is not available, although many insurance companies do offer specific disaster insurance, such as for floods or earthquakes. The federal government makes flood insurance available through the National Flood Insurance Program. It is sold through insurance firms and will fully repay covered losses.

Psychological Consequences

Disasters often leave victims feeling disoriented and helpless. Although this applies to disaster victims of all ages, the severity increases when individuals are physically incapable of rebuilding, especially the elderly and the disabled. For the elderly, damage of home or personal property, financial losses, new surroundings, strange faces, and disruption of daily routine may cause great psychological stress. Some stress can be ameliorated by preparedness measures that instill feelings of confidence and success in coping with disaster. Mental preparedness, therefore, may be as important as financial and property preparedness to prevent feelings of helplessness in older victims.

Largely as a result of insights gained from the experience of catastrophic disasters since 1989, awareness has increased of the need for special attention to the adequacy, promptness, and manner of delivery of the financial assistance and social services available to the elderly. Advance arrangements for helping elderly persons evacuate, get to shelters, and receive the care they need once they are in shelters are becoming more widespread. Innovations by state and local emergency management agencies and other social service organizations, especially in Florida and California, have led the way in helping elderly people establish eligibility for various kinds of assistance. (See also ACCIDENT INSURANCE, ASSISTED LIVING, HOMELESSNESS AMONG THE ELDERLY, HOMEOWNERSHIP, HOUSING, LONG-TERM CARE INSURANCE: A CONSUMER'S GUIDE, and NURSING HOMES.)

Organization
Federal Emergency Management Agency

Suggested Readings
Federal Emergency Management Agency. 1983. *Tips on Handling Your Insurance Claim.* Washington, DC: U.S. Government Printing Office.
Federal Emergency Management Agency. 1985. *Action Guidelines for Senior Citizens (for Hurricanes).* Washington, DC: U.S. Government Printing Office.
Federal Emergency Management Agency. 1987. *Guide to Federal Aid in Disasters.* Washington, DC: U.S. Government Printing Office.
Federal Emergency Management Agency. 1988. *Digest of Federal Disaster Assistance Programs.* Washington, DC: U.S. Government Printing Office.
Federal Emergency Management Agency. 1993. *Citizen's Guide to Disaster* (home study course). Washington, DC: U.S. Government Printing Office.

References
Dynes, Russell R., and Kathleen J. Tierney. 1994. *Disasters, Collective Behavior, and Social Organization.* Cranbury, NJ: University of Delaware Press.

Riley, M. W., R. L. Kahn, and A. Foner, eds. 1994. *Age and Structural Lag.* New York: John Wiley & Sons.

U.S. Congress, Senate Committee on Agriculture, Nutrition, and Forestry. *Oversight of the Disaster Assistance Programs.* Washington, DC: U.S. Government Printing Office.

U.S. Small Business Administration, Office of Disaster Assistance. 1994. *Disaster Loans for Homes and Personal Property.* Washington, DC: U.S. Small Business Administration.

Ralph B. Swisher

DIVORCE AND THE ELDERLY, dissolving a marriage after age 65. Early in this century, divorce was uncommon and difficult to obtain. In 1900, only one divorce occurred in 13 marriages, but by the 1990s, divorce was commonplace, with one divorce for every two marriages. The most dramatic increase in divorces occurred between 1965 and 1980, when the divorce rate more than doubled. Since 1980, divorce rates have persisted at a high level, and the increased incidence of divorce over time has important implications for all segments of the U.S. population, including the elderly.

Few studies have focused on the significance of divorce for the elderly; one reason for this neglect among researchers may be the relatively small proportion of divorces that occur within the elderly population. In 1990, fewer than 2% of the 2.3 million persons receiving divorces were over age 65. Further, a relatively small number (5 or 6%) of all older persons currently are divorced. Despite these statistics, a growing proportion of older persons is affected by divorce, and divorce has significant consequences for the elderly.

Changes in the Divorce Rate over Time

One way to view the impact of divorce trends on the elderly is to observe changes over time in the proportion of persons who have experienced a divorce before reaching old age. Since the majority of divorces occur in the early years following marriage, the most critical determinant of divorce for people entering old age is the divorce rate that existed 30 or 40 years earlier. The majority of divorces experienced by the people reaching age 65 in 1990, for example, occurred between 1950 and 1965 (when they were between age 20 and 35.) About 20% of persons reaching age 65 in 1960 had divorced, compared to 30% of those reaching age 65 in 1990. For those reaching age 65 in 2020, it is expected that nearly 50% will have divorced. From these statistics, it is obvious that the upsurge in divorces after 1965 has not yet had a major impact on the marital history of the elderly, but rapid changes will occur in coming decades as the baby boomers enter old age.

The Currently Divorced

A second perspective on divorce in later life looks at the proportion of people who are currently divorced when reaching old age. Due to remarriages, the proportion who are currently divorced is significantly lower than the proportion who have ever divorced. The number of divorced women reaching age 65 tripled between 1960 and 1990, but this only meant a growth from 2% to 6% of the relevant population. Projections by the Social Security Administration suggest that 16% of women entering old age around 2020 will be divorced. The actual percentage may exceed this projection, however, since divorced persons are remarrying at significantly lower rates than this projection anticipated. Changing marriage, divorce, and remarriage experiences of the baby boomers will lead to large changes in the marital and family characteristics of the future older population.

Divorce and Well-Being

The significance of divorce for well-being in later life has been demonstrated in three areas of study—mortality and morbidity, economics, and intergenerational support. A number of studies have examined the relationship between marital status and mortality. These studies consistently find that both men and women who are married experience lower death rates than their unmarried counterparts. Among the unmarried, the divorced have higher death rates than the widowed or the never-married.

The survival disadvantage of divorced compared to married persons is greater among men than women. Marital status differences in mortality are greater among middle-aged than older persons, but divorced elderly people still have significantly higher death rates than the married elderly. The high death rate of those divorced is especially strong for causes of death related to lifestyle and psychological state—suicide, homicide, accidents, and cirrhosis of the liver. Studies of morbidity also find that divorced persons are the least healthy of any marital status category, and are more likely to suffer from both acute illnesses and chronic diseases.

Financial Consequences of Divorce

Cross-sectional studies of the divorced elderly reveal they have the lowest income of any marital status category. Divorced females over age 65 are more than four times as likely to be in poverty than married females (26% versus 6%), and divorced males are about three times as likely to be in poverty (19% versus 6%). The disadvantaged economic status of the divorced persists in multivariate analyses, which control for factors correlated with poverty, such as race and education level. The divorced also are relatively disadvantaged with respect to assets. For example, about 80% of married and widowed older women live in homes they own, compared to 50% of divorced women.

Most elderly persons who are divorced experienced their divorce earlier in life. Longitudinal analyses shed light on why the negative consequences of divorce tend to persist into old age, especially for women. At the time of divorce, both partners usually experience a loss of wealth (frequently associated with loss of home equity). Following the divorce, men are often able to recover their former standard of living within a few years. Women, however, tend to have lower earning potential and are much less likely to experience economic recovery; upon reaching old age, they are less likely to have accumulated significant assets and are less likely to have adequate pension incomes.

The Social Security* program, technically sex neutral, also contributes to the lower economic status of older divorced women. At retirement, any worker retains the right to the primary benefit he or she earned as a covered worker. Social security benefits for most men are unaffected by divorce, but for women who have depended on their husband's income after marriage, divorce can have a significant impact. If the marriage lasted for less than 10 years, a divorced spouse is not entitled to any spouse benefit. If the marriage lasted for more than 10 years, a divorced spouse (at age 65) is entitled to 50% of her former spouse's primary benefit (or her own primary benefit if it is greater), while her former spouse receives 100% of the benefit. Thus, a divorced woman who has not had earnings equal to her former spouse's will receive a smaller social security benefit. In many cases there is also an unequal splitting of private pension benefits that were accumulated prior to divorce.

Research documents the important role that adult children play in the lives of most elderly persons. Elderly persons who have a high level of contact and interaction with their adult children receive much of their instrumental assistance and emotional support from their children. Divorced persons do not experience the same quality of intergenerational relationships as the nondivorced. Whether or not they have remarried, older men who are divorced from the biological mother of their children are much less likely to maintain contact with these children. Also, divorced men are less likely to receive help from these children or to view their adult children as a potential source of support in case of need. Further, stepchildren do not fill this vacuum, since divorced men do not have stronger ties with their stepchildren than with their biological children. Divorce also negatively affects mother-child relationships in later life, although the effect is not as striking for mothers as fathers.

The proportion of persons entering old age who are divorced or who have experienced an earlier divorce is increasing and will continue to increase for several decades. Approximately one-half of the baby boomers who will enter old age between 2010 and 2030 will have experienced a divorce from their first marriage. As discussed above, evidence suggests that divorce has negative consequences for well-being in later life. Compared to those who are married, those divorced on average experience greater poverty, have higher death rates, and receive less support from adult children. Negative effects of divorce on economic status are greater for women than men, while negative effects on social support networks are greater for men. If the current relationship between divorce and well-being persists, divorce will play an increasingly important role in shaping aging experiences and a growing number of elderly people will experience adverse consequences associated with marital instability. (See also COHABITATION, ECONOMIC HARDSHIP MEASURES IN THE OLDER POPU-

LATION, ECONOMIC STATUS OF THE ELDERLY, ECONOMIC STATUS OF ELDERLY WOMEN, MARRIAGE AND THE ELDERLY, PENSION FUND TRENDS, and SOCIAL SECURITY.)

Suggested Reading

American Association of Retired Persons. 1994. *Women, Pensions and Divorce: Small Reforms That Could Make a Big Difference.* Washington, DC: AARP.

References

Cherlin, Andrew J. 1992. *Marriage, Divorce, Remarriage,* Revised and Enlarged Edition. Cambridge, MA: Harvard University Press.
Cooney, Teresa M., and Peter Uhlenberg. 1990. "The Role of Divorce in Men's Relations with Their Adult Children after Mid-Life." *Journal of Marriage and the Family* 52: 677–88.
Fethke, Carol C. 1989. "Life-Cycle Models of Saving and the Effect of the Timing of Divorce on Retirement Economic Well-Being." *Journal of Gerontology* 44: S121–S128.
Hu, Yuanreng, and Noreen Goldman. 1990. "Mortality Differentials by Marital Status: An International Comparison." *Demography* 27: 233–50.
Uhlenberg, Peter, Teresa Cooney, and Robert Boyd. 1990. "Divorce for Women after Mid-Life." *Journal of Gerontology* 45: S3–S11.

Peter Uhlenberg

DRUGS AND THE ELDERLY, the relationship of older persons to drug utilization, insurance coverage for drugs from private and public funds, compliance with drug regimens, and biological changes affecting drug metabolism.

The elderly account for about 12% of the U.S. population, yet they consume more than one-third of outpatient, retail prescriptions. There are more than 33 million elderly persons (age 65 and older) enrolled in the Medicare* program, and in 1992 about 85% of them used prescription drugs. Medicare pays for prescription drugs used in the hospital; however, there is no outpatient prescription drug benefit.

Drug Utilization

Each year, Medicare beneficiaries on average purchase about 15 prescription drugs. Beneficiaries with functional impairments use 24 prescriptions per year, and those in particularly poor health average more than 30 (Lee 1994). This compares with an average of four prescriptions per year for persons under age 65. At any given time, the elderly take an average of 2.1 prescription drugs. About 26% of older persons take three to five different prescription medications (Amerian Association of Retired Persons [AARP] 1992).

In terms of usage of nonprescription or "over-the-counter" (OTC) drugs, a 1992 survey of Medicare beneficiaries found that they averaged 3.3 nonprescription drugs per year. The elderly self-medicate with OTC drugs, but these medications do not include special labeling for geriatric use, nor have persons age 65 and older usually been part of clinical trials. Further, few prescription benefit plans cover OTCs, although for some illnesses a nonprescription drug may be more efficacious, and probably more economical, than a prescription product. Regardless of what medication they are taking, elderly persons using multiple drugs simultaneously increase their chances of suffering an adverse drug reaction or drug interaction (Johnson 1992).

Insurance Coverage

Although Medicare does not cover outpatient prescription drugs, some elderly have a variety of financial resources to cover drug purchases. These include the Medicaid* program (for indigent persons) and state-sponsored pharmaceutical assistance programs in New Jersey, Maine, Maryland, Delaware, Pennsylvania, Illinois, Rhode Island, Connecticut, New York, and Vermont. In addition, 37% of Medicare beneficiaries have prescription drug coverage through employer-sponsored postretirement health insurance*. Medicare beneficiaries may also purchase Medicare supplemental insurance* (Medigap) policies, although only one-fifth of Medigap policyholders obtain prescription drug coverage (Lee 1994). Despite these options, only 55% of persons between 65 and 74 surveyed by the American Association of Retired Persons had prescription drug coverage, and only 40% of persons age 75 or older did (AARP 1994).

A 1994 report by the AARP reveals some characteristics of persons with prescription drug coverage. Elderly men are more likely to have insurance policies through their employers with associated drug coverage. Elderly women are more likely to have individual plans, and thus would not have drug coverage. Also, AARP found that African Americans are more likely to be covered by Medicaid and not have a Medicare supplemental drug benefit (Long 1994).

In 1992, the average out-of-pocket drug cost for Medicare beneficiaries was $604 (Lee 1994). This amount includes an average drug deductible of up to $200 per year. The top 11% of elderly who spent more than $1,200 on prescription drugs in 1991 accounted for nearly half of the total spending for prescription drugs (Long 1994).

Since 45% of the elderly have no insurance for prescription drugs, and as there is increased uncertainty about drug coverage under employer-sponsored retiree health insurance and limited Medigap coverage, drug benefits for the elderly remain an important policy issue for the future.

Compliance

Even if universal, first-dollar coverage of prescription drugs existed, many elderly would still experience drug use problems. To the degree that broader drug insurance coverage would increase overall drug utilization, drug-related medical problems could also increase. Problems may stem from biological changes common in the elderly, poor compliance, lack of information, multiple providers who unknowingly prescribe conflicting prescriptions, pharmacists* unable to communicate with elderly patients or caregivers, or other causes.

One recent study of Medicare beneficiaries found that only 19.5% have no drug interactions; 40% experience between one and three significant drug interactions; and 18% take at least one geriatrically inappropriate drug (Johnson 1992). As an AARP trustee testified before Congress, "The adverse reactions that can result from inappropriate prescribing can lead to drug-induced illness, hospitalization, and even death, not to mention unnecessary and wasteful health care expenditures" (Perkins 1994). Another U.S. study found that over 28% of elderly hospital admissions were drug-related (Col et al. 1990). Elderly persons now anticipate problems when taking their medications. An AARP survey found that among older respondents, the major reason for not complying with their medication regimen was "side effects of the drug" (AARP 1992).

Biological changes that are part of the natural aging process can inhibit a drug's efficacy and/or create more or different side effects than those that may be experienced by a younger person on the same medication. An elderly person's stomach lining may become more susceptible to injury from vitamins and antiinflammatory drugs such as those prescribed for arthritis. Two-thirds of the elderly have reduced kidney function that slows the body's ability to eliminate drugs. Brain receptors in an older person may become more sensitive, making some psychoactive drugs too powerful (AARP 1994).

Changes in body composition—a decrease in total body water and lean body mass, and an increase in body fat—can also affect how drugs are absorbed, distributed, metabolized, and excreted. Elderly persons on prescription drugs must also be mindful of proper nutrition and maintain a healthful diet. A study of geriatric physicians and nurses in 1993 estimated malnutrition among their elderly patients to be between 26 and 28%. Malnourishment among elderly hospital patients has been estimated at 43% by physicians, and at 57% by nurses. These physiological conditions may require a physician to alter the dosage strength or frequency of a drug prescribed for an elderly patient, and monitor drug tolerance during the course of therapy. Such monitoring can be performed by the physician or, in many cases, the pharmacist. Many pharmacists routinely monitor patients who suffer from asthma, diabetes, or high blood pressure.

Elderly patients with multiple health problems may seek care from more than one physician, each of whom may prescribe medications. If the patient does not provide a complete and accurate listing of all current medications (prescription and over-the-counter) to each physician and pharmacist, his or her risk of drug-induced side effects and complications—and expenses associated with seeking additional medical care—increase dramatically.

Importance of Drug Utilization Review

Achieving optimal medication results, and thus the best health outcome, requires regular, responsible communication between the patient, a caregiver, all prescribing physicians, and pharmacists. Fortunately, systemic drug utilization review (DUR) programs that further this goal are becoming more common in pharmacies and managed care organizations.

A DUR safeguard already present in many pharmacies is computerized tracking of prescription (and in some cases, OTC) drugs. Unfortunately, few systems can currently exchange data with other pharmacies or track the drug data of patients seeing multiple physicians. If an elderly person is enrolled in a health maintenance organization*, such a record may be maintained automatically by both the physician and pharmacist.

Active patient counseling by pharmacists and physicians is another component of DUR. A federal law implemented in 1993 requires pharmacists to offer counsel to Medicaid patients about their prescription medications, and more than 40 states have extended the mandatory counseling offered by pharmacists to all patients. This counseling is part of pharmacists practicing ''pharmaceutical care,'' which includes: (1) identifying potential and actual drug-related problems, (2) resolving actual drug-related problems, and (3) preventing potential problems.

As states collect more information about drug utilization by their populations, more information will surface concerning trends of overuse or underuse of certain drugs within a therapeutic class: opportunities for more economical generic drug prescription, drug interaction, new drugs from which patients may experience unanticipated side effects, and other problems and related issues. Educational campaigns will improve prescribing practices of physicians and educate patients about more appropriate drug use. Finally, as consumers are making increasingly educated choices about their health care, elderly persons are also taking more responsibility for ensuring the appropriateness of their medications. (See also HEALTH MAINTENANCE ORGANIZATIONS, MEDICAID, MEDICARE, MEDICARE SUPPLEMENTAL INSURANCE, PHARMACISTS, PHYSICIAN-ELDERLY PATIENT RELATIONSHIPS, and POST-RETIREMENT HEALTH INSURANCE.)

Organizations

American Pharmaceutical Association
National Council on Patient Information and Education

References

American Association of Retired Persons. 1992. ''Survey on the Need for a Prescription Drug Benefit under the Medicare Program.'' Washington, DC: AARP.

American Association of Retired Persons. 1994. ''Drugs Fighting Drugs Pose Growing Threat.'' *Bulletin* (January), 2,16.

Col, N., J. E. Fanale, and P. Kronholm. 1990. ''The Role of Medication Noncompliance and Adverse Drug Reactions in Hospitalizations of the Elderly.'' *Archives of Internal Medicine* 150: 841–45.

Johnson, Kathleen A. November 1992. ''The Determinants of Medication Use and Misuse in the Ambulatory Elderly.'' Presentation at the Annual Meeting of the American Public Health Association. Washington, DC.

Lee, Philip R. February 8, 1994. "Statement Before the Subcommittee on Health and the Environment." Committee on Energy and Commerce, U.S. House of Representatives. Washington, DC: U.S. Department of Health and Human Services.

Long, Stephen H. 1994. "Prescription Drug Coverage and the Elderly: Issues and Options." Washington, DC: AARP.

Perkins, Joseph. 1994. "Statement of the American Association of Retired Persons on the Prescription Drug Benefit Provisions of the President's Health Security Act." Subcommittee on Health and the Environment, Committee on Energy and Commerce, U.S. House of Representatives. Washington, DC: GPO.

N. Lee Rucker

DURABLE POWER OF ATTORNEY, a legal document in which an individual (the "principal") appoints and authorizes another to act as his or her agent ("attorney-in-fact"). The power of attorney is durable, because it remains in effect if the principal becomes ill or mentally incapacitated. The power can be general, rather than specific to a certain transaction such as an authorization to sign on another person's behalf in a real estate settlement. A general durable power of attorney (DPOA) is typically very broad, authorizing the attorney-in-fact to make medical decisions if necessary, sign checks, cash in savings or investment accounts, buy or sell a home or other assets, and in general do anything that the principal could do. Other DPOAs are more narrowly drawn, such as a durable power of attorney for health care, a type of advance directive* for use in a medical emergency. Nondurable powers of attorney automatically become invalid upon the death or incapacity of the principal, but DPOAs remain effective if the principal becomes completely incapacitated. "This power of attorney . . . shall not terminate on disability of the principal," effectively distinguishes a nondurable power of attorney from one that is durable. As in all powers of attorney, the power is revoked upon the death of the principal.

Assuming a person is fortunate enough to have a completely trustworthy person to act on his or her behalf, a DPOA is an excellent way to plan for the management of financial, medical, and/or practical affairs in the event of temporary or permanent disability. It can spare loved ones trauma, expense, and the red tape of a guardianship* or conservatorship proceeding. The choice of attorney-in-fact (not necessarily professional attorneys*) is typically a spouse, adult child, or close friend. In drafting a DPOA, critical issues arise and must be considered carefully. It may be quite inappropriate, for example, to grant fiduciary powers to the same person empowered to make medical decisions.

Nondurable powers of attorney did not contemplate the types of functions today's guardianship-avoidance instruments may usefully permit. It took more than three decades for every jurisdiction to enact legislation permitting DPOAs, and until every jurisdiction had taken such action, most nationwide organizations refused to accept them. Today, the DPOA has become an essential part of estate planning*, but acceptance of DPOAs by financial institutions and other organizations can still pose practical problems. Some financial institutions will request an affidavit executed by the attorney-in-fact that states the power of attorney has not been revoked and that the principal is still living. In an increasing number of jurisdictions, problems have been resolved by statutes that indemnify against the risks of persons relying in good faith on a DPOA after revocation of the DPOA or after the death of the principal.

Generally, any power of attorney will be construed narrowly and should contain an explicit recitation of the powers granted by the document. Gifts might be designated as *$10,000 per year, per donee "annual exclusion"* and recipients limited to *children and grandchildren.* Or, a DPOA may be drafted broadly so that all assets may be given in the sole judgment of the attorney-in-fact to someone else, including the attorney-in-fact. Broad powers are often essential for married couples when planning for the possibility of long-term illness or incapacity. A spouse, acting as attorney-in-fact for an institutionalized spouse, needs a broad power of attorney in order to take advantage of laws permitting the "community spouse" of an institutionalized Medicaid recipient to preserve assets and protect against impoverishment. Gift-giving power under a DPOA should be carefully considered in light of the specific potential needs of the individual who will grant such power.

Whether estate planning, planning for charitable contributions*, or for Medicaid* eligibility, careful consideration must be given to defining the extent of the power and the class of donees. DPOAs may be beneficial for estate tax and Medicaid planning purposes. In the case of a wealthy individual, removing assets from the principal's taxable estate while he or she is incapacitated may save otherwise unnecessary estate taxes. If someone is a candidate for care under Medicaid, it is essential to consider whether authorization of asset divestment is appropriate. Anyone considering granting a DPOA must realize, however, that a power of attorney in the wrong hands is an invitation for financial elder abuse*.

Depending on who is serving as attorney-in-fact, an individual may wish to include protective language requiring recordkeeping and reporting. If one adult sibling is serving as attorney-in-fact, other siblings may wish to require a copy of the DPOA and all copies of financial and other records periodically. When a non-relative is named as attorney-in-fact, he or she may have to account to the principal's family members. Particularly when asset divestment powers are included, an agent must be trusted to act in the same manner in which the principal himself or herself would act under the circumstances. Keeping everything "out in the open" may help avoid potential abuse and animosity among family members. Finally, even the most beloved adult child may not be a good candidate for attorney-in-fact if he or she has problems such as drug or alcohol abuse or is frequently on the edge of financial problems.

Although most forms of DPOA do not include provisions for compensation, payment may be appropriate in certain cases. Compensation may protect the principal, for example, by providing an incentive to the attorney to handle duties that become burdensome. For principals who are also parties to recoverable trusts*, parallel provisions should be included in both the trust document and the DPOA to accomplish the coordination of objectives.

A Case Illustration

Drafted properly, the DPOA can be the single most important legal instrument anyone can execute. The following example illustrates its usefulness. Mrs. Murphy's husband has been in a nursing home with Alzheimer's Disease for four years. Two years ago, Mr. Murphy qualified for Medicaid, after most of their savings had been spent on his care. Mrs. Murphy is now in bad health and wishes to move to a continuing care retirement community*. In order to afford her new living arrangement, Mrs. Murphy must sell her house and invest the proceeds from the equity to supplement her income. She and her husband are both owners of the house as "tenants by the entirety," however, so the house cannot be sold without her husband's signature. But he is not competent to sign the required legal papers. If Mrs. Murphy had obtained a broadly drafted DPOA from her husband while he was still capable of executing one, she could proceed with the sale. If she does not have a power of attorney, she must spend thousands of dollars in legal fees obtaining the permission of a court to sell the house. Because her husband has been receiving Medicaid in the nursing home, and depending on the state in which she resides, the court might order that one-half of the proceeds from the sale of the house be turned over to Medicaid and/or the nursing home, leaving her with inadequate resources. The importance of a carefully drafted durable power of attorney simply cannot be overstated. (See also ADVANCE DIRECTIVES, ATTORNEYS, CHARITABLE CONTRIBUTIONS, CONTINUING CARE RETIREMENT COMMUNITIES, ESTATE PLANNING, FINANCIAL ELDER ABUSE, GUARDIANSHIP, KING LEAR SYNDROME, MEDICAID, MEDICAID PLANNING, NURSING HOMES, and TRUSTS.)

References

Alexander, George J. 1988. *Writing a Living Will: Using a Durable Power-of-Attorney.* New York: Praeger.
Berg, Adriane G. 1993. *Financial Planning for Couples.* New York: Newmarket Press.
Cohen, Elias. 1984. *Durable Power of Attorney: An Important Alternative to Guardianship, Conservatorship, or Trusteeship.* Washington, DC: U.S. Department of Health and Human Services.
Haman, Edward A. 1994. *The Power of Attorney Handbook: With Forms.* Clearwater, FL: Sphinx Publishers.
Levitin, Nancy. 1994. *Retirement Rights: The Benefits of Growing Older.* New York: Avon Books.

Janet L. Kuhn

E

EARLY RETIREMENT. See Corporate Elder Care Programs; Early Retirement Incentive Programs (ERIPs); Employment of Older Americans; Individual Retirement Accounts (IRAs); Keogh Plans; Pension Fund Trends; Retirement, History of; Working Retirees.

EARLY RETIREMENT INCENTIVE PROGRAMS (ERIPs), plans that extend the incentives already offered to workers through pensions and other employee benefits. Early Retirement Incentive Programs offer workers ''an opportunity of limited duration to leave the company with higher benefits than would normally be available'' (Hewitt Associates 1986). Three characteristics define these plans.

First, participation in ERIPs is voluntary. In order to avoid charges of age discrimination, companies are careful to define eligibility to embrace an entire class of employees, or those in a particular location. A study of 100 firms with at least one such plan between 1983 and 1985 found that nearly six out of 10 offered the program to all those who met minimum age and service requirements (Bureau of National Affairs [BNA] 1986).

Second, ERIPs are short-term. Often called ''open window plans,'' these offers are made and must be accepted during a limited time period. Although it is most effective to make ERIPs available only once, when confronted with a continuous need to trim costs and personnel, many organizations offer them periodically. A survey of nearly 700 companies (Hewitt Associates 1992) found that 20% offered two programs since 1988; 7% offered three; and 3% offered four or more. Repeated offers threaten programs' objectives, since they induce workers to wait for the next, hopefully more generous, program.

Third, these plans provide one-time cash and/or pension plan adjustments. Some also provide continuation of other benefits such as health and life insurance for a specified time period. As Lublin (1991) noted, "Today's packages . . . bear little resemblance to those from the corporate cutbacks of the '80s." Instead, their designs and eligibility requirements increasingly have grown more selective, and in many cases, less generous.

Recent surveys by several benefits consulting firms have provided widely ranging estimates of the prevalence of these plans over the last two decades. One study of Fortune 100 companies found that eight out of 10 had offered ERIPs (BNA 1989). Charles D. Spencer and Associates (1992), surveyed 362 firms and found that 13% of private-sector and 28% of public-sector employers had offered an ERIP in 1991, and that nearly nine out of 10 who had not offered a plan in 1991 had done so in prior years. Hewitt Associates (1992) found that 25% of 700 firms had offered an ERIP within the past five years. Other surveys (Graffagna 1993; Buck Consultants 1989) had rates closer to 40%, while the Towers Perrin (1993) study of 534 firms found that only 20% had offered ERIPs in the prior four years. Various studies in the mid-1980s reported that over 33% of the largest U.S. firms had offered at least one incentive program to retirement-eligible employees.

Companies using ERIPs to reduce or restructure work forces are perceived as humane. Three concerns influence organizations when considering whether to offer such programs: their likely economic impact, reception by employees and their representatives, and public perception. Some firms who want to achieve greater diversity in their work forces make reductions to create opportunities for hiring new workers.

The American Management Association (1993) reported that between 1988 and 1993, between 36 and 56% of companies took steps to downsize work forces. "An actual or anticipated business downturn was the sole reason behind 32% of the reported reductions," the report said, but automation, information technology, and mergers also led to personnel cuts. "For the first time in [seven years] a majority of the jobs eliminated belonged not to hourly workers, but to . . . supervisors, middle managers, professionals and technicians" (AMA 1993). After workforce reductions, according to the AMA, operating profits increased for 45% of firms, but 80% experienced declining morale among those workers who survived the cuts.

Organizations offering ERIPs want to avoid lowered morale, and benefits consultants agree that "windows" are a humane and cost-effective way of downsizing. Early Retirement Incentive Programs preserve the morale of current workers and prevent the sense of crisis or panic that often accompanies layoffs. Using favorable incentives, a company is able to announce a carefully planned, generous act, and the firm is seen as being in control of its destiny. Finally, unions have responded favorably to ERIPs, viewing them as an extension of benefits for members.

Firms are exercising caution in targeting their ERIPs to define the target group narrowly. Fear of losing needed workers motivates companies to become more sophisticated in crafting programs, preferring to target positions, or even particular individuals, they want to eliminate. Most organizations offering ERIPs rely on age and years of service to determine who is eligible. Minimums for age and service reflect corporate pension guidelines, liberalized for the incentive program. The most prevalent combinations are age 55 with 10 years service (23%), age 50 with 10 years service (13%), and age 55 with 15 years service (10%). Sixteen percent of those in the Hewitt (1992) survey allowed workers to participate at ages 50 and younger, and 27% set eligibility criteria to include workers with fewer than ten years service. Some companies, particularly those with "30 and out" rules for regular pension receipt, relied only on service requirements, while a few allowed workers of any age, with as few as five years service, to qualify for program participation.

Federal workers and employees of other governmental entities frequently have regular retirement benefits that entitle them to retire with full benefits when they reach age 62 with five years of service, age 60 with 20 years service, or age 55 with 30 years service. After many years of discussion, Congress approved "early outs" that were offered to those who had reached 50 with 20 years service, or to those of any age who had 25 years service.

There is considerable variety in ERIPs offered, and employers often attempt to meet employee needs when designing programs. Most companies offer a combination of cash payments, pension plan adjustments, and other benefits, such as continued medical insurance coverage. Cash payments consist of either salary continuance or severance pay, which typically range from six months to two years. Sometimes there is an option to receive a lump sum, but more often payments are made periodically. "Bridge" payments are a form of salary continuance, typically replacing some portion of earnings until a worker becomes eligible for Social Security benefits at age 62.

Pension plan adjustments usually take one of two forms. Either the actuarial adjustment (penalty) is reduced or eliminated for early retirement, or years are added to an employee's age or length of service (or both) in calculating pension benefits. One such adjustment, called "the 5 plus 5 plus 4," adds five years to a person's age, five years to length of service, and provides four weeks of severance pay. While adding five years is commonly done, some companies target workers who are close to normal retirement age, offering only two to three weeks of severance pay.

Clearly, when incentives are generous, eligible employees are more likely to take early retirement. Acceptance rates vary as much as benefits provided, however. While some plans entice 10% or fewer employees to leave, others succeed in retiring 70 or 80% of an eligible group. In recent years, one in three workers offered early retirement accepted, and companies planning ERIPs have been advised to target three times as many employees as needed and to offer moderate incentives. The Older Workers' Benefit Protection Act (OWBPA) of 1990 requires that workers have sufficient time—at least 21 days—to consider an ERIP offer, if their decisions are to be considered voluntary. If employees leaving the firm are asked to sign waivers holding the employer harmless, the plan is subjected to increased scrutiny. Waivers are enforceable only if workers are given at least 45 days to consider their participation, and companies that decide to use waivers set their window period accordingly.

For most firms, window periods during which incentives are offered run from 60 to 90 days, although these periods can be as short as one month or as long as one year. Companies prefer short periods because media coverage is reduced and added benefits are less likely to go to workers already planning to retire.

These programs are costly, but companies report recovering the costs within two years. Expenses depend on the size of the target group, the rate of acceptance, and the generosity of the benefits offered. Special benefits costs, including pension plan adjustments offered on a one-time basis, must be accounted for during the quarter in which they are incurred. Consequently, profits may temporarily dwindle or disappear.

Several laws must be taken into consideration by employers wishing to offer an ERIP. The Age Discrimination in Employment Act (ADEA) and its 1990 amendment, the OWBPA, may pose age discrimination challenges. The Consolidated Omnibus Budget Reconciliation Act of 1987 (COBRA) also affects these plans by specifying that ''in the event of certain types of separation from service, the exiting employee must be provided with the opportunity to participate in the employer's health care plan for up to 36 months.''

The Employee Retirement Income Security Act (ERISA)* regulations must also be considered. A plan design may require that if severance pay is provided, the plan must meet the requirements of a welfare benefit plan. If it uses pension plan assets to fund the buyouts, plan fiduciaries must demonstrate that they have not violated their responsibilities to all pensioners. Plans offered to union members must comply with federal labor laws; state contract law may need to be considered as well. Finally, financial considerations are addressed by Section 415 of the Internal Revenue Code, which addresses the maximum early retirement pension allowed.

The extensive use of ERIPs by so many large employers has created a new ''retirement ethic.'' Rather than pitying the person ''put out to pasture,'' many envy the leisure* and other opportunities ERIP retirees can enjoy. These perceptions of lucrative ERIPs, in turn, encourage arguments to reduce entitlements for all older people. This sea of change in public opinion may require careful thought about ways that income and leisure are distributed. Routine use of ERIPs, then, may spawn new work opportunities in industries not downsizing and greater efforts in retraining individuals throughout their work lives. (See also AGE DISCRIMINATION IN EMPLOYMENT ACT; EMPLOYEE RETIREMENT INCOME SECURITY ACT; RETIREMENT; HISTORY OF; LEISURE; SOCIAL SECURITY; and WORKING RETIREES.)

References

American Management Association. 1993. *AMA Survey on Downsizing and Assistance to Displaced Workers.* New York: AMA.

Buck Consultants, Inc. 1989. *Pre-Retirement Planning Survey.* New York: Author.

Bureau of National Affairs. 1986. "Employer Rates Plans Successful in Meeting Objectives, Survey Finds." *BNA Pension Reporter* 13 (February 10): 277.

Bureau of National Affairs. 1989. "Despite Legislative Encouragement, Workers Reluctant to Stay on the Job." *BNA Pension Reporter* 16 (May 15): 854.

Graffagna, David. 1993. *Employer Experience in Workforce Reduction.* Lincolnshire, IL: Hewitt Associates.

Hewitt Associates. 1986. *Plan Design and Experience in Early Retirement Windows and in Other Voluntary Separation Plans.* Lincolnshire, IL: Author.

Hewitt Associates. 1992. *Early Retirement Windows, Lump Sum Options, and Post-Retirement Increases in Pension Plans.* Lincolnshire, IL: Author.

Lublin, Joann S. 1991. "Bosses Alter Early Retirement Windows to Be Less Coercive and Less Generous." *Wall Street Journal* (April 1), B1, B3.

Spencer, Charles D. and Associates, Inc. 1992. *Survey of Early Retirement Incentives 1991* (April 24), 1–10, 10A. New York: Author.

Towers Perrin. 1993. *Open Window Survey Results Report,* Mimeo.

Phyllis H. Mutschler

ECONOMIC HARDSHIP MEASURES IN THE OLDER POPULATION, measures used to assess the lack of basic material necessities or the experience of serious financial difficulties of the elderly. Unlike the official poverty threshold, which is based on household income, measures of economic hardship use non-income items to determine levels of privation. Economic hardship measures probe such things as whether individuals have adequate food, housing, access to medical and dental care, and clothing; whether they can pay for their necessities each month; and how satisfied they are with their financial situation. The study of economic hardship is still fairly new in the United States, and the corresponding body of literature is small and exploratory.

Determining the level of economic hardship among the elderly is important because many of the major social welfare programs they use provide in-kind benefits rather than income, such as food, medical care, housing, and utilities. Economic hardship measures give a more accurate indication than income of the success with which these public programs provide for persons age 65 and older. As the work of Holden and Smeeding (1990) has shown, there are older persons whose incomes are too high to qualify for public programs but too low to provide security against potentially devastating life events.

Economic hardship measures are a purer measure of the factors associated with standard of living than income-based measures. The amount of food families can buy, the kind of housing they can afford, or the extent to which they can access medical care and transportation can only be approximated from income. With economic hardship measures, however, these capacities can be measured directly.

Reports of income and living standards are particularly disparate among the elderly. Comparing reports of hardship in a number of economic areas to official poverty thresholds, Mayer and Jencks (1989) found that a family's official income-to-needs ratio explains less than one-fourth of the variance in material hardship. Similarly, there was little overlap between level of income and level of satisfaction with financial well-being among the elderly. Income and financial assets explain only about 25% of older adults' reports of financial satisfaction (George 1993). The apparent discrepancies between income and perceptions of financial well-being, and between the poverty line and consumption patterns of older adults, emphasize the need for alternative measures of economic well-being among the elderly.

Economic Hardship Measures versus the Official Poverty Threshold

Economic hardship measures and the official poverty threshold both try to determine what proportion of society is marginalized by a low standard of living. Both attempt to define a minimum standard below which hardship occurs, and both measure resources; however, the similarities end there.

Economic hardship measures typically define *minimum standard* as lacking adequate levels of certain necessities, such as inability to purchase needed food. Minimum standard definitions may vary, however, depending on the survey and the domain studied. Measures of economic hardship use reports of consumption and consumptive capacity to determine *resources*. For example, respondents are asked if there were times they had no food or were unable to pay bills. In contrast, the official poverty threshold is set at a minimum standard, three times the amount of money the U.S. Department of Agriculture (USDA) estimates is required for a family to purchase a minimally nutritious diet. This minimum standard calculation is adjusted for household size and for heads of households age 65 and older. Household income is then compared to the minimum standard, and households with incomes less than the minimum standard are considered to be living below the poverty threshold.

There are several problems with the poverty threshold as a measure of economic well-being among the elderly. Originally, adjustments in the official poverty threshold for age of household head were justified on the basis that older persons had fewer dietary requirements, thus lowered food costs, and a lower minimum standard. This assumption is problematic for several reasons. Studies of consumption have found that persons age 65 and older spend the same or greater proportions of their income on food than younger households (Cook and Settersten 1995). Additionally, these studies have found that persons over age 64 spend a higher proportion of their income on housing, health care, and utilities than younger households, even when controlling for income levels.

Economic well-being is a concept based on consumption—whether individuals have, or think they have, access to adequate levels of goods and services. The poverty threshold measures income, or resources, which is at best only an indirect measure of consumption. Persons may be able to consume beyond their income by borrowing, drawing on savings, or using nonmonetary exchanges. Conversely, those who have adequate income may choose not to spend it on necessities, thereby ending up with inadequate levels of consumption. Finally, households also have different needs, tastes, priorities, and levels of efficiency that may alter the relationship between income and consumption. Since income is only an indirect indicator of consumption, alternative measures of economic well-being that are not income-based are needed.

Measuring Economic Hardship

Although alternative measures have been part of the European statistical literature for almost 30 years, they have only recently been used in the United States. Some studies of economic hardship measure material hardship or lack of needed goods and services. Other studies look at "level of living," which includes nonmaterial components, such as access to education, working conditions, family relations, and measures of material needs. Still other studies focus on subjective financial well-being and measure how satisfied people are with their financial situation. Though the methodology differs, all of these studies have a common goal: to determine levels of hardship and deprivation through the use of nonincome measures.

Finding measures of economic hardship that compare households of different sizes and different needs is difficult. Although it is obvious that people of different ages and health statuses have different needs, it is not obvious what kinds of measures can be used to standardize the ratio of resources to consumption. The first major study to use nonincome measures of economic well-being, the Swedish Level of Living Survey, outlined nine areas of living conditions: (1) health and access to care, (2) employment and working conditions, (3) economic resources, (4) knowledge and educational opportunities, (5) family and social integration, (6) recreation and culture, (7) housing and neighborhood facilities, (8) security of life and property, and (9) political resources. Most work on *material hardship* has concentrated on basic necessities—food, housing, clothing, access to medical and dental care, and transportation—while recognizing that there are other items that contribute to quality of life, the lack of which may also cause considerable hardship.

To determine adequate levels of these factors, *hardship* is defined differently depending on the survey questions asked. Most surveys question whether respondents could not afford what they needed. Other surveys ask if there was a time in the past year when respondents had to go without items that they needed, could not afford to buy needed food, or could not afford to pay the rent or mortgage; if they had no access to medical insurance; or if there were times when they had to go without needed medical attention. Some researchers look at housing conditions, such as levels of disrepair, or at the presence of durable goods such as dishwashers, automobiles, and air conditioners, as indicators of well-being. Some studies also use subjective assessments of economic well-being, which generally ask the respondents about their levels of satisfaction with income, financial resources, current living standards, or the extent to which they worry about making ends meet.

Empirical Data

Studies consistently have found that persons over the age of 64 report fewer material hardships than younger adults. For example, Mayer and Jencks (1989) reported findings from the Chicago Hardship Study showing that, on average, families with heads age 65 and older had 36% as much income as younger families of the same size who reported the same number of hardships.

Also using Chicago Hardship Study data, Cook and Kramek (1986) found that households with heads age 65 and older were the least likely age group to report experiencing one or more hardships in the areas of food, rent, housing conditions, medical, dental, or utilities. Fewer adults age 65 and older said grocery spending was inadequate, and less than one-half as many reported a time when they needed food but could not afford it as adults under age 65. Very few age 65 and older reported a time they could not afford to pay the rent, they had been evicted, or had utilities discontinued. The 65 and older sample was less than half as likely as younger age groups to report having two or more physical housing problems.

Lower levels of hardship among older adults, however, does not mean they are universally better off than younger adults. Without controlling for income, Cook and Kramek also found that older adults spent less on groceries than those aged 50–64, and a higher percentage of adults over age 65 spent less than USDA minimum than adults aged 50–64. Older persons in the Chicago Hardship Study reported more medical problems than younger adults. They were as likely to say they had been sick and needed help, but were less likely than younger adults to say they went without medical care or dental care because of lack of money. The data show that the domains in which persons age 65 and older are most likely to experience hardship are medical, food, and housing.

Subjective assessments of economic well-being were measured in the Chicago Hardship Study by asking respondents to express feelings about their standard of living and making ends meet. Without controlling for income, those aged 65 and older were less satisfied with their standard of living than those aged 18–49, but more satisfied than those aged 50–64. Similarly, of persons reporting no hardships, those aged 65 and older were less satisfied with their standard of living than those aged 18–49, but slightly more satisfied than those aged 50–64. However, persons aged 65 and older who had experienced at least one hardship had the lowest satisfaction with their standard of living of any age group. Members of the oldest group were the least likely to be worried about making ends meet, regardless of whether they had experienced a hardship. Reviewing the literature on subjective assessments of economic well-being, George (1992) found that even though older adults had lower income on average than younger adults, older adults consistently reported higher levels of satisfaction with their income, financial resources, and standard of living than younger adults.

Although the poverty threshold adjusts over time for changes in consumer prices, it does not account for changes in consumption habits and priorities of society. Changing priorities in society are not captured by a poverty threshold based on income alone. In 1963, when the poverty line was being developed, it was considered unnecessary for households to have a telephone, whereas in 1995, this need is seen differently. Thus, alternative measures of deprivation that are based directly on consumption are important supplements to the poverty thresholds. Several studies suggest that widely used economic indicators may be misleading in terms of the overall living conditions in society. Although conventional wisdom has maintained that the U.S. standard of living declined in the 1970s, measures in four areas (health, housing, transportation, and food) have shown that conditions in these areas actually improved (Jencks 1984).

The relationship between changes in income and objective and subjective measures of economic hardship over the past three decades is less clear. Objective income levels of older persons have increased since 1973. There is no evidence, however, that subjective reports of financial satisfaction have increased among older adults despite improved objective economic status.

Explaining Levels of Economic Hardship among the Elderly

Although age differences in reports of material hardship have been found consistently, little work has attempted to untangle the effects of age and other factors on reports of economic hardship. The factors that put some elderly at risk for economic hardship and those that make others resilient to it have also not been explored in detail. Studies asking individuals to state an amount of money they perceive as a ''just sufficient'' level of income or ''enough income to make ends meet'' may provide some clues to the reasons for age differences in reports of economic hardship. These studies have found that the elderly have lower expectations of their economic resources, which suggests that they may report fewer economic hardships than younger adults because their idea of a sufficient level of income is lower than non-elderly adults. Perceptions of poverty may change little over a lifetime, and older persons experiencing lower incomes in the 1920s, 1930s and 1940s may have unchanged criteria for what constitutes an adequate standard of living.

Some researchers suggest that the elderly may report fewer hardships because they are more likely to have assets than younger adults. They are more likely to own their homes, and elderly homeowners are less likely to have mortgages. Several studies have found that, in general, the elderly underreport income and assets, making them seem objectively less well-off than they are. Other possible explanations are more speculative. Some suggest that the elderly are better managers of money, or that the elderly have different tastes, but these explanations have not been investigated empirically. Others propose that measures of past hardships do not capture economic worries of the elderly, which may have more to do with future ability to pay bills, especially large medical expenses, as their health deteriorates (George 1992; Holden and Smeeding 1990).

Since the study of economic hardship is a new field, there is simply not an adequate amount of research to understand specifically why elderly persons report different levels of economic hardship from those reported by younger adults. Yet this focus of inquiry has been valuable in bringing to light some of the complexity of the levels of well-being across age categories. (See also AS-SETS ALLOCATION AFTER RETIREMENT, ECONOMIC STATUS OF THE ELDERLY, ECONOMIC STATUS OF ELDERLY WOMEN, EDUCA-TION OF OLDER ADULTS, HEALTH AND LONGEVITY, HOUSING, LEI-SURE, and WEALTH SPAN.)

References

Cook, Fay Lomax, and Lorraine M. Kramek. 1986. "Measuring Economic Hardship among Older Americans." *Gerontologist* 26: 38–47.

Cook, Fay Lomax, and Richard A. Settersten, Jr. 1995. "Expenditure Patterns by Age and Income among Mature Adults: Does Age Matter?" *Gerontologist* 35: 10–23.

George, Linda K. 1992. "Economic Status and Subjective Well-Being: A Review of the Literature and an Agenda for Future Research." In *Aging, Money and Life Satisfaction: Aspects of Financial Gerontology,* ed. Neal E. Cutler et al. New York: Springer.

George, Linda K. 1993. *Financial Security in Later Life: The Subjective Side.* Philadelphia: Boettner Institute of Financial Gerontology.

Holden, Karen C., and Timothy M. Smeeding. 1990. "The Poor, the Rich, and the Insecure Elderly Caught In Between." *Milbank Quarterly* 68: 191–219.

Jencks, Christopher. 1984. "The Hidden Prosperity of the 1970s." *Public Interest* 77: 37–61.

Mayer, Susan E., and Christopher Jencks. 1989. "Poverty and the Distribution of Material Hardship." *Journal of Human Resources* 24: 88–114.

Fay Lomax Cook and Anne S. Welch

ECONOMIC SECURITY. See Introduction; Pension Fund Trends; Social Security; Supplemental Security Income (SSI); Wealth Span.

ECONOMIC STATUS OF THE ELDERLY. Per capita incomes of older persons rose substantially during the 1970s and early 1980s and are now similar to those for the general population. From 1970 to 1989, real median income of older households increased 41%, and composition of income sources changed substantially as well. In 1970, elderly households received 25% of their income from Social Security*, 14% from assets, 13% from employer pensions, 47% from earnings, and about 1% from other sources. By 1988, the share of income received from Social Security had risen to 38%, asset income increased to 25%, employer pension income increased to 18%, earnings decreased to 17%, and about 3% of income came from other sources. Improvements in economic status of the elderly have resulted from increases in Social Security, asset, and pension income. These percentages, of course, differ for subgroups within the older population. While Social Security benefits account for 80% of income among recent retirees in the lowest one-fifth of the income distribution, they compose only 10% of the highest one-fifth (National Academy on Aging [NAA] 1994).

The increasing importance of Social Security in the income composition of elderly families is of particular interest from a policy standpoint. Most of the increase occurred as a result of the 1972 Social Security amendments. In 1970, prior to the amendments, poverty among the elderly stood at 25%; by 1974, it had fallen to about 15%. The percentage of the older population in poverty continued to decline slightly in the early 1980s, but has remained fairly constant since (12.4% in 1991). While today the elderly are less at risk of falling below the poverty threshold, they are likely to be barely above it. Many older Americans have escaped poverty, but as many as one-half have not escaped it by much (NAA 1993).

The risk of poverty is uneven within the elderly population. The poverty rate for married couples over 65 is low—about 5% in 1990; among the unmarried, for men it is 14% and for women it is 22% (NAA 1993). In 1991, the poverty rate among single black women aged 75 and older was 62%. Considerable differences are evident between age brackets: In 1990, households in which the head was 65 to 69 years old received a median income between $20,000 and $23,000, while units headed by persons age 80 and older commanded only between $11,000 and $13,000. Twenty percent of those aged 85 or over fell below the poverty threshold (Steuerle and Bakija 1994). Thus, significant pockets of poverty remain among various elderly subpopulations.

Substantial real growth in the average economic status of older persons has resulted in an important policy consideration: equity between older and younger age groups in the population. In contrast to the 41% increase in real median income of older households during 1970–1989, real incomes of younger households increased by less than 4%. Even more alarming was the rapid increase in the proportion of children living in poverty (22% in 1991). As with the elderly, in some subgroups of children, the poverty rate is even higher. Yet federal tax rates on Americans age 65 or over on average are lower (16.3%) than those on the non-elderly (24.7%) (Steuerle and Bakija 1994).

High poverty rates among children have led some to argue that the improving economic status of the elderly has come at the expense of children. Others dispute this viewpoint, arguing that trends in relative economic status of younger and older persons are largely unrelated. Regardless of which viewpoint is correct, measures to improve the economic status of the elderly will be an unlikely priority policy emphasis in the foreseeable future in light of large federal government budget deficits and concerns about financing retirement and health benefits for the aging baby boom cohort.

The Aging of the Baby Boom Cohort

Formulation of retirement income policy requires a variety of assumptions about future economic growth and the characteristics of future retirees. The group that most concerns policymakers is the enormous 1946–1964 baby boom cohort, whose members are just now entering middle age. Characteristics of this middle-aged population will have far-reaching implications for public policy and the future economic status of older persons.

Conventional wisdom is that baby boomers are headed for tough economic times in retirement because of possible future financing difficulties in the Social Security system and conditions in the labor market that have kept real wage growth low. Weak earnings have certainly been a reality for part-time employees, whose ranks swelled from 10.8 million in 1969 to 20.7 million in 1993; 6.1 million of the latter total are workers who would prefer to work full-time but can only find part-time employment (Employee Benefit Research Institute [EBRI] 1994a). Also worrisome are growing signs of financial stress among middle-aged individuals who face involuntary early retirement. Too young to qualify for Social Security and unable to find work, many of them use up savings intended for their older years. Yet, there are some predictions that baby boomers will enter retirement in better economic shape than pre-boom retirees. Reasons for this stem from economic and demographic adjustments made by the middle aged, including deferred marriages, reduced child rearing, and increased labor force participation by women.

Aggregate Income and Asset Holdings

In considering the economic status of the current and future elderly, few would argue that money income is the best measure. Another approach, however, is to use household wealth as a measure of economic status where wealth is defined as the total market value of such assets as home equity, stocks and bonds, and savings accounts. Housing is a major form of equity for recent retirees, accounting for more than one-half of the total wealth of those close to and just entering retirement. Median wealth for non-homeowners aged 55 to 65 in 1989 was $800; for homeowners it was $115,000 (NAA 1994).

Wealth is a conceptually important variable because it reflects having met consumption needs in the past (wealth will be positive if income has been higher than expenditures in one's life) and the capacity to finance future consumption by drawing upon wealth.

A theoretical explanation of the relationships among income, consumption, and savings is provided by the life cycle hypothesis, which begins with the assumption that consumption needs and income are unequal at various points in the life cycle. Younger people have consumption needs that exceed their income (housing and education). In middle age, as earnings rise, debts can be paid off and savings accumulated. Finally, in retirement, incomes decline and individuals consume out of previously accumulated savings.

The empirical literature concerning the life cycle hypothesis, however, has been inconclusive with regard to the savings behavior of older persons. Although there is some evidence of dissaving among the elderly, other studies have found that the elderly continue to save in retirement. Saving in retirement is not necessarily inconsistent with the life cycle hypothesis if one considers an individual's aversion to uncertainty and a preference to consume in the present versus save for the future (King 1985). In addition, it is likely that dissaving in retirement would be much more evident if it were defined more broadly to include the diminution of claims on pension wealth.

Radner (1990) and Hurd (1990) provide overviews of the different ways in which researchers have used current income and wealth to measure economic status. The usual approach is to convert wealth into an equivalent income stream (based on life expectancy and interest rate assumptions) and add this income stream to current income, excluding the income already being received from assets. These studies consistently show that the income stream generated from assets is modest for most elderly, especially those who have low incomes to begin with. In the recent past, change in wealth has been a direct function of initial status measured by average income. During the mid-to late-1980s, a period of significant economic growth, households in the lowest one-fifth of the income distribution (with incomes less than $12,000) suffered actual declines in real net worth. The middle 50% of households saw virtually no change, whereas the richest 30% (with average incomes over $36,000) enjoyed asset increases of 40% to 80% (NAA 1993).

Policy Implications

Growing concerns about potential labor shortages and the ability of the economy to support retirement benefits for an aging population are causing policymakers to reconsider income maintenance policies for the older population. These concerns are heightened by the size of the current federal deficit and the recognition that other population groups have not experienced income gains comparable to those of the elderly. Consequently, some have concluded that public benefits for the elderly have been too generous, and have come at the expense of other population groups.

Unfortunately, aggregate income statistics that are the basis for such conclusions mask much more than they reveal. Although it is true that the income distribution of the elderly is now more similar to that of the general population, among certain subgroups of the older population the poverty rate is still extremely high.

Rising per capita incomes of the elderly did not stem from Social Security, as many assume. They resulted, instead, from the expansion and maturation of the employer pension system in the 1960s and 1970s, coupled with high interest rates in the late 1970s and early 1980s, but favored those lucky enough to have these particular income sources. Since the early 1970s, pension coverage has remained at about 50% of full-time workers, declining slightly in recent years. The mix of expected pension income is changing as more plans shift from defined-benefit to defined-contribution formats and as employment relationships become restructured, especially regarding the growth of part-time and other contingent employment (EBRI 1994b). More financial responsibility is transferred to employees, including the necessity to plan independently for one's income in retirement. Meanwhile, low personal saving rates in this country (4 or 5% of income) are considered insufficient to provide for long-term old age provision.

Despite the rising average income of the elderly population as a whole, older persons without employer pensions or financial assets are in a precarious situation. Prospects are gloomy for future retirees who are poorly educated and have not had marketable labor force skills (NAA 1994). (See also ASSETS ALLOCATION AFTER RETIREMENT, ECONOMIC HARDSHIP MEASURES IN THE OLDER POPULATION, ECONOMIC STATUS OF THE ELDERLY, ECONOMIC STATUS OF ELDERLY WOMEN, PENSION FUND TRENDS, SOCIAL SECURITY, and WEALTH SPAN.)

References

Employee Benefit Research Institute. 1994a. "Characteristics of the Part-Time Work Force." *EBRI Special Report SR-22* and *EBRI Issue Brief 149.*
Employee Benefit Research Institute. 1994b. "Employment-Based Retirement Income Benefits: Analysis of the April 1993 Current Population Survey." *EBRI Special Report SR-25* and *EBRI Issue Brief 153.*
Hurd, Michael. 1990. "Research on the Elderly, Economic Status, Retirement, and Consumption and Saving." *Journal of Economic Literature* 28: 565–637.
King, M. 1985. "The Economics of Saving: A Survey of Recent Contributions." In *Frontiers of Economics,* ed. K. Arrow and S. Houkapohja. New York: Blackwell.
National Academy on Aging. 1993. *Poverty and Income Security among Older Persons.* Washington, DC: NAA.
National Academy on Aging. 1994. *Old Age in the 21st Century.* Washington, DC: NAA.
Radner, David. 1990. "Assessing the Economic Status of the Aged and Nonaged Using Alternative Income-Wealth Measures." *Social Security Bulletin* 53: 2–14.
Steuerle, C. Eugene, and Jon M. Bakija. 1994. *Retooling Social Security for the 21st Century: Right and Wrong Approaches to Reform.* Washington, DC: Urban Institute Press.

William H. Crown

ECONOMIC STATUS OF ELDERLY WOMEN. In 1990, there were 31.1 million people aged 65 or older in the U.S. population. Of these, 18.6 million (60%) were elderly women (Taeuber 1992.) Among them, the census counted 2.2 million women age 85 and older making this group the fastest growing segment of the aged population.

The socioeconomic status of elderly women is influenced by their health status, as the financial burden of health care can create serious economic hardship. While most of the elderly have Medicare* coverage (94.8% in 1989), the system covers only about 45% of personal health expenditures. According to one estimate, initial out-of-pocket payments for long-term care, particularly, lead to poverty in about 25% of all cases (Allen and Pifer 1993). Compared with rapidly rising costs of nursing home care, private pension resources of the elderly do not increase much. A pension would typically lose two-thirds of its purchasing power over 20 years if it needed to be spent on nursing home care (Steuerle and Bakija 1994).

Despite their longer life expectancy, elderly women have a higher prevalence of chronic disability and more acute illnesses and injuries than elderly men. Elderly women have more chronic health problems and suffer more symptoms and physical limitations in their daily lives, whereas elderly men are more prone to life-threatening ailments. Elderly women visit physicians more frequently and use more days of hospital and nursing home care than men. Ultimately, women die from the same diseases as men, but at later ages (Verbrugge 1984).

Economic Status

Circumstances of the elderly have improved over the last two decades, to the extent that they are now perceived as being economically well-off. This assumption may not be true for women who are living alone, widowed, divorced, part of a minority group, living in a nonmetropolitan area, or older than 75. The material well-being of elderly women is conditioned by the economic gender gap among the elderly and shortcomings in social policies.

Economic characteristics of the elderly when examined by gender reveal sizeable differences. In 1990, the median income for elderly women was $8,044, compared to $14,183 for elderly men. The poverty rate for elderly women was 15%, compared to 7.8% for elderly men. These differences become more dramatic when controlling for living arrangements, marital status, minority status, and being among the oldest-old (U.S. Senate Select Committee on Aging 1991).

Unmarried older men experience a poverty rate of 14.4%, whereas unmarried older women face poverty at the rate of 22.1% (National Academy on Aging [NAA] 1993). Measured differently, the death of a spouse prompts a drop below 150% of the median income-to-needs ratio for 59.6% of men aged 50 years or over; in contrast, 79.3% of women in the same age group experience such an income decline upon death of a spouse. Most serious are the consequences of divorce: for women age 50 and above, divorce is likely to cause a 50% drop in the income-to-needs ratio in 23.7% of cases, whereas such a dramatic loss confronts only 8% of male divorcees age 50 and above (NAA 1993).

Differentiated by race and ethnicity, older women's lower economic status is reflected in the following median income figures for 1990: White men earned $14,839, white women $8,462, black women $5,617, and Hispanic women $5,373 (Gerontological Society of America 1991). Drastic contrasts are revealed by figures for persons 65 years and older and the risk of poverty. In 1990, a married older American living in a family household faced poverty at the rate of 3.8% if white, but 21.5% if black. In the case of a black woman living alone, the poverty risk was as high as 60.1% (Taeuber 1992).

Finally, women living in nonmetropolitan areas have suffered historically lower wages than men, and are more vulnerable when interruptions in normal life cycle patterns occur. Divorced or separated women in these areas have poverty rates almost double those of their counterparts in cities (McLaughlin and Holden 1993).

Labor Market and Policy Issues

The low economic status of elderly women reflects a lifetime of inequity created by labor market experiences and social and economic policy. Women's lives often combine careers in the paid work force, lengthy nonpaid caregiving periods, and marital changes that make it hard for them to accumulate adequate retirement benefits, either their own or derived from spouses (NAA 1994).

In 1980, women had a work life expectancy of 29 years, compared with 39 years for men (U.S. Senate Special Committee on Aging 1991). Although the number of women in the labor force has doubled in the last 50 years, there is inequity by sex with regard to employee benefits. And women, as compared to men, continue to be employed in larger proportions in lower income jobs that offer fewer employee-related benefits. Thus, women enter retirement with less than one-half the pension income of retired men. In 1991, 49% of men age 65 and older received a pension, with an average pension income of $9,855, while only 22% of women age 65 and older received an average pension income of $5,186 (Glasse 1993).

Policies on old-age provisions still assume that women are economically dependent on the primary wage-earning male head of the household. Consequently, retirement, pension, and Social Security* benefits have not sufficiently alleviated the low economic status of elderly women. Women age 65 and older are more likely to rely on Social Security as their sole source of financial support than are elderly men. Social Security provides about 90% of all income for one-third of elderly unmarried women.

Marriage permits elderly women with limited or no labor force activity access to Social Security and retirement benefits accrued by the work activity of their spouses, much as they shared in the earnings of their spouses throughout their lives. But following a divorce, an older woman has access to spousal and survivor benefits from Social Security only if she had been married for 10 years or more. She receives that benefit or the benefit for which she is eligible based on her own work record, whichever is higher. With the death of the covered worker, the Social Security benefit paid to the survivor, if based on the worker's benefit, will be equal to only two-thirds of the total benefit paid to the couple prior to widowhood. Pension income paid to a retired worker may be lost entirely, depending on the form of pension selected. Selection of a single-life pension (or a lump sum payment) ends all payments to the survivor when the worker dies (McLaughlin and Holden 1993).

Poor women would benefit from more equal sharing in the Social Security and pension benefits that were earned by their spouses. Indeed, for all women who for some portion of their lives shared in the income of their spouses, it is the degree to which those resources are shared over their remaining lifetimes, including the years they are widowed, that determines how well they fare when alone (McLaughlin and Holden 1993). Thus, to date, women go into old age and retirement with a greater possibility of impoverishment than do men. (See also COHABITATION, DIVORCE AND THE ELDERLY, ECONOMIC HARDSHIP MEASURES IN THE OLDER POPULATION, ECONOMIC STATUS OF THE ELDERLY, MARRIAGE AND THE ELDERLY, OLDEST OLD, MEDICARE, SOCIAL SECURITY, and WIDOWDHOOD.)

Organizations

The Older Women's League
American Association of Retired Persons

Suggested Reading

Doress, Paula Brown, Diana Laskin Siegal, and the Midlife and Older Women Book Project. 1987. *Ourselves, Growing Older.* New York: Simon and Schuster.

References

Allen, Jessie and Alan Pifer. 1993. *Women on the Front Lines: Meeting the Challenge of an Aging America.* Washington, DC: Urban Institute Press.
Gerontological Society of America. 1991. *Minority Elders: Longevity, Economics, and Health.* Washington, DC: Author.
Glasse, Lou. 1993. "Pension Policy in Changing Times." *The OWL Observer* (Winter),1–4.
McLaughlin, Diane K., and Karen C. Holden. 1993. "Nonmetropolitan Elderly Women: A Portrait of Economic Vulnerability." *Journal of Applied Gerontology* 12: 320–34.
National Academy on Aging. 1993. *Poverty and Income Security among Older Persons.* Washington, DC: NAA.
National Academy on Aging. 1994. *Old Age in the 21st Century.* Washington, DC: NAA.
Steuerle, C. Eugene, and Jon M. Bakija. 1994. *Retooling Social Security for the 21st Century: Right and Wrong Approaches to Reform.* Washington, DC: Urban Institute Press.
Taeuber, Cynthia M. 1992. *Sixty-Five Plus in America.* Current Population Reports Special Study P23–178. Washington, DC: Bureau of the Census.
U.S. Senate Select Committee on Aging. 1991. *Aging in America: Trends and Projections.* Washington, DC: U.S. Government Printing Office.
Verbrugge, Lois M. 1984. "A Health Profile of Older Women with Comparisons to Older Men." *Research on Aging* 6: 291–322.

Julia E. Bradsher and Carroll L. Estes

EDUCATION OF OLDER ADULTS, persons 55 and older participating in some type of organized instruction. Some are enrolled in institutions of higher education for credit, but the majority are more interested in noncredit courses offered by a variety of providers—continuing education programs of four-year colleges and universities, community colleges, adult education programs of the public schools, parks and recreation departments, public libraries, and senior centers, to name a few. Older adults also engage in self-directed learning projects. They are involved in an average of 3.3 learning projects per year and spend an average of 324 hours on each project. A learning project includes a series of related episodes that add up to at least seven hours, and may include a combination of learning modes (Bolton 1985).

Studies indicate that the more formal education a person has received previously, the more likely he or she is to participate in some type of organized educational program. In 1950, the median years of schooling for persons age 65 and older was the eighth grade; in 1989, it was over twelve years. Eleven percent of this population group in 1989 completed four or more years of college; by the year 2010, this figure will increase by 20% (Manheimer 1994).

As the education level of future cohorts of older persons increases, we can predict that there will be a steady growth in the number of older persons interested in participating in educational programs. Overall, the future seems bright for institutions and organizations that sponsor lifelong learning programs and services.

Implications for Financial Gerontology

The projected growth of education for older adults has financial implications for both the public and private sector, and for older learners themselves. Policymakers have debated whether society should finance and support education for older persons. In 1971, the White House Conference on Aging was a benchmark event for those who believed that education should be considered a ''right'' for older adults. This concept was inspired by the passage of the Older Americans Act* in 1965, which legislated basic rights for older adults in areas such as health, housing, and income security.

A majority of states enacted legislation during the 1970s permitting older students to enroll in state universities and colleges for waived or reduced tuition. Community college and university education programs mushroomed, with many providing no- or low-cost noncredit, short-term courses and educational programs in locations where elderly people congregate, such as senior centers, churches, and libraries. The Lifelong Learning Act (Education Amendments of 1976) was passed, but not funded.

Times have changed. The elderly are now seen as a group that is relatively well-off. Concerns focused on reducing the national deficit and eliminating government waste have eliminated some educational programs subsidized by the public sector. Some programs are kept afloat by institutional commitment or creative public-private partnerships. Still others operate on a marketplace philosophy, serving those who are able to pay a fee.

Tuition and/or Fee Waivers

Despite the present lack of policy support for older adult education, growth in programs and participants continues. Many community colleges, state colleges and universities, and some private institutions sponsor tuition and fee waivers for older persons. The College Board (1994) lists nearly 1,000 campuses that offer such programs. These programs can be administered with relatively low overhead since older persons generally enroll on a space-available basis only after matriculated students have selected classes. The most effective are those that have institutional commitment and offer "wrap-around" services to promote the program, assist older students with registration, and provide some academic or social support; however, there are not many of these special services now.

Tuition waiver programs appeal to a small number of older people. Data indicate that seniors participate primarily in short-term courses and educational offerings, and prefer informal settings with opportunities for involvement and discussion. Joining a fast-paced, semester-long course with degree-seeking younger students, completing term papers and homework, and sitting in large lecture halls does not seem as attractive as other alternatives.

The Educational Marketplace and Older Learners

Most expansion of older adult educational programs is taking place among the more entrepreneurial institutions of higher education. As the number of "traditional age" students on campus decreases and the number of adult students increases, these institutions are taking another look at older adult learners. They now consider this group as a potential market and are developing specially designed programs that meet their wants and needs. Facing financial realities, many colleges and universities have their eye on better-educated and more affluent seniors who can afford to pay tuition.

Colleges and universities are only one type of institution that has recognized the growing market for lifelong learning programs. Other settings include senior centers, department stores, and other community-based organizations. The programs they are establishing are self-supporting, operate on a pay-as-you-go basis, or are privately funded. Several national organizations have built successful educational enterprises. Elderhostel, a nonprofit educational vacation program where older people, in residence for a week or more, participate in classes and other activities, is expanding to include intergenerational educational programs, study tours, and community service opportunities. There are currently 1,200 locations with 250,000 older persons participating annually. Elderhostel has also established the Elderhostel Institute Network, which consists of approximately 200 independent Learning in Retirement Institutes. These institutes are based on campuses, usually four-year universities, and attract retired professionals and other educated retirees who play an active role in the institute's governance and/or instruction.

Another successful learning network is OASIS, a nonprofit organization sponsored by the May Department Stores Company. There are nearly 30 OASIS centers, which are based in stores and, with community support, provide educational, health promotion, and cultural programs for older adults. SeniorNet, a national organization of computer-using seniors with over 15,000 members, is expanding rapidly. It sponsors 60 Learning Centers throughout the country, and also provides classes online.

These networks and organizations are privately administered and do not rely solely on governmental or institutional support for their daily operations. Other self-supporting, locally-based innovative educational programs—in senior centers, museums, hospitals, and chapters of the American Association of Retired Persons—show that lifelong learning opportunities for older persons are burgeoning (albeit in a fragmented and uncoordinated way) without a national older adult education policy.

Some of these organizations, particularly university-based programs, have found an additional bonus in sponsoring educational programs. Active older learners often develop institutional loyalty and willingly contribute to college and university building or alumni funds. Members of the Institute for Learning in Retirement at California State University in Fullerton, for example, raised the funds needed to build the Ruby Gerontology Center.

In a marketplace approach, however, older people who are poor, disabled, and/or members of minority groups and who lack formal education are underrepresented or invisible. Although they reach only a few, many programs mentioned here have experimental scholarship funds or have tried other methods to involve less advantaged seniors. However, they are clearly an underserved group in education.

Student Aid

Older students are eligible for financial aid, although such aid is geared to full-time matriculated students and most adults, including older adults, enroll part-time. According to the College Board, $42 billion in student aid funds was available to students in public and private higher education in the academic year 1994–95. This included grants, loans, and work-study programs; 54% represented money for loans (Brouder 1994).

There are several federal financial aid programs available. The criteria, in most cases, are demonstrated financial need and full-time enrollment. On the federal level, part-time students might be eligible for the Pell Grant Program (a small percentage of funds is available for part-time students), the Supplemental Educational Opportunity Grant Program (institutions can decide whether to use funds for full- and/or part-time students), the Perkins Loan Program, the Stafford Loan Program, or work-study jobs.

A few states permit students who are enrolled at least half-time to borrow money, but most require full-time matriculation. As with the federal programs, older students are as likely to be considered for funds as any other age group if they meet the basic criteria. There are also private scholarship funds available, although most are for full-time students.

Job Training and Education

Many older persons wish to remain in the workforce to maintain income and remain active. As a result of layoffs and early retirement, growing numbers of men and women are unemployed and cannot find work. Others are looking for part-time employment to make ends meet, and they are likely candidates for job-related education and training. Adult education programs, sponsored by the public school systems and community colleges, offer vocational training in areas such as automotive repair, computer skill building, culinary arts, resume writing, and other job readiness courses. Although they are offered to adults of all ages, many older adults feel discouraged from taking job-related courses because of age discrimination in hiring practices. They believe retraining is not worthwhile if jobs are not available.

Some industries—particularly in service areas—need skilled workers, and employers are recognizing that many older adults bring solid reading, writing, and communication abilities to the workplace, and that they are proven, reliable workers. Some new educational programs have been developed specifically for older persons. Adult schools in Orange County, Florida, for example, train older persons to serve as home-health workers and place them in part-time jobs. McDonald's has developed the "McMasters" program to train and employ older workers in local outlets. Trainers indicate that once they make slight adjustments for cognitive and physical changes, older persons learn quickly and are conscientious workers.

Education for Community Service

Some people seek education for employment. Others look for opportunities to provide community service and to volunteer. With years of experience and time available in retirement, older people can provide valuable assistance in solving some of the nation's problems. Some organizations offer training for community volunteers. Literacy Volunteers of America, the American Association of Retired Persons, and some Institutes for Learning in Retirement on campuses, offer training and become volunteer centers for a variety of community projects. All such educational enterprises contribute to "productive aging" and should be considered especially worthy of public and private support because of the pay-back to society.

Baby Boomers and the Future

As baby boomers start to retire, it is likely that they will seek out continuing opportunities to learn. This bodes well for educational institutions and other organizations that offer lifelong learning programs. Boomers, more familiar with technology and distance learning than earlier retirees, may look to education for new ways of community involvement, to start new careers, or to find new meaning in life. It will be up to future providers of education to prepare for these exciting possibilities by becoming aware of physiological, psychological, and sociocultural changes associated with aging; learning what motivates adults to participate in education; experimenting with new delivery systems; and incorporating sound adult learning principles and techniques in their programs. (See also MARKETING TO ELDERS, LEISURE, OLDER AMERICANS ACT, TRAVEL, VOLUNTEERING, and VOLUNTEERS, OLDER.)

Organizations

Elderhostel, Older Adult Education Network
U.S. Department of Education, Federal Student Aid Information Center

Suggested Readings

Moskow-McKenzie, Diane, and Ronald J. Manheimer. 1994. *A Planning Guide to Organizing Educational Programs for Older Adults.* Asheville, NC: Center for Creative Retirement, University of North Carolina-Asheville.

Older Adult Education Network. *The Older Learners* (newsletter.) San Francisco: American Society on Aging.

Peterson, David A. 1988. *Facilitating Education for Older Learners.* San Francisco: Jossey-Bass.

U.S. Department of Education. 1994–1995. *The Student Guide.* Washington, DC: Federal Student Aid Information Center.

References

Bolton, Christopher R. 1985. "Alternative Instructional Strategies for Older Learners." In *Introduction to Educational Gerontology, Second Edition,* ed. R. H. Sherron and D. B. Lumsden. Washington, DC: Hemisphere Publishing, 125–47.

Brouder, Kathleen. Director, CSS Information Services, The College Scholarship Service, College Board. Interview, October 27, 1994.

College Board. 1994. *College Costs and Financial Aid Handbook-1995.* New York: College Entrance Examination Board.

Kampf, Leslie. 1994. "Educating Generation X." *Inside Colorado* (December) 20.

Manheimer, Ronald J. 1994. *The Handbook of Older Adult Education.* Unpublished Manuscript. Asheville, NC: Center for Creative Retirement, University of North Carolina-Asheville.

Sandra Timmerman

ELDER LAW PRACTICE, the legal practice of counseling and representing older persons or their representatives. It is the only area of law that is described by the clientele that is served rather than by the substantive area of law involved. Most clients are aged 55 and older. They range from the worker about to take early retirement to the frail elderly. The elder law attorney assists the senior citizen in a wide range of financial concerns, from basic estate planning to asset protection for long-term care.

Health and Personal Care Planning

Elder law attorneys advise clients about and help prepare advance directives* for health care. These documents are also known as medical powers of attorney*, living wills*, or health care declarations. All 50 states and the District of Columbia have laws permitting advance directives. These laws are based on the constitutional right to privacy. Through an advance directive a person sets forth his or her intentions regarding medical treatment in the last stages of life. An advance directive is usually accompanied by the appointment of a health care representative to act on behalf of the person. Elder law attorneys* also counsel health care representatives and families about medical and life-sustaining choices. It is sometimes necessary to go to court to enforce an advance directive, or to obtain an order to terminate life in the absence of an advance directive.

Pre-Mortem Legal Planning and Fiduciary Representation

This area of elder law, commonly called estate planning*, includes giving advice and preparing documents concerning: wills*; trusts*; durable, general, or financial powers of attorney; gifting; and the financial and tax implications of proposed actions. The attorney's role is to assist in the development of a plan for distribution of a person's assets to plan for avoidance of federal and state taxes upon the transfer of assets, to avoid probate* where appropriate, and to provide protective measures for the client that would be triggered upon disability.

Fiduciary representation includes seeking the appointment of, giving advice to, and representing persons serving as executor, personal representative, attorney-in-fact, trustee, guardian, conservator, representative payee, or other formal or informal fiduciary. An elder law attorney gives such legal advice as may be necessary to the fiduciary in performing his or her duties. Advance care planning for the appointment of and instruction to fiduciaries adds to flexibility and reduces costs in carrying out the wishes of the elderly person who may no longer be able to care for himself or herself. In the absence of a power of attorney, a guardian may have to be appointed to manage the affairs of an incompetent adult.

Legal Capacity Counseling and Protective Arrangements

Unfortunately, some older persons become incognizant and incapable of understanding the nature and consequences of particular acts or decisions. The medical community has developed client capacity screens that can be helpful in identifying whether a person is competent to act. The legal community also has developed a number of tests or standards to determine what level of capacity is needed for various acts.

On occasion, a person may seek to become appointed guardian for a parent or other older person over that person's objection. If the older person is competent, it is inappropriate to appoint a guardian. Another concern is whether the person applying to be appointed guardian is best suited to act as such. A close living relative, for example, is not always the best choice to handle the affairs of the elderly person. The elder law attorney may be called upon to represent the person who is the subject of the guardianship* proceeding or other family member. In the case of guardianship or conservatorship, an elder's financial resources should be protected.

Public Benefits and Insurance Advice

One of the most dynamic areas of elder law involves devising plans for assisting the elderly in obtaining or dealing with Medicare*, Medicaid*, Social

Security*, Supplemental Security Income (SSI)* benefits, veterans benefits, and food stamps. Perhaps the largest single area in public benefits advice for elder law attorneys involves protecting the family's assets in situations requiring long-term care.

The elder law attorney designs a plan that may involve the use of trusts, annuities*, or transfers of assets within the framework of the Medicaid law that makes a nursing home* patient eligible for benefits. Usually the family depletes some of its own assets prior to Medicaid eligibility, but the spouse remaining at home is able to save some assets, and assets can also be protected for children. Elder law attorneys also advocate for clients in obtaining Medicare benefits or assist in dealing with the administrative apparatus when problems arise.

The elderly have special needs relating to insurance that range from health and life insurance to long-term care, home care, Medicare supplemental insurance (Medigap)*, and long-term disability insurance. Clients often call upon elder law attorneys to analyze the various types of policies that are available and to make recommendations about what is needed and affordable.

Resident Rights Advocacy

Patients and residents in hospitals, nursing facilities, continuing care retirement communities*, assisted living* facilities, adult day care* facilities, and those cared for in their homes by others have certain rights. On occasion, the rights of the patient are ignored by the hospital or the nursing home*. Problems may involve financial elder abuse*, or range from the use of unlawful restraints to sexual abuse by members of a nursing home staff. Older persons entering continuing care retirement communities often require the assistance of an elder law attorney to review the contract, and occasionally to resolve disputes that arise between the community and the resident. An elder law attorney may be called upon to interpret the contract and help enforce the rights of the resident.

Nursing homes and other elder facilities may become aggressive in attempting to discharge patients when the insurance available to pay for a patient's care expires. The elder law attorney enforces the rights of the patient to prevent unlawful discharge. The financial issue of who will pay—the patient, a public assistance program, or the institution—is typically the issue to resolve.

Housing Counseling

Most elderly persons prefer to live in their own homes. Unfortunately, many do not have sufficient income to pay taxes, insurance, and maintenance, and sustain a lifestyle that affords dignity. Elder law attorneys often are able to assist such clients in obtaining reverse annuity mortgages. Under a reverse annuity mortgage, the homeowner receives a monthly check from the lender. The amount of the check is based on an appraisal of the property, the prevailing rate of interest, and the life expectancy of the borrower. The mortgage contract calls for repayment under certain terms and conditions. The attorney must review the documents to be sure the homeowner is protected. Reverse mortgages* can make an older person financially independent.

Many communities have loan programs available to older homeowners for purposes of rehabilitating their homes. The programs often provide that after a certain period of years, the loan is forgiven. Other programs do not forgive the loan, but make funds available at a below-market rate of interest. An attorney can be helpful in assisting a client in obtaining such loans. Many communities have subsidized senior citizen housing available, which an elder law attorney can assist low-income older persons to obtain.

Employment and Retirement Advice

At the time of retirement, questions arise about options relating to pensions, retiree health benefits, and unemployment benefits. There are often substantial tax consequences and significant financial considerations involving the retiree and the retiree's spouse. An elder law attorney is in a position to advise retirees on the options available and how they will financially impact the retiree and spouse.

Income, Estate, and Gift Tax Advice

A substantial amount of advice that elder law attorneys give their clients relates to passing assets from one generation to another. Federal estate tax, inheritance tax, and gift tax affect these transfers. Elder law attorneys develop plans for transferring assets in such a manner as to minimize or, if possible, eliminate transfer taxes. Proper income, estate, and gift tax advice can enable older persons to stretch their dollars to remain independent and pass assets on to future generations.

Tort Claims against Nursing Homes

On occasion, patients in nursing homes are illegally restrained or neglected, or they fall or are injured in some other way. They may be subjected to mental, physical, sexual, or financial abuse by nursing home staff. These cases are difficult because often the only witness is the elderly person, and in some cases the capacity of the elderly person is diminished and his or her testimony may be suspect. Litigation can be successful in protecting the rights of nursing home patients and in gaining compensation for physical and mental injuries suffered. An elder law attorney is often able to represent the nursing home patient or family members in this regard. Tort claims against nursing homes may result in compensation or even punitive damages.

Discrimination in Employment and Housing

As American businesses downsize and restructure, the victims are often aging workers. In many cases early retirement programs are structured in such a way as to compensate older workers for the rights they are relinquishing. Those who accept early retirement packages usually sign a written waiver of any rights they have based on age. However, older persons may be discriminated against through early termination or failure to hire, based solely on age. There are a number of elder law attorneys who specialize in age discrimination cases.

Elder law is a relatively new area of law, and most people are not aware of it. The National Academy of Elder Law Attorneys was established in 1988. The organizations listed below can provide help in learning about and obtaining an Elder Law attorney. (See also ADVANCE DIRECTIVES, ATTORNEYS, CHARITABLE CONTRIBUTIONS, DURABLE POWER OF ATTORNEY, ESTATE PLANNING, KING LEAR SYNDROME, MEDICAID, MEDICARE, PROBATE, SOCIAL SECURITY, SUPPLEMENTAL SECURITY INCOME, TRUSTS, and WILLS.)

Organizations

Commission on Legal Problems of the Elderly
National Academy of Elder Law Attorneys
Elder Law Section of State and County Bar Association
Legal Counsel for the Elderly (AARP)
National Senior Citizens Law Center

Suggested Reading

Regan, John J. 1989. *Your Legal Rights in Later Life.* Washington, DC: AARP.

References

Margolis, Harry S. 1995. *The Elder Law Portfolio Series.* Boston: Little Brown.
Mezzullo, Louis A., and Mark W. Wolpert. 1992. *Advising the Elderly Client.* New York: Clark, Boardman and Calaghan.
Regan, John J. 1982ff. *Tax, Estate and Financial Planning for the Elderly.* New York: Matthew Bender.

Thomas D. Begley, Jr.

ELDER TAXPAYER ISSUES, tax counseling services and tax preparation assistance for elderly persons; federal policies that affect the elderly; and the age factor in audits, collection, and enforcement practices of the Internal Revenue Service (IRS). Government at all levels, federal, state, and local, is financed through a variety of taxes administered through a complex web of regulations that change frequently, and usually require interpretation by tax professionals. While effective personal financial management requires familiarity with the U.S. (and local) tax environment, certain issues are of particular concern to older persons.

Tax Planning

Tax law has become so complex that tax counseling constitutes a large, if not the largest, component of financial and estate planning. Selecting the right tax professional is crucial, and choosing a tax professional is like choosing any expert: ask for recommendations from friends, colleagues, community members, bankers, attorneys, and other financial advisors*; investigate the credentials of candidates; and interview several candidates before choosing. Tax advisors should be in business all year, not just during tax season, since tax planning should be conducted on an ongoing basis.

A successful relationship with a tax counsellor will be built upon a compatible financial philosophy, mutual comfort in setting and achieving clear goals, and the confidence that the advisor will provide competent representation before the IRS should an audit occur. It is important to determine—*before selecting a tax advisor*—that he or she will not be intimidated by an aggressive revenue agent, since some representatives are more nervous about a confrontation with the IRS than their clients are.

Income Tax Filing Assistance for the Elderly

Free help is available *from the IRS* and from many other seniors' organizations for those who need tax filing assistance. The IRS provides training and technical assistance to prepare volunteers of private and public nonprofit agencies and organizations to assist persons who are 60 and older with their federal income tax returns. Reimbursement for transportation, meals, and other expenses incurred by volunteers* during training and while providing tax counseling assistance may be paid by the IRS.

Through the Tax Counseling for the Elderly (TCE) program, IRS-trained volunteers assist individuals who are 60 and older, and taxpayers who are disabled or have special needs, with their tax returns at many neighborhood locations. Also, certain Volunteer Income Tax Assistance (VITA) preparers are trained to help older Americans and others who cannot afford professional tax help with their tax returns. Volunteers who provide tax counseling frequently are retired individuals associated with nonprofit organizations that receive grants from the IRS. The grants help pay out-of-pocket expenses for volunteers for travel to older people's homes, to retirement or nursing homes, or special TCE sites. One such organization is the American Association of Retired Persons (AARP), responding to concerns that elderly taxpayers were overestimating and overpaying their taxes.

Under a cooperative agreement with the IRS as part of its TCE program, AARP began its Tax-Aide program in 1968 to provide free income tax assistance to older people. Each year, AARP volunteers, trained to understand the provisions of the tax code that affect older people, help more than one million taxpayers nationwide. Tax-Aide volunteers are available from February 1 through April 15 each year and can be located through the local IRS information office.

In addition to these counseling services, IRS provides toll-free telephone assistance, tax information publications, tax assistance and educational programs, and audiovisual instructional materials that are available for individuals and groups. While the IRS position is that most tax questions can be answered by reading the tax forms and reviewing the instructions, many taxpayers of all ages and older taxpayers in particular find the forms and the instructions burdensome and difficult to understand. Professional tax advisors, including income tax service companies, accountants*, and other qualified tax preparers such as *enrolled agents*—often former IRS employees who have passed a comprehensive series of tests—are available as paid private tax return preparers.

The law requires a paid preparer to sign the return and to complete the "Paid Preparers Use Only" section at the bottom of the form, just below the taxpayer's signature. The taxpayer, however, remains responsible for the accuracy of every item entered on his or her return. If a mistake occurs, the IRS will require the taxpayer, not the preparer, to pay any additional required taxes, penalties, and interest. Obtaining qualified tax preparation assistance is an important consideration. The ability to locate the preparer should the IRS have a question about the return is also important. Since tax laws change frequently, one should never rely on information booklets, pamphlets, or taxpayer instructions that are not current.

Audits and Collections

Breakdowns of the numbers of audits conducted by the IRS are published in the annual Report of the Commissioner by income and geographic location, but not by demographics, and it is generally unknown whether age is a factor in audits. In IRS collections procedures, it is presumed that actions are based on ability to pay. Since the IRS assumes that younger people have a longer working life, and the potential to earn more money than older persons, age is considered only indirectly (Carlson 1994).

Elderly persons who can afford to hire a representative should never speak directly to an IRS employee about either an audit or a collection matter. Unfortunately, while free advice from IRS and IRS-trained volunteers provide needy elderly taxpayers information about preparing and filing tax forms, no special help is available to them in the face of audit and collection procedures. Although hundreds of reputable books are published each year about taxes, audits, and how to deal with the IRS many older taxpayers who cannot afford to hire competent tax advisors experience anxiety, fear, and even abuse by aggressive revenue agents. Ironically, the only assistance available for troubled elderly taxpayers without resources may be the IRS itself.

Congressional hearings in recent years on the subject of IRS abuses led to legislation to protect taxpayer rights, and guidelines have been issued by the IRS for collection personnel to follow. Elderly taxpayers who believe they have been treated discourteously or unfairly should write to the chief of the examination or collection division at their local IRS district office. If a problem persists, contact the IRS's Problem Resolution Office (PRO) and ask to have a PRO officer assigned to resolve the case. When all else fails, an elderly person or representative should seek help through the local office of his or her member of Congress.

IRS's own investigations into compliance with income tax laws, according to Martin Kaplan and Naomi Weiss, authors of *What the IRS Doesn't Want You to Know,* have revealed what tax professionals have known all along: "taxpayers want to file their taxes correctly, but complex laws, badly designed forms, indecipherable instructions, and an adversarial relationship . . . stand in their way." Efforts are underway within the IRS to improve both its image and its collection strategies. The size of the IRS, however, and the difficulties inherent in bringing national policy changes down to grass roots levels are unlikely to bring relief to many deserving elderly taxpayers without outside intervention or organized advocacy. (See also ACCOUNTANTS, ATTORNEYS, CASH FLOW PLANNING FOR RETIREES, CONSUMER PROTECTION FOR THE ELDERLY, ELDER LAW PRACTICE, FINANCIAL ADVISORS, OMBUDSMAN.)

Organizations

American Association of Retired Persons
National Taxpayers Union

References

American Association of Retired Persons. 1988. *Tax Aide: A Program of People Helping People.* Washington, DC: AARP.
Boardroom Classics. 1992. *The Book of Tax Knowledge.* New York: Author.
Boardroom Classics. 1994. *Tax Loopholes: Everything the Law Allows.* Springfield, NJ: Author.
Carlson, Robert C., ed. 1993. *Tax Wise Money.* Vol. 2, No. 6 (June).
Carlson, Robert C. December 5, 1994. Letter to author.
Daily, Frederick W. 1992. *Stand Up to the IRS: How to Handle Audits, Tax Bills and Tax Court.* Berkeley, CA: Nolo Press.
Internal Revenue Service. 1993. *Guide to Free Tax Services.* Washington, DC: Department of the Treasury, Internal Revenue Service.
U.S. Library of Congress. 1992. "Federal Income Tax Treatment of the Elderly." *CRS Report for Congress.* Washington, DC: Congressional Research Service.
U.S. Senate. Special Committee on Aging. 1994. *Protecting Older Americans against Overpayment of Income Taxes.* Washington, DC: U.S. Government Printing Office.

Lois A. Vitt

EMPLOYEE RETIREMENT INCOME SECURITY ACT (ERISA), statute that federalized the law of employee benefits in the private sector. ERISA substantially modified the federal tax treatment of pension plans; introduced a federal fiduciary law of employee benefit plans, created federal jurisdiction for most employee benefits litigation, expanded disclosure and reporting requirements for employee benefit plans, preempted most state laws relating to employee benefits, vastly extended the scope of Department of Labor regulation of employee benefit plans, and created the Pension Benefit Guaranty Corporation, which insures pension benefits in most defined benefit pension plans.

Congress enacted ERISA in 1974 primarily as a response to grass-roots pressure to provide greater federal protection of pension benefits. The statute covers not only pensions, but all employee benefit plans. While the statute enhanced federal protection for pensions, it also pushed aside state law protection of employee benefit rights, leaving some employees with reduced, rather than increased, rights.

Structure of ERISA

ERISA has four sections. Title I amended the labor laws of the United States. The title includes six parts: (1) reporting and disclosure, (2) participation and vesting, (3) funding, (4) fiduciary responsibility, (5) administration and enforcement, and (6) continuation of health coverage.

Title II of ERISA amended the Internal Revenue Code (IRC). Certain amendments to ERISA parallel provisions in Title I. For example, Title I and Title II include identical vesting requirements. But other provisions of Title II have no analogue in Title I. These latter requirements reflect tax policy goals rather than employee protection goals. Among these provisions are the rules in IRC Section 415, which restrict the size of contributions to defined contribution plans and benefits from defined benefit plans. The policy basis for this rule is that the tax benefits enjoyed by participants in pension plans should be limited to the creation of reasonable levels of retirement savings. The IRC and regulations also include complex rules requiring tax-qualified pension plans to cover reasonable levels of rank-and-file employees and prohibiting discrimination in favor of highly compensated employees.

There are important differences between Titles I and II. A participant in a pension plan may bring a civil action to enforce any of the rules in Title I of ERISA; actions to enforce Title II generally must be initiated by the Internal Revenue Service (IRS). A plan's failure to follow rules in Title II can lead to the plan's loss of tax benefits, imposition of penalty taxes, or both, depending on the particular rule and its sanctions; no such penalties generally attach to a plan's failure to comply with rules in Title I.

Title III of ERISA includes miscellaneous provisions, statements of primary jurisdictional authority between the IRS and the Department of Labor, and the creation of a certification process for pension actuaries.

Title IV of ERISA establishes the Pension Benefit Guaranty Corporation and the defined benefit plan termination insurance program. There is a separate insurance program for single-employer and multiemployer defined benefit plans. Additionally, Title IV governs other aspects of defined benefit plan termination and, in 1980, was amended to impose "withdrawal liability" on employers who withdraw from underfunded multiemployer pension plans.

ERISA's Vesting and Participation Rules

ERISA's most notable contribution to employee benefit protection was its establishment of minimum vesting standards for retirement benefits. It requires most plans to provide that employees obtain a nonforfeitable right to their benefit at least as quickly as would occur in either of two statutory standards. The first standard provides that employees must have a nonforfeitable right to 100% of their benefits after five years of service. The second standard provides that employees must have a nonforfeitable right to 20% of their benefits after three years, and then increasing by 20% per year, so that after the seventh year, employees will have a 100% interest in their benefits. The first standard is commonly referred to as "cliff vesting," the latter standard as "graded vesting." ERISA also has rules to prevent evasion of the vesting standards. Rules defining service and the accrued benefit to which the vesting rules apply are most important. ERISA also prohibits a plan from conditioning participation on more than one year of service or attaining an age greater than 21.

Title I of ERISA also includes a special rule that prohibits employers from discharging, disciplining, or discriminating against employees for exercising rights under the plan or the statute, or for the purpose of interfering with the attainment of any right to which such participant may become entitled under the plan. An employer violates the statute if it fires employees for the purpose of preventing them from vesting in their benefits. The vesting and participation rules appear in both Title I and Title II of ERISA.

Fiduciary Standards

Title I of ERISA creates an elaborate set of fiduciary rules for most employee benefit plans. ERISA's legislative history indicates that Congress intended to adopt "principles of fiduciary conduct . . . from existing trust law, but with modifications appropriate for employee benefit plans." At the plan level, ERISA section 403(a) requires that employee benefit plan assets be held in trust, with certain limited exceptions. Moreover, ERISA's substantive fiduciary provisions apply to all plans, even those not structured in trust form.

At the individual level, ERISA defines fiduciaries broadly as persons or entities who exercise discretionary authority or discretionary control over the management, administration, or disposition of plan assets, or render investment advice for a fee. The definition of fiduciary is broadly encompassing, and the courts and the Department of Labor have interpreted the term liberally. As noted, ERISA's legislative history indicates that its fiduciary section "in essence, codifies and makes applicable to . . . fiduciaries certain principles developed in the evolution of the law of trusts." ERISA effects this codification with two related sets of fiduciary standards, the first a series of general trust principles, the second a list of specifically proscribed activities.

The general trust principles provide that plan fiduciaries must discharge their duties solely in the interests of the plan's participants, act prudently, diversify plan investments, and act in accordance with plan instruments. The statute's legislative history indicates an expectation "that courts will interpret the prudent man rule and other fiduciary standards bearing in mind the special nature and purposes of employee benefit plans intended to be effectuated by the Act."

The second set of standards is a more particularized set of prohibitions against fiduciaries causing the plan to enter transactions with parties already related to the plan ("transactional prohibitions"), using plan assets for the fiduciary's own account, or acting on behalf of a party with respect to a transaction involving the plan. The transactional prohibitions are broad and explicit, proscribing dealings with "parties in interest," a term encompassing most individuals and entities with preexisting relations with the plan. ERISA includes statutory exemptions from the prohibited transaction rules and establishes a procedure in which the Department of Labor can create further exemptions administratively.

The Department of Labor, a plan fiduciary, or the participant may bring an action on behalf of a plan against a fiduciary who breaches its obligations under the statute. Moreover, the IRC imposes a tax on a party who has engaged in a prohibited transaction with a plan.

Employee Civil Actions for Benefits and Other Relief

ERISA has by and large federalized jurisdiction over employee benefit claims. Section 502(a)(1) provides that a participant may bring action in federal court to recover benefits under the plan, to enforce rights under the plan, or to clarify future rights to benefits under the terms of the plan. Thus, a participant may bring an action to recover benefits under the plan. Courts, however, have generally refused to award punitive damages or damages to compensate employees for other injuries. Courts have also held that a plan's decision to deny benefits generally is entitled to deference from the courts (if the plan includes language indicating that such deference was intended by the plan's drafters), making it more difficult for employees to recover benefits arguably due them under plan language.

ERISA Preemption

ERISA preempts state laws that relate, directly or indirectly, to employee benefit plans, with only a few exceptions. The scope of ERISA preemption is broad; courts have held that state law rights to punitive and extracontractual damages are preempted; that state wrongful discharge law is preempted to the extent the discharge related to an employee benefit plan; that state law actions for misrepresentation are preempted when the misrepresentation involved a plan; that state law garnishment exemptions for employee plan benefits are preempted; and that a state law prohibiting a pension plan from offsetting benefits by a worker's compensation award is preempted.

There are exceptions to ERISA preemption, most notably state insurance law. Thus, a health benefit plan funded through an insurance policy is subject to state insurance law. ERISA has thereby encouraged employers to self-fund health plans in order to escape state regulation.

Funding and Protection of Defined Benefits

ERISA has attempted to protect employee interests in defined benefit plans in two distinct ways. First, ERISA imposes minimum funding rules for pension plans. Employers who fail to fund in accordance with the rules are subject to excise taxes. The minimum funding rules, however, have been criticized as too lenient, particularly in allowing plans to base benefits on past service and then amortizing those liabilities over relatively lengthy periods of time.

Second, Title IV of ERISA established the Pension Benefit Guaranty Corporation (PBGC) to strengthen retirement security by guaranteeing some benefits for defined benefit plan participants. The PBGC insures that payment of a specified portion of promised benefits from private defined benefit plans will be paid to the participants regardless of the status of the sponsor or the level of funds in the pension plan. The PBGC is funded by premiums paid by private sponsors of defined benefit plans, but the agency has been the focus of attention because of potential program deficits and the exposure faced by the PBGC in underfunded plans. Other critics of the PBGC program have contended that the effect of requiring all sponsors to pay premiums, even those whose plans are adequately funded, has the effect of shifting wealth from healthy to unhealthy sectors of the economy. Since ERISA's enactment, the PBGC premium structure has been reformulated to add a component that varied with the amount of plan underfunding and is now partly based on the risk of termination with insufficient assets.

Title IV provides a special program for multiemployer plans that become insolvent. The multiemployer premiums are set lower than the premiums for other plans; the PBGC benefit guarantees are also generally lower than those applicable to other plans. In 1980, Title IV was amended to impose withdrawal liability on employers that cease contributing to an underfunded multiemployer plan. The withdrawal liability equals the withdrawing employer's share of the plan's unfunded vested benefit obligations.

Reporting and Disclosure

Title I of ERISA imposes reporting requirements on employee benefit plans. In addition, Title II imposes reporting requirements on employee benefit plans, and Title IV imposes reporting requirements on defined benefit plans subject to the PBGC plan termination rules. Generally, a plan may satisfy the primary reporting requirements with a single form developed by the Department of Labor, the IRS, and the PBGC. Plans are generally required to prepare a summary annual report. There are also numerous specific reporting obligations imposed by the different ERISA titles.

Plan administrators and sponsors must make disclosure to participants in employee benefit plans. The most important disclosure requirement is that the plan sponsor or plan administrator must prepare a summary plan description and distribute it to plan participants. The summary plan description must be written in a manner that is comprehensible by a participant. On request, the plan must also provide participants with a benefits statement and certain other information. Failure to comply with a request for information within 30 days can lead to a penalty of up to $100 per day.

Spousal Protections

Title I and Title II of ERISA require in certain retirement plans that married pension participants be paid their benefits in the form of a joint and survivor annuity, unless the participant's spouse consents to a different form of distribution. Additionally, retirement plans must provide a preretirement survivor annuity in most cases.

COBRA

In 1985, Congress amended ERISA to provide that sponsors of employee health benefit plans must give former participants and their beneficiaries an opportunity to purchase continued coverage from the plan at the time their coverage under the plan would otherwise end because of death, divorce, termination of employment, loss of dependency status, or reduction of hours. The period of continuation is 36 months, except on termination of employment or reduction of hours, in which case the coverage period is 18 months.

Special Tax Provisions

The IRC includes a number of rules that reflect tax rather than employee protection concerns, and thus have no analogue in Title I of ERISA. Among these provisions are limitations on benefits from defined benefit plans and on contributions to defined contribution plans; rules requiring that plans cover at least a minimum number of non-highly compensated employees; rules that prohibit plans from discriminating against non-highly compensated employees; rules imposing excise taxes on certain preretirement distributions from retirement plans or excessive distributions from retirement plans; and rules that require pension plans to begin paying out benefits after employees attain age 70½.

ERISA and Its Critics

Consumer groups have criticized ERISA as not adequately living up to its promise to enhance protection of employee benefits. Such groups argue that a hostile federal judiciary has distorted the statute to dilute employee protections intended by Congress. Among the specific complaints is the deferential standard courts generally use to review plan denials of employee benefits, the restrictive reading of ERISA's remedial provisions, and the broad reading of ERISA's preemption provisions to deprive employees of state law rights they enjoyed before passage in ERISA. In the area of health benefits, where the statute creates few federal rights but preempts most state law rights, employees often find themselves stripped of most rights. In one case, *McGann v. H & H Music Co.,* an employer amended a health plan to cap benefits for AIDS at $5,000. ERISA preempted state law that would have made the cap illegal, but provided no federal remedy for the employee.

The business community also is critical of ERISA, whose complexity and compliance costs dampen employer enthusiasm toward sponsorship of employee benefit plans. This is especially the case with ERISA's tax provisions, which have spawned hundreds of pages of detailed regulation that is often unfathomable except to highly trained experts.

These disparate lines of criticism reflect a fundamental tension in ERISA: government regulation is necessary to ensure that private law adequately delivers benefits, but too much regulation diminishes the willingness of employers to sponsor plans at all. If this tension is intractable, the next decades may find the nation moving toward either direct government provision of health and retirement benefits or, alternatively, the abandonment of the notion of providing benefits through regulated, tax-subsidized private plans. (See also AGE DISCRIMINATION IN EMPLOYMENT ACT, EARLY RETIREMENT INCENTIVE PROGRAMS, EMPLOYEE STOCK OWNERSHIP PLANS, HEALTH MAINTENANCE ORGANIZATIONS, INDIVIDUAL RETIREMENT ACCOUNTS, KEOGH PLANS, PENSION FUND TRENDS, POSTRETIREMENT HEALTH INSURANCE, and RETIREMENT, HISTORY OF.)

Organization

Employee Benefit Research Institute

References

American Bar Association, Section of Business Law. 1994. *ERISA Basics: A Two-Part Primer on ERISA Issues: An ABA Satellite Seminar.* Chicago: American Bar Association.

Salisbury, Dallas L., and Nora Super Jones, eds. 1994. *Pension Funding and Taxation: Implications for Tomorrow.* Washington, DC: Employee Benefit Research Institute.

Stein, Norman. 1993. "ERISA and the Limits of Equity." *Law & Contemp. Prob.* 56: 71.

U.S. Congress, Senate Committee on Labor and Human Resources. 1994. *Recent Court Decisions Affecting ERISA and Executive Annuities.* Washington, DC: U.S. Government Printing Office.

Norman Stein

EMPLOYEE STOCK OWNERSHIP PLANS (ESOPs), employee benefit plans that are qualified for tax-favored treatment under the Internal Revenue Code (IRC) of 1986, as amended. A plan is qualified if it complies with various participation, vesting, distribution, and other rules established by the Tax Code to protect the interests of employees. An ESOP is classified as a type of deferred compensation plan which invests primarily in stock of the corporation that sponsors the ESOP. An ESOP also must comply with various reporting and disclosure requirements and fiduciary responsibility rules of the Employee Retirement Income Security Act (ERISA)* of 1974, as amended.

An ESOP is a "defined contribution plan," because the employer's contribution is defined and the employee's benefit is variable. Each participating employee's account is credited with a certain number of shares of company stock over the period of his employment. Upon retirement, death, disability, or other termination of service, the employee's account is distributed to him (or his beneficiary) in shares of stock or in cash, the dollar amount determined by applying the current fair market value of the stock in his account to the number of shares. An employee's benefit, thus, is not defined—as with a defined benefit pension plan—but is dependent upon the value of his stock.

What Do Employees Receive from an ESOP?

All ESOP assets (company stock and other investments) are allocated each year to the accounts of all employee participants in the ESOP by a formula usually based on the proportion of an employee's salary to total covered payroll. Assets of the ESOP are held in an ESOP trust established under a written trust agreement and administered by a trustee and/or administrative committee responsible for protecting the interests of employees and their beneficiaries.

An employee is not taxed on contributions to his ESOP account (or income earned in that account) until the employee's benefits are actually received. Even then, "rollovers" (into an IRA, for example) or special averaging methods can reduce or defer the income tax consequences of distributions.

An ESOP, like most employee benefit plans, generally is designed to benefit employees who remain with the employer the longest and contribute most to the employer's success. Therefore, an employee's ownership interest in company stock and other assets held in the ESOP usually is based on his or her number of years of employment. The employee's ownership interest in the ESOP is called his "vested benefit," and the provisions that determine the employee's vested benefit are called the "vesting schedule." Although there are various vesting schedules that may be used (extending for periods up to seven years), most are designed so that the longer the employee stays with the employer, the greater his vested benefit becomes.

If an employee terminates employment for any reason other than retirement, death, or disability, his vested benefit under the ESOP will be determined by referring to the vesting schedule. All company stock in which the employee does not have a vested benefit (because he has not worked long enough) will be treated as a forfeiture, which is allocated among the ESOP accounts of the remaining employees on the same basis as employer contributions. If an employee retires (e.g., at age 65), dies, or is disabled, he or she usually will be 100% vested in the total account balance.

After an employee's participation in the ESOP ends, the employee (or beneficiary) is eligible to receive a distribution of the vested benefit. There are many permissible times and methods for making this distribution. For example, it may be made as soon as possible after an employee's termination of employment, or it may be deferred for a period of up to six years. However, distribution of a former employee's vested benefit must start in the year following retirement, disability, or death. Payment may be made in a lump sum or in installments over a period of up to five years. In a closely held company, distributions are usually made in cash or in shares of stock that may be sold back to the company.

How Does an ESOP Benefit Employers?

As a technique of corporate finance, the ESOP can be used to raise new equity capital, to refinance outstanding debt, or to acquire productive assets through leverage with third-party lenders. Because contributions to an ESOP are fully tax deductible, an employer can fund both the principal and the interest payments on an ESOP's debt service obligations with pre-tax dollars.

An institutional lender may be able to exclude 50% of the interest received on an ESOP loan from its taxable income. Accordingly, interest rates on ESOP loans may be lower than on normal corporate loans. The 50% interest exclusion also may be available to an institutional lender that makes a loan to a company that, within 30 days, contributes an equivalent amount of its stock to an ESOP. This tax benefit is available only when an ESOP owns more than 50% of the employer's common equity.

Federal Income Tax Consequences of an ESOP for the Employer

Employer contributions to an ESOP are tax deductible within the limitations of the IRC. An employer may contribute to an ESOP and deduct up to 25% of covered payroll per taxable year. If the ESOP has borrowed and is leveraged, the employer may increase contributions beyond the 25% level to the extent that the excess is used to pay the ESOP's interest expense. In addition, cash dividends paid on ESOP stock are deductible if applied to the repayment of ESOP debt or if currently distributed in cash to ESOP participants. Under Section 415 of the Tax Code, the annual additions that may be allocated to the account of an individual ESOP participant each year normally may not exceed the lesser of 25% of his covered compensation or $30,000. The annual additions include employer contributions, any employee contributions, and certain forfeitures that are allocated to the employee's account, although contributions used to pay loan interest will usually not be considered annual additions.

Tax Benefits to Selling Shareholders

ESOPs provide a significant tax incentive for a shareholder of a closely held company who plans to sell his company and retire. An ESOP provides a market for the stock of such a closely held company. The IRC provides a special tax incentive for certain sales of stock to an ESOP, subject to satisfying a number of specific rules. Thus, a shareholder of a closely held company may be able to sell stock to an ESOP, reinvest the proceeds in other securities, and defer taxation of any capital gain resulting from the sale. As a result, the retiring shareholder can derive substantial financial security and liquidity for purposes of retirement. Because the tax liability from the sale is merely deferred, however, the shareholder's subsequent sale of the securities purchased with the proceeds from the sale to the ESOP will trigger a recapture of the deferred tax. If such securities flow through an estate, the step-up in basis that occurs will help the shareholder and his heirs avoid the tax permanently.

Voting Rights

In a closely held company, unless otherwise determined by the board of directors, employees have voting rights on allocated shares only with regard to certain major corporate issues, such as merger, certain sales or liquidation of the company, and recapitalizations. On other matters, ESOP shares are usually voted by the ESOP trustee or administrative committee that has been appointed by the company's board of directors. In order for the lender's 50% interest exclusion to be available with respect to an ESOP loan, however, the ESOP must pass through to participants' full voting rights on shares (acquired with the proceeds of such a loan) allocated to participants' accounts. In a publicly traded company, employees have voting rights on all shares allocated to their accounts under the ESOP.

Diversification

Unlike other qualified retirement plans, which typically diversify their holdings by investing in various assets, an ESOP, by law, must invest primarily in the stock of the corporation that sponsors the ESOP. Because ESOPs must invest in the stock of one company, there is a higher risk for the employee. Nonetheless, employees approaching retirement age qualify for a limited exception, which permits diversification of their ESOP accounts. Participants who are at least age 55 and have completed at least ten years of participation in the ESOP are eligible to make annual elections over a period of five years to diversify 25% of their ESOP stock account balance (on an aggregate basis) and at the end of the sixth year to make a final election to diversify up to 50% (again, on an aggregate basis). This does not apply, however, to certain "de minimis" amounts in participants' ESOP accounts.

To meet the diversification requirement, the ESOP must offer at least three investment options other than employer securities. Alternatively, the ESOP may satisfy the diversification requirement by distributing to the participant the portion of the account balance that the participant elected to diversify or allowing a transfer to another plan.

The diversification rules are applicable only with respect to stock acquired by the ESOP after December 31, 1986. However, the plan may permit diversification of stock acquired before that date and may permit diversification of a greater percentage of the participant's account balance.

Intangible Benefits of an ESOP

For the retiring employee or the selling shareholder, the financial and tax benefits may not be the only important aspects of an ESOP. The retiring employee may derive great satisfaction from receiving evidence (in the form of monetary rewards) of ownership in a company that he or she helped build. The selling shareholder may feel more at ease by placing company stock in the "friendlier" and certainly more familiar hands of the employees. These intangible elements may prove to be as rewarding to the retiring employee and/or selling shareholder as the financial security ESOPs may provide. (See also ASSETS ALLOCATION AFTER RETIREMENT, EMPLOYEE RETIREMENT INCOME SECURITY ACT, EQUITY SECURITIES, PENSION FUND TRENDS.)

References

National Center for Employee Ownership. 1993. *How Small Is Too Small for an ESOP?* Oakland, CA: Author.

National Center for Employee Ownership. 1994. *Employee Ownership Fact Sheet.* Oakland, CA: Author.

Rosen, Corey, and Michael Quarrey. 1987. "How Well Is Employee Ownership Working?" *Harvard Business Review,* (September/October).

David R. Johanson

EMPLOYMENT OF OLDER AMERICANS, labor force involvement in relation to the aging process. The employment of older workers is best examined in terms of the history of work and present-day economic, social, and organizational employment barriers faced by the elderly.

Historical Development of Work

Work has had meaning, value, and status since the beginning of civilization. The concept of work as toil to be avoided emerged from the earliest formation of class structures. The landholding aristocracy believed that any form of work was ignoble. A contrasting view developed during the Middle Ages, when the church taught that manual and intellectual labor were religious duties. As the feudal system disintegrated, work became more differentiated and formed the basis for new social classes.

During the Protestant Reformation, work was promoted as a virtue. Environmental conditions in early America further solidified the notion that work was a moral obligation connected to salvation. Anyone who was nonproductive or not socially responsible was considered a liability. Yet the elderly, even if no longer engaged in productive work, often maintained their status in society and continued to be venerated.

Great changes in the nature of work in the United States began with the shift from an agrarian to an industrialized economy after the Civil War. Machines replaced skilled labor with semi-skilled and unskilled labor. In the twentieth century, Frederick Taylor's theory of scientific management endorsed the notion that workers could be likened to machines. Efficiency was the goal; speed and physical stamina replaced skill and experience as the criteria for the ideal worker. Industrialization brought workers greater fragmentation and specialization but also higher wages, a decrease in manual labor, a reduction in hours worked, and an increase in leisure time.

An elaborate division of labor and the rise of bureaucratic economic organization began to devalue the status of the elderly in American society. The institution of retirement was created to control entry into and departure from the working world. Companies wanted to attract "ideal" candidates (primarily the young for speed and physical stamina), but needed to guarantee promotion and advancement by appealing to the individual achievement motive. The advent of Social Security* provided retirement income and encouraged labor force participation by fewer older persons.

Industrialization has given way to a postindustrial period, essentially a shift from an industrial economy to a service or information economy. Workers are now further removed from the production process, the traditional work ethic, and concrete individual achievement. They have more difficulty finding intrinsic value in work, and early retirement (long before age 65) has been the answer for many workers who have the financial security to leave the labor force.

Current Employment Status of the Elderly

Americans aged 65 or older represent a little more than 12% of the U.S. population. Currently, there are about 3.5 million elderly in the labor force, only 2.8% of the total (*Statistical Abstract* 1993). Moreover, 56% of workers aged 65 and older work part-time (Employee Benefit Research Institute 1994). The importance of older persons in the labor force will decline through the remainder of this century. The reasons for this are twofold: (1) the increase in workers' average age is due to the aging of the baby boomers and not to an increase in the size of the group of older workers; and (2) the population differs from the labor force. Since most people over 65 are not working, their greater numbers have little effect on the composition of the labor force.

The economic participation of older men has declined drastically, while labor force participation of older women has remained relatively constant. The drop in participation of older men can be attributed to increases in early retirement and declines in self-employment. There is no indication that labor force participation rates for older men or women will increase in the near future. Early retirement trends, before age 65, will continue for all workers. Statistics show that the median age of retirement in 1963 was 65; today it is 62 (Bureau of Labor Statistics 1992).

Generally, labor force participation tends to be high until age 50, after which it declines. For men, significant drops in participation occur at age 62 and at age 65, corresponding to eligibility ages for Social Security retirement benefits and the age of eligibility for full benefits. Lifetime labor force participation patterns for women are similar.

Elderly Employment: Forces for Change

The issue of elderly employment has taken on greater significance as changes in social attitudes have begun to challenge traditional elderly employment prac-

tices. Simultaneously, however, broad structural trends in the labor market continue to encourage the majority of older workers to leave the labor force as soon
as financially possible. These workers are pressured to leave the workplace as
employers reduce wage and benefit costs to meet competitive demands (National
Academy on Aging 1994). This paradox is at the root of the debate over the
employment of older Americans. Prevailing forces for change in the employment
of the elderly are: (1) demographics, (2) growth in the service sector, 3) concern
about Social Security and the cost of retirement, (4) economic needs of the
elderly, and (5) increased education of the elderly.

Shifts in U.S. demographics undoubtedly lie behind the biggest push for
change. Unlike the traditional population pyramid, the American age structure
now resembles a pillar composed of equal age groups—youth, middle-aged, and
the mature. Demographers agree that the greatest future increases will be in
older cohorts. By 2030, the population aged 65 and older will represent over
19.8% of the total population, compared with 12% today. With the retirement
of the baby boom generation, the United States will face the longest period of
retirement for the largest and best-educated generation in history. Questions
concerning the ability of the labor force to support extended retirements, and
the rise of life expectancy, surround discussions of elderly employment.

Serious work force issues are posed by population aging as well. Predictions
about the future of the labor force are difficult to make, but the aging of the
potential labor force as a whole is certain. Demographers predict that three key
trends will continue: (1) a decline in the proportion of youths in the labor force,
(2) an increase in the proportion of women, primarily between the ages of 25
and 55, and (3) a decline in the proportion of older persons, primarily older
men, in the labor force (Mitchell 1993).

Another driving force for change is the growth of services. More than 75%
of all workers are employed in the information and service sector (non-goods
producing). Service work usually requires reduced manual, strenuous effort and
offers relatively better working conditions. The concept of the ideal worker
created during industrialization does not necessarily fit the employment needs
of a service economy. Therefore, service work may create numerous new opportunities for older workers, including part-time work and flexible working
hours.

Concern about the integrity of the Social Security system by the general
public and worry about the cost of retirement may seem to require a push for
the employment of older persons. In a survey in 1985, 66% of younger workers
thought it somewhat or very likely that Social Security would no longer be
available when they reached retirement age (Atchley 1988). If this perception
persists as these workers age, they may be motivated to stay in the labor force
longer. Additionally, retirement projections for baby boomers suggest that the
increased burden of the Social Security system will require financing of annual
deficits equal to 3 or 4% of taxable payroll once this cohort is fully retired.
Thus, there is concern about the fiscal challenge of an aging population. An
increase in the normal retirement age under Social Security from 65 to 67 has

already been enacted for gradual implementation after 2000 in anticipation of these fiscal problems (Mitchell 1993).

Economic need, however, is an even stronger force for change. Although the majority of older persons living on retirement incomes today enjoy a middle-class existence, there is a substantial number who need, but cannot earn, additional income. Social Security provides nearly 40% of income for current retirees and is expected to be of similar importance to baby boomers. But workers, predominantly minorities and women, who have not been employed in core industries, are usually without pension plans and receive fewer Social Security benefits. They also experience the greatest labor market problems, such as discrimination and lack of training and skills, and these problems are likely to continue for poorly educated baby boomers. As these persons age, however, they will want and need to remain in the labor market (National Academy on Aging 1994).

The prevailing perception of older workers seeking employment is that they are marginal labor force participants. Many cite financial or personal gain (boredom reduction) as motives for employment. [Contrary to this stereotype, older persons looking for work are far less likely to have pensions than are retired persons the same age who do not seek employment.] Unemployed older workers are least able to afford retirement. The majority of older job seekers under age 62 are persons who begin looking for work immediately after losing a job; they are not leaving retirement to look for work (U.S. Department of Labor 1989).

Recent surveys reveal that many older Americans wish to return to work. A Commonwealth Fund report (1993) states that more than one-half of workers aged 50 to 64 would extend their careers if their employers provided training for a different job, continued pension contributions past age 65, or offered a position with fewer hours and responsibilities and reduced pay.

Increased education is likely to play a major role in future employment of the elderly. Currently, employers are reluctant to hire older workers due to the cost of training or retraining, since many lack the skills and competencies for new, service sector jobs. Projections of future educational attainment, however, indicate that older persons will become more highly educated (Atchley 1988), and these older workers will have more options to remain in the labor force. Part-time work and flexible hours are easier to coordinate and cost-justify for professional workers (accountants, attorneys, etc.) than for unskilled shift workers.

Of those forces pushing for change in employment practices concerning older workers, demographic change appears to be most significant, since there are and will be more older persons available for work. The extent to which older persons will be employed, however, is still unknown.

Elderly Employment: Resisting Forces

Prevailing forces resisting change are: (1) the institution of retirement, (2) age discrimination, (3) corporate structure and values, (4) Social Security, (5) types of available jobs, and (6) employability of the elderly. Retirement is a major institutional impediment to the employment of older workers. The age of retirement has steadily fallen, and early retirement is becoming the norm. Retirement decisions are based on preferences for leisure over work, on health status, on Social Security benefits, and especially on other income sources (private pensions). For many people, retirement is more attractive—financially, socially, and psychologically—than remaining in the labor force. The fact that retirement is so entrenched in the fabric of American society will make it difficult to change. The switch from the labor force to retirement is often abrupt—from full-time career employment into complete retirement without a phase-out period—and the institution of retirement is structured to remove older workers quickly.

Preretirement workers have indicated a preference to phase into retirement through part-time work with the same employer, but health issues, management policies, or prohibitive pension rules often make this impossible. The biggest obstacle to phased retirement is lack of meaningful part-time work opportunities. Most older workers who do enter the part-time job market find their value eroded to the point where employment is not a viable option. Older persons wishing to stay employed should try to continue employment with their long-term employers, with whom they may have the highest value.

The literature on discrimination against older workers identifies wage earnings and unemployment rates as key measures that lead to discrimination. Research findings suggest that age is not a major discrimination variable; rather, inadequate education, skill level, and job changes affect wages and length of unemployment. However, the unemployment rate among the elderly is deceiving, since statistics do not exist on whether abandonment of a job search was due to discouragement or to retirement. There are basically three positions researchers take when reviewing age discrimination:

1. Human capital theorists would argue that if discrimination exists, it is not related to age but to lowered productivity due to skill obsolescence and lack of investment in upgrading skills.
2. Equity theorists would argue that declining wages reflect a legitimate lifetime earnings profile. Older people want more leisure time and therefore work fewer hours.
3. The high cost of job switching for older workers encourages them to accept lower wages. Employers assume that older workers will accept lower levels of salary increases, or fewer of them, because their ability to find comparable alternative employment is low.

Whether discrimination against the elderly can be argued to be quantitatively based on wage scales and unemployment rates, older people face significant labor market problems. Age discrimination is found in corporate America. Employers' perceptions of older workers have been slow to change. Although most employers overtly support nondiscriminatory business practices, their hiring, promotion, discipline, and training decisions continue to adversely affect older workers.

Discussion of age discrimination leads to corporate structure and values, a broader obstacle to the employment of the elderly. The structure of business in the United States remains hierarchical. Compensation, career, promotion, and pension systems are designed to encourage older workers to leave an organization and make room for younger employees. Restructuring and downsizing of firms have also minimized job opportunities for the elderly. Some companies and management consultants find that older workers can make superior employees, particularly in jobs requiring customer interaction. They often are more loyal, motivated, dependable, and conscientious than younger workers. Companies, in general, are doing little to attract older workers, however, and changes are needed in structure, values systems, attitudes, and management practices to induce them to do otherwise.

Another obstacle to the employment of the elderly is Social Security itself. Social Security is both an incentive and a disincentive to the employment of older workers. The Social Security amendments of 1983 include several reforms designed to reduce disincentives to work and to encourage older persons to remain in the labor force. Most analysts believe that, even with the amendments, the Social Security system still provides disincentives to work. Researchers (U.S. Department of Labor 1989) have found that, although benefit levels increase for each year of additional work, gains from higher benefits were more than offset by the fewer number of years benefits were received. In fact, they found that the present value of total future benefits for a person who worked until age 68 was only 90% of that for a worker who retired at age 60.

The research concluded that the amendments have had little or no influence on the average retirement age (U.S. Department of Labor 1989). Any changes in Social Security regulations probably have been offset by private pension plan provisions that encourage retirement or penalize work activity. Recently, private pension plans have become increasingly liberal, allowing full benefits at earlier and earlier ages. Early retirement is used as an attrition technique to minimize the number of layoffs large companies would otherwise make.

Another obstacle is the type of jobs available to older workers. The growth in the service sector has generated low-wage, entry-level, transient, or temporary service work that requires little human capital. Older workers often have the greatest chance of being hired for these positions, yet they are considered unattractive by most skilled or semi-skilled older workers. Aside from wages, self-esteem and status issues are involved.

Finally, the employability of the elderly is sometimes viewed as an obstacle. Health and disability are key determinants of continued employment; health problems and work disabilities increase with age. Older persons use health care services more often than younger workers, which makes this a legitimate concern for an employer, given health insurance costs. Providing retiree health insurance is a strong disincentive to hiring older workers, and employers are often more comfortable hiring the elderly for part-time work to avoid paying health benefits. There is variability, however, in the health status of older people, and many are healthy. The stereotype of all older persons being sickly and incapable of working should be challenged.

Future Employment of the Elderly

Increasingly, government and private sector retirement policies and philosophy are in conflict. The projected fiscal burden on government programs has many in Congress advocating employment of older persons, while private sector policy is headed in the direction of early retirement. Employment of older persons seems to hinge on whether older workers' economic value is great enough to overcome the obstacles to hiring them. Employers must see an economic benefit before they become willing to alter drastically those corporate systems that currently make employment unattractive to the majority of the elderly. (See also ECONOMIC STATUS OF THE ELDERLY; ECONOMIC STATUS OF ELDERLY WOMEN; EDUCATION OF OLDER ADULTS; RETIREMENT, HISTORY OF; SOCIAL SECURITY; and WORKING RETIREES.)

Suggested Readings

Bluestone, Irving, Rhonda J. V. Montgomery, and John D. Owen. 1990. *The Aging of the American Workforce: Problems, Programs and Policies.* Detroit, MI: Wayne State University Press.

"Institutional Barriers to Employment of Older Workers." 1989. *Monthly Labor Review* 112 (April).

Rix, Sara E., ed. 1994. *Older Workers: How Do They Measure Up?* Washington, DC: AARP Public Policy Institute.

Schulz, James. 1992. *The Economics of Aging.* Westport, CT: Auburn House.

References

Atchley, Robert C. 1988. *Social Forces and Aging.* Belmont, CA: Wadsworth Publishing.

Bureau of Labor Statistics. 1992. *Outlook 1990–2005.* BLS Bulletin 2402. Washington, DC: GPO.

Commonwealth Fund. 1993. *The Untapped Resource.* Final Report of the Americans Over 55 At Work Program. New York: Author.

Employee Benefit Research Institute. 1994. "Characteristics of the Part-Time Work Force." *EBRI Special Report.* SR-22. Washington, DC: EBRI.

Mitchell, Olivia S., ed. 1993. *As the Workforce Ages: Costs, Benefits and Policy Challenges.* Ithaca, NY: ILR Press.

National Academy on Aging. 1994. *Old Age in the 21st Century.* Syracuse, NY: The Maxwell School.

U.S. Department of Commerce, Bureau of the Census. *Statistical Abstract of the United States.* 1993. Washington, DC: GPO.

U.S. Department of Labor. 1989. *Labor Market Problems of Older Workers. Report of the Secretary of Labor.* Washington, DC: U.S. Department of Labor.

Nancy Dailey

ENTREPRENEURSHIP, the initiation and assumption of the financial risks of a business and its management. The decision to start a business is often complex.

Many factors, including the need for achievement, the need for control over one's destiny, the willingness to take risks, the loss of one's job, and other forms of displacement may prompt a person to start his or her own business. While some writers see no link between age and the decision to start a new business, others have found close links. When age is a significant factor, it is often for psychological reasons.

Entrepreneurial opportunities are most likely to be pursued by people with a college education who are in their late thirties and have established careers. Age is relevant to entrepreneurship, and entrepreneurship is important for the aged. Of those who are employed at age 65 or older, 27% are self-employed (Maddox 1985). It is useful to examine the relationship between entrepreneurship and aging through the internal or psychological aspects of a person's decision to become an entrepreneur.

The Entrepreneur and Hero Compared

Joseph Campbell believed that the entrepreneur was the real hero in our society. Although he never systematically compared the entrepreneur and the hero, it is interesting to do so. Heroes and entrepreneurs are called to take part in an adventure that is a simultaneous journey of self-discovery, spiritual growth, and the personal creativity they make possible. An entrepreneur's journey closely resembles the journey of the hero in mythology as outlined in Campbell's book, *The Hero with a Thousand Faces* (1968). There is a strong similarity between the journey that entrepreneurs take and the adventure of heroes. Entrepreneurs and heroes also have similar personality traits. Myths describe the universal human desires and conflicts we see played out in the lives of entrepreneurs. Ian MacMillan and Rita Gunther McGrath (*Wall Street Journal* 1992) of the Wharton School's entrepreneurial center found that entrepreneurs, no matter what country they call home, think alike. Campbell found that the basic pattern in the hero's journey is the same in every culture.

Heroes bring change. Campbell (1968) refers to the constant change in the universe as "The Cosmogonic Cycle" that "unrolls the great vision of the creation and destruction of the world which is vouchsafed as revelation to the successful hero." This recalls Joseph Schumpeter's theory of entrepreneurship as creative destruction. A successful entrepreneur simultaneously destroys and creates a new world, a new way of life. Henry Ford destroyed the horse and buggy age while creating the world of the automobile. Campbell's hero finds that the world "suffers from a symbolical deficiency" and "appears on the scene in various forms according to the changing needs of the race." Changing needs and deficiencies correspond to the changing market conditions or the changing desires for products. The entrepreneur is the first person to perceive changing needs. Campbell believed that people become creative when they engage in an activity, pursue a career or entrepreneurial venture, because it is what one loves to do and because it bestows on one a sense of personal importance and fulfillment. It is not the social system that dictates that it be done; rather, the drive comes from within. It is this courageous action that opens up doors and creative possibilities that did not previously exist.

Relationship of the Hero's Journey to Aging

The hero's goal is now to find a purpose in life. Campbell's and Erik Erikson's (1963) heroes are similar, because the hero's journey is a quest for personal identity that can be found in service to others or to society, or in finding and delivering a boon. During the generativity versus stagnation stage, which comes in the second half of life, in Erikson's eight ages of man, people become willing to take risks in order to be creative or make their mark upon society. Generativity involves establishing and guiding the next generation, but it also includes productivity and creativity, which, along with the willingness to take risks, are essential to entrepreneurship. For Campbell, the act of creating involves the willingness to take a risk and cross a boundary into a new domain of ideas. To be unwilling or afraid to do so is to be controlled by what he calls ''the elder psychology,'' or the unwillingness to strike out on one's own and take risks.

The paradox, then, is that although entrepreneurship may be an important path for people to discover themselves and ''do something meaningful for society'' as they become older, they must resist this ''elder psychology,'' which Campbell believes blocks risk taking, creativity, and entrepreneurship. When a person is able to champion things becoming, he or she can achieve generativity by making a significant and unique contribution to society. If one is able only to maintain the status quo, he or she will stagnate and will remain self-centered and unable to contribute to society. Almost by definition, entrepreneurs are champions of things becoming.

In counseling and advising the elderly in the area of entrepreneurial activity, it is useful to keep these insights from mythology and psychology in mind. They deal with the deepest of needs and forces in the human psyche. For an older person contemplating a new business venture, it will be helpful to recognize that it is not just the potential financial gains or losses involved that are important. The entrepreneurial act may be a life-defining and self-defining act, one with deep personal and perhaps even spiritual implications for the individual and his or her relationship with society. Entrepreneurs are often seen as having different attitudes toward risk: what a nonentrepreneur might view as a great financial risk, the entrepreneur may see as a cost of learning and adventuring. The venture is an end in itself, more than the profit. People who start new businesses in the second half of life may view risk in this way, because they feel such a strong need to define themselves and contribute to society. (See also BUSINESS SUCCESSION PLANNING, EMPLOYEE STOCK OWNERSHIP PLANS, EMPLOYMENT OF OLDER AMERICANS, ESTATE PLANNING, MARKETING TO ELDERS, MASS MEDIA AND THE ELDERLY, LEISURE, and RETIREMENT, HISTORY OF.)

References

Campbell, Joseph. 1968. *The Hero with a Thousand Faces.* Princeton, NJ: Princeton University Press.

Erikson, Erik H. 1963. *Childhood and Society.* New York: W. W. Norton.

Jung, Carl G. 1956. *Symbols of Transformation.* New York: Harper Torchbooks/Bollingen Library.

Maddox, George L., et al. 1985. *The Encyclopedia of Aging.* New York: Springer.

Wall Street Journal. 1992. 6 February: A1.

Cyril Morong

EQUITY SECURITIES, ownership investments including shares in the ownership of corporations as well as in many forms of pass-through securities. They may represent shares (stock ownership) in a corporation or in certain designated assets of a corporation or other entity. Shares in investment companies (mutual fund shares) are also broadly referred to as equity securities or equity funds when the investment objectives are to own and hold stocks. Two types of equity security represent ownership in corporations: preferred stock and common stock. The key distinction between these types of stock ownership is the manner and form in which each class of shareholder participates in corporate earnings.

One advantage of these corporate forms of ownership is that shareholders have limited liability from transactions gone wrong in a corporation. Unlike other forms of business ownership such as sole proprietorships or general partnerships, corporate shareholders are shielded from exposure to loss in the event that firms cannot meet financial or other obligations. In unincorporated businesses, owners may be held personally responsible for payment of unsatisfied claims, for example, and creditors may file claims against owners' personal assets: houses, cars, bank accounts. This is not the case for corporate shareholders. While they can experience a complete loss of their investment, corporate shareholders are protected from further personal liability beyond the value of their investment in the stock.

Common Stock

Unlike general partners in a partnership or an owner in a sole proprietorship, stockholders have little or no control over management decisions affecting the corporation or whether and when they will be paid a return on their investment in the company. Shareholders, in sufficient numbers, elect a board of directors to manage the company for them and through the exercise of voting rights affect management's policy decisions. Elections for board of director positions and amendments to corporate charters are typically done at annual shareholders meetings. Although some shareholders choose to vote in person, most shareholders prefer to vote by proxy. A proxy is a power of attorney* appointing a specific agent for the specific purpose of voting at the annual meeting.

Shareholders have a preemptive right to purchase new shares of company stock before they are offered for sale to the general public. If a shareholder currently owns 5% of the outstanding stock of a firm, the preemptive right entitles the shareholder to purchase 5% of the new stock issue. This preemptive right allows shareholders to maintain a fixed percentage of ownership in firms if they wish. If not, their ownership in the firm declines, or is "diluted."

Investors in common stock have a residual claim on earnings distributions and receive their income only after all other claims have been satisfied. Income is either paid out in the form of dividend payments or is reinvested in the business as retained earnings. The immediate cash benefit to dividend pay-outs is obvious; however, shareholders also benefit when firms retain earnings and reinvest them. By reinvesting earnings, research and new projects can be funded, production capacity increased, facilities built or renovated, and other activities undertaken to increase future value of the stock. These investments in the firm can then result directly in new cash dividends or indirectly in future stock value and increased stock prices.

Additionally, by having residual claims on a firm's income, stockholders have residual claims on the firm's assets in the event of liquidation. This means that if a firm goes into bankruptcy and the courts decree that its assets must be liquidated in order to satisfy outstanding claims, then stockholders end up with whatever is leftover after all other claims have been satisfied. The residual value is often only a small fraction of the shareholders' initial investment. One of the benefits of stock ownership is that when the market is doing well the potential returns can be large. However, a disadvantage is that when the market is doing poorly, stock returns can be meager (or even negative if the stock price drops significantly).

The return on an investment in common stock can be broken down into two components: dividend yield and capital gain. The dividend yield is calculated by dividing the dividend paid at the end of the period by the stock's price at the beginning of the period. Although firms do not have to pay dividends, the historical trend has been that once a firm sets a level of dividends, then only in cases of extreme financial distress will it reduce the dividend level. Thus firms where a large percentage of the stock return comes from dividend payments (utilities, for example) can be attractive investments for individuals who rely on investment income for their livelihood.

Capital gain is the other component in the return on a stock investment. Capital gain reflects the appreciation in the firm's stock price: If stock is sold for a price that is higher than the purchase price, sellers realize a capital gain on the investment.

Much has been written about whether shareholders prefer to receive their income from dividends or capital gains. One classic theory is the bird-in-hand theory of dividend payments, which stems from the old adage, "A bird in hand is worth two in the bush." This theory states that shareholders prefer firms to pay out their earnings as dividends rather than retain them, because dividends represent income that is paid out as cash now, whereas capital gains (the result of plowing the income back into the firm) may take a long time, if ever, to be realized. Thus, with dividends there is no risk of the shareholders not realizing their income, while with capital gains there is the risk that the stock price will not appreciate once the money has been plowed back into the firm.

Preferred Stock

Preferred stock has characteristics of both common stock and debt securities, such as bonds. Like common stockholders, preferred stockholders receive dividends, but preferred dividends, like rates of interest, are set at a specified percentage called the dividend rate, although the rate may float with the market.

It is crucial that before making investment decisions, investors carefully gauge what their time horizon is, how much risk they are willing to take, and whether they need the investment income to finance their daily activities. Investors must also be aware that stocks are risky investments and that they may not be an appropriate investment choice for everyone. As discussed above, when firms go bankrupt, a substantial portion of stockholders' initial investments may be lost. It would therefore be advisable for novice investors to seek the advice of certified financial planners before investing a sizable proportion of their wealth in equity securities. (See also AGENTS AND BROKERS, ASSETS ALLOCATION AFTER RETIREMENT, CASH FLOW PLANNING FOR RETIREES, EMPLOYEE STOCK OWNERSHIP PLANS, FINANCIAL ADVISORS, and MUTUAL FUNDS.)

References

Brigham, Eugene F. 1992. *Fundamentals of Financial Management,* Sixth Edition. Orlando, FL: Dryden Press.
Haugen, Robert A. 1990. *Modern Investment Theory,* Second Edition. Englewood Cliffs, NJ: Prentice-Hall.
Reilly, Frank K. 1989. *Investment Analysis and Portfolio Management.* Third Edition. Orlando, FL: Dryden Press.

Ben J. Sopranzetti

ESTATE PLANNING, the process of creating an estate, preserving the estate, and transferring it to survivors (Amling and Droms 1986.) An estate is composed of all of a person's assets when that person dies. As people get older, estate planning becomes an important issue for them to address. Three stages are involved in estate planning: (1) creating the estate through saving, investment, inheritance, or some combination of these; (2) preservation of the estate; and (3) transferring the estate either during the owner's lifetime or upon death (Amling 1986). Major goals of estate planning are the maximization of the estate and the assurance that the right people get the right assets after death. A good estate plan will avoid probate*, if possible, and minimize the payment of estate taxes, the marginal rate of which can be more than 50%.

There are four key documents that everyone should prepare to smooth the transfer of assets: a will*, a durable power of attorney*, a durable power of attorney for health care, and a final letter. Sometimes one or more trusts are also useful. These documents must be signed in accordance with state law, at a time when the person is legally competent to do so.

A *will* spells out what happens to financial assets upon death. A valid will can speed the handling of an estate and reduce both probate costs and estate taxes. A will should be drafted by an attorney and reviewed periodically, especially when personal circumstances or tax laws have changed. When a decedent does not have a will, state laws govern asset distribution.

A *durable power of attorney* is a specialized form of a power of attorney. It permits someone to make decisions and control assets only when the principal designator of the power is not able to do so.

A *durable power of attorney for health care* authorizes someone besides a physician, typically a family member, to make decisions about health care to be provided to the principal if the principal cannot do so.

A *living will* spells out the medical steps to be taken to prolong or terminate life, and it gives the physician the right to act on those instructions. Many states have developed standardized forms for use. Without a living will, someone could be given expensive medical care that could dissipate his or her assets, even if he or she would not have wanted the care.

A *final letter,* sometimes called a letter of last instruction, is a nonbinding and informal letter of instructions that can greatly help an executor or family. It may include burial instructions, people to be notified upon death, lists of professional advisors and assets, the location of critical documents and keys, and other personal guidelines or instructions for living.

A *trust* is a separate legal entity with its own assets and rules, spelled out in a trust document. It files and pays its own taxes and is administered by a trustee, who can be a friend, a relative, an institution such as the trust department of a bank, or some combination of these. The trust can be established during lifetime and take effect at that time, or may be established upon death through a will (testamentary trust.) A trust can manage investments for beneficiaries when they cannot manage investments on their own. The trust can also control the timing for the release of money to beneficiaries.

The use of an irrevocable trust (one that cannot be changed) can sometimes reduce estate taxes. Any assets (with one exception) in an irrevocable trust, which the principal does not control, are outside the estate of the deceased and are therefore not subject to estate taxes. The exception is a life insurance policy that is transferred to a trust within three years of death; in that case, the death benefit insurance proceeds get called back into the estate.

A revocable trust, sometimes called a living trust, is created during a person's lifetime and can be changed at any time. The principal is frequently the trustee. The revocable trust is a will substitute, because it describes what happens to assets upon death. It generally contains provisions for a successor trustee; this provision is equivalent to a power of attorney for assets in the trust. A will is frequently used in addition to a revocable trust, because a trust controls only its own assets, whereas a will disposes of other assets without a beneficiary.

Although a goal of estate planning is to transfer the maximum amount to the beneficiaries upon death, it may be more advantageous to transfer assets during lifetime. A gift is a transfer of assets during the lifetime of the principal for less than their current value. All transfers, both during lifetime and after death, are taxed, except for transfers to a spouse or to charity. There is an additional exception for lifetime transfers; each person can gift $10,000 tax-free to any recipient each year.

The Unified Credit is an automatic credit against gift and estate taxes. It permits an individual to transfer $600,000 above and beyond those transfers mentioned above. Without the unified credit, the tax on the first $600,000 of transfers during lifetime or at death would be $192,800; when the credit is used, the tax is $0.

There are five major types of taxes that an estate might face: federal estate tax, state inheritance tax, generation-skipping tax, income tax, and excise tax. Estate taxes range from 37% to 55%, depending on the size of the estate. The remainder of the Unified Credit that has not been used for lifetime gifting can be applied against estate taxes. Generation-skipping transfer tax, in addition to other gift and estate taxes, is paid at a rate of 55% on all money in excess of $1,000,000 transferred to any generation later than children (e.g., grandchildren).

Income tax is due on dividends, interest, and other income from assets that the estate holds before the estate is settled. Also, income taxes must be paid on deferred accounts (401[k]s and other pensions, annuities, and savings bonds), unless they are left to a charity or spouse. The only deferred tax the IRS will not collect is on capital gains (the gain from the sale of an appreciated asset), even if the value of the asset has been depreciated. An asset is revalued to its current value upon death, so there is no capital gains tax due.

State income tax may need to be paid on pensions, even if the deceased retires in a state without an income tax. Many states are now collecting income taxes if the pension money was earned in their state, and some states collect both income and estate (or inheritance) taxes. If an estate has property, particularly real estate, in more than one state, probate may be necessary and taxes may be incurred in multiple states.

There is also a 15% federal excise tax, called the Excess Pension Accumulations Tax, on distributions from pensions and IRAs that total more than $750,000. That tax is deferred if the pension beneficiary is a spouse.

Cash Needs in an Estate

Sometimes estates have liquidity problems—there is not enough cash on hand to pay the bills when assets are tied up in a business or property. Cash needs can include: payments for creditors, probate court, and taxes; living expenses for beneficiaries; money to keep a business running; and bequests to friends, relatives, or charities. The largest cash need is frequently money to equalize an estate, as when a will states, "I leave my property or business to my second son and $X to each of my other children."

If there is not enough cash, the executor of an estate must sell illiquid assets, sometimes at low "estate sale" prices. This happens most frequently when the largest assets in the estate are a private family business or real estate. The problem is exacerbated by the length of time it may take to settle an estate— which can be many months or even years.

Life Insurance

Life insurance, which provides cash when someone dies, is one of the most commonly used tools to solve estate problems, for several reasons. Arrangements can include cash payments, when one or both spouses die, and these cash payments can solve liquidity problems. Before death, cash grows tax-deferred in a life insurance policy, and if the policy is kept until death, the entire death benefit is excluded from income tax. The death benefit can be substantially greater than all payments into the insurance policy.

When deceased persons own life insurance, the death benefit is included in their estate and is subject to estate tax, but not income tax. In order to avoid estate tax on the life insurance, it can be purchased and owned by the trustee of an irrevocable trust. Premium payments are gifts from the principal to the trust, whose ultimate beneficiaries may be the children. Upon death, the death benefit of the life insurance policy is paid to the trust, free of income and estate taxes. The trustee can then use the cash to purchase assets from the estate. This accomplishes making assets available to beneficiaries and providing cash to the estate so it can pay its bills.

Having a will or avoiding probate through a revocable living trust does not necessarily reduce estate taxes. For example, money left to a spouse avoids taxes when the first spouse dies. Unless the spouse spends it all or gives it all away, however, the government will collect tax on the money when the surviving spouse dies.

If an estate contains more than $600,000 and both spouses are alive, it is important for each spouse to use the Unified Credit. This means that assets must be distributed so that they are not all in one name or jointly owned. Some of the assets could be left in trust for the children. Such an arrangement could permit a surviving spouse to use all income from the trust and even use trust principal assets if necessary, as judged by a separate trustee.

Gifting is the other main technique used to avoid estate tax. The best assets to gift are those that will be worth substantially more at death. These include premiums for life insurance policies and stock in rapidly growing businesses. Assets can be gifted directly to children, to a trust for their benefit, or to a *family limited partnership*. The family limited partnership permits the sharing of ownership and control of assets among family members.

Gifts can sometimes be discounted for gift tax purposes. A good example is the gift of a minority interest of a closely held business or property. The value of the gift is less because a new minority owner may not have much control over the asset and because there may be no marketability of such an asset. These discounts can amount to up to one-third of the value of the gift.

Sometimes people do not want to give assets away because they need the use of the asset or the income from the asset while they are still alive. In that case, they may transfer the asset to a trust that permits use of the asset until they die. Upon death, the asset is turned over to the beneficiary, such as a charity.

The most common example of this approach is the charitable remainder unit (or annuity) trust. The trust can provide: income from assets while alive, depending on how invested; designation of who receives the money; a charitable deduction for part of the money transferred, depending on the age of the principal and other recipient(s) of income; the elimination of capital gains tax if and when the trust sells an asset; control over how money from the sale of the assets is invested; and the elimination of estate taxes on money previously transferred to the trust. The remainder of the assets go to the charity upon death of the income recipient(s).

To replace money that would have gone to children but is instead going to a charity, some people set up a wealth replacement trust for the children. This may be an irrevocable life insurance trust paid for by some of the tax savings from the charitable remainder unit trust.

A *personal residence trust* can contain a home or cabin that the principal continues to live in for a fixed period of time or until death. If the principal survives the fixed period, the residence goes to the beneficiary(ies) (e.g., children). The value of the gift, upon which gift tax is calculated, is reduced by the probability of the donor surviving to the end of the fixed period. There are many other approaches that have been designed to reduce gift and estate taxes. Most of them use some a combination of gifts, trusts, and life insurance.

A *Qualified Terminable Interest Property (QTIP)* trust provides income for the spouse and conveys assets to the children, allowing a husband, for example, to balance financial obligations to his wife and his children from a prior marriage.

Estate planning is an important aspect of financial planning and should be started, and updated periodically, even when asset accumulation is modest. Large estates, of course, require careful planning, since virtually all estates large enough to pay estate taxes are audited by the IRS. The IRS tends to value property on the high side in order to collect the highest possible estate taxes. Obtaining independent appraisals of assets during planning or before gifting will help to resolve possible later disputes. (See also ADVANCE DIRECTIVES, BUSINESS SUCCESSION PLANNING, CHARITABLE CONTRIBUTIONS, DURABLE POWER OF ATTORNEY, INHERITANCE, KING LEAR SYNDROME, LIVING WILLS, TRUSTS, and WILLS.)

References

Abramson, Keith V. 1992. *Top Ten Estate Planning Techniques for the 1990s.* New York: American Legal Publishing.

Amling, Frederick. 1986. *Personal Financial Management.* Homewood, IL: Irwin.
Manheimer, Ronald J., ed. 1994. *Older Americans Almanac.* Detroit, MI: Gale Research, Inc.
Plotnick, C. 1991. *How to Settle an Estate.* Yonkers, NY: Consumer Reports Books.
United Seniors Health Cooperative. 1993. *Finances after 50: Financial Planning for the Rest of Your Life.* New York: HarperCollins.

Mark S. Fischer

ESTATE TAXES. See Capital Gain; Charitable Contributions Elder Law Practice; Estate Planning; Inheritance; Wealth Span.

ETHICS IN FINANCIAL PLANNING, standards or imperatives in dealing with finances in the lives of older adults. Ethical dilemmas range from questions of professional practice to issues of social responsibility and public policy. The published ethical standards of the financial planning industry provide the groundwork for an analysis of principles and rules to help clarify and distinguish acceptable from unacceptable conduct. Many issues remain to be addressed, however, as the field of financial gerontology emerges and matures, and all professionals or entities acting as financial advisors* to older persons must grapple with these principles and issues.

Professional Financial Planning

The Code of Professional Ethics of the International Association of Financial Planners offers seven canons or ethical imperatives. Several of the canons are quite straightforward, such as the injunction to put public interest above private gain, or the imperative to improve professional skills and knowledge. Other imperatives in the canon seem more obscure, for example, the provision encouraging obedience to the law in order to "avoid conduct or activity which would cause unjust harm" to those relying on financial planners. Still other canons are simply redundant, for instance, a requirement to comply with the code and to act according to the rules of the association itself.

Unfortunately, the canons avoid most of the serious dilemmas of financial planning: the need to avoid conflict of interest in giving advice; the requirement for truth-telling and disclosure of options and the level of risk; or the balance between paternalism and autonomy in financial decision making.

Financial Advising

All financial advisors find themselves in a position where advice to an elderly client could put the client's assets at risk, as financial decisions often do. Regardless of intention, a financial advisor is regarded as an expert. Vulnerable elderly people, both those with substantial means and those with modest means, will put their trust in a financial expert. In light of that trust, what advice is appropriate? Is the idea of a "risk-averse" elderly person simply a stereotype to be set aside in favor of customized advice to an individual rather than an "average" older person?

These questions invoke the classic dilemmas of autonomy and paternalism in professional ethics. The pure paternalist position will compel the planner to safeguard the welfare of the elderly client and tailor recommendations offered to consider the risk to capital. By contrast, a pure libertarian position will emphasize the complete autonomy of the client and favor complete fact-telling with the ultimate decision left up to the client alone. Both extreme positions have ethical arguments in their favor. But where a financial advisor has a bias toward one or the other side, it seems imperative to reveal that bias before entering into a contractual relationship to provide financial planning or financial advice.

Social Ethics

Financial advising on behalf of elderly clients takes place in a public context and therefore requires the vantage point of social ethics. A serious ethical issue for financial advisors concerns the public status and definition of the finance profession itself. Just who qualifies as a "financial advisor" or "financial planner?" In most states, the professional designation is quite loose and ill-defined, unlike that for physicians, lawyers, or architects. As a result, financial advisors with very different levels of competence, including those with serious conflicts of interest (e.g., stock brokers), may present themselves as financial planners to a poorly informed public.

Another ethical dilemma in financial planning arises from the interpersonal and multigenerational structure of the family. The financial planner typically encounters elderly individuals for whom inheritance is a major issue. The problem arises in Medicaid* planning, where financial planners, as well as attorneys in elder law practice*, must take account of the need to plan for long-term care expenditures. There has been strong criticism of middle-class elderly people who take advantage of spend-down "loopholes" to qualify for Medicaid and safeguard an inheritance for their children. To what extent should a financial advisor take account of such criticism or ethical concerns?

Another area of intersection between individual ethics and social ethics is the realm of financial elder abuse*. Does a financial planner have an obligation to protect an elderly client when the planner sees evidence of exploitation—such as occurs when a frail or cognitively impaired older person is giving large amounts of money to a younger caregiver or an affectionate companion? Does it matter if mental competency is in question or is there a "right to folly?" Guardianship statutes and programs in many states today are wrestling with this dilemma.

With increasing numbers of "oldest old*" people, including significant numbers with strong financial assets, the ethical dilemmas of financial planning, financial advising, and aging will surely loom larger. Instead of relying on abstract codes of ethics, it may be more helpful to follow the example of medical ethics in confronting problems of clinical care: namely, to recognize that ambiguity and uncertainty, including ethical dilemmas, are inherent in planning for all stages of life, including old age, and must rigorously and continuously be addressed. (See also ATTORNEYS, CRIME PROTECTION, ELDER LAW PRACTICE, ESTATE PLANNING, FINANCIAL ADVISORS, FINANCIAL ELDER ABUSE, GUARDIANSHIP, MEDICAID, and MEDICAID PLANNING.)

References

DeGeorge, Richard T. 1990. *Business Ethics.* New York: Collier Macmillan.

Kapoor, Jack R., Les R. Dlabay, and Robert J. Hughes. 1991. *Personal Finance,* Second Edition. Homewood, IL: Irwin.

Harry R. Moody

F

FEDERAL AGENCY SECURITIES, bonds*, debentures, notes, and other securities issued to raise funds in support of public functions. As people approach retirement age, they restructure their investment portfolio. Equity securities tend to become less important and fixed-income investments more important. As older persons become less willing to take risks, they try to find investments that provide a satisfactory rate of return and reduce the possibility of principal loss.

The Federal Financing Bank and the Government National Mortgage Association are federal agencies that issue securities backed by the full faith and credit of the U.S. government. Most agencies considered here, however, are Government-Sponsored Enterprises (GSEs); the securities they issue are not guaranteed by the U.S. government, but involve federal sponsorship. Government-Sponsored Enterprises are the largest issuers of agency securities and include the Federal Home Loan Bank (FHLB), Federal National Mortgage Association (FNMA), Farm Credit System (FCS), Student Loan Marketing Association (SLMA), and the Federal Home Loan Mortgage Corporation (FHLMC.) SLMA and FNMA are also publicly owned and have stock that trades on the national exchanges.

Agencies were created by Congress to meet the special needs of specific segments of the general economy. They can be divided into three broad categories: (1) agencies supporting the mortgage market—FHLB, FHLMC, FNMA, GNMA; (2) agencies supporting agriculture—FCS; and (3) agencies supporting student loans—SLMA. Several other small agencies sell debt securities for specialized purposes. It is useful to analyze agencies by the type of securities they issue. There are two broad categories: (1) agencies that issue notes, debentures, bonds, or discount notes (FCB, FHLB, FNMA, SLMA); and (2) those that issue mortgage-backed securities, primarily "pass-through" securities (FNMA,

FHLMC, GNMA). FNMA issues both types, depending on the financial purpose of the funds being raised. Each of these agencies sell securities to the public through a nationwide group of dealers and dealer banks or through individually negotiated or competitive bid transactions.

Over the years, agency securities have become very popular with older investors. Two reasons for this acceptance are their perceived high quality, which assures investors that their principal is relatively safe, and an active secondary market that allows investors to sell their securities quickly when necessary. The majority of agency issues are debentures or short-term discount notes with set maturity dates from 30 days to 20 years and a set coupon rate, which pay interest every six months. Newer issues have some additional features, such as call options and floating rates, but they are not as popular with individuals since they often require a minimum purchase of $100,000. Typically, agencies issue their debentures in denominations of $5,000–$10,000.

The fastest-growing segment of the agencies market is for mortgage-backed securities, primarily pass-through securities issued by FNMA, FHLMC, and GNMA. Of these agencies, only GNMA carries the guarantee of the full faith and credit of the U.S. Treasury, and because of this guarantee, GNMA securities are among the most popular fixed-income investments in the world.

The Government National Mortgage Association (GNMA)

The Government National Mortgage Association (GNMA) was created in 1968 when FNMA was rechartered as a private corporation (privatized). GNMA securities today are the most widely held and actively traded mortgage-backed securities. Through its Mortgage-backed Securities Program (MBS), GNMA guarantees securities backed by pools of mortgages, "passing through" the principal and interest payments to the security holder monthly. Since GNMA guarantees the timely payment of principal and interest, the investor takes no risk that the underlying mortgages will become delinquent. Interest paid on mortgage-backed securities is subject to state and local taxes, so investors need to consider this before purchasing them.

Federal Home Loan Bank (FHLB) System

The FHLB was created by an Act of Congress in 1932, and amended by the Financial Institutions Reform, Recovery, and Enforcement Act of 1989 (FIRREA.) There are twelve district banks comprising the system. These banks operate as a reserve system for the savings and loan and banking industries to stabilize the flow of mortgage credit. They provide a ready, low-cost source of funds to member institutions, which is then made available to the public. Unlike FNMA and FHLMC, which purchase and then pool mortgages, the FHLB makes advances to its members on the security of their mortgages. Since enactment of the FIRREA, the supervisory and regulatory functions of member institutions reside in the Office of Thrift Supervisor within the Department of the Treasury. Owned by member institutions, the FHLBs do not take deposits. Funds are raised by selling FHLB Consolidated Discount Notes and Consolidated Bank Notes. More than $135 billion of consolidated obligations were outstanding at the end of 1993.

Federal Home Loan Mortgage Corporation (FHLMC)

The FHLMC was chartered in 1970 as a government-sponsored enterprise. It was established to increase the funds available for residential housing by providing a national secondary market in conventional residential mortgages. The FHLMC accomplishes this by purchasing from bankers mortgages that are not guaranteed by any government agency, putting these mortgages into pools, and selling them as pass-through securities backed by such mortgages. Along with FNMA, FHLMC is responsible for maintaining an active secondary market for home sales. Besides the pass-through securities, FHLMC also issues discount notes and short-term debentures, but pass-through securities constitute the vast majority of outstanding debt. Like GNMA securities, FHLMC securities are not exempt from state and local taxes.

Federal National Mortgage Association (FNMA)

The Federal National Mortgage Association is one of the largest corporations in the United States, based on asset size, and is the largest supplier of funds for home mortgages. It was incorporated in 1938 as a corporation owned by the government. In 1954, it became a mixed public-private corporation and finally, in 1968, the U.S. Congress split FNMA into two separate corporations, the Government National Mortgage Association (GNMA), a government agency, and the Federal National Mortgage Association (FNMA), a federally chartered corporation owned by stockholders.

The FNMA supports savings and loan associations, mortgage bankers, commercial banks, and other banks primarily by buying mortgages from them. This availability of funds allows an active secondary market and enables capital to flow to those areas of the country that may need funds. FNMA offers debentures, short-term discount notes, and, since 1981, has supported the housing market by purchasing mortgages from originators and generating mortgage-backed securities, which it sells in the capital market. The FNMA has more than $700 billion of outstanding mortgage debt. Income from FNMA securities is subject to state and local tax.

Farm Credit System

The Farm Credit System is a cooperatively owned system of banks and associations that provide both short- and long-term credit to farmers, ranchers, rural homeowners, and agricultural and rural cooperatives. Twelve federal land banks and associations provide the funding for making long-term loans on secured first mortgages by selling debentures and short-term notes in the money and credit markets. The banks are not depository institutions and rely on the Federal Farm Credit Bank Funding Corporation to raise funds for them. The

Funding Corporation issues Farm Credit Consolidated Systemwide Discount Notes, Bonds, and Medium-Term Notes. The income derived from these securities is exempt from state and local taxes, which makes them especially attractive to investors on fixed incomes.

Student Loan Marketing Association (SLMA)

The Student Loan Marketing Association (SMLA), like FNMA, is a government-chartered, publicly held corporation that owns 30% of all U.S. student loans. Chartered in 1972, the SLMA was developed in response to problems in the Guaranteed Student Loan Program of 1965. Originally only educational or student loan institutions were allowed to own stock. This was later changed so that anyone could buy nonvoting stock. As a secondary market for student loans, SLMA lends funds for student loans to qualified institutions. The obligations of SLMA are exempt from state and local taxes and from SEC regulations. Obligations include discount notes, debentures, and floating rate bonds. Investments in SLMA's securities are without much risk because state and federal authorities bear the brunt of the defaults.

A potential investor in federal agency securities should always talk to a financial advisor* before committing funds to this large and complex segment of the financial market. There are numerous types of federal agency securities with varying issuers, terms, liquidity, and tax treatments. Only by closely scrutinizing and understanding both the market and one's particular investment needs can investors navigate toward the retirement years with confidence. (See also ASSETS ALLOCATION AFTER RETIREMENT, BONDS, EQUITY SECURITIES, HOMEOWNERSHIP, MORTGAGE INSTRUMENTS, and SENIORS HOUSING FINANCE.)

References

Bretthorst, Kenneth A. 1988. "Instruments and Markets for Federal Agency Securities." In *The Bankers' Handbook,* ed. William H. Baugh, Thomas I. Storrs, and Charles E. Walker. Homewood, IL: Dow Jones-Irwin.

Stuhldreher, Donald J. 1988. "Instruments and Markets for Government Securities." In *The Bankers' Handbook,* ed. William H. Baugh, Thomas I. Storrs, and Charles E. Walker. Homewood, IL: Dow Jones-Irwin.

Kenneth A. Bretthorst

FINANCIAL ADVISORS, a term applied to a wide variety of professional individuals who provide an even wider variety of financial services and products. Among the individuals who may be referred to as financial advisors are financial planners, stockbrokers, insurance agents, bankers, attorneys*, financial managers, and accountants*. While each of these categories represents a field of legitimate financial advice, the scope of services offered by each advisor must be measured according to his or her particular training and experience, and the emphasis of each of these professions. Choosing a financial advisor is similar to choosing any professional in whom a great amount of trust must be placed. Knowing the array of finance professionals and their area of expertise is key, followed by an understanding of financial needs, and knowledge of sources for personal and organizational referrals. Surrendering total responsibility for one's financial affairs to advisors is always unwise. It is especially important for older individuals to learn and to participate actively in as many details of their own financial management as possible, since doing so can improve one's sense of autonomy and increase feelings of personal accomplishment.

Stockbrokers and Commodities Brokers are registered representatives or principals of National Association of Securities Dealers (NASD) member firms, and they are licensed by the NASD after passing the appropriate set of examinations for the particular type of license they hold. In addition, they must pass state examinations and be licensed by the state or states in which they sell securities. The examinations are independent of any specified academic background, so it is not necessary for securities brokers to have any special training beyond what is required to pass the tests. Although some brokers do have advanced academic or other training in financial areas, many do not.

Securities—bonds*, equity securities*, commodities*, and mutual funds*— are purchased customarily through brokers who are paid a commission based on the dollar amount of each transaction and the number of securities involved. Brokers should be selected based on their honesty, efficiency, accessibility, and ability to provide clients with information about the investments that are being considered for purchase or sale.

Insurance Agents are licensed to offer life insurance* products to their customers on behalf of the insurance companies they represent. Many life insurance companies offer extensive training to their insurance agents in most of the areas discussed below, so that insurance agents with these companies can give a broad base of recommendations to their clients. Many insurance agents have obtained additional designations: Certified Financial Planner (CFP), Certified Life Underwriter (CLU), or Chartered Financial Consultant (ChFC), and have taken advanced training that enables them to provide more expert advice to their clients.

Financial Planners constitute a huge and growing population of persons from many different backgrounds with widely varying abilities. Use of the designation "financial planner" requires no specialized license or credential and has been assumed by many stockbrokers, accountants, and insurance salespeople (Savage 1994.) *Certified Financial Planners (CFPs)* have completed a degree course offered at more than 40 colleges and universities around the country or through home study courses. Six core categories comprise specialized academic training in subjects ranging from investment advice to tax and estate planning. In addition, to earn the CFP designation, a 10-hour examination given by the International Board of Standards and Practices for Certified Financial Planners, Inc. must be passed to demonstrate proof of financial planning–related knowledge.

Financial Planners are compensated in several ways, and persons seeking planning and investment advice should know in advance how they are being charged. For creating a financial plan, a straight fee is often charged, but commissions on products such as insurance and mutual funds are often charged as well. This poses a conflict of interest for financial planners, and it is important to understand a financial advisor's motivation for recommending the purchase of a particular insurance policy or investment.

Attorneys in most states must first obtain a law degree from a law school and then become licensed, after passing the state bar exam, to practice law. Some attorneys have highly specialized backgrounds in taxation and financial consulting, but it is important before engaging the services of an attorney to determine his or her specialized training and area of expertise. Some attorneys are able to offer very detailed advice on wills*, trusts*, and estates, but are inexperienced in investments*, pensions*, business succession planning*, and other areas that impact sound personal financial planning. Even an attorney specializing in the practice of tax law, for example, is likely to have further specialized training within the field of taxation—civil and criminal, personal or corporate—so vast is this and other specialized areas of law. It is the responsibility of a prospective client to ascertain the areas and level of experience that attorneys have, and it is the duty of an attorney to disclose this information to the client, but many attorneys will not volunteer their credentials unless asked.

Public Accountants and *Certified Public Accountants (CPAs)* have backgrounds in accounting and frequently in taxation. This background often affords them a good basis for advising clients on financial matters, although this does not always extend into every area of financial consulting, such as insurance or investments. The services that accountants* are best trained to render as financial advisors are those of tax planning, tax projections, tax return preparation, business valuations, and cash flow projections.

Money Managers typically charge a fee to manage large blocks of funds inside investment portfolios. These individuals have credentials and investment experience that vary, and it is always advisable to obtain an investment history for the firms they represent in order to determine the success of the managers. However, even successful money managers may not be appropriate for some clients, since the minimum amounts they typically accept for investment management are frequently much higher than most individual investors have available in their estates.

Areas of knowledge that individuals should seek in their financial advisors include knowledge of the law, of estate and income taxation, of investments with respect to performance and economic trends and forecasts, of Medicare* and Medicaid* issues, and sensitivity to the needs of older persons in general. Because these matters are diverse and complicated, it is rare that any one individual can satisfy all areas of need for financial advice. As a result, most individuals will find it necessary to engage the services of more than one person for financial advice and assistance.

Perhaps the most common error made by an individual seeking to implement personal financial objectives is to rely on a specialist in one area to provide services, products, or advice outside the specialist's field of expertise. As examples, most attorneys do not prepare tax returns, CPAs are neither trained nor licensed to prepare trust documents or other legal instruments, and investment advisors may not understand estate planning, goals, or techniques. Despite these limitations, individuals seeking financial advice should be aware that there is a significant population of financial advisors who do have backgrounds, training, and experience in specialized areas. Once financial objectives are identified, one should seek assistance from more than one professional in order to obtain the range of help needed for financial planning needs.

Financial Advisors Designations

CLU stands for Chartered Life Underwriter. This designation is awarded by the American College of Bryn Mawr, Pennsylvania and usually requires ten courses in such areas as law, finance, estate and income taxation, life insurance, and investments.

ChFC means Chartered Financial Consultant. This designation is also given by the American College (see CLU, above) and requires additional, advanced courses in taxation, finance, and investment topics beyond those included in the CLU. The American College primarily trains insurance professionals in the techniques of financial planning.

CFP, or Certified Financial Planner, is a designation that signifies a broad amount of training in financial planning, as discussed above. Financial Planners who have the CFP designation must earn continuing education credits in order to maintain the credential.

MBA is the Master of Business Administration, an advanced academic degree conferred by many schools of business within universities. MBA degrees vary widely in content, but most require core courses in accounting, finance, economics, management, business policy, and other business topics.

CPA is a designation for accountants that stands for Certified Public Accountant. CPAs have significant academic and on-the-job training and must qualify for the designation by passing rigorous examinations. In order to maintain the designation of CPA, a number of continuing education classes must be completed each year.

JD, or Juris Doctor, is the degree conferred by law schools after a three-year academic program. The law school curriculum, at schools jointly accredited by the American Bar Association and the Association of American Law Schools, requires a Bachelor's Degree from an accredited university and covers the wide range of legal subjects necessary to prepare for the practice of law.

LLM is the Masters of Law, a degree that allows a law school graduate to study areas of specialty within the law, such as taxation, labor law, or patent law. (See also ACCOUNTANTS, AGENTS AND BROKERS, ATTORNEYS, CASH FLOW PLANNING FOR RETIREES, ELDER LAW PRACTICE, ETHICS IN FINANCIAL PLANNING, FINANCIAL COUNSELING,

GUARDIANSHIP, KING LEAR SYNDROME, OMBUDSMAN, and WEALTH SPAN.)

Organizations

Institute of Certified Financial Planners
International Association for Financial Planning
International Board of Standards and Practices for Certified Financial Planners, Inc.
National Association of Personal Financial Advisors

References

Johnson, Dale S. 1988. *Financial Services: Environment and Professions.* American College: Bryn Mawr, PA.
Professional Development Series. Updated Periodically. Denver, CO: College of Financial Planners.
Savage, Terry. 1994. *New Money Strategies for the '90s.* New York: Harper Collins.

Donald A. Hunsberger

FINANCIAL COUNSELING, an interactive periodic exchange between professional financial counselors and older persons, with the goal of maintaining a person's desired quality of life and helping with information concerning lifestyle needs. Retirement years are a time for reevaluation of financial goals, needs, and wants, since for many it means a reduction of economic resources.

Professionals should consider income averages and age categories in regard to patterns of spending when working with older adults on resource management, since age and income level are considered to be the strongest predictors of spending patterns (American Demographics 1993). According to the Bureau of Labor Statistics (1990), the average annual dollar amount that all households spend is $29,614. Adults 65 and older spend less, which helps them maintain a balance with their reduced income. Average annual expenditures for heads of household ages 65 to 74 is $22,562, and for ages 74 and older is $15,782. As shown in Table 1, the age group of 65 and older experiences a decrease of expenditures in all categories except housing and health care, which are projected to increase as the twenty-first century approaches.

Financial counseling for older adults often focuses on budgeting issues associated with the reduction of disposable income. The following six steps can be incorporated into the counseling process: (1) relationship building, (2) diagnosing needs, (3) establishing financial goals, (4) discussing alternative solutions to the financial problem, (5) implementing the financial plan, and (6) evaluating the plan.

Relationship building is a crucial first phase to the success of financial planning, as many people feel that finances are very difficult to talk about with others. The characteristics needed by the counseling professional are a friendly, nonjudgmental disposition and responsiveness to clients. It is also beneficial to interact with clients in an environment that entails minimum threat (Pulvino and Lee 1990). Once a client trusts the counselor and feels comfortable sharing

Table 1
Expenditures by Age 65 and Older Consumers

Spending Categories	Dollar Amount and Percent of Annual Expenditures by Age			
	65-74	Percent	74 and Older	Percent
Food	$3,466	15	$2,548	16
Housing	6,849	30	5,871	37
Transportation	3,906	17	1,765	11
Apparel and Services	1,270	6	638	4
Entertainment	841	4	444	3
Health Care	2,300	10	2,197	14
Insurance	1,033	5	238	2
Other	2,897	13	2,050	13

Source: Consumer Expenditure Survey, Bureau of Labor Statistics, 1990

financial information, progression to the next step of planning can be accomplished.

Diagnosis of needs calls for information about the client's lifestyle, income, and living expenses, that is, information related to goals (travel, disposal of income), needs, and personal data such as age, marital status, cultural background, and number in the household. Income information includes amount of gross income, net income, and discretionary income. Living expense information includes how the client spends monthly income. The expenses can be divided into fixed expenses (housing, food, utilities, debt payments, insurance) and flexible expenses (gifts, clothing, entertainment, travel). Income expenses should be recorded on a living expenses form. Income expense forms include categories such as current net income, fixed expenses, and flexible expenses.

During this diagnostic phase, comparisons should be made between what the client is spending and the national averages listed in Table 1, or to current averages published by the Bureau of Labor Statistics. Using comparisons can help clients in the adjustment of expenditures if they are having a difficult time living on their actual personal net income. At this point, it is time to begin financial goal setting. Questions that should be posed are:

1. Where can expenditures be reduced?
2. Can income be increased?
3. Can debt payment be reduced?
4. What are the specific financial goals for the next five years?
5. What are the specific needs that must be met?

Answers to these questions are the keys to establishing a new, workable budget. During this step, the professional must allow the client to generate workable solutions.

Once alternatives are generated, a plan of action can be established. This new resource allocation plan (budget) must be documented, and the client can try the plan for a month. After a month, it is important to discuss the workability of the budget with the client. Changes can be made if needed, and the client should then try the revised plan.

Successful resource management is an ongoing process. Clients change at their own pace, and their personal values and goals must be taken into account. Working with clients in resource management requires understanding that change is a difficult and slow process. As changes occur, evaluations of personal budgets and needed adjustments should be undertaken with this in mind. (See also CASH FLOW PLANNING FOR RETIREES, ECONOMIC STATUS OF THE ELDERLY, ECONOMIC STATUS OF ELDERLY WOMEN, and WEALTH SPAN.)

References

American Demographics. 1993. *American Demographics Desk Reference Series.* 3:2–28.
Bureau of Labor Statistics. 1990. *Consumer Expenditure Survey.* Washington, DC: BLS.
Deacon, R. E. and F. M. Firebaugh. 1981. *Family Resource Management: Principles and Applications.* Boston: Allyn & Bacon.
Pulvino, C. J. and J. L. Lee. 1990. *Financial Counseling: Interviewing Skills.* Dubuque, IA: Kendall/Hunt.

Deborah G. Wooldridge and Linda Murphy

FINANCIAL ELDER ABUSE, the illegal or improper use of an older adult's resources or property. This type of elder abuse is committed by family members and others close to an older person who withhold or misuse the person's funds or other assets, or criminals whose crimes take a variety of forms: forgery, misappropriation of cash withdrawals, abuse of joint bank accounts, abuse of powers of attorney, abuse of automated teller machines, fraudulent use of credit cards, and abuse of a trust (Brookdale Center on Aging of Hunter College 1994). Statutory or other legal definitions of financial elder abuse vary from state to state.

There is a lack of public awareness of the issues surrounding financial elder abuse because financial exploitation of older people is underreported and there are few resources to deal with the problem. Available estimates of the extent of financial elder abuse vary widely: 20% of all elder abuse cases reported by authorities nationwide; 34% of all adult protective services cases investigated in Arizona; and 63% of cases reported by the Los Angeles District Attorney's Office (Los Angeles County District Attorney 1994). There is a lack of knowledge concerning the extent of the problem and resources available to deal with it, since there are no uniform definitions, reporting requirements, or data collection mechanisms specifically for financial abuse of the elderly. Also, the criminal justice system involved in serving victims of financial exploitation is fragmented.

A Case Illustration

An example of financial elder abuse follows: Ms. Adams's lifetime savings of $120,000 is kept in a savings account from which she rarely withdraws any money. Ms. Adams, who is 92 years old and lives alone in a small apartment, recently acquired a new friend, John, who lives in the neighborhood. He visits her frequently, escorts her to the bank, and occasionally does marketing for her. John asks for and receives Ms. Adams's power of attorney, and now has access to her checking and savings account, so that he can pay her bills and balance her checkbook. Without her knowledge, however, John steadily withdraws funds from her savings account. Once the account is depleted, Ms. Adams's "friend" moves and disappears from her life.

Factors Affecting the Problem

This is not an unusual situation. Ms. Adams's circumstances fit the general profile of risk factors that contribute to the potential for elder abuse: an elderly woman living alone in relative social isolation, having some physical and cognitive impairment, dependent on others for care and protection, with a "new friend" who provides informal care and help.

Other risk factors that do not apply in Ms. Adams's case are financial dependence by the abuser on the victim, substance abuse by the abuser, and a history of family dysfunction. More than two-thirds of elder abuse perpetrators are family members, most often a child or spouse.

A major issue in defining financial elder abuse is the decisional capacity of the victim and, thus, whether the delegation of fiduciary authority to another person is voluntary and informed. Although advanced age cannot be equated with mental impairment, the "oldest old*" are more likely to have some physical or cognitive impairment that manifests in an inability to pay bills or purchase the necessities of daily living. The making of uncharacteristically large gifts and/or an irrational belief that it is necessary to hoard or preserve assets to the detriment of personal health and safety adds to the problem. Ms. Adams suffered from short-term memory loss and was marginally able to manage her affairs. After John's disappearance she could not remember his name or where she had met him. She did acknowledge that he was her friend and that he helped her a lot. She was shocked to hear that he had depleted her savings account and said that she had not intended to make large gifts of money to him. It is unclear whether she had understood the consequences of executing a power of attorney or the risks associated with such an instrument.

Questionable mental capacity of the victim may impede the ability of the criminal justice system to prosecute cases of financial elder abuse. In Ms. Adams's case, "John" was known to law enforcement authorities as a con artist, and yet, because of his victims' frailty and alleged inability to testify, he had never been successfully prosecuted. Even when a victim's decisional mental capacity is not in question, it may be impossible to pursue the issue because victims are unwilling to report these incidents to law enforcement agencies. Victims of abuse may be dependent on the abuser or be fearful of reprisal. Most are embarrassed, ashamed, and unwilling to admit they were victimized.

Health care facilities, social services providers, and the banking industry complain that the confidential nature of their relationship with the suspected victim of financial elder abuse impedes their ability to report many incidents of abuse to the authorities in the absence of the victim's consent. The banking industry is reluctant to report suspected cases of financial elder abuse when the alleged abuser has a duly executed durable power of attorney* or other surrogate authority.

Prevention and Intervention

Eventually, involuntary legal interventions may become necessary to protect the older adult from self-neglect or abuse by others. Such interventions might be a court-ordered guardianship*, conservatorship, or referral to Adult Protective Services. In recent years, alternatives to guardianship have been promoted by advocates of the elderly, to reduce undue interference in the life of the allegedly incapacitated elderly, to enable elderly persons to maintain a lifestyle of choice consistent with their personal values and background, and to maximize their participation in financial or other personal decisions.

Alternatives to guardianship consist of daily money management (DMM) services or surrogate financial management services. DMM services include assistance with bill paying, credit management, applying for government and pension benefits, submitting health insurance claims, and banking. DMM services are frequently delivered as part of a broader case management function provided by social service agencies or private practitioners. Surrogate financial management services might be durable powers of attorney* and/or springing powers of attorney (powers of attorney that are inactive until a specific event occurs), trusts*, and joint bank accounts. These alternatives have in common that they are initiated and executed voluntarily when the principal has the mental capacity to do so, much like an advance directive* for health care decisions. Another involuntary surrogate service is representative payeeship under the Social Security Administration or the Veterans Administration, by which a third party receives the monthly government benefit check on behalf of the beneficiary.

As relative newcomers on the human services scene, DMM services are limited in that they can only be used while the elderly person has the cognitive capacity to direct the DMM personnel. DMM services may not be useful alternatives to guardianship in all cases, since court-ordered interventions may still be needed if the older person loses the capacity to direct the DMM provider and has not appointed a surrogate or proxy in advance to manage finances

(Wilber 1993). Notwithstanding their limitations, DMM services are critical for many older persons who need financial management assistance.

As is illustrated by the case of Ms. Adams, there is no guarantee that powers-of-attorney will be free from potential abuse. A recent study, "Abuse of Powers of Attorney," conducted by the Albany Law School Government Law Center in New York State (1994) uncovered substantial problems with abuse of powers of attorney. Abuse of joint bank accounts and other surrogate devices has also been noted by the Brookdale Center on Aging (1994).

Future Directions

Throughout the United States there is a growing concern about the incidence of elder abuse and financial exploitation of the elderly. Many jurisdictions are in the process of evaluating the use of mandatory reporting requirements, revision of criminal or civil remedies, revision of power of attorney statutes to build in safeguards, and revision of guardianship statutes to enable the courts to order limited or one-time interventions so that immediate action is possible pending a full proceeding.

In addition to statutory revisions, there is increased recognition that training programs on elder abuse must be developed and offered to law enforcement agencies, offices of district attorneys, banking institutions, health care facilities, Adult Protective Services, and the aging network. Training curricula must include: how to determine that abuse has occurred and whether the victim has decisional capacity, how to interview victims and family members (including the possible abuser), how to identify what remedies might be needed in each case, and how to assist individual victims of financial and other elder abuse.

Finally, corporations, human services programs, self-help groups, and attorneys who specialize in elder law practice* are increasingly providing preretirement seminars and counseling to middle-aged persons who are looking forward to their own retirement or who are caregivers for their parents or friends. Such consumer education models include information on the positive and negative aspects of various financial surrogate management devices and health care advance directives, in an effort to encourage the public to "plan ahead for incapacity." (See also ADVANCE DIRECTIVES; CRIME PROTECTION; DURABLE POWER OF ATTORNEY; ELDER LAW PRACTICE; ETHICS IN FINANCIAL PLANNING; FINANCIAL PLANNING; GUARDIANSHIP; SOCIAL WORK, GERONTOLOGICAL; TRUSTS; and WILLS.)

References

Albany Law School, Government Law Center. 1994. "Abuse and the Durable Power-of-Attorney: Options for Reform." Albany, NY: Author.

Brookdale Center on Aging of Hunter College, Jacob Reingold Institute. 1994. "Survey of Financial Institutions." Unpublished manuscript.

Los Angeles County District Attorney's Office, Consumer Protection Division, Elder Abuse Section. 1994. "Silent Suffering: Elder Abuse in America." Los Angeles: Author.

Wilber, Kate. 1993. "Daily Money Management: Re-Examining an 'Alternative.' " *Aging Today*. San Francisco: American Society on Aging.

                                                          Sia Arnason and Debra S. Sacks

FINANCIAL RESOURCES. See Accountants; Agents and Brokers; Attorneys; Financial Advisors; Major Post-ERISA Benefit Legislation—Appendix A; Organizations and Resources—Appendix B.

FOOD STAMPS. See Elder Law Practice; Minority Elders; Nutrition Programs; Social Work, Gerontological.

FUNERALS, serve as verification of death for society and provide closure for the deceased's life. The bereaved must deal with important matters and decisions at a time of potentially great emotional stress. Funeral arrangements and other personal and financial affairs of the deceased must be handled within just a few days after death, while survivors may be grieving and unable to think clearly enough to make wise decisions.

Criticism of Funeral Practices

Funeral practices have been a center of controversy, as funeral directors have been accused of exploiting highly vulnerable consumers by using unfair selling techniques. While lavish funerals are often used by families to convey wealth and status, naive or less affluent persons also may be manipulated into incurring excessive costs. Under circumstances of grief and bereavement one can feel compelled to spend more money on the funeral in an effort to provide a loved one in death what they did not enjoy in life (Kalish 1985). Spending large sums of money on a funeral to relieve guilt, however, may erode the purpose and meaning of last rites. Many people will deplete their savings or go into debt in an attempt to "do the right thing for the deceased."

Public attention to the widespread commercialism and extravagance of funerals came about in the early 1960s with the publication of two popular books: Jessica Mitford's *The American Way of Death,* and Ruth Harmer's *The High Cost of Dying.* Both were highly critical of the materialistic and euphemistic manner in which death was handled in American funeral practices, and funeral directors responded to the criticism by attempting to provide a greater degree of personal choice in selecting funeral services (DeSpelder and Strickland 1992).

Funeral directors, however, remained uniquely able to exploit bereaved consumers who lacked public knowledge about funeral services and costs. In 1984, the Federal Trade Commission (FTC) implemented its "Trade Regulation Rule on Funeral Industry Practices," requiring that consumers be given detailed information about financial and legal aspects of funeral services. The rule stipulates that all funeral providers must itemize price information on services offered. The key provision of the Funeral Rule requires that funeral goods and services be specified on a General Price List. The funeral provider is required by law to present his or her General Price List at the beginning of the funeral arrangements and disclose itemized price information, both over the telephone and in writing (FTC 1984). Thus, consumers can compare prices with other funeral providers. Additionally, they can select only those services that meet their individual needs.

Funeral Service Costs

The average cost of funerals today is approximately $3,500 (DeSpelder and Strickland 1992). However, total burial costs including cemetery plots, memorials, and other expenses run about $5,000 (Harris 1990). Although the FTC Funeral Rule requires that costs be itemized, comparing costs at different funeral homes is still difficult. Funeral providers may not offer the same goods and services or they may have different methods of presenting prices. However, it is important for consumers to be aware of what charges are allowed under the Funeral Rule. Actual prices will vary from region to region, and also between urban and rural locations.

Typical funeral service expenses provided by the funeral director and mortuary staff include professional service charges, intake costs, embalming and other body preparation charges, casket prices, charges for use of facilities and vehicles, outer burial container prices, and miscellaneous charges.

Funeral providers may charge a basic fee for professional services rendered, such as arranging for the funeral, consulting with family members, assisting with the visitation, and completing and filing necessary notices and authorizations associated with the disposition of the body. A part of this fee covers the cost of maintaining a facility and staff around the clock. There is also an intake charge for transporting the body from the place of death to the funeral home. A surcharge may be included for nighttime pickups to cover the cost of additional staff.

Embalming has become an accepted practice in American funerals and may be necessary if the body is to be viewed. Yet, there is no law requiring embalming anywhere in the United States, except in special cases. Laws vary by state, but embalming may be mandatory in some circumstances involving transportation and disease control. The FTC rule, however, gives consumers the right to choose other funeral arrangements, such as direct cremation or immediate burial. Most funeral homes can keep the body refrigerated for 48 hours. Refrigeration expenses are usually less than the cost of embalming.

Perhaps the most important funeral cost is that of the casket. The casket has symbolic and emotional value in honoring the deceased (DeSpelder and Strickland 1992), and options and prices range from relatively inexpensive cloth-covered plywood to solid mahogany, copper, or bronze caskets costing thousands of dollars. Prices of comparable caskets vary from one funeral home to another, and some funeral providers inflate prices substantially, while other funeral providers incorporate fees for professional services in the price of the casket. While this inclusion is allowed under the Funeral Rule, a description of services must be included in the prices quoted for caskets (FTC 1984). Additional charges include the use of facilities for visitation or viewing, and use of the chapel for the funeral ceremony. Similarly, charges for vehicles must be itemized separately on the General Price List.

If outer burial containers are provided by the funeral home, their prices must be listed. Although not required by state or local law in most parts of the country, many cemeteries require either a burial vault or a grave liner to support the earth above the grave. Many funeral providers offer exquisite burial vaults made of bronze, copper or stainless steel to complement the casket selected. While burial vaults may be necessary, the emphasis should be on their structural function and not their beauty.

Miscellaneous charges for goods and services provided by the funeral home or obtained from other sources on behalf of the customer must be shown on the General Price List. Under this category are such items as floral arrangements, newspaper death notices, acknowledgment cards, and honoraria for pallbearers and clergy. The charges for these items may be higher than if the family purchased them directly.

Body Disposition

Preferences for disposing of the body are based on social and cultural customs, philosophical beliefs, and religious values. In American society, burial, cremation, and donation to science are the most frequently approved choices. Of these methods, internment or entombment are the most popular choices. The cost of burial plots varies considerably, depending on the cemetery. Similarly, there are wide variations in the costs of entombment. Memorials such as grave-markers and cemetery endowment costs for ''perpetual care'' must also be considered.

Cremation is another choice growing in acceptance. The costs are likely to be much lower than burial or entombment. For example, the law does not require a casket in cases of direct cremation. The Funeral Rule requires only a cardboard box or unfinished wood casket for delivery of the body to the crematorium (FTC 1984). Even for those who choose cremation, some sort of memorial service might still be desired.

Donating the body to science is more difficult than most people think. Most medical schools have an abundant supply of cadavers and are selective in the bodies they accept from donations. Thus, donating the body to science is not a very plausible alternative.

Pre-Planned Funerals

Kalish (1985) suggests that people take steps to avoid the risk of exploitation and reduce the vulnerability of family members at the time of bereavement by making funeral arrangements in advance. He recommends either contacting the funeral home directly or communicating with loved ones about the kind of funeral desired.

As a result of changes within the funeral industry brought about by the Funeral Rule, people can request information about funeral services and pricing by telephone or in writing. Nevertheless, most funeral providers will not volunteer information on pricing unless it is specifically requested. Some funeral directors will instead attempt to have the person come to the funeral home to discuss funeral arrangements. Consumers are advised to know their rights and to deal only with reputable funeral homes.

Planning ahead allows people to control the costs by making selections based on their personal preferences and budget. Prearranged funerals may relieve some of the burden and confusion placed on the family in making these decisions. There is also greater assurance that the individual's wishes will be carried out, which reduces conflict among family members regarding arrangements.

Since older people are the major purchasers of funeral goods and services, marketing of prearranged or pre-need funerals is directed toward them. Funeral providers offer several ways of paying for funeral costs, including funeral insurance and living trust accounts. Funeral insurance is similar to life insurance, except that the proceeds are paid directly to the funeral home. Trust funds can be paid for in one lump sum or by making premium payments. The money is placed in a trust account until the time of death. However, some trusts are irrevocable and the money deposited cannot be refunded except for the purpose for which it was intended. Additionally, some contracts may guarantee prices, while others do not. Guaranteed prices ensure that the cost of the funeral arrangements will be covered. Nonguaranteed prices may mean that the family will be responsible for the extra amount if prices increase.

Consumers are advised to carefully review the arrangements and costs with their family lawyer before entering into any kind of pre-need contract or paying any money. Even though funeral establishments want people to pay now for future services, there is no obligation to pay in advance for prearranging one's funeral. Veterans are accorded special consideration for funerals.

Personal and Social Choices

Historically, families were personally involved in providing last rites for a deceased loved one, rituals were performed at home, and the family disposed of the body. These functions have been replaced by the funeral director in contemporary society, and the modern funeral ceremony is now conducted more formally.

Funeral homes are businesses that function for profit, and professional funeral directors are paid for the services they perform. Emotionally, however, people have mixed feelings about funeral services and costs, and it is essential for funeral directors to be ethical, and perhaps more sensitive than other service providers about the problems and negative emotions sometimes associated with the business side of the funeral experience. One way to avoid such discord is to prearrange the funeral.

Current funeral industry practices allow for individual choice and provide a wide range of services. The costs vary accordingly. There are certain basic expenses, but most are determined by the item selections made. Familiarity with the options and the costs in advance should enable informed decisions about the type of funeral ceremony one prefers. (See also DEATH BENEFITS, ELDER FINANCIAL ABUSE, SOCIAL SECURITY, and VETERANS' BENEFITS.)

References

DeSpelder, Lynne Ann, and Albert Lee Stickland. 1992. *The Last Dance: Encountering Death and Dying*, Third Edition. Mountain View, CA: Mayfield.

Federal Trade Commission (FTC.) 1984. ''Compliance Guidelines: Trade Regulation Rule on Funeral Industry Practices.'' Washington, DC: U.S. Government Printing Office.

Harmer, Ruth M. 1963. *The High Cost of Dying*. New York: Crowell-Collier.

Harris, Diana K. 1990. *Sociology of Aging*, Second Edition. New York: Harper & Row.

Kalish, Richard A. 1985. *Death, Grief and Caring Relationships*, Second Edition. Monterey, CA: Brooks/Cole.

Mitford, Jessica. 1963. *The American Way of Death*. New York: Simon & Schuster.

Weeks, John R. 1994. *Population*, Fifth Edition. Belmont, CA: Wadsworth.

William D. Bland

G

GERIATRIC CARE MANAGERS (GCMs), practitioners with a graduate degree in the field of human services (social work, psychology, gerontology) or a substantial equivalent (e.g., an RN) who specialize in assisting older people and their families with long-term care arrangements. [Care managers are certified by their professional organization and/or licensed to practice by their state.]

Increasingly, individuals and families are turning to geriatric care managers to obtain assistance in caring for frail older relatives. If an older person is experiencing difficulty in taking care of daily needs; is isolated from family, neighbors, and friends; is having difficulty knowing where to turn and what services can help; or wants to do preventive planning, the family may want to consider using the services of a geriatric care manager (Polich et al. 1993).

When an older person becomes frail and in need of assistance, families often face the difficult and time-consuming task of negotiating a complex array of public and nonprofit social service agencies, many of which have waiting lists. Other problems may arise in finding a social or medical service, uncertainty about what a service offers, the need to coordinate services unmet even after receiving support from several agencies, refusal of services or claims, considerations of nursing homes* versus alternatives, or help with locating a good facility (Polich et al. 1993).

Attempting to understand complicated eligibility requirements and locating the most suitable services for an elderly family member can create stress and conflict within families. Relevant questions include whether the older family member has trouble making formerly routine decisions or conducting routine financial affairs, and whether guardianship or conservatorship should be considered. Adult children or grandchildren faced with career and other responsibilities in addition to their caregiving* concerns can seek the assistance of qualified professional care managers.

Possible sources of referral for geriatric care managers are the National Association of Professional Geriatric Care Managers, area agencies on aging, physicians, or home care agencies. Since most family members want to remain involved in a caregiving role, they can use GCMs for initial assessment and periodic consultation. Others, especially those who live far from their aging parent or relative, might retain GCMs to oversee the long-term care plan that has been arranged.

When choosing a private care manager, a number of points merit consideration. Care managers should have training and experience, usually a nursing or social work background. Knowledge of long-term care services, financing mechanisms, and local community resources should be evident. Good communication skills are important, as is a caseload of no more than 50–75 clients. References should be requested from the care manager and investigated (AARP 1989).

The process of obtaining GCM services begins with an assessment of the client's situation, needs, and resources. Next, a service plan is designed and implemented. Services are provided directly by the care manager, the client is referred to another service provider, or the plan is coordinated with other professional resources, such as the family's attorney*, investment counselors, insurance specialists, accountants*, physicians, and hospital staff. During this period, results are monitored to ensure that the client's needs are met, that services are delivered, and that modifications are made as the client's status changes.

Services provided by GCMs include:

• Conducting care plan assessments to identify problems, eligibility for assistance, and need for services

• Screening, arranging, and monitoring in-home assistance or other services

• Reviewing financial, legal, or medical issues and offering referrals to geriatric specialists to avoid future problems and conserve assets

• Providing crisis intervention

• Acting as a liaison to families at a distance, making sure things are going well and alerting families to problems

• Assisting with moving an older person to or from a retirement complex, care home, or nursing home

• Providing consumer education and advocacy

• Offering counseling and support

The cost of geriatric care management can be substantial in the initial evaluation stage, depending on the geographic area serviced and the scope of services offered, and generally fall in the range of $60 to $150 an hour. Once the plan of care is designed, costs recede as the care manager monitors and maintains the services. Payment can be per hour or on a package basis for an assessment, in conjunction with a sliding-fee scale. Most payment for private care management is made directly by the client, family, or caregiver (Parker 1992).

GCMs have recently joined efforts with the National Academy of Certified Care Managers and the Case Management Institute to work toward a credential in geriatric care management. The first credentialing exam is slated for December 1995. Care management credentialing will ensure to consumers or purchasers a standard of quality, as well as provide care managers greater access to liability insurance. (See also ACCOUNTANTS, ATTORNEYS, CAREGIVING FOR THE ELDERLY, FINANCIAL COUNSELING, GUARDIANSHIP, LONG-TERM CARE INSURANCE: A CONSUMER'S GUIDE, and SOCIAL WORK, GERONTOLOGICAL.)

Organizations

American Association of Retired Persons (AARP)
Children of Aging Parents
National Association of Professional Geriatric Care Managers
National Family Caregivers Association

Suggested Reading

American Association of Retired Persons. 1994. *A Checklist of Concerns: Resources for Caregivers.* Washington, DC: AARP.

References

American Association of Retired Persons. 1989. *Care Management: Arranging for Long Term Care.* Washington, DC: AARP.
Cutler, Neal E. 1994. "Caring for Elderly Parents: Where Do You Look for Help?" *Journal of the American Society of CLU & ChFC* 48: 38–41.
Parker, Marcie. 1992. "Private Geriatric Care Management: How Families Are Served." *Journal of Case Management* 1: 108–12.
Polich, Cynthia, Marcie Parker, Deborah Chase, and Margaret Hottinger. 1993. *Managing Health Care for the Elderly.* New York: John Wiley & Sons.

Jihane K. Rohrbacker

GERIATRIC REHABILITATION, concerned with improving the functional status and independence of older persons following acute illness, trauma, or surgery. Rehabilitation is applied to single or multiple conditions. They may be the result of later-life effects of developmental or childhood disabilities, or the outcome of later-life accidents or diseases. The disabling conditions may entail loss of function or ability to care for oneself at home, to perform activities in the community, to work, or to fulfill social roles (Wray and Torres-Gil 1992). Geriatric rehabilitation encompasses services such as physical therapy, occupational therapy, speech therapy, respiratory therapy, and rehabilitative nursing provided to:

• Persons 65 and older, following an illness, trauma, or surgery, such as a stroke, hip fracture, or amputation; and

- Older persons with declining functional ability because of chronic, progressive diseases, such as arthritis, chronic heart disease, neurologic disorders, or chronic obstructive pulmonary disease.

There is a logical conformity between chronic condition rehabilitation and long-term disability rehabilitation, since both address functional deficits and seek to prevent further impairment and resulting disabilities. Given this similarity, geriatric rehabilitation can be described as the treatment of chronic disabilities (Morrison 1993). Ultimately, maintaining a high level of functioning while fostering a dimension of caring are the crux of rehabilitation. Rehabilitation may be considered as a process involving the concepts of prevention, maintenance, restoration, learning, and resettlement (Abdellah 1986), restoring maximum physical functioning through a comprehensive, integrated program of medical and social services.

Older patients receiving rehabilitative care in rehabilitation facilities primarily have diagnoses of cerebrovascular diseases and fractures. In such facilities, a multidisciplinary team of skilled rehabilitation professionals provides appropriate therapies and services. Team members are physiatrists, physicians specializing in rehabilitation, nurses, social workers, psychologists, physical therapists, occupational therapists, and speech therapists.

The most frequent diagnoses requiring physical therapy services are degenerative joint disease, stroke, and other paralysis or neurological disorders. Treatments rendered by a physical therapist may include resistive exercises and gait, transfer, or prosthesis training. Education and training of the patient and family are also important goals of the physical therapist. Occupational therapy services may include evaluating a patient's level of functioning through special testing procedures, teaching persons techniques to enable them to be independent in performing activities of daily living (ADLs), and designing or fitting self-help devices. Frequent diagnoses that lead to referral to an occupational therapist include Parkinson's Disease, arthritis, cardiac diseases, and respiratory diseases. Speech-language pathologists use a variety of clinical methods to restore communication skills.

Organization of Geriatric Rehabilitation

A comprehensive approach to rehabilitation requires coordination across two organizational systems—the health care system and the disability system. Despite increasing evidence of the efficacy and cost-effectiveness of medical rehabilitation in treating older people, few comprehensive geriatric rehabilitation programs exist today. The health care system is not properly structured to promote funding for such programs. Acute-care hospitals are the major source of referrals for individuals needing medical rehabilitation. Rehabilitation services are provided in a wide range of settings: acute-care hospitals themselves, rehabilitation hospitals (inpatient as well as outpatient), skilled nursing facilities (SNFs), comprehensive outpatient rehabilitation facilities (CORFs), physicians' offices, offices of physical therapists in private practice, adult day care facilities, and at home through home health agencies (Katov 1990).

There has been extensive growth in the number of post-acute facilities and institutions where medical rehabilitation services for the elderly are provided since the implementation of Medicare's Prospective Payment System (PPS) for hospitals in 1984. The introduction of PPS reduced hospital lengths of stay and thus increased the demand for post-acute rehabilitation for Medicare* beneficiaries. The number of Medicare-certified SNFs doubled between 1984 and 1993 to more than 11,000 units, and the number of rehabilitation facilities (RFs) rose by 300%. Even more rapid growth occurred in outpatient medical rehabilitation services, including those provided by private practitioners in physical therapy, occupational therapy, and speech pathology (Smith 1994).

The physician, social worker, or rehabilitation professional who determines the most appropriate place for services to be rendered considers several factors: severity of illness, the patient's ability to participate actively in a rehabilitation program, prognosis for improvement, types of facilities available, geographic location, and payment source. Placement of Medicare patients for rehabilitative care in either a rehabilitation facility (hospital or unit) or a skilled nursing facility frequently depends on availability of RF or SNF beds, and regional or physician practice patterns (Kramer et al. 1994).

Since 1987, the Older Americans Act (OAA)* has required states to place an emphasis on coordinating services for older persons with severe disabilities. While the community-based services provided through the OAA were intended to enhance the independence of older persons, rehabilitative care was not included until the 1992 OAA Reauthorization. Now references to rehabilitation specify that preventive health services include home injury control services, programs relating to chronic disabling conditions, and information concerning diagnosis, prevention, treatment, and rehabilitation of age-related diseases and chronic disabling conditions. However, programs addressing the problems of aging are constrained by the relatively small appropriations given to meet the goals of OAA.

Financing Geriatric Rehabilitation

Financing is the most critical issue in the provision of rehabilitative services. Financing refers to what works best and at what cost, that is, the appropriateness of specific treatments and therapies, and the effectiveness and duration of their benefit. Gaps in financing also constitute barriers to services access.

Health maintenance organizations (HMOs) and private health insurance plans generally limit coverage for rehabilitation to short-term physical, occupational, and speech services for up to two months, if it is determined that the patient is likely to show a significant improvement in functioning during that time.

Medicare is the single largest payer of medical care delivered by rehabilitation providers and accounts for almost 70% of rehabilitation facilities' revenue each year (Smith 1994). Medicare coverage for rehabilitation is largely limited to allied health services (e.g., physical therapy, occupational therapy, and speech pathology) deemed "reasonable and necessary" by a physician in terms of duration, efficacy, and frequency. The disability must be related to a recent acute illness or injury. Individuals receive rehabilitation only if their functions are potentially restorable; they must demonstrate steady improvement almost immediately. Once functional improvement ceases, reimbursement is discontinued because "maintenance" therapy is not covered (Katov 1990).

Rehabilitation services, if approved by a physician, can be delivered in a variety of settings, including on an outpatient basis, in a physician's office, or in the community. Medicare eligibility and payment for rehabilitative care differ depending on whether care is provided in a rehabilitation facility or skilled nursing home. In addition to the growth in skilled nursing facilities and rehabilitation facilities offering post-acute rehabilitation services, there are now "sub-acute" SNFs that offer more intensive rehabilitative care than SNFs. The continuum of post-acute rehabilitation providers serving the Medicare population is thus extensive, with differences in cost and intensity of services.

Medicare beneficiaries enrolled under Part A may receive coverage for skilled nursing rehabilitation care following a hospital stay of at least three consecutive days. Direct transfer from a hospital is not required, but admission to an SNF must occur within 30 days after hospital discharge. Physical, occupational, and speech therapy furnished by an SNF are covered if deemed reasonable and necessary, and ordered and reviewed by a physician. Physician visits are also covered. Medicare intermediaries determine coverage for the SNF rehabilitation benefits and services.

The emerging sub-acute units are currently reimbursed as Medicare SNF units. However, a limited number of facilities have been granted exceptions to the routine cost limits, based on case mix and the services provided in these units. To the extent that additional costs in these sub-acute units are the result of rehabilitation services or other ancillary services, reimbursement may be substantially greater because there are no cost limits for these services (Barnett 1994).

Eligibility for admission to a rehabilitation facility (in-patient rehabilitation hospital and units) is based on preadmission screening to select those cases with potential for significant improvement from an intensive rehabilitation program. The criteria are the need for 24-hour availability of rehabilitation physicians and nurses and their services and intensive therapies, as well as related services in a coordinated program. Patients must receive at least three hours a day of physical and/or occupational therapy in addition to any other required care (Katov 1990; Kramer et al. 1994).

Current cost-containment concerns have led to increasing interest by Medicare and managed care systems in providing rehabilitation services on an outpatient basis for persons who do not require nursing care but who have the potential for gains in functional ability. By allowing persons to receive comprehensive services near their homes, comprehensive outpatient rehabilitation facilities provide a good alternative to a full range of rehabilitation services. Medicare requires that CORFs provide physician care, physical therapy, and social or psychological services.

Regarding reimbursement for rehabilitation care, different strategies are currently under consideration for SNFs and RFs. The strategy of the Health Care Financing Administration for prospective payment for SNF services concentrates on payment based on costs *per day* and, for prospective payment for RFs, focuses on payment *per stay*. Given the potential substitution of these settings and the emerging continuum of rehabilitation providers, it would seem preferable to concentrate on a uniform reimbursement approach for rehabilitation diagnoses that could be used across settings (Kramer et al. 1994).

Conclusions

Geriatric rehabilitation is a fairly new health care issue in the United States. Concern about the costs of traditional medical care for older persons has stimulated interest in additional care options. Yet the move toward rehabilitation as a standard component of medical care for older persons has been slow. Historically, rehabilitation has been associated with younger people for whom rehabilitation meant an opportunity to return to work.

This historical bias against rehabilitation for older persons coincides with the tendency of the medical community to view illness or disability from an acute-care perspective. Despite the problems specific to older people, geriatric rehabilitation programs can reduce the incidence of institutionalization and hospitalization. While complete restoration of function may not be possible, rehabilitation often will allow the patient to remain in or return to the community (Katov 1990).

Access to rehabilitation services is restricted by reimbursement problems and a lack of knowledge of geriatric rehabilitation among consumers and health professionals. A recent example of how to improve that knowledge is the publication *Recovering After a Stroke* (Agency for Health Care Policy and Research 1995). This guide shows the merit of proper evaluation, choosing appropriate rehabilitation services, and careful coordination of such services.

A major difficulty with funding systems for geriatric rehabilitation is the lack of sufficient data that show how much money and effort must be applied for maximum rehabilitative results. Research is needed relating to effectiveness of rehabilitation, outcomes for specific diseases, and outcomes according to types of interventions. The trends in research point in the direction of comparative studies involving hospital and sub-acute settings, with a longitudinal perspective of up to three years rather than the 60 to 90 days in customary evaluations (Smith 1994). (See also DISABILITY PROGRAMS, FEDERAL; HEALTH MAINTENANCE ORGANIZATIONS; MEDICARE; OLDER AMERICANS ACT; and PHYSICIAN-ELDERLY PATIENTS RELATIONSHIPS.)

Organizations

American Rehabilitation Association
National Rehabilitation Information Center
Resources for Rehabilitation

Suggested Reading

Resources for Rehabilitation. *Resources for Elders with Disabilities.* Lexington, MA:
    Author.

References

Abdellah, F. G. 1986. ''Public Health Aspects of Rehabilitation of the Aged.'' In *Aging
    and Rehabilitation: Advances in the State of the Art,* ed. S. J. Brody and G. E.
    Ruff. New York: Springer, 47–61.
Agency for Health Care Policy and Research. 1995. *Recovering After a Stroke: Patient
    and Family Guide.* Washington, DC: GPO.
Barnett, Alicia Ault. 1994. ''Subacute Care: High Tech Nursing Homes.'' *Report on
    Long-Term Care* 23 (12 January).
Katov, C. 1990. *Access to Geriatric Rehabilitation Services: A Background Paper.* Wash-
    ington, DC: AARP.
Kramer, Andrew M., Theresa B. Eilertsen, Carol A. Hrincevich, and Robert E. Schlenker.
    1994. *Rehabilitation of Medicare Patients in Rehabilitation Hospitals and Skilled
    Nursing Facilities.* Denver: Center for Health Services Research, University of
    Colorado.
Morrison, Malcolm H. 1993. ''Rehab for an Aging Population.'' *Rehab Management* 6
    (June/July), 36–40.
Smith, Rich. 1994. ''Trends in Medical Rehab.'' *Rehab* (October/November), 33–38.
Wray, Linda A., and Fernando M. Torres-Gil. 1992. ''Availability of Rehabilitation Serv-
    ices for Elders: A Study of Critical Policy and Financing Issues. In *Aging and
    Disabilities: Seeking Common Ground,* ed. E. F. Ansello and N. M. Eustis.
    Amityville, NY: Baywood Publishing, 55–67.

Coral S. Carey

GERONTOLOGICAL NURSE PRACTITIONERS (GNPs), advanced practice
nurses who assess health status and functional abilities; perform and interpret
selected laboratory tests; diagnose common acute and stable chronic illnesses;
develop and implement treatment plans to promote, maintain or restore health;
educate and counsel patients and families; collaborate with other health care
providers as needed; and act as advocates for older adults to improve health
status (American Nurses' Credentialing Center 1994). GNPs base decisions on
scientific data and interpret and use research as a basis for practice. The unifying
theme in all of these functions is a focus on health rather than disease, and an
emphasis on holistic care.

Gerontological nurse practitioners, as advanced practice nurses, are licensed
registered nurses who have a graduate degree in a nursing specialty and are
certified through a recognized certification program. This training prepares them

to provide a full range of health services to older adults and their families. The current expectation is that educational programs for GNPs are at the master's degree level and include academic and clinical practice requirements. Upon completion of an approved educational program, GNPs are eligible to apply for national certification and formal recognition of the nurse practitioner role by state licensing agencies.

Of the 1.8 million nurses employed in 1992, it was estimated that 176,000 were advanced practice nurses (APNs), although a smaller number had positions with this specific title. Of the total, 48,237 were nurse practitioners, but again only 22,000 functioned under this job title. About 58% had national certification, and one-third had a master's degree. As a subcategory, certified geriatric nurse practitioners numbered 1,232, according to the American Nurses Association. Even though there is a strong demand for GNPs, a scarcity of educational and training programs persists (McDougall and Roberts 1993).

History, Scope, and Practice Settings

The nurse practitioner model was initially developed in 1965 by Loretta Ford and Henry Silver at the University of Colorado. At first, it was limited to pediatrics, but quickly expanded to include other specialties, necessitated by population shifts and health care needs. Likewise, the initial development of the GNP role was intended for primary care settings. However, its expansion and the needs of select populations such as older adults, have changed this exclusive focus. Gerontological nurse practitioners now often practice in long-term care and traditional primary care settings, in community-based clinics, health maintenance organizations (HMO)s*, or home health care. In 1981, the American Nurses Association established certification for GNPs.

Gerontological nurse practitioners implement practice arrangements in a variety of ways, including collaborative practice with physicians, as a member of a geriatric consult team, through in-home health agencies, as an employee of a long-term care facility, in an assistive care facility, in an HMO, and in independent nursing practice. In these practice arrangements, GNPs may provide direct care to patients, work with families to improve care or resolve problems, serve as case managers to coordinate a variety of services, consult with or refer to other nurses, physicians, and a variety of health care providers or community agencies, develop or participate in research, or teach students in the health professions. Practice is governed by the standards and ethics of the nursing profession and by standards specifically relating to gerontology and the role of the nurse practitioner.

With the continuing health care crisis and the focus on health care reform at the state level, cost and quality of care have been major issues for many health care providers. Repeatedly, studies have shown that nurse practitioners provide quality health care and perform successfully within an expanded scope of practice. The Office of Technology Assessment (1986), after analyzing numerous studies of nurse practitioners and other providers, concluded that "within their

areas of competence nurse practitioners . . . provide care whose quality is equivalent to that of care provided by physicians.'' Further, the study stated that
''nurse practitioners . . . are more adept than physicians at providing services
that depend on communication with patients and preventive services.'' A study
of GNPs who were employees of nursing homes suggested that GNPs were able
to improve the quality of nursing home care in several areas, including activities
of daily living, nursing therapies, and drug therapies (Kane et al. 1989). This
study also ascertained that GNPs had the potential for reducing costs of hospitalization through lowering the number of hospital stays and decreasing emergency room use.

Barriers to Practice

A recent survey has summarized the most frequently reported barriers to practice as follows: lack of public knowledge about nurse practitioners, resistance
from physicians and psychologists, lack of third-party reimbursement, limitations of facilities, prohibitions on prescribing medication, lack of positions and
peers, and inadequate administrative support (Health Resources and Services
Administration 1993). Certain formal restrictions to practice also exist, many of
which have direct economic consequences. Nurse practitioners are regulated by
professional licensing boards in each state; consequently, practice restrictions
vary greatly (Pearson 1994). The most common restrictions to practice are in
the area of prescriptive authority and third-party reimbursement. Both of these
can have significant impact on access to care.

Prescriptive authority for nurse practitioners varies greatly in the type of drugs
that may be prescribed and the degree of independence of the nurse practitioner.
Three states permit prescribing a full range of drugs without physician involvement, while other states permit prescribing from a formulary of approved drugs
or using developed protocols. Certain states have restricted prescribing by geographic area or to specific underserved sites or populations. There are six states
where no form of prescriptive authority currently exists for nurse practitioners
(Pearson 1994). These restrictions are considered by some to have detrimental
consequences to the advanced practice nurse's professional stature and to the
public's access to health care (Safriet 1992). The need to continually consult
with a physician or seek a physician's signature limits access to care and increases the cost of health care for the public. A recent study (Mahoney 1994)
of geriatric prescribing decisions by nurse practitioners and physicians stated
that the nurse practitioners ''achieved a higher level of appropriate prescribing
than physicians,'' regardless of the nurse practitioner's prescriptive authorization
status. Thus, nurse practitioners can correctly prescribe drugs, enhancing health
care for older adults and increasing access to the health care system.

Additionally, third-party reimbursement has direct financial consequences that
affect the nurse practitioner and the consumer. The federal government, through
the Medicaid* and Medicare* programs, sets standards for reimbursement that
are followed by the states and private insurers. Many nurse practitioners are

eligible for Medicaid reimbursement. Still, there are common restrictions, such as reimbursement at a percentage of the rate that is paid for the same physician service, or the rule that only services that fall within the scope of practice of a pediatric or family nurse practitioner are reimbursed. A GNP's services fall within the scope of practice of a family nurse practitioner working with older adults.

The Medicare program also has permitted reimbursement for services performed by gerontological and other nurse practitioners. Nurse practitioners must be certified to receive direct reimbursement from Medicare or to have prescription-writing authority, which varies by state and drug. Certified nurse practitioners can receive direct reimbursement under Medicare in rural, underserved areas. Thus, the reimbursement is limited to specific situations and requires collaboration with a physician. The reimbursed services include those incident to a physician's services, services through a contract with an HMO, services occurring in a skilled nursing facility, and services performed in a rural area (Safriet 1992). These services are relatively limited in view of the full scope of practice offered by gerontological nurse practitioners. Medicare reimbursement also occurs at a percentage of the fee paid to physicians, and only in rural areas may the nurse practitioner be directly reimbursed.

Outlook

Given the demographic imperative and the importance of deterring institutionalization and improving the effectiveness of nursing home* and community-based care, there is a great need for gerontological nurse practitioners. "Advanced practice nurses are proven providers, and removing the many barriers to their practice will . . . increase their ability to respond to the pressing need for basic health care." (Safriet 1992).

Their role is also an active concern of future research, since HMOs and other managed care settings use GNPs to facilitate effective nursing home and home health care continuity, reduce emergency hospitalization, and monitor medication use. Finally, there is substantial promise in collaborative practice arrangements, in which physicians and GNPs no longer relate hierarchically, which allows independent practice for the GNP, and which permits independent reimbursement. A move toward such formalized, customary collaboration is also serving the primacy of patients' needs. (See also ASSISTED LIVING, CAREGIVING FOR THE ELDERLY, HEALTH MAINTENANCE ORGANIZATIONS, HOME CARE SERVICES FOR THE ELDERLY, MEDICAID, MEDICARE, and NURSING HOMES.)

Organizations

American Academy of Nurse Practitioners
American Nurses Association
National Conference of Gerontological Nurse Practitioners

References

American Nurses' Credentialing Center. 1994. *Certification Catalog.* Washington, DC: Author.

Health Resources and Services Administration, Bureau of Health Professions. 1993. *Registered Nurse Chart Book.* Rockville, MD: Author.

Kane, Robert, Judity Garrard, Carol Skay, David Radosevich, Joan Buchanan, Susan McDermott, Sharon Arnold, and Loyd Kepferle. 1989. "Effects of a Geriatric Nurse Practitioner on Process and Outcome of Nursing Home Care." *American Journal of Public Health* 79: 1271–77.

Mahoney, Diane Feeney. 1994. "Appropriateness of Geriatric Prescribing Decisions Made by Nurse Practitioners and Physicians." *IMAGE: Journal of Nursing Scholarship* 26: 41–46.

McDougall, Graham, and Beverly A. Roberts. 1993. "Gerontological Nurse Practitioners in Every Nursing Home: A Necessary Expenditure." *Geriatric Nursing* 14: 218–20.

Office of Technology Assessment. 1986. *Nurse Practitioners, Physicians Assistants, and Certified Nurse Midwives: A Policy Analysis.* Washington, DC: GPO..

Pearson, Linda. 1994. "Annual Update of How Each State Stands on Legislative Issues Affecting Advanced Nursing Practice." *The Nurse Practitioner* 19: 11–13, 17–18, 21.

Safriet, Barbara. 1992. "Health Care Dollars and Regulatory Sense: The Role of Advanced Practice Nursing." *Yale Journal on Regulation* 9: 417–87.

Linda R. Rounds

GOVERNMENT PROGRAMS. See Age Discrimination Employment Act (ADEA); Disability Programs, Federal; Disaster Assistance and the Elderly; HUD-Assisted Rental Housing; Medicaid; Medicare; Nutrition Programs; Older Americans Act (OAA); Social Security Program of the United States; Supplemental Security Income (SSI); Veterans' Benefits.

GUARDIANSHIP, the legal relationship between a ward and a guardian, usually authorized by the probate or equity divisions of a state court. Wards are persons who have been declared by the courts to be incompetent to make particular decisions on their own behalf. Court-appointed guardians act as surrogate decision makers for the ward.

The underlying rationale for guardianship is the legal doctrine of parens patriae (literally, "father of the land"), the inherent authority and responsibility of a benevolent society to intervene, even over objection, to protect people who cannot protect themselves. Thus, instead of abandoning cognitively incapacitated individuals to a superficial autonomy to make self-harmful decisions or neglect their own basic needs, the state may exercise its authority to protect even unwilling disabled individuals from their own folly or intellectual deficits.

Every adult is presumed to be legally competent to make individual choices. This presumption may be declared invalid and a substitute decision maker appointed only upon a sufficient showing that the individual is mentally unable to take part in a rational decision-making process. A legal ruling of incompetence signifies that a person, because of a lack of capacity to contemplate and weigh choices rationally, cannot care adequately for his or her own person or property.

Guardianship historically has been a matter of state jurisdiction. Every state has enacted statutes that empower the courts to appoint guardians for decisionally incapacitated persons. Most state guardianship statutes are similar in content because they are based on the Uniform Probate Code (UPC), Article 5, although certain variations in the law and its application exist in the United States. These interstate variations have prompted calls for, and the introduction of, federal legislation that would compel states to enact minimum procedural protections for wards and proposed wards, at least where someone other than a family member is the potential or actual guardian. Such federal legislation has not yet been enacted.

The past decade has been a period of substantial reexamination and revision of existing state guardianship statutes on the part of many legislatures. Several states have made substantive changes in their guardianship laws by substituting more objective standards for traditional definitions of incompetence that rely heavily on diagnostic labels (e.g., the person is ''depressed'' or ''demented''). These objective standards are designed to focus on the individual's functional ability to manage personal care or finances on a daily basis. In other words, there is now more focus on the person's ability to meet basic needs rather than just on his or her clinical ''condition.''

State guardianship statutes today typically contain a two-step definition of competence. First, the individual must fall within a specific category, such as old age, mental illness, or developmental disability. Second, the individual must be found to be impaired functionally—that is, unable to care appropriately for his or her own person or property—as a result of being within that category. Incompetence cannot be equated with categorical condition (such as advanced years) alone, so the determination of functional, behavioral, or adaptive disability is essential.

A variety of procedural reforms concerning guardianship have been enacted by the states. They are aimed at assuring potential wards greater due process protections against the unnecessary, premature, or improper loss of decisional rights. These procedural reforms deal with such matters as: who should perform assessments of capacity, with a marked preference for the multidisciplinary and interdisciplinary perspective; the content of the assessor's report to the court; the appointment of outside visitors to supplement the formal assessment; the right to counsel as advocate; the ward's presence at the hearing; more rigorous requirements with regard to petitions; enhanced notice requirements; formalized hearing procedures and rules; and more specificity in the court's findings and in the order appointing the guardian. Reforms have been passed in the spheres of limited and temporary guardianship as well.

States are moving away from referring to the legal status of the ward as ''incompetent,'' and toward the language of ''decisional capacity,'' which reflects movement away from emphasis on diagnostic category or label toward more proper emphasis on an individual's current functional abilities and deficits.

Terminology regarding the judicially created relationship between a decisionally incapacitated person and a surrogate decision maker, however, still varies somewhat among jurisdictions. Although the most common general designation for the court-appointed surrogate is "guardian," some states refer to this entity as a "conservator" (e.g., California). In a majority of states, a court-appointed surrogate with total authority over the ward's personal and financial affairs is called a "plenary" guardian. A surrogate with power over solely financial issues—the disposition of the ward's income and assets—usually is termed a "guardian of the estate" or "conservator." A surrogate decision maker concerning personal (such as medical, residential, and matrimonial) questions only is referred to in most states as a "guardian of the person."

Judicial appointment of a guardian to make decisions on behalf of a person who has been judged incompetent or incapacitated means that the ward no longer retains the legal power to exercise those decisional rights that have been delegated by the court to the guardian. The legal system historically has treated guardianship as an all-or-nothing proposition, with global findings of incompetence accompanied by virtually complete disenfranchisement of the ward. Plenary guardians ordinarily are awarded total power to control all of the ward's financial and personal matters.

The trend lately, however, has been toward statutory recognition of the concept of limited or partial guardianship and toward the encouragement of judicial deference to this concept. Limited or partial guardianship accounts for the decision-specific, waxing and waning nature of mental capacity for many persons and the ability of some people to make certain kinds of choices rationally, but not others. State statutes also have been widely amended recently to permit judges to grant guardianship on a temporary, time-limited basis, rather than the prevalent indefinite orders that shift the burden of proof regarding regained capacity and termination of the guardianship to the ward.

These trends reflect legislative deference to the least restrictive alternative (LRA), sometimes called the least intrusive alternative, principle concerning state impingement of an individual's rights to personal autonomy. Under limited, partial, or temporary guardianships, courts fashion their orders to delineate explicitly the particular and exclusive types of decisions that the ward is incapable of making and over which the guardian may exercise proxy authority, with the remaining powers residing with the ward. Limited, partial, or temporary guardianship statutes may be permissive, allowing but not requiring courts to carefully tailor the guardian's power to the ward's needs, or they may mandate that the powers of the guardian be drawn as narrowly as possible. Even in the absence of legislation, state courts have general equity jurisdiction to create limited, partial, or temporary guardianships sua sponte (on their own initiative.)

A number of policy considerations argue against overuse of the formal legal mechanism of guardianship. Guardianships frequently are expensive, time-consuming, emotionally draining, and result in unnecessary deprivation of basic civil liberties. In many cases, guardianships provide the ward with little meaningful protection against abuse and exploitation.

Much attention has been devoted recently to exploring and developing viable alternatives to guardianship that strike an acceptable accommodation between protection and independence. In the past decade, there has been a significant movement toward greater reliance on these less restrictive and intrusive alternatives to guardianship for older individuals with compromised cognitive and emotional abilities.

Mechanisms that may delay or obviate the need for guardianship to manage one's financial affairs include, but are not limited to: joint bank and other financial accounts, case management, daily money management programs, living or *inter vivos* trusts, durable powers of attorney*, and representative payee designations for government benefit checks. (See also ADVANCE DIRECTIVES, DURABLE POWER OF ATTORNEY, ELDER LAW PRACTICE, ETHICS IN FINANCIAL PLANNING, FINANCIAL ELDER ABUSE, LIVING WILLS, and TRUSTS.)

Organizations

American Bar Association
Legal Counsel for the Elderly
National Academy of Elder Law Attorneys
National Senior Citizens Law Center

References

Foehner, Charlotte, and Carol Cozart. 1988. *The Widow's Handbook.* Golden, CO: Fulcrum.

Maddox, George L., ed. 1987. *The Encyclopedia of Aging.* New York: Springer.

Stiegel, Loria A. 1992. *Alternatives to Guardianship: Substantive Training Materials and Module for Professionals Working with the Elderly and Persons with Disabilities.* Washington, DC: American Bar Association.

U.S. Congress, Senate Special Committee on Aging. 1993. *Innovative Approaches to Guardianship: Workshop Before the Special Committee on Aging.* Washington, DC: U.S. Government Printing Office.

Marshall B. Kapp

H

HEALTH AND LONGEVITY, population characteristics with significant social and economic implications, as a result of medical advances and improved living conditions and lifestyles.

Life Expectancy and Mortality Patterns

The U.S. population aged 65 and older has grown rapidly, which is attributable to declining mortality rates across the entire life span, improved life expectancy, and improved health care. In 1900, a 65-year-old person could expect to live 11.9 additional years to age 77; by 1992, life expectancy at age 65 increased 17.5 years to about age 82. Comparison of life expectancy tables with other industrialized nations shows that the United States ranked 23rd for men and 16th for women in 1990 (National Center for Health Statistics [NCHS] 1994a), suggesting room for even more improvement.

Mortality rates have declined for all persons. Women and blacks have shown the most rapid decreases and greatest relative gains in life expectancy. Between 1950 and 1992, women gained 7.9 years of life expectancy compared with 6.7 years for men. Blacks gained 9.1 years compared with 7.4 years for whites.

In 1991, deaths of persons aged 65 and older totaled 1.6 million, or 78.6% of all deaths. The leading causes of elderly deaths are heart diseases, malignant neoplasms, cerebrovascular diseases, chronic obstructive pulmonary diseases, and pneumonia and influenza (NCHS 1994a). Death rates for all causes, except cancer, have been declining. Factors responsible for the substantial declines in mortality from heart disease and stroke during the past three decades include improved medical care and interventions, greater availability of coronary care units, advanced surgical and medical treatment of coronary heart disease, improved control of high blood pressure, decreased smoking, modified eating habits, increased exercise, and healthier lifestyles.

Health Status

The health status of the elderly can be measured by their own perception of their health, limitations in their usual activities, and restricted-activity and bed-disability days. In 1991, more than 35 million persons, 14.3% of the noninstitutionalized population, reported limitations of activity due to chronic diseases. The rate of activity limitation increases with age, from 5.8% for those under age 18 to 44.2% for persons over age 75. Among persons aged 65 and older limited in activity due to chronic conditions, more than half reported fair or poor health compared with others their age, and they reported 72 restricted-activity days per person per year and 32.6 bed-disability days, a subset of restricted-activity days.

The prevalence of specific, chronic conditions causing limitations of activity among the noninstitutionalized elderly is high. In 1992, 48% had arthritis, 36% had hypertension, and 32% had heart conditions. Many elderly persons suffered from impairments: 32% had hearing impairments, 19% had orthopedic impairments, and 17% had cataracts (NCHS 1994b).

Many elderly suffer from multiple chronic conditions (MCCs) and disabilities. These activity-limiting conditions increase with age. About 9% of people have one condition and 5% have two or more conditions, but the proportion with two or more conditions increases more rapidly with age. For those under age 18, 5% have one condition and fewer than 1% have two conditions; by age 75 and older, 22% have one condition and an equal proportion have two or more conditions.

The numbers of restricted-activity and bed-disability days are significantly affected by the number of conditions. Persons with one chronic condition causing activity limitation report 47 restricted-activity days and 18 bed days per person per year. Those with two or more conditions report about twice that amount (NCHS 1994b).

Medical Care Use

Use of health services increases with age, and the elderly consume health services in amounts disproportionate to their numbers in the population. Elderly people visit physicians and are hospitalized more frequently than younger people. In 1992, persons aged 65 and older comprised 12.2% of the noninstitutionalized population, but they had 21.6% of 1.5 trillion physician visits, 29.1% of 27 million short-stay hospital discharges, and 38.7% of 163 million hospital days. Less than 5% of the civilian noninstitutionalized population was 75 years and older in 1992, yet this group accounted for 9.9% of all physician visits, 13.9% of hospital discharges, and 20.2% of the hospital days (NCHS 1994b).

Older persons who suffer from chronic and disabling conditions heavily utilize medical resources. In 1991, noninstitutionalized elderly people with chronic conditions causing activity limitation saw physicians on average 15.3 times a year, in contrast to 8.7 times for persons under age 18. Multiple chronic conditions cause the number of physician visits to rise to over 50%, from 11.1 visits for those reporting one cause of activity limitation to 17.2 for those with two or more causes.

The number of hospital days varies with age and the number of conditions. The elderly with two or more chronic conditions causing activity limitation had 47.5 hospitalizations per 100 persons per year, in contrast to 35.5 for those with one condition. Combinations of these patterns support the hypothesis that multiple chronic conditions create a significantly greater burden than one condition, and that the burden increases with age.

According to the 1991 National Health Provider Inventory, about 4.2% of the elderly aged 65 and older and 17.5% of persons aged 85 years and older (the "oldest old*") are in nursing homes (NCHS 1994c). An additional 413,040 people were in board and care homes*, of which half were elderly persons. Other chronically ill elderly persons were in psychiatric or other chronic disease hospitals, Veterans Administration hospitals, and other long-term care facilities. Generally, elderly residents of nursing homes suffer from multiple chronic conditions and functional impairments. The elderly's risk of institutionalization is estimated at about 40% (Kemper and Murtaugh 1991).

Long-Term Care Needs

Most elderly persons who have lost some capacity for self-care require a wide range of social, personal, and supportive services. Long-term care (LTC) is defined as physical care over a prolonged period for those persons incapable of sustaining themselves without this care. Long-term care includes a spectrum of services responding to different needs across a range of chronic illness and disability. To address the multiple and varied LTC needs of the aged population, services must cross the boundaries between income maintenance and health, social, and housing programs.

About 12 million persons require LTC, when defined as needing assistance in either activities of daily living (ADLs) or instrumental activities of daily living (IADLs.) ADLs include basic tasks of everyday life such as eating, bathing, dressing, toileting, and getting in and out of bed; IADLs encompass a range of activities such as handling personal finances, preparing meals, shopping, traveling, doing housework, using the telephone, and taking medications. Approximately 43% of LTC users are working-age adults or children, and 57% (7.3 million persons) are elderly. Of the 12.8 million persons who need LTC, 10.4 million live in the community and 2.3 million live in institutions such as nursing homes*, chronic care hospitals, or other facilities (General Accounting Office 1994). Family and friends, rather than paid personnel, provide the bulk of LTC services on an informal basis. The availability of home care services for the elderly* often plays a significant role in sustaining the capacity of the elderly and disabled to maintain their personal independence and often determines admission into institutions. Caregiving* is assumed to be women's responsibility because the home has traditionally been considered the women's domain and caring a natural female characteristic.

A wide range of organizations, professionals, and paraprofessionals are involved in the delivery of LTC. Long-term care services can be delivered in a variety of settings: a client's own home, community foster homes, multipurpose senior centers, day hospitals, day programs*, and residential settings, including sheltered housing, board and care homes, residential hotels, old-age homes, nursing homes, rehabilitation centers, and mental hospitals.

With growing numbers of chronically ill elderly and disabled adults, increased consideration is being given to alternatives in providing LTC services and preventing the need for high cost institutionalization. Research and demonstrations in the United States have focused on LTC needs, service systems, and financing for the elderly. Recent years have seen the development of a variety of community services such as day care, home health, meals-on-wheels, and respite care. Most of these services are aimed at maintaining the independence of the aged or disabled person at home to avoid institutional placement, often viewed as a measure of last resort.

Research studies in the United States have suggested that the provision of community-based, noninstitutional services has generally raised health care costs because limited reductions in institutional care are more than offset by the increased demand for and use of community-based care. Others suggest that evaluation of community-based care should consider the benefits associated with reinforcing existing informal support networks and meeting the preferences of the elderly and their caregivers, in addition to the cost-effectiveness of the services provided.

According to the Health Care Financing Administration, about 11% of the $884.2 billion national health expenditures in 1993 were spent on LTC. Of this total, 36% comes from personal resources and the remaining 64% from public sources—41% from Medicaid*, and 23% from other public sources, such as Medicare*. Private LTC insurance* represents only 1 to 2% of total LTC dollars. In 1993, more than twice as much was spent on institutional care as on community-based care. Expenditures for home health care are the fastest-growing component of national personal health care expenditures. In 1993, $24.9 billion, 3% of the total, was spent for home health care services (Levit et al. 1994).

Financing Medical Care of the Aged

Although 12% of the population was aged 65 and older in 1987, this group accounted for 36% of all personal health expenditures. Children and youth under age 19, 29% of the population, accounted for 12% of total spending; adults aged 19 to 64 comprised 59% of the population and accounted for 52% of total spending. For the elderly, private funds paid 35% of personal health care spending and public funds paid 65%, of which Medicare paid for 42%, Medicaid paid 16%, and the remaining 7% came from the Veterans Administration.

The idea that medical care is a basic right, along with food, clothing, and shelter, was greatly enhanced by the enactment of Medicare and Medicaid in 1965. Medicare is a national health insurance program for the aged and disabled that is administered by the federal government. It is the single largest health insurer in the country, covering virtually all elderly persons 65 years and older and certain persons with disabilities or kidney failure. Medicare outlays in 1993 amounted to $151.1 billion (Levit et al. 1994). Over 32 million elderly persons were enrolled in the Medicare program, and about 80% (25.2 million) used Medicare services. Medicare covers less than one-half of the total medical care expenses of the elderly. To pay for medical coinsurance and, in some cases, uncovered benefits, about 75% of the elderly Medicare beneficiaries have Medicare Supplemental Insurance (''Medigap'')*. Despite all these sources, the elderly spend an increasing share of their after-tax income on health expenses, increasing from 7.8% in 1972 to 12.5% in 1988 (De Lew et al. 1992). The burden of increasing health expenses as a share of after-tax income is even greater for the oldest old due to their higher utilization of home health services.

Medicaid covers low-income aged, blind, disabled, pregnant, and dependent children, and is jointly financed by federal and state governments. Of the 31.2 million Medicaid recipients in 1992, 12% were age 65 and older, accounting for 32% of the expenditures under the program (NCHS 1994a).

Expenditures in the Last Year of Life

Various studies have shown that elderly people approaching death or institutionalization have high expenditures for medical care. In 1978, the 1.1 million Medicare enrollees in their last year of life represented 5.9% of all enrollees, but accounted for 28.2% of program expenditures. Medicare users who died in 1978 were reimbursed for all covered services in their last year, about four times the amount reimbursed for services provided to survivors. Lubitz and Riley (1993) found that Medicare payments per person increased nearly fourfold among all elderly persons and among decedents between 1976 and 1988. However, the percentage of total dollars spent for decedents changed little, fluctuating between 27.2% and 30.6%, and the percentage that decedents represented of all enrollees fluctuated between 5.1% and 5.4%. The high medical costs preceding death are not a new phenomenon, and available data do not support the assumption that high medical expenses preceding death are due largely to aggressive, intensive treatment of patients who are moribund. The data suggest that most sick people who die are given the medical care generally provided to the sick, and sick care is expensive.

Future Morbidity Patterns

The incidence of chronic illness increases with age and becomes a major cause of disability requiring medical care. The cost of care for chronic illness sufferers accounts for a large proportion of national health care expenditures. Health trends of middle-aged and older persons beginning in the late 1950s paradoxically include longevity and declining health. Declining health, as reflected in the increasing prevalence of many chronic conditions, is attributed to greater awareness of diseases due to earlier diagnosis and earlier accommodations to disease. Longevity, as reflected in decreased mortality rates, may be attributed to earlier and more effective diagnosis and treatment, earlier and more effective self-care after diagnosis, and possibly lower incidence of some chronic diseases. Changing morbidity and mortality play an important part in estimating future illness patterns and in developing population projections, and considerable conjecture and controversy have arisen about future morbidity patterns. A review of the evidence suggests that the number of oldest old is increasing rapidly, the average period of diminished vigor will probably rise, chronic diseases will probably occupy a larger proportion of our life span, and the needs for medical care in later life are likely to increase substantially. Also possible are increases in the number of individuals in good health nearly up to the point of death and an increasing number with prolonged severe functional limitations, with a decline in the duration of infirmity. The effect on the prevalence of morbidity would depend on the relative magnitude of the various changes. Models linking morbidity and mortality can be developed to predict how healthy or ill the older population will be in the future.

A recent study indicates that the prevalence of chronic disability in the elderly may have declined from 1984 to 1989 (Manton et al. 1993), due to increased education and income among the elderly and improvements in mortality rates. Despite the 1984–1989 disability decline, the aging of the population will have a significant absolute impact on medical care use and future health expenditures. Applying current age-specific rates of use of physician services, hospital days of care, and per capita health expenditures to the Bureau of the Census population projections shows that more than one in five persons (20.7%) will be aged 65 and older by the year 2040 and will utilize 37% of physician visits, 53% of the hospital days of care, and comprise 54% of the nation's total personal health care expenditures.

How closely these population projections will correspond to future demographic changes is uncertain. Several demographers question the assumptions made by the Bureau of the Census and the Social Security Administration, and they project more elderly persons in the future. The interaction of future demographic changes and changing disability prevalence is unclear. Whatever else happens, however, the projected growth in the number of very old persons would have a significant impact on the need and demand for medical and long-term care services. (See also ADVANCE DIRECTIVES, BOARD AND CARE HOMES, CAREGIVING FOR THE ELDERLY, HOME CARE SERVICES FOR THE ELDERLY, LIVING WILLS, LONG-TERM CARE INSURANCE: PRIVATE MEDICAID, MEDICAID PLANNING, MEDICARE, and NURSING HOMES.)

References

De Lew, Nancy, George Greenberg, and Kraig Kinchen. 1992. "A Layman's Guide to the U.S. Health Care System." *Health Care Financing Review* 14: 151–69.

General Accounting Office. 1994. *Long Term Care: Diverse Growing Population Includes Millions of Americans of All Ages.* Washington, DC: GAO.

Kemper, Peter, and Christopher M. Murtaugh. 1991. "Lifetime Use of Nursing Home Care." *New England Journal of Medicine* 324: 595–600.

Levit, Katherine R. et al. 1994. "National Health Expenditures, 1993." *Health Care Financing Review* 16: 247–294.

Lubitz, James, and Gerald F. Riley. 1993. "Trends in Medicare Payments in the Last Year of Life." *New England Journal of Medicine* 328: 1092–96.

Manton, Kenneth G., Larry S. Corder, and Eric Stallard. 1993. "Estimates of Change in Chronic Disability and Institutional Incidence and Prevalence Rates in the U.S. Elderly Population From 1982, 1984, and 1989 National Long Term Care Survey." *Journal of Gerontology: Social Sciences* 48: S153–66.

National Center for Health Statistics (NCHS.) 1994a. *Health, United States 1993.* Hyattsville, MD: Public Health Service.

National Center for Health Statistics (NCHS.) 1994b. "Current Estimates from the National Health Interview Survey: United States, 1992." *Vital and Health Statistics,* Series 10, No. 1890. Washington, DC: GPO.

National Center for Health Statistics (NCHS.) 1994c. "Nursing Homes and Board and Care Homes: Data From the 1991 National Provider Survey." *Advance Data from Vital and Health Statistics* 244. Washington, DC: GPO.

Dorothy P. Rice

HEALTH CARE. See Board and Care Homes; Day Programs for Adults; Drugs and the Elderly; Geriatric Care Managers (GCMs); Geriatric Rehabilitation; Gerontological Nurse Practitioners (GNPs); Home Care Services for the Elderly; Hospice Care; Mental Health among the Elderly; Nursing Homes; Nutrition Programs; Pharmacists; Physician-Elderly Patient Relationships; Social Work, Gerontological.

HEALTH INSURANCE. See Health Maintenance Organizations (HMOs); Long-Term Care Insurance: Private; Medicaid; Medicare Supplemental Insurance; Medicare; Post Retirement Health Insurance (PRHI).

HEALTH MAINTENANCE ORGANIZATIONS (HMOs), health care option combining insurance and the provision of medical care in one entity. Instead of separate roles for the insurer and provider, a Health Maintenance Organization vertically integrates these functions. Enrollees are provided with comprehensive health care in exchange for a prepaid premium. Care is typically available through a limited number of providers at selected sites. HMOs have been operating in the U.S. health care market for several decades and this industry has rapidly grown, particularly in the 1990s.

The organizational structure of HMOs varies. Some HMOs hire physicians who then function as employees. This type of organization is called a staff-model HMO. Others provide managed health care for their members through the use of contract physicians. Physician remuneration in these organizations is usually determined on a capitation basis and consists of a fixed, prearranged fee for each patient. The physician is contracted to provide a certain level or specific types of care, but is not put at risk in the event of catastrophic illness, for example. An HMO that contracts with a single group practice of physicians is called a group-model HMO, whereas one that contracts with a network of group practices is a network-model HMO. Independent practice associations (IPAs) are HMOs that contract with a large number of small group practices of physicians. In 1993, IPAs accounted for more than 60% of all HMOs.

Another type of HMO that is increasingly offered for active worker health care coverage is known as a point of service plan. It incorporates some of the elements of traditional fee-for-service (FFS) coverage into the HMO framework and may become part of the Medicare HMO offerings as well.

More and more Medicare* beneficiaries are joining managed care plans, either HMOs or Competitive Medical Plans (CMPs). Both HMOs and CMPs contract with Medicare and follow the same contracting rules. Medicare enrollment in HMOs has grown since the first demonstration plans were initiated by Medicare in 1982. By 1995, 3.2 million beneficiaries were members of Medicare HMOs, almost one-half of them in IPAs. These enrollees account for about 9.0% of the total Medicare population (General Accounting Office [GAO], 1995).

The following discussion addresses the risk contract program offered to Medicare enrollees, the largest Medicare HMO program, which served 76% of all beneficiaries in HMOs in 1994. It covers about 7% of Medicare beneficiaries. Another 2% of Medicare beneficiaries belong to HMOs with cost contracts or health care prepayment plans that reimburse HMOs on a cost basis (GAO 1995).

HMO Advantages and Disadvantages

Medicare enrollees in HMOs enjoy several advantages. In most cases, Medicare Part A (hospital insurance) and Part B (medical insurance) deductibles and coinsurance are covered. There are no 20% Part B copayments; instead, HMOs may charge a modest per-visit fee. HMOs, by definition, "accept assignment" or agree to charge no more than Medicare's approved amount. They usually include coverage of preventive health services, such as physical examinations, immunizations, and eye exams. In some cases, coverage of outpatient mental health services is extended. There also may be coverage for prescription drugs or eyeglasses, with copayment. Finally, reduced paperwork is a clear advantage, since claim forms are not required.

Medicare recipients often purchase supplemental health coverage, called Medigap insurance, to cover some of the costs not paid by Medicare (copayment and deductibles). Enrollment in an HMO is a low-cost alternative to buying Medigap insurance that can reduce the out-of-pocket cost of health care. Approximately half of Medicare HMOs charge no monthly premium for the additional coverage of copayments and deductibles. Most plans charge a monthly premium.

There are several disadvantages associated with Medicare enrollment in HMOs. Restrictions on choice of provider are always present. Beneficiaries must use only doctors and hospitals associated with the HMO, except in emergencies. If a beneficiary has a regular physician not associated with the HMO, he or she must leave that physician and choose another affiliated physician in order for medical visits to be covered. HMOs require selection of a primary care physician who will be responsible for care management and will control referrals to specialists. Some HMOs have relatively little experience serving the needs of older people. Some may be newly organized with an uncertain or unproven future. Spending longer than three months of the year outside of the service area may cause termination of membership. If a Medicare beneficiary takes long trips or travels frequently, Medicare HMO enrollment is not a good choice. A disadvantage for the rural elderly is that HMO-affiliated providers and hospitals are typically located in urban areas.

Background and Trends

The Tax Equity and Fiscal Responsibility Act (TEFRA) of 1982 provided greater incentives for HMOs to enroll Medicare beneficiaries than had previously existed under the 1972 amendments to the Social Security Act. Under TEFRA, HMOs can be reimbursed under two types of contracts: cost contracts and at-risk contracts. Cost contracts pay HMOs for reasonable costs up to 100% of the adjusted average cost per enrollee. TEFRA risk contracts represent a major change. They pay HMOs prospectively for their enrollees at a rate of 95% of the adjusted average per capita cost (AAPCC). The AAPCC is the actuarially estimated per capita amount that would be payable if Medicare services for HMO members were provided by fee-for-service insurance. In addition to the AAPCC, another key cost estimation is based on the adjusted community rate, or ACR. The ACR is equivalent to the premium that the HMO would have charged Medicare enrollees for an equivalent benefit package. If any surplus arises between the 95% of the AAPCC paid to the HMO and the HMO's ACR, the health maintenance organization must use these funds to either provide additional benefits or to lower premiums.

TEFRA risk provisions did encourage growth in Medicare HMO enrollment. During 1993–1994, TEFRA risk enrollment grew at a rate of 23%. The growth rate of enrollment of Medicare beneficiaries in HMOs in 1995 is expected to be 30% (GAO 1995).

Characteristics of Enrollees

An evaluation of TEFRA risk contracts completed in 1992 identified characteristics associated with beneficiaries who enrolled and did not enroll in Medicare HMOs. Responses to a survey of enrollees indicated that HMOs were more likely to appeal to Medicare beneficiaries who were younger, who had lower income, who lacked Medigap insurance, and who did not have a regular provider (Brown et al. 1993).

Empirical evidence suggests that basic differences in health status and utilization do indeed exist between beneficiaries who do and do not enroll in HMOs. Studies have consistently found that, relative to beneficiaries with non-HMO coverage, Medicare HMO enrollees typically have lower Medicare expenditures in the years prior to their enrollment (Brown 1988). Healthier persons tend to join HMOs. A comparison of differences in mortality rates between HMO and fee-for-service (FFS) enrollees also suggests biased selection. A study by the General Accounting Office (1986) of enrollees in Florida HMOs concluded that the mortality rates for HMO enrollees were nearly 25% lower than those of FFS enrollees.

Satisfaction and Consumer Issues

An HMO must maintain the satisfaction of its members in order to maintain enrollment. A survey of 1,957 Medicare beneficiaries in 1988 asked the recipients to rate satisfaction levels regarding a number of aspects of their HMO and FFS plans. Approximately 80% of the respondents from both plan types reported being ''very satisfied'' overall, with no significant difference between the two groups (Rossiter et al. 1988). There were specific areas in which the beneficiaries had significant differences in satisfaction levels by type of plan. For example, HMO enrollees were less satisfied with the perceived professional competence of their providers and with the willingness of HMO staff to discuss problems with them. On the other hand, HMO enrollees were significantly more satisfied than FFS patients with waiting times and with the effort required to process claims. When HMO members were asked whether they were more satisfied now than with prior care, 29% said yes, while 9% said satisfaction had declined. These results support the view that those who join and maintain enrollment in HMOs enjoy an overall improvement in satisfaction and are as satisfied as those who remain in FFS plans.

Another way in which satisfaction with HMOs would be demonstrated is through persistence in enrollment. Medicare enrollees are free to disenroll from an HMO and join an FFS plan. Two surveys of HMO demonstration enrollees, conducted one year apart, revealed that 15% of the sample had disenrolled from their original HMO by the time of the second survey. Of these, almost 25% had subsequently joined another HMO (Langwell and Hadley 1989).

Disenrollees tended to be poorer, more likely to prefer seeing the same physician, more likely to rate their prior source of care as excellent, and generally in worse health. These are characteristics of Medicare beneficiaries who have higher utilization patterns, and therefore present the possibility of adverse selection to the subsequent FFS plan. Adverse selection means enrolling good risks at the expense of other health insurers.

Individuals first enrolling in HMOs may want to keep their Medicare supplemental policy or Medigap coverage until they are comfortable with the plan. Should they choose to disenroll for whatever reasons, then Medigap coverage would be available. Medicare beneficiaries can disenroll from a risk-contract HMO at any time by submitting a signed and dated request for disenrollment to the HMO or to a Social Security Administration office. Regular fee-for-service Medicare coverage will be effective the following month. HMOs or CMPs serving Medicare enrollees are required to have an appeals procedure for enrollees who request reconsideration for denied services or claims. HMOs must complete reconsideration requests within 60 days. Medicare HMO enrollees also have the right to request immediate review by a Medicare Peer Review Organization for claims of early discharge from hospitals. Enrollees can appeal to HCFA and also have a right to judicial-level appeals.

Health Outcomes and Cost Effectiveness

Studies examining whether HMO enrollees have functional outcomes similar to those of FFS enrollees have found no significant health care differences between the two populations (Brown et al. 1993). Comparing several measurements of functional capacity and health care outcomes, such as activities of daily living, mortality, readmissions, and status at discharge, studies suggest that the quality of care provided by HMOs is similar to that provided by FFS plans.

With regard to the cost impact of HMO enrollment on the Medicare program, researchers have concluded that, as a result of the favorable selection into Medicare HMOs, the Health Care Financing Administration is spending approximately 5.7% more than it would have spent if HMO enrollees had been in a fee-for-service plan (Brown et al. 1993). HCFA pays HMOs 95% of the AAPCC, and therefore expects to save 5% in cost of care. The presence of favorable selection results in enrollees' utilization patterns that are, on average, 10% less than their FFS counterparts. The program requires that the HMO use excess payments to lower premiums or increase benefits, and they do, in fact, fulfill that requirement. Thus, the TEFRA risk contracts seem to have had the net effect of subsidizing health benefits for some elderly Medicare enrollees; they have not had the effect of saving Medicare the intended 5% of cost.

Summary

HMO enrollment for Medicare beneficiaries is an attractive, cost-saving option for many elderly. Restrictions on provider choice and hard-to-access locations remain drawbacks, but out-of-pocket savings can be significant. Quality of care, as evidenced by health status outcomes and satisfaction levels, is comparable to fee-for-service plans. The number of Medicare enrollees in HMOs continues to grow.

From a policy perspective, the cost-saving effectiveness of the Medicare HMO capitation scheme is doubtful. Cost impact studies have estimated Medicare program overpayment for health care as compared with FFS payment. Better risk adjustment for underlying health status is essential for improving the fairness, viability, and participation of Medicare managed care plans. Medicare may consider providing incentives to increase the number of enrollees in an HMO plan, as well as increasing higher-risk enrollment, in order to neutralize selection. Also of importance for the future is how to effectively manage the treatment of chronic disease in managed care and maintain the quality of care. (See also MEDICARE, MEDICARE SUPPLEMENTAL INSURANCE, POST-RETIREMENT HEALTH INSURANCE, and SOCIAL SECURITY.)

Organizations

Group Health Association of America
Health Care Financing Administration
Medicare Beneficiaries Defense Fund

Suggested Readings

Brown, Randall S., Dolores G. Clement, Jerrold W. Hill, Sheldon M. Retchin, and Jeanette W. Bergeron. 1993. "Do Health Maintenance Organizations Work for Medicare?" *Health Care Financing Review* 15: 7–24.
Medicare Beneficiaries Defense Fund. 1994. *Medicare Health Maintenance Organizations: Are They Right for You?* New York: Author.

References

Brown, Randall S. 1988. *Biased Selection in the Medicare Competition Demonstrations.* Washington, DC: Mathematica Policy Research.
Brown, Randall S., Dolores G. Clement, Jerrold W. Hill, Sheldon M. Retchin, and Jeanette W. Bergeron. 1993. *The Medicare Risk Program for HMOs.* Report prepared for HCFA. Washington, DC: Mathematica Policy Research.
General Accounting Office. 1986. *Medicare Issues in Florida Health Maintenance Organizations.* Washington, DC: GAO.
General Accounting Office. 1995. *Enrollment Growth Underscores Need to Revamp HMO Payment Methods.* Washington, DC: GAO.
Langwell, Kathryn M., and James P. Hadley. 1989. "Evaluation of the Medicare Competition Demonstration." *Health Care Financing Review* 11: 65–79.
Rossiter, Louis F. et al. 1988. *Analysis Report of Patient Satisfaction for Enrollees and Disenrollees in Medicare Risk-Based Plans.* Washington, DC: Mathematica Policy Research.

Monica Cain

HOME CARE SERVICES FOR THE ELDERLY, services provided in the home to promote, maintain, and restore health, or to minimize the effects of illness and disability. Home care encompasses a broad continuum of medical, therapy, and social services, ranging from high-technology medical services, such as intravenous therapy and other skilled medical and therapy services, to low-technology, nonmedical services, such as homemaker services and personal care. Home care can be for short-term purposes, such as postacute or rehabilitative care after a hospital discharge or care for the terminally ill, or for long-term purposes, such as assistance with activities of daily living (ADLs) for persons with chronic disabilities.

The Home Care Market

Much of the existing information focuses on the medically oriented market segment of the home care market; less information is available concerning non-medical home care. To provide this wide range of services, there are various types of home care personnel, such as registered nurses, home health aides, social workers, physical, occupational and speech therapists, personal assistance attendants, and homemaker and chore workers. The medically oriented services are more likely to be covered by insurance. There appears to be a trend toward increasing medicalization of home care, even though there is a clear role for nonmedical services.

Although home health care accounts for only a small portion of national health expenditures (less than 3%), it has been one of the fastest growing categories of personal health care expenditures in recent years. A total of $24.9 billion was spent in 1993 on home health care (Levit et al. 1994). However, this amount does not include nonmedical home care services such as homemaker or social services. Also excluded are nursing services from nurse registries that are part of temporary help agencies.

A more comprehensive estimate of home care expenditures is available from the National Medical Care Expenditure Survey (NMES), which uses a broader definition of home care services. The 1987 NMES estimated that $11.6 billion was spent on home care. If one compares this amount with the revised 1987 estimate of $6.9 billion for medically oriented care from the National Health Expenditure Accounts, the medically oriented home care expenditures represent only 60% of all home care expenditures. It is unknown what the relative proportions of medical and nonmedical home care are currently, because national data are not available on the nonmedical segment. Two studies have updated the 1987 NMES expenditure number, based on different assumptions about the rates of growth. The estimates for all home care are $23.7 billion and $29.9 billion in 1994, respectively (National Association for Home Care [NAHC] 1994). However, these estimates would seem to be low, given that the 1993 estimate for medically oriented care alone is $24.9 billion and given that medically oriented care was only 60% of the total market in 1987.

A number of factors account for the tremendous growth of home care services. There are demographic changes, such as the increasing number of elderly 85 years or older; technological advances that have made home care more feasible for many services formerly delivered in inpatient settings; and policy changes, such as increased public financing through the Medicare and Medicaid programs and the implementation of the Medicare Prospective Payment System (PPS). Finally, surveys and polls indicate that the elderly prefer to receive care in the home if possible.

Home Care Providers

Providers of home care services can be classified into the following categories: (1) agencies certified by the federal government; (2) uncertified agencies, which may or may not be licensed; (3) home care workers from employment or temporary personnel agencies or nurse registries; and (4) independent providers, either through a formal contract or an informal arrangement. These provider types have differing regulatory requirements, payment arrangements, and care characteristics. For example, only agencies certified by the federal government can receive Medicare reimbursement. These agencies must provide skilled nursing services and at least one therapy service and meet other conditions of participation. Home health agencies are the market segment typically licensed by states, even if they are not federally certified. Many agencies that are licensed are also certified, but not all; one study estimated that about 70% of licensed home health agencies in 1993 were also certified. Certified agencies may have higher charges than noncertified agencies due to more stringent training and supervision requirements (Harrington et al. 1994).

Statistics on the first two categories (agency providers) exist but vary depending on the criteria used to define home care; statistics on the other categories, specific to home care, are nonexistent. Using a broad definition to include both medical and nonmedical providers, the National Association of Home Care (NAHC) identified 15,027 home care agencies in the United States as of March 1994, of which 7,521 were Medicare-certified home health agencies (HHAs), another 1,459 were Medicare-certified hospices*, and the remaining 6,047 were home care providers and hospices not participating in the Medicare program (NAHC 1994). Thus, Medicare-certified agencies account for 60% of the official home care agency providers.

In addition to Medicare patients, certified agencies serve Medicaid and private-pay clients, which can account for a sizeable percentage of their total patient load. The numbers of Medicare-certified agencies have increased substantially, from 2,924 in 1980 to 7,521 in 1994. One major impetus for growth in Medicare-certified agencies was a change in law in 1980 that permitted proprietary HHAs to furnish Medicare-covered services in states not having licensure laws. Despite the growth in Medicare home health agencies, there is some evidence of uneven access to certain types of home care services (e.g., therapies) in rural areas.

There are several reasons why an agency may not be certified. It may not provide all or any of the services that Medicare requires. Even if certification requirements are met, noncertified home care agencies may simply choose to serve private-pay, Medicaid, or other public program clients instead of Medicare clients. State programs may reimburse uncertified agencies and independent providers as well as certified providers for home health and personal care services.

The 1991 National Health Provider Inventory, sponsored by the National Center for Health Statistics (NCHS), provided the first national data on certified and uncertified HHAs in the medically oriented segment of the market. Only 15% of all HHAs were not certified by either Medicare or Medicaid. HHAs that were certified by both Medicare and Medicaid were more likely to offer four or more specialized services compared with two or fewer by uncertified agencies (Delfosse 1994).

A recent study in three metropolitan areas, using a broader definition to include nonmedical home care, identified six general types of uncertified providers: home health, home care, referral/case management, home-delivered meals, high-tech durable medical equipment (DME), and general DME (Estes 1994). The study found that uncertified agencies are mostly proprietary (57%). However, about two-thirds of the uncertified agencies are licensed. The largest revenue source for uncertified providers was private out-of-pocket (49%), followed by HMOs (24%), and public payers (16%). The most common barriers to certification cited were bureaucracy (e.g., paperwork), costs of the process, regulation, and perceived inadequate reimbursement levels. Some incentives for certification were seen, such as enhanced credibility, greater revenue, and client referrals.

Apart from these agencies, persons may also procure home care workers from employment or temporary help agencies, nurse registries, as individual independent contractors, or through private, informal arrangements. It is not known what proportion of the home care market these sources represent. The informal arrangement is an acknowledged ''gray'' market, similar to that for child care.

Client Characteristics

The 1987 NMES estimated that 5.9 million individuals, or 2.5% of the non-institutionalized population, receive some type of formal home care service, either medical, nonmedical, or both (Altman and Walden 1993). Of this number, 50% were aged 65 or older, with the likelihood of use increasing with age. Women, unmarried persons, and persons living alone were more likely to use home health care than men, married persons, and those living with someone; no racial differences were found. The likelihood of use increased sharply with the level of disability as indicated by the number of IADL or ADL problems. Among the elderly with some IADL/ADL difficulty, a prime target group for home care, only 36% used some type of formal home care service. Functionally impaired elderly persons who are female, living alone, older, and more impaired are more likely to use home care services than those who are male, living with someone, younger, and less impaired. These client characteristics hold true for the more medically oriented home care sector as well, as indicated in the 1992 NCHS National Home and Hospice Care Survey. Looking at data only for elderly home health patients, 73% of them received help with either an ADL or IADL and 61% received help with at least one ADL. About 80% of elderly home health clients received skilled nursing services, almost 50% personal care services, about 16% therapy services, and 11% homemaker or companion services.

Financing

There are several sources of payment for home care: public programs such as Medicare*, Medicaid*, veterans benefits*, private insurance, or out-of-pocket. The 1987 NMES estimated that, for all age groups, home care users paid out-of-pocket the largest share of total home care expenses (43%), with Medicare contributing about 19%, Medicaid almost 25%, and private insurance and other sources about 13% (Altman and Walden, 1993).

The 1987 NMES data are the latest available combining both medical and nonmedical home care. However, there appear to have been financing shifts since 1987. According to estimates from the National Health Expenditures accounts, which include only medically oriented home care, Medicare and Medicaid accounted for 63% of expenditures by 1993 as compared with only 53.5% in 1987 (Levit et al. 1994). The share of other revenue sources (including out-of-pocket spending, private health insurance and other nonpatient revenue sources) has declined from 46.5% in 1987 to 38% in 1993.

Medicare. The largest public payer of home health services for the elderly is Medicare. Its coverage is designed for treatment of acute-care conditions and for postacute care, and is medically oriented. The main requirements are that the person must be certified by a physician to need skilled nursing services on an "intermittent" basis and he or she must be "homebound." In 1993, Medicare home health expenditures were $9.7 billion, as compared to only $1.9 billion in 1988, almost a fivefold increase. Much of this growth is attributable to increases in the number of visits per person served (Bishop and Skwara 1993), growing from 24 visits in 1988 to 57 in 1993. In response to this tremendous growth, the Health Care Financing Administration (HCFA) has launched the Medicare Home Health Care Initiative: Policy, quality assurance, and operational elements of the home health benefit are under review and ongoing research will continue to guide the direction of improvements. Both short-term (e.g., procedural changes) and long-term strategies (e.g., statutory change or additional research) are being considered.

Medicaid. State Medicaid programs, a second major public funding source, may provide home care services in four ways: home health care services as a mandatory benefit, personal care services, home and community-based care services as optional benefits, and home and community-based care services as waivers. In fiscal year 1993, HCFA statistics indicate that $6.8 billion was spent by Medicaid on home care services, distributed as follows: (1) $1.4 billion on home health, (2) $2.5 billion on personal care services, (3) $55.3 million on optional home- and community-based services, and (4) $2.9 billion on home and community-based waiver services.

Medicaid home health services are generally similar to the services provided under Medicare and often are offered by a Medicare-certified home health agency. Medicaid personal care services cover assistance with basic ADL provided in a recipient's home. Services must be prescribed by a physician, supervised by a registered nurse, and provided by an individual who is not a family member. Thirty-two states provide personal care services as part of their state Medicaid plan.

Section 2176 of the 1981 Omnibus Budget Reconciliation Act established the Medicaid home and community-based waiver service program. Its intent was to provide noninstitutional services, not otherwise available under Medicaid, to individuals who would require institutional care. The program has permitted states flexibility to cover a broader number of non-medically oriented services (e.g., adult day care, homemaker services, respite care) and to extend the benefit package for waiver participants compared to those under the regular state plan. In 1993, 48 states had one or more waiver programs. However, only about 28% ($807 million) of the total expenditures was for the disabled elderly.

Section 4711 of the 1990 Omnibus Budget Reconciliation Act established Home and Community-Based Care Services for the Functionally Disabled Elderly as an optional service under Medicaid, also known as the "frail elderly" benefit. Eligible Medicaid recipients can be over or under age 65 and either be functionally disabled or have Alzheimer's disease. Services include homemaker, home health aide, chore, personal care, nursing, respite, caregiver training, and adult day care. The services must be provided under a care plan approved by a case manager. One major disadvantage of this program is that states choosing this option must serve all eligible people regardless of the extent of federal funds available. Only one state, Texas, has implemented this program; the benefits expire on September 30, 1995.

Social Services Block Grant (SSBG) or Title XX Program. States may also fund home care services through this program. Forty-one states and the District of Columbia used it in 1992 to partially finance a variety of home services. Approximately 21% of funds are used for home services. In fiscal year 1993, SSBG appropriations totaled $2.8 billion.

Title III of the Older Americans Act (OAA).* This is another funding source for home care. Any person aged 60 and older is eligible for services, but the program targets funds to the most vulnerable elderly. A 1987 amendment to the act authorized in-home services specifically for frail older individuals. Supportive services (in-home services such as homemakers and home health aides, transportation, health education and screening, transportation, home repairs/ maintenance, and information and referral) accounted for one-third of expenditures in fiscal year 1989. Half of the expenditures were for nutrition, either for congregate meals or for home-delivered meals. In 1992, less than $200 million was spent by Title III, with about 1.7 million persons served.

State-Only Long-Term Care Programs. States also devote their own funds to support long-term care services, by allocating funds required by Medicaid and OAA federal matching rules and by subsidizing optional Medicaid services and supplemental services by their own choice. A recent survey by the Administration on Aging (1994) found that almost all states provided funding for home and community-based care services for the elderly through a distinct state general revenue program. Total expenditures from these state-source programs were approximately $700 million in 1992, with an average state program expenditure of $4.6 million. However, four state programs were substantially larger: Massachusetts ($96 million), Illinois ($83 million), Florida ($49 million), and Pennsylvania ($47 million). About 60% of the programs use some form of financial eligibility standard and 80% use some needs criteria such as IADL/ADL.

The Department of Veterans Affairs (VA). This health system provides noninstitutional long-term care services as part of an extensive continuum of veterans benefits. VA-operated community-based services include the Hospital-Based Home Care (HBHC) program, homemaker/home health aide services, home medical equipment, home improvement and structural alteration program, hospice consultation teams, and adult day care.

The HBHC program provides hospital discharge planning and comprehensive primary health care to homebound veterans delivered by a hospital-based interdisciplinary team led by a physician. It was available at 77 of the 171 Veterans Administration Medical Centers in FY 1994. Eligible veterans for the HBHC program must be homebound, living within the program service area of the VA medical center, living with a caregiver, have multiple diseases or terminal illness, or be short-term patients needing postacute rehabilitation care. There are no financial eligibility criteria or cost sharing.

Private Sources. Private funding sources for home care include out-of-pocket payments of either the home care recipient and/or family members, private health insurance, long-term care insurance*, and Medicare supplemental insurance*. Out-of-pocket costs are not an insignificant component of home care expenditures. One study found that the elderly disabled (with at least 1 ADL problem), an important subgroup of home care users, paid 35% out-of-pocket for their home care costs compared to 14% by nonelderly disabled (Pollack et al. 1993).

Employer-sponsored postretirement health insurance* often provides home health benefits and accounts for approximately 12–13% of home care expenditures. Many long-term care insurance and Medicare supplemental insurance policies provide home care benefits. Four of the ten standard Medigap plans offer an at-home recovery benefit linked to the Medicare home health benefit. However, based on a sample of insurance companies representing about 30% of the Medigap market, only about 7% of persons purchased policies with the at-home benefit (Fox et al. 1995).

Research Issues

Two major research issues in home care have been: (1) the effect of formal (paid) home care use on informal (unpaid) home care provision; and (2) the relationship between home care and nursing home care. An emerging research issue is consumer satisfaction and quality in consumer-directed home care.

A large number of persons with disabilities use only unpaid home care but are potential users of formal home care. The effect of receipt of paid care on the provision of informal care is an important policy concern because of the potential cost implications if the level of informal care is not sustained with the introduction of an expanded home care benefit. Most studies, based on demonstrations or programs of expanded home care benefits, suggest that the effect is either insignificant or small. One example found that a 5% increase in disabled elderly receiving formal home care resulted in a 1% decrease in those receiving informal care (Christianson 1988).

A basic assumption is that, for many chronically disabled persons, formal home care (usually combined with informal care) and nursing home care are substitutes for each other. McBride et al. (1989) found that one indication of home health availability—number of Medicare home health visits per enrollee by state—had no effect on the time that the disabled elderly spent in the community prior to nursing home admission. It did, however, have an effect on shortening the time spent in the nursing home for those discharged back into the community. Demonstrations have been conducted to test whether community care can substitute for nursing home care; results have shown that provision of expanded, case-managed home care benefits does not significantly reduce nursing home use (Kemper et al. 1987).

Research that reveals the value that older clients attach to home health services and their own abilities to cope with chronic illness is extremely important in improving the design and provision of home health care. Greater understanding of the race-, gender-, and class-associated cultural differences in services to clients and families would improve recipient-defined quality of care. Consumer empowerment needs to be an integral part of the design and payment of home care; greater empowerment would be through vouchers or cash purchases of home care, allowing more direct consumer control of the purchase and quality of home care services.

Issues in Choosing and Managing Home Care Services

There are two major considerations for consumers and their family members in choosing home care services: (1) selecting and locating the appropriate level and payment sources for home care, and (2) managing home care services and monitoring quality.

Selecting and Finding the Appropriate Level of Care. The variability in home care services offers consumers and their families a wide range of choice of providers. Choices include certified and uncertified home health agencies, homemaker-home health aides from an agency or registry, independent providers, and other paid home care workers. However, the types of home care available vary by areas; one is likely to have less choice in more rural areas.

A consumer and his or her family should first obtain an assessment of the various types, amount, and duration of home care services they will require from outside sources. The consumer should consider what informal assistance will be available from family members and friends that would complement formal services to provide the appropriate level of care needed. Physicians, other health care personnel, and social service and home care agencies can be helpful in assessing the appropriate home care. If a person is being discharged from a hospital, care needs may be extensive and are likely to require skilled home health care. Prior to discharge from the hospital, patients should talk to the discharge planner and receive a written plan of care from their physician for posthospital home care. Part of the care plan may also include unskilled tasks such as assisting with ADL or IADL, which can be performed by home health aides. If one is living at home and needs assistance, an assessment is also recommended. One should contact the local Area Agency on Aging (AAA) or the Eldercare Locator for information on assessments and services available. When selecting an independent worker, the consumer should interview the care worker and check on references and training.

In developing the plan of care, one needs to determine if any of the care can be paid by federal, state, or other programs or insurance, or if one must pay for any or all of the care out-of-pocket. When home care services are covered by Medicare, Medicaid, private insurance, the Veterans Administration, or Medigap insurance, the choice, amount, and duration of services are determined by the program requirements. Support through the AAA or the state for frail elderly may include household help, home repairs, meals on wheels, transportation, and senior centers. Payment for services may be determined by ability to pay or based on degree of impairment.

When payment for home care is out-of-pocket, the consumer may need to rely on income or assets. Alternatives for financing home care can be the use of reverse mortgages for home owners and home sharing in exchange for services.

Managing Home Care Services and Monitoring Quality of Services. The consumer or family member who is arranging for the care also needs to manage the care arrangements. The most important issue is to have a clear understanding through a signed agreement about the responsibilities of home care workers, whether they are hired through an agency or are independent providers; a sample is included in USHC (1994). The agreement between the provider and the consumer should specify: the types and amounts of home care services, the associated charges, the role of the consumer in decision making, and expectations about worker performance and quality of services delivered. Clients also have responsibilities, including treating providers with respect and providing accurate information on service needs. If there are problems with home care, one may contact the home care supervisor or agency or the Long-Term Care Ombudsman* in the state or county. (See also also DAY PROGRAMS FOR ADULTS; GERONTOLOGICAL NURSE PRACTITIONERS; HOSPICE CARE; MEDICAID; MEDICARE; OLDER AMERICANS ACT; OMBUDSMAN; SOCIAL WORK, GERONTOLOGICAL; and TRANSPORTATION.)

Organizations

Eldercare Locator
National Association for Home Care
Visiting Nurse Association of America

Suggested Reading

National Association for Home Care. 1993. *How to Choose a Home Care Agency*. Washington, DC: Author.

References

Administration on Aging. 1994. *Infrastructure of Home and Community Based Services for the Functionally Impaired Elderly: State Source Book*. Washington, DC: Author.

Altman, Barbara, and Daniel Walden. 1993. *Home Health Care: Use, Expenditures, and Sources of Payment*. National Medical Expenditure Survey Research Findings 15. Rockville, MD: Agency for Health Care Policy and Research.

Bishop, Christine, and Kathleen Skwara. 1993. "Recent Growth of Medicare Home Health." *Health Affairs* 12: 95–110.

Christianson, Jon. 1988. "The Effect of Channeling on Informal Caregiving." *Health Services Research* 23: 99–117.

Delfosse, Rence. 1994. "Home Health Agencies and Their Certification by Medicare and Medicaid." Paper Presented at the Annual Meeting of the American Public Health Association.

Estes, Carroll. 1994. *Uncertified Homecare: Structure and Performance*. San Francisco: UCSF Institute for Health and Aging.

Fox, Peter, Thomas Rice, and Lisa Alecxih. 1995. "The Medigap Reform Legislation of 1990: Implications for U.S. Health Care Reform." *Journal of Health Politics, Policy and Law* 20: 31–48.

Harrington, Charlene, Richard DuNah, Barbara Bedney, and Helen Carrillo. 1994. *The Supply of Community-Based Long Term Care Services in the States in 1993*. Report to HCFA and HUD. San Francisco: University of California, San Francisco, Department of Social and Behavioral Sciences.

Kemper, Peter, Robert Applebaum, and Mary Harahan. 1987. "Community Care Demonstrations: What Have We Learned?" *Health Care Financing Review* 8: 87–100.

Levit, Katharine, et al. 1994. "National Health Expenditures, 1993." *Health Care Financing Review* 16: 247–94.

McBride, Tim, Korbin Liu, and Teresa Coughlin. 1989. *Surviving Analysis of Nursing Home Risk and Length of Stay: Methodological Issues and Findings*. Working Paper. Washington, DC: Urban Institute.

National Association for Home Care. 1994 *Basic Statistics about Home Care, 1994*. Washington, DC: Author.

Pollack, Ron, et al. 1993. *The Heavy Burden of Home Care*. Washington, DC: Families USA.

United Seniors Health Cooperative. 1994. *Home Care for Older People*. Washington, DC: Author.

Judith A. Sangl and Linda A. Siegenthaler

HOME EQUITY CONVERSIONS. See Home Modifications Finance; Home-ownership; Introduction; Reverse Mortgages.

HOMELESSNESS AMONG THE ELDERLY, a form of extreme poverty among the elderly, characterized by no access to shelter, or shelter that is so inadequate that life itself is threatened. In the United States, the elderly homeless include those on the streets and in homeless shelters. Whether people living in single-room-occupancy units (SROs), such as "flophouses" on skid row (often rented on a daily basis), or more permanent housing in a single room with shared bathroom and cooking facilities, should be considered homeless, is debatable. One way to understand homelessness is to consider the characteristics of adequate shelter: having protection from the elements, access to potable water, provision for removal of human wastes, protection from intruders, and freedom from sudden removal.

The 1990 Census counted 190,406 individuals living in emergency shelters for homeless persons (this category included persons lodging in hotels, motels, missions, and flophouses charging $12 or less per night) and 49,734 persons visible in street locations (U.S. Department of Commerce 1992). However, there are no age data for these populations. The 1990 Census homeless count did not include the population who slept in other people's housing on a temporary basis and did not have security of tenure.

Although it is impossible to speak of the numbers of elderly homeless with any precision, it is possible to discuss poverty (a major risk factor of homelessness) among the elderly. Although the elderly are underrepresented in the poverty population (they comprise 12.2% of the total population, but 10.8% of the poor), they are overrepresented in the near-poor population (100% to 125% of the poverty threshold), comprising 18.9% of this category (U.S. Department of Commerce 1993). Further, specific groups of elderly tend to be poor. Elderly blacks are three times more likely to be poor as elderly whites, and 43% of the elderly living alone are poor or near poor, which is five times the poverty rate of elderly couples. In one ethnographic study of elderly homeless men, Cohen and Sokolovsky (1989) estimated that there were 2,700 men aged 50 and older living in flophouses and apartments in the Bowery of New York. They argued that, although 50 years old is not "old" for most of the U.S. population, 50 was indeed old in terms of deteriorated health and general physical conditions for the Bowery population.

Historically, homelessness was a term closely associated with elderly men. The term conjures up an image of the single, unconnected individual, perhaps sleeping over a heating grate in a large industrialized city. In that perspective, the homeless man has variously been viewed as a saintly mendicant, a fiercely independent traveling man, a sick and lonely (often alcoholic) creature, or a drug-addicted or psychotic threat. By the 1960s, the term *homeless* came to be used for families living in squatter settlements of the developing world, and families in shelters and shared accommodations in the industrialized world.

Causes of homelessness may be conceptualized as belonging to either the "personal pathology" or the "lack of housing" school of thought. Until recently, homelessness in the industrialized nations has been understood in terms of personal pathology, that is, it was viewed as a result of alcoholism, mental illness (exacerbated by deinstitutionalizing the hospitalized mentally ill), drug addiction, and family disintegration. But by the 1980s, homelessness in the industrialized world was also seen as prompted by a lack of adequate and affordable housing, the deterioration of housing stock in cities, the "gentrification" of existing housing (i.e., upgrading the housing to such as extent that former poor occupants can no longer live in it) and the withdrawal of government-sponsored housing.

The rise of the elderly homeless on the streets is often viewed as one consequence of deinstitutionalization, which refers to releasing patients from psychiatric hospitals to the community, having shorter duration of hospitalization for only acute episodes, and preventing initial hospitalization. The push toward deinstitutionalization resulted from the increase in psychotropic medications, an insistence on the civil rights of the mentally ill, a belief in the least restrictive environment for psychiatric patients, and a desire to save money. Between 1955 and the early 1980s there was a reduction of three-quarters of the population residing in state mental hospitals (Hope and Young 1986). Once in the community, however, many of the chronically mentally ill found it extremely difficult to cope. Comprehensive services were not provided by group homes, day centers, and community mental health workers. People "fell through the cracks" and were lost to follow-up services. Families, who were supposed to become involved again, often did not. If the mentally ill did not pay their rent, they were evicted. If they were fearful of the place in which they stayed (such as rooms in hotels), they took to the streets. Once on the street, elderly people tended to be frightened of the large and dangerous shelters. Some elderly preferred to roam the streets at night and try to sleep during the day, in order to avoid being attacked (Baxter and Hopper 1981).

Single Room Occupancy units are inexpensive housing that usually lack private cooking and bathroom facilities. They are accessible housing for those who cannot get anything else. Many of the residents of SROs pay for the rent with a form of public money (the average SRO rent has been found to be almost 75% of the individual's check), yet SROs are privately owned. This situation of public monies and private ownership affords little public accountability for the conditions in the hotels. There have been some social service projects that bring health, dental, mental health, recreational, and supportive services into the hotels. Throughout the 1980s and 1990s, the SRO population has become increasingly elderly.

Coincidental with the era of deinstitutionalization was the push toward revitalizing the downtown core of cities through urban renewal programs of the 1950s to the 1970s. The SRO hotels, which had been housing many of the nation's poor elderly, were either demolished or rehabilitated for upper-middle-class use or for office space. The remaining SRO buildings continued to decay, and there was little government money for preventing the deterioration of the buildings. Estimates show that between 1970 and 1980 more than one million SRO units were lost (Ovrebo et al. 1991).

In addressing elderly homelessness, the emphasis must be placed on prevention of the individual's initial loss of housing. This can be accomplished by the building of publicly subsidized housing, rent subsidies, and mediation efforts to prevent eviction. An interesting architectural development is the Affordable by Design Single Room Dwelling (Davey 1994) which is a 225 square-foot unit with full living, sleeping, eating, cooking, and sanitation facilities, which can be sold for under $10,000, depending upon geographic location, and if built in conjunction with a community agency purchase of the land. It would need to be built near public transportation, so that the elderly could continue to meet their daily living needs.

Once on the street, homeless people may have access to food and shelter from soup kitchens, traveling vans, respite day centers, or temporary shelters. However, homeless people on the street find that it becomes more and more difficult to reenter permanent housing, due to the person's "undesirability" as a renter and the kind of survival independence that people develop from adapting to sleeping outside. Another level of help involves transitional housing, which consists of longer-term temporary accommodations that enable a person to leave the streets.

In developing countries, there have been numerous projects to upgrade squatter settlements, often with material provided by governmental or nongovernmental organizations and labor provided by the people themselves. Advocates for the homeless in the industrialized world are now recommending similar self-help and political empowerment as strategies to address homelessness. An example of an adaptation of the idea of self-help in addressing the elderly homeless is the Veteran's Memorial Manor in Vancouver, British Columbia, Canada. Here, elderly men (many of whom were alcoholics), who were living on the streets of Vancouver, were invited to help plan permanent housing for themselves. The men said that they did not want to leave the inner-city area that had been their home, and they wanted a safe environment, with freedom to come and go as they pleased. The result was the Veteran's Memorial Manor, which houses 124 men and even has a garden built on the roof of the building.

It has been observed that most of the services for the elderly in the United States have been "life enhancing" services that favor the downwardly mobile (due to income and health deterioration) elderly, in contrast to the "life supportive" services needed by the elderly poor. The middle-income elderly are politically well organized, and can enlist the support of their adult children, but the elderly poor and homeless have little political influence or family support. (See also CRIME PROTECTION, ECONOMIC HARDSHIP MEASURES IN THE OLDER POPULATION, ECONOMIC STATUS OF THE ELDERLY,

ECONOMIC STATUS OF ELDERLY WOMEN, HOUSING, and VETER-
ANS' BENEFITS.)

References

Baxter, Ellen, and Kim Hopper. 1981. *Private Lives/Public Spaces: Homeless Adults on the Streets of New York City.* New York: Community Service Society.

Cohen, Carl I., and Jay Sokolovsky. 1989. *Old Men of the Bowery: Strategies for Survival Among the Homeless.* New York: Guilford Press.

Davey, Dennis. 1994. *The Maximum Density Lot-Single Room Dwelling (MDL-SRD).* Tolland, Connecticut: Dennis Davey, AIA.

Hope, Margorie, and James Young. 1986. *The Faces of Homelessness.* Lexington, MA: Lexington Books.

Kreigher, Sharon M., Rebecca Hanson-Berman, and Madelyn A. Iris. 1990. "Personal Coping Strategies of the Elderly in Housing Emergencies: Clues to Interventions to Prevent Homelessness and Institutionalization." In *Optimizing Housing for the Elderly: Homes Not Houses,* ed. Leon A. Pastalan. New York: Haworth Press.

Ovrebo, Beverly, Meredith Minkler, and Petra Liljestrand. 1991. "No Room in the Inn: The Disappearance of SRO Housing in the United States." In *Housing Risks and Homelessness among the Urban Elderly,* ed. Sharon M. Keigher. New York: Haworth Press.

U.S. Department of Commerce. Bureau of the Census. 1993. *Poverty in the United States: 1992.* Washington, DC: Government Printing Office.

U.S. Department of Commerce. Bureau of the Census. 1992. *Statistical Abstract of the United States.* Washington, DC: Government Printing Office.

Irene Glasser

HOME MODIFICATIONS FINANCING, resources for older and disabled persons on limited incomes who require home modifications to remain living independently. Living in the familiar surroundings of one's own home fosters feelings of comfort, belonging, and peace of mind. In 1991, 66% of older homeowners had lived at the same address for more than 16 years (U.S. Bureau of the Census 1993). A survey by the American Association of Retired Persons (1990) confirmed that 86% of older Americans preferred to remain in their own homes and never move. Home represents one's identity, and is a symbol of one's roots, history, and family.

Notwithstanding the feelings of attachment to home, the living arrangements of many older individuals must be reevaluated from time to time. A number of factors may precipitate this: the house is too large or too difficult to maintain; age-related, declining physical and cognitive abilities make a house less accessible, more difficult to use, or unsafe; or health care and required daily assistance necessitate home modifications. The net result is obstacles and mismatches in the way people interact with their living space.

There are numerous ways of modifying or adapting one's home environment, but expenses associated with such projects may be prohibitive. Limited postretirement income may prevent maintenance or modification projects from being considered.

However, financial and labor assistance programs do exist. Although the pool of resources has shrunk, so has the number of applicants. Most programs offer funds on a first come, first served basis (Malizio et al. 1993). Eligibility requirements, policies, and procedures for obtaining financial assistance for home modifications and repairs differ among states and municipalities, and as government and agency administrations change, so do the criteria and availability of the programs. The administration of resources is specific to local areas. Most have qualification guidelines with which applicants must be familiar before applying for aid.

Financial resources are available in many forms. Traditional bank and home equity loans represent the more common ways of financing home modifications, adaptations, and repairs. Homeowners, however, must meet certain guidelines, and many older adults on fixed incomes will find themselves ineligible for these loan instruments. For low-income and disabled people, there are low-interest loans from federal and state agencies, deferred payment loans, reverse mortgages*, volunteer labor services, donated material and supplies, and grant programs. Funds provided through grants are given directly to an agency or other entity on behalf of the individual or family in need. There are also income tax incentives available for adaptations and the cost of any assistive equipment, products, or apparatus.

When contacting a federal, state, private, or community agency about financial assistance programs for home modifications, it is useful to obtain a copy of the program's policies, procedures, eligibility requirements, program options, and application forms. An applicant should be prepared to furnish all pertinent information required before approaching the agency: (1) name of the person applying; (2) pertinent financial eligibility criteria; (3) medical or other appropriate documents to support eligibility; (4) reason(s) for the modifications, adaptations, and/or repairs; (5) project plans and the intended outcome and benefits; (6) itemized costs, including the price of materials, purchases, labor, and other expenses with copies of itemized estimates from qualified contractors; and (7) method of repayment (if a loan is sought).

Tax Deductions for Seniors and Persons With Disabilities

According to the Internal Revenue Service, tax deductions for modification costs may be taken if a physician certifies that they were incurred for health reasons and were medically necessary. Deductions for such modifications must be itemized as an expense under medical deductions on federal income tax form 1040 Schedule A. Generally, medical expenses must exceed 7.5% of the adjusted gross income in order to be deductible.

Examples of deductible expenses include the cost of special telephone equipment or specially equipped television for the hearing impaired. Capital expenses incurred for home modifications or the installation of special equipment may be deducted if the cost of the improvements or equipment installation is for the purpose of medical care and the value of the property is not increased as a result of the improvements or new equipment. If the value is increased, the deductible amount of the cost is reduced by the increased property value. Other modifications and adaptations that the government identifies include, but are not limited to, the following:

1. Constructing entrance or exit ramps
2. Widening doorways at entrances or exits
3. Widening or otherwise modifying hallways and interior doorways
4. Installing railing, support bars, or other modifications in bathrooms
5. Lowering or modifying kitchen cabinets and equipment
6. Moving or modifying electrical outlets and fixtures
7. Installing porch and other forms of lifts (but generally not elevators)
8. Modifying fire alarms, smoke detectors, and other warning systems
9. Modifying stairways
10. Adding handrails or grab bars anywhere (not just in bathrooms)
11. Modifying hardware on doors
12. Modifying areas of front entrance and exit doorways
13. Grading the ground to provide access to the residence

Under current federal tax codes, income tax credits are available for persons aged 65 and older if adjusted gross income meets certain income guidelines. The tax credit also applies if a physician has certified that a permanent and total disability exists. Part 2 of Schedule R (Form 1040) or Schedule 3 (Form 1040A) must be completed. For veterans, if the Department of Veterans' Affairs has certified that there is a permanent and total disability, VA Form 21–0172, *Certification of Permanent Total Disability,* may be filed for a tax credit instead of the physician's statement. According to the IRS, there are certain special items, equipment, and capital expenses that may be tax-deductible under the medical expenses line on Schedule A (Form 1040). Renters who pay for costs of materials, equipment, or installations without reimbursement or rent reductions from a landlord may deduct them as well. Modifications and adaptations a family member makes to accommodate an older person's physical and health conditions may be deducted, provided the older person meets the criteria as a dependent.

Municipal and Community Resources

Local resources that offer financial assistance for home modifications include municipal housing authorities, elderly services or senior coordinator programs, grants, low-cost loans, and free and low-cost home modification labor services. Local home health care agencies and senior centers offer additional information and provide basic home evaluation and repair services. Although civic, fraternal, and religious organizations are apt to have limited funding, they may prove to be useful for finding volunteer laborers and handymen, and/or for obtaining materials.

Each state government maintains a department that focuses on senior affairs. The National Association of State Units on Aging has information and can refer callers to state agencies on aging. State units on aging can provide information on programs for home modifications, financial assistance, counseling, weatherization and energy assistance, in-home services, and property tax relief, through a network of aging councils or state agencies on aging.

Typical programs through state offices and community agencies include low-interest loans or grants for home modifications. Information or referrals may be available for emergency home repair and rehabilitation programs, and for energy conservation loan programs.

Loans from state and federal loan programs generally range from $1,000 to $10,000. Applicants must meet certain age and income qualifications, and own and live in a one- or two-family house that requires repairs. Depending on the government agency administering the program, loans are provided at a lower interest rate with repayment up to 30 years. Repayment of the loan's principal and interest may be deferred until the property is conveyed. The terms of the loan and conditions of repayment may be adjusted according to the borrower's ability to pay.

State agencies on aging will have information on Reverse Annuity Mortgage Programs (RAM). These allow lower-income seniors who live in the home they own to use the equity to receive a monthly tax-free cash payment for up to ten years. Generally, the homeowner must be 65 years old or older. The property may be a one- to four-family structure or condominium unit, and there are certain income eligibility requirements. The state receives repayment for the reverse annuity mortgage at the time the house is sold or transferred. (See also CONDOMINIUMS, HOMEOWNERSHIP, HOUSING, MORTGAGE INSTRUMENTS, and REVERSE MORTGAGES.)

Organizations

National Association of Area Agencies on Aging
National Council on Independent Living
National Eldercare Institute on Housing and Supportive Services
Corporation for Independent Living

References

American Association of Retired Persons. 1990. *Understanding Senior Housing.* Washington, DC: AARP.

American Association of Retired Persons. 1993. *Home Made Money: Consumer's Guide to Home Equity Conversion.* Washington, DC: AARP.

Malizio, E., R. Duncan, and J. Reagan. 1993. *Financing Home Accessibility Modifications.* Raleigh, NC: Center for Accessible Housing, North Carolina State University.

Pirkl, J., and A. Babic. 1988. *Guidelines and Strategies for Designing Transgenerational Products: An Instructor's Manual.* Syracuse, NY: Department of Design, Syracuse University.

U.S. Bureau of the Census. 1993. *American Housing Survey for the United States in 1991.* Current Housing Reports, Series H150/91. Washington, DC: U.S. Government Printing Office.

U.S. Senate Special Committee on Aging. 1991. *Aging America: Trends and Projections*. Washington, DC: U.S. Government Printing Office.

Jeff L. Lefkovich

HOMEOWNERSHIP, the predominant housing tenure arrangement of the 95% of elderly Americans living outside nursing homes. In 1991, a historically high 77% of heads of households aged 65 and older owned their homes. Only those aged 55–64 were more likely to be homeowners (80%). Homeownership was especially high among young-old (ages 65–74) households (81%) and even for the very old (ages 85 and older), it was the dominant form of tenure (67%).

Certain groups of elderly Americans were less likely to own their homes than others. Only 64% of African-American, and 59% of Hispanic elderly households, were homeowners, compared with 79% of non-Hispanic white elderly households. Similarly, only 64% of older persons living alone compared with 91% of older married couples owned their dwellings. Homeownership rates were also related to household income. Among lower-income elderly households (under $10,000 a year), 61% owned homes, compared with 91% of higher income elderly households ($25,000 a year or more). Elderly homeowners were also not equally found in all U.S. locations. In central cities of metropolitan areas, 65% of elderly households were homeowners compared with 81% of elderly households in the suburbs of metropolitan areas, and 82% of elderly households in nonmetropolitan (primarily rural) areas. The disproportionate presence of older homeowners in lower-density, primarily automobile-oriented locations is significant because it may suggest potential transportation and service accessibility problems for this group if they lose their ability to drive.

Most elderly homeowners (86%) occupied single-family detached or attached dwelling units while smaller percentages occupied mobile homes (7%), low-rise (2–49 units) multifamily buildings (6%), and larger (50 units or more) multifamily buildings (1%). Less than 6% of older homeowners specifically lived in cooperatives* or condominiums*.

Homeownership as a Liability

Elderly homeowners had median monthly housing costs of $239 (including debt service on mortgage, real estate taxes, property insurance, homeowners association fees, cooperative or condominium fees, mobile home park fees, utilities, and garbage collection). About 24% were paying over 30% of their monthly household incomes on their housing costs, a usual indicator of a housing expense burden. This expense burden ranged from 22% for homeowners aged 65–74 to 31% for homeowners aged 85 and older. Homeowners with such excessive housing costs run a greater risk of having to deprive themselves of other necessary consumables.

The majority of older homeowners (82%) owned their homes without mortgages, and the mortgage status of the dwelling was an important predictor of housing costs and expense burdens. Older homeowners with mortgages had median monthly housing costs of $549, compared with $217 for those without mortgages. About 48% of older homeowners with mortgages, compared with 20% of those without mortgages, spent 30% or more of their household incomes on housing expenses. In either instance, however, elderly homeowners were less likely to have excessive housing costs than renters, 66% of whom paid 30% or more of their income on their dwelling expenses. Older homeowners, however, were more likely to have excessive housing expense burdens than younger home-owners, but this disparity disappeared when controlling for the income levels of the two groups. Focusing only on households below the poverty level, 67% of elderly homeowners, but over 70% of younger homeowners, spent over 30% of their incomes on housing costs.

After mortgage debt service, property taxes are usually the largest dwelling expenditure of older homeowners, and these taxes may be especially burden-some to the poor. Property taxes are often unpopular with seniors because they can increase more quickly than inflation, threaten their ability to afford their homes, and are perceived as funding projects (e.g., schools) from which they derive few benefits. Elderly homeowners have higher property tax burdens than non-elderly homeowners because on average they live in higher-valued homes than non-elderly homeowners with similar incomes (Reschovsky 1994).

State governments have attempted to reduce the tax burden in several ways. Tax relief instruments have either lowered the assessed value of the property subject to taxation (homestead exemptions), or have provided a direct tax credit on the property tax bill (homestead credits or circuit-breaker rebates). In most states, circuit-breaker programs were the most important vehicle for providing property tax relief. A third approach is through property tax deferral programs that allow older homeowners to defer payment of property taxes until they sell the home or die. Deferred property taxes become a lien against the value of the taxpayer's home and have similar financial properties to reverse mortgages. While every state provides some type of property tax relief program, the extent of this relief varies greatly. Most states favor targeting relief to low income elderly households and most have more generous programs for elderly than for non-elderly homeowners (Mackey and Carter 1994). Property tax burdens re-main high for many elderly homeowners, however, because eligibility is often restricted to very low income or asset levels and participation by elderly home-owners in these relief programs is often low (Reschovsky 1994).

Costs of homeownership can be significantly reduced, since homeowners can reduce their federal income tax liabilities (by an amount proportional to their marginal income tax rate) by itemizing their deductible property taxes and mort-gage debt service costs. Older persons generally benefit less than non-elderly homeowners from this tax provision, because they own their homes free and clear, have lower incomes, and are less likely to itemize deductions (Reschovsky 1994). Nonetheless, most elderly persons have been homeowners throughout their adult lives and have reaped these tax savings over many years. Thus, from a lifespan perspective, they have clearly accumulated greater tax benefits from their homeownership status than younger homeowners. Homeowners aged 55 and older benefit from the additional provision that allows $125,000 of capital gains* from the sale of their final home to be tax exempted on a one-time basis.

An estimated one-third of elderly households pay unnecessarily high housing costs because, according to experts, they live in dwellings that are larger than necessary (Lane and Feins 1985). Ninety-four percent of elderly homeowners, compared with 64% of those aged 15–64, occupy dwellings with .5 or fewer persons per room, one measure of crowdedness. If these overhoused elderly households are also poor, the possibility exists that they must restrict their spending on other needed goods and services. This becomes a public issue to the extent that these homeowners are also receiving governmental subsidies (e.g., food stamps, Medicaid*, Supplemental Security Income*, and/or property tax relief) because they are identified as income poor.

Elderly homeowners who live in older dwellings may be disadvantaged. In 1991, 59% of elderly homeowners (ranging from 55% of those aged 65–74 to 69% of those aged 85 and above) occupied dwellings built prior to 1960. In contrast, this was true for only 45% of elderly renters and only 37% of non-elderly homeowners. Older homes are at greater risk of having physical deficiencies and being undermaintained, but the evidence on this question is equivocal. Data from the 1987 American Housing Survey indicated that the older the homes occupied by seniors, the more likely they were to need repair or upgrading. Home improvement data for the United States, on the other hand, emphasize that most elderly homeowners do maintain their dwellings and that while they may cut back on cosmetic aspects of home upkeep, they do not allow vital housing components to deteriorate (Reschovsky and Newman 1991). In 1987, homeowners aged 65–74 spent a median annual amount of $1,645, and homeowners aged 75 and older spent $1,281 on home improvements. Predictably, these expenses were disproportionately spent on upgrades and repairs as opposed to dwelling additions or remodeling (U.S. Bureau of the Census 1992). Older persons who cannot afford to make home repairs cannot rely on any single source of government subsidies. Local home-repair services for the poor are often supported in a piecemeal fashion by several federal funding sources (e.g., Community Development Block Grants, the Older Americans Act, and the Department of Energy), along with small programs funded by state and municipal governments (Pynoos 1993).

Older homes are generally less energy efficient and more expensive to heat than newer homes. Consequently, home heating costs may represent a larger expense item for elderly than non-elderly homeowners. This has public health implications, since older people are more vulnerable to hypothermia than younger adults. For those who are poor, the need for governmental assistance also increases. The Low Income Home Energy Assistance Program (LIHEAP) helps low-income homeowners meet unaffordable home heating costs and make their homes more energy efficient through cash benefits to the household or payments to the energy vendor. The U.S. Department of Health and Human

Services (HHS) administers LIHEAP as a state-run block grant program. In 1992, 37% of all households receiving LIHEAP heating assistance included at least one older (age 60 and above) person.

Even homes in good physical condition may prove hazardous to elderly occupants who have become physically frail. Accidents in the home (e.g., falls on stairways, floors, and bathtubs; burns or scalds from fires, hot liquids, and hot surfaces, such as heaters), are among the leading causes of death for older Americans. Despite these risks, only a fraction of noninstitutionalized seniors in the United States (7% of persons aged 65–74 and 14% of persons aged 75 and older) attempt to alleviate these potential problems. Most common adaptations are hand rails, raised toilets, ramps, and extra-wide doors; least common are slip-resistant floors or lowered counters. When home modifications are made, about 80% of the elderly pay for these modifications out of their own pocket. Unaffordable costs are the reason that 62% of aged 65–74 persons and 52% of age 75 and older persons give for why they have not made modifications, even though they have unmet needs (LaPlante et al. 1992).

The owned homes of elderly Americans may be interpreted as a liability in a final sense, one that may be difficult to measure objectively. Older persons who lack the health or energy to maintain their homes may perceive such failings as an unequivocal sign of their inability to live independently. Renters, on the other hand, may delay or avoid such harsh self-assessments. This is because older tenants in rental apartments have fewer or less demanding upkeep burdens, and when these tasks are necessary, they can often be assumed by a thoughtful or helpful landlord.

Homeownership as an Asset

Elderly homeowners had a median net worth of $88,192 in 1991, and all but $26,442 represented their home equity. Homeowners aged 65–69 had a median net worth of $104,354, but only $33,345 net of home equity. Median net worth declined after age 70, and homeowners 75 years of age and older had a median net worth of $76,541 and $22,866 net of home equity. On average, elderly homeowners had home equity in the amount of $87,383, ranging from $89,209 for dwellings occupied by aged 65–74 households to $86,162 for aged 75 and older households (Eller 1994). As was true for all age groups, home equity constituted the single largest component of the older population's wealth (about 42%). Home equity, however, represented a smaller proportion of the net worth of elderly than non-elderly households, because a larger share of the former group's net worth is comprised of financial assets such as stocks, bonds, and savings.

Older people can realize the equity in their home by selling it and then purchasing a lesser-valued property, or by renting. Elderly households, however, infrequently use moving as a means to utilize their housing equity. In 1991, 77% of age 65 and older households had lived in their dwellings for 12 years or more. They are apparently not strongly motivated to augment their cash income for the purpose of increasing current consumption. They may deem the costs of moving as too high relative to the remaining lifetime gains they would realize by changing their housing situation. Furthermore, even when older home-owners do move, most move into other owned units. Venti and Wise (1989) state:

The elderly with high income and low housing equity are the most likely to move; those with low income and high housing equity are less likely to move than the former group but more likely than other elderly families. . . . Moving by the elderly is just as likely to be motivated by the desire to reallocate more income to housing as to use housing wealth to finance current consumption. However, among homeowners who move, those with low income and high housing equity reduce housing equity the most; those with high income and low housing equity increase housing wealth the most.

The aversion older people have toward moving also points to their strong emotional and sentimental attachment to their homes. Many factors are influ-ential, but key is their stronger sense of control and mastery over their surround-ings than if they rented.

Older homeowners' apparent reluctance to release their home equity in order to finance other expenditures is further strengthened by several public policies designed to provide cash and in-kind income to poor older Americans. In most states, for example, the Medicaid* program's eligibility requirements of having almost nonexistent assets do not include the owned home in their computations. This is similarly true for the eligibility provisions of the Supplemental Security Income* and Food Stamp program. Thus, means tests for eligibility for social welfare benefits in the United States infrequently require older people to divest themselves of their homes.

Selling the home is also discouraged because of its increased importance as a setting where a growing population of frail older persons can receive services and care. Because older homeowners live in larger dwellings and are less likely to face occupancy restrictions, they can more easily accommodate a family member, housemate, or live-in who will provide caregiving or home upkeep assistance. There is also a greater prevalence of elderly homeowners who are providing temporary shelter to their unemployed or divorced adult children, or who are assuming new and demanding grandparent roles by raising their chil-dren's children.

Moving is also discouraged by factors that may be difficult to measure ob-jectively. Older persons find comfort, for example, knowing that when that "rainy day" comes, they have the option of selling or refinancing their homes for needed future income. Also, the emotional satisfaction and social status de-rived from homeownership clearly contribute to older people having a more positive self-image.

Older persons do not have to move in order to realize their housing wealth. They can access much of the equity in their dwellings by relying on such con-ventional financial instruments as a second mortgage, home equity loan, or home equity line of credit loan, which are available to homeowners of all ages. They can also avail themselves of a family of financial products known as reverse mortgages*, which are primarily marketed to older persons. These latter instruments may be more attractive because income level is usually not the basis for eligibility. Rather, loan feasibility depends on the size of their home equity positions and sometimes also on the future appreciation potential of their homes.

These instruments offer an important source of immediate and long-term income for older persons seeking to remain in their current homes. While the benefits of these financial instruments are often described in detail, it is prudent to identify some of their downsides. Foremost, borrowing against one's home is a risky endeavor, and paying back a loan too often means having to sell one's home. Reverse mortgages, in particular, present a complex and uncertain lending environment. The ultimate costs of borrowing are frequently not known until the end of the loan term and can vary dramatically according to the length of the loan term, the age of the borrower, the number of persons in the household, the extent that debt service is based on fixed or variable interest rates, the back-end loan charges, and whether the lender is entitled to all, part, or none of the appreciated value of the home at loan payback. Elderly consumers must be especially alert to how loan payback provisions will be influenced by their actuarial versus their actual life expectancy, the possibility that they may become institutionalized during the loan term, and the possible loss of decision-making powers due to mental incompetence. They must be sensitive to how inflation may substantially erode the purchasing power of their scheduled cash advances, and how these instruments will affect their own and their heirs' financial status at the end of the loan term. And finally, they must be wary of being victims of financial elder abuse* by scams or outright fraud.

There is a need for both financial advisors* and elderly consumers to assess under what social and economic circumstances each of these various home equity generating approaches is most appropriate. They should be compared with such obvious alternatives as moving to a lesser-valued dwelling or a rental apartment with the reinvestment of part or all of the home-sale proceeds in annuities*, the adopting of a sale-leaseback plan, perhaps with a family member as legitimate buyer, and the renting of the home to a boarder in return for some combination of cash income and in-kind services. However attached older people are to their homes, they must recognize that by borrowing against their home they are de facto increasing their real costs of homeownership and thus potentially reducing their expenditures on other, possibly essential, consumer products and services. Home equity conversion* approaches might prove to be especially expensive if older persons are already overhoused and utilizing only a fraction of their dwelling's living space. They are especially ill-advised for older persons who already have untapped alternative investment or savings income. Some groups of older homeowners will themselves be rejected as candidates for these financing instruments. These include cash-poor older persons who are also occupying homes with small equity positions. Homes occupied by elderly house-holders below the poverty level (about 13.5% of all elderly homeowners) had a median value of $49,004 (U.S. Bureau of the Census 1993).

While the popularity of reverse mortgages as home equity–generating approaches has increased, they have found favor with only a relatively small percentage of older homeowners. Negative attitudes toward debt, concerns about the size of their estate, preferences for greater financial return, no strong desire to increase their consumer spending, and the very complexity of these loan instruments are the usual reasons. Together with the recognition that older persons are reluctant to reduce their home equity by moving, some experts now question the validity of the life-cycle savings-spending theory promulgated by economists (Venti and Wise 1989). This predicts that individuals accumulate assets in their middle adult years when their earning capacities are highest, savings are increasing, and housing, family, and other consumer costs are declining, and after retirement they begin to gradually consume their wealth or dissave. Other experts argue that older people's low use of these financial instruments reflects a lack of availability of reverse mortgages and the ineffectiveness of current marketing efforts to communicate their potential. The resolution of these opposing positions is further complicated by researchers who suggest that current attitudes and behaviors towards saving and dissaving are generationally driven. They argue that when the baby boom generation (born between 1946 and 1965) turns age 65 (around the year 2011) and becomes the largest group of elderly Americans, they will be less adverse to accumulating debt, more receptive to these complicated financial instruments, and more disposed toward releasing the equity locked in their largest asset.

Issues for the Future

As increasing numbers and percentages of older people are staying in their homes or aging in place, traditional assessments of home affordability are becoming obsolete. This is a result of the home constituting shelter and a setting for special services and home care*. The conventional home is increasingly compared with supportive group housing alternatives, such as congregate living, shared group living, assisted living*, continuing care retirement communities*, and nursing homes*. Housing cost comparisons have become more complex and require computations that measure items such as the delivery of food, special transportation, chore services, personal care, and nursing services along with the traditional shelter attributes of the owned home. A central research and public policy issue is the cost-effectiveness of physically and mentally frail older persons receiving shelter and care in their own homes as opposed to relocating to these other settings. (See also ASSISTED LIVING, CONDOMINIUMS, CONTINUING CARE RETIREMENT COMMUNITIES, COOPERATIVE HOUSING, HOME MODIFICATIONS FINANCING, MEDICAID, MORTGAGE INSTRUMENTS, NURSING HOMES, and REVERSE MORTGAGES.)

References

Eller, T. J. 1994. *Household Wealth and Asset Ownership: 1991.* Current Population Reports, Series P-70, No. 34. Washington, DC: U.S. Government Printing Office.

Lane, Terry, and Judith D. Feins. 1985. "Are the Elderly Overhoused? Definitions of Space Utilization and Policy Implications." *The Gerontologist* 25: 243–50.

LaPlante, M. P., Gerry E. Hendershot, and Abigail J. Moss. 1992. *Assistive Technology Devices and Home Accessibility Features: Prevalence, Payment, Need, and Trends.* Advance Data 217: 1–12. Hyattsville, MD: National Center for Health Statistics.

Mackey, Scott, and Karen Carter. 1994. *State Tax Policy and Senior Citizens.* Second Edition. Washington, DC: National Conference of State Legislatures.

Pynoos, Jon. 1993. "Towards A National Policy On Home Modification." *Technology and Disability* 2: 1–8.

Reschovsky, Andrew. 1994. *Do the Elderly Face High Property Tax Burdens?* Washington, DC: American Association of Retired Persons.

Reschovsky, James D., and Sandra J. Newman. 1991. "Home Upkeep And Housing Quality Of Older Homeowners." *Journal of Gerontology* 46: S288–97.

U.S. Bureau of the Census. 1992. *Homeowners and Home Improvements: 1987.* Current Housing Reports, Series H121/92/1. Washington, DC: U.S. Government Printing Office.

U.S. Bureau of the Census. 1993. *American Housing Survey for the United States in 1991.* Current Housing Reports, Series H150/91. Washington, DC: U.S. Government Printing Office.

Venti, Steven F., and David A. Wise. 1989. "Aging, Moving, and Housing Wealth." In *The Economics of Aging,* ed. David A. Wise. Chicago: University of Chicago Press, 9–54.

Stephen M. Golant

HOSPICE CARE, specialized care for people during the last phases of illness, so that they may live as fully and comfortably as possible. Hospices provide constant palliative care (pain relief and symptom management) to terminally ill patients, and supportive services to patients, their families, and significant others in home-and facility-based settings. Hospice services focus on physical, social, spiritual, and emotional care during the final stages of illness and during bereavement by a medically directed interdisciplinary team consisting of patients, their families, professionals, and volunteers (National Hospice Organization [NHO] 1993b).

There are over 2,000 hospice programs in the United States. In 1993, they served 275,000 patients, of which approximately 70% were aged 65 or older. Of all hospice patients, 78% were diagnosed with cancer, 10% had heart-related diagnoses, 4% had AIDS, 1% had renal diagnoses, 1% had Alzheimer's Disease, and 6% had other diagnoses. The average length of time a patient receives hospice services is 64 days (NHO 1993a).

Hospice provides a coordinated program of services across a variety of inpatient and outpatient settings, including home health agencies, hospitals, nursing homes*, and free-standing or independent organizations. The primary setting for hospice care is the patient's home. The Medicare Hospice Benefit includes a comprehensive set of services in all settings. Covered services include nursing care (which may be continuous during periods of crisis to maintain a patient at home); medical social services; physician services; counseling services; pastoral care; short-term inpatient and respite care; medical appliances and supplies; drugs for symptom management and pain control; home health aide and home-maker services; physical, speech, and occupational therapies; and bereavement counseling. These services are coordinated by an interdisciplinary team of pro-fessionals and delivered according to the patient's individualized plan of care. Volunteers are also fundamental to the hospice philosophy and play an integral role in providing care. They may offer professional medical services, direct patient care, or provide administrative, counseling, or homemaker services. In a requirement unique to hospice programs, Medicare* asks hospices to use vol-unteers in administrative or direct patient care roles equal to 5% of the total patient care hours of all paid hospice employees (Lewin-VHI, Inc. 1994).

Hospice care is financed through a number of sources, including Medicare, Medicaid*, private insurance plans, patients, and charity funds. In 1992, Med-icare and Medicaid accounted for three-fourths of hospice revenues. Medicare reimbursement for hospices is on a prospective, per-diem basis, at four different rates relating to the amount of home or inpatient care involved. Medicare also imposes an annual aggregate cap on hospice care; in 1994, it was calculated on a per-patient basis of $12,846.

Medicare covers hospice services when the beneficiary elects the Medicare Hospice Benefit, is certified by a physician as terminally ill with a life expec-tancy of six months or less, and when care is provided by a Medicare-certified hospice program. Once hospice is elected, the beneficiary waives traditional Medicare coverage for the terminal illness and the hospice benefit covers the four levels of care-routine: home care, continuous home care, respite, and gen-eral inpatient care. All services are covered with the exception of the patient's attending physician, who bills directly to Medicare Part B. Hospices may require coinsurance from Medicare beneficiaries only for drugs and inpatient respite care. Coinsurance may not exceed 5% of the cost of a prescription (up to a $5 maximum) or 5% of the payment made by Medicare for an inpatient respite day (Lewin-VHI, Inc. 1994).

Interest in hospice care has grown because of its cost-effectiveness relative to conventional care. As has been widely publicized, 28% of all Medicare ex-penditures (more than $40 billion in 1992) are for people in their last year of life, and almost 50% of these costs are expended in the last two months of life. The federally sponsored evaluation of the first three years of the Medicare Hos-pice Benefit (Kidder et al. 1989) found significant savings for hospice care compared with conventional care. For example, for every dollar spent on hospice care, Medicare saved $1.26. During the last month of life, hospice care averages $3,069, while conventional care costs $4,071 (Lewin-VHI, Inc. 1994). Other data indicate that hospice patients paid significantly fewer out-of-pocket costs than conventional care patients. According to the National Hospice Study, hospice patients receiving waivered medical services under the hospice demonstration project paid about $6 per day in out-of-pocket costs, while hospice patients not receiving waivered services under the demonstration project paid $23 per day, and conventional care patients spent $46 per day (Mor et al. 1988).

Research on hospice care also has focused on quality. There is reasonably strong evidence that hospice care provides better quality of life for patients and caregivers. Although it is difficult to scientifically evaluate quality of life, based on available data, significant differences were found in five quality-of-life measures for hospice and conventional care patients. These include: measures of pain, satisfaction with interpersonal care, satisfaction with involvement with care, quality of care, and patient's social involvement with the support system. Significant differences were also found to favor hospice in four measures used to evaluate the quality of life of the primary caregiver. Hospice primary caregivers were less anxious and were more satisfied with their involvement in care than the conventional caregivers.

Hospice has been successful in today's health care environment because it addresses people's fears about dying in pain, alone, and without personal dignity. Hospice is particularly important because of its strong emphasis on coordination of services, patient participation in care planning, and patient choice. While the growth of hospice care has been steady over the last decade, its value is becoming more widely known and will undoubtedly increase as the population ages. A recent Gallup Poll suggested that almost 90% of Americans would prefer to use the services commonly associated with hospice care if they were terminally ill rather than undergo multiple hospitalizations, nursing home placements, or disorganized home-care treatment. Hospice provides a choice to the terminally ill patient for whom a traditional medical model, with its technological imperative, may no longer be appropriate. (See also ACCELERATED DEATH BENEFITS, GERIATRIC CARE MANAGERS, HOME CARE SERVICES FOR THE ELDERLY, MEDICAID, MEDICARE, and NURSING HOMES.)

Organizations

Hospice Association of America
Hospice Education Institute, "Hospice Link"
National Hospice Organization Hospice Hotline

Suggested Readings

Ahronheim, Judith, and Doran Weber. 1992. *Final Passages: Positive Choices for the Dying and Their Loved Ones.* New York: Simon & Schuster.
Health Care Financing Administration. 1994. *Medicare: Hospice Benefits.* Publication No. 607A. Consumer Information Center, Department 87, Pueblo, CO 81009.

References

Kidder, D., K. Merrell, and D. Dohan. 1989. *Medicare Hospice Benefit Program Evaluation: Final Summary Report.* Cambridge, MA: ABT Associates Inc.

Lewin-VHI, Inc. 1994. *Hospice Care: An Introduction and Review of the Evidence.* Arlington, VA: National Hospice Organization.

Mor, V., D. S. Greer, and R. Kastenbaum. 1988. *The Hospice Experiment.* National Hospice Study. Baltimore, MD: Johns Hopkins University Press.

National Hospice Organization. 1993a. "1992 Stats Shows Continued Growth in Programs and Patients." *NHO NewsLine*: Author. Arlington, VA.

National Hospice Organization. 1993b. "Hospice Philosophy." *NHO Standards of a Hospice Program of Care*: Author, p. 111. Arlington, VA.

Christine Cody

HOUSING, the living environments of older persons. The majority of the elderly reside in ordinary houses in community neighborhoods. Only about 5% are in nursing homes or other institutions, and a similar fraction are in special housing. Housing issues directly affect quality of life for the elderly and lie at the crux of financial gerontology. Housing often becomes complicated for older persons because it is influenced by other issues: financial constraints, changes in transportation* needs, health problems and medical care needs, maintenance, repairs, and modifications needed for physical limitations.

Financial Constraints of Aging at Home

The reduction of income at retirement affects the affordability of housing, and fixed incomes continue to decline over time due to inflation. Older persons spend a larger proportion of their incomes on housing than any other age group. They also have greater expenditures for medical care and medications. Since a large proportion of their income goes toward housing and medical expenses, those choosing to age at home tend to skimp on essentials such as food, clothing, and home heating. The elderly often eat poorly and live in dangerously cold environments in order to keep otherwise unaffordable homes.

Transportation

Housing and transportation become interrelated issues for elderly persons. Driving often becomes less of an option for the elderly due to loss of driver's licenses and the high cost of automobiles and maintenance. Public transportation is less available in the suburbs, and when available, is commonly designed to serve commuters, not the elderly. Older persons are often reluctant to use public transit because of physical limitations and embarrassment felt when younger commuters express impatience with them. Fear of crime and feelings of vulnerability deter elders from using public transportation as well. Since many older people walk as their primary means of transportation to shopping, banking, socializing, and other activities of everyday life, they are restricted in the amount and weight of items they can bring home.

Intergenerational Problems

Older persons prefer to live independently in their own homes, which can cause intergenerational problems. In some families, adult children urge parents to move to protected environments, such as their homes or retirement communities. Elderly persons, however, often experience difficulty adjusting to new home environments. Transitions to childrens' homes can be uncomfortable, because they sense adult childrens' reluctance to have parents live with them, and many parents—except those from cultures where multigenerational family living is common—are hesitant to live with their children. Widowers are more likely than widows to be taken into the homes of children, usually daughters. Research has shown that the physical condition of elders' housing is improved for those living with younger families (Lawton 1981).

On a societal level, the desire of older people to ''age in place'' may involve intergenerational conflict in terms of the housing stock. Older persons are sometimes considered to be ''overhoused'' when children move out or when one spouse dies. Some experts believe overhousing is an adverse influence on the well-being of older persons, but the elderly themselves do not perceive it to be so. Intergenerational equity issues may also be raised in these situations. One solution is for the older person (usually widowed) to give her home to an adult child in exchange for a life estate, but this has capital gains, estate tax, and other financial and emotional implications that should be considered carefully with the help of financial advisors*.

Housing Safety

Aging in place raises issues of home safety, since unsteadiness is common among older occupants. Falls, especially in bathrooms and kitchens, are special hazards for the elderly. Kitchen shelves exceed the reach of the average elderly woman, and stepping up on a stool or chair is hazardous because of diminished agility, strength, and balance (Czaja et al. 1993). Standard bathrooms do not provide secure handholds for entering and exiting the tub or shower, or for toileting. Frequent nighttime trips to bathrooms are more common among the elderly, compounding problems. A conference that focused on lifespan design of residential environments for a population that is aging concluded that many design features that older persons need (e.g., grab bars) are beneficial also for younger persons, and that original building designs should incorporate provisions for easy modification of other features as they become needed later (American Association of Retired Persons 1993).

Repair and modification programs designed to allow older persons to remain in their homes are increasing. Pynoos, Overton, Liebig, and Calvert (forthcoming) studied 300 such programs and found that evaluations of home environments tend to be slanted toward programs of the assessors (e.g., weatherization) rather than include the total needs of the home and its residents. They also found that occupational therapists were best trained to evaluate people-in-environment. In both home modification and home rehabilitation programs for older people, standard and coordinated procedures to assess both persons and environments are needed.

Possibilities for the Future

The oldest old*, the group most likely to live in institutions, is the fastest growing segment of the elderly population. This suggests a future need for more nursing homes, since the majority of institutionalized elderly suffer from Alzheimer's Disease or other dementing conditions. Awareness of the need to house them in Special Care Units (SCUs) is also increasing. Construction of new HUD-assisted rental housing* for the elderly is unlikely; local housing authorities have impossibly long waiting lists and are terminating receipt of new applications. Other federally funded elderly housing programs have decreased. Homelessness among the elderly* is difficult to measure, but it is obvious that the elderly are among the most vulnerable of that group. While the first shelter for homeless elderly in the nation opened in Berkeley, California, in January 1994 with 15 beds, more shelters are needed.

Retirement communities attract a minority of older people and probably will continue to do so, since their special attractions include security and country-club living style. As retirement communities age, however, the need for in-home and nursing home–type care among long-time residents increases. This is exacerbated by the rise in monthly ''dues'' over the years, and the relative decline in income for residents who retired long ago. Since these needs conflict with the image that attracts younger retirees (and that developers of such communities want to project), it is likely that more continuing care retirement communities* will be built in the future.

A majority of people undoubtedly will continue to remain in ordinary housing in neighborhood communities as they grow old. To support their well-being and the quality of their lives, such concepts as ''adaptable housing'' in new construction should include design features beneficial to all age groups that facilitate modifications over the lifespan. Better means of identifying person-environment incongruencies that impede needed and desired activities must be sought. In-home services for older persons should be expanded, coordinated, and made more equitably and widely available. In all of these efforts, housing the elderly must be viewed within the context of other environmental factors such as inflation, postretirement health insurance*, transportation, crime protection*, and other social forces. (See also CONTINUING CARE RETIREMENT COMMUNITIES, CRIME PROTECTION, HOMELESSNESS, HOME MODIFICATIONS FINANCING, HUD-ASSISTED RENTAL HOUSING, NURSING HOMES, POSTRETIREMENT HEALTH INSURANCE, TRANSPORTATION, and WIDOWHOOD.)

Organization

Lifease

References

American Association of Retired Persons. 1993. *Life-Span Design of Residential Environments for an Aging Population.* Washington, DC: AARP.

Carp, Frances M. 1966. *A Future for the Aged: The Residents of Victoria Plaza.* Austin, TX: University of Texas Press.

Carp, Frances M. 1988. "Significance of Mobility for the Well-Being of the Elderly." In *Transportation in an Aging Society: Vol. 1: Technical Papers, Transportation Research Board Special Report 218.* Washington, DC: National Research Council, 1–21.

Carp, Frances M. (Forthcoming). "Environment." In *Annual Review of Gerontology and Geriatrics, Volume 14: Assessment Techniques,* ed. M. Powell Lawton & Jeanne Teresi. New York: Springer.

Czaja, S. J., R. A. Weber, and N. N. Sankaran. 1993. "A Human Factors Analysis of ADL Activities: A Capacity-Demand Approach." *Journal of Gerontology* 48: 44–48.

Lawton, M. Powell. 1981. "Ecological View of Living Arrangements." *Gerontologist* 21: 59–66.

Pynoos, Jon, and E. Cohen. 1990. *Home Safety Guide for Older People.* Washington, DC: Serif Press.

Pynoos, Jon, and E. Cohen. 1992. *The Perfect Fit: Creative Ideas for a Safe and Livable Home.* Washington, DC: AARP.

Pynoos, Jon, J. Overton, P. Liebig, and E. Calvert. Forthcoming. "The Delivery of Home Modifications and Repair Services." In *Housing Adaptations to Meet Changing Needs: Research, Policy & Programs,* ed. J. Hyde and S. Lanspery. Amityville, NY: Baywood Publishing.

Frances M. Carp

HUD-ASSISTED RENTAL HOUSING, programs enacted under the National Housing Act (NHA) of 1937, as amended, and administered by the U.S. Department of Housing and Urban Development (HUD). Financial help is provided for older Americans through a variety of public, private, and nonprofit sponsorships where rent is based on a rent-to-income ratio for eligible tenants. Three HUD programs have provided the rent-subsidized housing units that serve the U.S. elderly population (aged 62 and older): Conventional Low-Rent Public Housing, Section 202, and the Section 8 Program.

Shelter is a basic need that can consume the major portion of a monthly budget. For older people on fixed incomes, housing costs can be overwhelming. Although regulations, requirements, and financing arrangements concerning housing development and tenant subsidies vary, the financial impact on older persons who participate in these rental assistance programs is essentially the same. It is this impact, rather than the subtle differences between programs, that is valuable to understand.

Over 1,433,000 elderly families are helped through HUD programs. As of 1993, HUD housing programs served approximately 35% of older American households believed to be income-eligible for assistance. Other pertinent characteristics of older assisted families are shown in Table 1.

Conventional public housing projects for the elderly in most communities are highrise or garden complexes owned, operated, and maintained by local public

Table 1
Characteristics of Elderly Families (Households in Thousands)

	Total Assisted		Total Eligible Unassisted		Total Eligible		Percent Served
Age of Householder							
65 to 74	617	43%	1264	47%	1881	46%	33%
75 and older	816	57%	1413	53%	2229	54%	37%
Median	75+		75+		75+		
Income Source							
Wages and salaries	121	8%	269	10%	390	9%	31%
Business	1	0%	17	1%	18	0%	6%
Social Security or pensions	139	97%	2506	94%	3898	95%	36%
Interest or dividends	145	10%	443	17%	588	14%	25%
Rental income	2	0%	36	1%	38	1%	5%
Welfare or SSI	306	21%	490	18%	796	19%	38%
Alimony or child support	3	0%	8	0%	11	0%	27%
Other	2	2%	108	4%	134	3%	19%
Regional Location							
Northeast	479	33%	638	24%	1117	27%	43%
Midwest	381	27%	719	27%	1100	27%	35%
South	378	26%	776	29%	1154	28%	33%
West	194	14%	544	20%	738	18%	26%

Source: U.S. Department of Housing and Urban Development, Report to Congress on Elderly Families, Families with Children, and Disabled Families Served by Federal Housing Programs, 1994.

housing agencies. There are about 3,000 agencies in various U.S. communities, not including American Indian housing authorities. These agencies may acquire, construct, modernize, or lease low-income housing for elderly individuals and husband-wife couples, and local agency-owners strive to make their developments appear no different from those offered by private owners at market rates. Financial assistance to subsidize operations and maintenance of these properties is funded by HUD to the local agency. In some areas, often large cities, housing supported under these programs is poorly regarded and sometimes badly managed, and has received negative press by the media. In other areas, particularly small- and medium-sized communities, local agencies provide quality programs and the housing developments they manage are favorably regarded.

The Section 202 program, enacted under the NHA in 1959, finances the construction, for nonprofit sponsors, of low-rent apartment developments for the elderly and the non-elderly disabled populations. Originally intended to serve older persons with incomes somewhat higher than Public Housing tenants, 202-funded apartment projects were combined with the Section 8 housing assistance program in 1974, making the units available to lower-income elderly. Tenants currently spend 30% of their income on rent and utilities, and operating deficits are covered by monthly subsidies from HUD. Many of the developments built under Section 202 contain community rooms and recreational services, and are outfitted with ramped entries, grab bars, and other design features necessary for elderly residents.

Under the Section 8 Certificate program, an elderly person or family is issued a certificate attesting to their qualifications for rental assistance. An eligible elderly person or family finds suitable housing in the private marketplace and can choose either 202-funded housing run by nonprofit sponsors for elderly persons or privately owned and operated houses or apartments. The Section 8 Certificate represents a commitment to the landlord in either case to pay the difference between what the individual or family can afford to pay and the market rent. Market rentals are determined and approved for housing unit types located within particular geographic areas or regions and represent the maximum rent that would be charged for an apartment by a private landlord. The local housing authority maintains a schedule of approved Fair Market Rents.

The Section 8 program also includes nonprofit or limited profit, privately owned and managed housing for elderly residents. The difference from the Certificate approach is that the subsidy is allocated to the individual units, and if a family qualifies, application is made directly to the owner or manager of the privately sponsored, assisted housing development. Services geared to the needs and concerns of an older community may also be provided and may include free, on-site medical screening, transportation services, meals-on-wheels, and recreation activities at low cost or even no additional cost to residents.

A Case Illustration

John and Mary Jones are former homeowners now in their late sixties. When their children were grown and gone, they sold their home and rented a two-bedroom apartment for $550 plus utilities that averaged $100 per month. A working-class family, home equity was their only asset, and the amount cleared from the sale of their home was $35,000. They gave their son $10,000 toward a down payment on his own house and saved $25,000, which now earns interest at the passbook savings rate of 3%. Their second-story, walk-up apartment consumes approximately 50% of their monthly income and their health costs are rising. Mary's arthritis is making it difficult for her to climb stairs, but rents are increasing in the community, and John and Mary can find no affordable ground-level alternative—even a smaller apartment.

To learn whether John and Mary Jones are eligible for federal assistance, their total annual income must be calculated. From combined Social Security* and pension payments, they receive income of $15,096 plus $750 in interest income, for a total of $15,846. Although the Joneses own a car, jewelry, and other personal effects, these are not counted within the asset definitions, which include only the $25,000 in savings.

Income is the major criterion that qualifies older persons for rental assistance, and amounts are based on the median income for the Standard Metropolitan Statistical Area in which the housing is found. Differences exist in income eligibility criteria throughout the United States. Eligibility income for New York City would be considerably higher than for Brownsville, Texas. Eligibility is based on personal income in relation to others' personal income in their particular geographic location. Conventional Public Housing apartments allow a family to earn as much as 80% of Median Income for their area and remain eligible. The Section 8 Certificate Housing Assistance program limits eligibility to 50% of Median Income for the area.

In almost all geographic locations, John and Mary Jones would qualify under the Conventional Public Housing Program. In many areas, they also would qualify for the lower income eligibility requirements of the Section 8 program. John and Mary would be eligible, under federal rules, for a one-bedroom apartment, and a rent-to-income formula would be used to determine the rent they must pay. Rent is based on a family's total annual income, less deductions for individual circumstances. Since most older people do not have children and are not working, two types of deductions are most applicable. The first is an Elderly Family deduction of $400 for a family head or spouse over age 62, and the second is for excessive medical costs. Medical expenses must be substantiated and nonreimbursable by medical insurance or other sources.

Mary's arthritic condition is likely to satisfy the excessive medical cost requirement, since she incurs out-of-pocket, nonreimbursed expenses of $500 a year for doctor visits, physical therapy, and over-the-counter drug purchases connected to her arthritis. After the medical deduction allowance is calculated, the Joneses may deduct $75 for allowable medical expenses plus the $400 allowance for elderly families. Their adjusted income is $15,731.

The formula that must now be applied to determine the family's rent is the greater of 30% of Monthly Adjusted Income ($384), or 10% of Monthly Income

($138). In a federally assisted apartment, John and Mary would be expected to pay $384 a month as rent.

The Joneses could explore the availability of housing under the Conventional Public Housing Section 8 Program or private, nonprofit-sponsored housing program using Section 8 federal assistance. In the case of Conventional Public Housing, the Joneses would apply to the local housing authority in their community. When occupying a public housing apartment, they would pay $384 for their shelter and utilities. Under the Section 8 Certificate program, the maximum local rent for a one-bedroom apartment by a private landlord would be about $625, including utilities.

If John and Mary decided to rent the unit, they would pay $384 as their contribution to rent and utilities, dividing the amount into a payment of $309 to the private landlord and $75 to pay for utilities.

If the market rent were $525, the difference between the $309 received from the Joneses and the monthly rent on the unit is $216, and this amount of federal subsidy assistance would be sent directly to the landlord by the agency administering the program.

Further information on available federally assisted public housing in a particular locality can be obtained from the local housing authority, the municipal government, or the local HUD field office. (See also FINANCIAL COUNSELING, HOUSING, SENIORS HOUSING FINANCE, and SUPPLEMENTAL SECURITY INCOME.)

References

Folts, E., and D. Yeats. 1994. *Housing the Aging Population.* New York: Garland Publishing.

Golant, Stephen M. 1992. *Housing America's Elderly.* Newbury Park, CA: Sage Publications.

National Association of Housing and Redevelopment Officials. 1981. *Public Housing Management Resource Manual.* Washington, DC: NAHRO.

U.S. Senate. Special Committee on Aging. 1993. *Developments in Aging: 1993.* Publication 103–403. Washington, DC: U.S. Government Printing Office.

U.S. Department of Housing and Urban Development. 1994. *Report to the Congress on Elderly Families, Families with Children, and Disabled Families Served by Federal Housing Programs.* Washington, DC: HUD.

U.S. Department of Housing and Urban Development. 1989. *Programs of HUD, 1989–1990.* Publication 214-PA(17). Washington, DC: HUD.

Veronica M. Bukowski and Richard H. Stanton

I

INFLATION. See Assets Allocation after Retirement; Bonds; Cash Flow Planning for Retirees; Cost-of-Living Adjustments (COLAs); Economic Hardship Measures in the Older Population; Equity Securities; Savings Investments; Homeownership.

INDIVIDUAL RETIREMENT ACCOUNTS (IRAs), a form of individual "defined contribution" pension or retirement account with a bank, savings institution, brokage firm, or insurance company. Establishing an IRA is straightforward and involves little paperwork. Before changes in the tax code (1986), the most frequently used retirement savings instruments were IRAs. Anyone with work-related income could establish an IRA and contribute up to the lesser of $2,000 or 100% of compensation per year. If both spouses had income, up to $4,000 could be deducted from their joint adjusted gross income. These funds thus escaped income taxes in the year earned as did the annual earnings on the money invested. The taxes were not eliminated, but rather deferred until the benefits were received by the contributors. If only one spouse was employed, a spousal IRA could be set up with an additional $250 contribution. This provided a valuable opportunity to split contributions to meet retirement and tax needs.

The 1986 tax reform legislation changed the nature of the IRA account and limited its benefits for many taxpayers. Currently, for people who are active participants in another qualified retirement plan (or are married to an active participant in another qualified retirement plan), full deductibility is available only for single taxpayers earning $25,000 or less and for joint filers earning up to $40,000. The deductibility of the contribution is phased out above these dollar amounts; a partial deduction is allowed for single taxpayers earning between $25,000 and $35,000, and for joint filers earning between $40,000 and $50,000.

Above these limits, contributions are not deductible. However, the $2,000/100% maximum contribution can still be made with after-tax funds, and the income accumulations are not taxed until benefits are received.

Benefits

Individual Retirement Accounts are available to anyone, even if they are already covered by a qualified retirement plan. All of the income the IRA account earns will compound with all taxes deferred until the individual withdraws funds from the account. The principal advantage of an IRA, along with the possibility of deductible contributions, is in the tax deferral of interest earnings.

To illustrate the compounding effect and impact of time on an IRA account, consider that a $2,000 contribution per year for 30 years invested at an average of 9% per year would grow to $320,202. A similar arrangement started 10 years later, a 20-year annual investment program of $2,000 per year invested at 9%, would accumulate to $116,815. Thus, the longer the money accumulates, the larger the benefit.

Plan Location

Individuals are not required to leave IRA funds with the same institution and may move the account from one place to another without tax penalty. However, the move may involve fees imposed by the institution from which the funds are being withdrawn, and the paperwork may take considerable time. One should be careful to retain all papers and documents related to the change in custodian for future references in the event of an Internal Revenue Service (IRS) audit.

Restrictions

IRA funds cannot be commingled (mixed) with other assets. The account may contain only IRA contributions and earnings, and qualified rollover contributions, which are discussed below. Funds deposited in IRA accounts cannot be used to purchase life insurance* or invested in collectibles, and funds may not be borrowed from IRA accounts. The regulations, in short, require that IRA accounts be maintained separately from other assets and that the accounts be left alone until withdrawn.

Withdrawals from IRAs

IRA funds may be withdrawn at retirement: (1) in one lump sum, (2) in installments over remaining life expectancy, or (3) in the form of an annuity that will provide a period of guaranteed payments. Distributions of deductible contributions and all earnings are taxable as ordinary income when received. Nondeductible contributions may be withdrawn without being taxed; however, the IRS requires that nondeductible contributions be withdrawn proportionately with deductible contributions and earnings. Thus, at least a portion of each withdrawal will be taxable.

When withdrawals are made before age 59, there is currently a 10% penalty tax in addition to ordinary income taxes due on the funds received. Funds must start being withdrawn by age 70½ or tax penalties occur. Since the tax code changes from time to time, it is extremely important to talk to one's financial advisor* or attorney* concerning specific circumstances.

Rollover IRAs

In addition to the annual contributions individuals make to their IRA accounts, distributions from an employer retirement plan occasioned by retirement, job change, disability, death of a spouse, or plan termination may be placed in IRA accounts. In these cases a ''rollover'' continues the tax shelter for the funds involved and avoids income taxes and penalties that would otherwise be assessed. The transaction must be completed within 60 days of the retirement plan distribution. Rollovers allow funds to continue to earn income on a tax-deferred basis until withdrawal becomes appropriate or necessary. This is especially valuable for individuals having no current need for the funds involved.

IRAs, like all tax deferral plans, are valuable in direct relation to the amount of time the savings program is in effect. If an IRA is started early in life, a considerable amount of funds can accumulate, but as retirement draws near, the opportunity for significant accumulation is no longer available. As retirement approaches, seeking professional advice from financial advisors is highly recommended. (See also ATTORNEYS, CASH FLOW PLANNING FOR RETIREES, EARLY RETIREMENT INCENTIVE PROGRAMS, ESTATE PLANNING, FINANCIAL ADVISORS, KEOGH PLANS, PENSION FUND TRENDS, SAVINGS INVESTMENTS, and WEALTH SPAN.)

References

Crowe, Robert M. 1990. *Fundamentals of Financial Planning.* Bryn Mawr, PA: American College.

Gitman, Lawrence J., and Michael D. Joehnk. 1990. *Fundamentals of Investing.* New York: Harper & Row.

Kapoor, Jack R., Les R. Dlabay, and Robert J. Hughes. 1991. *Personal Finance.* Homewood, IL: Irwin.

Ganas K. Rakes

INHERITANCE, the disposition of one's property upon death. Historically, inheritance was the passing of one's estate to his—rarely her—heirs. Heirs were strictly predetermined by established law, usually designating the decedent's eldest son. Today, there is a wide degree of latitude in one's options for disposing of property after death. Although most states guarantee a share to a surviving spouse, a person is otherwise free to dispose of his or her property as he or she chooses. Inheritance loosely applies to any disposition of property after death, whether by will*, trust*, or operation of law. There are a number of tools available to control who will inherit one's estate, varying in complexity, cost, and the degree of control the deceased can exercise from the grave.

The History of Inheritance

The inheritance system emerged from feudalism, in the early stages of which the strong man extorted or confiscated the land of the weak in return for protection. The lord then "lent" it back to his vassal as long as certain obligations were faithfully performed. After the Norman Conquest of 1066, William the Conqueror confiscated all land owned by the Saxons, redistributing it to his own barons. The king remained the true owner, and the barons held the land as "tenants in chief" as long as they remained obedient. These feudal tenures originally terminated upon death, but it soon became customary to regrant the land to the decedent's eldest son, although, of course, a fee was required. The system provided stability and predictability, and by the end of the twelfth century had "crystallized into a 'common law right of inheritance' " (Cribbet et al. 1990). The system was so stable and predictable, however, that the wishes of the deceased were unable to alter the scheme.

In England, where American law originated, the transfer of land (real property) by will was not allowed until 1540, although transfer of personal property by will was more or less unrestricted. In fact, the ecclesiastical courts had jurisdiction over the probate of wills for personal property, and by convincing its incredulous flock that a will was necessary for salvation, the Church guaranteed itself substantial fees. Though lawyers have replaced priests, remnants of the church's probate scheme remain today. A 1990 AARP study concluded that probate is "costly, slow, and outmoded . . . a sad state of affairs" (Budish and Clifford 1991).

The Social Merits of Inheritance

The social merits of inheritance have long been debated. Thomas Jefferson, in a letter to James Madison, said "that portion occupied by an individual ceases to be, and reverts to the society" (1789). The Soviet Union went so far as to ban inheritance, but the policy was abandoned as a failure after only four years, because it was felt that inheritance encouraged savings and incentives to work, and relieved the state of providing for dependents (Dukeminier and Johanson 1990). While a ban on inheritance has proven to be counterproductive, it is not unreasonable to expect a decedent to "pay his tab to society." The nation's estate tax policy is an attempt to balance these competing factors.

While defending the vast wealth he and other industrialists had accumulated, Andrew Carnegie was equally adamant that disparities in wealth should not be perpetuated through inheritance (Glastris 1990). The industrialists had earned their wealth, after all, but the social utility of leaving great wealth to family members who made no significant contributions to its accumulation was questionable. Does inheritance of wealth encourage the hard work, thrift, and initiative that helped to create it in the first place, or perpetuate a class of unproductive ingrates? Carnegie encouraged the altruistic use of one's excess wealth, funding projects that would benefit the public generally. To encourage such altruism, the government, said Carnegie, should impose severe estate taxes. While people may argue, "my family is my preferred charity," if asked whether higher taxes on income today or higher taxes after death is preferable, who doubts the likely response?

Intestacy

A person dying without a will or other estate plan leaves the state to determine who will inherit and prompts the involvement of a probate court, with its attendant costs and delays. Although "intestate succession" laws vary from state to state, they generally distribute specified shares to the spouse and children if they survive the decedent, or to other designated relatives if they do not. These laws entail a series of presumptions about how the decedent wanted his or her estate to be distributed—presumptions that may be entirely inconsistent with a person's wishes. After the estate is reduced by probate costs, attorney's fees, and estate taxes, the residue is distributed with no regard to what the decedent really wanted.

For all but the most meager estates, some form of estate planning is needed to ensure that the estate passes according to the decedent's wishes, that estate taxes are minimized, and that probate may be avoided. Traditional estate planning tools include wills and inter vivos trusts.

Wills

The will is the backbone of traditional, conservative estate plans. Through a will, one leaves his or her instructions for the distribution of his or her estate. While it does provide a means for expressing one's wishes, those wishes can only be executed by authority of the probate court. Being a judicial proceeding, probate is lengthy, costly, and intrusive. The costs of a simple probate vary, but the AARP found that they can deplete the average middle-class estate by as much as 10%, and costs can skyrocket if the will is challenged (Budish and Clifford 1991).

Inter Vivos Trusts

For many people, an inter vivos trust (living trust) is a better option: Trusts offer something for everyone. The primary benefit of an inter vivos trust is probate avoidance. Because the title to property is transferred into the trust *during the life* of the decedent, court involvement is usually not required. Living trusts have been used for centuries, but have only become popular as will substitutes since the middle of this century. The up-front costs of a trust are greater than for a will, since the trust is a more complex document than a will and title to assets must be transferred. However, the costs of settling a trust estate are generally much less than the costs of probate. Generally, trusts are cost-effective for estates of about $100,000 or more (Wasik 1993). Provisions can be included in a trust that can reduce the impact of estate taxes, though similar provisions can also be added to a will. While probate of a will is a matter of public record, a trust estate can generally be settled privately.

There has been a concern in recent years over the "selling" of living trusts by nonlawyers, and several states have taken measures to curb this "unauthorized practice of law" (Wasik 1993). In his 1993 *Consumer Digest* article, John Wasik also cautioned that "most of the fraudulent products were being sold by agents or financial planners, not lawyers." People should exercise care when preparing legal documents or taking advice from nonlawyers. A telephone call or letter to the state bar association is a good referral source for qualified estate planning attorneys.

Most people prefer to leave some sort of legacy to those they love: an inheritance. At the personal level, inheritance law offers the tools for a well-informed transfer. At the societal level, the magnitude of inheritance is growing rapidly. The $84 billion of wealth transferred per year at present will increase to $336 billion in the year 2015, and have a significant impact on the American economy.

Estate Taxes

Between now and the year 2040, baby boomers will inherit some $10 trillion: roughly $90,000 each (Stern 1993). This staggering sum will reshape the nation's social and business fabric, and may even become a potential source of revenue for politicians seeking solutions to the budget deficit. Legislators may look increasingly to estate taxes for a solution to counter the mounting deficit, since raising rates on income taxes is an increasingly unpopular move, and budget cuts seem even more elusive. As the debate over deficit reduction continues, society may ask, "Why not let parents and grandparents pay the deficit by increasing estate taxes?" Inheritance, after all, has always been subject to the debts of the decedent.

Current Law

The government has not, however, exacted an onerous burden on estates. Current estate taxes begin at 37%, and run as high as 55%, but only about 2% of all estates are large enough to be assessed any estate taxes at all. This is due primarily to the exemption of $600,000 from estate tax, which is doubled to $1.2 million for a married couple who plans properly. So while the federal government theoretically will take a substantial share of the nation's largest estates, the vast majority of estates are passed estate tax–free to heirs. Current capital gains tax is also structured to favor heirs. If an exempt $1 million inheritance is comprised of real estate purchased fifty years earlier for $100,000, and sold immediately by the heirs, the capital gains of about $250,000 that would otherwise be owed on the $900,000 appreciated value would be avoided.

Parents may place their $1 million primary residence or vacation home into a Grantor Retained Income Trust (GRIT), continue to use the home for the entire period, and reduce the value of the gift to $250,000 even though the house may actually appreciate in value over the years. While taxes on the $250,000 would be due at the time the GRIT was established, the size of the future estate may ultimately be reduced. There are several similar trusts available to reduce the size of one's estate.

Charities

When considering the sale of a highly appreciated property where capital gains taxes are daunting, people consider giving it away. By using a Charitable Remainder Trust, the appreciated property may be sold now, free of capital gains, and a guaranteed income for life retained from the proceeds. In addition, a current tax deduction is available for gifting the remainder to charity. These tax breaks, coupled with income from the untaxed proceeds of the sale, could pay for or exceed the actual gift to charity. Although the gift must go to the charity at death rather than to one's heirs, the overall tax consequences may dramatically improve the amount of one's net estate.

Life Insurance

Finally, life insurance is a tool many people use to provide an estate for the family, or to fund the ultimate estate tax bill. It is important to realize, however, that insurance proceeds may dramatically increase your estate tax bill if not handled properly. Insurance proceeds can be sheltered from estate taxes through use of an Irrevocable Life Insurance Trust.

Estate Tax Planning

If an estate is large enough that estate taxes could be a potential problem, it is imperative to consult an attorney who specializes in estate planning. Shop carefully, however, because it has been estimated that only 1% of all attorneys* can properly draft a living trust (Faltermayer 1991). And even fewer are capable of drafting the more advanced estate planning tools. Spending a little extra now for an attorney who is an expert on estate planning can save a family thousands of dollars later. (See also CAPITAL GAIN, CHARITABLE CONTRIBUTIONS, ESTATE PLANNING, KING LEAR SYNDROME, TRUSTS, WILLS, and WEALTH SPAN.)

References

Budish and Clifford. 1991. "The Multipurpose Trust." *Forbes* (August).
Cribbet, John E. et al. 1990. *Cases and Materials on Property,* Sixth Edition. Westbury, NY: Foundation Press.
Dukeminier, Jesse, and Stanley M. Johanson. 1990. *Wills, Trusts and Estates,* Fourth Edition. Boston: Little, Brown.
Esperti, Robert A. 1993. *Protect Your Estate: A Personal Guide to Intelligent Estate Planning.* New York: McGraw-Hill.
Faltermayer, Edmund. 1991. "The Financially Perfect Death: Adroit Moves While You're Still Around Can Shrink Estate Taxes and Spare Your Heirs the Long Wait of Probate." *Fortune* (February 25).

Glastris, Paul. 1990. "The New Way to Get Rich: Baby Boomers Will Inherit $8 Trillion." *U.S. News and World Report* (May), p.26.

Jefferson, Thomas. 1789. "Letter to James Madison, Paris, September 6, 1789." In *Social and Political Philosophy,* ed. John Somerville and Ronald E. Santoni. Garden City, NY: Doubleday, 261.

Stepanek, Marcia. 1994. "Deeper in Debt: The Rising Tab from Deficit Spending Is a Symbol of a Government Out of Control." *Arizona Republic* (March 20), C-1.

Stern, Linda. 1993. "Inheritances: Next Boom for Boomers." *Seattle Post-Intelligencer* (December 28).

Wasik, John F. 1993. "Living Trusts vs. Wills: Estate Planning Guide." *Consumer's Digest* (September/October).

Scott A. Miskiel

INSURANCE. See Accident Insurance; Liability Insurance; Long Term Care Insurance; Individual Disability-Enhancing Annuities (IDEAs); Long-Term Care Insurance: Private; Medicaid; Medicare; Medicare Supplemental Insurance; Postretirement Health Insurance (PRHI).

INTERGENERATIONAL ISSUES. See Business Succession Planning; Caregiving for the Elderly; Cohabitation; Estate Planning; Financial Elder Abuse; Geriatric Care Managers; Guardianship; Housing; Inheritance; Medicaid Planning; Trusts.

INVESTMENTS. See Annuities; Bonds; Commodities; Derivatives; Equities; Federal Agency Securities; Mutual Funds; Savings Account Trusts; Savings Investments.

K

KEOGH PLANS, also known as HR-10 plans or self-employed retirement plans, are "qualified" retirement plans for self-employed individuals and their employees. When designed and operated in compliance with Internal Revenue Service (IRS) guidelines, qualified retirement plans are afforded special tax treatment, and contributions plus account income enjoy tax deferral until benefits are received. The plans can be either *defined benefit* or *defined contribution* in concept. Each limits the allowable amount of tax-deductible contributions. The IRS imposes penalties on early withdrawals and on certain withdrawals not taken by age 70½. Keogh plans are sufficiently complex to require the advice of financial advisors* or financial counselors before establishing them.

Defined Benefit Plan

A defined benefit plan is based on an anticipated level of benefits to be paid to an individual at retirement. Annual contributions in this type of Keogh plan are actuarially determined, based on the particular formula and plan used. Defined benefit plans may be designed to provide a benefit of up to $124,000 (indexed for inflation) per year or 100% of final compensation. Frequently, the number of years of service an individual has worked for the sponsoring company and some percentage of average or final salary are the principal variables. The key factor is that while annual contributions may vary, the retirement benefit is a function of a specified formula.

Defined Contribution Plans

A defined contribution Keogh Plan allows the lesser of $30,000 (indexed for inflation) or 25% of salary to be contributed annually. Because the contributions vary, the benefits at retirement may vary as well. There are several types of defined contribution plans. *Target benefit pension plans,* for example, have some of the features of defined benefit programs in that a formula is used to determine the annual contribution, but thereafter the investment and actuarial risks shift back to the employee. This plan design works particularly well for business owners near the end of their careers. The benefit formula used in a target benefit pension plan requires larger contributions for older employees because there is less time to fund the target benefit.

Another form of defined contribution plan is a *money purchase pension plan,* where the company commits to make annual contributions based on a percentage of each participant's compensation. Some plans of this type will be limited to salary only and others will include overtime, bonuses, and other compensation.

Profit sharing plans are also considered defined contribution plans. These plans involve an allocation formula or a straight percentage of compensation formula. In the latter case, the company is allowed to make contributions regardless of profits in any given year.

401(k) Plans

Among the most popular types of qualified Keogh plans is the 401(k) plan. A 401(k) plan allows employees to elect to defer taxes on a part of current income simply by placing the money into such a plan. Typically, employers match employees' contributions in so-called ''thrift'' plans. Companies with defined benefit, target benefit, or money purchase plans may also provide for a complementary 401(k) plan. The employee's contribution in this later case is limited to a maximum of $7,627 (indexed for inflation). This program is available regardless of income level or participation in other retirement programs and vests immediately. However, 401(k) salary reductions may marginally reduce the amount of benefits an individual could receive through other benefit programs such as group life or health insurance.

403(b) Plans

Employees of public schools and specific types of tax-exempt organizations are eligible for a 403(b) plan. These are sometimes referred to as a tax-sheltered annuity (TSA) or tax-deferred annuity (TDA), and are similar to the 401(k) plan. Both plans enable employees to defer taxes on income by permitting before-tax contributions to employees' individual accounts. While 403(b) plans are not viewed as qualified plans, since distributions from these plans are not eligible for lump-sum averaging, they offer many of the same benefits, such as before-tax contributions. In the event a salary reduction is used, the amount of the 403(b) contribution made by an employee is generally restricted to $9,500 per year. (See also CASH FLOW PLANNING, ENTREPRENEURSHIP, ESTATE PLANNING, FINANCIAL ADVISORS, FINANCIAL COUNSELING, and INDIVIDUAL RETIREMENT ACCOUNTS.)

References

Crowe, Robert M. 1990. *Fundamentals of Financial Planning.* Bryn Mawr, PA: American College.
Gitman, Lawrence J., and Michael D. Joehnk. 1990. *Fundamentals of Investing.* New York: Harper & Row.
Kapoor, Jack R., Les R. Dlabay, and Robert J. Hughes. 1991. *Personal Finance.* Homewood, IL: Irwin.

Ganas K. Rakes

KING LEAR SYNDROME, a predicament illustrated in Shakespeare's play, *King Lear,* and used as a teaching tool for financial educators, financial advisors*, and planners. Nearly 500 years after it was first created, Shakespeare's *King Lear* holds relevant estate planning lessons for preretirees today. According to this teaching viewpoint, King Lear has little right to consider himself ''a man more sinned against than sinning,'' when considering the manner in which he planned and executed the disposition of his estate. Although Lear is in his senior years, he has neither ill-health nor failing mental powers to excuse the way he chose to distribute his worldly goods among his three children. His estate planning errors included falling prey to manipulative declarations of love from his children and planning more for his physical comfort than his financial security.

Familiarity with the King Lear Syndrome can help seniors preserve both their financial and personal integrity in planning for their later years. Some practical suggestions to be gleaned from *King Lear* include how financial provisions for children can be made while providing for one's own financial security—particularly payment for long-term residential health care should the need arise.

Lear's Errors

As a father who relied on the compassion of his children, King Lear would have been better off relying on the kindness of strangers, since with only one exception, those who came to the elderly king's aid were not related by blood. Lear's mistakes included pride and the refusal to look beyond the appearance of things to their substance.

Lear wanted to divide his wealth and lands among his three heirs to avoid the responsibilities of managing his kingdom in his later years. At the same time, he desired to provide for himself. As Lear puts it in the beginning of the play:

Know that we have divided in three our kingdom; and 'tis our fast intent to shake all cares and business from our age, conferring them on younger strengths while we unburdened crawl toward death.

Lear's motives were clearly reasonable, but the manner in which he planned to divide his estate was unreasonable. Although the king had a court of advisors, none were consulted about the crucial issue of how and among whom his wealth was to be divided. Lear relied instead on his childrens' verbal professions of love for him to measure how significant a child's inheritance should be:

> Tell me, my daughters—
> Since now we will divest us both of rule,
> Interest of territory, cares of state—
> Which of you shall we say doth love us most,
> That we our largest bounty may extend
> Where nature doth with merit challenge.

In response to their father's request, both of Lear's older daughters are eloquent in their verbal expression of love for their father, one of them claiming to love Lear more than her own husband. In his pride and vanity, Lear eagerly accepts the accolades and professions of love from his two elder children. He does not consider whether their past actions actually reflect this love or whether their future actions are likely to match their flowery words. Thus, Lear's two elder children secure their inheritance. Turning to his youngest and favorite daughter, he bids her to speak:

> Now, our joy,
> Although our last and least,
> To whose young love
> The vines of France and milk of Burgundy
> Strive to be interested,
> What can you say to draw
> A third more opulent than your sisters?
> Speak.

Lear's third daughter finds she cannot "heave her heart up into her throat" to flatter her father with empty words of love and praise. She tells her father merely that she loves him "according to her bond." The King becomes enraged when she remains adamant in her refusal to flatter him. He thus disinherits the only child who really loves him, banishing her and dividing her portion of the kingdom between her two unworthy sisters. Further, he expels the court advisors who try to dissuade him from his foolish course of action.

Lear has been prideful, refused wise counsel, and made rash judgments. He is soon made to pay, for in their greed, his elder daughters deny him the luxuries to which he has become accustomed. He eventually is denied even a roof over his head, and ultimately pays for his follies with his life. Even the court fool realizes that the King himself has acted foolishly and tells him so:

> If thou wert my fool, nuncle,
> I'd have thee beaten
> For being old before thy time.
> How's that?
> Thou shouldst not have been old till
> thou hadst been wise.

Lear's Lessons

The lessons from *King Lear* are harsh. Many who read and study this play and see it performed believe the punishments meted out to Lear are disproportionate to the poor property decisions he has made. While such a reaction may be based on the certainty that one's own children would not behave in a similar manner, wise counsel and proper estate planning should still be employed. Gifting estates to children to avoid taxation, for example, might backfire as it did for Lear. In an emergency, medical or otherwise, one may need to access that money, and children to whom it has been given may not be able to give it back. The desire to make gifts to children is shared by many Americans. Preliminary results of a nationwide survey conducted by the National Institute on Aging (NIA) illustrate this. More than 12,000 adults aged 51–61 were surveyed in this study, and more than one-third expressed a desire to be generous to their families, all having given at least $500 to a child in 1992 (AARP 1993). This kind of gift-giving reflects the generosity Americans feel for their offspring.

Such generosity, however, must be tempered with common financial sense under the guidance of professionals in order not to fall prey to the second major error made by Lear. He failed to understand the relationship between money and power, believing he could give away his property and money to his three daughters and still wield the power and command the respect to which he was accustomed. Gerontologist Robert Atchley (1985) comments on the relationship between money and power, using the example of a modern head of state:

Former President Eisenhower had a great deal of prestige and influence in old age, not because he was old but because he had been both a president and a military chief. A great many of the richest and most influential Americans are old, but their age is not the reason why they are rich or influential. In fact, their wealth and influence discounts their age, in that rich and powerful people are much less likely than others to be disqualified from participation purely on account of age. Age discrimination happens mainly to people who are already disadvantaged.

Lear found that his money and lands were his power base, and when gone, he no longer was respected by others. Thus, protected assets may help insulate an aging person from age prejudice. Like racism and sexism, ageism is an opinion that stereotypes elders as unproductive, old-fashioned in their ways, and outdated in their perspectives (Pai 1990).

Lear's third error was his failure to consult advisors when planning to distribute his wealth. The services of an objective, knowledgeable estate planner can help guide one to a middle course between giving away assets to protect them from taxes or a health care agency, and turning over these assets prematurely to well-intentioned children or others. Even if adopting a more optimistic view, the King Lear example can point the way to a proactive stance. According to the King Lear Syndrome, assets can help protect against ageism in one's later years. Today's seniors have the opportunity to discover that power lies not so much in the ability to control others but in the ability to control one's own destiny. Approaching financial planning in an analytical and objective way can be of great benefit in later life for everyone involved. (See also ETHICS IN FINANCIAL PLANNING, ESTATE PLANNING, FINANCIAL ADVISORS, INHERITANCE, and SAVINGS INVESTMENTS.)

References

American Association of Retired Persons. 1993. ''Middle Americans Glum about Prospects.'' *AARP Bulletin.* (September), 15.

Atchley, Robert C. 1985. *Social Forces and Aging,* Fourth Edition. Belmont, CA: Wadsworth.

Pai, Young. 1990. *Cultural Foundations of Education.* New York: Merrill.

Shakespeare, William. 1980. *King Lear.* New York: Bantam Books.

James A. Anderson

L

LEGAL ISSUES. See Advance Directives; Attorneys; Bankruptcy; Divorce and the Elderly; Elder Law Practice; Elder Taxpayer Issues; Ethics in Financial Planning.

LEISURE, non-work activities having a recreational function that counterbalances work at a trade or occupation and routine everyday chores. Leisure patterns of older persons are related to socioeconomic status. Middle-class elderly people tend to be more community-oriented in their leisure, preferring clubs and organizations, cultural events, parties, and travel, whereas the working class tends to be more home-centered, preferring family socializing, television, and hobbies. Reduction in income for some older persons who formerly had middle-class incomes may create a barrier to their previous activities.

Leisure is intuitively understood as a personally fulfilling experience. Gerontologists have recognized the broader importance of leisure in maintaining positive well-being (Cutler and Hendricks 1990). Leisure plays a major role in people's lives in terms of how they spend their time and the benefits derived from leisure.

Concepts of Leisure

The study of leisure has resulted in a number of different conceptualizations. *Leisure as a state of mind* is the classical view that emerged in Ancient Greece. It is perceived to be a mental and spiritual attitude, representing a state of freedom and characterized by calm, openness, and contemplation. Leisure in this context provides an opportunity for spiritual and intellectual enlightenment. *Leisure as discretionary time* is a common conceptualization in the sociological literature, representing the time remaining after subsistence (working) and existence (meeting biological requirements of eating, sleeping, etc.) have been satisfied. *Leisure as functional activity* refers to needs. The psychological function of leisure is to enhance life satisfaction for individuals through participation in activities that satisfy subjective needs. The function of leisure in society is to reward individuals for having met societal obligations of occupation, family, and so on.

Leisure is *perceived freedom* in each of these conceptualizations—a state of mind free from work or other obligations, discretionary or "free" time. The most comprehensive conceptualization of leisure in the gerontological literature was developed by Gordon et al. (1976), who built on the distinction between *instrumental activity* (work and other necessary activity oriented toward the attainment of gratification at a later time) and *expressive activity* (symbolic and material interchanges with the environment that involve intrinsic, immediate gratification). A continuum of expressive intensity involves five functions of leisure activities: relaxation, diversion, development, creativity, and sensual transcendence. Using this continuum, Gordon et al. (1976) define leisure as personally expressive discretionary activity, ranging in intensity of involvement from solitude, quiet resting, taking a nap (relaxing) to sexual activity, highly competitive games or sports, dancing (sensual transcendence) at the highest levels of cognitive, emotional, and physical involvement.

Leisure and the Elderly

Leisure activity patterns of the elderly vary by demographic, environmental, and social factors (age, gender, mobility, and socioeconomic status). Older persons engage in many of the same activities as younger people, but there are some differences. Activities such as reading, sitting and thinking, gardening, walking, sleeping, participating in fraternal or community organizations, doing volunteer work, and participating in political activities do not considerably decrease when persons age. Older respondents, however, were less likely to socialize with friends, participate in recreational activities and hobbies, or participate in sports such as golf, tennis, and swimming, and were more likely to watch television.

There is little variation in the decline of leisure participation with age for women and men. Solitary activities, however, significantly increased for women, whereas cooking increased for men but declined for women (Gordon et al. 1976). Overall, the findings that men increased their participation in home embellishment, cooking, and solitary activities supported the earlier findings of Zbovowski (1962) that men appear to become more home-centered in their activities.

Mobility deficiencies may severely limit leisure participation. Clubs, church activities and socials, libraries, theaters, restaurants, parks, recreation centers, sporting events, and visiting may not be convenient because of physical limitations to mobility or because of lack of transportation.

The impact of leisure on personal adjustment in old age is a key issue in retirement. In an often quoted article, Stephen Miller (1965) argued that retirement is a degrading and traumatic experience because it means the loss of the work role, that is, the major source of identity-providing, essential benefits. According to Miller, leisure roles cannot replace this lost identity because society does not generally consider leisure to be a legitimate source of identity.

But a frequently cited critic of Miller, Robert Atchley (1980), found that leisure can be a legitimate source of identity after retirement. Although the work role is important, identity loss is offset by continuity in other roles such as those provided by families, friends, church, and community. These roles create retirement companions for individuals and provide identity continuity. Prime predictors of retirement adjustment were an adequate retirement income and retired friends with whom to share the leisure role, suggesting that loss of income, not loss of work, accounts for negative retirement effects.

Practical Suggestions and Policy Issues

An important factor across adulthood is the *quality* of leisure activities rather than *quantity* (Kelly et al. 1987). It is not how many leisure activities one engages in that matters, but how much one enjoys them. As one's sense of self changes with age, what one does to seek affirmation changes. Lawton (1985) suggested that personal expectations affects what older persons do for leisure activities. Older persons, for example, may not think that physical leisure activities (such as aerobics) are appropriate and may prefer not to participate.

Given the wide range of leisure options, how do people choose their activities? Each of us has a leisure repertoire, that is, a personal library of intrinsically motivating activities that we do regularly (Mobily et al. 1991). The activities that comprise our repertoire are determined by two things: *perceived competence* (how good we think we are at the activity compared with other people our age) and *psychological comfort* (how well we meet our personal goals for performance). Other factors are also important: income, interest, health, abilities, transportation, education, and other social characteristics.

The Older Americans Act (OAA)* of 1965 supports the right of older persons to leisure. Under Title I, Section 101, the right of older persons to the "pursuit of meaningful activity within the widest range of civic, cultural, and recreational opportunities" is stated in Objective 7. The guarantee of an adequate income is a prerequisite for a leisure-oriented retirement. OAA, Title I, Section 101, Objective 1 states that older persons are entitled to "an adequate income in retirement in accordance with the American standard of living." A leisure-oriented retirement thus requires more than a subsistence level of income.

Support of guaranteed, adequate leisure education through the life cycle was affirmed by the 1971 White House Conference on Aging (1973). A public policy statement in support of qualified leisure service specialists asserted that "training and research agencies, including university programs which relate to recreation and leisure, should be encouraged to concern themselves with the needs of older persons as an integral part of their training curriculum."

The articulation of a concise, integrated, and realistic public policy agenda on leisure and aging is a challenge for the future. Service providers, researchers, and policy specialists in the area of leisure and aging need to take up the challenge of such a task. (See also ECONOMIC STATUS OF THE ELDERLY, OLDER AMERICANS ACT, RETIREMENT MIGRATION, TRAVEL, and VACATION HOMES AND RECREATIONAL PROPERTY.)

Organizations

National Institute of Senior Centers
National Recreation and Park Association

Suggested Reading

Fogg, George E. 1994. *Leisure Site Guidelines for People Over 55.* Arlington, VA: National Recreation and Park Association.

References

Atchley, Robert C. 1980. *The Social Forces in Later Life.* Belmont, CA: Wadsworth.
Cutler, Stephen J., and Jon Hendricks. 1990. "Leisure and Time Use across the Life Course." In *Handbook of Aging and the Social Sciences,* Third Edition, ed. R. H. Binstock and L. K. George. San Diego: Academic Press, 169–85.
Gordon, Chap, Charles Gaitz, and J. Scott. 1976. "Leisure and Lives: Personal Expressivity across the Life Span." In *Handbook of Aging and the Social Sciences,* ed. R. H. Binstock and E. Shanas. New York: Van Nostrand Press, 310–41.
Kelly, J. R., M. W. Steinkamp, and J. R. Kelly. 1987. "Later-Life Satisfaction: Does Leisure Contribute?" *Leisure Sciences* 9: 189–200.
Lawton, Mortimer P. 1985. "Activities and Leisure." In *Annual Review of Gerontology and Geriatrics.* Vol. 5, ed. M. P. Lawton and G. L. Maddox. New York: Springer, 127–64.
Miller, Stephen J. 1965. "The Social Dilemma of the Aging Leisure Participant." In *Older People and their Social Worlds,* ed. A. M. Rose and W. A. Peterson. Philadelphia: F.A. Davis Co., 77–92.
Mobily, K. E., J. H. Lemke, and G. J. Gisin. 1991. "The Idea of Leisure Repertoire." *Journal of Applied Gerontology* 10: 208–23.
White House Conference on Aging. 1973. *Toward A National Policy on Aging,* Vol. 2. Washington, DC: U.S. Government Printing Office.
Zbovowski, M. 1962. "Aging and Recreation." *Journal of Gerontology.* 17: 302–9.

Joseph D. Teaff

LIABILITY INSURANCE, a contract that insures a person against losses from being held legally responsible for injury or damage to another. It also covers costs of lawsuits arising from claims of negligence or other civil wrong. Liability coverage specifies the insured person(s), types of insurance provided, limits of coverage, source of liability, and costs of legal defense. Liability insurance also contains provisions that require reporting the occurrence of a loss or the filing of a lawsuit to the insurer in a timely manner. Companies that insure against liability losses employ the law of averages to spread their risks among many individual policy owners.

Liability Coverage in General

Liability coverage may constitute the entire policy, such as malpractice insurance, or comprise one element of insurance in a comprehensive policy that insures against other types of loss as well, such as automobile or homeowners insurance.

Sources of liability include motor vehicle use; property; daily activities including employment, professional, and business activities; and use of watercraft, aircraft, or other special possessions. Common sources of liability are automobile accidents that might cause personal injuries or property damage. While most people do not face all of these potential sources of liability, a part of personal financial management is assessing whatever risks may be present at any given time. Risk avoidance ranges from not engaging in risky activities to simply exercising great care and loss prevention. The purchase of liability insurance transfers the potential burden to the insurance company.

Coverage may include protection against damages because of bodily injury, defined in one personal auto policy as "bodily harm, sickness, or disease, including death, that results"; against property damage, defined in the same policy as "physical injury to, destruction of, or loss of use of tangible property"; or against personal injury, which may include libel, slander, defamation of character, invasion of privacy, or assault and battery. Because definitions in policy forms may vary, it is important to determine exactly what coverage is provided under each policy being considered for purchase.

Limits of coverage specify how much a policy will pay if one is found legally obligated to pay. Limits can be stated as "combined single limits" or "split limits." The limits can apply to single coverages or to multiple coverages. Combined single limits typically refer to a specified maximum amount of coverage (e.g., $100,000) for bodily injury and property damage combined. Split limits typically refer to a maximum amount per person for bodily injury, a maximum amount per occurrence for bodily injury, and a maximum amount per occurrence for property damage. For example, a policy designating limits of $100,000/300,000/50,000 would pay a maximum of $100,000 to any one individual, a maximum of $300,000 to all individuals sustaining bodily injury, and a maximum of $50,000 for property damage arising from a single occurrence.

Insurance coverage of defense costs is an important element in a liability insurance policy. If wrongdoing is alleged against an individual and a lawsuit is filed, potentially high costs of defense will be incurred, whatever the outcome of the lawsuit. While most personal liability insurance covers defense costs, all policies should be checked for special requirements or limitations of this type of coverage.

The designation of the person(s) insured in a liability contract is also important. A husband and wife who are residents of the same household may both be insured under personal liability policies, and resident children of the household may also be named as persons insured. In any liability policy, it is important to know exactly who is insured, for failure to do so could result in an uninsured loss.

Reporting requirements to the insurance company are also specified under the terms of a legal liability contract. If an individual is in an accident, the loss must be reported to the insurer promptly. The time specified may be 30 days, immediately, or "as soon as practicable." Any notice of a lawsuit should also be delivered to the insurer promptly.

Specific Liability Insurance

Types of liability insurance most often carried are included in automobile insurance, homeowners insurance, and the personal umbrella policy. While the following descriptions may not fit all policies, the forms chosen were published by the Insurance Services Office (ISO) and are used by many companies. The elements contained in these descriptions should be used as guidelines only.

Automobile insurance contains a liability insurance component and typically provides protection against liability resulting from bodily injury and/or property damage that may occur in an accident or other mishap. The source of liability for the person named on the policy (declarations) and, if residents of the household, the spouse and family members is "any auto." The "covered auto" is also a source of liability for other persons using it with permission or other organizations who incur liability because of its use by a person insured. "Covered auto" will be defined in the policy. A covered auto is typically defined as the auto named in the declarations, a trailer owned by the insured, an additionally acquired automobile, or a temporary substitute auto. As with all liability insurance, automobile coverage should be carefully reviewed to ascertain the exact types and limits of coverage.

Generally excluded sources of liability are intentional acts, use of automobiles owned but not listed in the policy, newly acquired automobiles, vehicles used in the automobile business, use of an auto as a public or livery conveyance, motorized vehicles with fewer than four wheels, and automobiles available for regular or frequent use. Share-the-expense car pools are *not* typically excluded.

Driving without automobile insurance is a violation of most state financial responsibility laws and may result in suspension of driving and registration privileges. Most drivers purchase complete automobile insurance that includes coverage against bodily liability, property damage liability, medical payments, uninsured motorists protection, collision, and comprehensive physical damages. Of these types of coverage, bodily injury and property damage liability are most important.

Some states have enacted "no-fault" laws to counter the expense and time-consuming process of determining who is legally liable for damages suffered in automobile accidents. No-fault insurance, where available, requires costs of bodily injury and property damage losses be paid by the injured person's insurance company, regardless of who is at fault for an accident. Theoretically, the need for long and expensive court proceedings should be eliminated in no-fault states, but in practice, injured persons are able to pursue recovery of damages in court that exceed no-fault insurance payment limitations.

Homeowners insurance protects owners (and renters) from bodily injury and property damage liability arising from the residence itself (the "dwelling") and any other buildings on the property—garages, toolsheds, or other structures. Comprehensive policies cover activities on the property itself and activities on properties away from home. Sources of liability include negligent acts or omissions, such as failure to maintain a property or carelessness that results in injury or damage to another. Certain perils may be specifically excluded, and as with all insurance, it is important to understand which risks are covered.

Persons covered, called "insureds" in most forms, include the person named in the declarations; the spouse of that person, if a resident of the household; and members of the household who are either relatives or persons younger than 21 who are in the owner's care. Exclusions are used to remove some sources of liability. The exclusions include motor vehicle liability; aircraft liability; business and professional liability; intentional acts; some watercraft; liability under workers compensation laws; owned or rented locations not included as insured locations; or any loss charged as an assessment by an association, corporation, or community of property owners.

As with automobile insurance, a homeowners policy also provides comprehensive coverage of other perils such as other property coverage and additional living expense coverage. As a package, the cost of comprehensive coverage is usually less expensive than buying the coverages individually.

Personal Umbrella Policy

A personal umbrella liability policy features two distinct provisions. First, it offers bodily injury and property damage coverage beyond the underlying limits and also covers some exposures not otherwise insured. For example, if an individual has $300,000 in automobile liability insurance, $50,000 in homeowners liability insurance, and a $1,000,000 personal umbrella policy, the resulting combined limits of coverage become $1,300,000 automobile, $1,050,000 homeowners, and $1,000,000 on other covered risks. Exposures covered, other than those requiring underlying insurance, apply after a specified limit is reached. Second, the umbrella provides coverage for personal injury such as libel, slander, defamation of character, and so forth.

Exclusions include obligations under workers compensation, disability benefits or benefits under similar laws; autos owned by other family members or furnished for regular, frequent use; intentional acts; aircraft; some boats; and an act or failure to act as an officer of a corporation or association. This latter exclusion does not usually apply to officers or directors of nonprofit corporations or associations.

The personal umbrella policy is an effective and economical way to increase liability insurance coverage, but other sources of liability requiring coverage not included in the policies discussed here are liability arising from investment property, watercraft, aircraft, workers' compensation for household workers, business; and professional liability.

Potential Liability for the Elderly

As society becomes more litigious, the likelihood of a liability claim against every individual increases, and the cost of defending the claim alone may justify liability insurance. Certainly the potential size of a liability settlement or judgment requires serious consideration of liability insurance.

Planning for liability coverage by older persons, however, must be balanced against the income and assets one possesses and stands to lose. For many older persons, lifestyle choices may be increasingly risk-averse. However, motor vehicle operation in advanced old age actually may have the opposite effect, increasing chances of accidents. Although liability insurance is an important protection to consider, the decision to buy such coverage must be weighed carefully within the overall framework of an older person's lifestyle, and his or her financial needs and resources. (See also ATTORNEYS, FINANCIAL ADVISORS, FINANCIAL COUNSELING, and HOMEOWNERSHIP).

References

Amling, Frederick, and William G. Droms. 1986. *Personal Financial Management.* Homewood, IL: Irwin.

Rejda, George E. 1992. *Principles of Risk Management and Insurance,* Fourth Edition. New York: Harper-Collins.

Dorfman, Mark S. 1994. *Risk Management and Insurance,* Fifth Edition. Englewood Cliffs, NJ: Prentice Hall.

Launie, J. J., George E. Rejda, and Donald R. Oakes. 1987. *Personal Insurance,* First Edition. Malvern, PA: Insurance Institute of America.

Green, Mark R., James S. Trieschmann, and Sandra G. Gustavson. 1992. *Risk and Insurance,* Eighth Edition. Cincinnati: South-Western.

Mars A. Pertl

LIFE ESTATES, land estates whose duration is measured or limited by the life of an individual. A life estate is a legal arrangement whereby the beneficiary, that is, the life tenant, is entitled to the income from, or the possession of, property for his or her lifetime. Upon the death of the life tenant, the property goes to the holder of the remainder interest or to the grantee by reversion.

The law of land estates differs by state. The general legal concepts were brought to America by English settlers. Some states chose to adopt certain concepts while others did not. Since the creation of life estates is complex, it is recommended it be done under the direction of licensed attorneys in the state where the real property is located. Familiarity with the law regarding life estates can help: (1) preserve seniors' rights, (2) avoid liability for damage to estates, (3) ensure harmony between the parties involved with the land's ownership, and (4) seniors make educated decisions on whether to create or accept a life estate.

Life estates may be created expressly, implicitly, or by operation of law.

Express life estates may only be created by will or deed. Because a life estate is an interest in land, it must be documented in writing. There are two recognized express life estates: those for the life of the grantee, and those for the life of another. Express life estates for the life of the grantee include conveyances such as: By and from Albert "to Betty for her life." In this example, Betty will have an estate in land for her own life. When Betty dies, the land will revert back to Albert. Thus, Albert is said to have a reversionary interest in the land.

Another example of an express life estate would be: By and from Albert "to Betty for her life, then to Charles." Betty will have an estate in land for her life, but when she dies, the property will go to Charles, not Albert. Upon Betty's death, Charles may do with the land as he pleases, and there are no restrictions on his ownership. The law recognizes Charles as a "remainderman," which means that Charles is not entitled to the land until the death of the measuring life. Thus, remainder interests, like reversionary interests, are a future estate in land, and are known in the law as a "future interests." The law considers remainder and reversionary interests as present legal rights that are entitled to protection.

The second type of express life estates are life estates for the life of another. These are called "estates pur autre vie," and are created in the following manner: By and from Albert "to Betty for the life of Debbie." In this example, Betty will have an estate in land only so long as Debbie lives. When Debbie dies, the land will revert to Albert.

Life estates also may be created by implication. In this category, the interest will be created in wills or deeds using language such as: By and from Albert "to Betty after the life of Charles." In this example, a life estate will be implied in Albert until the death of Charles. At Charles' death, the land will go to Betty. Another example would be if Albert wills his land "to Betty from and after the death of Betty's brother, Charles." Here, the life estate cannot be with Albert because he is dead, nor with Betty because Charles is alive; therefore, the law implies a life estate to Charles and a remainder interest to Betty. Implied life estates are rare and occur mainly as a result of poorly drafted wills and deeds.

The third and last category of life estates are those that occur by operation of law. Legal life estates are created out of the marital relationship. There are two types of legal life estates: curtesy and dower. These are recognized only in a minority of states and the District of Columbia, and can be an unexpected trap for the uninformed. Only dower has any significance today. Although a common law dower only applied to the wife and curtesy to the husband, some states have eliminated the distinction between the two and collapsed them into one concept, called dower. At common law, upon the death of her husband, a widow was entitled to receive a life estate in one-third of the lands owned by her husband during the marriage. Before her husband's death, the wife had only an expectancy of dower, because if she died before her husband, her potential or inchoate dower interest was eliminated.

An example of when dower operates is where Albert buys a tract of land, then marries Betty, and several years later sells the tract to Charles without getting Betty's signature on the deed. If Albert dies before Betty, Betty will be entitled to a one-third life estate in the land currently owned by Charles or his successors. If, however, Betty consented to the sale and signed the deed, she would not be entitled to dower because by signing the deed she waived her dower rights. Dower also operates in the situation where Albert buys a tract of land while married and does not sell it, but upon his death, wills the land to Charles, leaving his wife, Betty, nothing. In such a case, Betty would be entitled to a one-third life estate in the land despite being intentionally left out of the will.

Seniors in states that recognize dower should be aware that if their spouse cuts them out of a will, they may still be entitled to a one-third life estate in real estate their spouse owned at death or sold without permission. If dower has been abolished in the state, "elective share" statutes have generally replaced it to protect the widow or widower from being totally disinherited. If dower exists in a state, buyers should be careful to get the signature of both spouses when buying land from a couple. Otherwise, there may be an unexpected visitor demanding a one-third life estate in the land years later.

Before seniors create life estates, they need to be aware of the rights, duties, and obligations attached. Also, seniors who have acquired life estates should be aware of the legal implications that attach to the land. Those who have remainder or reversion interests in life estates should also be aware of their rights. Generally, life tenants are entitled to all the ordinary uses and profits of the land; however, they cannot lawfully do any act that will injure the interests of the person who owns a remainder or reversion interest in the land. A life tenant is analogous to a trustee of the land because he or she owes certain duties to preserve it for the remainderman. If life tenants injure the land, future interest holders may sue for damages or enjoin the life tenant's actions. Damage to life estates by life tenants falls into one of three categories: (1) affirmative (voluntary) waste, (2) permissive waste, or (3) ameliorative waste.

Affirmative waste applies to structures and natural resources on the land. As a general rule, life tenants may not consume or exploit natural resources on the property, such as, timber, coal, oil, and gas. For example, if Albert deeds his land, Blackacre, "to Betty for life, then to Charles," and it turns out that there is a valuable coal deposit under the property, Betty may not open a mine and extract the coal. If she does, Charles, the remainderman, may bring a suit to enjoin the activity and receive damages for the coal removed. In other words, Betty can use the estate, but cannot consume the estate. Life tenants, however, are allowed to utilize the natural resources for repair and maintenance of the land. They may cut trees for fences, or mine coal for heating a house on the land, but may not cut trees or mine coal to sell, unless given an express right to exploit these resources.

Permissive waste occurs when the life tenants allow the land to fall into disrepair or fail to take reasonable measures to protect the land. This concept imposes several affirmative obligations on life tenants. First, life tenants have an obligation to preserve the land and structures in a reasonable state of repair, to the extent of the income or profits derived from the land or, if the life tenants are living on the land themselves, to the extent of the reasonable rental value of the land.

The next obligation is to pay interest on encumbrances to the land to the extent of income or profits produced by the land. Life tenants must pay all ordinary taxes on the land to the extent the income or profits from the land permit. If, however, the tax is for a public improvement such as a new curb, sewer, or sidewalk that will last longer than the life estate, the tax or assessment is apportioned equitably between the life tenant and the future holder of the land. There is generally no obligation on life tenants to insure the premises for the benefit of the remaindermen. Both the life tenants and the remaindermen, however, have an insurable interest in the land.

The final category of damages is ameliorative waste, which is counterintuitive and thus a trap for the uninformed. Ameliorative waste occurs when the use of the property is substantially changed, but the change increases the value of the property. At common law, any change to existing buildings or other improvements was always actionable, even if it improved the value of the property. Because of the unexpected harshness of this rule, modern courts have modified it in the following instances. First, if the market value of the remainder interest is not diminished and the remainderman does not object, the use of the property may be changed. Second, if a substantial and permanent change in neighborhood conditions has deprived the property in its current form of reasonable productivity or usefulness, the use may be changed without the remainderman's permission. The classic example of this is where the life estate consists of a single house that is on a piece of prime real estate in Manhattan, New York. If this should occur, the life tenant may be allowed to tear down the old house and build a skyscraper.

Life estates normally terminate upon the death of the measuring life; however, in certain instances, a life estate may terminate earlier. Life estates may be sold by the life tenant. Such a sale, however, does not lengthen the duration of the life estate but merely creates an estate pur autre vie. For example, if Betty has a life estate and sells it to David, David will have a life estate for the life of Betty. Because of the uncertainty of such an estate, David will probably not pay top dollar for the land.

The doctrine of merger is one way life estates may terminate earlier than the death of the measuring life. This doctrine applies where life tenants sell their interest to the remainderman. For instance, if Albert grants Blackacre "to Betty for life, then to Charles," Betty will have a life estate and Charles will have a remainder interest. Thus, if Betty sells her life estate to Charles, Charles will hold the land in fee simple (own all the rights) because Betty's life estate and Charles' remainder interest will merge, and Charles will hold all the interest in the land. A person who buys the land from Charles would therefore be willing to pay full price.

Awareness of the rights, duties, and obligations imposed upon life tenants and remaindermen can help seniors plan for their future or take care of their current obligations. Therefore, seniors who are not already aware of the legal implications of this unique form of land ownership should consult an attorney in the state where the land is located before creating a life estate or before proceeding with any improvements or other changes to the life estate. (See also ATTORNEYS, ESTATE PLANNING, INHERITANCE, and TITLING AS-SETS.)

References

Lawler, John J., and Gail Gates Lawler. 1940. *A Short Historical Introduction to the Law of Real Property.* Chicago: Foundation Press.

Moynihan, Cornelius J. 1962a. *Introduction to the Law of Real Property.* St. Paul, MN: West.

Moynihan, Cornelius J. 1962b. *A Preliminary Survey of the Law of Real Property.* St. Paul, MN: West.

Powell, Richard R. 1993. *Powell on Real Property.* New York: Matthew Bender.

Thompson, George W. 1979. *Commentaries on the Modern Law of Real Property.* New York: Bobbs-Merrill Co.

Christopher R. McDowell

LIFE INSURANCE, a contractual relationship under which an insurance company promises to pay a specified sum of money upon the death of the insured to the person or persons designated as the beneficiary(ies). Life insurance contracts represent a fairly simple legal relationship among the insured, the insurance company, and the beneficiaries. However, the purchase and maintenance of, and claims made under, life insurance policies comprise a complex area within law, finance, and consumer decision making.

Life insurance contracts are written by insurance companies in simple and complex situations. Millions of parents insure their lives to protect against their untimely deaths for the benefit of young children. Older parents maintain life insurance to provide financial security for their families. Businesses and governments rely on life insurance contracts to protect against the loss of key executives and officials, and banks often require insurance on the lives of borrowers to assure repayment of loans.

Careful attention is required by anyone purchasing a new life insurance contract, or before amending or liquidating an existing policy. As one ages, life insurance becomes more expensive to acquire, and any changes to an existing life insurance contract must be made carefully. Life insurance can be a key tool in financial planning. Insurance proceeds may provide retirement income, accumulated savings, or the payment of estate and death taxes, or may be used to make charitable bequests after death.

Life Insurance Terminology

Actuarial cost is based on the scientifically calculated probability that an individual of a certain age will die within any given year. Life insurance premiums are based on actuarial cost, and the method for calculating actuarial cost is determined by mortality tables derived from the statistical experience of thousands of individuals over time. Mortality tables tell insurance underwriters the number of years that an individual of any age can expect to live, and enable insurance companies to price the required insurance.

A *life insurance application* begins the process of entering into a life insurance contract, and becomes part of the physical life insurance contract. Usually, it will be affixed to the life insurance contract issued to the insured. Information entered into the agreement must be accurate and complete, or it may provide the life insurance company with an excuse to terminate the agreement. The application includes information about the proposed insured's date and place of birth, his or her marital status, profession or occupation, health history, and sometimes the reason for purchasing the life insurance policy—referred to by individuals in the insurance industry as the insurable interest.

Cash surrender value is the account value of permanent life insurance and is the guaranteed cash value of the policy plus premium dividends, if any, paid by the life insurance company. Cash surrender value in a life insurance policy is similar to equity in one's home. To realize the equity, a policyholder may surrender the life insurance policy to obtain the cash value. Both a life insurance policy and a home offer collateral value against which the owner may borrow. For both, value is likely to continue to increase even though the asset has been pledged as collateral.

Endowment occurs when a life insurance contract fully matures and the cash surrender value equals the death benefit. Originally, endowment occurred at age 100, but it occurs at earlier ages under modern policies.

Insurable interest is the policyowner's reason for buying life insurance. The financial loss that would be suffered upon the death of one spouse constitutes the other spouse's insurable interest. Similarly, financial loss that might occur when a partner dies constitutes the insurable interest for the partnership. Employers insure key employees based on their insurable interest in the employee. If an insurable interest is absent at the time of issuance, the life insurance company is not legally able to issue a policy.

The *Medical Information Bureau (MIB)* is a nonprofit trade association, comprised of member life insurance underwriters. It maintains a large database that gathers and distributes information on the health histories of individuals. The purpose of the MIB is to protect the insurance consumer and insurance company against applicants who shop for favorable coverage without disclosing their medical histories. In most states, if a life insurance company refuses to issue a life insurance policy on an individual's life, it must disclose its reason for denying coverage.

The *medical questionnaire,* sometimes referred to as "Part 2" of the application, is often the most important part of the life insurance application procedure. Life insurance underwriters use this information to determine whether a life insurance policy will be issued. Often the medical questionnaire will prompt an underwriter to require additional information from doctors and hospitals, or from the MIB.

Policy dividends represent the return of unused premiums by mutual life insurance companies. Dividends are not guaranteed, but are merely projections of anticipated payments. Thus, if interest rates vary from the projections of the insurance company, or if mortality costs are higher than expected, the rate of return for the life insurance policy may be lower than projected at the time of the proposal.

Premiums are payments by the policy owner to the insurance company to issue the life insurance contract and keep it in force. Premiums are determined using the actuarial cost of the life insurance contract. Life insurance premiums can vary even with a fixed death benefit for individuals of the same age, depending on the type of life insurance contract.

Mutual or *stock companies* are terms that refer to stock life insurance companies owned by shareholders, and mutual life insurance companies owned by their policyholders. About 94% of U.S. life insurance companies are stock companies, and about 6% are mutual companies. Mutual companies sell participating policies, for which individuals pay a somewhat higher premium, but overpayments are returned to policyholders in the form of policy dividends. Profits of the stock life insurance companies go to shareholders, while the "profits" of mutual companies go to the policyholders. In the United States, the largest life insurance companies are mutual companies, and frequently, but not always, the word mutual appears in the company name.

Term insurance is designed to protect dependents and others with an insurable interest against lost income. It is most affordable for the young and becomes increasingly expensive as the insured ages. After age 65, the cost of term insurance may be prohibitive, especially when health problems exist. With ordinary term insurance, premiums increase each year as the likelihood of dying increases. Term insurance builds no cash surrender value, and wide variations in periodic premiums can occur depending on the insured's health habits and history, age, sex, and the pricing policies of the insurance company. Premiums are paid periodically and the insurance stays in force for the time the premium covers. When the premiums stop, the policy is cancelled. Term insurance can remain in force for many years or for the duration of a trip or vacation.

There are many types of term insurance, and choices must be made at the time of purchase about level versus increasing premiums, payment, renewal and conversion options, and age of expiration. A term rider can be added as a benefit to permanent life insurance. *Periodic term* is a type of term life insurance that is written for a fixed period of time, such as five, 10, or 20 years. The periodic term is the time an insurance company guarantees to insure an individual, after which the company often will require a physical reexamination or medical questionnaire. *Convertible term* refers to a term life insurance policy that provides for conversion to permanent or cash-value life insurance without any proof from the insured that he or she is still healthy enough to purchase the permanent life insurance.

Permanent life insurance refers to life insurance policies that have the following characteristics: (1) premiums are calculated based on keeping the policy in force for the life expectancy of the insured, (2) contracts are written and premiums are calculated based on creating cash surrender values, and (3) premiums are calculated so the policy will endow at a specific age.

Permanent life insurance policies offer several options to policyholders. Permanent life insurance provides a way for policyholders to ensure that life insurance benefits will not terminate before life expectancy. For permanent life insurance policies, cash surrender values accumulate on a tax-deferred basis, and enable policyholders to gain access to cash surrender value by borrowing against it. While some question the value of being able to "borrow" one's own money, this may be a significant advantage to others who regard the accumulating cash value in life insurance as "forced savings."

Permanent life insurance policies offer the option of terminating life insurance premiums after a given number of years, at which time policy dividends (see definition above) will take over the payment of premiums. This concept affords policyholders a potentially valuable planning tool. Types of permanent life insurance include universal life, whole life or ordinary life insurance, and endowment and variable life insurance contracts. All permanent life insurance contracts offer cash value, loan provisions, and a guarantee to insure until the end of the insured's life.

Rating systems analyze the financial status of life insurance companies and offer a basis for comparing the financial stability of companies. Most rating systems examine the investments of insurance companies, their capital reserves, and their ability to pay outstanding liabilities for potential death claims. Insurance rating systems use A+, AAA, superior, or other valuative terminology.

The analysis of ratings is only one variable, however, in choosing a life insurance company and the agent that represents it. Other considerations include the honesty, efficiency, and responsiveness of the agent; the quality of service by local or regional offices of the insurance company; and most importantly, the appropriateness of the insurance policy under consideration. (See also ACCELERATED DEATH BENEFITS, AGENTS AND BROKERS, ANNUITIES, DEATH BENEFITS, ESTATE PLANNING, and FINANCIAL COUNSELING.)

Organizations

American Council of Life Insurance
National Association of Insurance Commissions
National Insurance Consumer Organization

Suggested Readings

American Council of Life Insurance. 1994. *A Consumer's Guide to Life Insurance.* Washington, DC: Author.

Davis, Kristin. 1994. "Buying Life Insurance: What the Numbers Don't Show." *Kiplingers Personal Finance Magazine* 48 (6): 49–52.

Travis, Dale. 1994. "How Much Life Insurance Do You Really Need?" *Real Estate Today* 27 (7): 35–37.

References

Black, Kenneth, Jr., and Harold D. Skipper, Jr. 1994. *Life Insurance.* Englewood Cliffs, NJ: Prentice-Hall.

Budin, Beverly R. 1994. *Life Insurance.* Washington, DC: Tax Management.

Crawford, Michael L., and William T. Beadles. 1989. *Law and the Life Insurance Contract.* Homewood, IL: Irwin.

Donald A. Hunsberger

LIVING WILL, a type of advance directive* used to give instructions about future medical care in the event of serious illness or injury. A living will allows an individual to document his or her wishes about future medical care and thereby maintain some control at the end of life.

How Living Wills Work

A living will, also sometimes called a directive to physicians, health care declaration, or medical directive, is used to guide physicians and family members in deciding how aggressively to use medical treatments to delay a person's death. Every state except Massachusetts, Michigan, and New York has passed legislation regulating the use of living wills (Choice In Dying 1994). Even in states without living will statutes, living wills are valid following the 1980 U.S. Supreme Court *Cruzan* decision that competent adults have a constitutional right to make medical treatment wishes known and have them honored. State laws and rules governing the use and implementation of living wills vary. Usually a living will goes into effect only when the person who signed it becomes incompetent. Frequently, a law requires that a second doctor confirm the person's condition before a living will can be given effect.

A legally valid living will must be signed by its originator in the presence of witnesses who indicate that they believe the person signing the document is of sound mind and acting under no duress. Restrictions requiring that witnesses have no interest in the estate of the person making a living will frequently apply, and some states require the attestation of a notary public. Witnessing requirements must be followed exactly, or the validity of the living will can be challenged.

Most states have a standard living will form that is available from health care facilities, state departments of health, or organizations concerned with issues affecting the aging. There are also generic (non-state-specific) living wills, but state-authorized forms help ensure that state requirements are met and that health care providers will honor the document. Since most living wills contain relatively simple checklists or fill-in-the-blanks to indicate one's medical treatment preferences, a lawyer may not be needed.

Historic Development

Living wills were developed because modern medicine's ability to sustain life, in some cases, has exceeded its ability to cure. As chronic and degenerative diseases became a more common cause of death, and as more people began dying in hospitals rather than in home settings (President's Commission 1983), people looked for ways to regain control of the dying process. At a meeting of the Society for the Right to Die in 1967, the first living will was drafted as a way for people to indicate a wish to avoid life-prolonging treatment in the event there was no hope for recovery. While a property will becomes effective upon the death of the person making it, a living will becomes effective while its originator is alive, and is used solely for making decisions about medical care and treatment.

In 1976, California became the first state to pass legislation that directly addressed the issue of end-of-life decision making, allowing individuals to plan in advance for the treatment they would receive at the end of life. Other states followed with living will statutes. Early statutes tended to be limited. Under California law, for example, a person had to be diagnosed as terminally ill and expected to die within six months before a legally valid living will could be made.

Current Legal Issues

New laws and revisions of older laws currently allow individuals more freedom to specify medical treatment through living wills. A competent adult in any state may complete a legally valid living will, but some restrictions still exist, and the most troublesome is the definition of "terminal condition." When narrowly defined by state law, the applicability of a living will is limited. Many living will statutes, for example, define terminal condition such that persons permanently unconscious, or who could be maintained for a substantial period of time on life-support without hope for improvement, could be unprotected from unwanted treatment.

Artificial nutrition and hydration (tube feeding) present another problem area. Although the United States Supreme Court's *Cruzan* decision determined that artificial nutrition and hydration is a medical treatment that may be refused, many states require specific wording in a living will if tube feeding is not desired. Often all that is required is the additional statement: "I do not want tube feeding." The discontinuation of artificial nutrition and hydration has been the focal point of most of the major right-to-die court cases. Since terminal patients can frequently be maintained for long periods of time on tube feeding, any instructions accompanying the living will form should be reviewed to see if there are special provisions regarding tube feeding.

Most states allow competent adults to appoint a health care agent, who is authorized to make medical decisions in the event of incompetence. Some states allow such an agent to be appointed within the living will form, while others require a separate form, called a durable power of attorney* for health care. Where the option is available, experts advise executing both a living will and a durable power of attorney, since both forms work together. The living will can guide the agent in the decision-making process, and if the agent is unavailable or unable to make decisions when the time comes, the living will can stand on its own. (See also ADVANCE DIRECTIVES, AGENTS AND BROKERS, DURABLE POWER OF ATTORNEY, and WILLS.)

References

Brown, Carolyn. 1992. *Decide for Yourself: Life Support, Living Will, Power of Attorney for Health Care.* Atlanta, GA: Pritchett & Hull.

Choice In Dying, Inc. 1994. *Right-to-Die Law Digest.* New York: Choice in Dying.

President's Commission for the Study of Ethical Problems in Medicine and Biomedical and Behavioral Research. 1983. *Deciding to Forego Life-Sustaining Treatment.* Washington, DC: GPO.

U.S. Senate, Subcommittee on Medicare and Long-Term Care. 1990. *Living Wills Hearing.* Washington, DC: U.S. Government Printing Office.

Ann E. Fade

LOANS. See Banking Services for the Mature Market; Bonds; Credit Cards; Home Modifications Financing; Homeownership; Mortgage Instruments; Reverse Mortgages; Seniors Housing Finance.

LONG-TERM CARE INSURANCE: A CONSUMER'S GUIDE. Although almost two million people have purchased long-term care insurance, many have discovered some disheartening surprises about their policies. Given today's improved choices and flexibility, consumers are becoming more interested in long-term care insurance, but persons who choose this method for financing long-term care must determine whether it is appropriate and know what to look for in a policy.

Problems

Based on findings from two reports, insurance agents are not providing complete and accurate information to consumers. Research by *Consumer Reports* (1991) revealed numerous problems associated with deceptive sales practices by representatives from even the largest insurance companies. Some agents selling long-term care insurance were either unaware of important aspects of the policy they were selling, or were unwilling to disclose vital information.

Many of the insurance agents who were evaluated did not rank well in the areas of clarity, honesty, thoroughness, length of visit, and overall knowledge of the policy. Not all insurance companies offering long-term care products were financially secure or even reputable at the time (Polniaszek 1992). Even today, prospective policyholders should review an insurance company's rating. Cost is another problem associated with long-term care insurance. Policy affordability is influenced by age at time of purchase, the length of time and amount of coverage selected, and the types of benefits and additional options purchased.

As more states institute tougher regulations and public-private partnerships for long-term care, an increasing number of consumers will be able to make informed purchasing decisions. In a public-private partnership, insurance companies and state agencies work together to offer state residents higher-quality, affordable long-term care financing options. In addition to this model, insurance companies must recognize the need to educate and train their sales agents adequately in the following areas: (1) policy knowledge, (2) interpersonal communication skills, (3) buying behaviors of mature consumers, and (4) state regulations. Consumer perception of long-term care insurance policies can be significantly influenced by the way policies are represented by sales agents.

Wider Social Acceptance

Despite the problematic history of long-term care insurance policies, the concept and the industry have made significant improvements. Among the driving forces influencing these positive changes are: (1) government and industry regulations requiring that higher standards be met, (2) increased consumer demand as result of a more informed and educated market, and (3) an increasing competitive environment among insurance companies. The following six points offer an explanation of why long-term care insurance has gained wider social acceptance.

1. *Personal family experience.* Several studies demonstrate that a large percentage of families have had personal experience with long-term care. The financial and emotional strain of long-term care are likely to impact most families.

2. *Fear of dependency.* The fear of becoming dependent on others is a highly rated concern among most older adults, especially when there may be no family members or friends available to provide needed assistance.

3. *Lack of available family caregivers.* Cutler (1992) demonstrates that, while the growth of the majority of caregivers (women aged 55–64) is projected to climb by 58.1% from 1980 to 2010, the population of individuals who receive most of the care (adults aged 85+) is projected to explode by 173.2%. Adding to this demographic trend are the lifestyles, attitudes, and personal limitations of prospective caregivers.

4. *The cost of long-term care.* Like traditional health care, the costs associated with long-term care have escalated over the years and will continue to increase. It is estimated that, based on the national average cost of nursing home* care ranging between $36,000 to $50,000, a person who begins a stay as a private-pay patient exhausts his or her financial resources in an average of 13 months.

5. *Preferences for the type and location of care.* Long-term care insurance policies of today usually cover most or all of the charges for nursing home stays so long as the charges are reasonable and customary. With this flexibility, policyholders may have a wider range of options in choosing the type and location of these institutions. Most policies pay for all levels of care (skilled, intermediate, and custodial). Costs for home

care services* are also covered. This includes skilled care; physical, occupational, speech, and respiratory therapies; homemaker services; and other personal services such as respite care and adult day care*. Again, policyholders, with the aid of a case manager, can select from a wide range of services and resources—providing of course that eligibility requirements are met first.

6. *Asset protection.* The model of the Connecticut Partnership for Long-Term Care envisions private coverage of the front-end costs of long-term care, while the public part of the partnership provides asset protection equal to insurance payouts, and lifelong coverage of necessary care, once Medicaid* eligibility is established. Several states have moved forward in adopting similar public-private partnerships, including California, Indiana, and New York. A review of long-term care insurance policies that are "precertified" through a partnership program shows higher quality products that offer broader coverage, valuable options, and an asset protection feature. These policies, however, may come with a higher price tag.

In recent years, policies have increased in quality and affordability. But long-term care insurance can be complex and confusing. Potential purchasers should consider the following issues: first, is long-term care insurance affordable, and second, what provisions should one look for?

When Is Long-Term Care Insurance Right for a Consumer?

The Connecticut State Department on Aging (1992) has developed a user-friendly, comprehensive guide primarily for adults aged 50–70. Four sections guide the consumer through a series of assessments: health risk, family support, assets, and income.

1. *Assessment of health risk* determines the risk for developing disabling conditions later in life. Consumers are encouraged to assess any current or past acute or chronic health conditions experienced by them or by a close family member.

2. *Assessment of family support* helps the consumer determine the extent to which family members and friends would be available to provide personal assistance and support should one become disabled later in life. How the consumer personally feels about receiving such care is also explored.

3. *Assessment of assets* raises questions of asset protection. Does a consumer have enough assets to protect? What does he or she ultimately wish to do with assets? Are assets sufficient to pay for long-term care and still pass some on to heirs? How long will it take to spend down assets before being eligible for Medicaid? Connecticut's guide suggests using an average cost range of $35,000 to $50,000 a year for nursing homes, and about $15,000 a year for home health care services when making these assessments.

4. *Assessment of income and cash flow* currently and in later life will answer the most important question: Can long-term care insurance premiums be paid from income? If it turns out that assets must be used to pay insurance premiums, the next question should be: Given income projections and level of assets, is long-term care insurance affordable?

What to Look For in a Long-Term Care Insurance Policy

Knowing what to buy, and understanding the policy's terms, are as important as knowing whether a policy is affordable. The guide of the Connecticut State Department on Aging (1992) defines the more common terms used in long-term care policies, such as age requirements, authorized agent, benefit period, community-based services, daily benefit rate, exclusions or exceptions, ''free look'' period, grace period, home care option, level of care, lifetime maximum benefit, non-forfeiture value, and preexisting condition. Statements on how a term affects the policyholder are also provided. Following are four recommendations for determining whether a particular policy matches one's needs, and the financial stability of the insurance company offering the product.

1. Review policy features and know what to look for. Higher-quality long-term care insurance policies will provide coverage for the following, or make such benefits available as optional riders:

a. 100% coverage for nursing home care (skilled, intermediate, and custodial care)

b. At least 80% coverage for home care (skilled and personal care, physical therapy, occupational therapy, speech and respiratory therapy, visiting nurse, home health aid, delivered meals, adult day care, respite care, durable medical equipment, emergency response system, and some coverage for home modifications)

c. A broad range of age eligibility

d. A selection of premium payment options (lifetime, 20-year payment period, or lump sum)

e. Inflation protection

f. Discounted provider network

g. Options available for level premiums or increasing premiums

h. Options available for the elimination period (also referred to as the deductible or waiting period)

i. Premiums waived if the policyholder becomes disabled (or at least after spending 90 days in a nursing home or receiving home care services for 90 days)

j. Non-forfeiture rider

k. A wide selection for lifetime maximum benefits and/or coverage periods

l. Guaranteed renewable

2. The purchaser should check the insurance company's ratings for financial position through such publications as A. M. Best Company (a rating of A or A+ is recommended) or Standard and Poor's (a rating of A to AAA is recommended)

3. Several policies using the same criteria for each (lifetime maximum benefit, options, and so forth) should be compared when assessing policy provisions

4. The consumer should be critical of representations made about long-term care insurance, ask questions, and take time to decide which policy to purchase.

Long-term care insurance policies of today have emerged with significant improvements as policy benefits and features have undergone significant enhancements. Three factors that will impact the quality and success of long-term care insurance are: (1) state insurance commissioners cracking down on misleading sales tactics and poor products, (2) public-private "partnerships" for long-term care, and (3) insurance companies adequately training their sales agents. If a consumer can afford long-term care insurance and can pay the premiums out of his or her present and projected future income without having to dip into savings or other assets, long-term care insurance can be a valuable source of protection. (See also AGENTS AND BROKERS, CAREGIVING FOR THE ELDERLY, ETHICS IN FINANCIAL PLANNING, GERONTO-LOGICAL NURSE PRACTITIONERS, HOME CARE SERVICES FOR THE ELDERLY, LONG-TERM CARE INSURANCE: PRIVATE, MEDICAID, MEDICAID PLANNING, MEDICARE, and NURSING HOMES.)

Organizations

Connecticut State Department on Aging
National Association of Insurance Commissioners
United Seniors Health Cooperative

Suggested Reading

Connecticut State Department on Aging. 1993. *Is Long-Term Care Insurance for Me?* Hartford, CT: Connecticut State Department on Aging.

References

Connecticut State Department on Aging. 1992. *What to Look For in a Long-Term Care Insurance Policy.* Hartford, CT: Connecticut State Department on Aging.
Consumer Reports. 1991. "Empty Promises to the Elderly?" *Consumer Reports* 56: 425–42.
Cutler, N. E. 1992. "Long-Term Care Insurance: National Trends in Personal Care." *Journal of the American Society of CLU & ChFC.* 46: 23–26.
Firman, James P., Judith Walsh, and Bonnie Burns. 1994. *Private Long-Term Care Insurance: To Buy or Not to Buy?* Washington, DC: United Seniors Health Cooperative.
Mahoney, K. J., and T. Wetle. 1992. "Public-Private Partnerships: The Connecticut Model for Financing Long-Term Care." *Journal of the American Geriatrics Society* 40: 1026–30.
McConnell, S. 1990. "Who Cares about Long-Term Care?" *Generations.* 14: 15–18.
Norman, Albert, Susan Polniaszek, and James P. Firman. 1995. *Long-Term Care Insurance: A Professional's Guide to Selecting Policies.* Washington, DC: United Seniors Health Cooperative.
Polniaszek, S. 1992. *Insurance to Pay for Long-Term Care.* Washington, DC: United Seniors Health Cooperative.

Jeff L. Lefkovich

**LONG-TERM CARE INSURANCE: INDIVIDUAL DISABILITY-ESCALAT-
ING ANNUITIES (IDEAs)**, financing proposed for long-term care, based on
the principle that the financial risk of becoming functionally impaired during
retirement may be reduced by spreading it three ways simultaneously: (1) over
people, through insurance contracts; (2) over time, through sales to those under
age 60; and (3) against the inversely related risk of extended longevity (the peril
covered by annuities and pension plans).

Overview

Demand for long-term care services will rise dramatically in the decades
ahead. The supply of public funds is inadequate even to meet today's long-term
care needs. Traditional long-term care insurance product offerings in the private
sector have yet to cover even 5% of today's loss exposure.

Unlike acute-care Medicare supplemental insurance*, long-term care insurance policies provide nursing home and/or at-home benefits for those suffering
from chronic disabilities during their retirement. Since the prototype long-term
care policy was first introduced by Mark Meiners (1983), about 150 insurers
have sold more than two million such plans. But ideally, long-term care contracts
should be purchased by individuals well before they retire, since time can enhance the cost-effectiveness of any insurance plan that spreads risk financing
responsibility over a large number of people.

Proposed IDEAs

Conceivably, the risk of functional dependence during retirement be reduced
by spreading it, not just over people and time, but also against an opposing, or
inversely related risk. The premise underlying Individual Disability-Escalating
Annuities (IDEAs) is that disability among the elderly tends to be life-
shortening, that is, that the risks of functional dependence and extended longevity are inversely related. The central working hypothesis is that for both men
and women over 65, as levels of impairment increase, life expectancy and the
risk of superannuation decrease.

Since the primary purpose of annuities* is to protect against the peril of
outliving one's income, the risk of becoming functionally dependent might be
cut by packaging disability insurance coverage *with* annuity protection. A single
insurance policy might then cover the joint-peril of "superannuated-disability."
Under such a contract that would cover two opposing risks simultaneously, the
more disabled annuitants become, the more monthly cash they could receive to
help them pay for long-term care services of their choice, since, on average, the
shorter would be their remaining survival time.

Disability-Escalating Retirement Annuities call not only for monthly annuity
payments to continue to a retiree whose living status remains positive, but also
for benefit levels to escalate as the disability status of an annuitant worsens.
Cash benefits for elderly disability, unlike those meant to indemnify insureds

for lost income or for specific service expenses, would be ones of status, like those paid out under annuities.

Research Findings

Selected for analysis by Christopherson (1992) was the longitudinal Aging in Manitoba Study (Manitoba Department of Health & Social Development 1973). The government of Manitoba conducted the study to assess the needs of the elderly and the resources available to meet those needs. Follow-up interviews of original respondents still living were completed during the summer of 1983. Dates of death were recorded for those who died during the intervening twelve years. The principal research findings and conclusions from Christopherson's (1992) analysis of the Aging in Manitoba survey data include the following:

1. Each of the nine activities of daily living (ADL) physical dependency indicators is a more powerful predictor of mortality than virtually any health status or history question

2. For both men and women aged 65 or over, as levels of functional impairment increase, life expectancy decreases

3. The nine ADLs studied can be most closely grouped into three disjoint "factors" that largely reflect dependencies within three distinct ADL activity clusters (related to arms, legs, and the body)

Providing actuarially equivalent, disability-escalating, extra cash benefits to disabled insureds starts with a definition of the help they need in performing basic self-care activities at two different levels:

Level 1—Needing help with at least two of the nine Activities of Daily Living, so long as those activities are from at least two different clusters.

Level 2—Needing help with at least five of the nine ADLs, so long as those activities are from all three clusters.

Supplemental cash benefits payable to functionally dependent annuitants may be expressed as percentages of the basic monthly benefits they receive under their annuities. Christopherson (1992) recommends a unisex schedule of extra benefits that escalate not only with the level of impairment, but also with the original age of transition to that functionally impaired state, from 20% below age 75 at Level 1 to 70% at age 85 or over at Level 2.

Several IDEA pricing assumptions are intentionally conservative. Yet the maximum probable "net cost" of providing this unisex schedule of extra disability benefits is extremely low. Depending on the assumed interest rate used to price an annuity, it may cost as little as a 2% reduction in basic benefits for men and less than a 4% reduction for women to pay for these supplemental disability benefits. For example, a man may choose to finance a $1,000 monthly retirement income under a traditional annuity. For the same total premium contributions during his working years, he could fund an IDEA basic benefit of 2%

less than that amount, or $980. But that monthly annuity would escalate should he become disabled during retirement. The total net cost to annuitants might be reduced further, or even eliminated, by increasing charges payable by those who surrender their deferred annuities prior to retirement.

Policies for the Future

In the development of any new insurance products there are concerns about pricing assumptions. But a significant degree of security has been introduced into the calculation of the levels and costs of the disability benefits suggested here. Spreading against each other two inversely related risks (disability and superannuation) should lower the overall variability of survival projections. Eventually, new research data about ADLs and their effects on longevity should become available. Until then, it seems safest to use conservative assumptions when generalizing from the Manitoba study findings about impairments and their effects on survival times to current annuitant mortality projections.

The IDEA concept offers real advantages to both consumers and insurers. First, the product protects against the economic consequences of extended longevity by providing monthly benefits guaranteed for life. Second, disability-escalating contracts should be viewed as much more than traditional annuities. Historically, private disability insurance products have been designed to replace a percentage of one's working income lost due to accident or sickness prior to retirement. By contrast, IDEAs would protect against the peril of disability after retirement by paying escalated cash benefits, not only unrelated to lost income, but also regardless of the incurrence of any specific expenses caused by the disability.

By introducing waiting periods before considering claims for escalated benefits, insurers can minimize both their adverse selection risks and policy costs. With a maximum issue age of 60, the joint-peril of superannuated-disability could be effectively spread over time as well as over insureds. Insurers' verifications of the impairment status of claimants can be combined with active case-management assistance to disabled annuitants in finding cost-effective rehabilitation possibilities or in otherwise optimizing their escalated benefits.

By attracting attention to the real retirement planning and estate preservation needs addressed by Individual Disability-Escalating Annuities, insurance companies should realize better persistency for their annuity line than they currently do when speaking to those obsessed with merely finding the highest current and tax-deferred interest rate haven for their money. By advocating a comprehensive estate-preservation planning program, including the need to protect against the peril of needing long-term care, agents should also realize increasing levels of collateral life policy sales. Furthermore, by bundling together protection against two risks in one product, insurers can overcome the stigma and the psychological barriers of trying to sell stand-alone ''nursing home'' or even ''long-term care'' policies. Perhaps the peril most of us dread the most is outliving our income while becoming functionally dependent on others.

In the last two years, the first versions of disability-escalating annuities have been developed and introduced into the American and Canadian markets. Interested consumers who are approaching retirement age should ask their independent agents if the insurers they represent are offering protection against the joint-peril of superannuated-disability. When reviewing competing disability-escalating annuity alternatives, prospective policy purchasers should compare, not simply current interest rates and length of guarantee differentials, but also contract deferral periods, maximum issue ages, underwriting restrictions, waiting periods, surrender charge levels and durations, settlement rate guarantees and options, impairment group definitions, and related benefit-multiplier schedules. (See also ANNUITIES, LONG-TERM CARE INSURANCE; PRIVATE, MEDICARE SUPPLEMENTAL INSURANCE, and NURSING HOMES.)

References

Christopherson, David L. 1992. "New IDEAs for Insuring Long-Term Care." *Journal of the American Society of CLU & ChFC.* 46: 42–53.

Lieberman, T., ed. 1991. "An Empty Promise to the Elderly?" *Consumer Reports* 56: 425–42.

Manitoba Department of Health & Social Development. 1973. *Aging in Manitoba: Needs and Resources.* Winnipeg: Division of Research, Planning and Program Development.

Meiners, Mark R. 1983. "The Case for Long-Term Care Insurance." *Health Affairs* 2: 55–79.

David L. Christopherson

LONG-TERM CARE INSURANCE, PRIVATE, financial protection against medical and personal care expenses associated with chronic disability that are not covered by the Medicare* program. While most policies primarily cover nursing home* care, an increasing number also include home care services*. For long-term care insurance (LTCI), an age-related level premium is the norm—the older one is, the more a policy costs.

Private LTCI policies were first offered in the mid-1980s. Increasing wealth among the elderly, greater longevity, changing family structures, and lack of public financing have all contributed to an expanding and rapidly changing market for LTCI. The Health Insurance Association of America (HIAA) reports that the number of companies selling long-term care insurance increased from 75 in 1987 to 118 in 1993, while the number of policies sold increased from 815,000 in December 1987 to more than 3.4 million in December 1993 (HIAA 1995). Despite this growth, only 1% of all nursing home expenditures are paid by private insurance (Letsch et al. 1992).

The LTCI market has three components: the individual market, the employer-sponsored market and the life insurance rider market. At present, the individual market, where policies are sold on a one-on-one basis, overwhelmingly dominates private LTCI. Although much smaller, sales through employer-sponsored and life insurance markets are increasing and some believe represent the greatest potential sources of future growth.

Demand and Supply Barriers

Despite promising growth, the market for private LTCI exhibits both demand- and supply-side barriers. On the demand side, there are at least three major obstacles: affordability, lack of knowledge about the risks of long-term care, and misinformation about current coverage.

Historically, the elderly have been disproportionately poor and unable to afford significant premium payments. Although elderly income has risen substantially in the last 20 years, in part due to improvements in public and private pensions, LTCI remains expensive for most elderly people. The average annual premium for high-quality individual LTCI offered by the 15 leading sellers in 1991 was $2,525 at age 65 and climbed rapidly to $7,675 at age 79 (HIAA 1993). Most studies of LTCI demand find that only a relatively small minority of the elderly, 10 to 20%, can afford private LTCI (Rivlin and Wiener 1988; Families USA Foundation 1993).

By modeling the market for private and group LTCI under differing affordability assumptions, Wiener et al. (1994) found that the employer-based market of younger purchasers has the greatest potential for expansion. Using the Brookings-ICF Long-Term Care Financing Model to simulate the market for long-term care insurance through the year 2018, they found that while only 20% of the elderly might purchase long-term care insurance under existing market conditions (assuming premiums are no more than 5% of annual income), up to 76% of the elderly could afford coverage if the market were expanded to include substantial numbers of non-elderly policyholders.

Encouraging younger individuals to purchase insurance through employers would significantly reduce the price of premiums, but there may be barriers preventing expansion of the employer market. Many employers already face large, unfunded liabilities for retiree acute health care, and are not eager to commit to additional costs for long-term care. Challenges arise in stimulating demand among the non-elderly who face competing and more immediate financial needs—child care, mortgage payments, children's college education, and their own retirement. Although affordability estimates of LTCI are subject to somewhat arbitrary assumptions regarding an individual's willingness to pay, the number of policies sold remains far below even conservative gauges.

Misinformation about the need for long-term care insurance may help explain why relatively few elderly individuals purchase LTCI. Many elderly believe that Medicare* or Medicare Supplemental Insurance* covers extensive nursing home and home health services, when they do not. Medicaid* is the payer of last resort and will cover nursing home care only after an individual is impoverished. The risks associated with long-term care appear to be largely unrecognized by the elderly, yet research suggests that 40% of those who live to age 65 will spend some time in a nursing home in later life (Kemper and Murtaugh 1991).

Insurers of long-term care confront three barriers in bringing their product to market. First, most disabled persons receive no paid services, and how much demand would increase if services—especially home care—were covered by insurance is unknown. Second, a disproportionate number of high-risk individuals may purchase policies, pushing premiums ever-higher and causing low-risk policyholders to drop their coverage as prices rise. To protect against adverse selection, insurers usually screen out people with health problems and exclude coverage for preexisting conditions. A third barrier is the lack of claims experience for long-term care, since LTCI is relatively new and use patterns are still developing. This problem is compounded by the length of time between policy purchase and the filing of claims. Even when the purchaser is older, that individual may not need care for 20 years or more. Moreover, changes in disability or mortality rates, utilization patterns, or the rate of return on financial services can dramatically change a profitable insurance product into an unprofitable one.

Consumer Protection Issues

Long-term care policies have changed dramatically in a short period. Faced with great uncertainty, companies initially tried to anticipate and protect against financial loss by imposing restrictions and limitations on services covered and eligibility for reimbursement. The net effect was to lessen substantially the probability that an insured person who used a nursing home or home care would actually receive insurance benefits.

Over time, policies have improved substantially. While the average policy in force still has restrictions, newer policies provide significantly better coverage. In newer policies, prior hospitalization requirements have been eliminated, policies are guaranteed renewable, Alzheimer's Disease is explicitly covered, all levels of nursing home care and more home care are covered, indemnity levels are sometimes indexed for inflation, and a few policies provide some residual benefits to people who discontinue their policies.

Although the quality of policies has improved greatly, problems remain. Consumer protection issues include the absence of adequate inflation protection, high lapse rates, lack of nonforfeiture benefits, variation in how disability is determined, and agent and marketing abuses. While high-quality policies are available, current regulations also permit lower quality policies to be sold as well.

Features such as inflation protection, nonforfeiture benefits, and guaranteed renewability are particularly important to look for in a policy, although these features will raise its price. Given the rising costs of long-term care, adequate inflation protection is essential to assure that benefit levels will keep pace with rising prices for long-term care services. Also, most insurance underwriters assume that a majority of policyholders will drop their policies within five years of the initial purchase. Thus, nonforfeiture benefits enable individuals who allow their policies to lapse to recoup some of their investment.

The National Association of Insurance Commissioners (NAIC) has developed model standards requiring insurers to offer their customers the option to purchase policies with inflation protection. However, this model regulation does not prohibit the sale of policies that do not provide adequate inflation adjustments. By July 1992, 31 states had adopted this standard or some variation.

The Future of Long-Term Care Insurance

Private long-term care insurance offers the possibility of prefunding the inevitable societal burden that will occur when the aging baby boom generation needs long-term care. The classic virtue of the competitive market model is that it has the flexibility to adapt to individual needs and wants and to local conditions. Moreover, the large federal budget deficit and general concerns about government competence have made large-scale expansion in almost any public program difficult to enact. The marked improvement in the financial position of the elderly in the past twenty years has also made it more plausible to argue that private LTCI might be more widely affordable in the future. Likewise, increased awareness of financing long-term care is likely to reduce misinformation among the elderly about the need to reduce their risk exposure.

Despite recent growth in the market for private insurance, a number of formidable barriers to expansion remain. Good quality private LTCI is too expensive for most elderly people. Although the employer-based market exhibits the greatest potential for providing widespread affordable premiums, many employers are likely to resist adding long-term care benefits to employee compensation packages in the near future. Although reforms have helped to improve the quality of long-term care policies, it is unlikely that these reforms will rid the market of policies that exclude individuals with preexisting conditions. Finally, when long-term care coverage is funded privately through the market, rather than through a public program, individuals who can afford higher premiums and better-quality policies will purchase policies, while those with more modest means may be priced out of the market. This scenario raises questions of equity that are not addressed by market-based approaches. (See also HEALTH AND LONGEVITY, HEALTH MAINTENANCE ORGANIZATIONS (HMOs), HOME CARE SERVICES FOR THE ELDERLY, INSURANCE, LONG-TERM CARE INSURANCE: A CONSUMER'S GUIDE, MEDICAID, MEDICARE, MEDICARE SUPPLEMENTAL INSURANCE, NURSING HOMES, POST-RETIREMENT HEALTH INSURANCE and WEALTH SPAN.)

Suggested Readings

Firman, James P., and Susan Polniaszek. 1993. *Long-Term Care Insurance: A Professional's Guide to Selecting Policies.* Washington, DC: United Seniors Health Cooperative.

Polniaszek, Susan. 1993. *Long-Term Care: A Dollar & Sense Guide, Revised.* Washington, DC: United Seniors Health Cooperative.

References

Families USA Foundation. 1993. *Nursing Home Insurance: Who Can Afford It?* Washington, DC: Families USA.

Health Insurance Association of America. 1995. *Long-Term Care Insurance in 1993.* Washington, DC: Health Insurance Association of America (HIAA).

Kemper, Peter, and Christopher M. Murtaugh. 1991. ''Lifetime Use of Nursing Home Care.'' *New England Journal of Medicine* 324: 595–600.

Letsch, Suzanne W., Helen C. Lazenby, Katharine R. Levit, and Cathy A. Cowan. 1992. ''National Health Expenditures, 1991.'' *Health Care Financing Review* 14: 1–30.

Rivlin, Alice M., and Joshua M. Wiener. 1988. *Caring for the Disabled Elderly: Who Will Pay?* Washington, DC: Brookings Institution.

Wiener, Joshua M., Laurel Hixon Illston, and Raymond H. Hanley. 1994. *Sharing the Burden: Strategies for Public and Private Long-Term Care Insurance.* Washington, DC: Brookings Institution.

Joshua M. Wiener and Catherine M. Sullivan

M

MARKETING TO ELDERS, efforts by business to reach the aging population. As the number of elderly consumers with higher incomes and special needs increases, marketers become more responsive to their discretionary spending for goods and services. This mature market segment is expected to increase as baby boomers reach middle and old age. Marketing is the social and managerial process by which individuals and groups are provided with what they need and want through the creation and exchange of products and values. To facilitate this process, marketers employ strategies known as the four Ps: product, pricing, promotion, and place. These are also known as marketing mix strategies, establishing the bases that enable marketers to provide products and services to selected groups at a profit. A discussion of each of these strategies will serve to explain the financial impact of the senior consumer on product design, pricing, promotion, and retailing/distribution.

Research, Segmenting, Targeting, and Positioning

Successful marketing strategies begin with knowledge of the consumer. Market research and "marketing intelligence," obtained formally through research procedures, such as surveys and focus groups, or informally by listening to the needs and wants of the consumer, generally provide this knowledge. Tom Peters (1987) emphasizes that marketers who listen and respond most intently will be most successful, and maintains that marketers should be "in the field" at least 25% and preferably 50% of the time.

Once information about consumers is gathered, market segmentation allows the marketer to divide the market into smaller groups who share common needs and wants. For the aging population, the following segmentation variables are often used: geographic location, age, gender, income, family, education, religion, and race. Social class, lifestyle, and personality may also be considered. San Francisco–based Royal Cruise Lines, for example, is moving beyond price discounts to attract older consumers. To target older vacationers, Royal consulted with the American Heart Association and became the first in its industry to develop a health-conscious menu and to offer a lecture series on senior-oriented health issues.

When market segmentation is completed, market targeting begins. The marketer identifies certain segments with possible opportunities. Targets refer to one segment, such as vitamins for those over fifty, or multiple segments, such as the variety of leisure activities. Regardless of the targeting strategy chosen, products and services must reflect the life focus of persons in certain age brackets. For example, persons between the ages of 50 and 64 generally are primarily interested in products that promote health, comfort, leisure, and self-fulfillment (Dychwald 1989).

Following targeting, product positioning ensues. David Ogilvy (1985) defines positioning as ''what the product does, and who it is for.'' Positioning is successful when it brings about a competitive advantage. Typical positioning variables include price, quality, and service. Choice Hotels International found from its research that older patrons desire more than just discounts on room prices. In response, the chain now advertises that all first-floor, nonsmoking rooms have been reserved for seniors.

Product Strategies

The marketer formulates marketing mix strategies comprised of product, price, distribution, and promotion. Marketers have altered product strategies to attract older consumers. Their distinct needs and wants in reference to goods and services have prompted marketers to relabel, rebrand, and modify existing products or develop new ones. As an example, Buick's attempt to attract an older market by equipping its 1991 Park Avenue model with flat, plush seats, air bags, easy-to-use door handles, and other safety features received favorable comment from prospective older purchasers.

Pricing Strategies

Once the product mix is set, the marketer must develop appropriate pricing strategies consonant with the product perception of each target market. In setting price it is important to consider factors such as costs, marketing objectives, market demand, competitor's prices, and marketing mix strategy. Once these factors are assessed, the marketer determines the exact pricing strategy(ies) to use. These include market skimming, market penetration, product-line pricing, optional product pricing, captive product pricing, and product bundle pricing.

Market skimming is a strategy used for an innovative new product where a high initial price is set to skim the market, so that profits can be maximized quickly. Market penetration is another strategy used for new products, but a low price is set in order to penetrate or capture a large share of the market. Here the objective becomes market share, not profit. In product line pricing, the product to be marketed is priced in relation to an entire product line. Features and value determine the location of the new product on the spectrum of the product line. For optional product pricing, specific additional features or options are priced separately. This can be very useful in catering to the specific and varied needs of older customers. Captive product pricing is a strategy used for products that are dependent in their use upon another product. The captive product is the one that must be used with the main product. In product bundle pricing several products are marketed together at a reduced price rather than being sold separately. Discount pricing, discriminatory pricing (not to be confused with price discrimination), and promotional pricing are also options (Kotler and Armstrong 1994). For the older consumer, pricing strategies concentrate on discretionary income typically made possible by the absence of mortgage payments, education expenses, and child support.

Distribution Strategies

Distribution strategies are among the most important decisions facing a marketer. Distribution involves getting the right product, at the right time, at the right place into the hands of the consumer. The mechanism for accomplishing this goal is a distribution channel, a network of organizations working together to move the product from the producer to the consumer. These channels are most effective when they best satisfy customer needs.

Distribution also incorporates retailing and retail decisions involved in selling goods and services directly to final consumers for their personal, nonbusiness use. Major retail decisions include store or outlet location, product type and assortment, and pricing. K-Mart, for instance, has been successful with its formula of low prices, convenient locations, and customer service. Most stores have a ''greeter,'' usually a cheerful retiree, who welcomes shoppers, responds to questions, and is familiar with store layout. For the older shopper, this friendly, courteous service is helpful and welcomed.

A form of distribution that is growing among older consumers is television home shopping which, while providing convenience for some, does not appeal to those customers who still enjoy shopping. This consideration is particularly important for older consumers who have considerable leisure time.

Promotional Strategies

Tools used in marketing are sales promotion, publicity, and advertising, and the most used and readily recognized is advertising. Little is definitively known about effective advertising, as it remains an art, not a science. Success generally results when painstaking planning and implementation strategies are developed. These include formulating realistic objectives, establishing feasible budgets, conceiving and creating the right image and message, selecting the appropriate means for delivering the message, and determining effective bases for evaluation. Outstanding ads are rare, but have a huge impact.

Marketers attempting to reach the growing elderly market can no longer over-look this population's self-image in developing advertising objectives, message content, and media strategy. Marketers are successful when they portray older persons as they see themselves (Dychwald 1989). Advertisements that depict this market segment using and enjoying products in a true-to-life manner have a greater impact than those that stereotype elders in an unfavorable way. Show-ing older consumers as responsible, competent adults who continue to make intelligent marketplace choices leaves a more positive impact than commercials that portray the elderly as incapable of sound purchasing decisions.

Business has only recently been awakening to the marketplace power of the older consumer. Companies that once catered exclusively to younger markets are now redirecting or refocusing their efforts toward mature individuals. On product development, pricing, distribution, and advertising, older buyers now exert considerable marketing influence. Marketers are redesigning traditional strategies to target older consumers. Success will be measured by how well these strategies accommodate the needs, wants, and desires of this growing market. (See also HEALTH AND LONGEVITY, LEISURE, MASS MEDIA AND THE ELDERLY, TRAVEL, and VACATION HOMES AND RECREATIONAL PROPERTY.)

References

Dychwald, Ken. 1989. *Age Wave: The Challenges and Opportunities of an Aging Amer-ica.* Los Angeles: Jeremy A. Tarcher, Inc.
Kotler, Philip, and Gary Armstrong. 1994. *Principles of Marketing.* Englewood Cliffs, NJ: Prentice-Hall.
Ogilvy, David. 1985. *Ogilvy on Advertising.* New York: Random House.
Peters, Tom. 1987. *Thriving On Chaos.* New York: Alfred A. Knopf.

Christopher S. Alexander and Thomas Visgilio III

MARRIAGE AND THE ELDERLY, marriages occurring after the age of 65. More than half (56%) of the population over age 65 is married. But this general statistic does not reveal important information about marital status in old age, such as marital status differences across age and sex categories, the change in marital status of the older population over time, and differences between married and unmarried groups.

The effects of gender and age on marital status in later life are shown in Table 1. The majority (80%) of men aged 65–74 are married, compared to 54% of women. This difference is not due to differences in the proportion who ever married—only 4 or 5% never married. More women than men have been wid-owed, reflecting the higher death rates of men. Fewer women have remarried after divorce. Among the oldest old*, the gender gap is even greater. It is five times more likely that a man over age 85 is currently married than a woman.

Marriage after age 65 is uncommon. Fewer than 2% of all marriages in 1990 were to persons over age 65. The structure of the Social Security* program does

Table 1

Marital Status of the Older Population, by Age and Sex, 1993

Marital Status	Age and Sex							
	65+		65-74		75-84		85+	
	M	F	M	F	M	F	M	F
Married	76.8	42.2	80.2	54.0	74.0	31.3	56.1	10.8
Widowed	14.3	47.6	9.4	35.2	19.3	59.2	38.5	79.2
Divorced	4.5	5.8	5.6	7.1	2.7	4.5	2.5	3.2
Never Married	4.4	4.4	4.8	3.7	4.0	5.0	2.9	6.8

Source: U.S. Bureau of the Census 1994a.

not discourage remarriage for older persons, although some recent tax changes may. Remarriage after age 60 does not reduce any Social Security benefit to which one is entitled. There is evidence that adult children often oppose the potential remarriage of their aging parents since a remarriage could reduce or eliminate their expected inheritance. The odds of an unmarried person marrying after age 65 are six times higher for men than women. This reflects both the large gender imbalance in the older unmarried population and the propensity of older men to marry younger women.

Given historical change in patterns of marriage, divorce*, remarriage, cohabitation*, and mortality, change over time in the marital status distribution of the older population is expected. Data in Table 2, showing marital status of the older population in 1960 and 1990, and projecting marital status to 2020, confirm this expectation. Consider, for example, changes among women aged 65–75. The large decline in death rates produces an expected 50% decline in proportion of widowed women between 1960 and 2020. The increase in divorce rates is even more marked, leading to a 650% increase in the proportion of women who are divorced over this time period. The net effect of these trends results in a moderate increase over time in the proportion of older women who are married. For men, the increase in the proportion divorced about equals the decrease in proportion widowed, so little change occurs in those married over time.

Later-life marriage has economic implications. As shown by data in Table 3, older unmarried persons are more likely to be living in poverty than married persons. Widowed and divorced men over age 65 are two to three times as likely as their married counterparts to be impoverished, while for women the economic disadvantages of being unmarried are even greater. Higher poverty rates among elderly widows suggest that women are especially vulnerable to economic losses associated with losing a spouse.

Being married in later life provides an informal (unpaid) caregiver in case of

Table 2
Marital Status of the Older Population, by Age and Sex: 1960, 1990, 2020

Age and Marital Status	Age and Sex					
	1960		1990		2020	
	M	F	M	F	M	F
65-74:						
Married	78.9	45.6	80.2	36.1	6.9	21.5
Widowed	12.7	44.4	9.2	36.1	6.9	21.5
Divorced	1.7	1.7	6.0	6.2	8.8	12.9
Never Married	6.7	8.4	4.7	4.6	7.8	7.7
75+						
Married	59.1	21.8	69.9	25.4	69.9	28.9
Widowed	31.6	68.3	23.7	65.6	21.0	55.5
Divorced	1.5	1.2	3.1	3.6	5.9	11.7
Never Married	7.8	8.6	3.4	5.4	3.1	3.9

Source: U.S. Bureau of the Census 1994b.

disability. Research on caregiving* indicates that spouses are the preferred and most common caregivers for dependent elderly persons. Those who do not have a spouse often deplete their assets paying for home health care and are more vulnerable to institutionalization. There are more never-married than married persons living in nursing homes, while among the noninstitutionalized population married persons outnumber never-married by a ratio of 12–to–1. The economic and caregiving advantages of older married persons help explain why the married have lower death rates than the unmarried.

An additional implication of entering later life with a spouse relates to retirement. Studies find that the work histories of married women affect couples' retirement incomes. Over the past several decades an increasing proportion of married women have participated in the labor force, and a growing proportion of working women hold jobs with pension coverage. These trends suggest future growth in the proportion of retired couples with multiple pension incomes. Couples that approach old age with both spouses in the labor force also face unique issues related to retirement planning. Research finds that decision making on simultaneous retirement or sequential retirement of husband and wife is complex. This decision depends on later-life family and health events as well as the earnings and pension eligibilities of husband and wife.

Both men and women who are married in later life tend to be economically advantaged, compared with those who are unmarried. Since fewer women than men are married in later life, and since unmarried women suffer greater eco-

Table 3
Poverty Rates by Age, Sex and Marital Status, 1992

Sex and Marital Status	Age			
	65+	65-74	75-84	85+
Male:				
Total	8.9	8.1	9.7	13.2
Married	6.6	6.0	7.5	10.5
Widowed	15.0	13.7	15.7	16.7
Other*	17.6	18.1	16.5	N/A
Female:				
Total	15.7	12.7	18.9	22.7
Married	6.4	5.6	8.0	N/A
Widowed	21.5	18.9	23.2	23.8
Other*	26.0	25.6	27.0	N/A

Source: Social Security Administration 1994.

nomic problems than unmarried men, there is a significant gender gap in economic status within the elderly population. This gap leads to discussions of how social policy might be employed to reduce gender inequality in old age. The 1983 Retirement Equity Act, requiring workers to get spousal approval before selecting a pension option not providing for survivor's benefits, is an example of trying to obtain greater protection for older women. Increasing attention is being given to the treatment of married and unmarried persons by the Social Security program. The program, enacted in 1935, assumed stable marriages with a working husband and a homemaking wife. Given the current reality of high rates of divorce and high rates of female labor force participation, it may be desirable to change the benefit formula. (See also CAREGIVING FOR THE ELDERLY, COHABITATION, DIVORCE AND THE ELDERLY, ECONOMIC STATUS OF THE ELDERLY, ECONOMIC STATUS OF ELDERLY WOMEN, SOCIAL SECURITY, and WIDOWHOOD.)

References

Burkhauser, Richard V., and Greg J. Duncan. 1991. "United States Public Policy and the Elderly: The Disproportionate Risk to the Well-Being of Women." *Journal of Population Economics* 4: 217–31.

Goldscheider, Frances K. 1990. "The Aging of the Gender Revolution." *Research on Aging* 12: 531–45.

Meyer, Madonna Harrington. 1990. "Family Status and Poverty among Older Women:

The Gendered Distribution of Retirement Income in the United States.'' *Social Problems* 37: 551–63.

O'Rand, Angela M., John C. Henretta, and Margaret L. Krecker. 1992. ''Family Pathways to Retirement.'' In *Family and Retirement,* ed. M. Szinovacz, D. J. Ekerdt, and B. H. Vinick. Newbury Park, CA: Sage, 81–98.

Social Security Administration. 1994. *Income of the Population 55 or Older, 1992.* Washington, DC: GPO.

United States Bureau of the Census. 1994a. *Current Population Reports.* Series P-20, No. 478. Washington, DC: U.S. Government Printing Office.

United States Bureau of the Census. 1994b. *Current Population Reports.* Series P-23, No. 178. Washington, DC: U.S. Government Printing Office.

Peter Uhlenberg

MASS MEDIA AND THE ELDERLY, media influences on individual and societal consumer trends as well as attitudes, beliefs, and perceptions regarding aging and the elderly population. Literary works that focus on the philosophical, psychological, and sociological aspects of aging date back to 700 B.C. The elderly have paradoxically been depicted as weak, dependent, and feeble-minded, focusing attention on the negative aspects of aging; or as honorable, revered, and wise. The modern mass media have also engaged in this dual portrayal using cinema, theater, television programming, literature, and television and magazine advertising as their palette. Although the popular media are still slanted toward the young-to-middle-aged audience, producers, writers, and publishers are recognizing both the needs and market appeal of an aging population. Accordingly, more salient topics are being featured. Large-print books and books on tape, for example, accommodate older readers.

Over the past decade, challenges to negative elderly stereotypes have been made by scholars in the fields of mass media and gerontology (Davis and Davis 1985). They asserted that such characterizations of older people perpetuate the negative view of aging. These challenges and advances in health, increases in life expectancy, and the growing number of older persons have motivated marketers and advertisers to focus positively on the elderly and their needs. If the elderly retain their consumer habits and appetites for spending (which they exercised during middle-age), then an increasingly good use of advertising budgets will, in all likelihood, present an accurate, favorable image of the elderly. It has been suggested that the elderly have more disposable income than any other age group, and this income may be increasingly targeted by the media.

Television

Persons over age 55 watch more television than persons under 55 (see Table 1). Programmers at CBS, realizing this trend, have focused their prime-time programming on this audience. Persons over 50 enjoy national and local news shows, television and news magazines, and mystery shows, such as *Murder, She Wrote; Matlock;* and the *Cosby Mysteries.* These shows have helped to change the public image of the elderly.

Table 1
Television Viewing Behavior

Age Group/Sex	Prime Time	Viewing Hours Per Week
Teens/female	6.23	21.59
Teens/male	6.28	21.58
18-49/female	9.49	32.48
18-49/male	9.14	28.27
50 + /female	11.58	42.19
50 + /male	11.12	36.18

Source: Nielsen Television Audience, 1993.

Television programmers also have been charged with neglecting the needs of the elderly. Factual data, however, shows that television programming is based on viewer behavior that translates to consumer behavior. For example, ABC (ranked first in prime-time programming for the years 1992–1994) and NBC focus their prime-time programming on the 18–49 year-old audience that spends the most money on products offered by the largest advertisers. Programming decisions are based on the premise that families headed by television viewers aged 18–49 buy more general goods (such as toothpaste and cereal) than singles or couples, even though singles and couples, especially elderly couples, may have a greater disposable income. Prime-time programming on CBS is focused on the 55+ age group. Advertising directed at persons over 55 occurs during news shows, news magazines, and other shows created to specifically appeal to that age group.

Television programming also reveals differences in commercial advertisements. For example, commercials during shows for the 55+ age group promote products that this age group can afford or use frequently. During a recent world news program and a recent television magazine show, frequent advertisers promoted arthritis pain medication and luxury cars. During prime time, commercials advertise general goods—orange juice, sausage, soda, mayonnaise, mid-priced restaurant chains, and mid-priced automobiles. Content analysis of the commercials did not reveal age stereotyping or ageism. For example, actors used to sell arthritis pain medication range in age from a 30-year-old woman to a 60-year-old man, all of whom illustrated how they remain active by taking the medication.

Past studies suggest that negative stereotyping of older persons occurred on television, and that they were excluded from programming, although older persons watch the most television (Nielsen 1993). Studies found that: (1) elders were presented in disproportionately small numbers, (2) the reality of their lives tend to be distorted, and (3) older women tend to be depicted less favorably than older men (Vernon et al. 1990).

While in the past the elderly may have been excluded from attending the cinema because of lack of transportation and inadequate facilities (uncomfortable chairs, inaccessible rest rooms, ticket prices, crowding), home videos now offer the opportunity to view current productions. Movie theaters also offer senior discounts, and many nursing homes and retirement communities provide transportation to local cinemas on a regular basis. The plots of several recent movies that have positively depicted older persons include *Batteries Not Included, Cocoon, Dad, Driving Miss Daisy, Fried Green Tomatoes, Golden Years, Grumpy Old Men,* and *On Golden Pond.* Many actors have pursued their careers past the traditional retirement age. These actors, including Angela Lansbury, Andy Griffith, George Burns, Bob Hope, Katharine Hepburn, Lauren Bacall, Clint Eastwood, Sean Connery, Paul Newman, Jessica Tandy, and Hume Cronyn, are role models for all generations.

Educational Literature

The American Association of Retired Persons (AARP) provides educational information regarding aging, and its Research Information Center offers information to government agencies, the news media, and institutions. *Ageline*, a public on-line database, includes business topics related to marketing to older adults. The AARP also offers the *Selling to Seniors Senior Media Guide,* which lists over 200 national and regional magazines, newspapers, and mailing lists that target the $800 billion (and growing) elderly market. (See also EDUCATION OF OLDER ADULTS, LEISURE, MARKETING TO ELDERS and APPENDIX B ORGANIZATIONS AND RESOURCES.)

Suggested Reading

American Association of Retired Persons. *Selling to Seniors Senior Media Guide.* Washington, DC: AARP.

References

Bell, John. 1992. "In Search of a Discourse on Aging: The Elderly on Television." *Gerontologist* 32(3): 305–11.

Davis, Richard H., and James A. Davis. 1985. *TV's Image of the Elderly.* Lexington, MA: Lexington Books.

Nielsen Television Audience. 1993. Dunedin, FL: Nielsen.

Powell, Lawrence A., and John B. Williams. 1985. "The Media and the Elderly." *Social Policy* 16(1) (Summer), 38–49.

Vernon, Joetta A., J. Allen Williams, and Terri Phillips. 1990. "Media Stereotyping: A Comparison of the Way Elderly Women and Men Are Portrayed on Prime-Time Television." *Journal of Women and Aging* 2(4): 55–68.

Mary Phillips Coker

MEDICAID, the nation's major entitlement program that matches federal and state resources for providing health care coverage to low-income families as well as long-term care coverage to low-income elderly and disabled people. Over the past two decades Medicaid has become the insurer of last resort for the elderly, filling a crucial need for a substantial number of older persons. Medicaid makes Medicare* work for low-income elderly who cannot afford Medicare's financial requirements and need benefits outside the Medicare package.

History and Scope

Medicaid, enacted under Title XIX of the Social Security Act, is the sister program of Medicare. The latter provides health benefits for the elderly and disabled (or their dependents) having work records sufficient to obtain retirement or disability benefits through Social Security. Supplemental Security Income (SSI)* is the income benefit for blind, disabled, or elderly people who lack a sufficient work record to qualify for Social Security, or whose Social Security benefit is below the SSI standard. Medicaid was to be the health care system for SSI recipients, analogous to Medicare. It also meant to provide benefits for people who were in an SSI category (e.g., blind, disabled, or elderly) but whose earnings were slightly over scale, or whose incomes were high but offset by medical expenses.

Medicaid's responsibilities have gradually expanded and become more complex since its beginnings as a health care financing program mainly for welfare recipients. It is today the key provider of health insurance for four very distinct population groups: low-income families lacking insurance; low-income elderly people who need help with filling gaps in Medicare benefits; disabled elderly people who need long-term care services; and the non-elderly disabled population who needs acute and long-term care services. Medicaid supplements Medicare coverage for about four million elderly and disabled persons and is the only substantial source of financial assistance for long-term care provided primarily in nursing homes*.

In 1965, Medicare and Medicaid offered comparable hospital and nursing home benefits. Medicare, even with Medicare Supplemental Insurance*, might pay for nursing home care if a number of requirements are met, but for no more than 100 days of a continuous stay. It is thus of limited use for people suffering from Alzheimer's Disease or any other long-term disabling condition that renders them unable to maintain themselves at home for months or years.

Poor people who remained in hospitals or skilled nursing home beds for lack of a place to return presented a different problem. Since the early 1970s, Medicaid has expanded coverage to include "intermediate" care to move beneficiaries out of high-cost hospital or skilled-care beds. Thus was born the long-term care* benefit. Medicaid pays for nursing home care in all states when it is medically necessary. Medicaid also pays for home health services. The increased demand for long-term care services reflects the increased longevity of the elderly, resulting in part from Medicare's success in delivering medical care to older Americans.

In fiscal year 1993, about 3.9 million people (about 12.6%) aged 65 and older were Medicaid recipients, but expenditures for these elderly persons were relatively large, accounting for approximately 28% of total Medicaid spending. Of Medicaid expenditures for the elderly, 69% go to nursing homes. Other categories (prescription drugs, home health, hospitals, and other expenditures) each absorb 7–8% of the total (Health Care Financing Review 1991). Government support for long-term care comes from Medicaid, which alone covered 51.7% of total nursing home expenses, in 1993 (Waid 1994).

Payments for institutional services (inpatient hospital services and long-term care institutions) have consistently accounted for the largest share of total Medicaid expenditures. But since 1981, payments for noninstitutional services (e.g., home health services, outpatient hospital services, and prescription drugs) have increased substantially. By now, payments for services provided in the home and community comprise 16% of Medicaid long-term care expenditures. Medicaid has been one of the fastest-growing government programs in recent years—spending increases averaged 12.2% annually between 1986 and 1990, and rising costs are expected to continue. They reached $125.8 billion in 1993 ($72.3 billion in federal and $53.5 billion in state monies) (Waid 1994).

Administration and Benefits

Medicaid is a program of unique complexity. While Medicare is administered exclusively by the Health Care Financing Administration (HCFA) through "fiscal intermediaries" (private insurance companies), Medicaid is administered by states under a federal statute supplemented by HCFA regulations and oversight. This system introduces variation in three ways:

1. The federal government sets broad eligibility criteria specifying what categories of individuals are eligible for federal matching payments. These categories are then further defined by state policy.

2. The federal government provides states with matching funds for certain other eligibility groups if the state chooses to cover them. One of the major options is to cover medically needy persons who meet the categorical requirements but have incomes that exceed welfare income levels.

3. Although required to have a "single agency" operating the program, many states have a central agency writing standards and program materials, while county or city social services departments administer eligibility standards such as processing applications and determining eligibility.

Depending on the economic strength of a state, 50 to 83% of Medicaid expenses are shouldered by the federal government. Medicaid pays directly to service providers. In each state, Medicaid determines the payment rate for services and contracts with providers willing to accept established rates. Medicaid recipients can obtain health care only from these providers. Beyond that, some variability results from major congressional amendments, which sometimes revamp substantial parts of the system or work themselves through to operational levels over time.

For the elderly, the most significant benefit is nursing home care, but various noninstitutional services at the state level are also important. All states must have programs to make home health services available to certain eligible Medicaid beneficiaries. Thirty-two states include personal care as part of the home and community-based service mix. In 1981, Congress established a home and community-based service waiver program, which allowed states greater flexibility in developing cost-effective alternatives for delivering social services beyond the traditional focus of medical benefits (i.e., housekeeping assistance, personal care, or adult day care), and for individuals whose incomes were above the usual Medicaid eligibility standard, but less than the higher income standard used for nursing facility residents. Under the waiver program, services are directed to persons who, without the provision of such services, would require hospital or nursing facility care. One result of the shift to home and community-based care is that states serve more beneficiaries with the Medicaid and state dollars they have available (General Accounting Office [GAO] 1994). These options have introduced a great deal of variation into the Medicaid benefit profile and the financial and functional eligibility criteria from state to state. New York, for example, provides a substantially more generous state home-care benefit permitting many disabled individuals to remain in their homes. Extensive shifts of long-term care from nursing home to home and community-based services are occurring in Oregon, Washington, and Wisconsin (GAO 1994).

Individuals seeking Medicaid benefits must apply, either in person or through an agent or representative. The application requires disclosure of complete financial information for the applicant and spouse, including asset transfers made in the previous three to five years. A medical report is required from the applicant's physician, and nursing home. The completed Medicaid application is the starting point from which a technician will make an initial determination of eligibility. Federal law requires that in most cases decisions be made within 45 days; some states have shortened (but cannot lengthen) that time period.

If benefits are denied, the state must provide a detailed explanation for the adverse decision and the procedure for appeal. The state is then required to hold a hearing before an impartial administrative judge. These hearings are informal, although "on the record" with a tape recording, but strict rules of evidence do not apply. If this decision is adverse, further appeals may be pursued administratively and when they are exhausted, an applicant may seek review in state or federal court.

Eligibility

Non-Financial Requirements. These include legal U.S. residence (i.e., citizenship or resident alien status), state residency where benefits are sought, and the need for "nursing facility services" or other medical services. Individuals must meet functional impairment criteria to qualify for services under long-term care programs. Functional impairment generally is determined by a detailed assessment of the need for assistance in activities of daily living and other factors, including medical, cognitive, social, and living conditions (GAO 1994). Congress has generally prohibited limitations on establishing eligibility in a state, such as duration of prior residence, so that an individual can establish residence upon his or her arrival in the state, even if it is to enter a nursing home and qualify for Medicaid benefits on the first day. The situation is somewhat problematical where the applicant for benefits lacks the competence required to establish residence.

Medicare-Medicaid Relationship. Older adults with limited financial resources may be eligible for Medicaid in addition to Medicare. Medicaid then pays Medicare deductibles, coinsurance amounts, and Part B premiums, in addition to providing needed medical care not covered by Medicare. Medicaid thus provides assistance with cost sharing and premium payments under Medicare as well as meeting the long-term care needs of beneficiaries. It also expands the Medicare benefits package for SSI recipients by covering such items as prescription drugs and dentures. In addition, Medicaid has developed ways to protect spouses from impoverishment as they pay for the nursing home requirements of partners.

Financial Requirements. Medicaid is a "means-tested" welfare program that determines eligibility by whether a person or family lacks the financial means to provide for themselves. Means testing evaluates both income and financial resources.

A majority of states have an eligibility income cap: If the nursing home resident's income is more than a fixed percentage of the federal SSI rate (but no more than 300%), then he or she cannot qualify for benefits, no matter what his or her nursing home costs. Forty-one states and the District of Columbia have "medically needy" programs that extend Medicaid eligibility to additional qualified persons who have income in excess of the mandatory or optional categorically needy levels. This option allows such persons to "spend down" to Medicaid eligibility by incurring medical and/or remedial care expenses to offset their excess income, thereby reducing it to a level below the maximum allowed by that state's Medicaid plan.

California, Connecticut, Indiana, Iowa, and New York take a different approach in offering easier access to Medicaid for purchasers of a state-approved private long-term care insurance policy. These states allow nursing home patients with approved insurance to be eligible with substantially higher levels of assets (Wiener at al. 1994).

All states have resource limitations that appear severe: the applicant is entitled to own no more than $2,000 to $3,400 (the amount varies from state to state) in "non-exempt" resources. If he or she is married, and the one partner seeking Medicaid benefits resides in a nursing home, the other spouse (called the "community spouse") is subject to a resource limit determined in one of three ways, but the standard formula, and the one most known, limits the community spouse to half of their combined resources at the time of eligibility, but not more than an inflation-adjusted amount set at $74,820 in calendar 1995.

States must permit an individual to retain his or her home so long as he or she intends to return to it, and that intent need not be "medically reasonable"; there is no dollar limit on the value of the home. Moreover, asset limitations only apply to those resources that belong to the individual, and that are "available." Jointly owned real estate or assets in a properly drafted trust do not belong to the individual, or may not be available.

Efforts to fit a person within these and other constraints are sometimes referred to as "Medicaid Planning.*" The term, analogous to tax planning, is often used pejoratively. Yet Medicaid planning simply assists elderly middle-class individuals who, after a lifetime of conscientious work and bearing the burden of both taxes and insurance premiums, find themselves unable to preserve a modicum of the resources that they spent a lifetime acquiring, whether to protect their own remaining time in this life, or to pass to their children and grandchildren.

Accomplishments and Outlook

Medicaid has emerged as our national safety net for long-term care services. Medicaid legislation over the years has played a role in increasing access to services, reducing the number of service limits, improving the quality of care, and enhancing outreach to persons requiring support.

A review of Medicaid's history reveals a program constantly struggling with rising costs. Expenditures nearly doubled from fiscal year 1987 to 1991; they are projected to double again by the end of 1995. Major factors contributing to the rapid growth in Medicaid expenditures are federally mandated program eligibility expansions, higher nursing home reimbursement, and improved standards of care for nursing homes. Additionally, changes in the economy can increase or decrease the number of people who meet income and asset requirements. Some changes in expenditures represent the net effects of program decisions taken by the states (Health Care Financing Review 1993). Current congressional proposals to balance the budget target the Medicaid program through limits on spending. Under consideration are greater use of managed care for the elderly and reductions in provider payments. Overall, though, Medicare and Medicaid costs are symptoms, not the cause, of uncontrolled health care spending. Medicaid makes good use of its public funding. It meets the most urgent needs of the low-income disabled population at the lowest possible public cost. Although targeted to the poor, Medicaid also provides a safety net for middle-income people with high long-term care expenses. Spend-down requirements ensure that the program finances only that part of the care that is beyond the resources of the elderly (Wiener et al. 1994).

Medicare coverage of all elderly people assures full program participation and provides a broad and powerful constituency to ensure that program benefits are maintained and improved. In contrast, the means-tested Medicaid program has been vulnerable to cutbacks and is subjected to frequent criticism. Yet Medicaid has very limited ability on its own to control health care cost increases, and when it restricts payment levels in an effort to contain costs, access to care is often reduced. There is ultimately no way to deny the fact that chronically ill and disabled patients are expensive to care for in our health system, and that the cost of any program covering their health needs will reflect these higher expenses (Rowland 1994). (See also LONG-TERM CARE INSURANCE: PRIVATE, MEDICARE, MEDICARE SUPPLEMENTAL INSURANCE, NURSING HOMES, SOCIAL SECURITY PROGRAM OF THE UNITED STATES, and SUPPLEMENTAL SECURITY INCOME.)

Organizations

American Association of Retired Persons
Kaiser Commission on the Future of Medicaid

Suggested Readings

Congressional Research Service. 1993. *Medicaid Source Book: Background Data and Analysis.* Washington, DC: Congressional Research Service.
Kaiser Commission on the Future of Medicaid. 1992. *Medicaid at the Crossroads.* Washington, DC: Kaiser Commission.

References

Folkemer, Donna. 1994. *State Use of Home and Community-Based Services for the Aged under Medicaid.* Washington, DC: AARP Public Policy Institute.
General Accounting Office. 1994. *Medicaid Long-Term Care: Successful State Efforts to Expand Home Services While Limiting Costs.* Washington, DC: GPO.
Health Care Financing Review. 1991. ''Trends in Medicaid Payments and Utilization, 1975–1989.'' *1990 Annual Supplement.* Baltimore, MD: HCFA.
Health Care Financing Review. 1993. ''Medicare and Medicaid Statistical Supplement.'' *1992 Annual Supplement.* Baltimore, MD: HCFA.
Rowland, Diane. 1994. ''Lessons from the Medicaid Experience.'' In *Critical Issues in U.S. Health Reform,* ed. Eli Ginzberg. Boulder, CO: Westview, 190–207.
Waid, Mary O. 1994. ''Health Care: Medicaid.'' *Social Security Bulletin Annual Statistical Supplement,* 97–102.
Wiener, Joshua M., Laurel Hixon Illston, and Raymond J. Hanley. 1994. *Sharing the Burden: Strategies for Public and Private Long-Term Care Insurance.* Washington, DC: Brookings Institution.

Ronald M. Landsman

MEDICAID PLANNING, a process prompted by the income and asset eligibility rules that individuals must meet to qualify for Medicaid nursing home benefits. The process is most often guided by financial advisors* and attorneys*, especially those in elder law practice*.

A Case Illustration

Mr. and Mrs. Jones were elder law clients seeking advice on health care payments. Mrs. Jones and her institutionalized husband were in their eighties.

They had worked hard for most of their lives, lived frugally, and had saved regularly for their retirement. Seven years earlier, Mr. Jones suffered a massive stroke, forcing Mrs. Jones to place him in a nursing home*. From accumulated savings of $450,000, Mrs. Jones had been paying for nursing home care and a part-time aide for seven years, but nearly all of her money was gone. The prospect of her husband being evicted from the nursing home when she could no longer pay the bills terrified her. Mrs. Jones was elderly, frail, and emotionally and physically exhausted. She knew she could not care for her husband at home, and at age 85, faced a prospect of becoming penniless. The system had failed Mrs. Jones and was about to strip her of her financial and emotional dignity.

Had Mrs. Jones known about the Medicaid* laws seven years ago, her impoverishment could have been prevented and her husband would have received the medical and nursing home care that he needed. For example, in New York, Mrs. Jones would have had a community spouse resource allowance of $72,660 and a community spouse income allowance of $1,817 per month, and would have been allowed to keep whatever resources were necessary to generate the community spouse income allowance. With proper advice, Mrs. Jones could have been secure in the knowledge that she would have sufficient income to pay her bills without jeopardizing her husband's care.

The story of Mrs. Jones explains why Medicaid is so important today to middle-and low-income Americans. The cost of long-term care, whether home health care or nursing home care, has skyrocketed in recent years. The average cost of nursing homes in the United States is about $37,000 per year and can exceed $10,000 per month for select nursing homes, making uninsured long-term care expenditures affordable for only the truly wealthy. Medicare covers acute care and post-acute care but will not pay benefits for long-term custodial care. Individuals with chronic long-term illness, such Alzheimer's Disease or related dementias, must look to private funds or insurance. If such funding is not available, middle- or lower-income persons have no alternative but to seek assistance from Medicaid for these expenses.

Medicaid Planning

Attorneys in elder law practice work with individuals to create financial plans that will help them qualify for Medicaid benefits. Gifting resources (assets that count in calculating eligibility level), spending down assets, and transferring assets to exempt persons or trusts are some of the strategies employed in Medicaid planning.

There is general consensus among elder law attorneys that ethical issues arise in the case of affluent individuals who can afford to pay for uninsured long-term care expenses, but seek ways to utilize Medicaid payments. If the emphasis is appropriately put on long-term health care planning instead of Medicaid eligibility in these cases, it is usually possible to effectuate an estate plan in which expenses are paid solely from asset-generated income. Thousands of dollars in estate taxes can be saved by using estate planning techniques.

On August 10, 1993, President Clinton signed the Omnibus Budget Reconciliation Act of 1993 (OBRA 93), which contained sweeping changes to Medicaid eligibility rules and estate recovery laws. These changes have the effect of limiting Medicaid eligibility and providing for mandatory estate recoveries. Unfortunately, the language in many relevant sections of OBRA 93 is ambiguous, making it difficult to determine its precise meaning and impact. The following explains and analyzes some important provisions of OBRA 93. Despite changes established by OBRA 93, planning opportunities still exist for older persons who are urged to plan ahead for possible long-term care needs.

Look-Back Period. In order to become eligible for Medicaid benefits, an individual may decide to transfer or gift his or her assets to third parties, but consequences result for a Medicaid applicant who has made such gifts or transfers. Federal legislation imposes a penalty or waiting period in which an individual must privately pay for nursing home care after gifting assets to nonexempt persons. With regard to assets transferred (gifted) on or after August 10, 1993, the look-back period is 36 months; for transfers of assets from trusts, the look-back period is now 60 months. Any asset transfers discovered during this look-back period will be used to calculate a penalty period. The penalty period is calculated by taking the cumulative uncompensated value of the gifts by the Medicaid applicant and spouse and dividing that number by the average monthly cost to a private patient of a nursing facility in the state (or, at the option of the state, in the community). The resulting number is the penalty period, which runs from the date of the transfer. There is no longer a ''cap'' on the period of ineligibility.

This rule may trap those unfamiliar with the new law. For example, if an older person living in New York transferred $300,000 to his son during Month 1, and applies for Medicaid benefits for nursing home care during Month 37, barring other factors, he or she would be Medicaid eligible, as transfers prior to the look-back period will not be considered. However, if the same person applied during Month 36, then the transfer would have occurred during the look-back period, and the penalty period would be calculated without a ''cap.'' In this example, there would be a 51-month penalty period ($300,000 ÷ $5,864 = 51.16). By not waiting one extra month to apply for Medicaid benefits, this individual must pay privately for nursing home care for an additional period of 15 (51 − 36) months. The look-back period commences from the time an individual is institutionalized and applies for Medicaid.

Waiting Period for Community Care. OBRA 93 gave states the option to impose penalty or waiting periods for community-based Medicaid services, such as for a home health aide, provided these penalty periods do not exceed those established for institutional care.

Estate Recoveries. Under OBRA 93, the states are mandated to seek recovery from estates for Medicaid payments, and the age where recovery must be sought has been lowered from 65 to 55. The law requires that recovery be sought from the estates of individuals who were 55 or older at the time Medicaid benefits were received. In a few states, older persons can avoid estate recovery by buying long-term care insurance. States now have the option to expand the definition of "estate" for Medicaid recovery purposes to include "assets in which the individual had any legal title or interest at the time of death (to the extent of such interest), including . . . assets conveyed . . . through joint tenancy, tenancy in common, survivorship, life estate, living trust, or other arrangement." Further, states have the option to recover against the individual's interest in the asset at the time of death to the extent of such interest. The decedent's interest in a life estate, as a life tenant of a trust, or as a joint tenant of a bank account extinguishes at the time of death, however. And even if this OBRA 93 provision were to be interpreted as meaning an individual's interest in such assets immediately prior to death, the value of the life estate of an elderly individual would be relatively low.

Assets/Income. OBRA 93 now defines assets as "all income and resources of the individual and of the individual's spouse, including any income or resources that the individual or the individual's spouse is entitled to but does not receive because of action by the individual or the individual's spouse." Under the previous law, transfers by an individual of resources, not income, determined the penalty period. Now, transfers of income will also subject transferors and spouses to a penalty period. For example, under the prior law, an inheritance or a tort settlement was often considered income during the month received and a resource in subsequent months, and therefore could be transferred without penalty during the month received. This is no longer possible, and if a Medicaid recipient transfers his or her inheritance or tort settlement in the month it is received, he or she will be subject to the applicable period of ineligibility.

California, Connecticut, Indiana, Iowa, and New York allow nursing home patients who purchased state-approved, long-term care insurance to be eligible for Medicaid with substantially higher levels of assets than are permitted in other areas. They exclude insurance-related assets from their definition of resources that must be used in determining Medicaid eligibility (Wiener et al. 1994).

Return of Assets. Medicaid applicants may reverse the penalty period by returning assets transferred. In order to obtain such reversal of the penalty period, however, the law requires that *all* assets transferred for less than fair market value must be returned to applicants, which may create severe consequences if assets previously transferred cannot be fully recovered. The law does provide that a transfer for less than fair market value is exempt from a penalty or waiting period if a "denial of eligibility would cause an undue hardship."

Trusts. In the case of revocable trusts, the trust corpus is still considered to be an available asset, and payments made to the settlor are considered to be available income. Payments from the trust to third parties are considered transfers of assets. With regard to irrevocable trusts, the new law eliminates the "Medicaid Qualifying Trust" provisions that have become familiar to elder law attorneys. Prior law provided that if there was no discretion to pay the trust corpus to the individual, then the corpus would not be deemed an available resource. The new law does not look to discretion as a test of availability, but provides that any portion of the trust corpus (and income generated by the trust corpus) that under any circumstances could be paid to or for the benefit of the individual, will be considered an available resource or available income.

OBRA 93 provides that a 60-month look-back period will apply "in the case of payments from a trust or portions of a trust that are treated as assets disposed of by the individual." The Health Care Financing Administration (HCFA), the agency that administers the Medicaid program on the federal level, has issued an opinion letter stating that the look-back period of 60 months will be triggered even upon the transfer of assets into an irrevocable income-only trust. HCFA's letter, however, directly conflicts with the language contained in OBRA 93, which states that the 60-month look-back applies to payments *from* trusts, not *into* trusts. In any event, careful planning can limit the size transfers into such trusts, thereby reducing the look-back period to 36 months if so desired. OBRA 93 has also provided for exempt trusts containing only the income of an individual. These *Miller v. Ibarra* trusts are used in income cap states to permit an individual with excess income to obtain Medicaid.

Disabled Individuals. The new law created two types of exempt trusts for disabled individuals that provide new planning options. In both of these trusts, if any assets remain upon the death of the individual, the state will receive all such remaining amounts up to the total value of medical assistance paid on behalf of the individual. As opposed to third-party supplemental needs trusts, these new trusts are funded with the disabled individual's own assets. Several large nonprofit organizations have established and are managing pooled asset trusts to conform with these OBRA 93 provisions.

Joint Assets. In the case of assets held jointly by an individual in common with another in a joint tenancy, tenancy in common, or similar arrangements, the asset or the affected portion of the asset will be considered transferred when either party takes any action that reduces or eliminates the individual's ownership or control of the asset. Therefore, the withdrawal of money from a joint account by any tenant of that account, such as a nonexempt child of the Medicaid applicant, will be subject to the transfer of asset rules and will create a waiting period for a Medicaid applicant.

Knowledge is the key to effective planning for long-term care expenditures that are now out of reach for most Americans. Of course, the Medicaid program was not meant for use by the wealthy who can afford long-term care costs or those who can purchase generous long-term care insurance. However, middle- and lower-income Americans who have worked and sacrificed most of their lives to build up a sense of financial security must not be led to believe that it is a crime to utilize the Medicaid program in an honest and forthright way in order to pay for long-term care expenses, and avoid severe financial hardship. (See also ASSETS ALLOCATION AFTER RETIREMENT, ATTORNEYS,

ETHICS IN FINANCIAL PLANNING, HOME CARE SERVICES FOR THE ELDERLY, ELDER LAW PRACTICE, LONG-TERM CARE INSURANCE: PRIVATE, MEDICAID, NURSING HOMES, and TRUSTS.)

Organization

National Academy of Elder Law Attorneys

Suggested Reading

Budish, Armond. 1995. *Avoiding the Medicaid Trap: How to Beat the Catastrophic Costs of Nursing-Home Care.* New York: Henry Holt.

References

General Accounting Office. 1993. *Medicaid Estate Planning.* Washington, DC: GAO.

"Omnibus Budget Reconciliation Act of 1993" (OBRA 93). 1993. *Health Care Financing Review* 15: 177–216.

Schlesinger, Sanford J., and Barbara J. Scheiner. 1993. *Planning for the Elderly or Incapacitated Client.* Chicago: Commerce Clearing House.

Wiener, Joshua M., Laurel Hixon Illston, and Raymond J. Hanley. 1994. *Sharing the Burden: Strategies for Public and Private Long-Term Care Insurance.* Washington, DC: Brookings Institution.

Ronald A. Fatoullah

MEDICAL DIRECTIVES. See Advance Directives; Durable Power of Attorney; Elder Law Practice; Living Will.

MEDICAL SAVINGS ACCOUNTS (MSAs) and MEDICAL IRAs, two recent innovations in health care financing that combine a high-deductible health insurance policy with an individual savings account. The savings account or IRA portion of the plan is designed as a source of self-insurance to cover small medical expenses. The insurance policy portion of the plan provides protection against large medical expenses. By reducing the frequency of insurance claims while providing major medical coverage, MSAs and Medical IRAs are expected to reduce an individual's health care expenses, provide for future medical needs, and reduce periods of noncoverage.

MSAs and Medical IRAs are similar. Regular payments are made into either account by an employer and participants. With an MSA, funds in the savings account can be used for expenses only. With a Medical IRA, at 59½ years old, funds can be withdrawn for any reason, just as in a conventional IRA.

Current tax laws discourage MSA and Medical IRAs. No federal tax exemptions are granted for deposits into the savings account portion or on the interest earnings of an MSA. The only federal tax exemptions granted for deposits into the retirement account portion of a Medical IRA are exemptions covering ordinary IRAs, making accountholders subject to taxes and penalties for withdrawing funds, even to pay medical expenses. The insurance policy coupled with the account, on the other hand, receives the same tax treatment as other types of health insurance. If paid by an employer, the insurance premium portion of the MSA or Medical IRA is not considered taxable compensation for the worker. Employer contributions toward the savings plan portion of an MSA are also taxable. For an employee, federal, state, and local taxes are paid on deposits in addition to taxes on interest earnings from the account.

Despite these tax disadvantages relative to conventional health insurance plans, some companies have still opted to offer Medical IRA and MSA plans— Golden Rule Insurance Co., Dominion Resources, Inc., and Forbes, Inc., are three. Although experience with these plans has been limited, some corporations report advantages over their previous insurance arrangements, including health expenses falling well below the national average, significant premium savings, and a high percentage of employee participation in such plans.

There is considerable support for legislation in the 104th Congress to grant more favorable tax status to MSAs, allowing employers and employees to make tax-free contributions into the accounts. Under most current proposals, funds not spent from a given year's contributions to the savings account portion of the plan would become the individual's to use for medical expenses or to purchase health insurance during any period of unemployment. Account balances would be the sole property of the accountholder, and at death would become part of his or her estate.

An example of how these plans would work shows the potential for such accounts to provide health insurance benefits today, while controlling costs and providing for health care expenses tomorrow. Currently, the average employer spends about $5,300 annually to provide family health insurance coverage to an employee (Gabel et al. 1994). To establish a Medical IRA or MSA with similar expenditures, the employer could spend about one-third of that amount for a high-deductible insurance policy (e.g.,a $2,500 deductible). Although the premium for a family policy with this deductible would vary with the particular demographics of the insured, in most areas the cost would be between $1,200 and $2,100 (see Table 1). At the end of the year, any unspent balance in the MSA/Medical IRA would carry over and accumulate interest the next year. This ''use-it-or-keep-it'' feature would give many individuals a strong incentive to purchase health care services wisely.

Medical IRAs and MSAs provide several advantages over conventional insurance products. First, by empowering the consumer to decide whether and how much to pay for medical services, the accounts have the potential to foster healthy competition among health care providers, keeping medical expenses at a competitive level. Over the last two decades, health care expenses have grown about twice as fast as the gross national product (Goodman and Musgrave 1993). MSAs and Medical IRAs empower patients to become prudent consumers.

Second, Medical IRAs provide another way to save for retirement, and both plans provide a way to save for future medical needs. In any given year, many Americans incur few or no medical expenses, and many go for several years without significant medical costs.

Assuming an 8% annual interest rate, a $3,500 yearly deposit, and no with-

Table 1

Individual Health Insurance Annual Family Premium with $2,500 Deductible

Area		Washington National	Pyramid Life	Times Insurance	American Community
Cincinnati	City	$1,369	$1,622	$1,310	$1,083
	Suburb	1,469	1,622	1,310	1,032
Indianapolis	City	1,369	1,537	1,404	1,259
	Suburb	1,213	1,451	1,216	1,135
Peoria	City	1,542	1,622	1,572	1,032
	Suburb	1,542	1,622	1,572	1,032
Portland	City	N/A	1,878	1,253	N/A
	Suburb	N/A	1,878	1,164	N/A
Des Moines	City	1,369	1,451	1,123	N/A
	Suburb	1,213	1,281	1,123	N/A
Dallas	City	1,836	2,135	1,872	N/A
	Suburb	1,680	1,281	1,123	N/A
Richmond	City	1,525	1,622	1,497	N/A
	Suburb	1,525	1,537	1,497	N/A

Note: These policies reflect per-person deductibles. Cents have been truncated.
Source: (Craig 1993).

drawals for medical expenses, a Medical IRA would grow to more than $500,000 after 35 years. With yearly withdrawals of $2,500 to pay medical expenses, the account would grow to more than $170,000 in the same period. The potential for long-term savings is the strongest advantage of MSAs and Medical IRAs compared to conventional insurance arrangements.

Third, MSAs and Medical IRAs provide a source of insurance protection during periods of unemployment. Many periods without health insurance are precipitated by a loss of employment. During periods of unemployment, income typically decreases dramatically, making it difficult for a family to replace lost coverage. With an MSA/Medical IRA plan, however, it often takes only a short time to create a healthy balance in the savings account portion of the plan, and the funds could be used to purchase insurance in the insured's own name, or purchase COBRA continuation coverage through the previous employer. If they were common, MSAs and Medical IRAs would provide a source of bridge insurance during periods when coverage would otherwise be unaffordable.

The key advantage of Medical IRAs and MSAs, for many individuals, is that these plans guarantee as much financial protection as conventional insurance plans, and potentially provide retirement income and funds to pay future medical expenses. The funds accumulated in these accounts could be used in addition to, or in place of, Medigap coverage, that is, to pay for services not covered by

Medicare. Potential concerns about MSA plans include the effects of tax exclusions on government revenues, risk selection effects if only healthier employees choose MSAs, and whether MSAs reduce health care costs (Polzer 1995). (See also HEALTH MAINTENANCE ORGANIZATIONS, MEDICARE, PENSION FUND TRENDS, SAVINGS INVESTMENTS, SOCIAL SECURITY, and POSTRETIREMENT HEALTH INSURANCE.)

References

Craig, V. 1993. "Medical Savings Accounts: Questions and Answers." Alexandria, VA: Council for Affordable Health Insurance.

Gabel, J., D. Liston, G. Jensen, and J. Marsteller. 1994. "The Health Insurance Picture, 1993: Some Rare Good News." *Health Affairs* 13.

Goodman, J., and G. Musgrave. 1993. "Personal Medical Retirement Accounts (Medical IRAs): An Idea Whose Time Has Come." *NCPA Media Backgrounder No. 128,* National Center for Policy Analysis.

Monheit, A., and C. Schur, "The Dynamics of Health Insurance Loss: A Tale of Two Cohorts." 1988. *Inquiry* 25: 315–27.

Polzer, Karl. 1995. "Medical Savings Accounts: Analyzing Potential Impacts." National Health Policy Forum Issue Brief No. 669. Washington, DC: George Washington University.

Robert J. Morlock

MEDICARE, a nationwide health insurance program for the elderly, certain disabled persons under 65, and persons of any age with kidney failure, authorized under Title XVIII of the Social Security Act. It consists of two parts: hospital insurance (Part A) and physician and other provider services (Part B).

Eligibility and Coverage

Most Americans aged 65 or older are automatically entitled to protection under Part A. Persons aged 65 or older who are not "fully insured" (i.e., not eligible for monthly Social Security or railroad retirement cash benefits) may obtain coverage, providing they pay the full actuarial cost of such coverage. Also eligible, after a two-year waiting period, are disabled people under 65 who are receiving monthly Social Security benefits and disabled railroad retirement system annuitants. Part B is voluntary. All persons age 65 or older may elect to enroll in the supplementary medical insurance program by paying the monthly premium, which in 1995 is $46.10. The deductible is $100 per year, with a copayment of 20%.

Most individuals establish entitlement to Part A on the basis of work in employment covered by either the Social Security or railroad retirement systems. Medicare covers individuals who have end-stage renal disease if they are: (1) fully insured for old age and survivor insurance benefits, (2) entitled to monthly social security benefits, or (3) spouses or dependents of individuals described in (1) and (2).

Medicare is primarily an acute-care program with limited coverage for nursing-home care and no coverage for outpatient drugs, hearing aids, eyeglasses, or dental care. Since Medicare covers 45% of total personal health care expenditures, beneficiaries can limit the burden of out-of-pocket costs if they also enrolled in an employer-provided health insurance plan after retirement, a Medicare Supplemental Insurance Plan (Medigap)*, a managed-care plan, or a long-term care insurance policy. Over 75% of Medicare beneficiaries have private supplemental health insurance to cover Medicare coinsurance deductibles and noncovered services (Chulis and Epping 1993).

In 1989, a new benefit became available to low-income Medicare beneficiaries. Under the Qualified Medicare Beneficiary (QMB) program, those whose incomes are at or below 100% of the national poverty level, but are not low enough to qualify them for regular Medicaid benefits, can have their Medicare premiums, deductibles, and coinsurance paid by the Medicaid program. Income limits for the QMB program are $633 per month for individuals and $840 per month for married couples (1994 figures). There are also asset limits of $4,000 and $6,000, respectively, excluding a home or automobile (Health Care Financing Administration [HCFA] 1994a).

A Specified Low-Income Medicare Beneficiary (SLMB) program is available to Medicare beneficiaries with incomes above 100% and at or below 110% (120% starting in 1995) of the federal poverty level. Under this program, the state pays the full cost of Medicare Part B premiums. Here, the income limits for eligibility are $695 per month for individuals and $992 per month for married couples, and asset limits are the same as for QMB. Applications for QMB and SLMB are through state, county, or local Medicaid offices. It is estimated that 1.8 million senior citizens are eligible for, but not enrolled in, the QMB program. Some reasons for this are perceived stigmas, the complicated application process, and a belief that the benefit is not worth much in monetary terms (General Accounting Office 1994).

Between 1975 and 1991, the number of persons covered by Medicare grew from 22.9 million elderly and 2.2 million disabled, to 31.5 million elderly and 3.4 million disabled. About 94% of persons enrolled in Medicare have coverage under Part A and Part B. Within the total, elderly persons aged 75 and older, who are generally considered as incurring higher health care costs, constitute about 43% of the elderly enrollees, a share that is expected to increase (Petrie and Silverman 1993).

Benefits

Part A of Medicare will pay toward inpatient hospital care, and some skilled nursing facility care, home health care, and hospice care.

Inpatient hospital care. Medicare pays all reasonable expenses for the first 60 days minus a deductible ($716 in 1995) in each benefit period. For days 61–90, a daily coinsurance amount ($179) is deducted. When more than 90 days are required in a benefit period, a patient may elect to draw upon a 60-day lifetime reserve. A coinsurance amount ($358) is also deducted for each reserve day.

Skilled nursing facility care. Coverage includes up to 100 days (following hospitalization of at least three days) in a skilled nursing facility for persons in need of continued skilled nursing care and/or skilled rehabilitation services on a daily basis. After the first 20 days, a daily coinsurance amount is deducted ($89.50 in 1995).

Home health care. Medicare covers unlimited home health visits provided to homebound persons who need skilled nursing care, physical therapy, or speech therapy on a part-time or intermittent basis, under the care of a physician who establishes and reviews a home health plan of services. The home health services must be delivered by an agency meeting Medicare conditions for certification.

Hospice care. Medicare will pay for hospice care services provided to terminally ill Medicare beneficiaries with a life expectancy of six months or less, up to a 210-day lifetime limit. A subsequent period of hospice coverage is allowed beyond the 210-day limit if the beneficiary is recertified as terminally ill.

Part B of Medicare generally pays 80% of the approved amount (fee schedule, reasonable charges, or reasonable cost for covered services in excess of an annual deductible of $100). Medicare-participating providers agree to accept assignment of Medicare claims and not to charge more than the Medicare-approved amount for services and supplies covered under Part B. There is a limit on the amount that a provider who does not accept assignment can charge for Part B services. That limit is set at 115% of the Medicare fee schedule for nonparticipating physicians. Services covered by Part B include the following:

Doctor's services. This includes surgery, consultation, home, office, and institutional visits. Certain limitations apply for services rendered by dentists, podiatrists, and chiropractors and for the treatment of mental illness. This coverage also includes Medicare-approved health providers who are not physicians.

Other medical and health services. Coverage includes laboratory and other diagnostic tests, X-ray and other radiation therapy, outpatient services at the hospital, rural health clinic services, home dialysis supplies and equipment, artificial devices (other than dental), mental health care, physical and speech therapy, and ambulance services.

Home health services. This includes an unlimited number of medically necessary home health visits for persons not covered under Part A. The 20% coinsurance and the $100 deductible do not apply for such benefits. In a review of Medicare services, it is this category that has received the most complaints. Certified home health agencies may not be available in some regions, or they may not provide as much care as needed; often the agencies, physicians, social workers, and beneficiaries lack understanding about the scope of the home health benefit (Archer and Burt 1994).

Service Use and Costs

Physicians' services are the most widely used Medicare benefit. Enrollees using physicians' services increased from 63% in 1980 to 81% in 1990. Next in frequency are hospital stays, but over time there has been an increase in the use of postacute care and a decline in inpatient care. The use of home health care services is increasing rapidly. Between 1989 and 1993, spending on home health care as a percentage of Medicare expenditures almost tripled (Prospective Payment Assessment Commission 1993).

As Medicare beneficiaries are entitled to decide how they will receive the services covered, they may choose a managed care plan (also called coordinated care plan), either in the form of a Health Maintenance Organization (HMO)* or a competitive medical plan having a contract with Medicare. Most Medicare HMOs or competitive medical plans have risk-based contracts with Medicare with lock-in provisions, requiring Medicare enrollees to receive all services from providers affiliated with the HMO. Risk-based HMOs receive a fixed payment from Medicare for each enrollee. Exceptions to the lock-in provisions are emergency and urgent care services. Also, HMOs serve Medicare beneficiaries through cost-based HMOs and Health Care Prepayment Plans. A broader range of managed care options will be available shortly. The choices include Medicare Select, a preferred provider Medigap plan, and a point of service options plan.

By 1994, 9% of Medicare beneficiaries had chosen a managed care option. To enroll with an HMO, beneficiaries must also be enrolled in Part B and continue to pay the Part B premium. Through risk-based contracts with the federal government, managed care plans provide all hospital and medical benefits covered by Medicare as well as additional benefits (routine physical examinations, preventive care, prescription drugs, dental care, hearing aids, eyeglasses). A network of health care service providers (doctors, physician assistants, therapists, hospitals, skilled nursing facilities) generally offers comprehensive, coordinated medical services on a prepaid basis. The federal government pays a fixed monthly amount for beneficiaries who are enrolled in a plan; enrollees are responsible for any copayments that are billed. Some HMOs may charge a monthly premium for additional benefits.

There are several advantages to Medicare HMOs, such as the elimination of paperwork for the beneficiary, no need for Medigap insurance, and the availability of services that Medicare alone does not cover (preventive, vision, and hearing care, or free transportation and prescription drugs). Services, however, may be obtained only through the HMO, and referrals are needed for specialists and for out-of-area care. An issue of concern is the adequacy of home health coverage for Medicare HMO members. Individuals enrolling in an HMO may wish to keep their Medigap policy until they decide they are comfortable with the plan. If they disenroll and are without a Medigap policy, it may be difficult to purchase another policy in case of serious health problems.

In 1993, Medicare spending increased 11.6% to $151.1 billion, and covered about 36.3 million beneficiaries. The distribution of payments by services included: inpatient hospital care, 61.3%; physician services, 23.0%; nursing homes, 4.0%; and home health care services, 5.4% (Levit et al. 1994). It is the latter two shares that have grown in importance, substituting for the greater dominance of hospital and skilled nursing facility care in the past (Petrie and

Silverman 1993). If current trends continue, Medicare expenditures are expected to increase to $259 billion in 1998. Future cost trends are difficult to predict because of the uncertainty of such factors as the role of health care technology in the years to come, and new efforts of cost containment. Some estimates forecast at least a doubling of the share of Medicare spending as a proportion of Gross Domestic Product by the year 2010, from 2.1% to 4.3% (Steuerle and Bakija 1994).

Financing

Medicare is financed by a combination of payroll taxes, premiums, and general revenue. The Medicare Part A Hospital Insurance Trust Fund (HI) finances inpatient hospital, skilled nursing facility, home health, and other institutional services. The Part B Supplementary Medical Insurance Trust Fund (SMI) finances principally physician and hospital outpatient services. The HI trust fund is financed primarily through Social Security payroll tax contributions paid by employers, employees, and the self-employed. Most financing for HI is derived from these payroll taxes. Part B is financed from premiums paid for the elderly, disabled, and chronic renal disease enrollees (about 25%), and from general revenues (about 75%). The premium rate is derived annually from projected costs of the program for the coming year. In 1995 the Medicare Boards of Trustees alerted the public of financing problems faced especially by the Hospital Insurance trust fund in the near future. They strongly recommended comprehensive Medicare reforms to make all of the program financially sound over the long term (Social Security and Medicare Boards of Trustees 1995). Various cost containment efforts that have been proposed include increasing deductibles and copayments in Medicare, means testing, reduced provider payments, and expanded use of managed care options.

Administration and Procedures

Responsibility for administration of the Medicare program has been delegated by the Secretary of Health and Human Services to the Administrator of the Health Care Financing Administration (HCFA). The Social Security Administration is responsible for determining Medicare eligibility and enrollment. It also provides general information on Medicare through its offices, publications, and information telephone number.

Much daily operational work of the Medicare program is performed by "intermediaries" and "carriers," which have responsibility for reviewing claims for fee-for-service coverage determinations and for making payments. Intermediaries are fiscal contractors with HCFA. The intermediaries determine reasonable costs for covered items and services, make payment, and guard against unnecessary use of covered services. Carriers handle administrative duties under Part B of Medicare, determine charges, make payments, and deal with claims for services provided by physicians and other suppliers under Part B.

Medicare's administrative costs are about 3% of expenditures, compared to about 10% for private health insurance. It has been successful in minimizing costs, particularly for hospital services in the late 1980s, when the Prospective Payment System for hospitals superseded the old cost-based system (HCFA 1994b). In 1989, Congress approved a new Medicare physician payment system that introduced a new Medicare Fee Schedule (MFS). The objective of MFS is to improve the balance between procedure-oriented services and primary care services. Its implementation started in 1992; by 1996 all Medicare physician services will be paid by MFS. Research on the early implementation of the new fee schedule found a shift in physician visits away from procedure-oriented services toward primary care services. Recent studies by the Health Care Financing Administration indicate that the assignment rates increased during the first year of the Medicare fee schedule and that, on unassigned claims, there was a reduction in extra billing (HCFA 1994b).

Consumer Issues

A number of issues and problems arise in the Medicare program because of complex billing and administration. Medicare offers beneficiaries who disagree with coverage decisions the right to appeal under Parts A and B and Medicare HMOs. Medicare beneficiaries under Part A can appeal early hospital discharges to the peer review organizations. Information on Part B appeals may be obtained from AARP. Medicare HMOs are required to have an appeals procedure for denial of coverage of services and questioning of charges.

Lack of consistency occurs in the application of Medicare rules and in HCFA policies throughout the country, mainly because of the diversity among carriers making coverage decisions. Another issue involves overcharges to Medicare patients by doctors. Legislation effective in January 1995 addresses overcharges and beneficiaries' understanding of physician charges. It enforces the 115% charge limit of the Medicare fee schedule applicable to nonparticipating physicians and requires insurance carriers to monitor Medicare claims for overcharges. Medicare beneficiaries are not required to pay fees in excess of charge limits.

Of further concern is the increasing burden of costs for services not covered by Medicare. Beneficiaries have been experiencing a higher burden of out-of-pocket costs, partly because they do not have limits on catastrophic expenses as the under-65 population does. Older Americans' out-of-pocket health costs (cost-sharing for Medicare-covered services, noncovered services and products, private health insurance premiums, and the Medicare Part B premium) are projected to be 23% of household income in 1994, compared with 15% in 1987 (AARP 1994). These costs are distributed unevenly throughout the population. The burden is especially serious for the oldest old*, whose use of prescription drugs and long-term care is highest when their incomes decrease.

There is a great need to strengthen acute-care coverage under Medicare by improving the coverage of prescription drugs and stressing preventive care; better coordination between acute and long-term care services is needed. (See also

HEALTH MAINTENANCE ORGANIZATIONS, HOME CARE SERVICES FOR THE ELDERLY, HOSPICE CARE, MEDICARE SUPPLEMENTAL INSURANCE, POSTRETIREMENT HEALTH INSURANCE, and NURSING HOMES.)

Organizations

American Association of Retired Persons
Health Care Financing Administration
Medicare Beneficiaries Defense Fund
National Committee to Preserve Social Security and Medicare
Social Security Administration

Suggested Readings

American Association of Retired Persons. 1993. *When Your Medicare Bill Doesn't Seem Right: How to Appeal Medicare Part B.* Washington, DC: AARP.
Health Care Financing Administration. 1994. *Medicare and Managed Care Plans.* Baltimore, MD: HCFA.
Health Care Financing Administration. 1995. *Your Medicare Handbook.* Washington, DC: HCFA.

References

American Association of Retired Persons. 1994. *Coming Up Short: Increasing Out-of-Pocket Health Spending of Older Americans.* Washington, DC: AARP.
Archer, Deane, and Anne Burt. 1994. "Systematic Problems in Medicare: Overview of Eight Critical Issues." *Journal of Long-Term Home Health Care* 13: 37–40.
Chulis, George, and Franklin Epping. 1993. "Health Insurance and the Elderly: Data from the MCBS." *Health Care Financing Review* 14: 163–82.
General Accounting Office. 1994. *Medicare and Medicaid: Many Eligible Not Enrolled in Qualified Medicare Beneficiary Programs.* Washington, DC: GAO.
Health Care Financing Administration. 1994a. *Medicare Savings for Qualified Beneficiaries.* Washington, DC: Author.
Health Care Financing Administration. 1994b. *Monitoring the Impact of Medicare Physician Payment Reform on Utilization and Access.* Report to Congress. Washington, DC: Author.
Levit, Katherine R. et al. 1994. "National Health Expenditures, 1993." *Health Care Financing Review* 16: 247–94.
Petrie, John, and Herbert Silverman. 1993. "Medicare Enrollment." *Health Care Financing Review,* 1992 Annual Supplement, 13–22.
Prospective Payment Assessment Commission. 1993. *Medicare and the American Health Care System.* Report to Congress. Washington, DC: Author.
Social Security and Medicare Boards of Trustees. 1995. *Status of the Social Security and Medicare Programs.* Washington, DC: Boards of Trustees.
Steuerle, Eugene, and Jon Bakija. 1994. *Retooling Social Security for the 21st Century.* Washington, DC: Urban Institute Press.

                                                                          Linda A. Siegenthaler

MEDICARE SUPPLEMENTAL INSURANCE, (also known as ''Medigap''), generically refers to any type of health insurance that supplements Medicare* benefits, including employer group health plans that supplement Medicare coverage for retirees, or hospital indemnity insurance and specified disease policies. The term applies to a specific type of Medicare supplemental insurance for purposes of federal insurance regulation.

The Medicare program was designed to provide baseline coverage for acute care services and was never envisioned to cover all the medical care costs of the elderly. It is estimated that Medicare covers 45% of personal health care expenditures of the elderly (Waldo et al. 1989). There are several types of exclusions or limitations to Medicare coverage. First, health care expenses such as custodial long-term care, prescription drugs, and dental care are not covered. Second, there are cost-sharing features such as deductibles and coinsurance for covered benefits. The Part B premium, which must be paid for enrollment, may also be considered as a gap. Finally, there is no out-of-pocket limit on covered expenses. Hence, Medicare's "gaps" have prompted the term "Medigap" to describe supplemental Medicare benefits.

The distribution of Medicare supplemental health insurance for the elderly in 1991 was as follows: approximately 75% of the elderly had private Medicare supplemental insurance, either individually purchased or provided through employer-sponsored insurance (Chulis et al. 1993). Of these, the predominant type was individually purchased, owned by almost 42%; 38% had only employer-sponsored coverage through a previous employer; and about 5% had both. Approximately 12% of all Medicare beneficiaries can be considered to have public supplemental coverage through Medicaid. Only about 11% had Medicare as their sole source of health care coverage. One study estimated that approximately 13% of elderly Medicare beneficiaries had multiple insurance coverage (Government Accounting Office 1994).

Characteristics Associated with Supplemental Insurance Status

The 1991 Medicare Current Beneficiary Survey (MCBS) shows that the type of supplemental insurance coverage varies by age, sex, race, income, and health status of the elderly Medicare beneficiary. Persons aged 85 and over are least likely to have private employer-sponsored insurance; the largest proportion was found among the youngest age group (65–69). Conversely, the proportion of persons with individual supplemental insurance increased up to age 85, when it declined. The oldest old* (85+) are more likely than other age groups to have only Medicare coverage or to have Medicaid coverage. The high percentage of the oldest old with Medicaid could exist because more are in nursing homes, often funded by Medicaid (Chulis et al. 1993).

Men were much more likely than women to have private employer-sponsored coverage; the reverse was true for private individual coverage, where women were more likely than men to have it. The proportion of women with Medicaid was double that of men; men were more likely to have Medicare only (Chulis et al. 1993).

Whites were much more likely than blacks or other races to have both employer-sponsored and private individual supplemental insurance. Black Medicare beneficiaries were more likely than whites or other races to have only Medicare coverage. Whites were least likely to have Medicaid, blacks had triple the proportion, and other races had the highest proportion, more than four times that of whites (Chulis et al. 1993).

As income increases, the percentage of elderly without private, employer-sponsored, or public supplemental health insurance (for example, Medicare only) declines. The percentage of persons with Medicaid coverage is greater at lower incomes, as expected. The relatively high percentage of low-income persons purchasing private Medicare supplemental insurance is surprising: 54% of persons with annual incomes below $5,000 have such policies. The pattern is similar for employer-sponsored insurance, but the percentages at the lower income levels are much smaller.

Persons with poor or fair health status are more likely to need supplemental health insurance, but are less likely to have private individual or employer-sponsored insurance than persons in excellent or very good health (52% versus 84%). Persons in poorer health are more likely to have Medicaid coverage or Medicare only (Chulis et al. 1993).

Regulatory History

In the late 1970s, various studies cited problems in the Medicare supplemental insurance marketplace related to the policies or the manner in which they were sold. The most common problems identified were: (1) marketing abuses, (2) inadequate information to permit informed choice, and (3) inadequate policy benefits, especially with respect to premiums paid. In response to these problems, Congress enacted the first federal legislation addressing Medicare supplemental insurance by establishing a "Voluntary Certification of Medicare Supplement Health Insurance Policies" (June 1980) program. This amendment to the Social Security Act (Section 1882) was also known as the "Baucus Amendment" after its chief sponsor, Senator Max Baucus.

The certification program encouraged states to adopt the 1979 National Association of Insurance Commissioners (NAIC) minimum benefit and performance standards. It allowed states to have their own regulatory programs and to be certified by a Supplemental Health Insurance Panel, consisting of state insurance commissioners and the Secretary of the Department of Health and Human Services (DHHS). If states did not become certified, companies could seek certification of their policies by the Secretary of DHHS. Only four states—Massachusetts, New York, Rhode Island, and Wyoming—have not approved programs; these four states operate under their own, different standards.

The 1979 standards included: minimum benefit requirements; "expected" minimum loss ratio requirements of 60% and 75% for individual and certain group policies, respectively (loss ratio is the ratio of benefit payments to premiums in the aggregate); limits in the duration of preexisting condition clauses;

various information and disclosure provisions, such as a buyer's guide and a 30-day "free look" period; and provisions against duplicative coverage. These (and subsequent) standards are not applicable to group policies established by employers or labor organizations for active or former employees or members, nor to plans administered by Health Maintenance Organizations (HMOs) or other direct service organizations; HMO supplemental products, however, are subject to the standards. Additionally, policies sponsored by association groups, such as the American Association for Retired Persons (AARP), are subject to the standards.

During the 1980s, several regulatory changes occurred as the NAIC updated its model regulations and acts, which were incorporated into the federal voluntary standards. In 1987, the NAIC enhanced its model regulation to require compliance of actual loss ratios and provided for enforcement mechanisms. Also, there were two main provisions of the Medicare Catastrophic Coverage Act (MCCA) of 1988 affecting Medicare supplement insurance. One required that all companies submit information on actual loss ratios on standard forms to the NAIC; the other required filing of all Medicare supplement advertisements with the state insurance departments. Even though MCCA was repealed in 1989, the Medigap provisions remained in effect. MCCA was expected to reduce the need for Medigap coverage since there would be an annual cap on Medicare cost-sharing and some coverage for prescription drugs. However, with the repeal it was realized that the Medigap industry would continue, and concern was raised about the need for additional regulation. The NAIC incorporated many consumer protection provisions into its 1989 Model Regulation, many of which were later codified in federal legislation, the Omnibus Budget Reconciliation Act of 1990 (OBRA 90).

Three aspects of OBRA 90 are significant: (1) federal, rather than state, government has the ultimate responsibility for overseeing the regulation of the Medigap market; (2) the provisions of this legislation are now mandatory rather than voluntary; and (3) up to 10 standard Medigap policies (with a few exceptions) are permitted to be sold. With respect to the first point, the Secretary of the Department of Health and Human Services, rather than the Supplemental Health Insurance Panel, is to approve state Medigap regulatory programs. An additional aspect of federal oversight is the monitoring of states' regulatory programs, including enforcement. Insurers wishing to sell Medigap policies in states with nonapproved programs must obtain certification from the secretary of HHS. As of December 1994, all of the states have approved regulatory programs.

Standardization was adopted to facilitate comparison shopping for Medigap policies. The NAIC designed 10 standard Medigap policies—a basic plan that must be offered by all companies selling Medigap products, and nine additional standard plans that offer other features. The basic benefits included in every plan are:

Table 1
Ten Standard Medigap Plans

	A	B	C	D	E	F	G	H	I	J
Basic Benefits	✓	✓	✓	✓	✓	✓	✓	✓	✓	✓
Skilled Nursing Coinsurance			✓	✓	✓	✓	✓	✓	✓	✓
Part A Deductible		✓	✓	✓	✓	✓	✓	✓	✓	✓
Part B Deductible			✓			✓				✓
Part B: Percent of Excess of Actual Charge Over Allowable Charges						100% ✓	80% ✓		100% ✓	80% ✓
Foreign Travel			✓	✓	✓	✓	✓	✓	✓	✓
At-home Recovery				✓			✓		✓	✓
Basic Drugs ($1,250 limit)								✓	✓	
Extended Drugs ($3,000 limit)										✓
Preventive Care					✓					

- Part A coinsurance
- Coverage for 365 additional hospital days after Medicare benefits end
- Part B coinsurance
- The first three pints of blood each year

Table 1 shows what features are in each of the 10 standard plans. Each of the plans has a letter designation ranging from ''A'' through ''J.'' Insurers are not permitted to change these designations or to substitute other names, but they may add names or titles to these designations. Insurers are not required to offer all of the plans; however, they must offer Plan A if they offer any of the other nine plans in the state. Delaware, Pennsylvania, and Vermont do not permit all 10 policies to be sold. As of July 30, 1992, these 10 policies are the only ones that can be sold (previously purchased policies that do not conform to one of these 10 standard plans generally can continue to be renewed). However, three states (Massachusetts, Minnesota, and Wisconsin) that had standardization programs in effect prior to the enactment of the program were permitted to continue under a waiver.

There are several other important provisions of OBRA 90; some of them are contained in the Social Security amendments of 1994. These provisions are:

- Policies must be guaranteed renewable

- Waiver of waiting period for preexisting conditions in a replacement policy, to the extent that time was spent under the original policy

- An increase in the loss ratio requirements from 60% to 65% for individual policies; the loss ratio remains at 75% for group policies. Insurers must provide for premium rebates or credits in any given year that a group or individual policy does not meet the minimum loss ratio on a cumulative basis

- Insurers must offer a six-month open enrollment period without any medical underwriting to beneficiaries who are age 65 or older after they first enroll in Medicare Part B. Although the Social Security amendments of 1994 do not extend this open enrollment to persons under age 65 who are eligible for Medicare due to disability or end-stage renal disease, the law does grant these persons a six-month open enrollment period when they become age 65. The law also permits a one-time open enrollment period if one had Part B coverage prior to age 65 and turned 65 between November 5, 1991, and January 1, 1995

- In OBRA 90, the sale of duplicative coverage was broadened to make it illegal to sell to a Medicare beneficiary any health insurance policy (other than an employer group health policy) that duplicates Medicare or any other private health insurance coverage, no matter how small the overlap. The sale of Medigap policies was also banned to anyone on Medicaid (unless the Medicaid program pays the premium). A purchaser of a Medigap policy must state in writing that he has no other Medigap policy (or is replacing a current policy) and is not entitled to Medicaid. Policyholders are permitted to suspend their Medigap policies during a period of Medicaid eligibility of two years or less.

The 1994 Social Security amendments changed the prohibition on duplicative insurance sales to allow duplication of Medicare coverage if a policy pays benefits directly without regard to other coverage, and if there is disclosure of the duplication on the application. In effect, the provision still prohibits the sale of duplicate Medigap policies, but not the sale of Medigap with some other form of health insurance, including employer retiree health coverage. The prohibition of Medigap sales to regular Medicaid beneficiaries continues, but the law allows two exceptions: (1) a Qualified Medicare Beneficiary (QMB) if the policy has prescription drug benefits, and (2) a Special Low-Income Medicare Beneficiary (SLMB), since SLMBs do not receive full Medicaid benefits.

OBRA 90 also created a demonstration program in 15 states, called Medicare Select. The only difference between Medicare Select and a standard Medigap policy is that the former pays full supplemental benefits only if covered services are obtained from a selected group of health care providers; otherwise, the Select policy may deny payment or pay less than full supplemental benefits. Because of this restriction to certain providers, premiums for these policies are expected to be lower than for standard Medigap policies. This option was designed as an intermediate choice between a Medicare HMO and a traditional combination of

Medicare fee-for-service and a standard Medicare supplemental policy. Approximately 450,000 Medicare beneficiaries have enrolled in this program. Congress recently expanded Medicare Select to 50 states and extended it for at least three years.

Another provision of OBRA 1990, Section 4360, authorized HCFA to award grants to states for health insurance advisory services. The grants program was intended to create and, in those states with existing programs, strengthen their capability to provide health insurance information, counseling, and assistance (ICA) to Medicare beneficiaries. ICA services are provided through telephone and face-to-face counseling, group seminars, or presentations.

Considerations in Purchasing Private Medicare Supplemental Insurance

First, one should consider whether purchase of private supplemental insurance is necessary. If one has difficulty in affording a private Medicare supplemental policy, one should determine if one may be eligible for one of three Medicaid programs: regular Medicaid, the qualified Medicare Beneficiary program (QMB), or the special low-income Medicare Beneficiary program (SLMB). One may be eligible for the regular Medicaid program if one has low income, limited assets, and meets other criteria. In some states, one may also be eligible if high medical bills bring one's income and assets down to the same level. The QMB program (begun in 1989) is for Medicare beneficiaries who are not eligible for the regular Medicaid program but whose income is at or below the national poverty level, while the SLMB program (begun in 1993) is for those with incomes between 100% and 110% of the poverty level; it was expanded to 120% for 1995. Both programs require persons to have assets at or below the same level. The regular Medicaid and the QMB programs can function to fill all or part of the Medicare "gaps," and purchase of private supplemental insurance would generally be unnecessary.

Upon retirement, continuing health insurance coverage through a former employer may offer several advantages. The employer may pay all or part of the premiums, or the group rates may be lower than those for individual policies. There is also usually no waiting period for preexisting conditions, and benefits may be more generous than those offered under one of the 10 standard Medigap plans. Joining an HMO or other prepaid health plan is another alternative to consider, if one is available in the area. The plan will provide for all of Medicare Part A and Part B services (if covered for both) and some plans may also provide benefits beyond what Medicare pays. For more information, one should consult the government pamphlet, *Medicare and Coordinated Care Plans.*

Comparing private Medicare supplement policies should be simpler now that there are 10 standard Medicare supplement plans in almost all states. A careful examination of the 10 plans shown in Table 1, ranging from basic to comprehensive and/or specialized benefits, will help determine which plan would best meet one's needs. Several booklets or guides that provide assistance in choosing among these benefit plans are available. Comparison shopping is important, particularly outside of open enrollment, because policy premiums and terms (e.g., medical underwriting, waiting periods) can vary, even within the same plan type. Understanding how the policy premium is calculated is also important. A company may base its premium on: (1) issue age, (2) attained age, or (3) no age rating. A policy premium based on issue age will continue to base its premium on one's age when bought, whereas a policy premium based on attained age will increase as one grows older. Some companies may also vary premiums by sex or geographic location. The potential for cost increases should also be examined, especially since premiums usually are increased each year as the Medicare coinsurance and deductibles are changed. In addition to premiums, the company's reputation for service and its financial rating should be considered. Financial ratings may be obtained from sources such as A. M. Best.

A variety of written, telephone, and in-person counseling resources are available to assist persons with decisions to purchase Medicare supplemental insurance. For impartial and free information, health insurance counseling programs are available in every state. A toll-free phone line exists in all 50 states and the District of Columbia for finding the location of health insurance counseling. These phone numbers are listed in the *Guide to Health Insurance for People with Medicare,* which is available free from any Social Security office or by calling the toll-free Medigap information hotline: 1 (800) 638–6833. The local area agency on aging or the state insurance department may be called for the nearest counseling program. Applications for Medicaid, QMB, or SLMB programs must be filed at a state, county, or local medical assistance office. The same hotline phone number can be called to find the nearest medical assistance office. Several of the written guides and booklets are listed in the reference section at the end of this article.

Research Issues

There are two major research issues in the field of Medicare supplemental insurance: (1) the effect of supplemental insurance ownership on Medicare and other health care utilization, and (2) beneficiaries' understanding of Medicare and supplemental health insurance policies, including how their knowledge and decision making can be improved. Theoretically, insurance coverage may influence the decision to use health services and the level of use because it reduces the cost at the point of service. Cross-tabulations of data from the 1991 MCBS suggest that higher Medicare per capita spending was associated with greater Medicare supplemental coverage, including public and private (Chulis et al. 1993). Even after adjusting for self-reported health status, similar Medicare spending differences were found. There were two limitations to this study: the insurance data were not as detailed as one would like and the statistical model was not multivariate. A multivariate study in 1982 of persons residing in six states found that policy ownership had a substantial positive impact on service usage and costs, particularly for beneficiaries in fair or poor health (McCall et al. 1991). With its detailed data on insurance policies, the study found that the greatest impact was found for policies that provided first-dollar coverage.

Many Medicare beneficiaries are not knowledgeable about Medicare or their supplemental health insurance. There has been little formal evaluation of the effectiveness of health insurance information and educational programs to date. One quasi-experimental test of the Illness Episode Approach (IEA), a specific information intervention for Medicare beneficiaries, found that the IEA did not result in significant improvements in health insurance knowledge. However, IEA participants did show important differences in purchasing behavior—specifically, they were likely to drop their duplicative coverage and to spend less on premiums compared to persons receiving traditional information (Sofaer et al. 1992). There is increasing interest in determining what information would be useful for Medicare beneficiaries to understand the Medicare program itself as well as to decide about supplemental health insurance and HMO options, as well as how to present this information in a user-friendly way. (See also HEALTH MAINTENANCE ORGANIZATIONS, MEDICAID, MEDICARE, and POST-RETIREMENT HEALTH INSURANCE.)

Organizations

Health Care Financing Administration (HCFA)
American Association of Retired Persons (AARP)
National Association of Insurance Commissioners (NAIC)
The National Committee to Preserve Social Security and Medicare

Suggested Readings

Health Care Financing Administration. 1994. *Guide to Health Insurance for People with Medicare* (includes a list of all state insurance counseling programs). Baltimore, MD: Author.

National Committee to Preserve Social Security and Medicare. 1994. *Buying Your Medigap Policy*. Washington, DC: Author.

Polniaszek, Susan. 1994. *Managing Your Health Care Finances: Getting the Most Out of Medicare and Medigap Insurance*. Washington, DC: United Seniors Health Cooperative.

"Filling the Gaps in Medicare" 1994. *Consumer Reports* (August), 523–32.

References

Chulis, George, Franklin Eppig, Mary Hogan, Daniel Waldo, and Ross Arnett. 1993. "Health Insurance and the Elderly: Data from MCBS." *Health Care Financing Review* 14: 163–81.

General Accounting Office. 1994. *Health Insurance for the Elderly: Owning Duplicate Policies Is Costly and Unnecessary*. Washington, DC: GAO.

McCall, Nelda, Thomas Rice, James Boismier, and Richard West. 1991. "Private Health Insurance and Medical Care Utilization: Evidence from the Medicare Population." *Inquiry* 28: 276–87.

Sofaer, Shoshana, Erin Kenney, and Bruce Davidson. 1992. "The Effect of the Illness Episode Approach on Medicare Beneficiaries' Health Insurance Decisions." *Health Services Research* 27: 671–93.

Waldo, Daniel, Sally Sonnefeld, David McKusick, and Ross Arnett. 1989. "Health Expenditures by Age Group, 1977 and 1987." *Health Care Financing Review* 10: 111–20.

Judith A. Sangl

MEDIGAP. See Medicare Supplemental Insurance.

MENTAL HEALTH AMONG THE ELDERLY, the measure of individuals' mental capacity in later life to understand and function in society. Mental health can be conceptualized along a continuum, with mental illness on one end and mental wellness on the other. Mental wellness refers to the individual's mental ability to function fully. This is an active process characterized by the individual's openness to experience, his or her ability to focus attention in the present moment, and confidence in his or her ability to satisfy personal needs (Rogers 1961).

Definitions of mental illness often follow the guidelines established by the American Psychiatric Association (APA 1994). For example, definitions within the *Diagnostic and Statistical Manual of Mental Disorders* are the most frequently used in clinical and research settings. From an operational perspective, mental illness in older adults is characterized by patterns of disorders.

Patterns of Mental Disorders in Later Life

The Epidemiologic Catchment Area (ECA) study provides the most comprehensive description of older adults' patterns of mental disorders. Three important themes emerge from the data. First, mental illness is not a part of normal aging. Only approximately 12% of community-dwelling elderly have a diagnosable mental disorder. Older adults' rates of mental illness are the lowest of any age group.

Second, rates of disorders vary by setting. For example, older adults in institutional settings present a different picture: Between 40 and 50% of older adults hospitalized for medical conditions also have psychiatric conditions (Spar and La Rue 1990). Similarly, between 65 and 90% of nursing home residents have a diagnosable mental disorder, depending upon the methods used to assess and diagnose residents (Burns et al. 1993). These substantial rates of mental illness in institutional settings remind us that older adults and health care providers face issues of comorbidity—challenging combinations of more than one mental illness, physical illness, or combinations of both.

Three disorders are most frequent for older adults who are mentally ill: anxiety disorders; depression; and cognitive impairment, including the dementias. Anxiety disorders affect 5.5% of those over age 65. Depression in later life appears in several guises. At least 8% of community-dwelling elderly have serious symptoms of depression and approximately 19% have less severe dysphoric symptomatology (Blazer 1993). As with other disorders, issues of comorbidity are important in geriatric depression. For example, at least 25% of older adults in medical hospitals have diagnosable mood disorders. Psycho-pharmacologic and psychotherapeutic interventions are well established for the successful treatment of geriatric depression (NIH Consensus Panel 1992).

Depression in older adults is closely linked to suicide (Conwell 1994). Suicide among the elderly is associated with diagnosable psychopathology (most often affective disorders) in approximately 90% of cases. The threat of suicide is also substantial in later life, with the highest rates among those 80–84 years old (28.0 per 100,000 versus 12.4 per 100,000 for the general population). The group at highest risk is white men aged 80–84, with a rate of suicide six times the nation's age-adjusted rate. Sadly, the majority of suicide victims had seen their primary care physician within the month prior to suicide. Thus, there is a serious need for better preparation of physicians for screening and treatment of geriatric depression (Conwell 1994).

The ECA data highlight a third category of mental disorders among older adults: cognitive impairment, including the dementias. The prevalence rate among the oldest age groups follows a now-familiar pattern: increasing prevalence with increasing age—2.9% for those 65–74; 6.8% for those 75–84; and 15.8% for those 85 and older. The Advisory Panel on Alzheimer's Disease (1993) estimates that as many as four million Americans currently have Alzheimer's Disease and related dementias (ADRD), with 2.5 to 3 million of these patients suffering from Alzheimer's Disease (AD). Conservative figures suggest that the number of AD patients will increase to more than six million by the year 2040. Cognitive impairment among older adults is a challenge for diagnosis and treatment. Approximately 20% of dementias are reversible if promptly diagnosed and treated. Currently, resources are being invested in research on the biological bases of ADRD, the social impact of these diseases, and the potential for preventive interventions.

Financial Aspects of Mental Health and Aging: Insurance Coverage

The financial aspects of mental illness for older adults reflect the general patterns of treatment and funding for mental health care in America. Inpatient and outpatient care for persons with a mental illness diagnosis are often excluded from coverage by insurers. When covered, such care may be subject to incomplete coinsurance, higher deductible payments, stricter utilization review, and tighter lifetime limits on maximum expenditures. Additionally, as the public system of mental health care was dismantled, patients have had to rely more and more on a system of care that requires payment from private sources. To begin to understand the financial aspects of mental health and aging, it is necessary to examine the insurance coverage offered to older adults.

Medicare. Medicare* coverage of mental illness, while improved in recent years, is still restrictive. While general acute care for mental illness diagnoses are covered under Medicare Part A (Hospital Insurance), Medicare will pay for no more than 190 days of inpatient psychiatric care in freestanding public or private psychiatric hospitals during a person's lifetime. Medicare does provide limited coverage for care in skilled nursing facilities; however, strict conditions must be met for reimbursement. This benefit primarily targets posthospital subacute care, and is not a program for physically or mentally impaired older adults.

Outpatient care for mental illness diagnoses are covered in Medicare Part B (Supplemental Medical Insurance). This includes care that is given while in and out of psychiatric and general hospitals. Under Part B, the services of physicians, psychiatrists, clinical psychologists, and other mental health professionals (e.g., clinical social workers) supervised by a physician or psychologist are covered. For care given by these persons in an inpatient setting, Medicare will pay 80% of the allowed charge; for mental health care in an outpatient setting, however, Medicare pays only 50% of the allowed charge, unless the patient would have required inpatient admission without the treatment. Medicare does not provide any outpatient prescription drug coverage, including psychotropic drugs.

Medicaid. While the state mental health system is the safety net for younger persons with mental disorders, Medicaid* offers some limited security for mentally ill older adults. While Medicaid coverage of mental health care varies by state, all state Medicaid programs are required to pay for inpatient and outpatient hospital services, physician services, and skilled nursing facility care for persons over age 21. These programs pay for services regardless of diagnosis, including coverage of mental illnesses. In addition, more than 30 states cover hospital and nursing facility services for persons over age 65 in institutions for mental disorders, and all states provide some prescription drug coverage. Thus, the poorest elderly are offered some coverage of inpatient and outpatient mental health care through Medicaid.

In Medicare and Medicaid, however, low reimbursement levels for mental health care providers limit access to care. In 1990, Medicare and Medicaid payment rates for psychotherapy averaged less than one-half of median private fees for this service. Furthermore, in Medicaid programs, strict income and asset limits mean that few older adults can qualify for the program. Only 9% of the elderly have coverage through Medicaid (Piacentini and Foley 1992).

Private Insurance. Because of the gaps in Medicare coverage, many elderly persons purchase additional insurance. Private insurance coverage for mental health care among older adults comes from two main sources: privately purchased Medicare Supplemental Insurance (Medigap)* policies and postretirement health insurance* provided through former employers. The latter generally covers more services than the Medigap policies. Three of the ten standardized Medigap plans offer coverage of outpatient prescription drugs; none of them offers extra coverage extending beyond the limits on psychiatric hospitalization.

More than one-third of the elderly now have supplemental insurance coverage through a former employer (Shea and Stewart 1994). These policies typically mirror those of the younger employed population. Two key features of these plans are that they typically provide significant coverage of prescription drugs and often cover some psychologists' services as well. Furthermore, since many employer plans also provide some inpatient and outpatient mental health treatment, elderly persons with these policies will have increased access to such services.

Employer policies, however, often have more restrictive limits on use. Bureau of Labor Statistics studies of insurance coverage indicate that although 98% of firms cover mental health care, 77% of medium and large firms and 85% of smaller firms have separate limitations, including limits on days of inpatient care, total expenditures, different coinsurance, and no consumer out-of-pocket expense limit. Similarly, for outpatient care, 92% of medium and large firms and 95% of smaller firms have stricter limits on use of mental health care (Piacentini and Foley 1992).

Restrictions on mental health care use are also common in health maintenance organizations and other managed care arrangements. Almost 90% of HMOs limit mental health benefits, usually to 20 visits for outpatient care and 30 days of hospital care. Nearly 75% of HMOs require cost-sharing for outpatient care and 33% require cost-sharing for inpatient care (NAPPH 1991).

Total Costs

The most complete recent study indicated that direct health care costs of mental illness in 1985 was $42.5 billion, including $12.8 billion in specialty institutions, $10.6 billion in nursing homes, $8.8 billion in general acute care hospitals, and $10.3 billion in physician and other professional services, drugs, and support costs (Rice et al. 1992). Another $61.2 billion in indirect and related costs in 1985 was traced to mental illness. It has been estimated that direct costs in 1990 increased to $67 billion.

Rice et al. (1992) calculated only the core costs (direct costs plus indirect mortality and morbidity costs) by age and gender. Their results indicate that in 1985, $17.3 billion of core costs were for persons 65 and older, with more than two-thirds of this amount for women older than 65. For older adults, care in nursing homes constitutes the largest element of mental health care costs, since 90% of the mentally ill population are in nursing homes (Lair and Lefkowitz 1990). In contrast, adults over the age of 65 represent only 11% of the population receiving inpatient care in specialty institutions and general hospitals. They represent less than 8% of the population receiving outpatient or partial care.

This reliance on the nursing home for mental health care of older adults has important financial implications. At one time, state and county mental hospitals provided the bulk of care for young and old individuals with chronic mental impairments. That method relied almost exclusively on public sources of revenue. More than 80% of the financing in such institutions came from public sources, primarily state mental health agency funds.

The decline in the use of these public facilities for mental health care for the elderly changed the sources of funding for mental health care of older adults, as more care was given in general acute-care hospitals, private psychiatric facilities, and nursing homes. Since 1977, the number of patients with mental disorders in these three settings has more than doubled. Patients in these settings are far more likely to be paying for their own care. Private psychiatric hospitals receive more than two-thirds of their funds from client fees; general acute care hospitals and nursing homes receive 40% of their fees from patients. In 1987, of the nearly $11 billion spent on nursing home care for older adults, 42% was from patients and their families (Shea 1994).

Some payments for mental health care of older adults also flow from Medicare and Medicaid. These payments have increased in recent years. Medicare payment rules under the new Prospective Payment System (PPS) encouraged the development of private psychiatric hospitals and psychiatric wings or beds in general hospitals (Dada et al. 1992). Nonetheless, Medicare still represents only a minor source of payment for mental health care of older adults.

Medicaid already pays for a significant amount of the costs of nursing home care for older adults, including older adults with mental illnesses. Approximately 51% of total costs of care given to older persons with a mental illness in nursing homes was paid for by Medicaid. The exact financial responsibility for mental health care of older adults is subject to considerable disagreement between federal and state authorities. Medicaid does not separately reimburse for the costs of mental health treatment in nursing homes. Furthermore, states do not have targeted funding mechanisms for mental health care in this setting.

Perhaps as a result of the lack of clear funding authority for mental health care in nursing homes, two recent studies indicate that, although many nursing home residents have been diagnosed with a mental illness, few receive any mental health care. Burns et al. (1993) examined data from the 1985 National Nursing Home Survey. They found that fewer than 5% of older adults with a mental disorder received any mental health treatment in a one-month period. Data from the 1987 National Medical Expenditure Survey showed that fewer than one-fifth of nursing home residents with a mental disorder had received any treatment from a mental health specialist during their stay. Rates of treatment dropped significantly with increasing age. A 70-year-old female nursing home resident with minor activities of daily living (ADL) impairments and depression was predicted to have a 10% chance of any treatment by a mental health specialist during her nursing home stay.

Under the Nursing Home Reform Act of 1987, nursing homes were required to provide mental health services to residents. Several studies estimated the cost of this mandate to be between $1.4 and $1.9 billion or more (Shea et al. 1993). Many states objected to this federal mandate, especially since states and nursing homes must find new sources of funds (or channel existing sources from alternative uses) to pay for this care. Since much of the current funding for nursing home care comes from patients and their families, it is likely that this requirement will raise their costs.

In summary, the current structure of public and private insurance for mental health care of older adults, with strict limits on use of outpatient care, high coinsurance, and low reimbursement levels, limits the use of outpatient services.

More complete coverage of some inpatient care is available, but limitations on acute-care hospitalization generally encourage largely custodial care in long-term care settings; that is, care primarily for meeting daily living or personal needs, delivered by personnel without professional mental health skills or training. Since Medicaid and state programs do not explicitly target payments for mental health care in the nursing home, little quality mental health care is given. Furthermore, the costs of nursing home care and additional mental health care in the nursing home setting fall heavily on patients and their families. (See also HOME CARE SERVICES FOR THE ELDERLY, MEDICAID, MEDICARE SUPPLEMENTAL INSURANCE, NURSING HOMES, and POSTRETIREMENT HEALTH INSURANCE.)

Organizations

National Institute on Aging—NIA Information
National Institute on Aging—Alzheimer's Disease Education and Referral Center (ADEAR)
National Institute of Mental Health—Mental Disorders of the Aging Branch
National Institute of Mental Health—Public Inquiries Office
Mental Health Policy Resource Center
National Citizens' Coalition for Nursing Home Reform

Suggested Readings

Birren, J. E., and K. W. Schaie. 1990. *Handbook of the Psychology of Aging,* Third Edition. San Diego: Academic Press.
Lombardo, Nancy E. 1994. *Barriers to Mental Health Services for Nursing Home Residents.* Working Paper 9401. Washington, DC: AARP Public Policy Institute.
Smyer, M. A., ed. 1993. *Mental Health and Aging: Progress and Prospects.* New York: Springer.

References

Advisory Panel on Alzheimer's Disease. 1993. *Fourth Report of the Advisory Panel on Alzheimer's Disease, 1992.* NIH Pub. No. 93–3520. Washington, DC: Superintendent of Documents, U.S. Government Printing Office.
American Psychiatric Association. 1994. *Diagnostic and Statistical Manual of Mental Disorders: DSM-IV,* Fourth Edition. Washington, DC: American Psychiatric Association.
Blazer, D. G. 1993. *Depression in Late Life,* Second Edition. St. Louis, MO: Mosby.
Burns, B. J., H. R. Wagner, J. E. Taube, and J. Magaziner. 1993. "Mental Health Service Use by the Elderly in Nursing Homes." *American Journal of Public Health* 83 (3): 331–37.
Conwell, Y. 1994. "Suicide in Elderly Patients." In *Diagnosis and Treatment of Depression in Late Life: Results of the NIH Consensus Development Conference,* ed. L. S. Schneider et al. Washington, DC: American Psychiatric Press.
Dada, M., W. D. White, H. H. Stokes, and P. Kurzeja. 1992. "Prospective Payment for Psychiatric Services." *Journal of Health Politics, Policy, and Law* 17: 483–508.
Lair, T., and D. Lefkowitz. 1990. "Mental Health and Functional Status of Residents of Nursing and Personal Care Homes." In *National Medical Expenditure Survey*

Research Findings 7. Rockville, MD: Agency for Health Care Policy and Research.

National Association of Private Psychiatric Hospitals (NAPPH). 1991. *Trends in Mental Health Coverage.* Washington, DC: National Association of Private Psychiatric Hospitals.

NIH Consensus Panel on Depression in Late Life. 1992. "Diagnosis and Treatment of Depression in Late Life." *JAMA* 268: 1018–24.

Piacentini, J. S. and J. D. Foley. 1992. *EBRI Databook on Employee Benefits.* Washington, DC: Employee Benefit Research Institute.

Rice, D. P., S. Kelman, and L. S. Miller. 1992. "The Economic Burden of Mental Illness." *Hospital and Community Psychiatry* 43: 1227–32.

Rogers, C. R. 1961. *On Becoming a Person.* Boston: Houghton Mifflin.

Shea, D. G. 1994. "Nursing Homes and the Costs of Mental Disorders." Manuscript under review.

Shea, D. G., M. A. Smyer, and A. Streit. 1993. "Mental Health Care in Nursing Homes: What Will It Cost?" *Journal of Mental Health Administration* 20: 223–35.

Shea, D. G., and R. P. Stewart. 1994. "Ability to Pay for Retiree Health Benefits." *Inquiry* 31: 206–14.

Spar, J. E., and A. La Rue. 1990. *A Concise Guide to Geriatric Psychiatry.* Washington, DC: American Psychiatric Press.

Michael A. Smyer and Dennis G. Shea

MINORITY ELDERS, persons aged 65 and older who belong to ethnic groups regarded as social and cultural minorities. At present, the bulk of studies conducted on ethnic elderly have centered on black elderly and Spanish-speaking or Hispanic elderly (Barresi and Stull 1993).

Focusing on ethnic groups that have markedly different cultural traditions from white culture is important. Trends toward greater well-being, healthier lifestyles, and improvements in morbidity and mortality rates for older persons during the last decade have not held for racial or ethnic minority elderly, who continue to fare worse on most objective measures of health and well-being than their white counterparts. Although the leveling forces of American culture affect all groups, significant differences in fertility, family living arrangements, and possibly norms concerning children's responsibility for parents remain, thus resulting in different forms of social support for the elderly (Angel et al. 1992). A growing sensitivity to the ethnic and cultural diversity of older Americans has strengthened the mandate to differentiate models of health and social service delivery and to target needs accordingly (Mui and Burnette 1994). A major theme in research on the cultural diversity of America's aged has been ethnicity as a positive resource, a form of compensation for the problems usually associated with aging (Sokolovsky 1990).

Background

Blacks constitute the nation's largest and, in many ways, most underprivileged minority group (Markides and Mindel 1987). Blacks began to arrive in the

United States as slaves in the early 1600s with white settlers. For blacks, culture stems from their African heritage and the experience of slavery.

Americans of Hispanic origin constitute the nation's second largest minority group. Perhaps one of the best illustrations of the complexity of the problem is the common grouping of several Spanish-speaking groups under the caption "Hispanics" (Gerontological Society of America [GSA] 1991). The diversity of the Hispanic-American, or Latino, community is exhibited by the distinct Mexican, Puerto Rican, Cuban, and other Hispanic-origin groups (Applewhite 1988). These groups differ in the timing and pattern of their migrations to this country, their geographic locations, and their economic status. Within these clusters, some older Hispanic-Americans are characterized by economic disadvantage, high levels of cognitive and functional impairment, and above-average symptoms of depression.

Puerto Ricans who have migrated to the mainland United States have been predominantly, although not exclusively, of low socioeconomic status, have moved mostly to metropolitan New York, and have continued to migrate, often in both directions (GSA 1991). Studies indicate that Puerto Rican elderly residing in the United States have little formal education. The majority have finished some primary school grades, and the average years of education for those who attended school range from three to four. When elderly Puerto Ricans were children, elementary schools on the island reached the maximum level of fourth grade. Only large towns and cities had secondary schools. Puerto Rican elderly, like the majority of the elderly population in the United States, experience poor physical health and a lack of adequate income as two of their major problems (Applewhite 1988).

Income

According to census data, in 1989 the poverty rate among black elderly (30.8%, or 766,000 persons) was more than triple, and among Hispanic elderly (20.6%, or 211,000 persons) more than double, the poverty rate among white elderly persons (9.6%, or approximately 2.5 million persons) (Mui and Burnette 1994). Ethnic elders had lower personal incomes than whites. A breakdown by both ethnic and gender subgroups shows the following range of annual income in 1990: elderly white men, $14,839; elderly white women, $8,462; elderly black men, $7,450; elderly black women, $5,617; elderly Hispanic men, $9,546; and elderly Hispanic women, $5,373 (GSA 1991).

Wage and salary income is the most important component of income for both blacks and whites, but the proportion of adults receiving this type of income increased for whites and decreased for blacks (Luckey 1993). This discrepancy is not mediated by asset income, as only 27% of black and 37% of Hispanic elderly draw on asset income sources, in contrast to 72% of whites. Nor are pension* benefits substantial among older minority Americans. They thus rely more on social insurance and social assistance income (GSA 1991).

Social Security

The 1983 amendments to the Social Security Act anticipate a gradual increase in the eligibility age for full benefits from 65 to 67 years old between the years 2000 and 2027. As a result, one must work until age 65 to receive 80% of the primary insurance benefits. This legislation will have a disproportionately negative impact on older blacks (Luckey 1993). Poor health, low income, and low educational levels are primary reasons for their increased vulnerability. The changes as they relate to blacks do not address the objectives the amendments seek to meet, that is, to encourage private savings and to discourage early retirement. Older black workers have a lifetime history of low-paying jobs, many of which carry no benefits or retirement plans and are more sensitive to business cycles and longer periods of unemployment than most held by whites. This results in little or no savings or assets on which to rely in retirement. Evidence indicates that older blacks are not participants in the early voluntary retirement trend (Luckey 1993).

Differences between the general population and the Hispanic elderly seem to be greatest in terms of dependence on Social Security and Supplemental Security Income. There are fewer individuals drawing on Social Security among Hispanics than in the general population (approximately 50% of Hispanics as compared to almost 90% of others). The lower rate of Hispanic-American elderly participating in the Social Security program has at least three explanations: (1) misconceptions of citizenship requirements, (2) language difficulties, and (3) eligibility for benefits. Hispanic elderly are clustered predominantly in occupations that are transitory: nontransport operatives and farm and nonfarm unskilled labor. Many Hispanic women are employed as domestics and in service areas. Employers in these fields often do not withhold Social Security taxes, thus reducing eligibility in later life (Applewhite 1988).

Housing

Of homeowners aged 55–65, 17% of white women, 27% of African-American women, and 12% of Hispanic women spend at least 40% of their income on housing (AARP 1993). This compares with 8% of white men, 12% of African-American men, and 13% of Hispanic men. These discrepancies are due to the general, but differential, demographic shift among the elderly in the last 50 years: individuals, especially older women, live alone.

As blacks, Latinos, and whites differ on many dimensions, this variation translates into different living arrangements among the infirm elderly. In the event of serious declines in functional capacity, an unmarried individual who is living alone has three options: (1) He or she may continue to live alone despite diminished health, (2) he or she may live with others who can provide help with activities of daily living, or (3) he or she can enter an institution. For blacks and Latinos the last option is exercised much less often than among whites (Angel et al. 1992).

A common misconception about Hispanic elderly is that they are cared for by the extended family. Hispanic-origin elderly are three times more likely to live alone than in someone else's home (Applewhite 1988).

Health

In the United States, the health consequences of race and ethnicity are confounded with those of social class. Many of the health risks to which poor blacks and Latinos are exposed result from poverty. A growing number of studies have highlighted the problems of access to and utilization of health services by the poor and nonwhites.

Most studies that focus on age and retirement issues of nonwhites report that poor health is the most frequent reason for early withdrawal from the labor force, as blacks suffer disproportionately from physical disabilities and impairments that begin at earlier ages than do whites (Luckey 1993). There is also evidence that blacks have poorer health and greater limitations than Hispanics (Markides and Mindel 1987), but personal health is a principal area of concern for Hispanic elderly as well. A history of discrimination against Hispanics as a minority further restricts their access and utilization of health and human services (Applewhite 1988). Added to the structural, organizational, and sociocultural factors that are similar for blacks, is their preference for Spanish as the dominant language and use of folk medicine as an alternative treatment modality.

Social Support

Perhaps the greatest debate concerning similarities and differences in social support of minority and majority groups is whether the documented differences result from socioeconomic differences or have independent causes (GSA 1991).

In the African-American culture, kindred relationships are based on affection and mutual interests, criteria that also apply to friendships. When relations with friends compete with kin relations, friends are redefined as kin. Most blacks have active, ongoing friendships. In the inner city, a majority are in frequent contact with friends, and those friends are as likely as children to provide emotional support (Johnson and Barer 1990).

In addition to kinship, the black church congregation provides an effective social support network for elderly African Americans. Some churches create spiritual families and assign kinship terms to members. By custom, some churches have "church mothers," who function as lay therapists and confidantes to any member with problems (Johnson and Barer 1993). The church mother is often the center of a system in which resources are pooled and redistributed (Sokolovsky 1990). Understanding how such cultural traits affect health and living arrangements is important in addressing the needs of elderly minority Americans.

Studies of Puerto Rican elderly indicate that the family—particularly adult children—is still the predominant support network in daily life and during crises.

The family provides instrumental support (information, escort, shopping, chauffeuring, translation, errands, health assistance) and emotional support (companionship, advice-giving, listening to problems) (Appelwhite 1988). In turn, Puerto Rican elderly play important and active roles in providing assistance to families (Gelfand and Kutzik 1979). Almost daily contact with children living in the same city is the normal pattern for Puerto Rican elderly, whether through visits or telephone calls. Child care, cooking, counseling, and providing assistance during illnesses are among the supportive tasks Puerto Rican elderly frequently perform for adult children and grandchildren.

Minority families depend on the community for assistance as well. Although informal supports are present and provide some emotional and instrumental relief, they cannot meet all of the caregivers' needs. Health, social service, and income support programs, differentiated by subgroups in the elderly population, must continue to receive urgent attention. (See also ECONOMIC STATUS OF THE ELDERLY, ECONOMIC STATUS OF ELDERLY WOMEN, HEALTH AND LONGEVITY, HOUSING, OLDER AMERICANS ACT, PENSION FUND TRENDS, and SOCIAL SECURITY.)

Suggested Readings

Abeles, Ronald P., Helen C. Gift, and Marcia G. Ory. 1994. *Aging and Quality of Life.* New York: Springer.

Cole, Thomas R., W. Andrew Achenbaum, Patricia L. Jakobi, and Robert Kastenbaum. 1993. *Voices and Visions of Aging.* New York: Springer.

Gerontological Society of America. 1994. *Minority Elders: Five Goals toward Building a Public Policy Base.* Washington, DC: GSA.

References

Angel, Ronald J., Jacqueline L. Angel, and Christine L. Himes. 1992. "Minority Group Status, Health Transitions, and Community Living Arrangements among the Elderly." *Research on Aging* 14: 496–521.

Applewhite, Steven R. 1988. *Hispanic Elderly in Transition.* Westport, CT: Greenwood Press.

American Association of Retired Persons. 1993. *AARP Housing Report.* Washington, DC: AARP.

Barresi, Charles M., and Donald E. Stull. 1993. *Ethnic Elderly and Long-Term Care.* New York: Springer.

Gelfand, Donald E., and Alfred J. Kutzik, eds. 1979. *Ethnicity and Aging.* New York: Springer.

Gerontological Society of America (GSA). 1991. *Minority Elders: Longevity, Economics, and Health.* Washington, DC: GSA.

Johnson, Colleen L., and Barbara M. Barer. 1990. "Families and Networks among Older Inner-City Blacks." *Gerontologist* 30: 726–33.

Luckey, Irene. 1993. "Implications of Social Security Amendment of 1983 for Older Blacks." *Journal of Aging and Social Policy* 5: 9–21.

Markides, Kyriakos S., and Charles H. Mindel. 1987. *Aging and Ethnicity.* Newbury Park, CA: Sage.

Mui, Ada C., and Denise Burnette. 1994. "Long-Term Care Service Use by Frail Elders: Is Ethnicity a Factor?" *Gerontologist* 34: 190–98.
Sokolovsky, Jay 1990. *The Cultural Context of Aging: Worldwide Perspectives.* New York: Bergin & Garvey.

Lisa J. Edwards

MORTGAGE INSTRUMENTS, written, publicly recorded documents that provide the terms for financing real estate interests and secure payment of the mortgage debt incurred. For most people, the purchase of a home is their largest investment, and home purchases usually require a mortgage. The type of mortgage selected is an important financing decision in the home purchasing (or refinancing) process. Decisions regarding financing require an understanding about the types of mortgages that are available, and decisions made in later life especially impact retirement, financial planning issues, and future health care concerns.

Fixed Rate Mortgages

The most common financing used by residential borrowers is a fixed rated mortgage. The interest rate is fixed, a repayment period is specified, and the monthly payments are equal over the life of the loan. Unless otherwise specified, the fixed rate mortgage allows the borrower to prepay the outstanding principal before the maturity date. The constant monthly payments of a fixed rate mortgage make it an ideal instrument in periods when interest rate inflation is expected, as the borrower will actually repay the loan in cheaper dollars than borrowed. Its chief disadvantage is that fixed mortgage payments generally require a smaller percentage of income as one's career advances (although the opposite can be true after retirement). Thus, people can generally qualify for a larger loan if the initial mortgage payments are smaller, and a number of different mortgages have been introduced as alternatives to fixed rate mortgages. The most popular of these alternative mortgages is the adjustable rate mortgage (ARM).

Adjustable Rate Mortgages

Unlike fixed rate loans, flexible rate mortgages have variable interest rates that fluctuate according to the movement of some predetermined index. The index, to a large extent, represents the actual cost of funds to lenders. Widely used indices include the Federal Home Loan Bank Board (FHLBB's) Eleventh District cost of funds index, which includes the average mortgage rates for major lenders on existing homes. The FHLBB cost of funds is based on interest and dividends paid or accrued on the thrift institutions' liabilities. These indices are usually less volatile than the Treasury indices, which may be for six-month, one-year, or three-year Treasury notes.

In addition to indexing, a typical ARM also contains other features, such as margin, adjustment periods, and interest rate caps. A margin is a fixed percent-

inflation, the borrower's likelihood of default increases. With a PLAM, equity accumulates more slowly than with most other mortgage instruments. Finally, the total cost of the loan at the beginning of the term is unknown to the borrower since it is based on forecasts. (See also HOME MODIFICATIONS FINANC-ING, HOMEOWNERSHIP, HOUSING, REVERSE MORTGAGES, SENIORS HOUSING FINANCE, and VACATION HOMES AND RECREATIONAL PROPERTIES.)

Reference

Phillips, Richard A., and James H. VanderHoff. 1994. "Alternative Mortgage Instruments, Qualification Constraints and the Demand for Housing: An Empirical Analysis." *Journal of the American Real Estate & Urban Economics Association* (Fall), 453–77.

Andrew Quang Do

MUTUAL FUNDS, investment companies that raise money by selling shares to the public and investing the proceeds in other securities. The value of mutual fund shares fluctuate with the value of the securities in its portfolio. Professional managers select, purchase, trade, and manage diversified portfolios of stocks, bonds, and/or other securities, to achieve the financial objectives promised to the shareholders.

Each mutual fund is a separate company, and its investors are the shareholders or owners of the company. They are represented by an elected board of directors, which is legally responsible for fund management. A management company and investment advisor will organize and administer the fund and make investment decisions for a fee, in accordance with the fund's objectives. Despite the legal structure, the management company effectively controls the fund.

There are approximately 5,000 mutual funds in the United States, invested in about $2 trillion in assets. Although the first mutual funds began in 1924, they did not become popular until the early 1980s. All mutual funds are regulated by the Investment Company Act of 1940, and are registered and overseen by the Securities and Exchange Commission (SEC).

Mutual funds have been more popular with younger investors in the work force in the last decade. A major shift to "defined contribution" benefit plans (such as the 401k) in the 1980s made many millions of workers responsible for investing their own pension accounts. The most popular means of accomplishing this has been through mutual funds, resulting in a natural surge. However, mutual funds remain important to investors in their retirement years, particularly when considering the investment of a lump-sum retirement or other distribution.

The primary purpose of mutual funds is diversification. Investors seek high returns, but dislike high risk. Holding a single, typical stock implies two to five times the risk of investing in many stocks. By pooling funds to invest in a diversified portfolio of securities, mutual funds can produce investment returns at risk levels resembling the lower risks of the market overall. Small investors would be unable to achieve such diversification on their own.

Convenience, service, and liquidity are other reasons for the popularity of mutual fund investing. The management and administration of the fund reduces an individual's burden. Year-end statements summarize activity, making taxes easier to track. Funds will automatically reinvest dividends and other distributions if desired, and most have convenient retirement plans (such as IRAs) and systematic withdrawal plans. Many fixed-income and most money-market funds have check-writing privileges. Other popular services are automatic investment plans and telephone switching between funds. Large investment amounts can be purchased or sold without affecting the price (and without commission, for many funds).

Finally, there are benefits of having professional managers pursue and meet fund objectives. Superior performance is the most highly promoted, and most controversial, of these benefits. Cost savings result from high volume, superior information, and professional management. To pursue a specific investment objective and risk level without complicated research is another attractive quality of mutual funds.

Types of Mutual Funds

Most mutual funds are *open-ended* investment companies. Investors may buy new shares, increasing the size of the fund; likewise, the size of the fund is reduced when shares are sold. Shares are purchased at net asset value (NAV) plus any sales load; they are sold at the NAV, less any redemption fee or "back-end load." The NAV is simply each share's portion of the net value of the fund's assets: the total assets owned, less any accumulated expenses (liabilities), divided by the number of shares the mutual fund has outstanding. Some funds, called *closed-end* funds, have a fixed number of shares. These publicly traded investment companies' shares are bought and sold like regular stocks, usually on a major stock exchange. Their share prices are not necessarily close to the fund's NAV, as shares sometimes sell at deep discounts or steep premiums.

There are six general categories of mutual funds, differing primarily by underlying asset type. *Money-market* mutual funds invest in very short-term securities such as Treasury bills, large bank CDs, and commercial paper of large corporations. They aim for constant price stability ($1.00 per share), so their interest rate varies and they compete with banks for short-term funds. Like other mutual funds, money-market funds are not guaranteed, so asset quality is a key concern.

Fixed-income funds invest in government bonds, corporate bonds, mortgages, and sometimes preferred stock, in order to provide a good return and the safety of a diversified portfolio. *Equity funds* aim for capital growth by holding a diversified portfolio of common stocks. *Balanced funds* hold a mix of stock and bond investments, aiming for both income and growth with broader diversification.

Other types of funds include *international funds,* which invest in the stocks and bonds of companies and governments outside the U.S. If they hold significant U.S. assets as well, these funds are usually termed global funds. Finally, there are a wide array of *special purpose funds,* which offer a more focused portfolio (such as gold or technology stocks), at the expense of diversification.

The Investment Company Institute identifies at least 22 different categories of mutual funds, based on general type and investment objectives. Money-market and fixed-income mutual funds, for example, have taxable and nontaxable (municipal) versions. Bond funds may focus on government, high-grade, or high-yield corporate mortgages, or another category of fixed-income investment. Equity funds may range from medium-risk growth and income funds to high-risk aggressive growth funds. Index funds, which try to match closely the returns of one of many published investment indices, are also popular. These categories and investment objectives provide some information concerning the risk level of the fund, as well as its overall investment style. The categorizations reflect conscious choices of where the manager wants to position the fund along several investment dimensions, such as asset class, tax status, maturity, diversification, domestic versus international, income versus growth, turnover, and risk.

Mutual Fund Costs and Operations

The fund's prospectus is an important legal document that provides information concerning investment risks, objectives, fees, loads, and expenses; how to buy and sell shares; services and distributions provided; and many other facts. It is often written in such complex language that the SEC has begun an initiative to simplify prospectus texts and offer investors a one-page summary.

The convenience of professional management and service is costly. Costs of mutual fund investing are direct, indirect, and hidden. A direct cost is a front-end sales load to purchase fund shares, a one-time commission, or a redemption fee when selling, and primarily compensates the broker or salesperson. Front-end loads are typically 4–5%, but can be as high as 8.5%. If $10,000 is invested with a 5% load, only $9,500 goes to the fund; $500 is a sales charge. Some funds have back-end loads, many of which decline and even disappear as the fund is held for longer periods. There are many no-load funds directly marketed by the fund with no need for a sales load. No-load funds provide the most liquidity. They can be purchased and sold at their NAV.

The majority of mutual funds have 12b-1 fees, which are sales loads in disguise. Named for SEC Rule 12b-1, they allow funds to levy an annual amount (up to 1% of assets) to cover advertising and distribution. Like a one-time load, the 12b-1 fee is often used as compensation for the advice or service of the selling broker, but as an annual charge, it becomes a direct cost.

Indirect costs are paid from assets on an ongoing basis, and the major component of these ongoing expenses is the management fee, a part of every fund's cost structure. Whether a fund is a load fund or a no-load fund, its advisor or portfolio manager charges a fee as an annual percentage of assets on a continual basis. Most management fees range from .5% to 1%. Other expenses paid on an ongoing basis include shareholder services and reporting; custodial, legal and auditing fees; and directors' fees.

These costs comprise the fund's operating expenses. Stated as a percentage of the fund's NAV, these costs compromise the fund's expense ratio. The median expense ratio for bond funds is 0.85%; for equity funds it is 1.33%; for international funds it is 1.75%; money-market fund expenses are considerably lower. The expense ratio is an important number, as the fund's gross investment gains are reduced by this amount before arriving at the fund's actual return to the investor. All prospectuses include a detailed section and table covering the fund's direct and indirect costs, and their effect on a hypothetical investment. Some mutual fund costs are hidden, since they show up as neither a one-time load nor as a component of the expense ratio. Brokerage commissions and other transaction costs fall into this category, and these costs can be significant for funds that have a high turnover ratio (lots of trading activity). This multitude of fees, expenses, and other costs can be sizeable, and may do little to help the fund investor achieve high returns. Funds with higher cost structures must produce higher gross returns to stay even with lower-cost funds, but in practice, this has proven extremely difficult for fund managers to do.

Mutual Fund Performance

Fund performance is measured in terms of total return—the increase in fund price, plus any dividends or distributions paid out by the fund. If funds receive income, or realize capital gains by selling positions at a profit, they must pass the bulk of the net gains through to the shareholders. When dividends or distributions are paid, the NAV of the fund falls by the amount of the pay-out. These distributions are taxed at the personal level, not at the fund level. Investors must thus be cautious of profitable, high-turnover funds that are about to make a large distribution, as often happens at year-end. An unwitting buyer may purchase $10,000 of a fund in December only to have a $1,000 taxable distribution on December 31, paid from gains made earlier in the year. The investor could then be left with $9,000 of the fund, $1,000 in cash, and a large tax bill on the entire $1,000 distribution, despite making no profit.

Other key tax issues arise when mutual fund shares are sold. Investors may use several techniques to determine the tax basis (purchase price) of fund shares in order to calculate the profit on the sale. When selling shares, it is prudent to consult with a tax or financial advisor*. The reinvestment of dividends or distributions may present an even more difficult problem, since many investors forget to increase the tax basis of shares when reinvesting in new shares with already-taxed distributions. When shares are sold later, they pay taxes on the same money a second time. This is a costly mistake, and highlights the importance of keeping good records when dealing with mutual funds and other investments.

Mutual fund returns vary significantly by fund and by period. Long-term average returns are most comparable within fund categories and tend to vary with the risk profile of the fund. During long periods, higher-risk investments are expected to produce higher returns. In the ten years before mid-1994, domestic equity funds averaged 12–13% annual returns, domestic and global bond funds returned an average 10–11%, and international equity funds provided an average 16% return. Money-market fund returns were significantly lower, about 5%. Fund returns in the future are unpredictable, but these 10-year returns were very high. Several ranking services calculate risk-adjusted returns, or otherwise factor risk into their performance evaluations.

Attention paid to past returns may be of limited value, according to consistent findings of academic studies over the past 25 years. Two empirical facts generally issue from serious research: (1) many mutual fund managers fail to outperform comparable market averages, and (2) there is little consistency in the funds showing above-market performance. In an early study (Jensen 1969), and several later studies on mutual fund performance, researchers have found no evidence that fund managers have beaten the market on a risk-adjusted basis. The number of funds with above-average performance five years in a row is basically no higher than the laws of probability would determine. Several implications follow these findings. Investors wanting high returns must accept high levels of risk. Consistent above-average performance may be due to luck or skill. Another important implication is that past returns will tell little about future results.

A look at the cost structure of mutual funds provides information regarding returns. Several analyses have found that funds with higher expense ratios and higher turnover produce, on average, lower net investment results. This is not surprising, since it reflects the dual realities that costs reduce returns unless they are outweighed by additional gains, and that it is difficult to produce investment gains consistently. One industry development stemming from this research is the remarkable growth of index funds. Instead of trying to "beat the market," index fund managers attempt to closely match an index, such as the S&P 500. Most make an effort to keep expenses and turnover costs very low, thus surpassing the majority of other funds, but not achieving top performance. While a fairly new development, there are now almost 100 index funds tied to a wide variety of market indices.

There are two general types of mutual fund information sources, both of which can be found at most libraries. Most financial periodicals have quarterly or annual mutual fund surveys with a wealth of information on fund performance and fund categories. The second source is a mutual fund update service, guidebook, or directory, providing varying degrees of information and ratings on many popular mutual funds. (See also AGENTS AND BROKERS, ASSETS ALLOCATION AFTER RETIREMENT, CASH FLOW PLANNING FOR RETIREES, EQUITY SECURITIES, FINANCIAL ADVISORS, INVESTMENTS, TAX PLANNING, and WEALTH SPAN.)

References

American Association of Individual Investors. 1995. *The Individual Investor's Guide to Low-Load Mutual Funds.* Chicago: AAII.

CDA Investment Technologies. 1995. *Wiesenberger Investment Companies Service.* Rockville, MD: CDA.

Fredman, Albert J., and Russ Wiles. 1993. *How Mutual Funds Work.* New York: NYIF.

Investment Company Institute. 1995. *Directory of Mutual Funds.* Washington: ICI.

Jensen, Michael. 1969. "Risks, the Pricing of Capital Assets, and the Evaluation of Investment Performance." *Journal of Business* 42 (April): 2.

"Mutual Funds 1994." *Kiplinger's Personal Finance Magazine* 48 (September: 37–139.

Morningstar Mutual Funds. Updated twice yearly. Chicago: Morningstar.

Vujovich, Dian. 1992. *Straight Talk about Mutual Funds.* New York: McGraw Hill.

Michael E. Edleson

N

NURSING HOMES, residential care settings licensed by the state to provide nursing care. Most nursing facilities are also certified by the federal government so they can be reimbursed under the Medicare or Medicaid programs. Facilities certified for reimbursement from the Medicaid program are simply called nursing facilities; those certified for reimbursement from Medicare are called skilled nursing facilities. A number of facilities are certified for Medicare and Medicaid and are called dually certified. According to data from the Health Care Financing Administration (HCFA), as of 1993, more than 17,000 nursing homes were certified so they could be reimbursed from public funds for providing nursing care to Medicare or Medicaid beneficiaries.

The nursing home industry in this country was, until the mid-1960s, a cottage industry dominated by small "mom and pop" homes or denominational facilities. With the advent of Medicare and Medicaid in 1965, all of that changed. By 1987, nursing homes provided care to over 1.5 million Americans. For-profit providers dominated the industry. In 1985, three out of four nursing homes were owned by proprietary enterprises. Concurrently, multifacility systems (i.e., nursing home chains) began to provide more of the nation's nursing home care. By 1985, over 40% of nursing facilities were part of multifacility systems.

Currently, the average nursing home is a free-standing, for-profit enterprise that is probably affiliated with a chain. The average nursing home contains more than 100 beds, with an occupancy rate of about 90% (Harrington et al. 1993). However, the characteristics of nursing homes vary considerably by state. While almost 90% of Texas nursing facilities operate under for-profit arrangements and almost 80% are chain-affiliated (Phillips et al. 1991), some states have a not-for-profit sector that constitutes over one-third of all facilities, and other states (e.g., New York) actively discourage interstate chains.

Average occupancy in nursing homes across the country is about 90% in some states, and about 80% in others (e.g., Texas), partially depending on whether state approval is required before expanding the number of beds. Until recently, all states controlled the supply of nursing home beds through a Certificate of Need (CON) procedure, but some states have recently abandoned the CON requirement for new bed construction.

Although the nursing home industry varies from state to state, it is influenced by a number of national trends. Nationwide, services and functions are becoming more diverse. More facilities are beginning to specialize or engage in product differentiation. A number of hospital-based facilities now operate as "step-down" units that care for postacute Medicare patients requiring relatively heavy nursing care. Other facilities are starting Alzheimer's Special Care Units that specialize in treating private-pay residents with serious problems in cognitive functioning but less impairment in their Activities of Daily Living (ADLs). Probably 10–15% of facilities have at least one specialized unit, and the presence of such units seems to vary by state, ownership, and chain affiliation (Zinn and Mor 1994). Other nursing facilities offer special units operating within a setting that includes multiple care modalities, such as continuing care retirement communities or facilities that provide assisted or congregate living and nursing home care.

Expenditures for Nursing Home Care

While the nursing home industry expanded quickly, expenditures on nursing home care increased even more dramatically. In 1960, total expenditures on nursing home care stood at $1 billion. By 1980, that figure had increased to $20 billion, and by 1991 had increased to $59.9 billion. In the last three decades, per capita expenditures on nursing home care increased by 448%, from $5 to $229 per person. In 1960, less than four cents of every health care dollar was spent on nursing home care. In 1991, it was eight cents. Additionally, the nursing home sector experienced inflation equal to or greater than in other portions of the health care sector. From 1989 through 1991, expenditures for nursing home care grew more quickly than expenditures for hospital care, physician services, and dental services (Letsch et al. 1992).

A shift in sources of payment has accompanied this change. In 1960, 80% of expenditures for nursing home care were personal, out-of-pocket payments. By 1991, almost 60% of all long-term care expenditures were payments from third-party payors. By far, the public sector is the largest third-party payor. In 1991, third-party payors expended $34.1 billion on nursing home care. Of that, $32 billion came from public funds. In 1970, government provided $2.3 billion to pay for roughly one-half of nursing home care. In 1991, the federal government spent $12.8 billion. The ratio of federal to state and local spending has remained constant. For every $3 spent by the federal government, state and local governments spend $2. The Medicaid program, funded by the federal and state governments, has, since its inception, provided the major proportion of governmental funds for long-term care. In 1991, Medicaid expenditures of $28.4 billion constituted 47% of the total expenditures on nursing home care, and 88% of governmental expenditures on nursing home care (Letsch et al. 1992).

As the expenditure data suggests, two primary payors provide for nursing home care: individuals and their families paying out-of-pocket, and the Medicaid program. While Medicare is the program most people think of as providing coverage for health care of the elderly, it has restricted coverage for nursing home care. That coverage is limited to a specific number of days, and a Medicare beneficiary is eligible for coverage only if he or she will benefit from rehabilitative care. This latter restriction, in particular, has meant that Medicare actually pays only 2–3% of all money spent on nursing home care, with the exception of the one year for which expanded coverage of "catastrophic costs" was available under Medicare. Private long-term care insurance plays a similarly minor role in paying for nursing home care.

Medicaid Reimbursement for Nursing Home Care

Because Medicaid is the largest single payor for nursing home services, Medicaid reimbursement systems play a major role in determining our society's level of expenditures for nursing home care. These systems vary considerably from state to state. The most common categorization of reimbursement systems is along three dimensions: prospective versus retrospective, facility-based versus class-based, and case-mix versus flat-rate. But Medicaid reimbursement is complex, and most systems reflect some type of combined system. Within a single state, providers will be paid in different ways for different types of expenditures. Or, phrased differently, costs in different "cost centers" are reimbursed using different strategies. For example, a state may reimburse patient care costs using a case-mix system, pay capital costs on a historical basis, and pay administrative costs with a flat prospective rate. The flexibility within each of these strategies may be increased through the use of "floors," "ceilings," or "corridors."

As complex as these systems are, the general trend in nursing home reimbursement systems is clear. In the future, most states will move to some variant of a prospective, class-based, case-mix reimbursement system. Such systems will, for example, pay for patient care costs by setting a class-based "price" prospectively and adjusting it for each facility's case-mix. The most commonly used case-mix classification system for residents will probably be some variant of the Resource Utilization Group (RUG)-III model developed for HCFA's Multistate Nursing Home Case-Mix and Quality Demonstration.

States vary considerably in their level of payments for nursing home care. No matter what reimbursement system they use, "poorer" states usually pay less and "richer" states usually pay more. In 1992, the average Medicaid per diem for nursing home care was $77.45: Arkansas's Medicaid program paid $49 per resident day; Mississippi's program paid $58; Connecticut paid $118; and New York's Medicaid program paid $125.

Medicaid payments are an important part of state budgets. In 1989, almost

30% of Medicaid funds went into payments for nursing home care. In some states, the percentage is even higher. Many states have difficulty meeting their long-term care costs.

Nursing Home Residents

The discussion above notes some of the contextual factors that may affect nursing home expenditures. However, a substantial proportion of the variation in expenditures is associated with differences in the health and functional status of individual residents. Studies have documented the increase in the functional and medical needs of the nursing home population since the introduction of prospective payment in hospitals (Shaughnessy and Kramer 1990). The average nursing home resident today is an elderly woman suffering from a number of chronic medical conditions and has a series of functional problems. Over 45% of nursing and personal care home residents are among the oldest old* (i.e., age 85 or over). Three out of four residents are women. Less than 10% of residents are members of a racial or ethnic minority. Sixty percent suffer from some measure of cognitive impairment and over one-half from urinary incontinence.

Nursing home residents are also consumers of health services beyond those provided in the nursing home. Recent research indicates that over 20% of nursing home residents are hospitalized during any six-month period and that 5% are hospitalized more than once during that same period. The presence of advance directives*, a resident's race, their length of stay, their ADL status, and the state in which they reside significantly affect their comparative risk of hospitalization (Mor et al. 1993). Also, approximately 13% of the residents fall into the lightest-care group, showing few of the multiple impairments usually associated with a nursing home stay. Such residents may be viable candidates for discharge to another care setting.

Information on the status of individual residents has improved since the implementation in 1990 of the Minimum Data Set for Nursing Home Resident Assessment and Care Screening (MDS). This instrument is now in use in all Medicare or Medicaid certified nursing facilities. The items on the instrument provide data on a wide range of medical and functional problems that might be associated with expenditures. For all residents admitted to certified facilities since October 1990, an MDS completed at admission will be available in the resident's medical record. Additionally, an annual MDS with quarterly updates will be a part of every resident's record.

Choosing a Nursing Home

Several steps are recommended for planning a possible nursing home stay. One may begin with a list of several facilities in the area of choice and arrange for visits with a spouse and/or grown children. Valuable insight is gained by talking with residents of the home and with family members. Observe the interaction between staff and patients, notice responses to call signals, and check on activities and surroundings. Once a facility appears comfortable, ask about costs and services. Based on this information, one may be able to adjust financial resources and avoid the hardship of last-minute decisions. As many nursing homes have long waiting lists, ask to be placed on the list. In case of immediate needs, contacts with a physician, a social worker, the local Area Agency on Aging, or a hospital discharge planner will provide information about nursing homes that have available space (Polniaszek 1993).

The Future of the Nursing Home

Because of its high cost, policymakers are interested in minimizing nursing home use. Some analysts have begun to predict the demise of the nursing home. These predictions are premature. Currently, there is no proven lower-cost substitute for nursing home care. Our best current evidence indicates that only the rarest home care programs reduce nursing home utilization or costs. Also, acute care patients are, and will be, released from hospitals with higher levels of need, requiring considerable nursing oversight. Add to these trends the burgeoning oldest old population, which has the highest rate of dementia and uses nursing home care most heavily. In concert, these factors imply that the nursing home will remain an important care modality for many years to come. (See also AS-SISTED LIVING, GERONTOLOGICAL NURSE PRACTITIONERS, HOME CARE SERVICES FOR THE ELDERLY, LONG-TERM CARE INSURANCE: PRIVATE, MEDICAID, OLDEST OLD, OMBUDSMAN, and SOCIAL WORK, GERONTOLOGICAL.)

Organizations

National Association of Area Agencies on Aging
National Citizen's Coalition for Nursing Home Reform
American Association of Homes for the Aging
Concerned Relatives of Nursing Home Patients

Suggested Reading

Meshinsky, Joan. 1991. *How to Choose a Nursing Home: A Guide to Quality Caring.* New York: Avon Books.

References

Harrington, D., C. L. Estes, A. del la Torre, and J. H. Swan. 1993. "Nursing Homes under Prospective Payment." In *The Long-Term Care Crisis: Elders Trapped in the No-Care Zone,* ed. C. L. Estes, J. H. Swan, and Associates. Newbury Park, CA: Sage, 113–31.

Health Care Financing Administration. 1994. *Guide to Choosing a Nursing Home.* Baltimore, MD: Author.

Letsch, S. W., H. C. Lazenby, K. R. Levit, and C. A. Cowan. 1992. "National Health Expenditures, 1991." *Health Care Financing Review* 14: 1–2.

Mor, V., C. D. Phillips, J. N. Morris, B. E. Fries, and C. Hawes. 1993. "Predictors of Hospitalization in a Sample of Nursing Home Residents." Paper presented at the Annual Meeting of the Gerontological Society of America, New Orleans, LA.

Phillips, C. D., G. Zarkin, and C. Hawes. 1991. "Is Better Quality of Care in Nursing

Homes More Expensive and Less Profitable?'' Paper presented at the Annual Meeting of the Gerontological Society of America, San Francisco.

Polniaszek, Susan. 1993. *Long-Term Care: A Dollar & Sense Guide.* Washington, DC: United Seniors Health Cooperative.

Shaughnessy, P. W., and A. M. Kramer. 1990. ''The Increased Needs of Patients in Nursing Homes and Patients Receiving Home Health Care.'' *New England Journal of Medicine* 322: 21–27.

Smith, Lynn. 1992. *Right Choices: An Insider's Guide to Selecting a Home.* Staten Island, NY: Power Publications.

Zinn, J., and V. Mor. 1994. ''Nursing Home Special Care Units: Distribution by Type, State and Facility Characteristics.'' *Gerontologist* 34: 371–77.

Charles D. Phillips and Catherine Hawes

NURSING HOME PROFITS, a cause of controversy that arises in public policy discussions on long-term care, as nursing home operators and their representatives lobby state government for additional Medicaid* reimbursement. States rarely investigate nursing home profits and focus instead on controlling Medicaid costs and maintaining adequate levels of nursing home care quality. State health care administrators see nursing home profits apart from such concerns, but this view disregards connections among profits, costs, and quality. If quality is low, for example, is the Medicaid payment rate inadequate, or are profit requirements too high? As nursing home costs grow and public budget pressures continue, nursing home profitability may increasingly be addressed.

The reason states do not address this issue directly is that appropriate levels of profitability are difficult to assess. The U.S. nursing home industry has developed primarily as a private industry, and the business of providing nursing home care must remain profitable to induce owners to maintain an adequate supply of beds. Economic theory suggests that the optimum profit level is one that induces providers to supply all required nursing home care. For public entities, the main purchasers of nursing home services, the fundamental question of ''how much profit is enough?'' remains open.

Conservative estimates of profitability indicate that, on average, two cents of every dollar expended on U.S. nursing home care is retained by providers as profit (HCIA and Arthur Andersen 1992). Nonprofit nursing homes also realize profit in the form of ''fund balances in excess of expenditures for operations.'' In the following analysis, therefore, ''profit'' applies to both private and nonprofit nursing homes.

Analyzing Profitability

Available research on profitability indicates that private nursing homes generally make higher profits than nonprofits, as do facilities with high occupancy rates and those located in low wage areas (Phillips et al. 1991). However, there is considerable variation across states. Data from 1990 indicate that facilities in Texas average almost an 8% total profit margin, but facilities in Michigan average only .5% to 1%. Such variation is expected, since Medicaid rates, operating expenditures, and net patient care revenue vary from state to state. In 1992, the mean Medicaid per diem was about $77. Four states, however, had Medicaid per diem rates above $100 per resident day, while five states had rates under $60 per resident day. In 1990, seven states reported total operating expenses of more than $100 per resident day, and an equal number reported less than $50 (HCIA and Arthur Andersen 1992).

These estimates are conservative, since they are based on cost reports filed annually under state Medicaid programs. Not shown in these reports are related financial benefits derived from the operation of related enterprises, appreciated assets, excessive remuneration taken by owner-operators and other "off–balance sheet" sources of gain. For example, an operator may own three nursing homes, a linen supply firm, a real estate firm, a home health agency, and a health care management consulting firm, all of which form an interdependent web of financial relationships. Only the financial performance of the nursing homes, however, appears on the Medicaid cost reports.

Although incomplete, Medicaid reports provide the best available information on nursing home profits. To illustrate the data available, how these data might be used, and the general findings one can expect when investigating such data, Medicaid cost reports for facilities operating in New York during 1991 were analyzed. New York uses a case-mix reimbursement system in which it pays different rates for care based on a resident's characteristics. These data are part of a larger study on costs, profitability, and quality in nursing homes in New York (Rudder 1994).

Measures of profitability for nursing homes include: (1) return on assets, (2) return on equity, (3) return on revenues, and (4) return per unit of output. Each of these is based on a ratio in which profits are divided by equity, assets, revenue, or the total units of output or service. Ascertaining nursing home profitability as return on invested capital (equity) seems most ideal, but calculating this return can be difficult, since assets appearing on nursing home cost reports are inconsistently valued. The questionable validity of asset valuation in nursing homes makes calculating return on assets an inconclusive measure as well. Considering profitability as either a return on revenue (profit margin) or a return on services (profit per resident day of care), and for the present examples, profit margin has been used. The total margin indicates the amount of profit derived from each dollar of total income (e.g., patients, donations, investment income). The operating margin indicates the amount of profit derived from each dollar of operating revenue (e.g., patient care revenue, cafeteria revenue, gift shop revenue). Also, the analysis focuses on median levels for most indicators, rather than the mean or average, because cost report data always have some extreme cases of special circumstances. In the face of such potential variation, the median provides a much more stable and representative summary of a distribution than the mean.

Findings

During 1991, the median total margin for New York facilities was less than 3%. One-half of the facilities in the state kept at least three cents of every dollar of revenue. Median operating margin was about 1.9 cents in profit from each dollar of operating revenue. According to total margin, three-fourths of the nursing homes in the state made some profit; considering operating margin, two-thirds of the facilities were profitable. There were dramatic differences between facilities operating under different ownership arrangements, however. While private nursing homes made a profit of 5.25 cents for every dollar of revenue, both nonprofit and public facilities had operating losses and only nonoperating revenues gave them a positive total margin.

Analysis of profits in New York also showed that profit levels varied considerably across the state regions. Facilities operating in the Northeast region had a median total margin of only 1.57%, while New York City facilities had a median total margin of 3.72%. Again, profitability varied for different types of regional facilities. Downstate private nursing homes were most profitable, with a median total margin of 6.26%, and downstate voluntary and public facilities were the least profitable. The former had a margin of only .83%, and the latter operated at a loss.

A common complaint is that Medicaid payments do not cover the costs of care. Only one-third of facilities in New York made a profit by caring for Medicaid residents. Again, however, there are differences by type of facility. Only 13% of voluntary facilities were profitable, while 42% of private homes profitably cared for Medicaid recipients. Only 14% of facilities in Rochester, New York made a profit on Medicaid, but 61% in New York City did. Combining information on sponsorship and location, the differences are dramatic. The downstate (i.e., northern Metropolitan, Long Island, New York City) privately owned facilities had an operating margin of 2.2%, and almost 60% of them made a profit. In other words, 70% of all facilities that made a profit providing care to Medicaid recipients were downstate proprietaries. While these results indicate that it is possible to make a profit from caring for Medicaid recipients, they show that profits are far from evenly distributed within the nursing home industry.

A related issue is whether private-pay patients subsidize Medicaid residents in nursing homes. The argument is that since Medicaid rates are lower than private rates (and frequently lower than costs), private residents subsidize Medicaid patients. This view assumes that all payors, private or Medicaid, should pay the same rate. A counter, however, can rest on much that is seen in the pricing of other consumer services. Auto rental firms, for example, negotiate special auto prices because they are volume buyers, but outcries are rare from individual car buyers who pay higher prices. Insurance companies reduce prices for health care providers and pharmaceutical companies. From this perspective, some subsidization occurs simply because these are large buyers of products or services. The same case can be made for Medicaid programs.

Without Medicaid revenues, the nursing home industry would be a fraction of what it is today. It has been estimated that Medicaid pays about 47% of the money spent on nursing home care in the United States (Letsch et al. 1992). Since a major determinant of nursing home profitability is its level of occupancy, higher occupancy means more units of production across which to spread fixed costs. Today's high occupancy rates are due to the 60–70% of Medicaid nursing home residents (Lair and Lefkowitz 1990). While Medicaid rates decrease industry profits, it can be argued that the Medicaid program makes current profits possible.

The issue of profitability has sometimes been ignored in discussions of reimbursements for nursing home care. Given the increasing costs of care and the demographic shifts that foretell an increasing demand for care, it seems likely that future analyses will be forced to address issues of profitability. (See also MEDICAID, MEDICAID PLANNING, and NURSING HOMES.)

References

HCIA and Arthur Andersen. 1992. *The Guide to the Nursing Home Industry*. Baltimore, MD: HCIA and Arthur Andersen.

Lair, T., and D. Lefkowitz. 1990. *Mental Health and Functional Status of Residents of Nursing and Personal Care Homes*. National Medical Expenditures Survey Research Findings 7. Rockville, MD: Agency for Health Care Policy and Research.

Letsch, S. W., H. C. Lazenby, K. R. Levit, and C. A. Cowan. 1992. "National Health Expenditures, 1991." *Health Care Financing Review* 14: 1–2.

Phillips, C. D., G. Zarkin, and C. Hawes. 1991. "Is Better Quality of Care in Nursing Homes More Expensive and Less Profitable?" Paper presented at the Annual Meeting of the Gerontological Society of America, San Francisco.

Rudder, C. 1994. *New York State's Nursing Home Industry: Profit, Losses, Expenditures and Quality*. New York: Nursing Home Community Coalition of New York State.

Charles D. Phillips and Cynthia Rudder

NUTRITION PROGRAMS, federally funded programs intended to increase the food-buying power of low-income people or to provide food directly to elderly people in the form of nutritionally sound meals.

Food Stamp Program

This program provides low-income households with coupons that can be used like cash at most grocery stores to ensure access to a healthful diet. The U.S. Department of Agriculture (USDA) administers the program at the federal level through its Food and Nutrition Service (FANS). The Food Stamp Program served an average of almost 27 million people each month in 1993. State welfare agencies administer the program at the state and local levels.

Eligibility Requirements. The rules for the participation of aged (if at least one member of the household is age 60 or older) and disabled households are more liberal than those for younger and able-bodied households. There is no net income limit for participation by the elderly and disabled because high monthly costs for rent, utilities, and medical expenses (over $35 per month) can offset income well over the regular limits for other participants. Nevertheless, assets (such as automobiles, property other than a personal home and lot, and savings) of the aged and disabled are considered according to special rules. The value of the stamps received increases with the number of eligible people in the household and decreases with the net monthly income.

Items That Can Be Purchased. Food stamps can be used to buy any food or food product for human consumption, and seeds and plants for use in home gardens to produce foods.

Items That Cannot Be Purchased. Households cannot use food stamps to buy alcoholic beverages and tobacco, hot foods ready to eat and food intended to be heated in the store, vitamins or medicines, pet foods, or any nonfood items (except seeds and plants). However, restaurants can be authorized to accept food stamps in exchange for low-cost meals from qualified homeless, elderly, or disabled people. Food stamps can never be exchanged for cash.

Nutrition Program for the Elderly (NPE)

This program helps provide elderly persons with nutritionally sound meals in community senior citizen centers (congregate dining) or through local meals-on-wheels programs. The NPE is administered by the U.S. Department of Health and Human Services (DHHS), but receives commodity foods and financial support from USDA. Under provisions of the Older Americans Act* of 1965, USDA contributes commodity foods and/or cash to DHHS programs for the elderly. USDA provided reimbursement for an average of more than 900,000 meals a day in 1993. Congress appropriated $470 million for NPE for 1994 (AARP 1994).

Eligibility Requirements. Age is the only factor in determining eligibility for NPE. People 60 years or older and their spouses, regardless of age, are eligible. Indian tribal organizations may select an age below 60 for defining ''older'' persons for their tribes. There is no income requirement to receive meals under NPE. Each recipient can contribute as much as he or she wishes toward the cost of the meal, but meals are free to those unable to make any contribution.

Requirements for USDA Contributions to Local Programs. In order to qualify for cash or commodity assistance, meals served must meet a specified percentage of the nutritional Recommended Daily Allowance (RDA). States can take part or all of their subsidies in cash, rather than commodities. NPE has evolved from a program to distribute USDA commodities to senior citizen meal sites to primarily a cash subsidy program in which approximately 94% of program resources are distributed to meal providers in cash.

Many elderly people require diets and nutritional supplements that are tailored to meet specific needs, based on state of health, level of activity, and medical histories. Researchers who have conducted studies on the nutrient intakes and nutritional status of elderly participants in NPE programs have found that participants were more likely to have consumed two-thirds of the RDAs for calcium, vitamin A and vitamin C than nonparticipants, and that men and women aged 75 years and older who were regular participants had more favorable blood levels of hemoglobin, vitamin A, and proteins than nonparticipants or infrequent participants (Splett 1994). (See also DAY PROGRAMS FOR ADULTS, ECONOMIC STATUS OF THE ELDERLY, ECONOMIC STATUS OF ELDERLY WOMEN, ECONOMIC HARDSHIP MEASURES IN THE OLDER POPULATION, and OLDER AMERICANS ACT.)

References

American Association of Retired Persons. *Nutrition Assistance for Older Americans.* Washington, DC: Public Policy Institute.

Splett, P. L. 1994. "Federal Food Assistance Programs: A Step to Food Security for Many." *Nutrition Today* 29(2): 6–13.

James E. Konlande

O

OLD-AGE PROVISIONS AND ECONOMIC STATUS, the transition to economic status for determining benefits and burdens in U.S. old-age policies, beginning in the early 1980s. Incremental changes in policies have gradually eroded the traditional approach in many policies that relied primarily on specific elderly categories to determine eligibility for public benefits and the amount of those benefits. These changes have also introduced the principle of asking wealthier older persons to pay greater taxes or share more heavily in financing services and benefits than older people with less income and wealth. Some of these changes have been generated by direct concerns for the plight of poorer older people, but efforts to reduce large annual federal deficits have been a major factor.

The Specter of Unsustainable Old-Age Benefits

Concerns about the "graying" of the federal budget first surfaced in the late 1970s. Academicians and journalists identified a trend by which the proportion of federal expenditures for benefits to older persons had reached 26%, roughly equivalent to that spent on national defense. Today, as expenditures on aging are over 30% of the federal budget and defense has fallen to about 21%, doubts about the future economic and political viability of old-age benefits are frequently expressed by public policy analysts, political figures, and the media.

So far, federal benefits to the aging have not been an economic strain. Analyses by the Congressional Budget Office of the U.S. Congress indicate that Social Security*, Medicare*, and Medicaid* have not contributed to the deficit. Contrary to common assumptions, the growth of the elderly population has not contributed significantly to spiraling health care costs. Several studies indicate that even when health care costs are adjusted for inflation, population aging accounts for less than 10% of annual cost increases in the health sector (Mendelson and Schwartz 1993). And despite much rhetoric about cross-sectional issues of intergenerational equity—for example, pitting the welfare of children versus the welfare of the elderly—old-age benefit programs have remained politically viable.

Through what Robertson (1991) has termed "apocalyptic demography," foreboding scenarios have been generated for the aging U.S. society in the twenty-first century. They are constructed by plugging into existing policies and institutional arrangements the familiar projections regarding greater numbers and proportions of older Americans in the next 50 years. For instance, Schneider and Guralnik (1990) have projected that Medicare costs for persons aged 85 and older may increase sixfold by the year 2040, as estimated in constant, inflation-adjusted dollars.

Analysts such as Peter Peterson (1993), former U.S. Secretary of Commerce, warn that a substantial decline in the ratio of workers to retirees will make it impossible to maintain Social Security when the baby boom cohort reaches old age and one in five Americans will be aged 65 and older. Health policy experts and biomedical ethicists warn that health care expenditures on older people—already one-third of the national total—will become a great fiscal "black hole" that will consume an unlimited amount of our national resources.

Yet, the constructs through which these anxieties are generated overlook important considerations. The ratio of workers to retirees, children, and other categories of "dependents" has little to do with the capacity of an economy to transfer resources for their support through such mechanisms as Social Security. Far more important for the requisite national prosperity will be such factors as technological development, natural resources, capital investment, and balance of trade. And there is no inherent reason why Social Security must be financed by a payroll tax, levied on a worker-by-worker basis. Many nations rely on other sources of revenue to help finance Social Security payments.

Similarly, cross-national comparisons of industrialized countries, with respect to their proportions of older people and the amount of national wealth spent on health care, suggest that population aging, in itself, does not cause health care expenditures to be high or out of control. Much more important in determining costs are the structural features of health care systems, and behavioral responses to them by citizens and health care providers.

Assuming that the American economy in the decades ahead is sufficiently prosperous to afford governmental income transfers, the important question is: Is the political will to provide benefits to older persons going to be present?

The New Trend Based on Economic Status

A foundation for sustaining that will has already been laid. During the past 10 years a trend has been established through which Congress has reformed policies on aging to reflect the diverse economic situations of older persons.

The Social Security Reform Act of 1983 began this trend by making 50% of

Social Security benefits subject to taxation for individuals with incomes exceeding $25,000 and married couples with incomes over $32,000. The Tax Reform Act of 1986, even as it eliminated the extra personal exemption that had been available to all persons 65 years and older when filing their federal income tax returns, provided new tax credits to very-low-income older persons on a sliding scale. The Older Americans Act* programs of supportive and social services, for which all persons aged 60 and older are eligible, have been gradually targeted by Congress to low-income older persons.

Even a provision in the Medicare Catastrophic Coverage Act (MCCA) of 1988, one that was not repealed, followed this trend of sensitivity to economic status. The Qualified Medicare Beneficiary program established in the MCCA requires that Medicaid pay Part B premiums as well as deductibles and copayments for Medicare enrollees who have incomes that are below specific federal guidelines regarding income and asset levels for classifying individuals as poor. The Omnibus Budget Reconciliation Act of 1993 continued this decade-long trend by subjecting 85% of Social Security benefits to taxation for individuals earning over $34,000 and couples earning over $44,000.

In short, a substantial trend of incremental changes has already moved us toward balancing age and economic status in old-age benefit programs. Despite the protests of the American Association for Retired Persons (AARP) and other old-age interest groups, these changes have been politically viable. Ironically, the one such change that was repealed, the progressive surtax for catastrophic coverage in the MCCA, was favored by AARP, and that organization unsuccessfully opposed its repeal.

This trend of introducing policies that are sensitive to economic status has already established a workable political framework for maintaining governmental benefits to those older persons who truly need help through public programs—in the near term—and in several decades when the baby boom cohort retires. And it has managed to do so without stigmatizing the policies that it has affected as "welfare programs." (See also HEALTH CARE SERVICES FOR THE ELDERLY, MEDICAID, MEDICARE, OLDER AMERICANS ACT, SOCIAL SECURITY, and WEALTH SPAN.)

References

Mendelson, Daniel N., and William B. Schwartz. 1993. "The Effects of Aging and Population Growth on Health Care Costs." *Health Affairs* 12: 119–25.

Peterson, Peter G. 1993. *Facing Up: How to Rescue the Economy from Crushing Debt and Restore the American Dream.* New York: Simon & Schuster.

Robertson, Ann. 1991. "The Politics of Alzheimer's Disease: A Case Study in Apocalyptic Demography." In *Critical Perspectives on Aging: The Political and Moral Economy of Growing Old,* ed. M. Minkler and C. L. Estes. Amityville, NY: Baywood, 135–50.

Schneider, Edward L., and Jack M. Guralnik. 1990. "The Aging of America: Impact on Health Care Costs." *Journal of the American Medical Association* 262: 2335–40.

Robert H. Binstock

OLDER AMERICANS ACT (OAA), a law enacted in 1965 to assist elderly Americans in living independently in their own communities by removing barriers to independent living and providing a continuum of care.

The services of the OAA, designed to promote the independence and dignity of persons aged 65 and older, include the National Older Americans Volunteer Program; the Nutrition Program for the Elderly; information and referral services on home health care services; Medicare*, Medicaid*, Social Security*, and Supplemental Security Income (SSI)* benefits; and transportation* services. The OAA is also a conduit for connecting older persons with home modifications financing*, housing* programs, and senior employment opportunities, and is the source of community education opportunities for older persons.

The OAA is the funding source for the nursing home ombudsman* program. Through this program, nursing home* residents are provided an advocate for the resolution of concerns about quality of services and conditions of nursing facilities. Similarly, the OAA funds services and programs that prevent elder abuse, neglect, and financial elder abuse*.

The Older Americans Act is administered on the national level through the Administration on Aging (AoA), one of the service agencies of the Department of Health and Human Services (HHS). The AoA is headed by the assistant secretary for aging, who addresses the concerns of the elderly across program and agency lines. The AoA is responsible for the administration of the act, for setting policy and program direction, and for assuring that OAA requirements are met at the regional, state, and local levels. The AoA provides funding for OAA services and programs in several states through an interstate funding formula that is based on the population of persons 60 years old or older in a given state.

Funds are distributed within states based on an intrastate funding formula that is reflected in the state plan for delivering OAA services. The intrastate funding formula is a critical aspect of delivering OAA services by determining the apportionment of OAA funds to various geographic areas. It is based on the number of persons 60 and older in the state, the distribution of persons in rural and urban areas, and special factors and weights for older persons who are frail, isolated, low-income, or members of minority groups.

The OAA requires states to designate a unit of state government to serve as the State Unit on Aging (SUA) for purposes of the administration of OAA services. States must also create Planning and Service Areas (PSAs) that serve as geographic groupings within states (depending on the size of the state) for planning and administering OAA services. Within PSAs, the SUA is to designate one or more Area Agencies on Aging (AAAs or Triple As). Area agencies on aging are responsible for the daily provision of OAA services either directly or by contract with a host of service providers.

State Units on Aging and Area Agencies on Aging serve as advocates, commenting on state, local, and national legislative and administrative proposals that affect the elderly. They create advisory councils that comment on state and area plans, with a particular emphasis on assuring that state and local policy developments and administrative actions promote the interests of the elderly.

State and Area Agencies on Aging face decreasing fiscal resources. In an effort to extend the reach of the services of the OAA, many states use state Medicaid funds, federal community block grant funds, federal funds for transportation services for the elderly, and state public assistance funds in conjunction with OAA funds. A state may, for example, use some of its transportation funds to extend OAA-funded transportation services (trips to day health centers, doctors visits, shopping, etc.), or some of its Medicaid funds to supplement its efforts to provide home health care services, community-based adult day health care, or respite care services.

In most instances, Area Agencies on Aging contract with other service providers for the delivery of services. An Area Agency on Aging may, for example, contract with a catering company to provide meals-on-wheels as part of the nutrition services it funds. Similarly, it may contract with a publicly funded legal services entity, a private attorney, or a law school clinic for the provision of legal services. The area agency on aging is also charged with assuring that the providers of services adhere to the requirements of the OAA. Information and referral services and assessments for Medicaid qualification or in-home supportive services are often done by Area Agency on Aging staff itself.

OAA community services or in-home services are usually initiated through a telephone call to an area agency on aging or senior services agency. The phone number of the local Area Agency on Aging can be found in the local telephone directory. The Eldercare Locator, a service of the AoA, is a national toll-free number available to help families and friends locate information on community services and organizations for older persons. Often a referral to an appropriate social services agency is sufficient. Sometimes, though, the Area Agency on Aging will want to send a social worker or intake worker to the caller's home to make an assessment of the social and supportive services that are needed.

The services of the OAA are available without regard to income, although income-related questions may be requested as part of an assessment to determine whether a potential OAA services recipient might qualify for Medicaid or public financial assistance such as state general relief funds or the federal Supplemental Security Income program. Similar questions might be asked in determining whether an older person might qualify for public housing or a related federally assisted housing program.

OAA services are available at no cost to the older person. The Nutrition Project of the Older Americans Act does invite voluntary contributions toward the cost of meals. Similarly, federal regulations implementing the OAA provide for creating opportunities for recipients of services to make voluntary contributions. The opportunity to contribute to services broader than the nutrition project is somewhat controversial, given that the OAA only addresses contributions to services (voluntary or otherwise) in the context of the nutrition project. Nutrition sites and other providers who suggest opportunities for contributions to the cost of services must assure that potential services users do not forego services (or feel pressured to contribute) because of a contributions provision.

The OAA does not provide specific financial services. It can, however, through the local Area Agency on Aging referral services, refer older persons to attorneys, planners, and public benefits counselors who are able to address financial and health care planning concerns. In many states, Area Agencies on Aging, often through their legal assistance provider networks, have lists of attorneys who will prepare wills*, durable powers of attorney*, and other planning documents on a reduced fee or pro bono basis.

Area Agencies on Aging can also put older persons in touch with other OAA services that have an impact on finances. These services include health insurance counseling, particularly Medicare Supplemental Insurance* (Medigap) counseling, and assistance in obtaining Medicaid (health care coverage for persons with low incomes) and Medicare. Buy-In for persons whose low income qualifies them for the Qualified Medicare Benefits (QMB) or the Specified Low-Income Medicare Beneficiary (SLMB) program. Area Agency on Aging resource persons can also refer older persons to organizations that provide assistance in obtaining Supplemental Security Income* assistance, food and nutrition services, and housing.

The AoA is responsible for the overall administration of the OAA, including the approval or disapproval of the intrastate funding formula. Approving or disapproving intrastate funding formulas is a new AoA monitoring and enforcement tool and should be an effective vehicle for assuring that OAA funds are directed to areas of the state that are in greatest social and economic need. In a uniform fashion, AoA is to collect data from each state on the types of services and programs provided and on program utilization. This information is submitted to Congress as part of AoA reporting on OAA activities. States, on the other hand, are to collect data through their Area Agencies on Aging on program utilization and expenditures. Data of this sort are useful tools for program monitoring and planning. Additionally, states are to assure that area agencies on aging have in place monitoring and enforcement mechanisms to assure program compliance. These mechanisms include data collection and on-site program visits. A key concern in monitoring and enforcement activities is to assure client confidentiality in all enforcement and review procedures.

Over the years, Congress has been concerned with assuring ethnic and minority participation in the services and programs of the OAA. This has led to a greater emphasis on targeting services to low-income minority persons and to exploring better coordination of the activities of area agencies on aging with programs that serve older Native Americans. In many instances, targeting activities have focused on how to extend assistance to more people as resources remain stagnant or decline. A related task has been one of identifying organizations and focal points among minority populations for targeting and outreach efforts. Critical issues are the location of services, access to transportation, the availability of written resources in languages other than English, and the availability of oral translation services or staff fluent in languages relevant to targeted communities. (See also ATTORNEYS, DURABLE POWER OF ATTORNEY, HOUSING, MEDICAID, MEDICARE, MEDICARE SUPPLEMENTAL INSURANCE, NURSING HOMES, NUTRITION PROGRAMS, SOCIAL SECURITY, SUPPLEMENTAL SECURITY INCOME, WILLS, and WORKING RETIREES.)

Organizations

American Association of Retired Persons
Eldercare Locator
National Caucus and Center on the Black Aged, Inc.
National Association of Area Agencies on Aging
National Citizens Coalition for Nursing Home Reform (Ombudsman Program)
National Hispanic Council on Aging
National Association of State Units on Aging
National Senior Citizens Law Center
American Bar Association, Commission on Legal Problems of the Elderly
Center for Social Gerontology (legal program development and guardianship)
Pension Rights Center
AARP/Legal Counsel for the Elderly
National Consumer Law Center
National Council on the Aging
National Council of Senior Citizens
National Indian Council on Aging
National Asian/Pacific Center on Aging

References

Atchley, Robert C. 1985. *Social Forces and Aging,* Fourth Edition. Belmont, CA: Wadsworth.
Estes, Carroll. 1979. *The Aging Enterprise.* San Francisco: Jossey-Bass.
Ficke, Susan Coombs. 1985. *An Orientation to the Older Americans Act.* Washington, DC: National Association of State Units on Aging.
Gelfand, Donald E. 1988. *The Aging Network: Programs and Services,* Third Edition. New York: Springer.
O'Shaughnessy, Carol. November 27, 1991. "Older Americans Act: 1991 Reauthorization and FY 1992 Budget Issues." *Congressional Research Service Order Code 1391002.* Washington, DC: Library of Congress.
General Accounting Office. 1994. *Older Americans Act: The National Eldercare Campaign: Report to the Chairman, Subcommittee on Human Resources, Committee on Education and Labor, House of Representatives.* Washington, DC: General Accounting Office.

Alfred J. Chiplin

OLDER WORKERS. See Age Discrimination in Employment Act (ADEA); Employment of Older Americans; Working Retirees.

OLDEST OLD, a construct used in gerontology, demography, and public policy to describe the population aged 85 and older. By the early 1980s, it had become clear that differences within the rapidly growing elderly population were so dramatic that it was no longer analytically or programmatically useful to treat "the elderly"–those aged 65 and older—as a single category. Those who have more recently passed into official old age, the so-called "young old," aged 65–74 years, and the "old," aged 75–84, are dissimilar to the more senior "oldest old." Condensing 25 or more years of remaining life into a single descriptor of "elderly" can only prejudice the documentation and understanding of emerging facts about old people in American society and their health and functioning, use of services, living arrangements, and financial security.

Those 85 and older are more likely than younger people to be women, to be afflicted with several chronic illnesses, and to experience significantly higher levels of disability. They are more likely to have outlived their social and familial supports, to live alone in the community, or to be housed in an institutional setting. They consume higher amounts of health and social services, and receive benefits and transfer payments out of proportion to their numbers in the population.

Even more unrecognized about the oldest old, however, is their heterogeneity in sociodemographic and health characteristics. All very old people are not alike; they are as different as their accumulated life experiences (Binstock 1992; Taeuber 1993). Nor is their decline into frailty, disability, dependency, and institutionalization inevitable and irreversible. The degree to which members of this cohort exhibit robustness and mental and physical plasticity will depend, of course, on their own unique endowment of social and biological attributes. But it will also be influenced—as will each subsequent birth cohort—by the shared experiences of the march through "its own slice of historical time" together (Suzman et al. 1992).

Demographic Portrait

Size and Growth. Between 1900 and 1990, the proportion of the population that is elderly has more than tripled. But this rapid rate of increase—comparable to that seen in other developed countries—masked an even more dramatic and unique shift in America's population structure. The older population is itself becoming older, and people even at age 85 can anticipate another six years of life. At ages 65–74 the population had doubled between 1900 and 1990; it had quadrupled at ages 75–84; and the number of oldest old had increased sixfold to just over three million. Nearly one million of this latter group reported their age as 90 or older. Historically, high fertility levels of the past and the prior immigration of children and young adults set upper limits to the number of persons who could survive to age 85. But the more recent "aging of the aged" reflects a new population dynamic: disproportionate improvements in survival at very old ages (Taeuber 1993), which is expected to continue well into the next century.

By the year 2010, according to the consistently conservative "middle series" estimates produced by the Census Bureau, the number of persons aged 85 and older is projected to double to about 6.1 million. Alternative projections to 2040, the approximate year in which the baby boom generation will be fully enrolled in the ranks of the oldest old, are even more expansive; the Census Bureau's "high series" projects 18 million oldest old. If significant behavioral risk factors for premature death (e.g., smoking, obesity, high blood pressure) were to be controlled among the cohorts now in their early middle years, the ranks of the oldest old could swell to over 41 million by 2040.

Average life expectancy at older ages will continue to increase differentially for men and women. By 1990, 65-year-old men could expect to live an additional 15 years and women almost 19 more years. Men who survived to age 85 had an additional life expectancy of five years; six years for women. The rate of gain in life expectancy for aged persons has been most dramatic since 1980. Greater numbers and percentages of the population will be beneficiaries of Medicare*, Social Security*, and private pensions over longer periods of time. Much of the industrialized world can anticipate comparable growth. Historical vital statistics for Sweden, for example, which are arguably the world's most complete and accurate, show that death rates have fallen substantially for octogenarians, nonagenarians, and even centenarians since the 1940s.

Sex Composition. The increasing "feminization" of the oldest old is perhaps the most striking demographic imbalance. At every age, mortality among men exceeds that of women; with advancing age, the differential becomes wider. In 1990, between ages 65 and 69, the ratio of men to women was four to five; at ages 85 and above it was two to five. Beyond age 95, the ratio of men falls nearly one-half. By 2050, under the middle series of Census Bureau projections, there will be 58 men per 100 women aged 85 and older, a considerable gain from the current 39 men per 100 women (Day 1992). Despite such relative change, however, the women will outnumber men at very old age by 4.7 million.

Among analysts and advocates, the well-being of the oldest old is justifiably characterized as a women's issue for reasons beyond sheer numbers. Women at this advanced age are more likely to be unmarried (90% compared with fewer than 50% of the men); widowhood* is almost twice as common a current status among women, and remarriage after divorce is an infrequent option for older women. At any age, the loss of a spouse can be traumatic; for very old women, the consequences, whether through widowhood or divorce*, are more extreme. This signal event is likely to mark the loss of considerable social support and household help in daily living, to trigger a sudden diminution of income and accumulated assets, and to accelerate the loss of independence. Few women in the current group of the oldest old had been in the labor force long enough, or at high enough levels of wages and salary, to have earned significant pension and retirement benefits in their own name. For many whose husbands had retired before the modest spousal protection of the Employee Retirement Income Security Act (ERISA)* had been enacted, subsequent widowhood often led to poverty. Future cohorts of women are likely to reach age 85 with more financial assets having been protected by the spousal impoverishment rules under Medicaid* that protect against the costs of a husband's terminal illness. Nevertheless, unlike younger-old married women, who are quite affluent by international standards, oldest-old women living alone in the community are likely to be very poor (Holtz-Eaton and Smeeding 1994).

Racial and Ethnic Diversity. Increasing racial and ethnic diversity also characterize the oldest-old population. Almost 9 persons in 10 above age 85 were identified as white in 1990, and a high percentage had immigrated from Western Europe in the earlier 1900s. Blacks constituted almost 8% of oldest old; Asians were just about 1%, and Hispanics (of any race, but mainly from Mexico and South and Central America) were about 3% of the total. But changing immigration and fertility patterns, along with selective gains in survival, all point to a markedly different composition of the oldest old in future decades. By 2025, according to Census "middle series" projections, the proportion of non-Hispanic whites will decline to about 76%, and will be almost entirely native-born. In thirty years, then, one-fourth of the oldest old will be members of racial and ethnic minorities.

The racial and ethnic composition of the oldest-old population may suggest differential needs for, and utilization of, public and private service programs. Precise determinations for very old ages, however, cannot be inferred from existing data on the still relatively small numbers of minorities; the data also lack a necessary historical perspective.

Indirect measures commonly associated with racial and ethnic differences, however, may indicate trends for the future. Education, for example, is almost universally accepted as positively correlated with social status and an ability to optimize personal use of preventive, treatment, and restorative services. Better-educated persons remain healthier longer, are less likely to be irreversibly disabled, and are more stable economically, even at age 85 and older. The substantial differences in educational level seen among the current oldest old are less pronounced among younger cohorts. The oldest old in 2010 will be considerably better educated: two-thirds of the whites will have completed high school, as will one-third of the blacks (a twofold increase in the next 15 years). Among Hispanics at all ages, however, wider educational gaps persist, especially at the elementary and high school levels. Asians exhibit the largest proportional and absolute gains: They will surpass whites in number of years of high school and college completed.

Geographic Distribution. Not surprisingly, the oldest old population is distributed across all sections of the country in concentrations approximate to those of the younger old. Immigration by sun-seeking retirees is not the major factor contributing to concentrations of the very old. Rather, it is the nonmigration of aging persons who, through choice or circumstance, remain in their communities and "age in place." Actual postretirement relocation occurs well before age 85, most often at ages 65–74; such migrants subsequently age in place.

Persons aged 85 and older are found in every city, but their distribution is characterized by significant clustering of racial and ethnic subgroups. The populations of Baltimore, Maryland, and San Francisco, California, for example, although of comparable size, and each exceeding the average among cities in percentage at very old age, are otherwise dissimilar. One-third of the oldest old in Baltimore are black; San Francisco has few very old blacks, but one-fourth of its oldest old are Asian. In fact, four cities (Honolulu, Los Angeles, San Francisco, and New York) contain 40% of the nation's oldest-old Asians. Hispanics are somewhat more dispersed.

Living Arrangements

Community. Despite considerable differences by age, sex, marital status, ethnicity, and region of the country, more than three-fourths of all persons age 85 and older live in the community. About two-thirds of those aged 90–94, and more than half of those 95 and older, continue living outside of nursing homes*. This relative independence is closely associated with higher income, greater physical robustness, good cognitive functioning, and, perhaps above all, presence of spousal or family supports. Among the oldest old living in the community in 1990, differences between men and women were most striking. Almost one-third of men, and over one-half of women, lived alone (most of them near family members); this represents a 10% increase since 1980. (Over the past several decades it has become less common at all ages to live with relatives.) One-half of men—and only one woman in 10, the rare nonwidow—lived with a spouse. Adult children remain the largest source of nonspousal housing. An apparent cultural bias against institutional care of elderly family members may account for the significantly higher rates of oldest-old Hispanics and Asians being cared for in the community.

Nursing Homes. Nursing home services have not been a central theme in public policy discussions since the repeal of the Medicare Catastrophic Coverage Act of 1988. Yet they are of ever-increasing importance in the lives of the oldest old and their families. In 1960, before the enactment of Medicaid*, which has since become the primary source of payment for this care, only 14% of persons 85 and older lived in a nursing home; by 1990 the proportion had grown to 25%. The oldest old were almost twenty times more likely to reside in nursing homes than were persons aged 65–74. At ages 95 and older, the proportion institutionalized doubled again. However, this seemingly explosive increase in the use of nursing homes by the oldest old masks a number of significant underlying changes. A greater increase occurred between 1980 and 1985. At that time, changes in availability and coverage of skilled nursing facilities, along with the initiation of a national program of earlier hospital discharges (''quicker and sicker,'' it was alleged), stimulated a demand for nursing home care. The pattern established in that period—more nursing home admissions of the oldest old for short-term posthospital care—persists today.

An absolute increase in the numbers surviving to oldest-old age—an age at which one's caregiving adult children are themselves young old or even old—will continue to exert upward pressure on nursing home use. At any given level of physical and mental functioning, however, institutionalization can be deferred, shortened, or even avoided if home- and community-based services are available to complement family supportive care (Manton et al. 1993).

Health and Functioning

Recent data from 13 countries of Western Europe, Japan, and the United States offer clear evidence that mortality, illness, and disability do not increase exponentially at very old ages (Kannisto et al. 1994). In fact, the pace of improvement in mortality has accelerated over the past four decades. Sweden's highly reliable historical vital statistics for the oldest old are illustrative. Death rates for 85-year-old Swedish women are today less than one-half their level in the early 1900s and less than two-thirds their 1950 level. Nevertheless, poor health and impaired functioning, and the likelihood of a terminal illness, are increasingly concentrated at very old ages. The associated increase in use of expensive medical care services prompts intense discussion among medical, economic, ethical, social, and legal experts about the appropriateness of such resource allocation. Systematic data to inform such inquiry are not readily available. (See also DIVORCE AND THE ELDERLY, ECONOMIC STATUS OF ELDERLY WOMEN, MARRIAGE AND THE ELDERLY, MEDICAID, MINORITY ELDERS, NURSING HOMES, PENSION FUND TRENDS, RETIREMENT MIGRATION, SOCIAL SECURITY, and WIDOWHOOD.)

References

Binstock, Robert H. 1992. "The Oldest Old and 'Intergenerational Equity.' " In *The Oldest Old,* ed. R. M. Suzman, D. P. Willis, and K. G. Manton. New York: Oxford University Press.

Day, Jennifer C. 1992. "Population Projections of the United States, by Age, Sex, Race, and Hispanic Origin: 1992 to 2050." *Current Population Reports,* Series P25–1092. Washington, DC: U.S. Bureau of the Census.

Holtz-Eaton, Douglas, and Timothy M. Smeeding. 1994. "Income, Wealth, and Intergenerational Economic Relations of the Aged." In *Demography of Aging,* ed. L. G. Martin and S. H. Preston. Washington, DC: National Academy Press.

Kannisto, V., J. Lauritsen, A. R. Thatcher, and J. W. Vaupel. 1994. "Reductions in Mortality at Advanced Ages." *Population Development Review* 20.

Manton, Kenneth G., Larry Corder, and Eric Stallard. 1993. "Changes in the Use of Personal Assistance and Special Equipment from 1982 to 1989: Results from the NLTCS." *Gerontologist* 11: 168–76.

Suzman, Richard M., David P. Willis, and Kenneth G. Manton, eds. 1992. *The Oldest Old.* New York: Oxford University Press.

Taeuber, Cynthia M. 1993. "Sixty-Five Plus in America." Current Population Reports, Special Study P23–178RV. Washington, DC: U.S. Bureau of the Census.

David P. Willis

OMBUDSMAN, a mechanism for resolving grievances and providing personal advocacy for individuals dealing with complex institutions. The concept of the ombudsman, and the name, date from the mid-nineteenth century. The idea was developed in Scandinavian countries in order to give citizens a means of cutting through bureaucratic red tape to resolve personal difficulties with the political and administrative system (Gwyn 1980). The function of an independent advocate proved effective as a means of intervening in governmental processes on behalf of individuals.

Background

The ombudsman concept provided citizens a chance to address difficulties that previously were hard to resolve because the proper authorities could not be approached or accessed. Governmental regulations may cause hardships when applied to a specific personal situation, but often there is no way to discuss or cope with the difficulty. The individual may not know where to begin. This kind of challenge is what gives the ombudsman function its unique effectiveness. The ombudsman is accessible, and independent, serving as an outside-the-system but knowledgeable figure, appointed to represent the interests of those subject to institutional regulation. Sometimes the ombudsman is created by the very institution with which it intercedes, but the ombudsman's position must have integrity and autonomy in order to achieve its purpose.

When the ombudsman was first created, it was an empowering idea in representative democracies where sheer numbers generated anonymity and powerlessness for the average citizen. In the 1950s, the idea became more widespread in the Western world, and ombudsmen served in a variety of positions in the Commonwealth nations, in France, and in the United States. Their function as intercessors was extended to many more situations: federal, state, and local governments; newspapers; hospitals; and industries. The adaptive power of the concept is further illustrated by the use that the U.S. military makes of the idea. The U.S. navy, for example, uses an active volunteer ombudsman program to represent the concerns of the families of its military members in the command structure (Howe 1988).

Ombudsmen go by a variety of names, from public relations representative (in a corporate context) or reader advocate (for newspapers) to patient representative or patient advocate (in hospitals). To qualify as an ombudsman position, its function must be independent and include advocacy, policy explanation, and grievance presentation on behalf of the individual user vis-à-vis the institution or system.

Long-Term Care Ombudsman Programs for the Elderly

The ombudsman concept has proven particularly useful to the institutionalized in nursing homes* and board and care homes*. The 1978 amendments to the Older Americans Act (OAA) authorized Long-Term Care (LTC) Ombudsman

Programs to resolve complaints by nursing home residents, inform residents of their legal rights, provide information on resident needs and concerns of the community, and advocate on behalf of residents for changes in laws and regulations to improve long-term care services. As defined by OAA, the ombudsman function includes complaint settlement and consumer advocacy as well. This means that the ombudsman complements, but does not duplicate, the contributions of regulatory agencies, families, community-based organizations, and providers (Institute of Medicine [IOM] 1995).

State agencies on aging were required to establish and operate either directly, through contract, or by other arrangement an Office of the State Ombudsman. Subsequent amendments have strengthened the role of the program, extending the reach of ombudsmen to residents of board and care facilities and other group residential homes. Functions now include public education and outreach, training and technical assistance, referral of unlicensed homes, and the coordination of services. The coordination between ombudsman services, legal assistance, and protection and advocacy programs has become particularly important. Federal law allows each state to design a reporting system to meet the needs of its various constituencies and to collect data relevant to their needs (Netting et al. 1992). Today the LTC Ombudsman Program operates in all 50 states, the District of Columbia, and Puerto Rico. Paid staff number about 865 and volunteer ombudsmen about 6,750 (IOM 1995).

In considering the record of ombudsman programs for the elderly, reports demonstrate great variation from state to state. Overall, access via the ombudsman program has improved, because representatives have found it easier to contact residents and the homes themselves, and to gain access to resident records. Access to administrative records maintained by facilities still constitutes a problem in many states (General Accounting Office 1992). As of 1990, the distribution of major complaints ranged from resident care matters (38.1%) to the administration of facilities (21.5%), resident rights (18.7%) and nutrition (14.4%) (Netting et al. 1992). A measure of success is documented by the research finding that the existence of ombudsman programs is often associated with better nursing care, whereas mere volunteer programs are not effective enough to have an impact on quality (Cherry 1993). Earlier, it had been found that nursing home ombudsmen called attention to aspects of quality of care that were not currently assured by other protective mechanisms.

Outlook

The ombudsman role could also be utilized to include advocacy and explanation of financial issues in a variety of other situations affecting the elderly. Since the size of the older population is growing rapidly and its specialized financial needs are increasing, the concept of a dedicated financial ombudsman for senior citizens is timely. While financial complaints constitute a relatively small part of the actions dealt with by nursing home ombudsmen, financial questions are of great concern for older persons living at home. The banking system, for instance, might utilize an ombudsman to explain policies, savings strategies, or money management to the elderly, and intercede/mediate with bank officials.

Ombudsman-type representation to serve the needs of the older population may be considered by the institutions themselves and/or advocated by those who are concerned about the often complex financial needs of the elderly. Geriatric social workers with financial experience have an ideal background for this advocacy function. Ombudsman positions could be set up at the community level with local financial institutions or financial planners who are knowledgeable regarding elderly issues on a consultative or as-needed basis. Local accountants, banking executives, and others who understand the community's financial institutions and services and have cross-cutting contacts could volunteer to work on an on-call basis as ombudsmen when seniors need advice, assistance, or advocacy.

At this time the ombudsman model remains a valuable advocacy mechanism with an impressive record, waiting to be activated more extensively on behalf of those who need intervention with complicated institutions, including those of the financial world. (See also BOARD AND CARE HOMES, OLDER AMERICANS ACT, and NURSING HOMES.)

Organizations

National Citizens Coalition for Nursing Home Reform
National Eldercare Institute on Elder Abuse and State Long-Term Care Ombudsman
    Services
National Society for Patient Representation

Suggested Reading

Hunt, Sara, and Sarah Burger. 1992. *Using Resident Assessment and Care Planning as Advocacy Tools: A Guide for Ombudsmen and Other Advocates.* Washington, DC: National Citizens' Coalition for Nursing Home Reform.

References

Cherry, Ralph L. 1993. "Community Presence and Nursing Home Quality of Care: The Ombudsman as a Complementary Role." *Journal of Health and Social Behavior* 34: 336–45.
General Accounting Office. 1992. *Older Americans Act: Access to and Utilization of the Ombudsman Program.* Washington, DC: GAO.
Gwyn, William B. 1980. "The Discovery of the Scandinavian Ombudsman in English-Speaking Countries." *Western European Politics* 3: 317–38.
Howe, Harriet M. 1988. *Navy Ombudsman Training Manual.* Washington, DC: Department of the Navy.
Institute of Medicine. 1995. *Real People, Real Problems: An Evaluation of the Long-Term Care Ombudsman Programs of the Older Americans Act.* Washington, DC: National Academy of Sciences.

Netting, F. Ellen, Ruth Nelson Paton, and Ruth Huber. 1992. "Long-Term Care Ombudsman Program: What Does the Complaint Reporting System Tell Us?" *Gerontologist* 32: 843–48.

Harriet Howe

P

PENSION FUND TRENDS, current developments in the U.S. occupational pension system and their implications for employee retirement incomes. Employee pension plans are a major source of income for many retirees. More than 43% of private-sector employees are included in a pension plan, as are 83% of public employees. In the aggregate, in 1990, private pension benefits comprised 31% of total retirement benefit payments (up from 16% in 1970), and public pension benefits had a 20% share. Social Security* payments amounted to 48% of the total. From the individual's perspective, pensions provided on average 18% of a retiree's income, Social Security 37%, and income from earnings and assets 43%. These averages indicate that substantial numbers of retirees have no occupational pension benefits (Employee Benefit Research Institute [EBRI] 1994a).

Among the major types of pension plans, defined contribution plans are increasing in popularity and will soon have more assets than defined benefit pension plans. Unfortunately, employees may not be contributing sufficiently to their contribution plans. It is also possible that overall pension benefits may be inadequate for future retirees to maintain their standards of living.

Defined Benefit Pension Plans

In a defined benefit pension plan, the employer promises employees specific benefits at retirement age. The benefit is determined by a formula that includes an average of salary from recent years, the number of years worked for the employer, and a multiplier. Logue (1991) finds that a common benefit formula is number of years of service × average salary over the final three years × .015. For example, a retiring employee with thirty years of service and an average salary of $35,000 over the last three years would receive an annual benefit of

$15,750. Benefit formulas are different for each employer, and are sometimes integrated with Social Security. Integrated plans consider Social Security payments as part of the pension benefit; benefits paid by the employer are reduced when Social Security benefits comprise a larger share of the defined replacement income. Total benefits may be lower in integrated plans, but the employer is providing a kind of insurance against Social Security shortfalls.

Employees accrue pension benefits annually but do not receive them until retirement. To account for this future liability, the plan sponsor contributes the present value of the future benefits to the pension fund. When the present value of all future benefits is equal to the assets in the pension fund, the plan is said to be fully funded. Plans that have insufficient assets to meet the future liability are called underfunded plans. The funding status of defined benefit plans is of major concern to participants.

The defined benefit pension plans offered in the private and public sectors are technically similar. But the nature of the sponsor differs, which leads to different forces affecting future benefit levels.

The Private Sector

Historically, the major risks for retirees with private pension plans were the possibility of the sponsor defaulting on its pension obligation and the financial failure of the sponsor itself. Congress mitigated this risk by enacting the Employee Retirement Income Security Act (ERISA)* in 1974. This law provided federal insurance for private defined benefit plans through a new quasi-federal agency, the Pension Benefit Guaranty Corporation (PBGC). The PBGC insures and oversees private defined benefit pension plans. This insurance guarantees retirement benefits to a predetermined maximum, but does not cover cost-of-living adjustments, health insurance, life insurance, early retirement, or other supplemental benefits. Many companies promise pension benefits above the maximum insured by the PBGC, but the excess amount may not be realized if the PBGC is given administrative control of the fund. The PBGC administers the defined benefit plan when companies terminate it, often to start a defined contribution plan.

Overall, defined benefit plans are well funded, with $1.3 trillion in assets to support $900 billion in benefit liabilities; approximately 85% of pension plans had assets equal to or exceeding 100% of liabilities in 1992. But significant pockets of underfunding exist within the system. The PBGC estimates that there exists $40 billion in underfunding within single-employer plans; they are 75% funded in the aggregate (EBRI 1994a). Since companies can terminate their defined benefit pension plan at any time, it is important to follow the funding status of private plans. Recently, the PBGC has released a list of the 50 companies with the largest underfunded pension liability. Total underfunded liability in all plans increased from $27 billion in 1987 to $53 billion in 1992 and $71 billion in 1993 (Older Americans Report 1994).

One simple method companies can use to reduce the required contribution to their pension fund is to assume high investment returns for their pension assets. The investment return is used to discount future liabilities to present cost. Aggressive investment return assumptions decrease the present cost of future benefits owed and reduce the contribution of the company. If pension fund assets are invested to meet overly high expectations, the portfolio of investments will need to seek a high degree of risk. This strategy leaves the pension plan and retirees in a potentially risky situation.

To secure greater protection, Congress passed the Retirement Protection Act in December 1994, which provides for a 15-year period during which companies must reduce their pension deficits. Part of the requirements under the law is to inform employees about the funding and PBGC guarantees (Older Americans Report 1994).

The Public Sector

An array of public defined benefit plans are sponsored by federal, state, and local governments. The rules and laws governing public plans are different in each state and are not regulated by ERISA. Because these are public plans, they are exposed to political risk. The defined benefit pension plans for the U.S. military, U.S. legislators, and other federal employees are "unfunded." These are "pay-as-you-go" systems in which money is raised as needed to pay current retirement benefits. Thus, no money is set aside to pay future retirement benefits.

Other public pension plans are established as funded systems. The underfunding of state and local pension plans is not severe on average, but a few are seriously underfunded. Wilshire Associates (1990) reported that four state teacher retirement plans and two state employee plans lacked sufficient assets to pay current retirees their promised benefits. It appears that public pension plans are subject to underfunding problems to the same extent as private plans. But a larger issue for participants is the political considerations government sponsors introduce into the administration of their pension plans. This influence has fostered political abuses of pension assets.

Political abuses come in the form of mandated investments with concessionary returns. Some state legislatures have required or encouraged their pension fund trustee to invest in projects designed to help the local economy. These "investments" are called Economically Targeted Investments (ETIs) because they are designed to support a specific geographical area, population, or sector of the economy. Historically, ETIs have earned low returns with high risk (Marr et al. 1993).

Defined Contribution Pension Plans

In the defined contribution plan, the size of the pension benefit depends directly on the amount of contributions by the employer and employee, and the investment performance of the pension assets. Some defined contribution plans take the form of salary reduction plans (401[k] plans, 457 plans, and 403[b] plans). In 1993 almost three-quarters of participants reported such a plan as primary. Almost one-half of all salary reduction plan participants reported also participating in a defined benefit retirement plan (EBRI 1994b).

The risks of funding a defined contribution pension plan are borne by the employee. Historically, the defined benefit plan has been the dominant plan offered by employers. However, the popularity of defined contribution plans experienced tremendous growth over the past 20 years. Chernoff (1993) reports the number of defined contribution plans nearly tripled, from 208,000 in 1975 to 599,000 in 1989. The number of defined benefit plans increased from 103,000 in 1975 to a peak of 175,000 in 1983, then declined to 132,000 in 1989. At the end of 1992, the assets in private defined benefit plans amounted to $1.57 trillion, while private defined contribution plans held $911 billion. The Employee Benefit Research Institute predicts that assets of contribution plans will surpass assets in benefit plans after 2003. The Department of Labor believes this could occur by 1997. Thus, it appears that defined contribution plans will be the dominant plan offered in the future.

Problems of funding status and political abuses do not occur in defined contribution plans. Contribution plans are 100% funded by definition, and the participants control the investment choices in their own plans.

Fink (1993) states that less than 30% of defined contribution assets are invested in stocks and bonds*. Compared with the professional money managers who control defined benefit assets and who place roughly 80% in stocks and bonds, the majority of defined contribution pension assets are invested in cash instruments such as Guaranteed Investment Contracts, Certificates of Deposit, and money-market funds. Since pension benefits at retirement age directly depend on the investment rate of return on the pension assets, most participants will find that their conservative investment strategy will provide inadequate retirement income.

One advantage the defined contribution plans have over defined benefit plans is portability. When an employee changes employers, the pension benefit from the first employer has often become tied up in a defined benefit plan. Frequent job changes could reduce total pension benefits by 20% compared with remaining with one employer. In comparison, the assets in a defined contribution plan can be "rolled over" into the new employer's plan or an Individual Retirement Account*, using an electronic transfer of the assets from one trustee to another, or a lump-sum distribution to the employee who deposits the assets into another plan. The assets can be invested in a portfolio similar to the first employer's plan, thus allowing the assets to grow at the same rate. Defined contribution plans enhance job mobility.

Yet the theoretical mobility advantage of defined contribution plans can become a disadvantage for many. Most workers who change employers or retire early and receive a lump-sum payment from their pension plan spend the money instead of rolling it over into another retirement savings plan. According to a report by the Employee Benefit Research Institute in 1988, only 13% of the workers who received a lump-sum distribution rolled at least some of it into another retirement savings plan. Pension distributions for workers who are under age 59½ are subject to income taxes and a 10% penalty unless rolled-over into another pension plan.

Why are employers more likely to offer defined contribution plans? One answer is the increasing cost of defined benefit plans. According to Chernoff (1993), the administrative costs for defined benefit plans have increased from $162 per participant in 1981 to $455 in 1991. Additionally, the insurance premium to the PBGC is now between $19 and $72 per participant, up from the original $1. These higher costs and more stringent tax laws have made defined benefit plans impractical for small and medium-sized companies. (See also BONDS, EQUITY SECURITIES, EMPLOYEE RETIREMENT INCOME SECURITY ACT, INDIVIDUAL RETIREMENT ACCOUNTS, PENSION FUND TRENDS, and SOCIAL SECURITY.)

References

Chernoff, Joel. 1993. "Defined Contribution Soaring." *Pensions & Investments* (February).

Employee Benefit Research Institute (EBRI). 1994a. *Pension Funding and Taxation: Implications for Tomorrow.* Washington, DC: EBRI.

Employee Benefit Research Institute. 1994b. *Salary Reduction Plans and Individual Saving for Retirement.* EBRI Issue Brief No. 155. Washington, DC: EBRI.

Fink, Ronald. 1993. "Sound and Fury." *Financial World* (July 20), 20–22.

Logue, Dennis E. 1991. *Managing Corporate Pension Plans.* New York: Harper Collins.

Marr, M. Wayne, John R. Nofsinger, and John L. Trimble. 1993. "Economically Targeted Investments: A New Threat to Private Pension Funds." *Journal of Applied Corporate Finance* (Summer), 91–95.

Older Americans Report. 1994. "President Signs Pension Reform." (December), 416.

Wilshire Associates Inc. 1990. *1990 Report on Funding Levels for State Retirement Systems.* Santa Monica, CA: Author.

John R. Nofsinger

PENSIONS. See Employee Stock Ownership Plans (ESOPs); Employee Retirement Income Security Act (ERISA); IRAs; Keogh Plans; Pension Fund Trends.

PERSONAL SERVICES. See Caregiving for the Elderly; Financial Counseling for the Elderly; Geriatric Care Managers; Gerontological Nurse Practitioners (GNPs); Home Care Services for the Elderly; Service Credit Programs; Social Workers, Gerontological.

PHARMACISTS, trained professionals who are licensed to dispense medication. Pharmacists must pass a rigorous examination given by a state board of pharmacy, and display their licenses in the pharmacies in which they work. Not everyone behind the counter or dispensing window at a pharmacy is a licensed pharmacist. "When in doubt, ask for a pharmacist," is a good rule to follow.

Pharmacists practice in diverse settings. They are researchers, teachers, and hospital pharmacists. They may work in traditional drug stores or in chain pharmacies where the department is one section of the business. Professional pharmacies located in buildings occupied by physicians' offices have dispensing counters but usually do not sell other merchandise. Clinic pharmacies in managed care settings (e.g., HMOs*) are similar to professional pharmacies, since they are often located close to patient waiting rooms of hospitals or clinics. They provide prescription service but essentially no other merchandise. Mail-order pharmacies, where contact is mainly by telephone, are growing rapidly. The professional requirements for the pharmacist are the same in all of these settings.

When selecting a pharmacy and pharmacist, a number of practical, professional, economic, and medical factors should be considered. While the cost of the medications is a major concern, it is not the only one. Practical concerns include factors such as the location and appearance of the pharmacy and the services the pharmacy offers. The pharmacy should be conveniently located to home, work, and/or the physician's office. It should provide safe parking and be convenient to public transportation if needed. Another practical consideration in choosing a pharmacy is whether home delivery is provided.

The facility should appear clean and orderly. A private place to speak to the pharmacist and seating should be provided. For those customers who work or rely on others for transportation, the business hours of the pharmacy are a concern. The method of payment that the pharmacy accepts (credit cards, store credit, direct billing for prescriptions covered by insurance) is an important factor. Pharmacies with computerized records may offer annual medication expense reports that can be used for tax and insurance purposes. Mail-order pharmacies should offer fast service. Other practical concerns may include whether the pharmacy offers child-proof caps, easy-to-open containers, and large-print labels.

Pharmacies should offer a number of professional services. Pharmacists should be accessible in person or by phone, in the case of mail-order pharmacies. It is important for elderly customers to develop a relationship with their pharmacist because of possible long-term problems with medications. Literature on each prescription drug and instructions on what to do if adverse effects occur should be provided. Pharmacists should be informed of all medications (prescription or over-the-counter) that customers are taking. Information recorded on the pharmacist's computer may alert them to potential drug interactions or allergies. Many pharmacies offer an emergency phone number and access to the computer after hours, which could prove lifesaving in emergency situations.

Economic factors worthy of consideration when choosing a pharmacy include the cost of medications, the services offered, and the availability of generic equivalents. Pharmacists should offer customers the choice of brand-name or generic medication, and the option of special ordering the generic equivalent. They should be available to discuss the economic concerns of the customer and offer advice regarding Medicare coverage and state-sponsored insurance programs for the elderly.

Advice on medical concerns regarding prescription drugs* is a primary service that pharmacists offer. Pharmacists can determine whether a drug side effect, interaction, or reaction requires changes or modifications in the consumption of the medications. They can also counsel customers regarding the effectiveness of over-the-counter drugs, potential harm and side effects of those drugs, and interactions that may result from other prescription medications. If customers have questions regarding expiration dates on old medications, sharing medications, storage and potency of medications, directions for use of a prescription, or the appropriateness of over-the-counter drugs, they should consult their pharmacist.

Many factors influence the effective use of medications in disease therapy, prevention, and health promotion. Pharmacists play an integral role in the education of the public regarding the practical, professional, economic, and medical factors that affect the use of prescription medications. (See also DRUGS AND THE ELDERLY.)

Organization
National Council on Patient Information and Education

Suggested Reading
National Council on Patient Information and Education. 1994. *Consumer's Guide to Prescription Medicine Use.* Washington, DC: Author.

References
Blumenthal, Dale. 1991. *Pharmacists Help Solve Medication Mysteries.* Rockville, MD: Department of Health and Human Services, Public Health Service, Food and Drug Administration, Office of Public Affairs.
Mason, Pamela. 1994. *Nutrition and Dietary Advice in the Pharmacy.* Boston: Blackwell.
Tindall, William N., Robert S. Beardsley, and Carole L. Kimberlin. 1994. *Communication Skills in Pharmacy Practice: A Practical Guide for Students and Practitioners.* Philadelphia, PA: Lea & Febiger.

Steven R. Moore

PHYSICIAN–ELDERLY PATIENT RELATIONSHIPS, the interpersonal expectations, interactions, experiences, and emotional reactions that patients over age 65 and physicians rely upon to understand each other's behavior and bring about the patient's present or future health care. The relationship may be long-term if the elderly patient has maintained the same physician for many years, or it may be short-term, especially if the patient is seeking a second opinion or specialized care for an acute problem. When the relationship has been a long-term arrangement, it encompasses the cumulative information and emotional feelings that elderly patients and their physicians have developed for each other.

Features of the Elderly Patient–Physician Relationship

The number of contacts by elderly patients with the health care system will increase dramatically in the future. Persons aged 65 and older average eight visits to a physician each year, compared to an average of five physician visits per year by the general population. The number of physician visits by persons aged 65–74 is expected to double between 1980 and 2040, while visits by persons aged 75 and older are expected to quadruple (Manton and Suzman 1992).

Health care needs of elderly patients typically differ from, and are potentially more complicated than, those of younger patients. Although elderly patients see physicians to resolve acute medical problems, visits frequently result from the need to manage chronic diseases, such as arthritis, diabetes, hypertension, Alzheimer's Disease, Parkinson's Disease, or cancer. Since elderly patients often have multiple chronic diseases, the focus of their relationship with their physicians is on how to balance or coordinate treatment plans for multiple medical problems.

Elderly patients are less likely to participate actively in making health care decisions. They have a lower desire for health-related information and control than other age groups and feel they have less of a right to challenge a physician's authority. Even though older patients typically have more health concerns than younger patients, they do not ask significantly more questions unless they are given sufficient time in a medical encounter (Beisecker and Beisecker 1990). Older patients tend to give more socially desirable responses and show more gratitude, and are more fearful of expressing complaints.

Older patients focus their agendas for the encounter (the problems they intend to raise) almost exclusively on medical instead of psychosocial problems. Rost and Frankel (1993), studying patients aged 60 and older, found that 27% of the problems patients intended to raise were never discussed during their medical visits, and over half of patients had at least one important problem that was never addressed. For 70% of encounters, the problem that was identified by the patient as most important was not the problem mentioned first to the physician.

While less likely to ask for information from physicians, older patients receive more information, more total communication, more questions about medication, more courtesy, and fewer comments indicating tension release than younger patients. As the amount of information given to the patient increases, the percentage of information recalled by the patient decreases. Patients may obtain more information from physicians by asking questions and expressing opinions. Patients who volunteer information adhere better to the medical regimen.

Elderly patients are more likely to be accompanied by companions who bring additional interests to the physician–elderly patient relationship. Family members are more frequently involved in the care of older persons, often initiating contact with the physician. These companions, usually spouses or adult children, interact with physicians and influence the encounter. When patients have illnesses that affect cognition, such as Alzheimer's Disease, doctors may interact more with family members than with the patient.

Elderly patients may receive insufficient time during individual visits with their physicians to address their medical needs. If either party is in a hurry, or senses that the other is rushed, they may refrain from asking questions or bringing up a topic. Elderly patients also may need more time to process and respond to information given them by physicians. Radecki et al. (1988) found that older patients had shorter encounters for repeat visits, whereas encounter length did not differ by age group for initial visits. As the number of visits for a particular problem increased, the length of each visit decreased. Since older persons often visit physicians for management of chronic conditions, their repeat visits are frequent. Even though each visit may be shorter than that of younger adults, older patients may interact with a physician for a longer time during the course of a year.

Research on patient satisfaction indicates that although older patients should experience unmet expectations as many of their chronic conditions cannot be cured, patients express a high level of satisfaction with medical encounters, and older patients are more satisfied than younger adults. Patient satisfaction with medical encounters is higher than physician satisfaction. Higher physician satisfaction has been associated with positive attitudes toward patients, positive assessment of the patient's health status, positive expectations of the benefits of health education, and higher patient educational level.

Demographic variables, situational factors, and aspects of the physician-patient interaction process have been related to patient satisfaction with medical encounters. Older white women and patients with lower educational levels exhibit the greatest satisfaction. Sicker patients tend to be less satisfied. When physicians ask biomedical questions or patients talk about biomedical topics, patients are less likely to be satisfied. Patients are also less likely to be satisfied when physicians dominate the interview and more satisfied when physicians perceive the relationship to be a partnership. Patients do not like physicians who dominate the conversation; however, they do not feel comfortable asserting themselves by asking questions and assuming responsibility for medical decisions. While older patients tend to be satisfied with a physician's behaviors, their family caregivers are far less satisfied. The older the patient, the less satisfied the caregiver is likely to be (Bertakis et al. 1991).

Financial Implications

Features of the elderly patient–physician relationship include several financial implications. Some address the costs of maintaining the relationship itself while others address the costs of medical care. The average cost of maintaining an elderly patient–physician relationship is greater than maintaining a relationship between a physician and a younger adult patient. This difference exists because elderly patients on the average see their physicians more frequently each year, and they typically present more severe and complex medical conditions.

Since the number of elderly patients is growing, the medical system must cope with anticipated cost increases. One possible way to control medical costs for elderly patients is for physicians to provide health risk appraisals and emphasize preventive services. Physicians can assist elderly patients in maintaining their health by discussing with them the health effects of their habits and behaviors. Such habits include tobacco and alcohol use, maintaining a proper diet, and exercise. Behaviors include driving and using seat belts. Manton and Suzman (1992) calculated a potential savings of $3 billion in use of home health services per year by 2020 if disease and disability declined as rapidly as mortality due to the introduction of effective health promotion programs.

The medical decisions that result from elderly patient–physician interactions potentially carry considerable and long-term financial implications, including costs of medical treatment, drugs*, and other therapies. They also can result from lifestyle decisions, such as choosing to move to a nursing home* or to receive home health care. Drug costs, currently not covered by Medicare, are frequently of concern to older patients. Many elderly patients are either unable or unwilling to fill all their medication prescriptions because of costs. During interactions with elderly patients, physicians can determine whether a patient can afford costly prescription medications. A frank discussion with patients regarding the cost of alternate medications may cause a physician to prescribe an alternative, cheaper regimen that allows for a better health outcome than would be possible if the patient neglected to fill a more expensive prescription.

Of particular importance are the financial implications associated with end-of-life decisions. A large share of elderly persons' medical expenditures are incurred in the last year or even months of their lives. An increasingly popular way for elderly patients and their decision makers to control these costs is by executing advance directives*—instructions to physicians about when to use or withhold extraordinary medical care.

The financial implications of medical decisions for elderly patients are complicated by elderly patients' reluctance to make medical decisions and by the potentially competing interests of patients' companions or third-party payors. As a result, final financial decision-making authority may rest with neither the patient nor the physician. Medicare*, for example, establishes the physician's reimbursement schedule. The growing importance of Medicare managed care may also affect financial decision authority. If the elderly patient has insurance coverage for long-term nursing home care, the policy terms can limit the patient's options. Even when elderly patients use personal assets to finance their health care choices, family members or legal guardians may intervene, thus leaving elderly patients feeling powerless over their own health care wishes.

Payment limitations to physicians by Medicare and other third party payors may restrict the time physicians spend with elderly patients. By promoting shorter visits, Medicare reimbursements decrease the likelihood that physicians will spend enough time with their elderly patients. One result of current Medicare payment restrictions may be the development of alternative care providers with whom elderly patients interact when receiving health care advice. One proposal is for elderly patients to interact more frequently with physician extenders (i.e., physician assistants or nurse practitioners) during routine visits. The assumption is that, in situations not requiring changes in medical treatments, the elderly patient's condition can be adequately monitored by less expensive medical personnel, with more time available for counseling and advice on health promotion.

Advances in technology, such as CAT scanners, magnetic resonance imagers (MRIs), and lithotripters, will affect costs of maintaining the physician–elderly patient relationship. Future technological advances such as telemedicine, a two-way interactive television transmitted over telephone lines, will enable patients to interact with specialists over long distances while retaining visual and verbal contact. This will allow patients who otherwise are unable or unwilling to travel to obtain comprehensive health care even in rural areas. The expansion of telemedicine will depend on the rapidly decreasing costs of establishing a telemedicine system locally and the ability of physicians to be adequately reimbursed for services delivered via a telemedicine system. Early studies indicate that patients are satisfied with their physician visits via telemedicine (Allen et al. 1992).

Both physicians and their older patients should recognize the financial implications of their interactions and the decisions made regarding a patient's treatment options. Only when the financial ramifications are understood by both parties can they make fully informed decisions. A strong physician–elderly patient relationship is based in part on the physician's knowledge of the patient's financial constraints and a patient's understanding of the costs required by a proposed treatment regimen. (See also ADVANCE DIRECTIVES, CAREGIVING FOR THE ELDERLY, DRUGS AND THE ELDERLY, EDUCATION OF OLDER AMERICANS, HEALTH AND LONGEVITY, MENTAL HEALTH AMONG THE ELDERLY, MEDICARE, and NURSING HOMES.)

Suggested Readings

National Consumers League. 1993. *Questions to Ask: Taking Charge of Your Health.* A Guide to Help Consumers Talk with Health Professionals. Washington, DC: Author.

National Institute on Aging. 1994. *Talking With Your Doctor: A Guide for Older People.* Bethesda, MD: National Institute on Aging.

References

Allen, Ace, Robert Cox, and Calvina Thomas. 1992. "Telemedicine in Kansas." *Kansas Medicine* 93: 323–25.

Beisecker, Analee E., and Thomas D. Beisecker. 1990. "Patient Information-Seeking Behaviors When Communicating with Doctors." *Medical Care* 28: 19–28.

Bertakis, Klea D., Debra Roter, and Samuel M. Putnam. 1991. "The Relationship of

Physician Medical Interview Style to Patient Satisfaction." *Journal of Family Practice* 32: 175–81.

Manton, Kenneth G., and R. Suzman. 1992. "Forecasting Health and Functioning in Aging Societies: Implications for Health Care and Staffing Needs." In *Aging, Health and Behavior,* ed. M. G. Ory, R. P. Abeles and P. D. Lipman. Newbury Park, CA: Sage, 327–57.

Radecki, Stephen, Robert Kane, David Solomon, Robert Mendenhall, and John Beck. 1988. "Do Physicians Spend Less Time with Older Patients?" *Journal of the American Geriatrics Society* 36: 713–18.

Rost, Kathryn, and Richard Frankel. 1993. "The Introduction of the Older Patient's Problems in the Medical Visit." *Journal of Aging and Health.* 5: 387–401.

Analee E. Beisecker and Thomas D. Beisecker

POSTRETIREMENT HEALTH INSURANCE (PRHI), health care coverage provided to retired workers and their dependents by the retirees' former employers. For retirees not yet eligible for Medicare*, postretirement health insurance is a primary source of health care coverage. Among persons aged 55–64, approximately one out of four (5.5 million persons) are retired, and nearly three-quarters (3.8 million) now receive retiree health insurance. For retirees on Medicare, typically those age 65 and older, postretirement health insurance is coverage that supplements Medicare insurance. For these persons, PRHI often helps cover beneficiary copayments not reimbursed under the federal program, and provides insurance for several categories of care not covered by Medicare.

Among retirees aged 55–59, 71% have employer-sponsored PRHI coverage; among those aged 60–64, 67% have such insurance. Among persons aged 65 and older who are also eligible for Medicare, 28% carry PRHI as a second source of health coverage. The Consolidated Omnibus Reconciliation Act (CO-BRA) of 1987 accounts for 5% of retiree health insurance coverage, which is limited to 18 months beyond the date an individual retires (Monheit and Schur 1989; Zedlewski 1993).

Scope—A Range of Changing Issues

1992 and Prior Years. In data gathered through 1992, a high percentage of workers expect to receive future retiree coverage because employers have promised this benefit. Two-thirds of all current employees in medium and large private firms and 77% of all current nonfederal public employees work for employers that provide health care coverage to retirees (Jensen and Morrisey 1992). For about 11% of current workers in private firms, the coverage is without employer contributions. The long-run trend has been one of stability—the rate at which this fringe benefit is provided has remained steady since at least the early 1980s (Bureau of Labor Statistics 1989, 1993).

As more workers retire with coverage and enroll in Medicare, the proportion of elderly covered by an employer-sponsored supplement would normally be expected to grow. Among persons most recently enrolled in Medicare (those aged 65–69), the rate of Medicare supplementation through retiree coverage is significantly higher (33%) than among the Medicare elderly in general (28%).

Survivor's benefits are uncommon for PRHI. Only three of every 10 recipients receive benefits that continue indefinitely for the individual's dependent survivors. Sometimes, survivor's benefits are provided for a limited period. Premium and benefit levels almost always are the same as for the retirees (Jensen and Morrisey 1992). Health Maintenance Organizations (HMOs)* retiree options are available to more than one-half of workers who are promised PRHI coverage.

PRHI benefits are generous, with provisions similar to active worker benefits, that is, retiree plans cover the same services and stipulate the same deductibles and copayments.

Post-1992 Issues. PRHI benefits were the subject of a major change in the U.S. Accounting and Reporting Rules that became effective in 1993. The new rules, created by issuance of Statement of Financial Accounting Standards No. 106, "Employers' Accounting for Postretirement Benefits Other Than Pensions," required that the future costs of all PRHI benefits be calculated and accrued in advance as annual charges to expense during the years that employees were working and earned those benefits (Financial Accounting Standards Board 1990). These new rules resulted in major changes to balance sheet expense— for some individual companies in the multibillions—and altered the financial profiles of companies with PRHI plans. As a result of the increased awareness and focus on the costs of PRHI programs, some companies have curtailed or eliminated such benefits since 1992, a development which, if continued, could have significant impact on retiring employees and their families.

Companies confronting the financial reporting issues and the costs of their retiree health benefit programs must also examine the legal environment surrounding PRHI decisions and policy changes. The ability of a company to change or terminate benefits for current retirees is an uncertain and complex area. Conflicting court decisions indicate that, at a minimum, a company must have expressly reserved the right to modify or terminate these benefits in order to do so (Dankner et al. 1989).

Coordination with Medicare

Benefit levels alone do not describe the actual value of retiree coverage to persons who are also covered by Medicare. How such plans coordinate with Medicare is equally important. Most often, employers use a "carve-out" method to determine their payments as "second-payers" after Medicare. Of retirees who receive PRHI benefits, 67% are in plans that use carve-out coordination with Medicare (Morrisey et al. 1990). When expenses are incurred, the firm assesses reimbursements due the retiree, based solely on the provisions in its plan. This amount is then reduced by what Medicare pays toward the expenses. For example, a retiree may have $600 in bills for physician office visits in one year that are considered reasonable under the Medicare definition. Medicare would pay 80% of the amount over $100 (its annual deductible), or $400. Suppose that the firm's plan has a $150 deductible, an 80/20 coinsurance arrangement, and uses carve-out coordination. In this case the firm would have a potential liability of $360 minus Medicare (80% of ($600 – $150)). However, subtracting the Medicare payment ($400) from this amount leaves an actual employer liability of $0. The retiree is left with a $200 bill, the same out-of-pocket liability under Medicare-only coverage.

Under the less common coordination-of-benefits (COB) method, which applies to 15% of all retirees with postretirement coverage, the firm again first calculates its payment minus Medicare, but then applies Medicare's payment to satisfy the retiree's copayments under the employer plan. Consider the earlier example of a $150 supplement deductible, 80/20 coinsurance, and $600 in physician bills. Medicare continues to pay $400. In the absence of Medicare, the firm would pay $360 once the insured's copayments of $240 were satisfied. The firm using COB treats Medicare's payment as available to meet this $240 enrollee copayment. Thus, the retiree would pay nothing out-of-pocket. The firm's liability, however, would be $200. Thus the COB method results in near-complete coverage for those services dually covered by Medicare and the supplement.

A third method, exclusion, is relatively rare. With exclusion, the firm applies its plan's deductible and coinsurance schedule to the expenses uncovered by Medicare. In the above example, the retiree has an out-of-pocket obligation of $200. After subtracting the firm's $150 deductible and then applying its 80% coinsurance, the employer plan pays $40. The exclusion method typically yields an employer liability between that implied by either the carve-out or COB methods.

Benefits

Benefits provided include coverage for hospital care, physician visits, and outpatient prescription drugs in most plans. Extended care facility (ECF) coverage is common in retiree plans and is usually more generous than Medicare. Prior hospital stay rules are absent from most plans and, where present, usually only one or two days are required. Special day limits often apply—usually 100 days per year or 60 days per illness or confinement. But this coverage is not a substitute for long-term care insurance since it excludes custodial care or intermediate nursing care.

Home health care benefits are a recent addition to retiree plans; about two-thirds of private plans have this coverage. Hospice benefits, also fairly new with employers, are available to roughly one-third of those with coverage.

For physician care, most retiree plans apply an annual deductible and coinsurance. Few have a deductible lower than Medicare's, however, and most have the same 20% copayment above the deductible. Thus, under the common carve-out coordination method, most dually covered beneficiaries face the full Medicare physician deductible.

A majority of plans limit retirees' out-of-pocket expenses by either capping them directly, or by limiting the claims on which coinsurance is paid. With the latter, when covered expenses reach a certain threshold, the plan covers additional care in full. Seventy-four percent of private sector retiree plans and 65% of public plans have one of these ''catastrophic coverage'' provisions. Among those with a ceiling on out-of-pocket outlays, about one-half have annual limits of $500 or less, and few have limits as high as $2,000.

Many PRHI plans also cover several important non-Medicare covered services, such as nonhospital prescription drug expenses, which are substantial for many of the elderly. Private duty nursing care, when ordered by a physician, is also covered for most retirees (at the rate of 98% and 93% in private and public plans, respectively). Among public plan retirees, about 30% have this expense fully paid. Chemical dependency coverage is also now routine in retiree plans. Coverage for visits with clinical psychologists, or for hearing care, dental work, or eye exams, is less common.

Summary

Postretirement health insurance is an important source of insurance protection for early retirees and persons on Medicare. Through 1992, the benefits were largely paid for by the employers who offered it, and coverage was often continued for the remaining life of the retiree. For persons on Medicare, PRHI acts as a supplement to Medicare benefits. Coverage under PRHI is generally more extensive than privately purchased Medicare supplemental insurance (Medigap policies). PRHI often covers expenses and areas left uninsured by Medicare, while Medigap policies focus on covering gaps in Medicare such as copayments and deductibles.

For persons on Medicare, the value of PRHI depends on the methods used to coordinate the dual coverage. Under carve-out coordination, the most common method used by employers, the extra benefits that PRHI coverage affords Medicare beneficiaries come in seven areas: (1) elimination of most hospital cost-sharing, (2) lower overall out-of-pocket expense limits, (3) more relaxed eligibility standards for ECF and home care benefits, (4) partial coverage for most Part B balance bills, (5) more generous prescription drug coverage, (6) chemical dependency treatment coverage for care in substance abuse facilities, and (7) occasional coverage for psychologists' services, physical exams, and routine eye, hearing, or dental care.

Post-1992 reports indicate that employers are modifying coverage, shifting costs to retirees by increases in premiums and cost sharing, and some employers are discontinuing benefits entirely. These trends are due to the expenses of retiree health insurance to employers from the issuance of the Financial Accounting Standards Board Statement 106 (GAO 1993). Employers are also offering retirees the option of enrolling in HMOs that contract with the Medicare program, thus shifting costs. Therefore, the depth of coverage of retiree health insurance described here may overstate the generosity of benefits available (Jensen and Morrisey 1992). Research on these recent modifications is greatly needed. (See also HEALTH CARE, HEALTH MAINTENANCE ORGANI-ZATIONS (HMOs), LONG-TERM CARE INSURANCE: PRIVATE, MEDICARE, and MEDICARE SUPPLEMENTAL INSURANCE.)

References

Bureau of Labor Statistics. 1989. *Employee Benefits in Medium and Large Firms, 1988.* BLS Bulletin #2336. Washington, DC: U.S. Government Printing Office.

Bureau of Labor Statistics. 1993. *Employee Benefits in Medium and Large Firms.* BLS Bulletin #2422. Washington, DC: U.S. Government Printing Office.

Dankner, Harold, Barbara S. Bald, Murray S. Akresh, John M. Bertko, and Jean M. Wodarczyk. 1989. "Retiree Health Benefits: Field Test of the FASB Proposal." *Financial Executives Research Foundation.* Morristown, NJ: FASB.

Financial Accounting Standards Board of the Financial Accounting Foundation. December 1990. *Statement of Financial Accounting Standards No. 106: Employers' Accounting for Postretirement Benefits Other Than Pensions.* Norwalk, CT: FASB.

General Accounting Office. 1993. *Retiree Health Plans: Health Benefits Not Secure under Employer-Based System.* Washington, DC: GAO.

Jensen, G., and M. Morrisey. 1992. "Employer-Sponsored Post-Retirement Health Benefits: Not Your Mother's Medigap Plan." *Gerontologist* 32: 693–703.

Swain, Lloyd B., John A. Osborne, Craig C. Lindsay, and Fred Tromans. 1994. "Don't Wait for Washington." *Financial Executives Institute.* (July/August), 17–24.

Morrisey, M., G. Jensen, and S. Henderlite. 1990. "Employer Sponsored Health Insurance for Retired Americans." *Health Affairs* 9: 57–73.

Monheit, A., and C. Schur. 1989. *Health Insurance Coverage of Retired Persons.* National Medical Care Expenditure Survey Research Findings 2. Rockville, MD: National Center for Health Services Research and Health Care Technology Assessment.

Zedlewski, S. 1993. "Retirees with Employment-Based Health Insurance." In U.S. Department of Labor, *Trends in Health Benefits.* Washington, DC: U.S. Government Printing Office, 147–85.

Gail A. Jensen

POVERTY. See Economic Hardship Measures in the Older Population; Economic Status of the Elderly; Economic Status of Elderly Women; Homelessness; Medicaid; Nutrition Programs; Supplemental Security Income (SSI).

POWER OF ATTORNEY. See Advance Directive; Agents and Brokers; Durable Power of Attorney; Living Will; Trusts; Wills.

PROBATE, a court procedure by which a will is determined to be valid and that involves the orderly distribution of assets in an estate by a probate court. When a person dies, many of his or her assets may go through probate. A probate court approves the appointment of the executor if there is a valid will, or assigns an administrator if the person dies intestate—without a valid will. If there is no valid will, then the administrator uses the "default will" written by the legislators of the state—the laws of intestacy.

The responsibilities of an administrator or executor include: (1) identification of the state of domicile if the deceased lived or held assets in more than one state; (2) hiring an attorney and other professionals as needed; (3) identification of all assets; (4) pricing of all assets at death (and six months later if necessary); (5) safeguarding all assets, including investments, real estate, and businesses; (6) collection of all income from assets and payment of all bills; and (7) filing all appropriate forms, including those for the probate court and the federal and state governments involved. The probate court verifies that all of the above concerns have been dealt with properly. This formal scrutiny and control of the distribution of assets in the estate via probate can be helpful, because it assures that the law is followed and the estate is distributed properly. Because of its complexity, probate can be expensive and time consuming. Settlement time is measured in months for small estates and in years for larger ones. Costs depend on the size of the estate and the complexity of the assets and the situation.

Not all assets go through probate. The assets that go through probate are those that are individually titled to the decedent. For example, any asset that is owned jointly "with right of survivorship" goes directly to the joint owner upon death, by operation of law. Assets with a beneficiary (IRAs, pension plans, annuities, and life insurance), or those owned by a trust, go directly to the beneficiary upon death. (See also ANNUITIES, ESTATE PLANNING, INDIVIDUAL RETIREMENT ACCOUNTS, LIFE INSURANCE, PENSION FUND TRENDS, SAVINGS ACCOUNT TRUSTS, TRUSTS, and WILLS.)

References

Foehner, Charlotte, and Carol Cozart. 1988. *The Widow's Handbook.* Golden, CO: Fulcrum, Inc.

Henry, Ed. 1995. "When the Executor Is You." *Kiplinger's Personal Finance Magazine* (February), 107–9.

Ostberg, Kay. 1990. *Probate: Settling an Estate: A Step-by-Step Guide.* New York: Random House.

Mark S. Fischer

R

RELIGIOUS GIVING BY ELDERS, giving practices of the elderly based on theological teachings of Judaism, Christianity, and Islam. Theocentric economic theory suggests that the giving practices of persons who identify with one of these monotheistic traditions will follow one of two distinct patterns outlined in scripture.

From an economic perspective, the earliest documents of Western theism may be examined as "economic contracts." When God called Abraham the founding patriarch of Judaism, Christianity, and Islam, He required him to make certain religious and ethical commitments in exchange for the promise of economic prosperity. Abraham agreed that he would acknowledge that God was the only god, that he and his descendants would worship God alone, and that they would obey all the commandments of God—many of which had specific economic implications. In return, God promised that He would use His omnipotent power over all economic variables in the world He had created, to assure that Abraham and all of his descendants, biological and religious, would experience economic security. According to scripture, God said to Abraham, "I will make of you a great nation, and I will bless you, and make your name great, so that you will be a blessing. I will bless those who bless you, and him who curses you, I will curse; and by you all the families of the earth will bless themselves" (Genesis 12:2–3). Abraham responded by building an alter, making sacrifices to God, and promising God that he and his descendants would serve God in every aspect of their lives. The economic conditions of this contract are clear. As long as Abraham and his descendants obeyed the commandments of God, He would guarantee their ultimate economic success. However, if they broke one of God's commandments in the pursuit of economic gain, their project would eventually fail. The terms of this agreement are restated throughout the sacred documents of Judaism, Christianity, and Islam, and continue to form the basis of economic instruction for all who identify themselves with one of these monotheistic traditions.

Given the fact that the scriptures, and subsequent religious instruction, are clear on this matter, one would expect religious persons in society, most of whom say they are monotheist, to abide by the terms of this theocentric economic theory. One would expect them to act on the conviction that one's economic success or failure is directly related to obedience or disobedience of God's commandments. Specifically, one would expect that the budget of every religious household would include a portion for charity. (Most Christians agree that this portion should be 10% of one's annual income; most Muslims agree that it should be 1–3% of one's total assets annually.) Of course, all religious people do not follow God's instructions in this matter. One might also expect religious elders to follow this "ordinary pattern of religious charity." Some do, while others, because of their economic and personal circumstances, may not. The scriptures contain stories that offer economic instruction to the poor, the displaced, the outcast, and the disaffected. These stories usually contain economic instruction that is relevant to the elderly.

To better understand theocentric economics in relationship to those who experience a loss or significant decrease of economic power—those who appear not to be blessed by God—other stories need to be consulted. The story of "the Widow of Zarephath," found in I Kings 17:8–24, is a good example. A prolonged drought has caused all crops to fail, and the widow of Zarephath has only enough meal and oil to prepare a cake for herself and her son. She goes to the edge of the city to gather wood to cook what she believes will be their final meal. There she meets Elijah, a prophet of God. The prophet asks her to draw water for him. This she does, because she is a believer in the God of Israel and honors God's prophet. Then Elijah tells her to feed him. When she explains that she has only enough meal for one small cake for herself and her starving son, the prophet insists that she prepare a cake first for him and then cook for her family. Without dispute, she follows the instruction of the prophet, and to her delight, there is not only enough meal for that day, but enough for every day as long as the drought continues. According to I Kings 17:16: "The jar of meal was not spent, neither did the cruse of oil fail, according to the word of the Lord, which he spoke by Elijah." Thus, by obeying the prophet of God and giving everything she had to the cause of God, the economic future of her family was secured.

Some contextual factors need to be clarified before the full economic implications of this story may be understood. Without knowledge of context, one might conclude that God had failed in His economic obligations to the widow. The context of the story makes it clear that the widow and her family are not suffering the consequences of their own sin; rather they, and all the people of Israel, are suffering because of the disobedience of King Ahab. Ahab, against the specific instructions of God, had formed alliances, political and economic, with some of the nations around Israel, and hence by implication, had made contracts with the gods of these nations. In response to this royal apostasy, God caused a drought to afflict Israel and her neighbors, and He sent His prophet, Elijah, to tell the King and the people that the drought would continue until the apostasy had ceased. In ancient times, and even today in the understanding of many theists, the activities of leaders determine God's judgments on a nation. The widow was experiencing desperate economic circumstances because of the King's actions.

Without full knowledge of the context of the story, one might also conclude that the prophet was unreasonably selfish when he demanded that he be fed before the widow and her son. However, the opposite was true. According to theocentric economics, the prophet was doing the widow a special favor, for by allowing her to serve him, he was enabling her to indirectly serve God. Under the direction of God, he was calling the people of God to religious (and economic) reform. According to the promises of God, those who responded to His call would be blessed; those who failed to respond to the call would be cursed. The widow and her son were the first to join with Elijah in this divine warfare. Hence the widow, in contrast to the infamous Jezebel, wife of Ahab and the other Sidonite woman in the story, secured for herself a place of honor in the history of her people and secured the continuation of her progeny forever. From the perspective of secular economic theory, the widow made an irrational and foolish decision, but from the perspective of theistic faith, she made a wise choice. It would not be surprising that some economically disadvantaged devout persons would take instruction from the widow's example.

In summary, two models for religious giving are prescribed by scripture. Those blessed by God financially believe these blessings are directly related to obedience to God in all things including charity. Some theists believe, or are expected to believe, that future success is contingent on continued obedience. In contrast, some who feel they are not receiving God's economic blessings may attribute their misfortune to the religious apostasy of the nation's leaders. These theists, however, are also obligated to give a portion of their (sometimes meager) resources to the cause of God. But, following the implications of scripture, these people would be more likely than the affluent to give their support to some "prophet of God" who is calling for a reform of national policy that would be in compliance with God's commandments.

If there is validity in these conclusions, it would be reasonable to assume that religious elderly persons would allow these models for religious giving. It would also be reasonable to expect that those who remain attached to their religious communities and who, either because they are cared for by their communities as the scripture requires, or because they have sufficient personal economic resources to meet their needs, would be content with their economic circumstances and would follow the ordinary pattern of giving. To most this would mean continuing to give a portion of their economic resources to charity. Further, religious elders who experience displacement or disaffection from their religious community, for whatever reason, and who feel they are being treated unjustly in economic matters, would follow the pattern of giving prescribed by the story of the widow of Zarephath. To many of these "separated elders," this instruction would lead them to give to ministries that are clearly and aggressively prophetic. In our society, these "prophets of God" are most likely to be found in extremist evangelical churches and in almost all popular "media ministries."

Data to test the theocentric theory of giving by elders are unavailable. Future research could attempt to demonstrate that most elderly people, especially those who remain in contact with a religious community, continue the same patterns of charitable giving as they practiced in middle age, and to show that a significant portion of our elderly population, especially those who experience some sort of disaffection with society, change these patterns and follow the economic instructions in the story of the widow.

In the search for relevant data, several churches and religious charitable organizations were consulted. None kept specific data by which giving patterns could be correlated with the age of the donor. Some media ministries keep giving statistics that are age correlated (as one would expect from the theory outlined above), but the records of media ministries are not open to researchers. So, while giving patterns of religious elders appear to be predictable in theory, it is unclear just what those patterns are. (See also ASSETS ALLOCATION AFTER RETIREMENT, CASH FLOW PLANNING FOR RETIREES, CHARITABLE CONTRIBUTIONS, ESTATE PLANNING, FINANCIAL ELDER ABUSE, and INHERITANCE.)

References

Peters, F. E. 1982. *Children of Abraham: Judaism, Christianity, Islam.* Princeton, NJ: Princeton University Press.

National Opinion Research Center (NORC). 1991. *Emerging Trends.* Princeton, NJ: Princeton Religious Research Center.

Roschen, John F. 1991. *Baby Boomers Face Midlife: Implications for the Faith Communities in the 1990s and Beyond.* Minneapolis, MN: Adult Faith Resources.

Seeber, E. 1992. *Spiritual Maturity in the Later Years.* New York: Haworth Press.

Fischer, Kathleen. 1985. *Winter Grace: Spirituality for the Later Years.* New York: Paulist Press.

John Collins

RETIREMENT, HISTORY OF, the relatively new withdrawal from the labor force, from a historical perspective. Economic historians have traced the history of retirement primarily by examining labor force participation rates of men. They generally assume that individuals who have left the labor force in early old age are retired. Historians have found that labor force participation rates were considerably higher in 1900 than they are today; the average retirement age at the turn of the century was almost 75 (see Table 1). Even among men in poor health, labor force participation rates were very high. Among Civil War veterans who were receiving small disability pensions in 1900, with an average age of

Table 1
Estimated Labor Force Participation Rates of Men, 65 and Older, 1860–1992

Year	Rate (%)
1860	78
1880	78
1900	65.4
1930	58.0
1950	47.0
1970	27
1992	16

about 60 years, the labor force participation rate was just a little lower than average. Fewer than one in six who were categorized as "very disabled" had retired (Costa 1993). The growth in the retirement rate can be attributed to the increased wealth that the elderly have at their disposal. Costa (1993) found that 60% of the increase in retirement could be attributed to the greater lifetime incomes and wealth in today's economy. The retirement rate has also increased due to the effects of modernization: The shift of production out of the home, and from agriculture to manufacturing, reduced the employment opportunities of the elderly. Proponents of the modernization theory argue that this change pushed the elderly out of the labor force and onto the "industrial scrap heap."

The period between 1880 and 1930 brought shifts in traditional agriculture and changes within the nonagricultural sector. Among them were new production processes that prohibited workers from laboring at their own pace, rapid technological change and shifts in the occupational mix that made skills obsolete, higher capital-to-labor ratios that raised the cost of using less efficient workers, the rationalization of big business and the scientific management movement that sought efficiency at every margin and created mandatory retirement schedules and policies against hiring workers over a certain age, and increased competition from the young and immigrants who were willing to adopt a relentless work pace. These changes may have worsened the employment prospects of older workers, as did declines in possibilities for self-employment.

However, critics warn that the modernization theory should not be pushed too far. Carole Haber and Brian Gratton (1994), for example, argue that mandatory retirement was adopted jointly with seniority plans (and sometimes pensions) that protected older workers, even as they made it more difficult for unemployed older men to find new jobs. Moen (1989) concluded: "for many occupational categories, the age and occupation distributions showed little change in the representation of older workers.''

Older workers may have continued to work longer a century ago because retirement was a more gradual process. In jobs that required substantial brawn, many retired ''on-the-job'' by switching to less physically intense occupations. A century ago, in many manual occupations, workers reached their maximum earnings between the ages of 30 and 40. The decline in the length of the work week in the early twentieth century also helped keep the elderly in the labor market.

A less visible, but potentially important, set of changes involved society's attitudes toward work and retirement. Many historians argue that the prevailing attitudes of a century ago discouraged retirement. They suggest that the work ethic of the period marginalized those who sought to retire. Contemporaries claimed that resistance to retirement was ingrained in the national character. As Dahlin (1982) notes, ''men who were still able to work were expected to do so. Retirement for leisure's sake . . . was frowned upon.'' However, Costa (1993) estimates that the elderly of a century ago were more likely than today's elderly to retire when faced with an increase in retirement income, and cautioned that the changing rhetoric about retirement may not match the reality.

An additional concern is changing attitudes about the abilities of the elderly. According to cultural historians, attitudes toward the elderly worsened between the Civil War and the Great Depression. In or out of work, the elderly may have increasingly been viewed as peripheral, less capable members of society. However, these attitudinal shifts are difficult to document systematically. Indeed, Range and Vinovskis (1981) found little change in the images of the elderly in a content analysis of popular magazines.

Finally, there is the role of government in fostering the increase in retirement rates. The United States was later than most of the Western European nations in instituting a state-sponsored old age pension system when the Social Security Act was adopted in 1935. In its early years, Social Security's welfare component, Old Age Assistance (OAA), dominated the Old Age Insurance (OAI) component. Disability Insurance was added to the package in 1956. As the decades have progressed the fraction of the elderly population receiving Social Security benefits and the generosity of these benefits have increased. In 1950, only 37% of the population 65 years and older received Social Security benefits; by 1960, this rose to 72%, and by 1970 to 90%, as coverage was extended to groups initially excluded, including farmers, domestics, and the self-employed. Meanwhile, the inflation-adjusted average monthly benefits of a retired worker more than doubled between 1950 and 1975.

Up until a decade ago most observers thought that the development of Social Security was the critical force in explaining trends in retirement. But studies of the post-1930 period emphasize that, while Social Security has played a role in influencing retirement, it has been ''modest.'' Leonesio (1993) summarizes recent research by saying that, while ''the social security system has contributed to the popularity of retirement at ages 62 and 65, [it] appears to be a minor force in the long post-World War II trend to retire at earlier ages." Others give more credit to the role of Social Security. Parsons (1991) estimates that the expansion of OAA was responsible for half of the increase in retirement among men 65 and older between 1930 and 1950. Social Security has expanded concurrently with the rise in the wealth of the elderly, the rise of private-sector pensions, changes in the work environment, improvements in the health of the elderly, and the growth of mass entertainment and mass tourism. While the development of Social Security was important in spurring retirement, these other factors explain why it was not the watershed event earlier observers thought.

While the forces behind the adoption of Social Security are manifold and complex, most historians argue that Social Security was ultimately enacted because of society's persistent desire for security. Since the turn of the century, reformers began a campaign to solve the "problem of old age." They echoed and amplified the fear that old age would inevitably mean dependency, poverty, and worst of all, a trip to the poor house. Interestingly, much of the reformers' rhetoric (and perhaps public perception) was out of touch with economic reality. For example, Haber and Gratton (1994), have documented that, despite the misrepresentations of reformers, the proportion of the elderly in the poorhouse remained constant at about 2% throughout the late nineteenth and early twentieth centuries. Families adopted many strategies to avoid old age poverty during this era, including saving, insurance, pensions, working, and relying on the wages of children. However, the Great Depression changed everything. With it the savings and wealth of many elderly people evaporated, and unemployment among the elderly became a serious problem. Without the Great Depression, the country might never have adopted Social Security.

Social Security was designed to solve poverty and dependency by transferring wealth to the elderly and to combat unemployment among the young by luring the old out of the labor market (Graebner 1980). Its goal was to induce retirement. Initially, there was a limit of only $15 per month that retirees could earn in the labor market. If they earned more, they lost their Social Security benefits. The "retirement test," a legacy of the Great Depression, is still with us today. Postwar circumstances influenced the steady expansion of Social Security (Achenbaum 1986). Because of the low initial ratio between Social Security's beneficiaries and the number of taxpayers, large surpluses were generated by the system's pay-as-you-go financing scheme. This, plus the era's robust economic growth, allowed expanding the system without needing to raise taxes immediately.

At the same time that Social Security was conceived, established, and expanded, private pensions grew tremendously. The nation's first company pension was adopted by the American Express Company in 1875. It has been estimated that by 1913 about 9% of the nonfarm labor force was covered by a pension (Craig and Trawick 1993). This grew to nearly 14% in 1929, but collapsed to

4% during the Great Depression, before rebounding to 25% in 1950. By 1979, 60% of workers were included in a pension plan.

Companies originally supplied pensions to help cut down on costly labor turnover, to thwart unionization by rewarding loyal workers, and to ensure that older workers were not kept in jobs where they were overpaid. Since pensions attracted more stable workers and reduced turnover, they also encouraged more training on the job. Recent regulations that require pension vesting after shorter periods thus undermine the original intent of companies to cut turnover by using pensions.

Before employer-based pensions became widespread, many workers purchased annuities*, called tontines, directly from insurance companies. "However, in 1906, after a public scandal of alleged mismanagement and impropriety in the insurance industry and an extensive investigation which exposed abuses in the handling of tontine insurance funds, the State of New York prohibited any further issue of tontine insurance. Other states quickly followed suit and the individually-purchased pension disappeared" (Ransom et al. 1993). Company pensions arose to fill this void. The use of pensions was also accelerated by the federal government's creation of tax breaks for pensions, beginning in 1938 (Craig and Trawick 1993). Thus, workers who desired to save for retirement found that their best option was a company pension. (See also ANNUITIES, BUSINESS SUCCESSION PLANNING, ECONOMIC STATUS OF THE ELDERLY, ECONOMIC STATUS OF ELDERLY WOMEN, PENSION FUND TRENDS, SOCIAL SECURITY, VOLUNTEERING, and VOLUNTEERS, OLDER.)

References

Achenbaum, W. Andrew. 1986. *Social Security: Visions and Revisions.* New York: Cambridge University Press.

Costa, Dora. 1993. "Health, Income, and Retirement: Evidence from Nineteenth Century America." Working Paper No. 4537. Cambridge, MA: National Bureau of Economic Research.

Craig, Lee, and Michelle W. Trawick. 1993. "Federal Regulation and the Growth of Private-Sector Pensions, 1913–1950." Paper presented at the Gerontological Society of America Annual Meeting, New Orleans.

Dahlin, Michel. 1982. *From Poorhouse to Pension: The Changing View of Old Age in America, 1890–1929.* Ph.D. Dissertation, Stanford University.

Graebner, William. 1980. *A History of Retirement: The Meaning and Function of an American Institution, 1885–1978.* New Haven, CT: Yale University Press.

Haber, Carole, and Brian Gratton. 1994. *Old Age and the Search for Security: An American Social History.* Bloomington: Indiana University Press.

Leonesio, Michael. 1993. "Social Security and Older Workers." In *As the Workforce Ages: Costs, Benefits, and Policy Challenges,* ed. Olivia Mitchell. Ithaca, NY: ILR Press.

Moen, Jon. 1988. "From Gainful Employment to Labor Force: Definitions and a New Estimate of Work Rates of American Males, 1860–1980." *Historical Methods* 21: 149–59.

Moen, Jon. 1989. "The Disappearance of American Men from Different Occupations: 1860 to 1980." Paper presented at the Social Science History Association Meeting, Washington, DC.

Parsons, Donald. 1991. "Male Retirement Behavior, 1930–1950." *Journal of Economic History* 51: 657–74.

Range, Jane, and Maris Vinovskis. 1981. "Images of Elderly in Popular Magazines: A Content Analysis of Littell's Living Age, 1845–1882." *Social Science History* 5: 123–69.

Ransom, Roger, Richard Sutch, and Samuel Williamson. 1993. "Inventing Pensions: The Origins of the Company-Provided Pension in the United States, 1900–1940." In *Societal Impact on Aging: Historical Perspectives,* ed. K. Warner Schaie and W. Andrew Achenbaum. New York: Springer.

Robert Whaples

RETIREMENT MIGRATION, change of residence to new geographic locations offering more attractive living environments for older Americans. Geographic locations that attract retirees generally develop in areas with high-level tourism. Towns, counties, and states in the Sunbelt and the Northwest welcome and are beginning to recruit older interstate migrants. Rural communities that are favorably located are in a position to attract retirees as effective strategies for economic development. Some governmental units finance the marketing of their communities and provide technical assistance to their retiree attraction committees.

Older migrants in the United States have steady incomes not vulnerable to the normal down cycles in the national economy. Although income derived from interest or stocks can fluctuate with business cycles, government transfers and pension benefits are relatively stable. One-fourth of the income for the elderly in metro and nonmetro areas is produced by assets (Hoppe 1991). Most of this asset income comes from interest, with the largest source of interest coming from banks, savings and loan associations, and credit unions that are insured by federal agencies. Older migrants tend to have sizable amounts of discretionary income to spend locally, which leads to economic development and job creation in the community of relocation. They also have better health, better education, and earlier retirements than retirees who are aging in place.

Only about 5% of the retirement-age population move across state lines in any five-year period, but the advantages gained from recruiting retirees are many. They include increases in the tax base, no large investments in the infrastructure or tax abatements by governments, the addition of residents who are unlikely to pollute or destroy the environment, a growth in the number of volunteers and contributors in local philanthropic and service organizations, and benefits to churches. Since jobs tend to follow people with money to spend, retirement income can lead to job growth in the same way that industrial payrolls generate jobs. Although many of the jobs created are low-paying service jobs, there are also opportunities created for higher-income professionals.

A study by the Federal Reserve Bank of Kansas City found that rural counties whose incomes are based on retirees have out-paced all others in per capita income growth. Counties designated as retirement sites witnessed the largest increase in personal income and employment among all nonmetro counties, although it should be noted that per capita income in nonmetro retirement counties is still below average for all nonmetro counties (Glasgow and Reeder 1990; Reeder and Glasgow 1990).

Older migrants add to the existing mature market, increasing the importance of this market segment. The consumption potential of older households is seen in their incomes and in their accumulated assets, a resource that can be drawn on for large purchases. The balances in their savings accounts are also larger than average households, and their homes are worth 20% more than the U.S. average (Menchin 1989). Consumption studies have shown that older consumers purchase houses and other durable goods, as well as nondurable goods and services, including food, travel*, recreation, entertainment, and medical care.

Longino and Crown (1990) examined the 1979 incomes of all people aged 60 or older who reported in 1980 that they lived in a different state in 1975, using 1980 census microdata. These data do not include information on assets or on the multiplier effect of the income transfers into each state. In this examination, Florida topped the list of states benefiting from retirement migration, according to these estimates. It had a net gain of over $3 billion annually. Nine other states—Arizona, Texas, North Carolina, Arkansas, Oregon, South Carolina, Nevada, Georgia, and Washington—posted net gains of $100 million or more annually from their elderly migrants. These estimates further suggest that most of the states in the South and West benefited economically from retirement migration. The annual income transfer between states due to retirement migration can be substantial.

State-level analyses, however, cloak the major economic impact of older migrants on local communities. Convincing evidence of local economic impact has been turned up by several investigators. Guntersville, in the mountain lakes region of Alabama, for example, has a large river reservoir along with other recreational amenities appropriate for retirees. Fagan's (1990) data on 185 older in-migrants into this community suggest that these migrants had a positive influence on the local economy. Sometimes strong migration streams connect two specific locations. Such is the case with a stream of retired migrants from the Panama Canal Zone to Dothan, located in the southeastern corner of Alabama. Eighty-four retired households, all members of the Dothan Panama Canal Society, were surveyed in 1991 to estimate their local economic impact. The data suggest that current economic impact underestimates total or eventual impact because in-migrant retirees may encourage friends to follow them, thereby extending the economic benefits from retirees over time.

The Appalachian Regional Commission funded a study of retirees who had moved into western North Carolina. In this telephone survey of 814 retirees in 1989, which represents one of the most thorough surveys of in-migrants, Haas and Serow (1990) found that over three-quarters settled in nonmetro counties;

the average household bank deposits were over $40,000; the average investment portfolios were nearly $200,000; and reported mean home values were $108,000. The 630 households who kept spending records showed that they had collectively spent an annualized $22.6 million, not counting houses and cars, with a multiplier effect totaling $45 million annually. The researchers estimated that these retirees had the following measurable impacts on the economy: the creation of 943 jobs with an average annual salary of nearly $15,000; substantial local revenues in property and sales tax; and state revenues in income tax, intangible tax, and sales tax. Further, 77% of the retirees volunteered an average of 7.4 hours a week of community service, and 55% held positions of leadership in community churches and organizations. Over two-fifths (41%) had an opportunity to vote on a school bond issue and 82% supported the increase. From the perspective of direct public-sector receipts and expenditures, the retirees demonstrated that they were self-supportive through the indirect economic effects of their consumption expenditures. Migrant retirees represent an addition to the fiscal status of local governments.

Home ownership for migrant retirees can also have an impact on their newly chosen communities. Eighty percent of persons in the mature market own their homes, and 80% of those are mortgage-free. When retirees come into a community, most immediately purchase a home. They then invest the proceeds from their house sale at their last community into the host community's financial institutions.

Attracting retirees is a low-risk strategy for communities. Even if few retirees relocate to a community, promoting the community should increase curiosity and tourism, and enhance its image. Also, community promotion creates quality of life features that industrialists considering plant relocation may find attractive (Glasgow 1990). Green and Schneider (1989) estimate, however, that it takes 3.7 factory jobs to equal the same economic impact on a community of one new retiree household. (See also HEALTH AND LONGEVITY, HOUSING, LEISURE, TRAVEL, and VACATION HOMES AND RECREATIONAL PROPERTY.)

References

Fagan, Mark. 1990. "Economic Impact of Retirees on a Community." *Social Science Perspectives* 4(3): 72–81.

Glasgow, Nina. 1990. "Attracting Retirees as a Community Development Option." *Journal of the Community Development Society* 21: 102–14.

Glasgow, Nina, and Richard J. Reeder. 1990. "Economic and Fiscal Implications of Non-Metropolitan Retirement Migration." *Journal of Applied Gerontology* 9: 433–51.

Green, B., and M. Schneider. 1989. "Manufacturing or Retirement: A Comparison of the Direct Economic Effects of Two Growth Options." Unpublished paper, University of Arkansas.

Haas, William H., III, and William J. Serow. 1990. *The Influence of Retirement In-*

Migration on Local Economic Development. Unpublished Final Report to the Appalachian Regional Commission.

Hoppe, R. 1991. "The Elderly Income and Rural Development: Some Cautions." *Rural Development Perspectives* 7: 27–32.

Longino, Charles F., Jr., and William H. Crown. 1990. "Retirement Migration and Interstate Income Transfers." *Gerontologist* 30: 784–89.

Menchin, R. 1989. *The Mature Market.* Chicago: Probus Publishing.

Reeder, Richard J., and Nina Glasgow. 1990. "Nonmetro Retirement Counties' Strengths and Weaknesses." *Rural Development Perspectives* 6: 12–18.

Charles F. Longino, Jr. and Mark Fagan

RETIREMENT PLANNING. See Cash Flow Planning for Retirees; Continuing Care Retirement Communities (CCRCs); Estate Planning; Financial Counseling; Financial Advisors; Wealth Span.

REVERSE MORTGAGES, a method used to convert the equity value of a home into a series of nontaxable income receipts. The home is used to secure a series of payments a lender makes to a borrower (homeowner) during a period of time the home is occupied by the borrower. At a future date, the accumulated indebtedness is paid off, usually upon surrender of occupancy, and usually out of proceeds derived from sale of the home. Reverse mortgages are a family of loan types that vary by the form of the stream of receipts and by the timing of repayment. Their common characteristic is use of the equity value of the home to secure a stream of income on a repetitive basis.

Seniors who want to remain in their homes are the primary users of reverse mortgages. Their objectives are normally to supplement other income sources during retirement or to meet large cash requirements caused by events such as a major home repair or an unexpected illness. The potential need is sizeable (Trent 1994). While most older Americans own their homes and have paid off their mortgage debt, a significant percentage are cash poor. Homes occupied by older Americans had a median value of $70,418 in 1991, even as this group had a median income of only $18,375, and 2.1 million of this group (13.5% of elder homeowners) had incomes below the poverty line (Grall 1993).

Knowledge of the forms of reverse mortgages, their primary characteristics, and lenders who make these loans enables retirees and their financial advisors to investigate a potential income source that may provide incremental income to preserve financial independence and/or enhance quality of life in retirement. Such knowledge is also useful to attorneys who advise elderly clients about the legal implications of financial encumbrance relative to the benefits expected from the series of cash receipts.

Characteristics of Reverse Mortgages

All reverse mortgages entail a build-up of debt, which is the sum of the periodic principal amounts borrowed and accumulated interest. Since no payments are made to reduce indebtedness during the life of the mortgage, interest accrues on interest and increasing principal, which means the amount owed will increase at an increasing rate through time. A practical consequence is that reverse mortgages tend to generate small cash flows if the collateral value of the home is not large and/or if the borrower expects to reside in the home for more than a few years. Reverse mortgages are best suited to elderly borrowers who live in homes with adequate equity values and who expect to reside in their home for several years. A reverse mortgage is thus best suited to a retiree who may be characterized as "house rich" (in terms of market value) and "cash poor" (in terms of other income sources), and who does not expect to need the cash receipts for a long period. In areas of the country where housing prices have risen significantly, some homes with sizeable market values are owned by retired persons with low incomes.

Types of Reverse Mortgages and Their Attributes

Several reverse mortgage types are available to meet various forms of cash needs. Most common are annuity types that pay a fixed monthly amount to supplement other income sources. A term annuity reverse mortgage is the most direct form and pays a fixed monthly amount for a fixed number of years. The loan balance must be paid in full at the end of the term. If this requires selling and vacating the home prior to the time when the home would be vacated due to death or moving to a care facility, this form of loan arrangement is unsuitable. The borrower could hedge against this possibility by deciding on a longer loan term, but the longer term will create lower monthly cash receipts. One solution to this problem is the split-term reverse mortgage, where borrowers receive a fixed cash receipt for a fixed period, but are not required to repay the loan until they decide to vacate or sell the home. For most borrowers, a superior alternative to the term loan is a tenure reverse mortgage wherein the home owner receives a fixed monthly income for as long as the home is occupied. It is not possible to outlive the payment stream. Of course, the size of the receipts will be smaller than with a straight-term loan, since the lender must hedge against the possibility that the borrower will occupy the home longer than actuarially expected. Even so, the borrower has the security of knowing that he or she controls the decision of when to vacate, and that the income stream will continue until that time.

A shared appreciation reverse mortgage is intended to boost the monthly cash receipt by granting the lender all or part of any appreciation in the value of the home that may occur after the date of the market value appraisal used in the origination of the loan. This form of loan is not generally available, because lenders have not been willing to extend larger payments on the possibility that housing values will increase. When home prices are expected to increase, however, these loans are sometimes available and may be attractive to some borrowers.

Potential borrowers may not need a supplemental income annuity. Some homeowners may need a single large amount, some may occasionally need to receive irregular amounts for specific purposes, and some may wish to receive various amounts for unrestricted use at their discretion.

A deferred payment loan is designed to provide one large amount to meet a major need, with the expectation that the loan will not be paid off for many years.

A property tax deferral loan is intended to assist older homeowners on limited incomes by enabling a periodic draw against the equity value of the home to pay property taxes. Note that the use of funds is restricted to a single purpose.

The most flexible alternative to annuity loans is the line-of-credit mortgage, because the purpose for borrowing is unrestricted. The senior homeowner may borrow at irregular intervals for purposes such as property tax payments, home repairs, medical bills, travel expenses, and such. Of course, this form of loan should not be used as a source of income to meet regularly recurring living expenses (Higgins 1994).

Cautions

Reverse mortgages deplete the borrower's stock of housing wealth, so the first consideration is whether it is necessary to become a debtor again. Reverse mortgages are self-supporting financing programs, not government assistance programs. Low-income homeowners should first examine their eligibility for other government assistance programs, to preserve their home equity, and because the income stream generated by a reverse mortgage may make them ineligible for income-tested assistance programs. Second, if sizeable medical expenses or other costs are anticipated, it may be preferable to preserve the equity value of the home rather than deplete it for daily living expenses, because reverse mortgages can be expensive. A borrower must pay all normal loan origination costs, such as application and appraisal fees, loan interest points, mortgage insurance premiums, and closing costs. Reverse mortgages are not bargain arrangements.

Third, while the income received through a reverse mortgage is not taxed because the receipts are considered loans, there is no tax benefit to the accruing interest since interest is not tax deductible until the year in which it is paid. Thus, there is no tax advantage during the period of occupancy except in the case of a pure term loan, which must be repaid in full prior to vacating the home, and thus is likely to be a rare occurrence. Fourth, many elderly people desire to bequeath their property to their children or some other beneficiary, a goal that should not be surrendered without due reflection.

Fifth, other ways to extract the equity value of a home are available and may be more suitable for some senior homeowners. Generally, a reverse mortgage should be used only if it will help the homeowner remain economically independent or will materially add to the older person's quality of life.

Under a sale-and-leaseback agreement, the homeowner sells the home and then leases it back from the buyer. The lump sum received from the sale can be invested to generate an income stream. Most arrangements of this type involve a parent selling his or her home to an adult child. Since the child has the tax advantage of depreciating the property, it is often possible to charge the parent a modest rent, which still produces a break-even cash flow for the child. Under a life estate agreement, the owners exchange ownership, upon death, for the right to remain in the home for the remainder of their lives. Typically, the beneficiary is a charity or educational institution. The agreement entails no income stream, but the owner will receive a gift tax deduction based on the value of the home. Generally, the beneficial use of such an agreement is limited to those who have sufficient wealth to take advantage of the gift deduction or who have a philanthropic motive. Both sale-and-leaseback and life estate agreements should not be entered into without the advice of legal counsel (Higgins 1994).

Reverse Mortgage Programs

A variety of reverse mortgage programs have been funded by states and local governments, often to assist elderly people in refurbishing older homes that they wish to continue to occupy. Information on these programs is available through local Area Agency on Aging offices. Privately insured reverse mortgages are becoming more available through various financial institutions that have chosen to enter this market. The most active of these is Capital Holding Corporation of Louisville, Kentucky.

The program of most interest, however, is the HUD-FHA joint effort titled the Home Equity Conversion Mortgage (HECM) insurance demonstration, also known as the Federal Housing Administration (FHA) reverse mortgage program. Originally authorized by Congress in 1987, the program has been expanded and is now authorized through 1995. Any approved FHA lender may initiate a mortgage according to guidelines administered by the Department of Housing and Urban Development (HUD). Borrowers may choose among straight term, tenure, and line-of-credit mortgages; or they may combine either straight term or tenure with line-of-credit, representing five options. If a borrower combined one of the annuity forms with a line-of-credit by reserving a portion of the home's equity value to support the line-of-credit, the monthly annuity payment would be lower than otherwise possible. Borrowers under the HECM program must be at least age 62, own a home free of debt, and reside in that home. Payments to borrowers are based on the age of the youngest member in a married household, the interest rate on the mortgage, and an adjusted property value, which is defined as the lesser of the property's appraised value and the maximum mortgage on a one-unit residence as defined by FHA criteria. Currently, the adjusted property value varies between $67,500 and $124,875 depending upon geographic location. The adjusted property value acts to limit the size of the monthly payment that could be sustained by appraised values in excess of this amount. Borrowers may choose fixed or adjustable rate loans, and they must purchase mortgage insurance to protect the lender against the possibility that proceeds from sale of the home will be insufficient to retire the accumulated debt. This insurance premium is paid in two parts: 2% of the adjusted property value at closing, and a monthly premium equal to .05% of the outstanding principal owed. Both of these costs may be financed. All applicants are legally required to obtain counseling from a HUD-approved third party, independent of the lender, before loan closing to ensure that elderly borrowers understand the full implications of their decision. (See also CASH FLOW PLANNING FOR RETIREES, ELDER LAW PRACTICE, HEALTH AND LONGEVITY, HOMEOWNERSHIP, HOUSING, LIFE ESTATES, and LONG-TERM CARE INSURANCE: IDEAs.)

Organizations

American Association of Retired Persons
National Center for Home Equity Conversion (NCHEC)
American Bar Association's Commission on Legal Problems of the Elderly

Suggested Readings

Reverse Mortgage Locator. 1995. Apple Valley, MN: National Center for Home Equity Conversion.
Scholen, Ken. 1995. *Your New Retirement Nest Egg: A Consumer's Guide to the New Reverse Mortgages.* Apple Valley, MN: National Center for Home Equity Conversion.

References

Grall, Timothy S. 1993. *Our Nation's Housing in 1991.* U.S. Bureau of the Census, Current Housing Reports, Series H121/93–2. Washington, DC: U.S. Government Printing Office.
Higgins, David P. 1994. "Home Equity as an Income Source for Older Adults." In *Housing the Aging Population: Options for the New Century,* ed. W. Edward Folts and Dale E. Yeatts. New York: Garland, ch. 14.
Trent, Tina R. 1994. "Elderly Demographics and Preferences Indicate Need for Reverse Mortgages." *Housing Research News* 2 (3), (September), 4.

David P. Higgins

S

SAFETY. See Assisted Living; Crime Protection; Disaster Assistance and the Elderly; Elder Financial Abuse; Ethics in Financial Planning; Liability Insurance.

SAVINGS ACCOUNT TRUSTS, also referred to as "tentative trusts" or "totten trusts," are nominal trusts that operates like ordinary savings accounts, except that upon the depositor's death, the proceeds in the account pass directly to a beneficiary named on the account, rather than to the depositor's estate. The validity and operation of savings account trusts depend on the laws in each state.

Savings account trusts are an estate planning* tool available to persons who cannot afford the services of an attorney* to prepare a will*. Early in their history, savings account trusts were called "the poor man's will," although their use is not limited to the poor, and they are an appropriate way to dispose of small sums of money or small estates consisting of cash. Savings account trusts can be created at a bank or savings and loan association at the time a savings account is opened (or later) by a notation on the signature card that the depositor holds the account "in trust for (ITF)" or "as trustee for" a named beneficiary. The beneficiary designation is freely revocable. In some states, savings account trusts can be revoked by a provision mentioning the account in the depositor's will.

If the beneficiary dies before the depositor, the trust designation is automatically revoked and the account becomes an ordinary savings account payable to the depositor's estate. However, some financial institutions provide that if the beneficiary dies before the depositor, the account becomes payable on the depositor's death to the beneficiary's estate. Generally, the provisions printed on the signature card will govern. It is therefore essential to read and understand them before signing.

Savings account trusts have a number of features that make them attractive to elderly persons. They are easy to create and affordable compared to hiring an attorney to draft a will. Banks impose no special fees for opening these accounts or collecting the proceeds, unless payment involves closing a certificate of deposit before maturity. In that case, the bank may assess penalties for early withdrawal.

The convenience savings account trusts offer is another attractive feature. The accounts are available at the older person's financial institution, presumably a place they frequent and know the bank officers. It is not uncommon for elderly persons to have multiple savings account trusts at several different financial institutions. Often they will have several accounts with roughly equivalent sums for children, grandchildren, nieces, nephews, and so forth.

Savings account trusts can be created without consulting an attorney. Some elderly persons hesitate to hire attorneys because they are reluctant to discuss their financial affairs with strangers, uncomfortable with the formality of a lawyer's office, or fearful of entanglements or possible fraud, or they do not want to pay an attorney's fees for estate planning. For some there is an attempt to deny their own mortality by deferring estate planning, refusing to consider or talk about the financial consequences of death. As a result, many Americans die without a will and their estates are unplanned, devolving to heirs according to state statutes of intestate succession. From this perspective, savings account trusts constitute a useful and nonthreatening estate planning device.

There are disadvantages to engaging in estate planning without the supervision of an attorney or other qualified professional. The planning decisions involved in opening savings account trusts may be piecemeal without the advice of a professional who is knowledgeable regarding the individual's overall family situation and finances. Also, elders will not be aware of other options and alternatives as they pertain to their estate. Bank employees may not be well trained regarding estate planning in general or about their own products, and they may not have the ability or time to explain them fully to customers. Further, as members of a retail sales force for their bank, their recommendations may not always constitute disinterested estate planning advice. Probably the best use of savings account trusts is as one component part of a comprehensive estate plan that includes a will and other appropriate estate planning devices, such as insurance, and is reviewed in its entirety by an attorney or other estate planning professional.

The opening of a savings account trust will not, in most cases, entirely negate the need for a will. Most individuals will own some assets other than the cash in their savings account and will require a will to dispose of them.

Savings account trusts are deemed to be "testamentary substitutes" because they function like wills, channeling funds to a beneficiary at the depositor's death just as if the depositor had left the beneficiary a legacy for that amount in his or her will. Usually, a savings account trust will perform this function more efficiently than a will. The account is an asset that bypasses the depositor's estate and is deemed to pass directly to the beneficiary at the depositor's death. The beneficiary is often able to obtain the proceeds sooner than a legacy under a will since there is no need to wait for probate of the will nor to rely on the executor for payment. Instead, the beneficiary may obtain payment directly from the bank soon after the depositor's death by presenting the passbook, a copy of the death certificate, and in some cases, a waiver from state tax authorities.

In some instances, the executor of the depositor's estate may have a claim on part or all of the proceeds in a savings account trust that is superior to that of the named beneficiary. The executor can reach the proceeds when the depositor's other assets are insufficient to pay his debts. The proceeds are also reachable by a surviving spouse, even if disinherited by the depositor, if the proceeds are determined by court order to be needed for the elective or forced share of the estate to which the survivor is entitled by state statute.

Although the proceeds in the account bypass the depositor's estate for the purpose of administration by the executor, they are part of the estate for tax purposes. Thus, depending on the size of the depositor's overall estate, the proceeds in a savings account trust may generate federal and state death taxes. If, however, the beneficiary is the depositor's spouse, the account will pass tax free under the estate tax marital deduction.

Under most state statutes, death taxes generated by the account will be a charge against the proceeds, reducing the amount receivable by the beneficiary. To prevent this reduction, the depositor may direct in a will that all death taxes shall be paid from the general assets of the estate, including any death taxes attributable to nonprobate assets such as savings account trusts. Whether it is advisable to make such a direction, and what the impact will be on the beneficiaries of the general estate, are questions a client should address with an attorney or tax advisor in connection with the preparation of a will.

It must be noted that the terms ''trust'' and ''trustee'' in some respects are misnomers in this context. The opening of a savings account trust does not create a trust in the formal legal sense. No fiduciary relationship is established, no equitable rights are immediately conveyed to the beneficiary, and the depositor remains sole owner of the funds on deposit in his or her individual capacity until death. If any trust is created, it is only at the depositor's death when the account becomes payable to the beneficiary.

The use of trust labels in connection with savings accounts has caused confusion among the public, some lawyers, and judges. It is possible that depositors who open such accounts believe they have created ''trusts'' for their beneficiaries. This belief may be harmless, but in cases that have arisen after the depositor's death, courts have been called on to interpret clauses printed on signature cards that confirm the trust designation. The result in numerous states has been a line of sometimes inconsistent judicial decisions regarding the nature and operation of savings account trusts. These decisions do not provide clear instructions for the general public and for the bank officers, estate planners, and attorneys who attempt to advise them on estate planning matters.

With this background, the influential Uniform Probate Code (1990) recommended eliminating savings account trusts in favor of "payable on death" (POD) accounts. In opening a POD account, as when opening a savings account trust, the depositor indicates on the signature card the names of one or more beneficiaries to whom the proceeds in the account are to be paid at the depositor's death. However, no mention of a "trust" or "trustee" appears on the signature card. According to the UPC, POD accounts serve the same function as savings account trusts more directly, without the potential for confusion caused by the trust label. The UPC, therefore, seeks to discourage the creation of savings account trusts in the future. In states where all or part of the UPC has been adopted, financial institutions are complying by offering a form for creating a POD account instead of a savings account trust.

It is not uncommon for a depositor to name a minor as the beneficiary of a savings account trust. If, when the depositor dies, the minor has attained the age of majority, there will be no problem collecting the proceeds. If, however, the beneficiary is still a minor, problems may arise. The financial institution may be reluctant to release funds directly to a minor. State law may require the account to remain on deposit until the minor reaches majority, preventing ready access to the funds for many years except under court order in an emergency. State law may also prevent a parent from collecting the proceeds on behalf of the minor unless the father or mother is first appointed the minor's legal guardian. This requires a legal action and imposes annual accounting obligations by the parent.

State legislation to clarify the respective rights of the financial institution, on the one hand, and the minor's guardian, on the other, seems likely in the future. Meanwhile, elderly clients who wish to name grandchildren or other minors as POD or savings account trust beneficiaries should be aware of the potential problem. The savings account trust may not be suitable for large sums of money or for cases in which the depositor believes the funds should be withheld from the beneficiary after attaining majority. In such cases, engaging an attorney to draft a formal trust tailored to one's exact wishes may be preferable. If one decides to employ a savings account trust, then any trust agreement printed on the back of the bank's signature card must be scrutinized carefully. The purpose of the review is to ensure the fund will not be tied up at the financial institution under a successor trustee who is virtually powerless to take any action for years after the depositor's death. There should be a provision authorizing the bank to pay the funds to the minor's parent, custodian, or guardian without a court order.

As part of a comprehensive estate plan, savings account trusts remain in many jurisdictions a simple, inexpensive, and efficient estate planning device that elderly persons are able to access conveniently and without the services of an attorney. (See also ATTORNEYS, ESTATE PLANNING, ESTATE TAXES, GUARDIANSHIP, INHERITANCE, TRUSTS, and WILLS.)

References

Estes, R. Wayne. 1977. "In Search of a Less Tentative Totten." *Pepperdine Law Review* 5: 21–47.

Institute of Financial Education. 1990. *Insurance of Accounts: A Practical Guide to the FDIC Regulations* (First Edition). Chicago: Institute of Financial Education.

O'Connell, Vanessa. 1994. "When It Pays You to Wrestle with Your Banker." *Money* (September): 80–82.

Roth, Jeffrey I. 1993. "Successor Trustee of Tentative Trusts: Trust Law Phantoms." *St. Louis University Law* 38 (July): 407–67.

Uniform Probate Code: Official 1989 Text. 1990. St. Paul, MN: West.

Wittebort, Robert J., Jr. 1974. "Savings Account Trusts: A Critical Examination." *Notre Dame Lawyer* 49: 686–99.

Jeffrey I. Roth

SAVINGS INVESTMENTS, funds placed in investment instruments that involve virtually no risk of loss to principal or interest. The major investment alternatives for savings include accounts at banks, savings and loan associations, and credit unions; money-market funds; and U.S. Savings Bonds.

Objectives

Typical objectives for the use of these savings opportunities include the following:

1. To insure safety of the monies involved. Federally regulated depository institutions provide insurance of accounts up to a maximum of $100,000. Institutions are required to display the FDIC (Federal Deposit Insurance Corporation) or other agency seal to inform depositors of the coverage of accounts.

2. To provide income. Most savings accounts pay a fixed interest rate that will vary among institutions, type of account, and amount of money involved. Some savings investments pay variable interest rates, as described below.

3. To provide liquidity. Most savings alternatives allow immediate withdrawals. Most financial plans recommend that individuals retain some funds that are available on short notice to meet unexpected situations.

4. To provide convenience. The many branch office locations of financial institutions typically provide convenient access for most individuals.

5. To build savings balances. Funds can be accumulated gradually (and earn interest income) to meet future objectives that require larger amounts of money.

Banks, savings and loan associations, and credit unions are traditional favorite alternatives for mature individuals to save money. Convenience, safety, and immediate availability are frequently cited as significant reasons for selecting a depository institution. Increasingly, automatic teller machines are preferred by younger individuals; as a result, some experts project a decline in the number of physical banking offices.

Types of Savings Investments

The most frequently used savings investments or alternatives (and the major advantages and disadvantages associated with each) can be classified into seven types of accounts:

Regular savings accounts, statement or passbook accounts at banks, savings and loan association accounts, and share accounts at credit unions are the most frequently used savings investments. Low minimum balances are usually required in these insured arrangements and funds can be easily withdrawn. The principal disadvantage of this type of account is a relatively low rate of interest.

Certificates of deposit at banks, savings and loan associations, and credit unions are insured accounts that provide a guaranteed rate of return for the period of time involved. A possible disadvantage is a penalty for early withdrawal of funds.

Negotiable Order of Withdrawal (NOW) accounts at banks, savings and loan associations, or share draft accounts at credit unions, provide an insured, interest-earning account with check-writing privileges. The disadvantages include service charges if the account drops below a minimum balance, and other possible fees.

Super NOW accounts are similar to regular NOW accounts in terms of check-writing privileges and insurance, but pay higher returns. The disadvantage is the requirement for higher minimum balances; the account earns lower returns if the balance falls below a set amount.

Money-market deposit accounts at insured institutions are a relatively new type of savings investment. They provide a return that changes with the general interest rates in the economy. The returns can range from attractive to less-than-passbook rates. The usual disadvantages include high minimum balance requirements and lower income returns and/or service charges if the account balance falls below a specified level.

Money-market funds, which are available from most stock brokerage firms, are a similar type of savings investment. This alternative provides a relatively good return that varies with current market rates of interest. The major disadvantages of this investment are a lack of government-sponsored insurance and minimum balance requirements.

United States Savings Bonds are yet another savings investment alternative. This instrument, which involves a relatively low minimum deposit, provides a good return on a government-guaranteed investment. The return will vary with current interest rates in the economy and is exempt from state and local income taxes. The disadvantages include a long period to maturity and a lower rate of return when redeemed before a five-year holding period. (See also ESTATE PLANNING, FINANCIAL COUNSELING, SAVINGS ACCOUNT TRUSTS, and WEALTH SPAN.)

References

Cohn, R. A., W. G. Lewellen, R. C. Lease, and G. G. Schlarbaum. 1975. "Individual Investor Risk Aversion and Investment Portfolio Composition." *Journal of Finance* 30: 605–20.

Sciortino, J. J., J. H. Huston, and R. W. Spencer. 1988. "Risk and Income Distribution." *Journal of Economic Psychology* 9: 399–408.

Snelbecker, G. E., M. J. Roszkowski, and N. E. Cutler. 1990. "Investors' Risk Tolerance and Return Aspirations, and Financial Advisors' Interpretations: A Conceptual Model and Exploratory Data." *Journal of Behavioral Economics* 19(2).

Winger, B. J., and N. K. Mohan. 1988. "Investment Risk and Time Diversification." *Journal of Financial Planning* 1: 45–48.

Ganas K. Rakes

SENIORS HOUSING FINANCE, the system for providing equity and debt capital to acquire, develop, or maintain housing that meets the special needs of elderly persons. As used here, "seniors housing" refers to multiunit residences that provide ease of access, personal care, health care, and other supportive services and amenities designed for elderly persons. As with the rest of real estate finance, seniors housing finance experienced profound shocks and major institutional restructuring since the mid-1980s.

Seniors housing finance grows in importance with pressure to hold down the cost of health care and to serve growing numbers of frail elderly persons. Service-supported seniors housing is highly cost-effective in enabling frail elderly persons to live with maximum safety and independence. By the year 2030, the population aged 75 or older is expected to grow by approximately 20 million persons (U.S. Bureau of the Census 1993). To meet their needs, investment in specially designed residential structures will need to increase at unprecedented rates.

Seniors Housing and Other Real Estate Finance

Seniors housing, as other forms of multifamily rental housing, requires a large infusion of initial capital and generates steady revenues over many years. Because of that cash flow pattern, about 70% or more of the capital for seniors housing is typically provided by debt. The start-up phase of a project may be financed with construction loans, provided by a short-term lender such as a commercial bank. After project occupancy stabilizes, those loans are replaced by long-term mortgage lending, often from other lenders. The lender determines the loan amount after analyzing the property's projected revenues and related risks. A "debt coverage ratio" estimates the principal and interest payments that the property's revenues could support as a successful business, after operating expenses and an appropriate safety cushion. A "loan-to-value ratio" estimates the amount of loan principal that could be assured of repayment in the event of default. Interest rates reflect market forces and risks related to the mortgaged property. The remaining portion of the required capital is provided by the owner, other equity investors, various forms of subordinate loans, and government subsidies.

Recent History of Seniors Housing Finance

Between 1950 and 1980, the seniors housing industry, largely within the non-profit sector, grew steadily. Seniors housing was often financed with various forms of government assistance, and by lenders who had established business relationships with the housing sponsors.

In the early 1980s, a speculative boom in real estate spilled over into seniors housing production. Highly favorable tax incentives enacted in 1981 fed a rapid inflation in real estate values. Many developers new to seniors housing sought to capitalize on powerful demographic trends by providing upscale "retirement housing." Eager lenders, including newly aggressive savings and loans, made debt financing readily available on very favorable terms—often with "bullet loans" that had to be refinanced in fewer than 10 years.

The speculative bubble burst in the late 1980s, and real estate lenders suffered devastating losses from foreclosures. Seniors housing, a relatively small part of the total market, shared in the problem. Anticipated demand for retirement housing never materialized, vacancy rates soared, expensive projects failed, and high-leverage loans went into default. In reaction, virtually all sources of capital for seniors housing dried up for several years.

By 1994, inexperienced firms had left the seniors housing industry, and property values and financial structures had adjusted to harsh market realities. Rent revenues were increasing, and occupancy rates had increased to over 90% on average. Mortgage lenders and equity investors were starting to show renewed interest in seniors housing (National Investment Conference 1994). Nevertheless, over 20% of the seniors housing developed before 1991 remained in financial difficulty (American Seniors Housing Association 1995).

Special Underwriting Considerations for Seniors Housing

Seniors housing confronts unusual complexity within the financial system, because it must provide both residence and services. Loan servicing is more difficult than with other real estate lending. It is virtually impossible for a lender to force an unwilling or incompetent manager to control costs of labor and materials, to be known for friendly treatment of residents, to provide good meals, and to offer a variety of high-quality health care and social services, all at the same time. Potential lenders and investors must therefore evaluate a seniors housing facility as a complex business—looking primarily at the quality of the management company, rather than at the quality of the property as real estate.

Tighter Underwriting Requirements

In reaction to losses suffered in the late 1980s, lenders tend to apply stringent underwriting standards to all multifamily loans, including seniors housing. Although a wide range of financing terms and conditions was available in 1994, more than 80% of financial institutions surveyed (National Investment Conference 1994) would not make loans larger than 75% of a property's appraised value. Lenders often required debt service coverage of 1.3 or better.

A typical loan made at the time of the survey may have had an interest rate of 9.5% fixed for 10 years, with an amortization schedule of between 15 and 25 years. It would have yielded between 8.5% and 10%. The loan would have been underwritten with a loan-to-value ratio of between 70% and 75% and a debt coverage ratio between 1.25 and 1.3. The loan probably would have included recourse to the borrower in the event of default, and would involve about 1.3 points in upfront fees. On a typical construction loan, the interest rate would probably have floated at about 1.4 to 1.7 percentage points above the prime rate, and the lender would probably have required real equity equal to about 20% to 25% of the project costs.

Securitization

Perhaps the most striking development in seniors housing finance in the early 1990s has been the rapid development of a deep and liquid secondary market (U.S. Bureau of the Census 1993) in multifamily mortgage-backed securities. New sources of mortgage financing are opening for multifamily housing as a result. The total volume of multifamily mortgage-backed securities grew from about $2.9 billion in 1993 to about $4.2 billion on an annualized basis in 1994 (National Investment Conference 1994). Although available data do not show how much of these totals went to seniors housing, securitization is of growing importance to seniors housing finance.

In essence, securitization converts a group of mortgage loans into securities tailored to the financial risk and income preferences of various investors. The process gives the seniors housing sponsor access to the immense resources of the international capital markets, and gives investors a relatively good investment tailored to their risk and income preferences.

Mortgage-backed securities transactions take many forms, but it can be helpful, if overly simplified, to think of the securitization of seniors housing loans as a four-step process (Anthony 1994). First, a lender originates a mortgage loan so that a borrower can acquire or refinance a seniors housing facility. This creates a financial asset that will generate a specified series of payments of principal and interest, secured by the seniors housing property.

Second, that mortgage loan, either alone or in a pool of similar loans, is used to back a "pass-through" security. The borrowers' periodic payments on mortgage loans backing the security will be passed through periodically to holders of the security.

Third, one or more nationally recognized rating agencies evaluate the creditworthiness of the pass-through security. On the basis of that evaluation, the pass-through security is divided into several classes, or "tranches," with the holders of different classes having different rights to the stream of mortgage payments into the pool—some classes offer an investor higher risks and potential returns than other classes. The size and rating of each class is determined by the rating agency's analysis. The total face value of the pass-through securities is often smaller than the aggregate value of the mortgages in the pool. This "overcollateralization" or creation of residual collateral serves to increase the creditworthiness of the securities.

Fourth, the pass-through securities are sold, generally to institutional investors, who often are the only purchasers able to handle the complexity of mortgage-backed securities. Different classes of the security are marketed to different investors on the basis of the investor's risk and return preferences.

Despite its advantages, securitization also tends to increase pressures for standardization of product and resistance to lending for new construction, which may create special problems for seniors housing finance.

Government Impact on Seniors Housing Finance

Federal, state, and local governments affect seniors housing finance through an extraordinary variety of tax, spending, regulatory, and monetary policies. For example, regulations related to service-supported housing can make a specific investment more attractive by limiting potential competition, or they can make the investment unattractive by increasing costs or risks.

Elected officials have tended to consider seniors housing as meriting special support. For example, the Section 202 Housing for the Elderly program financed the construction of about 9,000 units of seniors housing in fiscal year 1994. Earlier, this financing took the form of direct federal loans and rent subsidies; more recently it takes the form of capital grants and operating subsidies. As congressional pressure builds to cut federal support for housing, continued federal assistance at past levels—let alone increased assistance to meet increased need—is not assured. Federal policy is likely to shift more responsibility for program design and funding to the state and local levels of government.

Emerging Concerns

Seniors housing finance can be expected to undergo constant and rapid change well into the twenty-first century. Whatever direction those changes take, the most difficult challenges for seniors housing are likely to be: (1) to provide the quality of performance data that future lenders and investors are likely to demand, and (2) to attract adequate financing for seniors housing that is affordable to frail elderly persons who are not among the very affluent. (See also ASSISTED LIVING, CONTINUING CARE RETIREMENT COMMUNITIES, FEDERAL AGENCY SECURITIES, HOME CARE SERVICES FOR THE ELDERLY, HOUSING, HUD-ASSISTED RENTAL HOUSING, MORTGAGE INSTRUMENTS, and NURSING HOMES.)

References

American Seniors Housing Association. 1995. *State of Seniors Housing 1994.* Washington, DC: ASHA.

Anthony, Raymond. 1994. "Financing Techniques for Skilled Nursing Facilities, Assisted Living Facilities and Congregate Care Retirement Residences." Washington, DC: National Investment Conference.

National Investment Conference. 1994. *Lender and Investor Survey Results.* Annapolis, MD: National Investment Conference.

U.S. Bureau of the Census. 1993. "Population Projections of the United States by Age, Sex, Race, and Hispanic Origin: 1993 to 2050." Current Population Report P-25, No. 1104. Washington, DC: GPO.

W. Donald Campbell

SERVICE CREDIT PROGRAMS (SCPs), programs that provide a variety of volunteer services to the elderly and disabled, and enable volunteers to help others while earning a credit for every hour of service they provide. People receiving services pay for them with credits they have earned earlier, or that have been donated to them by the program or other volunteers. The concept of service credits integrates elements of traditional volunteerism, barter, and co-op exchanges.

Service credit programs (SCPs) involve diverse groups of people, have developed intergenerational activities involving school children and senior citizens, and are sponsored by community centers, health maintenance organizations*, hospitals, public housing units, or churches. The size and emphasis of the program depends on the goals of the sponsoring organization.

About 85 SCPs currently operate in the United States, with at least 15 more being planned. A variety of services are offered by SCPs, ranging from respite care to guitar lessons to gutter repair. The key to a successful SCP is to help everyone understand that they have something valuable to contribute—not just money or material things, but time, experience, and goodwill. SCPs complement the formal, professional assistance that state and federal governments provide by encouraging people to provide for their own needs while helping others. Existing government resources can then be concentrated on individuals with advanced levels of need who have no other sources of care.

Payment for a wide range of formal, long-term care services is not currently available through insurance policies or most government programs. Additionally, many communities and charitable organizations are minimizing the provision of formal support services. Payment problems for noncovered services are regarded as health care access and delivery problems, and as a reimbursement problem. Noncovered services usually include transportation to the physician's office, chore service, translation and reading assistance, friendly visiting, and health education and screening.

The lack of these basic support systems can often lead to a person's situation deteriorating and contribute to the development of an acute illness that may involve hospitalization or institutionalization. Informal care by family and friends is one of the ways in which long-term care is provided at home in a financially manageable way. However, informal support systems available to people through friends and families are also changing as a result of demographic shifts, such as women working outside the home and adult children living far from their elderly parents. Service credit programs offer a way to supplement and complement formal and informal support networks at reasonable cost.

Key Issues in Service Credit Programs

Service Credits. Some sites consider service credits a closed system or an alternative currency. They carefully seed credits to participants who have not earned credits, but want services. They also monitor credit flow and issue monthly credit statements to participants. Others maintain an open system in which credit accounting and policies afford a more flexible approach.

Program Services. The community in which the volunteers are situated determines which services are important and provided. The varying socioeconomic, cultural, and geographic characteristics of the community are reflected in the volunteer pool.

Volunteering*. Traditionally, volunteering has been associated with institutions (e.g., hospitals). SCPs focus on specifically requested services. This creates an association between the type of need within a community and the services offered by the program.

Recruitment and Retention. Frequently, when people hear about SCPs, they assume that volunteers participate solely to earn service credits. In general, this is not the case. People volunteer because they desire to help others and provide community service. Credits do, however, appear to be a factor in a person's decision to volunteer. Volunteers appreciate their time being treated as a valuable commodity. Additionally, many programs have found that the credits attract people who do not ordinarily volunteer or who might be first-time volunteers, especially men. Most programs have also found that retention rates are higher in service credit programs than in more traditional volunteer programs. This may result from a volunteer's sense of truly being "invested" in the program.

Funding. Although SCPs depend almost entirely on volunteers, operating funds are needed for office space, equipment, and supplies. Some programs have closed because they could not find this funding to maintain or expand their operations. While volunteers can perform many administrative tasks, most sites have found that a paid staff member is essential for long-term program continuity. Because service credits imply a promise of future services, the long-term source of operating funds needs to be a central part of strategic planning.

Into the Future

Service credit programs have great potential to increase the resources available to help individuals in communities. The programs provide important services in a manner that encourages volunteers to prepare for their own needs by allowing access to future services. This is done through a sense of empowerment rather than entitlement. Work is underway to expand the use of SCPs by managed care and health maintenance organizations, and possibly to corporations that could offer SCPs as an employee benefit.

There is interest in the development of a national network of service credit sites. This network would encourage the transfer of credits across states. For example, children of elders would be able to volunteer in Montana and transfer their credits to their parents in Florida.

While this idea has great potential, SCPs are still developing, with fewer than 100 programs nationally; most are small. Programs have been developed to reflect and meet local needs and concerns. As a result, they differ greatly by locality. It is a part of the idea's strength to be able to meet local needs. Many supporters believe it is important to preserve this strength, even as a national network is being considered.

In the future, providing adequate levels of services will require the combined resources of government programs, individual savings, and community commitment. Service credits offer a proven and powerful way to supplement these resources. (See also DAY PROGRAMS FOR ADULTS, HEALTH MAINTENANCE ORGANIZATIONS, and VOLUNTEERING, VOLUNTEERS, OLDER.)

Organization
Service Credit Program Center on Aging

References
Coughlin, Teresa, and Mark Meiners. 1990. "Service Credit Banking: Issues in Program Development." *Journal of Aging and Social Policy* 2: 25–41.
Kahn, Edgar, and Jonathan Rowe. 1992. *Time Dollars.* Emmaus, PA: Rodale.
Oklahoma Aging Services Division, U.S. Administration on Aging. 1993. *Oklahoma Volunteer Service Credit Bank Program.* Oklahoma City, OK: Oklahoma Department of Human Services, Aging Services Division.

Mark Meiners, Kathleen Treat, and Hunter McKay

SOCIAL ASSISTANCE. See Medicaid; Nutrition Programs; Supplemental Security Income (SSI).

SOCIAL SECURITY PROGRAM OF THE UNITED STATES, the social insurance program officially designated as Old-Age, Survivors, and Disability Insurance (OASDI). The program covers most workers in paid employment and provides monthly cash benefits to retirees and their dependents, to disabled workers and their dependents, and to surviving dependents of deceased workers and retirees. Internationally, Social Security has a broader meaning, including pensions, medical care benefits, unemployment insurance, workers' compensation, and family allowances. Such programs can be of a social insurance nature or of a public assistance or minimum-benefit nature. Sometimes the Medicare* program is seen as part of Social Security because both OASDI and Medicare have the Social Security Act as their legislative base. Also, part of Medicare (the Hospital Insurance portion) is financed by the same payroll tax as is OASDI.

The Social Security program significantly affects the lives of a majority of Americans. About 43 million persons received monthly benefits under the program in July 1994, and about 115 million persons paid contributions (or taxes) in 1994. Millions of others are also affected by the program because they are potential beneficiaries in the event of the retirement, death, or disability of covered workers.

The financial impact of the program can be seen from the fact that total benefit disbursement in 1993 amounted to $302 billion, while total contribution income (including $6 billion from the income-taxation of benefits) was $328 billion. The administrative expenses involved in collecting the contributions, maintaining the earnings records, and paying the benefits were $3.0 billion, or 0.9% of the contribution income. The assets of the trust funds of the OASDI system amounted to $378 billion at the end of 1993 and earned interest income of $28 billion that year. In mid-1994, the average monthly benefit payable to retired workers was $676, while that for disabled workers was $642. The maximum benefit payable to a worker who retired at age 65 in January 1994 (and who never received disability benefits) was $1,147; some who worked beyond age 65 in the past received larger amounts. The average benefit for widows aged 60 or over at the time of initial claim was $634, while the average benefit for a widowed mother and two children was $1,291.

OASDI has several basic principles: (1) benefits are based on presumptive need, (2) benefits provide a floor of protection, (3) benefits are related to earnings, (4) a balance between social adequacy and individual equity is present, and (5) the financing is on a self-supporting contributory basis.

Benefits Based on Presumptive Need

Certain categories of social risk are established by the law, and benefits are paid accordingly. For example, old-age benefits are not payable automatically upon attainment of a given "normal" retirement age, such as 62 or 65, but only upon actual retirement (although they are payable at age 70 and older, regardless of retirement). Likewise, benefits for surviving widows are not payable for their lifetime, but only while they have eligible children present or are aged 60 or over (or aged 50 or over and disabled), and only so long as they are not remarried (except that remarriage after age 60 is not disqualifying), and are not employed with earnings above those permitted under the earnings test.

The retirement requirement is frequently misunderstood as being a means or needs test (i.e., a test of the individual's situation to make certain that he or she needs the income to meet subsistence-level economic requirements). From that viewpoint, some critics believe that the earnings test is unfair. This procedure, however, is essential if there is to be a system paying retirement benefits, and not a charity program based on individual needs. Furthermore, the elimination of the earnings test would be costly (about $10 billion annually at the present time), because of higher payments coming due longer-working beneficiaries later on.

Floor-of-Protection Concept

It is generally agreed that OASDI benefits should provide only a minimum floor of protection against various risks. However, many opinions exist on how far apart the floor and the ceiling should be. Some believe that the floor should be very low, or even that there should be no OASDI program at all. Still others believe that the floor should be high enough to provide a comfortable standard of living by itself, disregarding any economic security that individual or group methods might provide. A middle group believes that OASDI benefits should, along with other income and assets, be sufficient to yield a satisfactory minimum standard of living for the majority of individuals. Then, any residual needy population should be aided by supplementary public assistance.

Earnings-Related Benefits

As a consequence of the floor-of-protection concept, it seems desirable from a social standpoint that, compared with contributions, benefits should be relatively larger for those with low earnings than for those with high earnings. The benefit formula under the OASDI system has always been heavily weighted accordingly. A higher benefit rate applies to lower portions of earnings than to higher portions. Higher-income groups do receive larger benefits, but there is weighting in favor of low-income groups.

Individual Equity and Social Adequacy

Whenever a social insurance system involves contributions from potential beneficiaries, the question of individual equity versus social adequacy arises. Individual equity means the contributors receive benefit protection directly related to the amount of their contributions. Social adequacy means the benefits will provide, for all contributors, a certain standard of living. The two concepts are usually in direct conflict, and social insurance systems tend to have a benefit basis falling somewhere between complete individual equity and complete social adequacy. The tendency is generally more toward social adequacy than individual equity, and this is the case with the OASDI system. If individual equity prevailed when a system started, the benefits paid would be relatively small for many years, because they would be related solely to contributions paid, or to service rendered, after the effective date. Thus, many years would elapse before the system would meet the purposes for which it was established.

Self-Supporting Contributory Financing

The principle of self-supporting contributory financing means that no appropriations from general revenues will be needed to pay the benefits. Available for self-supporting financing under OASDI are the contributions (taxes) from workers and employers, a portion of the income taxes on benefits, and the interest earned on the trust funds that have resulted from the accumulated excess of income over outgo of the system (which, by law, must be invested only in U.S. government securities). Such interest does not represent "contributions" or "financial support" from either the treasury or the general taxpayer, because the interest on this type of investments must be paid, regardless of whether they are held by the trust funds or by private investors.

The employer and the employee share the cost of OASDI equally. Legislation in 1983 provided that the self-employed should pay the combined employer-employee rate (but with an allowance for one-half of the tax as a business expense for income tax purposes, just as employers receive).

The principle of self-supporting contributory financing was breached in 1983 through the introduction of indirect general-revenue financing in two respects. First, up to 50% of OASDI benefits received were subjected to income tax for persons with high incomes, and the proceeds are put in the OASDI trust funds. Second, the 1984 tax rate was increased for employers, but not for employees, and the OASDI trust funds received from general revenues what would have resulted if the employee rate had been increased.

Coverage Provisions

The majority of employed persons are covered under the OASDI program (or could be covered by election). The major exceptions are federal government employees under the Civil Service Retirement System (who were employed before 1984), low-income self-employed persons, and farm and domestic workers with irregular employment. Railroad workers have a separate system (the Railroad Retirement Act) but are, in essence, covered under OASDI because of close coordination.

Non-Farm Self-Employed. All non-farm, self-employed persons are covered—both nonprofessionals, such as store owners, and professionals, such as lawyers, physicians, and dentists, provided their net annual earnings are at least $400. Farm operators are covered on the same general basis as other self-employed persons, but with a special simplified reporting option based on gross income, for those with low net income. Ministers are covered on a compulsory basis, unless they object for conscience or religious reasons, to all public insurance which provides death, disability, or retirement benefits.

Employees of Non-Farm Private Employers. All employees in private industry and commerce are compulsorily covered, with no minimum restrictions on amount of earnings or length of employment. Coverage for employees of certain nonprofit organizations such as churches, private hospitals, and private schools is compulsory. (Before 1984 it was optional on the part of the organization.)

Employees of State and Local Government. As a result of legislation in 1990, all employees of state and local governments who do not have a retirement system are compulsorily covered. (Formerly this was on a voluntary elective group basis.) Employees of state and local governments who are covered by a retirement system can be covered at the option of the state and the employing unit. About 80% of all state and local government employees are covered under these procedures.

Employees of Federal Government. Most federal civilian employees not under an existing retirement system who were hired before 1984, all civilian employees hired after 1983, all members of the uniformed services, and all employees hired before 1984 who were under the Civil Service Retirement System but who shifted to the new supplementary retirement system established for new hires after 1983 are covered on a regular contributory basis.

Other Employees. Farm employment is covered if yearly cash wages from an employer amount to at least $150, or if the employer has a total payroll of $2,500 or more in the year. Domestic workers are covered if cash wages are $1,000 or more in a year from a single employer. Tips of $20 or more per month received by employees are included as wages and are reported through the employer. However, restaurant owners do not pay the employer tax on tips.

Employment Abroad. The preceding discussion relates to employment in the United States (including Possessions) and on U.S. vessels and airplanes, and applies to U.S. citizens and alien residents working abroad for U.S. employers. Totalization agreements have been reached with several countries so that (1) U.S. citizens and residents temporarily employed there by a U.S. company or affiliate are not subject to the social security taxes of the other country (and vice versa); and (2) covered employment in one country can be used to meet the eligibility requirements of the other country's program.

OASDI Insured Status Conditions. There are three kinds of insured status: fully, currently, and disability. Fully insured status provides eligibility for all types of old-age and survivor benefits. Currently insured status, in the absence of fully insured status, gives eligibility for certain young survivor benefits. Disability insured status is a partial requirement for the disability "freeze" and for disability monthly benefits. Insured status is defined in terms of quarters of coverage (QC). Since 1978, a QC is given for a certain amount of annual earnings ($830 in 1995), with a maximum of four QCs annually; the required amount is changed each year according to national wage increases. Fully insured status is achieved if the individual has at least as many QCs (acquired at any time) as the number of years elapsed after 1950 (or at age 21, if later) and before age 62. Thus, the maximum requirement is 40 QCs.

Currently insured status is achieved by having six QCs in the 13-quarter period ending with the quarter of death, attainment of age 62, or actual retirement if after age 62. Disability insured status is generally achieved by having 20 QCs in the 40-quarter period ending with the quarter of disablement, with a lower requirement for persons becoming disabled before age 30. Periods of qualifying total disability for individuals who have both fully insured and disability insured status are excluded in measuring the elapsed period at any later time for any of the insured status categories (the "disability freeze" provision).

OASDI Beneficiary Categories

Old-Age Beneficiaries. Fully insured individuals are eligible for a full old-age benefit if they claim benefits at the Normal Retirement Age (NRA). The NRA is 65 for persons who attain that age before 2003, and it gradually increases to 66 for persons who attain that age in 2009–2020 and 67 for persons who attain that age in 2027 and after. The amount of this benefit is 400% of the Primary Insurance Amount (PIA) (see explanation below). The old-age benefit can be claimed between age 62 and the NRA, with a reduction of 5/9% for each of the first 36 months below the NRA at time of retirement and of 5/12% for months in excess of 36. Thus, a person retiring at exact age 62 before 2000 faces a 20% lifetime reduction, which closely approximates an "actuarial equivalent" basis. A person retiring at age 62 who has an NRA of 66 will have a 25% reduction; when the NRA is 67, the reduction will be 30%.

Persons retiring after the NRA receive increases in the form of delayed-retirement credits. These are at the rate of 3% for each year of deferment for persons who attain age 65 in 1982–1989, and increase gradually according to year of attainment of age 65, until being 8% of those attaining the NRA in 2009 and after.

Disability Benefits. An individual is eligible for a disability benefit of 100% of the PIA if he or she is permanently and totally disabled and has been so disabled for at least five months, and has both fully and disability insured statuses.

Auxiliary Benefits. If the retired or disabled individual has a spouse at the NRA or over (or, regardless of age, has a child under age 16, or of any age who has been totally disabled since before age 22), an additional benefit of 50% of the PIA is payable. There is a similar benefit for each eligible child (subject to the family maximum provisions, when several persons in the family are eligible for benefits).

Survivor Benefits. Widow's benefits are payable at age 60 (or at ages 50–59 if the widow is disabled) if the deceased person was fully insured. This benefit is 100% of the PIA if first claimed at the NRA; the amount is 71.5% at ages 60 or under. Any delayed-retirement credits applicable to the worker are also applicable to the widow.

When a fully insured worker dies, parent's benefits are payable (upon attainment of age 62) to parents who had been dependent upon such individuals. When a fully or currently insured individual dies leaving an eligible child, benefits are payable to the children and the widowed parent in the same manner as for the children and spouse of a retired worker.

General Benefit Provisions. No individual can receive the full amount of more than one type of monthly benefit. Payments are made only after an individual files a claim, with retroactive payments of monthly benefits for as long as six months before filing.

OASDI Benefit Amounts

The PIA, from which all benefits are determined, is based on the average earnings of the insured individual. This section will describe the method of calculating the PIA that is applicable over the long run (several other methods are applicable for certain closed groups, such as those who attained age 62 before 1979).

Average Indexed Monthly Earnings. The Average Indexed Monthly Earnings (AIME) is based on the indexed earnings record (which, for any year, does not include earnings in excess of the Maximum Earnings Base) over the entire potential period of coverage, but with certain periods of low earnings disregarded. Generally, the average is computed from the beginning of 1951 (or at age 22, if later) to the beginning of the year of death, attainment of age 62, or disability, whichever is first applicable. In computing this average, five calendar years are dropped from consideration (for those disabled before age 47, fewer than five drop-out years are allowed). Further, years with high earnings beginning with the year of attainment of age 62 (or before age 22) may be substituted for years at ages 22–61 with lower earnings.

The past earnings record is indexed (i.e., brought up to date, to alleviate the effects of inflation). Such indexing is done up to age 60 (or to two years before the year of disability or death, if prior to 62). The indexing is based on nationwide average wages.

Benefits Formula. After the AIME is determined, it is entered into the PIA benefit formula applicable to the particular "cohort" to which the individual belongs. A cohort relates to persons attaining age 62 in a particular year (or becoming disabled or dying before age 62 in that year). The formula for the 1995 cohort is: 90% of the first $426 of AIME, plus 32% of the next $2,141 of AIME, plus 15% of AIME in excess of $2,567.

The PIA formula for cohorts of subsequent years is derived from the 1995 formula. The percentage factors remain the same, but the "dollar bands" are increased on the basis of the relative changes in nationwide average wages from year to year. Individuals who do not receive retirement benefits for months after the NRA (primarily because of the earnings test, described hereafter), receive an increase in the PIA, termed "delayed-retirement credits," as described earlier. A special minimum benefit is provided for persons with long periods of coverage at low earnings.

The PIA is automatically adjusted for changes in prices, as measured by the Consumer Price Index for All Urban Wage Earners and Clerical Workers. Such adjustment is made for benefits for each December (paid at the beginning of the following month). The adjustment is determined from the percentage increase in the CPI from the third quarter of the previous year to the third quarter of the current year; such adjustment was 2.8% in 1994.

Income Taxation of Benefits. Beginning in 1994, OASDI benefits have, for

high-income persons, become subject to income tax. The proceeds are transferred to the trust fund that paid the benefits on which income taxes were levied.
If the sum of (1) Adjusted Gross Income (AGI) (as customarily determined for
income tax purposes), (2) interest on tax-exempt bonds, (3) certain foreign-
source income, and (4) 50% of OASDI benefits exceeds the basic threshold
amount ($25,000 for single persons, $32,000 for married persons filing a joint
return, and zero for married persons filing separate returns who lived together
at some time in the year), then 50% of the ''excess''—but not more than 50%
of the OASDI benefits—is added to the AGI in computing income tax liability.
Note that the threshold amounts are not indexed for future years.

Beginning in 1994, a second threshold ($34,000 for single persons and
$44,000 for married persons filing a joint return) is in place; when the foregoing
''excess'' carries beyond the second threshold, then 85% of the ''excess'' beyond such threshold (as well as 50% of the difference between the thresholds)
is added to the AGI in computing income tax liability—but not more than 85%
of the OASDI benefits can be so added (with equitable transition provisions for
those who are just above the second threshold). The additional tax proceeds are
transferred to the Hospital Insurance Trust Fund.

Earnings Test. Benefits for retired workers and their eligible spouses and
children, for eligible spouses and children of disability beneficiaries, and for
survivors are usually not paid when the beneficiary is engaged in substantial
employment, nor are benefits paid to the eligible spouse and children of a retired
worker who is engaged in substantial employment. In 1995, benefits are payable
for persons aged 65 and older for all months in a year if the annual earnings
from all types of employment (regardless of coverage) are $11,280 or less. If
earnings exceed $11,280, then $1 of benefits is withheld for each $3 of such
''excess earnings.'' For beneficiaries under age 65, the annual exempt amount
in 1995 is $8,160, with $1 of benefits withheld for each $2 of earnings above
such amount. In the first year of benefit receipt, benefits are never withheld for
a month in which the individual had wages of 1/12 of the annual exempt amount
or less and does not render substantial self-employment services. The earned-
income restriction is not applicable at all after the individual reaches age 70.
The annual and monthly exempt amounts are adjusted annually in the same
manner as the earnings base.

Elimination of Windfall Benefits for Retired and Disabled Workers. A different method of computing the PIA is applicable generally for persons who receive
pensions based wholly or partially on earnings from noncovered employment.
The percentage factor in the PIA formula applicable to the lowest band of earnings is 40% (instead of 90%), but this procedure will not reduce the PIA by
more than 50% of the pension based on noncovered employment. This provision
is phased in for those with 21–29 years of coverage (defined as the special-
minimum benefit).

Offset of Governmental Pensions for Spouses and Widow(er)s. Two-thirds of
the amount of any pension received by individuals for their service under a

public-employee retirement system under which the members are not also covered under OASDI as of the last day of the individual's service is offset against any OASDI spouse or widow(er) benefit.

Coordination with Workers' Compensation and Other Governmental Disability Benefits. OASDI benefits are reduced when they, plus Workers' Compensation and other government disability benefits, exceed 80% of average recent earnings.

Payment of OASDI Benefits Abroad. Benefits are not payable in the case of deported persons whose rights are terminated until they are subsequently lawfully admitted. In the case of persons residing in certain countries where there is no reasonable assurance that checks can be delivered or cashed at full value, the benefits are withheld, but can subsequently be paid if conditions change. For aliens residing outside the United States who came on the roll after 1954, benefits are payable only if the insured worker has 40 or more quarters of coverage or has resided in the United States for 10 or more years, or if the country of which they are citizens has a reciprocity treaty with the United States or has a general social insurance or pension system that will continue full benefits to U.S. citizens while outside the foreign country.

OASDI Financing Provision

The benefits and administrative expenses are paid out of two separate trust funds. The old-age and survivor benefits come from the Old-Age and Survivors Insurance Trust Fund, while the monthly benefits for disabled workers and their auxiliary beneficiaries come from the Disability Insurance Trust Fund.

In considering the financial impact and burden of the OASDI program, it is necessary to consider also the payroll taxes that support the Hospital Insurance (HI) portion of the Medicare program. The combined employer-employee tax rate is scheduled to be level at 15.3% (1990 and after), of which 2.9% is for HI. The rate began at 2% for 1937–1949 and then increased in most subsequent years—for example, to 3% in 1950–1953, 7.25% in 1963–1965, 8.4% in 1966 (when HI first went into effect), 11.7% in 1973–1977, and 13.4% in 1982–1983.

The trust funds are invested in interest-bearing debt obligations of the United States. These can be either marketable issues or special issues bearing an interest rate approximating the average market yield on all government obligations having at least four years to run until earliest maturity as of the issuance date of the special issue. In actual practice, most of the assets have been in special issues.

The tax rates are levied only on earnings up to the applicable maximum taxable and creditable earnings base. This base is automatically adjusted upward, in accordance with changes in average wages in nationwide employment. The base was $60,600 in 1994 and $61,200 in 1995. The maximum base for the HI program was always the same as for the OASDI during 1966–1990, but in 1991 it was made significantly higher, and in 1994 it was eliminated.

The latest official cost estimates indicate that the OASDI program should be self-supporting from the contributions of covered workers and their employers, according to the intermediate-cost estimate. The intermediate-cost estimate in the 1994 *Trustees Report* shows a negative actuarial balance for OASDI (i.e., the financing provided is less than sufficient to meet obligations during the full 75-year valuation period—an average amount of 2.13% of taxable payroll).

This discussion of the financial status of the OASDI program indicates that some changes in the benefit structure and/or the financing are necessary. However, from a cash-flow standpoint, no problems exist for the next 10–15 years. The HI program, however, will probably have severe problems in 5–10 years.

Possible Changes in OASDI Program

Currently, some people advocate reducing OASDI benefits to alleviate the national budget-deficit crisis, now and in the future. They propose such changes as reducing the cost-of-living adjustments (COLAs) and means testing the benefits (so that high-income people will receive much smaller benefits, or even none at all). But changes in OASDI for budget purposes may be ill-advised, because that program has not been the cause of the deficits. Reduction of COLAs is not desirable because it would affect the oldest beneficiaries. Also, means testing would encourage income manipulation, as well as destroy confidence in the program.

It is suggested that changes in the Social Security system should include an increase in financing and a reduction in benefit outgo, beginning in 2005, using a phasing procedure. The additional financing could come from a small increase in the contribution rates; the benefits reduction could best come from an increase in the normal retirement age, such as, from 67 to 70 years.

If this procedure is followed, Social Security will continue to serve as the basic floor of economic protection against the risks of old-age retirement, permanent and total disability, and death of the primary wage earner. This is not to say that other changes in the Social Security program are not necessary. It is a flexible program that can, should, and will be altered occasionally to meet changing demographic, economic, and social conditions. So, confidence in Social Security's future is justified. (See also DISABILITY PROGRAMS, FEDERAL; ECONOMIC STATUS OF THE ELDERLY; ECONOMIC STATUS OF ELDERLY WOMEN; SOCIAL SECURITY: BENEFITS FOR DISABLED INDIVIDUALS; SOCIAL SECURITY: SPECIAL MINIMUM BENEFITS, and WIDOWHOOD.)

References

Beedon, Laurel. 1994. *Administering Social Security.* Washington, DC: AARP Public Policy Institute.

Board of Trustees, Federal Old-Age and Survivors Insurance and Disability Insurance Trust Funds. 1994. *Annual Report.* Washington, DC: U.S. Government Printing Office.

Detlefs, Dale R., and Robert J. Myers. 1995. *Mercer Guide to Social Security and Medicare.* Louisville, KY: William M. Mercer (updated annually).

Myers, Robert J. 1992a. *Social Security.* Philadelphia: University of Pennsylvania Press.

Myers, Robert J. 1992b. *"Within the System:" My Half Century in Social Security.* Winstead, CT: ACTEX Publications.

Myers, Robert J. 1994. "The Role of Social Security in the Smoke-and-Mirrors Budget Deficit." *Benefits Quarterly* (First Quarter), 17–21.

Rejda, George E. 1991. *Social Insurance and Economic Security.* Englewood Cliffs, NJ: Prentice-Hall.

Steuerle, C. Eugene, and Jon M. Bakija. 1994. *Retooling Social Security for the 21st Century: Right and Wrong Approaches to Reform.* Washington, DC: Urban Institute Press.

Robert J. Myers

SOCIAL SECURITY: BENEFITS FOR DISABLED INDIVIDUALS, benefits payable to individuals who are unable to engage in any substantial gainful activity because of a severe, medically determinable disability that has lasted or is expected to last for at least 12 months or to result in death. For blind individuals over age 55, benefits are payable if the individual is unable to engage in a usual occupation. During the first two years, benefits are paid regardless of earnings. Thereafter, disability beneficiaries may have small earnings and continue to receive benefits as long as they are considered unable to engage in any substantial gainful activity. The disability benefits terminate at the Normal Retirement Age, when the beneficiary goes on the old-age benefit roll.

Disabled Widows

It was not until the 1967 amendments that survivor benefits were provided for disabled widows and widowers. Even now, widow protection is severely restricted.

To qualify for disabled widow benefits, the widow must:

1. Be at least 50 years old
2. Become disabled within seven years of the spouse's death or within seven years of being eligible for a mother benefit based on care of an eligible dependent child of the deceased worker
3. Meet the same severe, medically determinable disability criteria applicable to disabled workers or disabled children.

Widows who successfully pass the three-part test and become eligible for disabled widow benefits face one more barrier to economic security: Benefits are reduced for early retirement. Initially, the reduction was for each month the widow was younger than 65. If benefits began at age 50, for example, a widow received only 50% of the benefit that would have been payable at age 65.

The 1979 Advisory Council on Social Security, which in its deliberations gave significant attention to women's Social Security issues, recommended eliminating the age 50 requirement and the early retirement benefit reductions. The 1983 Social Security amendment partially rescinded the reduction by establishing a minimum disabled widow benefit of 71.5% of the deceased spouse's full benefit. This is identical to the benefit payable to a nondisabled widow who elects to begin widow benefits in the month she reaches age 60. While amelioration of the reduction was a significant improvement, disabled widows remain the only disabled individuals covered by the Social Security Act whose benefits are reduced as if early retirement were voluntary.

Before 1991, a disabled widow had to satisfy separate, more stringent disability criteria in order to receive benefits. Because of the harsher standard, more than 20% of disabled widow applicants annually were judged not disabled for widow benefits, even though, based on the regular disability criteria, they either qualified for disability benefits on their own earnings records or would have qualified if they had sufficient recent Social Security earnings credits.

Disabled Spouses

The 1979 Advisory Council on Social Security also recommended the extension of spouse benefits to a disabled spouse of a retired or disabled worker. The council report pointed out that ''just as is the case of the disabled widow, the disabled spouse of an annuitant is by definition unable to work'' (Advisory Council 1979).

The council's disabled spouse recommendation was never implemented. Disabled spouses are still ineligible for reduced spouse benefits until they reach age 62.

Medicare Eligibility

One of the most advantageous aspects of eligibility for disability benefits is that a disabled individual entitled to cash benefits does not need to wait until age 65 to become eligible for Medicare. As Medicare was extended to disabled workers, disabled adult children, and disabled widows effective in 1973, Medicare coverage became available in the 25th month of cash benefit entitlement. For many disabled persons, particularly dependents, access to Medicare is likely to have a greater financial value than the monthly cash benefit received. Similarly, a disabled spouse's lack of access to Medicare is likely to be a greater financial burden than lack of eligibility for monthly cash benefits. (See also DISABILITY PROGRAMS, FEDERAL; SOCIAL SECURITY PROGRAM OF THE UNITED STATES; and WIDOWHOOD).

Reference

Advisory Council on Social Security. 1979. *Social Security Financing and Benefits.* Washington, DC: Author.

Mary Jane Yarrington

SOCIAL SECURITY: SPECIAL MINIMUM BENEFIT, a benefit providing extra protection for workers with low earnings. The Social Security benefit computation formula was designed to provide proportionally higher benefits to low earners than are provided to high earners. However, approximately 200,000 long-term, low-wage workers and/or their dependents or survivors receive extra protection under a provision of law called the Special Minimum. Modest change could make this Special Minimum a more effective tool for strengthening the retirement income of low earners.

The Special Minimum, enacted as part of the 1972 Social Security amendments, is an alternate method for determining the amount of the monthly benefit. Instead of basing the monthly benefit on average indexed monthly earnings over the worker's lifetime, the Special Minimum looks at the length of a work career. The retiree receives whichever is greater—a benefit determined under the regular benefit method or a benefit determined under the Special Minimum method.

As is true with regular benefits, the amount of the Special Minimum benefit is reduced for each month a benefit is paid before age 65. Special Minimum benefits are never increased by delayed retirement credits if the recipient waits until after age 65 before receiving monthly benefits, which is different from regular benefits.

Targeted to Long-Term Workers

To insure that the principal beneficiaries of the Special Minimum are persons with a long-term attachment to the work force, a base of ten years is required before the Special Minimum computation can be used. The amount of the monthly benefit payable then is determined by multiplying a set dollar amount by the number of earning years over 10 and up to 30 (i.e., a maximum of 20 years) in which the worker had substantial creditable earnings. When the Special Minimum began in 1973, the monthly multiple was $8.50. The maximum Special Minimum benefit payable at age 65 for 30 years of substantial earnings was $170 a month. The 1972 act, which provided automatic cost-of-living adjustments (COLAs) for regular benefits, stipulated that COLAs would not apply to Special Minimum benefits. An ad hoc adjustment, effective March 1974, raised the monthly multiple amount to $9.00. It remained at that level through 1978 (maximum benefit $180).

The Social Security amendments of 1977 raised the Special Minimum multiple to $11.50, partially restoring its 1973 value. More importantly, the 1977 amendments provided that, effective June 1979, the maximum amount payable would increase automatically by the same percentage and at the same time that COLAs became effective for other Social Security beneficiaries. COLAs since 1979 have raised the Special Minimum benefit payable to a 1994 maximum of $505.30—roughly equivalent to the regular benefit payable to a retiree whose lifetime indexed earnings average $10,000 a year.

Qualifying Earnings

For Special Minimum purposes, annual earnings had to sufficiently indicate more than a casual attachment to the work force. To be creditable, annual earnings after 1950 had to equal at least one-fourth of each year's maximum taxable Social Security wage base. Earnings from 1937 through 1950 count toward the

Special Minimum benefit, but because the Social Security Administration maintains those earnings as a dollar total instead of yearly, the number of creditable years is determined by dividing total 1937–1950 earnings by $900, up to a maximum of 14 years.

The one-fourth requirement for earnings to be creditable for Special Minimum purposes was continued through 1990. Effective in 1991, the creditable earnings requirement was reduced to 15% of the maximum taxable wage base. The change from one-fourth to 15% of the wage base was a response to the fact that, in the 1980s, the federal minimum wage remained unchanged for so long that earnings from full-time, full-year minimum wage employment did not satisfy the Special Minimum definition of substantial earnings.

A Practical Vehicle for Improvement of Benefits to Low Earners

The Special Minimum establishes a floor below which monthly Social Security benefits will not fall for long-term, low-wage workers, but the maximum payable benefit is only 85% of the federal poverty level for a single person.

Two changes could be made to insure long-term workers at least a poverty-level retirement income. One would be to increase the multiple amount so that anyone with 30 years of creditable earnings would receive a monthly benefit equal to the poverty level. An alternative would be to increase the number of years of earnings accorded Special Minimum consideration. Many of the individuals who now qualify for higher benefits under the Special Minimum—or who would qualify if more years were considered—have worked in excess of 30 years. Consideration of even five additional years of earnings would bring the maximum Special Minimum benefit to the poverty line. (See also SOCIAL SECURITY PROGRAM OF THE UNITED STATES and SOCIAL SECURITY: BENEFITS FOR DISABLED INDIVIDUALS.)

References

Detlefs, Dale R., and Robert J. Myers. 1995. *Mercer Guide to Social Security and Medicare.* Louisville, KY: William M. Mercer (updated annually).
Rejda, George E. 1991. *Social Insurance and Economic Insurance.* Englewood Cliffs, NJ: Prentice-Hall.

Mary Jane Yarrington

SOCIAL WORK, GERONTOLOGICAL, a specialty within the profession of social work in response to the increasing health and social service demands of our aging society. Over the last twenty years, social workers in health, mental health, and community development have reshaped their expertise for older adults whose numbers are increasing. It was once uncommon to work with an 80-year-old client at a mental health clinic; now mental health agencies have social workers whose specific jobs are to serve older clients and their families. Thus, a specialized body of social work knowledge and skills in gerontology has emerged, and the demand for gerontological social workers will continue to increase.

Gerontological social workers provide clinical services to elders and their families, develop programs to serve the elderly, administer social and health care facilities, advocate on behalf of elderly citizens, and participate in the development of social policies. Gerontological social workers are found in health care (hospitals, home health agencies, hospices); residential care (congregate housing, nursing homes); mental health services (geropsychiatric units of acute care hospitals, mental health clinics); specialty nonprofit organizations, and community development organizations (the Alzheimer's Association; Housing Options Provided for the Elderly, Inc.); and public agencies (State Units on Aging, Area Agencies on Aging). Social workers are distinguished from other professionals in gerontology because of their knowledge of community resources and the range of options available to ameliorate problems and their skills in engaging the elderly person, family, and community in aspects of problemsolving. In fact, so many elders and their families request help finding solutions to problems associated with aging that many gerontological social workers are opening private practices. These clinicians often help families understand the situation, access in-home services, or make nursing home decisions.

Social work interventions with older adults usually begin with a psychosocial assessment. Due to the close interconnections of the biological, psychological, and social aspects of aging, assessment can be complicated (Kane and Kane 1981). For example, an elderly person may lose the ability to drive because of sensory loss; this person then becomes socially isolated and eventually depressed; this depression can lead to problems with confusion. If not assessed thoroughly, it could be concluded that this person has an irreversible dementia, when the confusion is a result of other psychosocial problems that can be addressed. An assessment completed by a gerontological social worker will often be multidimensional and cover physical functioning, health conditions, mental status, emotional health, social resources, physical environment, and financial resources. Other professionals are involved as needed or permitted by a client. For example, a neurologist should provide the diagnosis of dementia of the Alzheimer's type. However, the social worker often is the professional with the broadest knowledge of the client. Social workers most frequently work with family or friends of the elderly client.

Financial resources are often an important part of a complete psychosocial assessment. Sometimes, this is a sensitive area of questioning, but a good social worker will allay the client's fear regarding misuse of information. The development of service arrangements depends on a client's resources and entitlements, which must be accurately understood. The assessment must also reveal what informal (family and friends) and formal (paid or from an agency) services are already in place for a client. It is often difficult to get a clear picture of what agencies are involved and who is paying. Providers and funding streams are largely invisible in some cases. The client may know that someone comes three times a week to help, but it is difficult to ascertain, for example, that the local Area Agency on Aging is supplying a person to help with personal care through monies from the Older Americans Act*. Some older adults and families still mistakenly believe that Medicare* is paying for such services. (This mistake is being made less frequently, given an increased knowledge about long-term care.) A thorough assessment of financial resources is also needed to ensure that older adults are taking advantage of resources available to them. Surprisingly, only 50% of poor older adults who are eligible for Supplementary Security Income (SSI)* are certified to receive those benefits (Berman and Gelfand 1993).

Based on information gained from a psychosocial assessment, social workers can choose from a variety of interventions. Clinical case management is often the treatment of choice. Case management is an intervention aimed at organizing an effective and efficient package of long-term care services to a client. Case management functions include casefinding (conduct outreach, eligibility determination, intake), assessment (current status, problem identification), care planning (develop plan based on needs), coordination (arrange delivery of services), follow-up (monitor client and services), and reassessment (reevaluate) (White 1987). The term *clinical case management* is used because counseling is important in this process; it is more than just arranging services. Some clients present complex psychosocial situations, and some clients are reluctant to accept services. There is also the need to balance family care and assistance from formal sources. Sometimes clients are in degenerative situations, so service needs are continually changing. Thus, social workers' clinical skills are needed to provide effective case management to elderly clients.

Case management can also have a financial function. There are models in which social workers authorize funding and waive eligibility criteria. Sometimes, these workers must contain the cost of a service package to a predetermined amount of money (which will assure that in-home care is less than nursing home care). There are models in which case managers approve the expenditure of money for a package of client services and monitor this package but have little direct client contact. These models are common among HMOs and commercial insurance carriers, but social workers are less likely than nurses to be employed in these positions. Different models of case management call for different amounts of client contact and different degrees of authority to purchase and allocate resources. Social workers are most likely to perform case management roles where there is maximum client contact, given their professional expertise in clinical and family work.

The assessment and care arrangement functions are also the key components of discharge planning, and many social workers provide discharge planning services to patients in hospitals and nursing homes. Workers assist elders and families in identifying care needs and options, in making decisions about informal and formal care arrangements, and in establishing such arrangements. Social workers thus play a role in ensuring continuity of care between hospital, nursing home, and home.

Gerontological social workers provide a range of clinical interventions with older adults and their families. They organize and lead therapeutic groups that address all types of challenges posèd in later life, such as widowhood, caregiving, or recovering from/adjusting to stroke or Parkinson's Disease. Often these groups are offered free of charge through nonprofit associations such as the Alzheimer's or Parkinson's Association. Social workers also counsel clients individually and assist with problems of depression or adjustment to the multiple late-life losses (Knight 1986). Families often need assistance in dealing with an aging relative's increasing dependence, and family therapy around issues of aging is a growing demand (Rathbone-McCuan 1991). Medicare can be billed for counseling services (although current reimbursement rates are low). Many agencies have a sliding scale fee schedule.

Understanding who pays for which services is critical and difficult in gerontological social work. There are 80 federal programs that address long-term care of the elderly through cash assistance, in-kind transfer, and provision of goods and services (Monk 1990). Social workers must know the programs that affect their clients. The core policies that affect gerontological social work practice are Social Security*, Medicare, Medicaid*, SSI*, Older Americans Act* services, food stamps, and housing* subsidies. Medicare is intended to pay for acute care; social workers often help clients understand coverage and work with the bureaucracy to organize bills. Medicaid, the federal-state program that covers medical care for the poor, covers long-term care in the home, in day care centers, and in nursing homes. Social workers assist clients in obtaining Medicaid coverage and using these benefits to meet their care needs. Social service block grants and Older Americans Act funds are used at the local level to provide in-home and meal services to elders in need.

Social workers play key roles in accessing these subsidized services on behalf of their clients. Yet most of the money spent on services by elders and their families comes from private funds. Thus, social workers must educate clients and help make decisions about using money to meet care needs. To help them achieve this expertise, the Boettner Center at the University of Pennsylvania, affiliated with the School of Social Work, plans to offer course work in Financial Gerontology for Social Workers. (See also BOETTNER CENTER OF FINANCIAL GERONTOLOGY, HOUSING, MEDICAID, MEDICARE, MENTAL HEALTH AMONG THE ELDERLY, NUTRITION PROGRAMS, OLDER AMERICANS ACT, and SUPPLEMENTAL SECURITY INCOME.)

References

Berman, J., and D. Gelfand. 1993. "Age, Employment, and Income Maintenance." In *The Aging Network,* ed. D. Gelfand. New York: Springer, 29–47.

Kane, R., and R. Kane. 1981. *Assessing the Elderly: A Practical Guide to Measurement.* Lexington, MA: Lexington Books.

Knight, R. 1986. *Psychotherapy with Older Adults.* Newbury Park, CA: Sage Publications.

Monk, A. 1990. "Gerontological Social Services." In *Handbook of Gerontological Services*, ed. A. Monk. New York: Columbia University Press, 3–26.
Rathbone-McCuan, E. 1991. "Family Counseling: An Emerging Approach in Clinical Gerontology." In *Serving the Elderly: Skills for Practice*, ed. P. Kim. New York: Aldine de Gruyter.
White, M. 1987. "Case Management." In *Encyclopedia of Aging*, ed. G. L. Maddox. New York: Springer.

Nancy Morrow-Howell

SUPPLEMENTAL SECURITY INCOME (SSI), a means-tested, federally administered income assistance program. Established by the 1972 amendments to the Social Security Act and begun in 1974, SSI provides monthly cash payments in accordance with uniform, national eligibility requirements to needy aged, blind, and disabled persons. At the outset, it was envisaged that the SSI program would "provide a positive assurance that the nation's aged, blind and disabled people would no longer have to subsist on below–poverty level incomes" (Social Security Administration [SSA] 1992). The number of recipients on SSI has increased from nearly 4 million in 1974 to 5.6 million in December 1992. Total annual benefits paid under the SSI program increased from about $5.3 billion in 1974 to $21.8 billion in 1992; after adjusting for inflation, annual increases were 2.2%. The monthly federal benefit for individuals rose from $140 ($210 for couples) in 1974 to $434 ($652 for couples) in 1993.

Eligibility

To qualify for SSI payments, a person must satisfy the program criteria for age, blindness, or disability. The aged are defined as persons 65 years and older. A person also must be needy, that is, have limited income and resources, to be eligible for SSI. Additionally, to qualify for SSI, a person must: (1) be a U.S. citizen or an immigrant lawfully admitted for permanent residence or otherwise permanently residing in the United States under color of law, and (2) be a resident of the United States. Since SSI payments are reduced by other income, applicants and recipients must apply for any other money benefits due them. The Social Security Administration works with recipients and helps them receive other benefits for which they are eligible. People who receive SSI checks also may receive Social Security* checks if they are eligible. Social security benefits are the highest source of income for SSI recipients. However, a person cannot get SSI payments and participate in the Aid to Families with Dependent Children (AFDC) program. Since its inception, SSI has been viewed as the "program of last resort," that is, after evaluating all other income, SSI pays what is necessary to bring an individual to the statutorily prescribed income floor.

Under the program, $20 of monthly income from most sources is excluded from countable income. The first $65 of monthly earned income plus one-half of remaining earnings are excluded. The value of any in-kind assistance is counted as income unless such in-kind assistance is specifically excluded by statute (for example, nutrition, food stamps, housing, or social services). If an SSI applicant or recipient is living in the household of another and receiving in-kind support and maintenance from them, the SSI benefit standard for such an individual will be reduced by one-third of the federal SSI benefit standard. Living in a publicly operated community residence that serves no more than 16 people, living in a public institution mainly to attend approved educational or job training, or living in a public emergency shelter for the homeless may allow low-income persons to receive SSI. As countable income increases, a recipient's SSI benefit amount decreases. Ineligibility for SSI occurs when countable income equals the federal benefit standard plus the amount of applicable state supplementation.

SSI eligibility is restricted to qualified persons who have countable resources (assets) not exceeding $2,000 (or $3,000 for couples). In determining countable resources, a number of items are not included, such as the individual's home and household goods, personal effects, an automobile, and a burial space. The value of property that is used in a person's trade or business, or by the person as an employee, is also excluded.

Although most low-income elderly have few assets, "the asset test for SSI is so stringent that some people with inadequate incomes are denied assistance because of small amounts of savings and other resources" (Schulz 1992).

Benefits and Costs

The regular federal SSI benefit for an individual for 1993 was $434 per month and $652 for a couple. Most states supplement the regular federal SSI benefit. For example, there is a state supplement (for individuals) of $186 in California, $93 in Wisconsin, and $2 in Oregon (1993 figures). Some states also link their SSI supplement to state-only funding of aging services. It is the combined regular federal SSI/state-supplemented benefit against which countable income is compared in determining eligibility and benefit amount. The regular benefits are indexed to the Consumer Price Index (CPI). Maximum potential SSI and food stamp benefits, combined, are of interest: They were at least $516 per month (for individuals in 1993) in most states, with a few states providing about $100 more. Finally, it is worth comparing the combined benefits to the poverty threshold of $6,931 per year (individuals in 1993): The federal SSI benefit alone reached about 90% of poverty, and with Social Security benefits added, 92%. Only as food stamps were taken into account did the support exceed the poverty threshold at 102%. A study of the adequacy of SSI benefits in light of real costs for basic needs (shelter, food, clothing), rather than the abstract poverty threshold, made them appear even less sufficient; only about 85% of these costs could be covered by program benefits on average. "Even when food stamps and social security insurance benefits are considered, . . . the income package fails to meet basic needs" (Meyer and Bartolomei-Hill 1994).

Federal SSI benefits and the cost of administering the program are financed from general funds from the U.S. Treasury. The Social Security Administration also administers the payment of approximately $3.2 billion of state-financed state supplementary payments. In fiscal year 1991, of $14.6 billion in federal SSI benefits, approximately 80% went to those who were eligible on the basis of disability, 18% to the aged, and 2% to the blind. The higher percentage of federal SSI payments for the disabled is due to the fact that only 35% of the disabled have other income in the form of Social Security benefits, compared with 68% of the aged.

SSI Beneficiaries

The number of SSI recipients declined from 1975 to 1983. However, in the years 1984–1992 the number has increased from about 3.9 million to more than 5.5 million. About two million of them are elderly, or about 7% of Americans who are 65 and older. Still, since 1975, the number of elderly persons receiving SSI has declined from 2.3 million to 1.5 million in 1992, primarily because of increasing incomes among seniors. But not all elderly have done well. Of those SSI recipients receiving benefits on the basis of age (i.e., age 65 or older), 37% were 80 years of age or above, that is, in the category of the oldest old. But even as needs increased for some, the rate of participation in SSI among the poor elderly dropped from about 75% in 1975 to between 55% and 60% since 1980. It is estimated that about one-third of aged persons eligible for SSI do not participate in the program (Meyer and Bartolomei-Hill 1994).

Outreach and Adequacy Issues

The 1983 Social Security amendments mandated that the Social Security Administration conduct two separate outreach activities aimed at the aged population. The first was a one-time notice mailed to those aged individuals and couples whose Social Security benefits were less than the SSI eligibility levels. The second outreach activity is an ongoing effort to notify two groups of Social Security beneficiaries: those about to reach age 65, and disabled individuals who have been receiving Social Security benefits for 21 consecutive months and will soon be eligible for Medicare.

The goal of the SSI outreach strategy is to reduce the barriers that prevent or discourage potentially SSI-eligible individuals from participating in the program. Common barriers include a lack of information or a misunderstanding about the program, a perception that program participation results in stigma, and the inherent difficulties of the application process for persons who are elderly or disabled. Obstacles within the application process include complex forms, the absence of "one-stop shopping," transportation difficulties, long waiting times, and poor attitudes of intake workers (Kassner 1992). Duplication of other SSA procedures, lack of publicizing the program, and insufficient referral to and complicated application modalities for food stamps at the state level were criticized independently (General Accounting Office 1992).

The Social Security Administration seeks to overcome barriers by providing better information, alleviating stigma surrounding the program, and making the process of applying for benefits easier. It tries to accomplish this through direct action and cooperative efforts with other government agencies and private-sector organizations that have links with individuals whom SSA is trying to reach.

In 1990, the Social Security Administration established the SSI Modernization Project, comprised of 21 experts on SSI and related policy areas, to determine the effectiveness of the SSI program. The project experts urged priority for the following four recommendations: (1) increase benefit guarantees, (2) increase resource limits, (3) eliminate in-kind support and maintenance from consideration as income, and (4) increase the number of SSA staff. A reform, according to this opinion, would bring the benefit level to 120% of the poverty guideline, lower the eligibility age from 65 to 62, eliminate income verification in situations when such verification would not be cost effective, and personalize and individualize contact and service by SSA staff. (SSA 1992).

Program costs associated with these recommendations were estimated at $3.5 billion in fiscal year 1993 and were to increase to $32.5 billion by 1997 as the improvements would gradually be implemented. Bills dealing with these issues were introduced in the 102nd Congress, but none were passed. Because of the budget deficit, many policymakers viewed the legislation as too costly and expansive, and some were concerned that it provided preference to one group of needy persons (aged, blind, and disabled individuals) over another (families with children) with generally higher rates of poverty. The outlook for aged persons in need is thus not very bright. One suggestion that would entail an improvement is to combine the benefits reviewed here with federal housing assistance (not an entitlement), a "kind of program linkage [that] could vastly improve the economic well-being of many lower-income aged people without the need to create or alter existing programs" (Meyer and Bartolomei-Hill 1994). (See also SOCIAL SECURITY PROGRAM OF THE UNITED STATES, SOCIAL SECURITY: BENEFITS FOR DISABLED INDIVIDUALS, and SOCIAL SECURITY: SPECIAL MINIMUM BENEFIT.)

Organization
Social Security Administration, Office of Public Inquiries

Suggested Reading
Social Security Administration. 1994. *SSI—Supplemental Security Income.* Washington, DC: SSA.

References

General Accounting Office (GAO). 1992. *Social Security: Need for Better Coordination of Food Stamp Services for Social Security Clients.* Washington, DC.

Kassner, Enid. 1992. *Falling through the Safety Net: Missed Opportunities for America's Elderly Poor.* Washington, DC: AARP.

Meyer, Daniel R., and Steve Bartolomei-Hill. 1994. "The Adequacy of Supplemental Security Income Benefits for Aged Individuals and Couples." *Gerontologist* 34: 161–72.

Schulz, James H. 1992. *The Economics of Aging,* Fifth Edition. Westport, CT: Auburn House.

Social Security Administration. 1992. "SSI Modernization Project: Final Report of the Experts." *Social Security Bulletin* 55: 22–35.

U.S. House of Representatives, Committee on Ways and Means. 1993. *Overview of Entitlement Programs.* 1993 Green Book. Washington, DC: U.S. Government Printing Office.

Jurg K. Siegenthaler

SURVIVOR'S BENEFITS. See Death Benefits.

T

TAX PLANNING. See Capital Gains; Charitable Contributions; Elder Taxpayer Issues; Estate Planning; Homeownership.

TAX SHELTER. See Condominiums; Cooperative Ownership in Housing; Employee Stock Ownership Plans (ESOPs); IRAs; Keogh Plans; Homeownership; Reverse Mortgages.

TITLING ASSETS, the means whereby the owner of property has the just possession of the property under the law. The *title* is the evidence of ownership of the property. There are a number of different ways to hold title to property whether real (such as houses, land, buildings), or personal (such as stocks, cash, furniture, etc.).

In *tenancy in common,* each owner, whether two or more, holds title to an undivided interest in the property. The interests may or may not be equal, depending on how the owners acquired the property. In most jurisdictions, title to real property inherited by children will be held as tenants in common, with each child owning an equal undivided interest. The distinctive characteristic of tenancy in common is that each owner's interest can be severed from the others and sold or bequeathed under a will. As a practical matter, there may not be a big market for partial ownership interests, but an individual owner may force the sale of the property by filing a court action. The other tenants in common do not become owners of another's tenancy-in-common interest upon that owner's death.

Joint tenancy, another way to hold title, means that the last surviving joint tenant (i.e., joint owner) will own the entire property. This is known as the "right of survivorship." Although the use of the word *joint* automatically includes the concept of right of survivorship in many states, this is not always the case. In Virginia, for example, the words "with common law right of survivorship" must be included in the instrument of conveyance or a so-called joint tenancy will actually have the effect of a tenancy in common. Joint tenancies can be of equal or unequal interests, depending on how the joint owners took title. For married couples, joint tenancy automatically assumes equal ownership by each spouse. An ordinary joint tenancy with right of survivorship can usually be severed by the unilateral act of one joint tenant, such as by filing a court action or by taking any other action inconsistent with right of survivorship.

A third way to hold title is *tenancy by the entirety,* which is joint tenancy with a common law right of survivorship for married couples only. Generally, property owned by married couples as tenants by the entirety enjoys protection against creditors if the debtor is only one of the two spouses. For example, the husband may be a physician with a large malpractice judgment; his insurance does not cover the entire liability. If he owns his home with his spouse as "tenants by the entirety" the judgment creditor cannot take the house.

Holding title by means of a *life estate/remainder interest* is best explained by understanding the two concepts that make it up. A life estate is ownership for the lifetime of the life estate title holder. What is left upon that person's death is the entire property—that is, the "remainder." The "remainderman" becomes the sole owner of the property automatically upon the death of the life estate holder. For federal estate tax purposes, life estates are generally not counted as "resources." The life estate holder is liable for all taxes and expenses on the property and is also entitled to any income produced by the property, such as rent. When the life estate holder dies, the remainderman automatically owns the property with a "step-up" in tax basis. Thus, if the property had originally been purchased for a low price, for example, $20,000, and is worth $100,000 when the life estate holder dies, the remainderman can sell the property for the $100,000 and not pay any capital gains tax.

A final way to hold title is by *community property.* Community property is property owned by married couples in community property states, such as California. Community property presupposes equal ownership by each spouse of property acquired during the marriage. People residing in community property states should consult with local counsel with respect to both their ownership interests and their ability to leave such property under their wills*. The law is not the same in every jurisdiction.

Every jurisdiction has variations on each of the above methods of holding title to property. It is imperative that readers check with an attorney in their own jurisdiction to determine precisely what their rights are as owners. (See also ELDER LAW PRACTICE, ESTATE TAXES, INHERITANCE, LIFE ESTATES, PROBATE, TRUSTS, and WILLS.)

References

Dukeminier, Jesse. 1993. *Property,* Third Edition. Boston: Little, Brown.

Harvey, David C. B. 1966. *Harvey Law of Real Property and Title Closing.* New York: C. Boardman Co.

Maisel, Sherman J. 1992. *Real Estate Finance,* Second Edition. Orlando, FL: Harcourt Brace Jovanovich, Inc.

Savage, Terry. 1993. *New Money Strategies for the '90s.* New York: Harper Business.

Janet L. Kuhn

TRANSPORTATION. The aging of society is a profound demographic change that has important implications for transportation planning and decision making. There is little doubt that the growing number of old and very old Americans will require changes in the ways in which we predict travel patterns, estimate transportation service requirements, and design transportation systems.

The Aging of the Population

There are six major elements of the aging of society that have important transportation implications; they are briefly outlined below. First, the sheer number of elderly travellers is increasing rapidly. The elderly are the fastest growing component of the U.S. population—the number of those over age 65 increased more than 20% between 1980 and 1990. Also, the number of the very old has increased; in 1990 more than 6.2 million Americans were 85+, a number the Census Bureau expects to increase by over 400% by 2050. By the first decade of the twenty-first century, almost one-half of all elderly people will be over 75—and almost 5% of the entire U.S. population will be over 80. As a result of these trends, the Census Bureau expects the median age in the United States to climb to almost 40 by 2035—up from 32.8 in 1990 (Taeuber 1993).

Second, the aggregate trends hide important differences between women and men that have transportation implications. Because women live longer, they outnumber men by 3-to-2 and are overrepresented among the very old (Taeuber 1993). In 1991, almost 46% of women (but only 37% of men) over 65 were over 75, while more than one in four older women were over 80 (compared to less than one in five men). The Census Bureau predicts that by 2010 more than one-half of all women (but only 41% of all men) will be over 75.

Partially because of the age gap between men and women, older women are substantially more likely to be unmarried or to live alone; in 1990 almost 54% of women (but only 19% of men) over 65 were widowed or divorced, while 16% of men (but over 42% of women) over 65 were living alone. But the age gap does not explain all the differences between the sexes, among those over 85 more than 57% of women (but only 28% of men) were living alone; moreover, men over 85 not living alone were almost twice as likely to be living with a spouse or relative than comparably aged women.

Third, the geographic distribution of the elderly has transportation implications. Despite popular views to the contrary, the U.S. Census Bureau (Taeuber

1993) has concluded that "most elderly people stay put." Between 1986 and 1987, less than 2% of those over 65 moved far enough to change counties, and fewer than 1% moved to another state. In fact, among the elderly who do move, the largest percentage stay within the same region but change counties—for example, 60% of all moves by those over 65 living in the Northeast in 1986 and 1987 were to another county within the same state.

Fourth, the geographic concentration of elderly people is also relevant. In 1990, 23 million seniors lived in metropolitan areas, while 8.2 million lived in nonmetropolitan or rural regions. Because the rural elderly also age in place, while younger residents have migrated to metropolitan areas, the actual concentration of rural elders has increased. Nationally, the rural elderly constitute more than 15% of the population in the areas where they live, and there are a number of states and individual counties where they comprise more than 35% of the rural population. Moreover, the oldest old (over 85) are more concentrated in rural areas (Taeuber 1993).

In 1990, almost two-thirds of all seniors living in metropolitan areas were in the suburbs, and until 1980, the majority of seniors living in urban places lived in central cities. Although younger seniors were more likely to live in suburbs than older elderly, the differences were smaller in 1990 than in 1980. Little of this increasing suburban concentration represents moves by the elderly; it is another facet of the aging-in-place phenomenon.

Fifth, the diversity seen among younger Americans is increasingly considered among those now elderly, and there is little doubt that it will increase in the future. Cultural and ethnic preferences have important transportation implications. There is a growing body of literature that shows that cultural or ethnic differences may create variations in the driving patterns of younger and older people, the kind and amount of ride giving either requested by or provided to them, and their attitudes about safety and security (Bengston, et al. 1976; Ho 1994; Miller et al. 1986; Wachs 1976).

Finally, arguably the most important change among the elderly is the rapidly increasing rate of driver's licensing. Between 1984 and 1992, licensing rates increased substantially for every cohort of the elderly, and faster for women than for men. In 1992, over 98% of men and over 80% of women aged 60–69 had a driver's license, but women's rates had increased 50% faster than men's. Since licensing is almost universal among younger cohorts of women, the gap between the sexes among older people has and will continue to decrease; by 2010, 90% of women and almost 100% of men over 65 will be licensed drivers—with over thirty years of driving experience.

Transportation Implications

Those who will be elderly in the next four decades will differ notably from previous generations in many important ways: They will be wealthier and better educated, substantially more diverse, and much more likely to be living in the suburbs, and most will be drivers. At the same time, a major subset of the elderly will be poor—generally older women living alone—requiring substantial assistance. All of these patterns will create important transportation differences and desires among older Americans in the future.

Possession of a driver's license is associated with substantial increases in the number of trips and miles travelled by the elderly. For example, in 1990 the trip rates of men with licenses was almost double those of men without. The impact was especially important for very old men—men over 85 with licenses made three times as many trips as comparable men without.

Regardless of license status, the elderly have become increasingly more reliant on cars. In 1990, less than 75% of all trips taken by the elderly were in private vehicles. Conversely, the elderly were even less likely to use public transit for their trips than ever before; no cohort of the elderly used public transit for more than 5% of their trips and the average was substantially less. Although walking was the mode of second choice, its importance decreased by one-third in urban areas and one-fourth in rural areas since 1983.

Linked to the use of the car is the increasing distance covered by the elderly. The elderly drove 20% more miles than they had in 1983, while those over 70 drove 40% more. Even the very old were driving over 80 miles per week.

The elderly population includes pockets of much older women living alone, many below poverty level, many of whom cannot or will not drive, or cannot or will not obtain rides from others. Given their economic status and household situation, it is not surprising that there are important differences in the travel patterns of older men and women. For example, in 1990, elderly men took 24% more personal trips, travelled 19% more miles, and made 94% more vehicle trips than elderly women. However, despite these differences, and although fewer older women have licenses, women took almost as great a percentage of their trips in a private vehicle.

The residential patterns of the elderly significantly impact travel behavior. Older people living in the suburbs or rural areas must travel farther and have few alternatives to the car. For example, all suburban women over 65 drive 6% more than central city women, while suburban men drive 14% more than comparable central city men. The patterns are even sharper when the elderly are grouped by cohort; for example, suburban men aged 75–79 drive 20% more than their central city counterparts.

Changes in the American population structure has important societal implications, which in turn have transportation impacts. Older people need services and support—which can include or take the place of transportation. These services can be provided by individual family members and neighbors or by society as a whole.

The dependence of the elderly on the car creates substantial safety concerns. Today the per capita accident rate of the population decreases substantially as the age of the driver increases; that is, older people are much less likely to have accidents than younger people. But when their accident rate is calculated by exposure, that is, by miles driven, the result is the well-known U-shaped curve;

older and very young drivers have more accidents per mile driven than those in the middle. This means that older drivers have lower overall accident rates simply because they drive less. Moreover, even on a per capita basis, older drivers have more serious injuries and higher fatality rates when involved in accidents than other age groups. Preliminary studies indicate that younger old drivers have better driving records than older drivers did at the same age. Even if all older drivers reduced their driving as they aged, or newer generations of older people had driving records per mile driven, the large number of older drivers will still increase the total accident rate.

The Implications for Transportation Planning

To respond to the growing segment of the population who are over 65, society must offer older people realistic ways to meet their mobility needs. This includes options or policies that: (1) improve the safety of cars and the road network; (2) improve the driving abilities or coping mechanisms of the driver; (3) offer safe, reliable alternatives to the car by making transit and paratransit more effective and reliable; (4) make pedestrian travel safer and more practical for either recreation or mobility; and (5) address the safety, and other special, concerns of the elderly.

While the elderly as a group have many of the same needs as other travellers—for safety, security, convenience, and reliability at cost-effective prices—they may value some system attributes more than other members of society (security, for example); they may have disproportionate requirements for other attributes (reliability or convenience, for example); and they may make different assessments of the cost-effectiveness of various transportation systems and services because the cost of transportation may constitute a greater percentage of their disposable income.

Therefore, the effectiveness of any policies or programs aimed at the elderly will be reduced if they: (1) believe themselves to be safer or better drivers than they are, (2) cannot afford or find themselves unable to use any new transportation systems or services, (3) are put in situations where they feel unsafe or are more likely to be victimized, or (4) are not offered reasonable or realistic alternatives to driving alone.

Transportation programs and policies can be a powerful force in increasing the mobility and independence of the elderly—but only if these services are developed and implemented with special attention to the particular needs of this growing segment of society. (See also BANKING SERVICES FOR THE MATURE MARKET, DAY PROGRAMS FOR ADULTS, DISABILITY INITIATIVE, FINANCIAL COUNSELING, LEISURE, OLDER AMERICANS ACT, RETIREMENT MIGRATION, TRAVEL, and VACATION HOMES AND RECREATIONAL PROPERTY.)

References

Bengtson, Vern I., Fernando Torres-Gil, Deborah Newquist, and Mary Simonin. 1976. *Transportation: The Diverse Aged.* National Science Foundation Report. Washington, DC: U.S. Government Printing Office.

Cerrelli, Ezio C. 1992. "Crash Data and Rates for Age-Sex Groups of Drivers, 1990." *Research Note.* U.S. National Highway Safety Administration (May: Fig. 1–4.) Washington, DC: U.S. Department of Transportation.

Ho, Amy. 1994. "Understanding Asian Commuters in Southern California: Implications for Rideshare Marketing. Paper Presented at the 1994 Annual Conference of the Transportation Research Board, January 9–13, Washington, DC.

Millar, M., R. Morrison, and A. Vyas. 1986. *Minority and Poor Households: Patterns of Travel and Transportation Fuel Use.* Argonne, IL: Argonne National Laboratory.

Rosenbloom, Sandra. 1994. *Travel by the Elderly.* Final Report, 1990 NPTS Subject Area Report. Tucson, AZ: Federal Highway Administration.

Taeuber, Cynthia M. 1993. *Sixty-Five Plus in America.* U.S. Bureau of the Census Current Population Reports, Special Study. P23–178RV. Washington, DC: GPO.

Wachs, Martin. 1976. *Transportation for the Elderly: Changing Lifestyles, Changing Needs.* Berkeley: University of California Press.

Sandra Rosenbloom

TRAVEL, activity connecting the person to the environment outside the home by offering the experience of distance, movement, and encounter. Opportunities for travel are important if older persons are to be socially integrated. Travel is a supportive resource linking older persons with life's necessities, and it also is a life-enriching resource. Travel expands the social world of older persons, while lack of travel can cause disengagement and social isolation.

Importance and Modes of Travel

Travel is an important indicator in life satisfaction of older persons. Cutler (1972, 1975) found that 58% of older persons with some type of personal transportation had high life satisfaction scores, while only 37% of those without personal transportation had high scores. Even after socioeconomic status and health were accounted for, transportation was still the most important factor in determining life satisfaction scores.

The automobile is an important mode of travel for older persons. The Federal Highway Administration (1973), in a study that excluded walking, found the automobile to be the dominant mode of travel for all ages, with the majority of all trips for those 65 years of age or older involving the older person as the driver. Many more trips are made by those who drive automobiles than those who are passengers. Carp (1974) found frequency of trips to be associated with car ownership, good health, and distance from the center city. Mass transit is another mode of travel available to older persons. Lawton (1980), in a review of a number of studies, concluded that only in New York City is mass transit the dominant mode of travel. Carp (1974) found use of mass transit to be highly associated with proximity to a bus stop, good health, and living in the center city.

Walking serves a variety of purposes for older persons. Eckmann (1974), in a study of pedestrian behavior in two cities, found that 32% of older persons were walking for pleasure, in contrast to 21% of persons of all ages; 34% walked for enjoyment; and 39% walked for "exercise," even though other modes of transportation were available. Carp (1974) found walking to be done mostly by older persons in good health, by men, and by those living in the center city. Among center city residents, 50% of the elderly walked daily, while 50% in the suburbs never walked.

Lawton (1980), in an examination of destinations associated with different modes of travel, concluded that the automobile was used most often by the elderly visiting children or relatives and attending entertainment and organizational functions. Mass transit was used most frequently to obtain health care and to shop for items other than groceries. Walking was most frequently used to visit friends, shop for groceries, and attend religious services.

Satisfaction differs with various modes of travel. Carp (1972) found that most older persons preferred private automobiles to mass transit because of convenience, speed, and sociability; drawbacks of using someone else's automobile were feeling obligated to or not trusting the driver. Cutler (1975) found that many older persons dislike mass transit because of crowds or the sense of being rushed.

Leisure Travel

Research shows that when people retire, travel is their top leisure priority (Supernaw 1985). People aged 55+ account for about 80% of all vacation expenditures in the United States (Shoemaker 1989). According to Rosenfeld (1986), "older Americans travel more frequently, go longer distances, stay away longer, and rely more on travel agents than any other segment of the population."

Research concerning the senior travel market is a relatively recent development. Tongen (1980) reported that 52% of the respondents 65 years of age and older planned three to four trips per year in retirement, 28% planned one or two trips per year, and only 6% planned an average of less than one trip per year. Three out of every four retirees used some type of travel service, but a variety of personal problems frequently resulted in changes in travel modes later on, for example, difficulties with airports, schedule problems, and health.

Another study provided useful comparisons between those nearing and those past the age of retirement. Anderson and Langmeyer (1982) profiled similarities and differences between travelers under and over the age of 50, and found that the over-50 travelers preferred leisurely, planned, group pleasure trips for rest and relaxation or for visiting relatives. Travelers under 50 also tended to travel for rest and relaxation, but were more likely to participate in outdoor recreation activities or to visit man-made amusement facilities.

Blazey (1992) examined the relationship between retirement status and constraints to travel activity. Retirees were more likely to be constrained by perception of age, disability, health conditions, and physical energy. Being too busy to travel discouraged the preretirees, while physical infirmity and less of an adventuresome spirit discouraged the retirees. Preretirees were more likely to travel for business or to include business with vacation, while postretirees emphasized family in their travel activity. Travel duration and mode of travel seemed linked to employment and its associated time constraints. Concerning travel-related activities that were linked with retirement status, only one activity, the package tour, was more popular with postretirees.

Ananth et al. (1992) sought to determine differences in the importance of hotel attributes between younger and older travelers, measuring the significance of 57 attributes for travelers above and below the age of 59. The attributes rated most important and that did not vary between age groups related to price and quality, that is, travelers in both age groups desired quality products and attractive prices, including special discounts and complementary services. Attributes more important to older travelers were: grab bars and supports in the bathroom; night lights in bathrooms; legible, visible signs in hallways, public areas, and restaurants; extra blankets; and legible, larger printing on schedules, information, and menus. It is interesting that information about the availability of specific hotel attributes important to older persons is not usually included in advertising and information listings.

Practical Suggestions for Successful Leisure Travel

Travel and travel destinations must be carefully evaluated. An appropriate choice requires the consideration of a number of essential travel components:

1. *Transportation.* The basic mode of transportation, whether bus, train, plane, or ship is only one of the considerations when planning transportation. Transportation must also be planned from place of residence to depot, station, airport, or dock, and back to place of residence.
2. *Accommodations.* Accommodations need to be planned from departure until the return. Because many travel packages are priced based on double occupancy of the room, travelers should also consider whether there is a need for a single room and whether the need warrants the added cost.
3. *Meals.* Meals must be planned based on an assessment of individual needs, cost, and travel package. Individual needs may require a special diet. It may be cheaper to purchase meals individually than as a part of a travel package, especially if there are dietary constraints. However, meals can often be purchased as part of a travel package more cheaply when international travel is involved.
4. *Sightseeing.* Sightseeing is an integral part of the travel experience. However, each day's schedule must be realistic, allowing time for meals, breaks, shopping, and free time.
5. *Step-by-Step Management.* The management of the travel process demands attention to certain details. Reservations must be made and confirmed, itineraries planned, luggage collected and dispatched, and so on. Management of these details may be an individual's responsibility or the responsibility of a tour director.
6. *Necessary Arrangements before Leaving.* Necessary arrangements include such routine matters as stopping mail and paper delivery, and obtaining passports and visas.

Traveling with a tour group has distinct advantages for the first-time traveler as well as the veteran traveler, particularly with international destinations. Group travel provides the services of a professional to integrate all of the necessary components of the travel experience, and is usually offered at lower costs. Group travel provides personnel to solve problems and make adjustments as needed in transportation, accommodations, meals, and sightseeing.

The fully escorted and all-inclusive tour has an escort available at all times to manage all details, and has few additional costs. This type of tour usually provides fewer group activities, such as meals and shows, but does have a full-time escort. The hosted tour provides transportation and accommodations, but no escort. Instead, an agent or employee of the wholesale tour operator is available to manage the details of arrival and departure; hear complaints; answer questions; and give advice concerning restaurants, shopping, sightseeing, and other concerns. The "throwaway" package includes economy air fare and other elements, such as some accommodations and meals. The cost is often less than an individually backed economy fare. It allows the traveler certain accommodations and meals, but the traveler is allowed or even required to plan other elements not included in the land portion of the package.

The older traveler should examine in detail what a tour includes before making a decision and paying a deposit. A list of the names, locations, and classes of hotels should be provided, along with the number of meals, form of land transportation, tipping expectations and procedures, and so on.

The older traveler should take health precautions and make certain health preparations before traveling. Travel should be matched to health status and physical ability before making the decision about a particular travel plan, examining, in particular, the number of travel days, pacing of days, and days free of scheduled activities. Health preparations should include having the names of physicians in an area or country, prescription slips with the generic names of medications, booster immunizations, insurance cards and/or funds to cover a medical emergency, and a list of precautions concerning particular countries.

Older persons will strongly influence the leisure travel market. They will have the time and the money for leisure travel. Consumers over 55 years of age spend 80% of their vacation dollars in the United States; people aged 50 or above earmarked approximately $20 billion for vacations in 1985 (Shoemaker 1989). The increasing longevity of older persons will allow them more leisure time to travel and to enjoy different destinations and activities. Although early retirement may not remain as popular as in the past, many Americans expect to be free from work demands. After their peak earning years, many persons will place more emphasis on leisure than on work. Others, while still working, will find ways to increase their leisure time.

Although the income of older Americans may be less than their income in their prime earning years, the senior travel market will be promising because of savings, investment income, and other assets. Many older persons will be discriminating spenders, focusing less on product status and more on quality and value. (See also HEALTH AND LONGEVITY, LEISURE, RETIREMENT MI-

GRATION, TRANSPORTATION, and VACATION HOMES AND RECRE-
ATIONAL PROPERTY.)

Organizations

Association of Community Travel Clubs
Elderhostel
Golden Age Passport
Grandtravel
National Tour Association
September Days Club

References

Ananth, M., F. J. DeMicco, P. J. Moreo and R. M. Howey. 1992. "Marketplace Lodging
    Needs of Mature Travelers." *Cornell Hotel and Restaurant Administration Quar-
    terly* 33: 12–24.
Anderson, B. B., and L. Langmeyer. 1982. "The Under-50 and Over-50 Travelers: A
    Profile of Similarities and Differences." *Journal of Travel Research* 20: 20–24.
Blazey, M. A. 1992. "Travel and Retirement Status." *Annuals of Tourism Research* 19:
    771–83.
Carp, F. M. 1972. "Retired People as Automobile Passengers." *Gerontologist* 12: 66–
    72.
Carp, F. M. 1974. "Transportation and the Older Person." Final Report, Grant AA-4-
    70-087. Washington, DC: Administration on Aging.
Cutler, S. J. 1972. "The Availability of Personal Transportation, Residential Location,
    and Life Satisfaction among the Aged." *Journal of Gerontology* 27: 383–89.
Cutler, S. J. 1975. "Transportation and Changes in Life Satisfaction." *Gerontologist* 15:
    155–59.
Eckmann, Alex. 1974. *The Behavior and Perception of Elderly Pedestrians and Appro-
    priate Accommodations.* Washington, DC: Institute of Public Administration.
Federal Highway Administration. 1973. *Mode of Transportation and Personal Charac-
    teristics of Tripmakers.* Washington, DC: U.S. Department of Transportation.
Lawton, Mortimer P. 1980. *Environment and Aging.* Monterey, CA: Brooks/Cole.
Rosenfeld, J.P. 1986. "Demographics on Vacation." *American Demographics* 8 (Janu-
    ary), 38–41, 58.
Shoemaker, S. 1989. "Segmentation of the Senior Pleasure Travel Market." *Journal of
    Travel Research* 27: 14–21.
Supernaw, Scott. 1985. "Battle for the Gray Market." In *The Battle for Market Share:
    Strategies in Research and Marketing.* Proceedings of the Sixteenth Annual Con-
    ference, Travel and Tourism Research Association, 287–90.
Tongen, H. N. 1980. "Travel Plans of the Over-65 Market, Pre and Post Retirement."
    Journal of Travel Research 19 (Fall), 7–11.

Joseph D. Teaff

TRUSTS, legal arrangements by which the legal and beneficial ownership of
assets are separated. A trust is normally established by a written agreement
between the grantor or settlor and the trustee, although a trust may be established

orally. For estate planning* purposes, a trust should be established by a properly written trust agreement.

To illustrate, John Brown, the grantor, conveys securities to Tom Smith, the trustee, with instructions that the securities should be invested and managed for the benefit of John Brown. Tom Smith is perceived as the owner of the securities and would have the right to manage them in any manner he deemed appropriate. However, by virtue of the trust arrangement between the grantor and the trustee, Tom Smith is legally obligated to administer the securities pursuant to the terms of the trust.

General Planning Issues

While numerous types of trusts target particular objectives, income, estate, gift, and generation-skipping tax considerations often play major roles in the design of trusts.

For income tax purposes, a trust may be treated as a separate taxable entity, depending upon the extent of the grantor's reserved powers. Trusts that are revocable by the grantor are generally not recognized as separate taxpaying entities. The income and deductions generated in revocable trusts are reported directly on the income tax return of the grantor.

Irrevocable trusts, however, are generally treated as separate taxpayers. Thus, transfer of an income-producing asset to an irrevocable trust moves the income from the grantor's tax return to the tax return of the trust. If the trust is in a lower marginal tax bracket than the grantor, the aggregate tax liability of the grantor and the trust will be lower than if the grantor had retained the asset and continued to report its income on his or her return. Changes in federal income tax rate brackets, however, may severely limit the ability of a family to reduce its overall tax liability by using trusts. For example, a trust now enters the maximum 39.6% marginal income tax rate once its income exceeds $7,500. A married couple would not enter the 39.6% bracket until their taxable income exceeded $250,000.

Trusts are often indispensable components of financial plans designed to reduce federal gift and estate taxes. Under current law, individuals have a $192,800 gift and estate tax credit, which effectively exempts $600,000 from tax. Thus, every individual may give away, during lifetime or at death, or in any combination, as much as $600,000 before incurring any gift or estate tax liability. Additionally, individuals may make annual gifts of up to $10,000 per year to as many individuals as they wish, which is not included in the $600,000 exemption.

Effective tax planning for a married couple requires that each take full advantage of the $600,000 exemption. Because this deduction totally eliminates tax on transfers between spouses (provided the recipient spouse is a U.S. citizen), there may be a temptation for each spouse to leave his or her entire estate to the survivor. No tax would be levied on that transfer, but it would have the effect of accumulating the entire joint estate in the estate of the survivor. Upon the survivor's death, only one $600,000 exemption would be available to shelter the joint estate from taxation.

The more effective plan would be for the first-to-die spouse to direct the first $600,000 of their estate (the tax exempt amount) into a trust for the benefit of the surviving spouse. If the surviving spouse's access to that trust is properly limited, the trust will not be considered part of the estate of the surviving spouse at his or her death and will therefore pass free of estate tax to children or other beneficiaries.

Trusts can also be employed to take advantage of the $1 million exemption currently available for "generation-skipping." Under present law, an individual may leave as much as $1 million to a grandchild or more remote descendant without imposition of a generation-skipping tax. Thus, as much as $1 million could be left to a grandchild without imposition of an estate tax in the generation of the child or the imposition of a generation-skipping tax. If the grantor wants his child to enjoy lifetime income of the trust for the lifetime of the child, while at the same time obtaining the benefits of the $1 million generation-skipping tax exemption for his grandchild, a trust must be employed.

In addition to the tax considerations involved, trusts can serve many other purposes. Situations frequently arise where the grantor wishes to provide income to a person for life, or a period of years, but thereafter wants the property to revert to other individuals. A typical example is a second marriage where each spouse has children from a prior marriage. Each spouse might want the surviving spouse to enjoy income from his or her estate for the spouse's lifetime. Upon the death of the surviving spouse, the first-to-die spouse might want an estate to revert back to his or her own children, not to children of their spouse. This can be accomplished through the use of a trust.

In another situation, the grantor of the trust may want to provide for an individual who does not have the skill and business judgment necessary to manage the gift or bequest. The grantor can give his estate to a trust for the benefit of the individual, naming a bank or trust company or other professional to manage the estate.

Similarly, the intended beneficiary may be a spendthrift. If that person were to inherit property outright, it might soon be dissipated through improvident expenditures. Rather than giving property outright to such an individual, a trust can be created with appropriate limitations and controls on the beneficiary's access to the funds.

Selection of a Trustee

Regardless of the type of trust, selection of a trustee is critical. First, the trustee must be a person who the grantor can trust, and possess the skills and experience to administer the trust. A trustee must be able to discharge these responsibilities competently and efficiently. Although there are methods by which grantors and beneficiaries can enforce the proper administration of a trust by a trustee, those remedies are poor substitutes for a trust that is properly administered in the first place. A dishonest trustee will have ample opportunity to misappropriate funds from the trust. Even though the trustee may ultimately be held accountable for the misappropriation, unless assets are available for a dishonest trustee to make restitution to the trust, the trust and its beneficiaries are essentially without remedy.

A trustee may be one or more individuals, a bank or trust company, or a combination of an individual(s) and a bank or trust company. Institutional trustees may have certain advantages. They are professionals in the business of administering trusts, and can do so in-house, while an individual may have to hire professional advisors to assist him or her in the administration of the trust. The relative costs of trustee selection must be carefully weighed in either case.

Most institutional trustees have the advantage of longevity, although after recent bank failures, this cannot be said with the same certainty as in the past. However, if a bank or trust company fails, assets that it holds and administers as trustee are not subject to the claims of creditors or shareholders. An institutional trustee should also have greater neutrality and impartiality than close family members. If it is possible that the administration of the trust will create hard feelings among members of the family, a grantor may prefer that the anger be directed outside the family.

It is often desirable, particularly in irrevocable trusts, to authorize a third person to remove the incumbent trustee and designate a successor. That power should not be included, however, without careful consideration of the potential tax consequences. Since the possibility exists that an individual trustee could die or become incapacitated prior to the termination of a trust, an alternative or successor trustee should be named.

Revocable Living Trusts

A popular form of trust is the revocable living trust. While much has been written about their advantages, these advantages have been exaggerated. Revocable living trusts offer no tax advantages that cannot be obtained through other types of planning. A will, for example, can be prepared to realize the same estate tax savings as a living trust.

Some advantages, however, are unique to living trusts. Perhaps the most important is protection against incapacity or incompetence. Although other means can provide for the management of one's estate in the event of incapacity (most notably, durable powers of attorney), none works as well as a revocable living trust.

A revocable living trust is an arrangement whereby the grantor transfers ownership of assets to a trustee and reserves the right to revoke the trust at any time, withdraw assets from the trust, and otherwise direct the trustee regarding the administration of the trust. When the grantor no longer wishes or is unable to exercise any of those rights, the trustee assumes more complete management responsibilities. Thus, if the grantor becomes incapacitated, the trustee assumes a more active role, managing trust assets for the grantor's benefit, paying bills, and otherwise attending to the grantor's business affairs.

A second advantage of a revocable living trust is avoidance of probate* to the extent that assets have actually been transferred to the trust during the grantor's lifetime. It therefore becomes important to go beyond merely creating the shell of the revocable living trust and to actually transfer ownership of assets to the trustee in order to avoid the time, expense, and other possible burdens of probate. A will must be probated to become operative and becomes a public record open to anyone wishing to inspect it. A trust remains a private document generally available only to the grantor, the trustee, and the beneficiaries of the trust.

Many argue that an estate plan embodied in a living trust is better protected from contest than a plan embodied in a will. This is a debatable proposition, but at least implementation of the plan through a living trust may shorten the time period in which a contest may be launched. The time period for contesting a will begins on the date of probate, whereas the time period for contesting a living trust begins upon creation of the trust, or at the latest upon transfer of a particular asset to the living trust.

Living trusts have some disadvantages. The implementation of an estate plan through a living trust normally will be more expensive than implementation of a plan by a will. Additional legal documents (trust agreements) must be prepared, which will make the legal fees higher.

Another disadvantage of a living trust is that assets must be transferred to the trust during one's lifetime in order to accomplish the intended benefits. This entails paperwork and administrative work. On the other hand, it is easier for the grantor to effect the change in ownership during his or her lifetime than it would be for an executor to administer those assets through the probate system after the grantor's death. In a sense, the creation and funding of a revocable living trust moves forward in time the transfer of title that would otherwise occur after death.

Bank Account Trusts

Most banks offer trust-type accounts. In this instance, the terms of the trust are established by the signature card for the account. Those terms are typically drawn in very broad fashion and should be reviewed carefully before opening such an account. Bank account trusts are to be distinguished from a true trust account, which might be opened by a trustee under a trust agreement. In the latter case, the terms of the deposit account would probably be identical to an individual deposit account except that the "owner" of the account would be designated as "John Smith, Trustee" rather than simply "John Smith."

Uniform Custodial Trust Act

Many states have adopted the Uniform Custodial Trust Act. This act creates a form of statutory trust that individual grantors may adopt. In appropriate circumstances, utilizing the uniform act could avoid the expense of having a trust document specially tailored to a person's particular circumstances.

Irrevocable Living Trusts

As the name suggests, an irrevocable living trust is a trust created during lifetime that cannot be amended or revoked. The fact that the document is irrevocable is a significant disadvantage, made acceptable only by other advantages gained. These advantages are all tax-related.

Most often, the tax benefit that is sought is removal of property from the taxable estate of the grantor. This would only be a consideration if the grantor otherwise would have a taxable estate in excess of the prevailing exemption equivalent (currently $600,000 for each donor). If the estate exceeds that threshold, ultimate tax liability can be reduced by taking advantage of the $10,000 per year gift tax exclusion. Gifts of $10,000 each year can be made to as many individuals as one wishes, and a married couple can make gifts of $20,000 per year to as many individuals as they wish. If, however, the individuals to whom they wish to make the gift are either too young to properly manage the property or if they lack the judgment and maturity to administer the property for some other reason, the gift can be to a trust for the benefit of that individual.

Irrevocable trusts can be used effectively in conjunction with life insurance. If an individual retains ownership of life insurance on his life until death, the full amount of the death proceeds will be subject to estate tax in his estate. However, if, before death, the insured transfers ownership of the policy to an irrevocable trust, and if the insured survives the transfer by at least three years, the policy proceeds will be exempt from estate tax, leading to very substantial reductions in estate tax.

Testamentary Trusts

Testamentary trusts are trusts created by will. The same estate tax savings that can be realized through proper use of revocable living trusts can likewise be realized through proper use of testamentary trusts. The major difference between the two is that a living trust can be created and funded without having to deal with the probate system. A testamentary trust, because it is created by will, takes effect once the will is probated, and funding of the trust is normally delayed until the probate process is completed. Further, in some states, a testamentary trust is required to report on an ongoing basis to the probate court. It remains under the supervision of the probate court throughout its term.

Charitable Trusts

Charitable trusts may be created during one's lifetime or by will. In order to obtain the tax benefits of charitable contributions*, a trust created during one's lifetime must be an irrevocable trust.

A purely charitable trust is a trust exclusively for the benefit of one or more charities. Contributions to a purely charitable trust are fully deductible for estate and gift tax purposes. For income tax purposes the deduction is subject to certain limitations based on the income of the grantor. A charitable trust is appropriate where the grantor wishes to benefit certain charities, yet does not want to entrust the investment and management of the gift to those charities. The grantor, in that case, may transfer the gift to a trustee directed to distribute trust income periodically to designated charities.

Trusts also allow a hybrid form of charitable giving. In "split-interest" trusts, both charities and noncharities have some beneficial rights. In a charitable lead trust, the grantor directs that an income stream be distributed to a particular charity or charities for a specific term of years. Then, the capital, or corpus, of the trust is distributed to a family member or noncharity. If drawn in compliance with the complex technical requirements of the Internal Revenue Code, the charitable lead interest reduces the value of the gift to the family member, thereby enabling the grantor to make a substantial gift at minimal tax cost.

A charitable remainder trust is the reverse of a charitable lead trust. A charitable remainder trust directs the distribution of an income interest to oneself, to a family member or noncharity for a term of years, or perhaps for the lifetime of the grantor or family member. At the conclusion of the term, or upon the death of the family member, the capital of the trust is distributed to one or more charities. In this case, the grantor is entitled to a charitable deduction for the value of the interest passing to the charity, which is calculated at the inception of the trust.

Pooled income funds are another way a gift can be made to charity with a reserved income interest for the grantor or family member. Pooled income funds are similar to charitable remainder trusts except that the grantor does not have the burden of establishing a private trust agreement. He or she simply buys into an existing pooled arrangement previously established by the particular charity. (See also ATTORNEYS, CHARITABLE CONTRIBUTIONS, ELDER LAW PRACTICE, ESTATE PLANNING, FINANCIAL ADVISORS, KING LEAR SYNDROME, PROBATE, and SAVINGS ACCOUNT TRUSTS.)

References

Berg, Adriane G. 1992. *Warning. Dying May be Hazardous to Your Wealth: How to Protect Your Life Savings for Yourself and Those You Love.* Hawthorne, NJ: Career Press.

Clifford, Denis. 1992. *Plan Your Estate with a Living Trust.* Berkeley, CA: Nolo Press.

Reutlinger, Mark. 1993. *Wills, Trusts, and Estates: Essential Terms and Concepts.* Boston: Little, Brown.

Shenkman, Martin M. 1993. *The Complete Book of Trusts.* New York: John Wiley and Sons.

Sloan, Irving J., ed. 1992. *Wills and Trusts: How to Make a Will and How to Use Trusts.* Dobbs Ferry, NY: Oceana.

C. L. (Tim) Dimos

V

VACATION HOMES AND RECREATIONAL PROPERTY, any of a number of types of real property when used primarily for recreational purposes, vacation accommodations, or seasonal living, rather than for primary housing or investment purposes. The term *recreational properties* encompasses a variety of property types, such as vacation homes, cabins, and condominiums; lots used for camping or held for future construction of a second home; timeshare condominiums and certain types of vacation clubs; and campground memberships.

Approximately 4.6 million of the 6.3 million recreational properties in the United States include some type of living unit, with the balance primarily undeveloped land, RV sites, or camping sites (Miner 1990a, p. 1). Little nonproprietary research of national or international scope is available for the recreational properties industry, when compared with other industries of similar size. However, due to the many developers, builders, realtors, marketers, and consultants involved in recreational properties, the dynamics of the market are well understood. While the following discussion applies specifically to the United States, many of the same trends apply to other Westernized industrial countries. Ownership patterns regarding recreational property are closely tied to the aging cycle. Because only the most affluent of households typically can afford recreational property or second homes when the household heads are young, just 3.2% of households with household head aged 25 or younger own any type of recreational property (Miner 1990a, p. 1). This proportion increases significantly with age, as income grows, assets accumulate, and children begin to appreciate outdoor recreation. Thus, the rate of recreational property and second home ownership jumps to 7.6% among households headed by a 35–44-year-old.

With advancing middle age often comes a further increase in household assets as the home mortgage matures and savings grow, making recreational property and second home ownership more affordable. At this age many homeowners also begin planning for retirement. This may take the form of a recreational property or vacation home purchase, with the idea of converting the acquisition to a primary or seasonal home upon retirement. The rate of recreational property and second home ownership jumps again among the 45–54 age group, reaching a peak of 13.7%. By the time households reach the 55–64 age bracket, they begin to show an average decline in the rate of recreational property and second home ownership, down to 11.8%. However, this overall statistic masks three different patterns typical of this age group: (1) some are purchasing second homes, primarily in anticipation of high-amenity retirement or seasonal living; (2) other households in this age bracket retire and convert their recreational property or second home into a primary residence; and (3) households of more moderate incomes begin to shed expensive luxuries or pass them on to children, including their second homes and other recreational property. After age 65 the rate of second home ownership declines precipitously, to just 6.0%. By the time households reach the early years of this age bracket, most retire and either sell their vacation home, or convert it to a residence and sell their former primary home. Few retirees can afford to maintain two homes. Upon death of the owners, recreational property is either sold or passed on to heirs. One in eight recreational property owners inherited their interest (Miner 1990a, p. 1). Although these are the main trends in ownership of recreational property and vacation homes, there is marked variation depending on the specific form of recreational property. For the four main categories of recreational property, the specific trends relating to the aging cycle are as follows:

Unimproved Land. A recent survey found that only 3% of households over age 40 are "very interested" in purchasing unimproved recreational land, as compared with 13% who are under 40 (Miner 1993). Land without a building typically is of greatest interest to younger households because of the low price and the romance of someday building a home. When unimproved land is purchased by the near-retiree or retiree, construction of a home normally is contemplated in the immediate future.

Vacation Homes, Cabins, and Condominiums. For these products, the primary difference between units purchased by the elderly and their younger counterparts is in design and location. Younger buyers may settle for a smaller unit with minimal storage or garage space to keep the price down, because they will be staying in the unit only for brief periods. Older buyers want more storage room, usually including a garage, to facilitate residential or seasonal living. Many prefer a minimum of stairs due to current or anticipated disabilities. Younger buyers purchase where they like to vacation, which may include exotic foreign locales and ski areas. Older buyers tend to prefer high-amenity areas near their primary home, or warmer Sunbelt locations.

Timeshares and Other Shared-Ownership Accommodations. Since the mid-1970s, the fastest growing segment of the recreational property market has been timeshares and related types of shared-ownership vacation accommodations, if measured in terms of number of households owning such an interest (Miner 1990a). About 35.5% of U.S. residents who own timeshares are 55 or older (Ragatz 1993). Timeshares represent an affordable type of second home that many of today's active retirees can enjoy. Lawrence Welk Resort Villas in northern San Diego County is one of several timeshare resorts that cater specifically to senior citizens.

Membership RV Parks. About 16% of households in the 55–64 age group, and 12% in the 65–74 age group, own recreational vehicles (Curtin 1994). With approximately 400,000 new recreational vehicles sold in the United States each year (Recreational Vehicle Industry Association 1994), the owners obviously need somewhere to park them. Over 500,000 households have elected to purchase memberships or other interests in private or semi-private RV parks (Miner 1990b). Of these RV park members, 73% are 50 or older, 50% are 60 or older, and 14% are 70 or older (Miner 1991). Many have even elected to relinquish homeownership entirely, becoming seasonal migrants who follow preferred weather conditions in an RV. It is noteworthy that some of these recreational property products, particularly timeshares and RV campground memberships, have developed only during the past 20 years. Recreational property products constantly are being invented and modified, both for the elderly and other markets.

In 20 years, more options may be available. Understanding the relationship between recreational property ownership and the aging process is increasingly important, because the number of Americans purchasing such property in anticipation of retirement or after retirement is expected to expand significantly over the next 20 to 30 years. This is due to such trends as: (1) the long-term increase in affluence among the elderly that facilitates ownership of this discretionary good, (2) the increased health and longevity of the population that generates more interest in maintaining quality of life and access to recreational opportunities during the senior years, and (3) the anticipated increase of the elderly population as the baby boom generation ages in coming years, potentially increasing demand for all types of goods and services desired by the elderly (Miner 1984). With the total value of all recreational properties located in the United States estimated at over $900 billion—plus another $46 billion in foreign locations owned by U.S. residents—small percentage changes in this market may have a large impact on the economy. Because households with heads who are 55 or older own about 37% of this property, or about $335 billion, trends in this segment of the market are significant (Miner 1990a). The best source of additional information on recreational properties and second homes is the American Resort Development Association. Other sources include the Urban Land Institute, the National Association of Homebuilders, and the National Association of Realtors. All of these are located in Washington, D.C. Regarding membership RV parks, the best source is Coast to Coast Resorts, in Englewood, Colorado. Some specialty consulting firms also conduct research regarding the recreational properties industry. (See also CONDOMINIUMS, HEALTH AND LONGEVITY, HOMEOWNERSHIP, HOUSING, LEISURE, MORTGAGE IN-STRUMENTS, RETIREMENT MIGRATION, and TRAVEL.)

Organizations

Escapees, Inc.
Recreational Vehicle Industry Association

References

Curtin, Richard T. 1994. *The RV Consumer: A Demographic Profile*. Reston, VA: Recreational Vehicle Industry Association.

Miner, Steven S. 1984. "Get Ready for the Baby Boom Generation." *Resort Timesharing Today* 8, (4).

Miner, Steven S. 1990a. *The American Recreational Property Survey 1990*. Washington, DC: National Association of Realtors, American Resort & Residential Development Association, National Foundation for Timesharing.

Miner, Steven S. 1990b. *The Private Outdoor Resort Industry in the United States*. Unpublished proprietary study.

Miner, Steven S. 1991. *Coast to Coast Members: 1991 Study of Characteristics and Purchase Motivations*. Englewood, CO: Camp Coast to Coast, Inc.

Miner, Steven S. 1993. *The American Recreational Property Survey 1993*. Washington, DC: Alliance for Timeshare Excellence, American Resort Development Association.

Ragatz, Richard L. 1993. *Timeshare Purchasers: Who They Are, Why They Buy,* 1993 Edition. Washington, DC: Alliance for Timeshare Excellence.

Recreational Vehicle Industry Association. 1994. *Profile: The RV Industry 1993*. Reston, VA: Recreational Vehicle Industry Association.

Steven S. Miner

VETERANS' BENEFITS, payments and services provided by the U.S. government to former or current members of the armed forces or their dependents. Eligibility for Veterans Administration (VA) benefits is based on discharge from active service under other than dishonorable conditions for a minimum period specified by law. Active service generally means full-time service as a member of the army, navy, air force, marines, coast guard, or as a commissioned officer of the Public Health Service, the Environmental Service Administration, or the National Oceanic and Atmospheric Administration. Completion of at least six years of honorable service in the selected reserves also entitles veterans to some benefits. Veterans Administration benefits are also provided for the Women's Air Force Service Pilots (WASPs), U.S. merchant seamen who served on block-ships in support of Operation Mulberry, honorably discharged members of the American Volunteer Group (Flying Tigers), and American merchant marines in ocean-going service between December 7, 1941 and August 15, 1945. Men and women veterans with similar service are entitled to the same benefits.

Disability

Disability compensation is money paid directly to veterans disabled by injury or disease incurred or aggravated during active military service in the line of duty. The amount of the benefit depends on the degree of the disability. Veterans whose service-connected disabilities are rated 30% or more are entitled to additional allowances for dependents. Disabled veterans evaluated 30% or more are entitled to receive a special allowance for spouses who are in need of the aid and attendance of another person. Disabled veterans may also be entitled to a grant from the VA for home modifications and may qualify for up to $5,500 toward the purchase of adaptive equipment for automobiles.

Veterans with a limited income may be eligible for support if they have 90 days or more of active military service, with at least one day during a period of war. These veterans must be permanently and totally disabled for reasons traceable neither to military service nor to willful misconduct. Payments are made to these veterans to bring the total income, including other retirement or social security income, to an established support level. The level of support is set by law and varies depending on number of dependents and if regular aid and attendance are needed. Pensions are not payable to those who have assets that can be used to provide adequate maintenance. Veterans aged 65 or older, or those who are blind or otherwise disabled, may be eligible for Supplemental Security Income (SSI)*.

Education, Housing, and Life Insurance

The VA administers a number of educational programs. If a senior has not already used his or her educational benefits and would still like to receive education assistance from the VA, the only service still available is vocational rehabilitation. Those eligible for vocational rehabilitation are veterans and service members who served in the Armed Forces on or after September 16, 1940, if three conditions are met:

1. Service-connected disabilities or disabilities in active service were suffered
2. Discharge or release occurred under other than dishonorable conditions or hospitalization occurred while awaiting separation for disability
3. The VA determines that vocational rehabilitation is necessary to overcome employment impairments

Enrollment in the program qualifies veterans for many other benefits programs, including some medical benefits for which they might not otherwise qualify.

Eligible veterans and unremarried surviving spouses may obtain VA-guaranteed loans for the purchase and refinancing of homes, condominiums, and manufactured homes. The VA guarantees part of the total loan so veterans may obtain mortgages on homes or condominiums with competitive interest rates. With VA guarantees, lenders are protected against losses up to the amount of the guarantee. To be eligible for a loan guarantee, applicants must have a good credit rating and have income sufficient to support the new mortgage payments. Applicants must also agree to occupy the property as a home. The amount of the VA guarantee is called the entitlement. The basic entitlement available to veterans is $36,000. Up to $46,000 of entitlement may be available to veterans purchasing or refinancing homes with a higher loan amount.

The VA also provides certain homeowner's safeguards to veterans. Homes that were completed less than one year before purchase with VA financing, and inspected during construction by the VA or the Department of Housing and Urban Development (HUD), must meet or exceed VA minimum property requirements for construction and general acceptability. HUD administers the Federal Housing Administration (FHA) Home Mortgage Insurance Program for Veterans. These home loans require less down payment than other FHA programs.

Depending on the date of service and the date of issuance of the policy, veterans are entitled to a variety of life insurance* policies. Veterans' life insurance is a complicated issue generally requiring the aid of professionals.

Most of the VA life insurance policies for seniors have closed. Generally, seniors must be enrolled in existing programs to be insured. These policies must be kept current, and collections on the policy should be made. For veterans who have life insurance under an existing plan and become totally disabled before age 65, the VA will pay the life insurance premiums. In order to qualify, veterans must be totally disabled and unable to work for six consecutive months or longer.

Dependents' Benefits

The U.S. government provides some special benefits to surviving spouses and minor children of veterans. Eligibility usually requires that the deceased veteran be discharged from active service under other than dishonorable conditions.

Dependency and Indemnity Compensation (DIC) benefits are paid to surviving dependents of veterans in certain circumstances. Benefits are paid for deaths due to service-connected disabilities, and non-service-connected causes. Those eligible to receive DIC benefits for a death due to service-connected disabilities are surviving spouses, unmarried children under 18, helpless children, those between 18 and 23 if attending a VA-approved school, and low-income parents of service personnel or veterans who died from: (1) diseases or injuries incurred or aggravated in the line of duty while on active duty or active duty training; (2) injuries incurred or aggravated in the line of duty while on inactive duty training; or (3) disabilities compensable by VA. DIC payments are not available if death resulted from willful misconduct.

Those dependents eligible for service-connected disability DIC payments may receive them for non-service-connected deaths if: (1) they were the dependents of veterans who suffered from totally service-connected disabilities at the time of death whose death was not the result of the service-connected disability, and

(2) either (a) the veteran was continuously rated totally disabled for a period of 10 or more years immediately preceding death; or (b) the rating was for a period of not less than five years from the date of discharge from military service. Payments for non-service-connected deaths are offset by any amount received from judicial proceedings. When death occurs after service, the veteran's discharge must have been under conditions other than dishonorable.

All surviving spouses of veterans who died after January 1, 1993, receive $769 a month. For deaths occurring before January 1, 1993, the amount paid is based on the veteran's rank at the time of death and on different programs.

A Non-Service-Connected Death Pension, or "widow's pension," is available to surviving spouses of deceased veterans with wartime service, and to their unmarried children under 18, or until age 23 if attending a VA-approved school. Pensions are not provided to those survivors whose estates are large enough to provide maintenance. The pension program provides monthly payments to bring survivors' incomes to a support level established by law.

Educational assistance benefits are available to spouses and children of deceased veterans under the following circumstances: (1) if the deceased veteran was totally disabled as the result of disabilities arising from active service; (2) if the veteran died from any cause while rated permanently and totally disabled from service-connected disabilities; or (3) the veteran was listed as missing in action or as a prisoner of war.

Burial Benefits

Most veterans are entitled to burial benefits including burial in national cemeteries, headstones and markers, Presidential Memorial Certificates, burial flags, and reimbursement of burial expenses. Qualified survivors may also be entitled to a one-time payment of $225 under social security. Burial benefits in VA national cemeteries include the gravesite, opening and closing of the grave, and perpetual care. Many national cemeteries have columbaria for the inurement of cremated remains or special gravesites for the burial of cremated remains. Headstones and markers and their placement are provided at the government's expense. Deceased veterans may be buried in one of 114 national cemeteries. Eligibility for burial in national cemeteries is limited to veterans and armed forces members who died on active duty. Veterans must have been discharged or separated from active duty under conditions other than dishonorable and have completed the required period of service. Spouses, dependents, and minor children of eligible veterans may be buried in national cemeteries. Gravesites in national cemeteries can no longer be reserved; however, those who made reservations under previous programs will have their agreements honored. Generally, funeral directors or others making burial arrangements must apply at the time of death. There are special eligibility requirements for Arlington National Cemetery.

The VA provides headstones and markers for the graves of veterans anywhere in the world, as well as headstones and markers for eligible dependents of veterans buried in national, state veteran, or federal cemeteries. Eligibility for a VA headstone or marker is generally the same as for burial in a national cemetery; however, the VA will not issue headstones or markers for spouses or dependents buried in private cemeteries. Presidential Memorial Certificates, expressing the nation's grateful recognition of the veteran's service, may be obtained through the VA. The VA provides an American flag to drape the casket of veterans who were discharged under conditions other than dishonorable and to persons entitled to retired military pay, including reservists. After the funeral service, the flag may be given to the next of kin or a close associate of the deceased. The VA will also issue a flag on behalf of service members who were missing in action and later presumed dead.

In certain cases, the VA will reimburse some burial expenses. The VA will also pay a $300 burial and funeral allowance for veterans who, at the time of death, were entitled to receive pension or compensation or would have been entitled to compensation but for receipt of military retirement pay. Eligibility is also established when death occurs in a VA facility or a nursing home* with which the VA contracted.

Health

The VA provides many health care benefits to veterans who qualify. Benefits include hospital and nursing-home care, mental health care, domiciliary care, outpatient medical treatment, outpatient pharmacy services, dental treatment, counseling services, substance abuse treatment, and prosthetic and blind aids services. Eligibility for VA hospital care and nursing-home care is divided into two categories: *mandatory* and *discretionary.* The VA must provide hospital care and may provide nursing-home care to veterans in the mandatory category. The VA may provide hospital and nursing-home care to veterans in the discretionary category if space and resources are available in VA facilities. The VA makes an income assessment to determine whether a non-service-connected veteran is eligible for cost-free VA medical care.

Those veterans in the mandatory category are patients who have non-service-connected injuries or illnesses and whose income is $19,912 or less with no dependents, or $23,896 or less if married or single with one dependent. The income maximum is raised $1,330 for each additional dependent. Some veterans must be provided hospital care and may be provided nursing-home care regardless of their income. These veterans are: veterans with service-connected disabilities, veterans who were exposed to herbicides while serving in Vietnam (e.g., Agent Orange), veterans who were exposed to ionizing radiation during atmospheric testing or in the occupation of Hiroshima and Nagasaki, veterans who are seeking treatment for a condition related to service in the Persian Gulf, former prisoners of war, veterans on VA pensions, veterans of the Mexican Border period or World War I, and veterans eligible for Medicaid. By law, hospital care in VA facilities must be provided to veterans who meet any of these criteria. If no VA facility is available, care must be furnished in a Defense

Department facility or another facility with which the VA has a sharing or contractual relationship. Also, nursing-home care may be provided in VA facilities to veterans who meet any of the above criteria provided that space and resources are available.

Veterans in the discretionary category are patients with non-service-connected injuries or illnesses and whose income is above $19,912 if single with no dependents, or $23,896 if married or single with one dependent, plus $1,330 for each additional dependent. The patient must agree to pay an amount equal to what would have been paid under Medicare. The Medicare deductible for 1994 is $696 and is adjusted annually. The VA may provide hospital, outpatient, and nursing-home care in VA facilities to veterans in the discretionary category, if space and resources are available.

Outpatient medical treatment for those who qualify includes medical examinations and related medical services, drugs and medicines, rehabilitation services, mental health services, and counseling. Also, as part of outpatient medical treatment, veterans may be eligible for hospital-based home health services and hospice care. Eligibility for outpatient medical treatment is limited. The VA must, however, furnish outpatient care without limitation to veterans for their service-connected disabilities, and for any disability to veterans with a service-connected disability of 50% or more. Further, the VA must provide unlimited care for any injury or condition resulting from VA hospitalization. A recent Supreme Court ruling found that the VA must pay disability benefits to veterans for injuries caused by VA hospitals even when the hospitals were not negligent.

Outpatient care without limitation is also available to veterans in a VA-approved vocational rehabilitation program, former prisoners of war, World War I or Mexican Border Period veterans, and veterans who receive increased pension or compensation based on the need for regular aid and attendance of another person, or who are permanently housebound. The VA may provide outpatient medical treatment for any condition to prevent the need for hospitalization, to prepare for hospitalization, or to complete treatment after hospitalization care to veterans with service-connected disabilities of 40% or less, and veterans whose annual income is not less than the maximum annual pension rate. Veterans exposed to a toxic substance during service in Vietnam, veterans exposed to ionizing radiation following the detonation of a nuclear device, and veterans exposed to environmental contaminants in the Persian Gulf, may receive outpatient medical treatment for conditions related to their exposure to these substances.

Veterans receiving medication for treatment of service-connected conditions, veterans rated with 50% or more service-connected disability, and veterans whose annual income does not exceed the maximum VA pension are not charged for pharmacy services. Veterans with a service-connected condition rated less than 50% receiving medication on an outpatient basis from a VA facility for treatment of non-service-connected disabilities or ailments are charged $2 for each 30-day supply of medication.

A full range of diagnostic, surgical, restorative, and preventative dental treatment is available to qualified veterans. Those eligible for full coverage include veterans whose dental condition or disabilities are service connected, veterans who have a dental condition upon discharge from the military and seek dental treatment within the requisite amount of time (up to one year), veterans who were prisoners of war for more than 90 days, veterans with 100% service-connected conditions, disabled veterans participating in a vocational rehabilitation program, veterans who have been admitted for inpatient medical treatment, and veterans whose dental condition can be shown to complicate a medical condition being treated by the VA. Other veterans may be eligible for some limited forms of dental treatment.

Veterans may apply for prosthetic services to treat any condition when receiving hospital, domiciliary, or nursing-home care in a VA facility. Veterans who meet the basic requirements for outpatient medical treatment may be provided needed prosthetic services for a service-connected disability or adjunct condition.

Veterans whose blindness is as a result of a service-connected disability, who are entitled to compensation from the VA for any service-connected disability, or who are eligible for VA medical services, are also eligible to receive VA aid for the blind. Blind veterans need not be receiving compensation or a VA pension to be eligible for admission to a VA blind rehabilitation center or clinic, or to receive services at a VA medical center.

The VA provides skilled or intermediate nursing care and related medical care in VA or private nursing homes for convalescents or persons who are not acutely ill and not in need of hospital care. Admission or transfer to VA nursing home care is the same as for hospital care. Direct admission to VA nursing homes is limited to: (1) veterans who require nursing care for a service-connected disability, (2) any person who will require nursing care upon discharge from active service, and (3) veterans who have been discharged from a VA medical center and are receiving home health services from a VA medical center.

The VA Civilian Health and Medical Program, known as CHAMPVA, shares the cost of medical services and supplies obtained by dependents and survivors of certain veterans. The following are eligible for CHAMPVA benefits, provided they are not eligible for medical care under CHAMPUS (Civilian Health and Medical Program of the Uniformed Services) or Medicare* Part A, as a result of reaching age 65: (1) spouses or children of veterans who have a permanent and total service-connected disability; (2) surviving spouses or children of veterans who died as a result of a service-connected condition, or who, at the time of death, were permanently and totally disabled from a service-connected condition; and (3) surviving spouses or children of a person who died while on active military service in the line of duty. Beneficiaries aged 65 or older who lose eligibility for CHAMPVA by becoming potentially eligible for Medicare Part A, or who qualify for Medicare Part A benefits on the basis of a disability,

may reestablish CHAMPVA eligibility by submitting documents from the Social Security Administration certifying their nonentitlement to or exhaustion of Medicare Part A benefits. Persons under age 65 who are enrolled in both Medicare Parts A and B may become eligible for CHAMPVA as a secondary payer to Medicare.

Monthly retirement, disability, and survivors benefits are payable under Social Security* to veterans and dependents if the veteran has earned enough work credits under the program. A one-time payment of $225 also is made upon the veteran's death and can be paid only to the veteran's eligible spouse or child who is entitled to benefits. Veterans may also qualify at age 65 for Medicare's hospital insurance and medical insurance. Medicare protection also is available to people who have received Social Security disability benefits for 24 months and insured people and their dependents who need dialysis or kidney transplants.

Active military service or active military service for training in the U.S. uniformed services has counted toward Social Security since January 1957, when taxes were first withheld from a service person's basic pay. Service personnel and veterans receive an additional $300 credit for each quarter in which they receive any basic pay for active duty or active duty for training after 1956 and before 1978. Retired veterans may be eligible for other credits depending on the time and type of service.

Veterans and their spouses should be aware of the location of their discharge and separation papers. Because most benefits programs require honorable discharge, these papers are very important. If these documents have been lost, duplicate copies may be obtained by contacting the National Personnel Records Center. Military records that are incorrect may be corrected to redress injustices. Applications for correction of military records, including review of discharges issued by court-martial, may be considered by a correction board.

The Defense Department issues veterans a military discharge form, identifying their condition of discharge: honorable, general, other than honorable, dishonorable, or bad conduct. Honorable and general discharges qualify veterans for most benefits, while other than honorable (dishonorable and bad conduct) generally disqualify veterans for most benefits programs. Veterans with disabilities incurred or aggravated during active military service may qualify for medical or related benefits regardless of separation and characterization of service. Because of the importance of the type of discharge, each of the military services maintains a Discharge Review Board with authority to change, correct, or modify discharges or dismissals that are not issued by a sentence of a general court martial. (See also DEATH BENEFITS; DISABILITY PROGRAMS, FEDERAL; EDUCATION OF OLDER ADULTS, FUNERALS, LIFE INSURANCE, MEDICARE, MENTAL HEALTH AMONG THE ELDERLY, NURSING HOMES, SOCIAL SECURITY, SUPPLEMENTAL SECURITY INCOME, and WIDOWHOOD.)

Organizations

Armed Forces Discharge Review Boards
CHAMPVA Center
Department of Veterans Affairs—Office of Public Affairs
Department of Veterans Affairs—Insurance Center
National Personnel Records Center
U.S. Soldiers' and Airmen's Home and U.S. Naval Home

References

Department of Veterans Affairs. 1989. *Veterans Benefits for Older Americans.* VA Pamphlet 27–80–2. Washington, DC: U.S. Government Printing Office.
Department of Veterans Affairs. 1991. *A Summary of Department of Veterans Affairs Benefits.* VA Pamphlet 27–82–2. Washington, DC: U.S. Government Printing Office.
Department of Veterans Affairs. 1994. *Federal Benefits for Veterans and Dependents.* VA Pamphlet 80–94–1. Washington, DC: U.S. Government Printing Office.

Christopher R. McDowell

VOLUNTEERING, work involving the donation of time to an organization, or taking the form of helping an individual or a group on an informal but regular basis. Over the past three decades, participation in volunteer work by older persons has changed. First, the proportion of elders involved in volunteering has increased markedly. In 1965, one in ten people over the age of 65 volunteered. By 1990, 41% of people who were 60 and older had volunteered at some point during the past year (Marriott Senior Volunteerism Study 1991). Recent research suggests a second important trend. People tend to continue to volunteer until much later in their lives than they did in the past. Almost one in three people over the age of 75 volunteered in 1990. Given the higher incidence of serious illnesses past age 75, and the fact that poor health is a major reason why older people stop volunteering, the current involvement of people over the age of 75 compares favorably with that of teenagers and young adults.

Cultural and Programmatic Factors

Social changes have contributed to the higher level of volunteerism by elders. Older people have been encouraged to become involved in volunteer work as a way to stay productive and contribute to their communities during retirement. The mass media underscore the positive aspects of volunteering, describing it as a way to "make a difference" and "be a hero." An increase in elders' involvement in volunteer work is also a reflection of demographic and economic changes. Older people are better educated and financially more secure today. There are also more opportunities to volunteer. Some organizations, such as the Red Cross, once had a retirement age for volunteers. For the past three decades, a number of government and private sector initiatives have recruited and placed older persons in volunteer jobs, provided them with incentives to participate, and reduced financial barriers that limited participation by reimbursing out-of-pocket expenses such as car fare and providing free lunches. Some programs offer volunteers stipends that reimburse costs and provide a small amount of income. The financial value of these types of payments is usually below the market value of the labor that people provide.

Cultural and demographic changes have increased the supply of elders interested in volunteer work and the demand for their services. In 1950, Robert Havighurst stated: ''Few old people have the vigor, or the money, or the skill to do in their later years what they have always wanted to do but somehow have not got around to doing in their earlier life.'' Starting in the mid-1960s, these views began to change, and new and existing programs began to offer opportunities for older people to be contributors rather than recipients of services. One, the Service Corps of Retired Executives (SCORE), tapped the skills of retired business executives who could offer advice to small business owners. Others, such as the Retired and Senior Volunteer Program (RSVP) and Foster Grandparent programs, placed elders in social service agencies. The development of these programs reflects major shifts in the paradigm of the aging process. Elders are no longer viewed as a problematic group in declining health with limited social contacts who require services, but as a diverse population, most of whom can be active contributors to society, sometimes with limited assistance.

Many public and private programs have been established. From 16 programs for older volunteers in the United States in the mid-1960s, the number of national and local programs has increased substantially. These efforts have expanded the supply of older volunteers by making volunteerism attractive; recruiting people and helping them find appropriate jobs; and sometimes, with programs like RSVP and Foster Grandparents, reducing economic barriers by providing stipends, car fare, or a free lunch. In 1974, only 10% of nonvolunteers over the age of 65 said they were interested in volunteer work (National Council on Aging 1975), compared with 25% in a recent survey (Princeton Survey Research Associates 1991) and 37% in another (Marriott 1991).

There are four programs sponsored by the federal government. The Service Corps of Retired Executives, with 13,000 members, provides management expertise to prospective or current small business owners. The Foster Grandparent Program, with 27,000 members, provides social and emotional support to children with special or exceptional needs, including autistic and physically handicapped, abused, and neglected children, teenage parents, and adolescents with substance abuse problems. The Retired and Senior Volunteer Program, with 410,000 members, sponsors volunteer placements in human services programs and office-type jobs, collaborates with the Volunteers in Tax Assistance (VITA) program, and offers technical assistance and consultation to organizations. The Senior Companion Program, with 10,000 members, provides a stipend to volunteers who visit frail elders in their homes and provide them with social support.

Although these four programs were originated by the federal government, local RSVP, Senior Companion, and Foster Grandparent programs are actually public-private partnerships, since some of them are sponsored by nongovernmental organizations and rely on private and local government funds.

Throughout the nation, there are also many privately sponsored efforts, some of them initiated by foundations. The Shepherds's Center, in Kansas City, Kansas, is a network of programs where elders function as collaborators in providing services to other elders. Family Friends matches older volunteers with families caring for mentally ill adults or retarded children. Linking Lifetimes includes a number of intergenerational efforts, such as telephone reassurance between elders and latchkey children. The National Executive Service Corps places professionals and business executives in consulting assignments with nonprofit organizations and in other appropriate settings. The National Retiree Volunteer Center (NRVC) offers technical assistance to corporations interested in establishing programs for retired employees.

Probably the largest private-sector initiative—involving about 400,000 people and 8% of older volunteers—are programs sponsored by the American Association of Retired Persons (AARP). AARP initiated or cosponsored such innovative programs as the Widowed Persons' Service and the Volunteers in Tax Assistance program. A nationwide Volunteer Talent Bank matches volunteers and jobs. AARP's widely disseminated publications, *Modern Maturity* and *50 Plus,* have played a crucial role in shaping people's perceptions about community service.

Although the above organizations are important vehicles for promoting interest and expanding participation, most older people volunteer outside of these programs and are involved in settings where there is a mix of age groups. A survey conducted in 1988 revealed that 4% of older volunteers worked for RSVP, 2% for Foster Grandparents, 4% for Senior Companion, and 8% were in AARP-sponsored programs (Hamilton and Schneider 1988). But the largest concentration of elder volunteering (57%) is in churches and synagogues (Marriott 1991). Some organizations rely heavily on older volunteers without necessarily designing programs just for them. More than one-half of Red Cross volunteers are older than 55, many of whom have been involved for several decades.

Continuity of Participation

Many of the programs designed to foster volunteerism by older persons assume that participation in volunteer activities is a way to keep active, particularly in the face of retirement and widowhood. There is limited empirical support for this idea, however. The evidence shows that people do not volunteer to become active, but their volunteer work is because they are more active. Older volunteers tend to be involved in a broader array of leisure* activities than their peers who do not volunteer. Past involvement in volunteer work is a significant predictor of current activity, and a large proportion of older volunteers are simply continuing a pattern of commitment.

A recent survey (Independent Sector 1990) found that 17% of older volunteers were involved because they had free time. Another study found that one-quarter of the older volunteers were seeking companionship or wanted to reduce their sense of loneliness (17%). But these were considerably less important motives than "fulfilling a moral responsibility" (52%) or a "social obligation" (30%). Rather than being people who have lost their main social roles and volunteer in order to keep active, older people are more often involved in volunteer work if they are married or if they are employed, irrespective of their age or health. Many people combine paid and unpaid work, especially if they work part-time: 58% of working people and 42% of retirees volunteered in 1990 (Marriott 1991).

While involvement in community work is often an extension of people's work and family obligations, this is much less common for seniors, since few of them (5%) indicate they volunteer to ensure the "continuation of activities or institutions I or my family benefit from," compared with one-third of all volunteers. Elders also report that they are less often asked to volunteer: 37% of people over 65, compared with 41% of all respondents, indicated that they were involved in their current activities because someone asked them (Independent Sector 1990). These findings should not be interpreted to mean that individuals cannot become involved during old age. Even though volunteer participation tends to be higher among elders with histories of community involvement, it is possible to attract new volunteers. Recruitment of retirees, in particular, is a cost-effective strategy because they devote more time than other groups when they do volunteer: 69% of retirees, 55% of working people, and 54% of homemakers devote ten or more hours a month to volunteer work (Princeton Survey Research Associates 1991).

Social Factors Associated with Participation

The strongest predictor of volunteering is a person's educational achievement. College graduates are twice as likely to volunteer as those who have graduated from high school; two-thirds of college graduates over the age of 60 volunteer compared with one-third of high school graduates (Marriott 1991). At present, racial differences in participation are not significant.

Although most older volunteers are women, which reflects the composition of the older population, past differences in men's and women's participation have shifted considerably. In 1965, 7.6% of men over age 65 volunteered, compared with 9.6% of women. By 1991, this pattern had reversed, and volunteering was more common for men (46%) than for women (38%) (Marriott 1991).

A considerable amount of research documents that older volunteers are healthier and express higher levels of life satisfaction than people who do not volunteer. Although helping others or participating in organizations would seem to improve a person's life satisfaction, sense of empowerment, and health status, it is difficult to determine whether volunteering is the cause or the consequence.

What Will the Older Volunteer Workforce Be Like in the Future?

Several demographic changes are altering the needs and interests of older volunteers. These need to be considered in designing future policies and developing new programs. The size of the older population will increase, which suggests there will be far more older volunteers. However, if changes in retirement patterns continue, particularly if the age for eligibility for full Social Security* benefits is increased, the expansion might not be so straightforward. Recent census data suggest that more people over 65 are remaining in the labor force. This would reduce the number of older volunteers available during the regular work day and the amount of time they work, but should not reduce the total number of older volunteers.

Several trends indicate that the overall supply of older volunteers is likely to increase in the future, particularly as their average education continues to increase. Currently, 10% of older people are college graduates, as compared with 16% of 55-to-64-year-olds and 22% of middle-aged people (45 to 54 years old) (U.S. Department of Commerce 1991). A better-educated older population will include more potential volunteers and a large number of people with valued skills and past experience in community work. These qualities suggest, however, that there might be fewer people interested in clerical and unskilled tasks. There will be a need to continue to expand volunteer opportunities for well-educated elders and to create work climates in which people can find gratification in performing tasks that might not fully use their skills but are needed to sustain organizations.

A larger number of elders live in suburban areas than in central cities. This change suggests a need to arrange transportation for older volunteers, not just to reimburse costs. In light of the suburbanization of the older population, a second strategy may be needed to create more jobs that can be done at home or close to home, such as telephone reassurance and neighborhood-based friendly visiting.

Summary

Changes in the number of older persons who volunteer and the types of activities in which they are involved are a result of shifts in the educational and income profile of the older population as well as new images and perceptions of later life. Older persons are currently the mainstay of many organizations because of the skills they bring and their availability during the 9-to-5 work day. There is little evidence, however, that volunteering is a substitute for paid employment or for a decline in family responsibilities. Rather, volunteering is a way elders continue and sometimes expand commitment and contributions to their communities and cope with the impact of changes in their lives. Elder volunteering responds to social issues and social forces, just as volunteer work does for people in all other age groups. (See also HEALTH AND LONGEVITY,

LEISURE, EMPLOYMENT OF OLDER AMERICANS, RETIREMENT, HIS-
TORY OF, VOLUNTEERS, OLDER, and WIDOWHOOD.)

Organizations

Service Corps of Retired Executives (SCORE)
Retired Senior Volunteer Program (RSVP)
Foster Grandparent Program
The Senior Companion Program
National Executive Service Corps

References

Hamilton, Frederick, and S. Schneider. 1988. *Attitudes of Americans over 45 Years of
    Age on Volunteerism.* Washington, DC: AARP.
Havighurst, Robert J. 1950. "Public Attitudes toward Various Activities of Older Peo-
    ple." In *Planning the Older Years.* ed. Wilma Donahue and Clark Tibbits. Ann
    Arbor: University of Michigan Press, 141–48.
Independent Sector. 1990. *Giving and Volunteering in the United States.* Washington,
    DC: Independent Sector.
Marriott Senior Volunteerism Study. Commissioned by Marriott Senior Living Services
    and U.S. Administration on Aging. Washington, DC: U.S. Administration on
    Aging.
National Council on Aging. 1975. *The Myth and Reality of Aging in America.* Washing-
    ton, DC: Author
Princeton Survey Research Associates. 1991. *AARP's 12th Annual Survey of Middle-
    Aged and Older Americans.* Princeton, NJ: Author.
U.S. Department of Commerce. Bureau of the Census. 1991. *Statistical Abstract of the
    United States.* Washington, DC: U.S. Government Printing Office.

Susan M. Chambré

VOLUNTEERS, OLDER, persons over 65 inclined to help others, acting not
primarily for material gain or out of a sense of obligation. There is enormous
diversity in the types of services provided by older volunteers. Older volunteers
help school children and frail elderly; they run cultural programs; they help to
build houses and repair leaky faucets for poor people. Older persons make substantial contributions to their communities, to charitable and cultural organizations, and to individuals.

Many of the financial aspects of volunteer activities for older persons are not
well defined and are poorly understood. Even estimates of the numbers or percentages of older people who volunteer are problematic. There is considerable
ambiguity in defining what kinds of activities to "count" as volunteering.
Should informal help given to neighbors, friends, or relatives be considered
volunteer work? Some surveys include informal volunteering; others only count
formal volunteering arranged through organizations.

How Many Older People Volunteer?

There is an astonishingly broad range of estimates on the numbers of volunteers. Among people aged 18–64, between 18 and 55% volunteer. For older

adults, the estimates range from 11 to 52%. Even surveys conducted in the same year report different numbers of volunteers. However, there does appear to be a consistent trend: rates of volunteering have increased, for both younger and older volunteers.

An important rationale for recruiting older volunteers is that retirees ought to have more time to do volunteer work than younger people who are in the paid work force. We might expect, then, that retirees would be more likely to volunteer than younger people. But this does not seem to be true. There appears to be an inverse, U-shaped relationship between volunteering and age: People in their thirties and forties are the most likely to volunteer. Younger people and older people alike have lower rates of volunteering. Moreover, studies have shown that most elderly volunteers do not spend large amounts of time on volunteer work.

There are a number of significant barriers to volunteering for older people. The elderly are much more likely than others to identify poor health and lack of transportation as reasons for not volunteering. Another problem is income level. Low income is likely to restrict a person's ability to volunteer time or to give money to charity. However, most elderly people are not too sick to volunteer, and having lower incomes does not prevent the elderly from giving to charity. In fact, people aged 65 and older give the highest proportion of income to charity. A recent report on charitable giving in the United States noted that, among the 56% of contributors who worried about having enough money in the future, only respondents 65 years of age or older gave an average of 2% or more of their household income to charity (Independent Sector 1988).

Even if rates of volunteering decline with age, there are still substantial numbers of elderly, even among the very old, who continue to volunteer. Interestingly, it appears that the age curve has changed, so that the decline in volunteering occurs at much later ages.

This suggests that postretirement "careers" (including volunteer careers) may last for many years. The implications are intriguing:

• There should be ample time for "career development" among retired volunteers. If retirees look forward to 10, 20, or 30 more productive years, this span of time is similar to a person's work-life. Retiree volunteers may need opportunities for growth and advancement to sustain a long-term involvement in volunteering.

• Periodic retraining may be important. Retirees are often stable, long-term volunteers. Just as paid employees in many fields require ongoing training, older volunteers may need further training to maintain their skills.

• The problems of aging in place may be a concern for older volunteers. Long-time residents of senior housing experience the effects of aging while continuing to live in their apartments; consequently, they may begin to have service needs like residents in long-term care facilities. Similarly, long-time older volunteers may experience a loss of physical capabilities, associated with the hazards of aging. Volunteer programs must develop strategies for accommodating age-related physical changes.

The Cost and Value of Older Volunteers

A recent report on using older volunteers to work with school children noted: "Elderly volunteers, like their younger but often unavailable counterparts, generally can help to improve learning without increasing costs" (Tierce and Seelbach 1987). This may wrongly imply that volunteers are free.

Few studies have systematically studied the costs of working with volunteers. One study gathered detailed data on how much time was invested in each volunteer by paid staff (Baker and Murawski 1986). On average, one hour of paid staff time supported 13.2 hours of volunteer service. But the ratios varied widely—from 1:1.4 to 1:33.5. That is, for every hour invested by paid staff, volunteers contributed between one and thirty-four hours. The researchers then estimated the cost and found that for every dollar of paid staff time, the average value of volunteer time was $9.33. But this estimate also showed a broad range—from $1.33 to $14.69. The study suggested that there were a number of factors that decrease efficiency: high turnover, having individual orientation and training for volunteers (rather than group training); having high-salaried trainers; giving infrequent assignments to volunteers so that they needed a lot of retraining; needing many paid staff per volunteer; and recruiting totally unskilled volunteers.

Another project followed an information and referral service as it was transformed from paid staff to volunteer staff. One component of this study was to assess the costs of volunteer versus paid workers. Indeed, volunteers cost less: a volunteer cost $4.17 per hour, which was $1.83 less than a paid worker. But although this represented a savings, it took the program a long time—almost two years—after it had been shifted to a volunteer base to break even and begin seeing a profit (Pizzini 1986). The findings from these studies are sobering. They suggest that volunteers are not "cheap" and are not necessarily an efficient source of labor. High turnover and ineffective management can raise costs to the point that volunteers cost more than they give.

Can we estimate a dollar value for the services of older volunteers? We might want to calculate the net benefit (the value minus the costs), or a ratio of costs and social benefits. According to a recent report, based on a national sample of older persons, older volunteers contribute about 3.6 billion hours of voluntary service to organizations yearly (Marriott 1991). If we multiplied this number of hours by the minimum wage ($4.25/hour in 1991), we could assess the contribution of older volunteers to society at about $15.3 billion. Is this an adequate assessment of the value of services by older volunteers? Is it really feasible or reasonable to place a dollar value on volunteer services? Volunteer service organizations often seem eager to count volunteer hours and translate them into equivalent dollar values. But there are a number of problems in estimating the dollar value of volunteer services. A minimum wage standard would seem to undervalue the market rate of many services provided by older volunteers. Thousands of volunteers are retired professionals (teachers, business executives, engineers, etc.) who would be surprised to see their hours valued at such a low rate.

Typically, volunteers are asked to estimate "how much time a month" (or a week or a year) they spend volunteering. But in addition to problems of memory, there is variability in the time structure of volunteer commitments. For example, a volunteer for a hospital auxiliary might make a commitment to spend 2, 3, or 4 hours a week performing a particular kind of service. For such regular volunteer work, it might not be difficult to count the number of hours. But many types of volunteering entail episodic commitments, for instance, contributing to a bake sale. If there are difficulties in accounting for time spent volunteering for formal organizations, it is virtually impossible to assess time spent in informal services, helping neighbors, friends and relatives. One of the characteristics of such informal helping arrangements is precisely that people do not count the time they spend.

There is a related problem in translating time to dollars for any form of volunteer service. Traditionally, the Gross Domestic Product is based on dollars spent. By definition, no dollars are expended for informal help (such as domestic work by family members) or volunteer services. By this standard, domestic labor and volunteer services are not counted as a component of national productivity. Some feminist scholars and others have attempted to rectify this neglect and calculate a dollar value for unpaid "women's work." At best, however, it is difficult to make "guesstimates" of dollar equivalents without actual expenditures.

There is one further complication: Volunteering tends to be different from paid work. First, volunteers are participants by choice in the sense that their activities are not driven directly by their work or family obligations. In most voluntary service, there is a component of altruism—helping, and "doing good." Volunteers, in a great variety of roles, function as "concerned citizens." This suggests that the value of voluntary service may be intangible and difficult to measure.

Second, the responsibilities of volunteers often are defined as doing what paid workers do not do. In hospitals, nursing homes, schools, or other institutions, for example, it is common to recruit volunteers primarily to spend time with patients/residents. They may have assigned tasks, but part of the rationale for using volunteers is that they are not bound by hourly wages. Conversely, staff typically do not have "extra" time just to be with clients beyond performing their required tasks. The implication is that no one is actually prepared to pay for the type of services provided by volunteers.

To the extent that volunteer service is different from paid work, we would expect that monetary value may be an inadequate yardstick for judging the work of volunteers. We might imagine, in fact, that older volunteers, in particular, add value to their communities in several symbolic ways: They offer a message of caring across generations. Their stake in the welfare of others is a statement of faith in a future that continues beyond their own lifetimes. Their roles as volunteers also provide models of a productive and meaningful lifestyle in later life.

Volunteering for Retirees: Work or Leisure?

In trying to measure the value of volunteer labor, we are implicitly assuming that volunteers are producers of services or commodities. But volunteering can be viewed in another way—as a form of leisure*. In this sense, retired persons presumably have more time for leisure than persons in the paid work force and, therefore, are prime consumers of volunteer opportunities.

In many ways, volunteering serves a leisure function for retirees. Older volunteers are more likely than working-age volunteers to say they volunteer because they have "free time." Retirees often say their motivation for volunteering is "self-fulfillment." They are also less likely to volunteer for instrumental reasons—for the sake of career development or to help their families. Yet volunteer activities are tied to work and family roles. Two of the most common types of voluntary associations to which individuals contribute their time are trade groups and civic organizations; both of these tend to attract membership through their occupations and professions; most volunteers in these associations are employed adults. There are also many programs associated with family roles. Older volunteers are far less likely than volunteers in their middle years to say they volunteer because they have a "child, relative or friend who was involved in the activity or would benefit from it" (Independent Sector 1990).

Older people who volunteer tend to be "joiners." Most older volunteers are younger volunteers who grew old. Most active volunteers tend to be active in other organizations as well. If volunteerism is a form of leisure activity, then volunteer activities compete with other opportunities for use of leisure time— sports, hobbies, reading, playing cards, watching television, and so forth. For retirees, volunteer work is their choice; it is enjoyable and meaningful to them. Some gerontologists have argued that older people constitute a new leisure class that has emerged in the second half of the twentieth century. As people live longer and retire at earlier ages, a substantial portion of the lifespan occurs in the postretirement years. One of the most important benefits of early retirement is that it gives workers a choice about how they spend their time and energy. (See also ECONOMIC HARDSHIP MEASURES IN THE OLDER POPULATION, ECONOMIC STATUS OF THE ELDERLY, ECONOMIC STATUS OF ELDERLY WOMEN, LEISURE, VOLUNTEERING, and WORKING RETIREES.)

Suggested Readings

Bull, C. Neil, and Nancy D. Levine. 1993. *The Older Volunteer: An Annotated Bibliography.* Westport, CT: Greenwood Press.

Fischer, Lucy Rose, Daniel P. Mueller, and Philip W. Cooper. 1993. *Older Volunteers: Volunteering by the New Leisure Class.* Lexington, MA: Lexington Books.

Friedman, Marc. 1993. *The Kindness of Strangers: Adult Mentors, Urban Youth, and the New Volunteerism.* San Francisco: Jossey-Bass.

References

Baker, B. J. and K. Murawski. 1986. "A Method for Measuring Paid Staff Support for Volunteer Involvement." *Journal of Voluntary Action Research* 15: 60–64.

Independent Sector. 1988, 1990. *Giving and Volunteering in the United States.* Findings from a National Survey Conducted by the Gallup Organization. Washington, DC: Independent Sector.

Marriott Senior Volunteerism Study. 1991. Commissioned by Marriott Senior Living Services and the U.S. Administration on Aging. Washington, DC: U.S. Administration on Aging.

Pizzini, M. 1986. "Volunteers: An Answer for Information and Referral in the 80s." *Information and Referral* 8: 58–80.

Tierce, J. W. and W. C. Seelbach. 1987. "Elders as School Volunteers: An Untapped Resource." *Educational Gerontology* 13: 33–41.

Lucy R. Fischer

W

WEALTH SPAN, a model introduced in 1987 by Davis W. Gregg for illustrating financial changes during phases of the human life cycle. Gregg ([1987] 1992) noted that while biologists, psychologists, and sociologists were examining human life from a developmental perspective, the past hundred years of developmental psychology revealed that ''development'' more often than not referred to children. Programs at the University of Chicago, under psychologist Robert Havighurst (1993), did not expand human development to more fully include maturation and change at the older end of the life cycle until 1941.

The basic developmental model of the life cycle in financial terms has two basic stages: the *Accumulation Stage* and the *Expenditure Stage.* Gregg and his colleagues fully recognized, of course, that human financial behavior is much more complicated than this. These two stages could easily be defined as shorter, more specific stages. Further, the dichotomy of ''accumulating when young'' versus ''spending when old'' is an oversimplification of the complex world of individual and family financial behavior, a fact recognized by the scientific controversies surrounding Modigliani's (1986) life-cycle theories of saving and dissaving. But Gregg's basic model, developed more for pedagogical purposes than as an empirical basis for scientific hypothesis testing, serves to introduce a number of key ideas of financial gerontology, and offers a lens through which we can view several issues of both theoretical and applied importance.

As a brief introduction to Gregg's idea of the human wealth span, the following discussion reviews four main elements of the model: (1) recent historical changes in the relative size or balance between the accumulation and expenditure stages, (2) increasing complexities during the accumulation stage, (3) increasing complexities during the expenditure stage, and (4) the wealth span model as an opportunity for proactive, positive changes in financial behavior even at older

Figure 1
The Human Wealth Span: A Heuristic Model

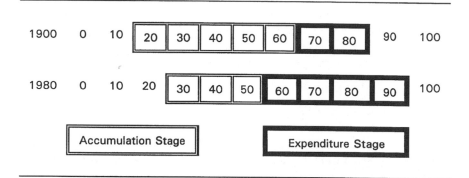

ages. The new complexities of the accumulation and expenditure stages, and the concomitant decisions that aging individuals and families are increasingly called upon to make because of these complexities, direct attention to another of Dr. Gregg's life-long concerns as a financial scholar and educator: the growing importance of *Financial Literacy*—the fact that such literacy is needed more and earlier in the human wealth span (Cutler 1992).

Historical Changes in the Human Wealth Span

Figure 1 displays the wealth span at two symbolic points in twentieth-century history: 1940 and 1990. The distinctions as to when the dynamics of accumulation and expenditure begin and end are suggestive rather than scientifically precise in this illustration. In the 1940s, people entered the labor force at a relatively young age, perhaps 17 or so, and could begin the process of accumulation fairly early. The Social Security system defined retirement at age 65, so the accumulation stage ended at about that age. Old-age life expectancy was comparatively low, so that the expenditure stage in this heuristic model was fairly short, with people living until age 70 or 75.

By contrast, the relative lengths of these two stages in recent times (*circa* 1990) are notably different. Young people stay in school longer, including graduate and professional training, so that full-time labor force entry into the accumulation stage does not begin until the mid- to late 20s. What used to be called ''early retirement'' is now the norm, and many private pensions build on the fact that Social Security provides reduced pension benefits as early as age 62. In the model, retirement in the 1990s is set at around age 61. These historical changes serve to shorten the accumulation stage.

What about the expenditure stage, fully recognizing that some accumulation continues in what is labelled the expenditure stage? With retirement at age 61, and with improvements in life expectancy, the expenditure stage is now substantially longer than it was in 1940 (Cutler 1994).

The general historical trend tends to shorten the accumulation stage of the human wealth span. At the same time, the expenditure stage is lengthened because of early retirement and greater old-age longevity. The typical pattern is clear: on average, people accumulate for a smaller number of years, and what is thereby accumulated must last for longer expenditure years. The accumulation of personal, governmental, and employment-related financial resources must be planned in a much more systematic way than in years past.

The Accumulation Stage is Not Only Shorter, But More Complex

The increased responsibility for informed and wise accumulation strategies, what Gregg referred to as the need for financial literacy (Cutler and Gregg 1991), is not only prompted by the shorter accumulation stage of the human wealth span. In the past, in what might be referred to as "the good old days," financial security was seen as a simple function of the "three-legged stool:" Social Security as a basic retirement income pension, an employer-provided pension whose dollar benefit was defined in advance, and savings.

But Social Security rules have changed many times in recent decades, including those on the taxation of benefits. The value of savings as an income-producing strategy has dramatically changed from the 14% interest rates of the 1970s to the 3% rates of the 1990s. And the most dramatic change is occurring in the financial structure of the American pension system. The trend from defined benefit to defined contribution pensions puts much greater financial responsibility on the shoulders of individual citizens (Salisbury 1993).

Where a defined benefit pension communicated to the worker and his family how much they would get upon retirement, defined contribution pension plans only identify what the employer and employee together provide as input into the investment process. What those invested funds financially produce 15 or 25 years later is the responsibility of the employer or union. Again, this requires substantial financial literacy on the part of the citizen: what investments to choose, what kinds of risk to absorb, how to manage risk and return, how to balance inflation-risk and capital-loss risk, and similar choices. The accumulation stage of the wealth span, therefore, is not only shorter than it used to be, but demands a much more literate understanding of financial dynamics and choices.

Additional Complexities of the Expenditure Stage

The balance between a shorter accumulation stage and a longer expenditure stage would seem enough of a financial challenge to aging individuals and families, but the situation is even more complex than that. Research points to two clusters of complexity connected with the changing relationship of families, finance, and aging. One of the basic principles of financial gerontology is that financial decisions are family decisions, and in this context the financial decisions of later life have become much more intricate than they used to be.

Who Are the Dippies? Dippies is an acronym for Double Income (DI) and

Plural Pensions (PP), and describes families in which both husband and wife are employed. While they are working they not only earn current double income, but also shares of future retirement income, their plural pension future. While having more money is not usually seen as a serious problem, from the perspective of financial gerontology the central characteristic of Dippies is the complexity of their current and future income profile.

Dippies are not necessarily wealthy. In many working-class and middle-class families, both husband and wife must work just to make ends meet. The issue here is not riches but complexity. Families characterized as Dippies have complex financial situations during their working years, but face even greater planning challenges as they anticipate their future retirement income profile. They must anticipate two Social Security benefits, two employer pensions (made even more complex if either or both pensions are defined contributions rather than defined benefit pensions), two sets of savings and investments, home equity, and perhaps supplemental retirement accounts. Not all families will have all of these future income streams, but the profile of complexity is potentially significant.

From the perspective of the human wealth span, the primary implication for Dippies is the challenge of complex financial planning for the future. Knowing that the family must anticipate this profile, certain choices must be made in advance. Issues of taxes, of investment strategies, of allocation of financial resources to different categories of risk and return, all direct attention to the critical importance of financial literacy.

Financially Complex Intergenerational Relations. Discussions of increased life expectancy typically focus on the implications of longevity either for individual older men and women (such as problems of health and illness, or their financial cost), or on the implications for society as a whole, such as the impact of population aging on the Social Security* and Medicare* systems. Typically overlooked is the impact of increased old-age longevity on the family as a social organization that has substantial financial decision-making responsibility. This role of the family takes on greater importance in the course of aging, when important decisions are made concerning long-term care, residential changes, intergenerational transfers, and other aspects of estate planning*.

A study of the impact on American families of increasing old-age life expectancy provides dramatic evidence of the linkages between longevity and family structure, with clear implications for the general principle that financial decisions are family decisions. Looking at increases in old-age longevity, Uhlenberg (1980) asked how family structures in 1900 might have differed from those in 1976 (see Table 1). His results offer insights also from the perspective of finances and the human wealth span.

In years past, middle-age couples might look forward to a period of an "empty-nest," income-providing years in which funds could be set aside for future income security. Now young-adult children will still be on the financial agenda of some 55-year-old parents who may also face responsibility for their

Table 1
Changing Family Structures

What are the odds that . . .	In 1900	In 1976
. . . a 15-year old would have 3 or 4 grandparents still alive?	17%	55%
. . . a middle-age couple would have at least 2 of their elderly parents alive?	10%	47%

own surviving elderly parents, a situation Brody (1985) has referred to as the sandwich generation phenomenon.

The lessons suggested by the model of the human wealth span are not only for the wealthy. Rather, the issues are best characterized in terms of financial complexity for both rich and middle-income households. During the accumulation stage of the wealth span one should anticipate and plan for changing family and demographic pressures. And even during the expenditure stage there are substantial and complex financial decisions to be made, many of which have become intergenerationally complex as well as financially challenging.

The Good News: It's Never Too Late to Start Planning

Despite these concerns, the wealth span model is not about "bad news." In fact, the intellectual origins of the model suggest a very optimistic message. Building from the general lifespan view of maturation from birth through multiple life stages to older age and death, physician John W. Rowe and psychologist Robert L. Kahn developed the "Health Span" model of "successful aging" (Rowe and Kahn 1987).

The essence of the health span model is two-fold. First, what happens earlier in the health span affects what happens later. But second, even changes that are initiated later in the health span can have positive effects on the rest of life. Research demonstrates that even when good health habits begin later in life, there likely will be positive effects on health for the rest of the individual's health span. In most cases, they suggest, health can be improved and some old health problems can subside.

In the human wealth span, the same logic applies. It would be best, of course, if individuals and families developed good financial habits early in their lives. But teaching young people good financial health habits is difficult. Saving for retirement involves seeing oneself as old, which is difficult for most young adults (Cutler 1992). So one may turn to Rowe and Kahn's logic of the health span. Better to start early, but if not early, then better late than never. Learning

the principles of compound interest, of tax-free accumulations in retirement accounts, of the differences between inflation risk and capital-erosion risk, are
important elements of financial literacy to know even if they cannot be implemented immediately. Even at age 40 or 50, or later, financial planning, saving,
and allocation are effective.

Summary

In sum, the wealth span model suggests three basic principles for improved
lifetime financial planning. First, a combination of demography and cultural and
economic trends has evolved to create a new balance (or imbalance) between
the relative amounts of time available for accumulation compared with expenditure. Despite differences among individuals and families, we generally have
less time to accumulate resources for a longer time spent in the later years of
our lives.

Second, within that shorter accumulation stage, financial life has become more
complex, requiring a higher level of financial literacy. We are now more individually responsible for decisions concerning our pensions, investments, and
savings strategies. And family-finance linkages have become more complex due
in part to more couples with dual incomes, and in part to the greater longevity
of our parents and grandparents.

Third, Davis Gregg's wealth span model suggests that the cliché of better late
than never does have validity for both health and wealth behavior. It is better
to be financially literate and to begin good habits earlier in life. But if circumstances do not allow an early start, even later implementation of good wealth
habits can have a positive influence on financial well-being in later life. (See
also BOETTNER CENTER OF FINANCIAL GERONTOLOGY, ESTATE
PLANNING, HEALTH AND LONGEVITY, HOUSING, KING LEAR SYN-
DROME, MEDICARE, NURSING HOMES, and SOCIAL WORK, GERON-
TOLOGICAL.)

References

Brody, E. M. 1985. "Parent Care as Normative Family Stress." *Gerontologist* 25: 19–
29.
Cutler, N. E. 1992. "Sex, Asset Accumulation, and Rock 'n' Roll: Introducing Retire-
ment Planning to Teenagers and Other Pre-Middle-Agers." *Journal of the Amer-
ican Society of CLU & ChFC* 46 (November), 36–39.
Cutler, N. E. 1994. "Live Long (90+ Years) and Prosper: The Personal Financial Im-
plications of Demographic Trends. *Journal of the American Society of CLU &
ChFC* 48 (November), 35–37.
Cutler, N. E., and D. W. Gregg. 1991. "The Human Wealth Span and Financial Well-
Being in Old Age. *Generations* 25: 45–48.
Gregg, D. W. [1987] 1992. "The Wealth Span: A Promising Dimension for Geronto-
logical Research." Invitational Symposium, Bryn Mawr, Pennsylvania, Reprinted
as: "Human Wealth Span: The Financial Dimensions of Successful Aging." In
Aging, Money, and Life Satisfaction: Aspects of Financial Gerontology, ed. N. E.
Cutler, D. W. Gregg, and M. P. Lawton. New York: Springer, 169–82.

Havighurst, R. J. 1993. ''History of Developmental Psychology: Socialization and Personality Development through the Life Span.'' In *Life-Span Developmental Psychology,* ed. P. B. Baltes and K. W. Schaie. New York: Academic Press, 3–24.

Modigliani, F. 1986. ''Life Cycle, Individual Thrift, and the Wealth of Nations.'' *Science* 234: 704–12.

Rowe, R. W., and R. L. Kahn. 1987. ''Human Aging: Usual and Successful.'' *Science* 237: 143–49.

Salisbury, D. L. 1993. ''Policy Implications of Changes in Employer Pension Protection.'' In *Pensions in a Changing Economy,* ed. R. V. Burkhauser and D. L. Salisbury. Washington, DC: Employee Benefit Research Institute.

Uhlenberg, P. I. 1980. ''Death and the Family.'' *Journal of Family History* 5: 313–20.

Neal E. Cutler

WIDOWHOOD, marital status and phase in the life cycle prompted by separation from one's husband by death. Often widowhood separates the woman from a large share of the resources upon which she depended while her husband was alive. Income flows (e.g., earnings from work and sometimes pensions) cease upon his death. The reasons why total income falls when husbands die despite large life insurance* and pension* industries, as well as social legislation attempting to increase protection against this contingency, are still not fully understood.

The continuing economic vulnerability of widows may be because of several factors. Coverage by public and private insurance programs and the receipt of survivor benefits may be limited by work, family status, or age restrictions. Couples may have chosen not to purchase supplementary protection, or the appropriate coverage against certain risks may simply not be available. Finally, the husband may have been permitted by law to will his assets to others or to restrict his widow's access to resources.

Measuring Change in the Economic Status of Widows

Widows have substantially lower incomes and assets than do women of the same age who are married. For widowed women aged 65 and older, the poverty rate is four times greater than that for married women of the same age (Burkhauser et al. 1991). The percentages of married and widowed women who are counted as being in poverty in cross-sectional data imply that over 20% of women who were not poor prior to their husband's death are plunged into poverty when their husbands die. Yet, data collected in a single survey or census provide information only on the percentage of widows and married women who are poor at the time of the survey (or during the relevant income reference period), but in fact give little information on how financial status changes when husbands die. Widows identified at any point in time are an aggregate of women with different histories of marriage* and widowhood. This and other factors may lead to biases of unknown magnitude and direction.

Only when women are followed from marriage into widowhood—as they can be with longitudinal panel studies—can the consequence of the widowhood event itself be observed and separated from other influences that may confound the measure of its economic effects. The availability of several major panel studies has advanced our understanding of the financial effects of widowhood. Yet even panel studies must take care to accurately assess the impact of widowhood itself on economic status. Examining financial changes only of couples in which the husband dies (we will call these "eventual widows"), without comparison to other marital status groups, implies that widowhood is the primary variable explaining changes in income in the years before and after the husband's death. Yet, over the same period, other women of the same age—those who remain married and those who were unmarried to begin with—may be experiencing similar changes. For example, job market conditions may lead to earlier retirements or layoffs among all women, inflation rates may increase, or the stock market or housing prices may fall; these factors will erode the real value of income and income-producing assets of all individuals. To capture these society-wide influences, comparisons are most often made with women who remained married during the same period (we will call these "intact couples").

Financial change may be captured by a variety of measures, although changes in poverty rates and changes in income relative to needs are the most often studied measures. Income-to-needs ratios adjust household income for the consumption needs of households of different sizes. Poverty thresholds have been used most often as the relative needs standard. Declines into poverty as the change measure identifies widows who become poor but not those who remain out of poverty yet experience income instability. Large changes in income are more prevalent at widowhood than declines into poverty, and distinguish a different group of women at risk.

While greater income as a couple reduces the chances of a widow becoming poor, it increases the chances of her suffering a major decline in income to needs. Women who were relatively better off when married experience larger average percentage income-to-needs changes when their husbands die than do widows with lower incomes as a couple. In part, this occurs because lower-income couples are less dependent on sources of income that may not continue automatically to the widow.

Studies using panel data document an important role for prewidowhood differences and postwidowhood changes in income in explaining observed cross-sectional differences between married and widowed women. Nevertheless, these studies also show that widowhood itself exacts a large economic loss (Holden and Smock 1991; Morgan 1991). These changes appear to be especially large for women widowed at younger ages, in part because of age-related eligibility rules in Social Security* and private pensions, but also because younger couples may underestimate the risk of widowhood and, although they have had less time to self-insure through their own accumulated savings, purchase far less insurance than is optimal against the loss of the husband's earnings. Zick and Smith (1991) report that average income-to-needs ratios five years after widowhood are more than 60% below the ratios for intact couples. For younger widows (under age

60), the drop in income at their husbands' death fully accounted for the difference between them and the comparable group of intact couples. For older widows (age 60 and above), lower prewidowhood income-to-needs ratios explained about two-thirds of the final difference between them and intact couples, implying a smaller effect of widowhood for these older women. This different situation for older widows is due to older couples having had more years to accumulate savings and to the greater dependence of the older couples on Social Security and pensions, some of which continues to be paid to the widow.

Protection against the Loss of Financial Resources

Widowhood presents a financial issue because both partners in a marriage will not usually survive for precisely the same number of years. Even if women and men had identical life expectancies, some women and men would lose their partners. As cohorts aged, they would be increasingly composed of widows (and widowers). Higher mortality among men than women and the average younger ages of wives makes outliving one's spouse a far more likely event for women than for men. Women are more likely to lose their spouses through death at younger ages than men, are far less likely to remarry after their spouses die, and to survive alone for a far longer period of time following their husbands' deaths. Although issues of survivorship are equally applicable to men and women, it is for women that protection against the loss of financial resources when their spouse dies is most important and most inadequate.

The greater dependence of wives on husband's income than vice versa makes the economic hazards of a spouse's death greater for women than men. The greater work participation of women will reduce this risk over time, but will not eliminate it. Even when earnings are equal over a couple's lifetime, the death of one is likely to reduce the income-to-needs status of the economic unit.

Pension Protection. Over recent decades, both Social Security and federal pension regulations have attempted to increase the security of women when husbands die. In 1974, the Employee Retirement Income Security Act (ERISA)* established minimum fiduciary, coverage, and vesting requirements for private pension plans. But ERISA covers only private pensions, excluding the 22% of pension participants in public plans from its protection. Also, private retirement plans that are not ''employee welfare benefit plans'' are not regulated by ERISA pension plan provisions (e.g., IRAs, 401(k)s, and annuities purchased from life insurance companies). Consequently, when an individual takes a lump-sum pension distribution at retirement and rolls it over into another retirement vehicle, the annuities are not subject to ERISA survivorship payout rules.

ERISA appears to have increased the chances that married men would choose a joint and survivor benefit. But obligations to ex-spouses may divert retirement resources from the second spouse. As second marriages become more prevalent among retiring couples, a growing proportion of widows may be exposed to a large income change in widowhood.

Pensions can reduce economic vulnerability for the widows only of the 50–

60% of men who are eligible for a pension when they retire. Even among this group, a survivor pension was chosen (in both the pre-and post-ERISA years) more often by couples who could afford to forego current income and whose pension wealth was a higher proportion of all wealth. These relationships are consistent with the hypothesis that couples who can afford to do so will purchase some desired insurance against the consequences of widowhood. Of course, high-income couples without pension income may seek other forms of insurance. Nevertheless, the incomplete protection of young widows against the loss of their husband's earnings, and the decline in income even among high-income widows, suggests generally low levels of insurance purchased among couples in general.

Social Security Protection. The basic structure for protecting widows through payment of an annuity based on insured workers, as designed in the 1930s, still remains. Eligibility for a survivor benefit is primarily a function of the age and motherhood status of the widow and of the survivor's eligibility for retired-worker benefits. These benefits are paid to nondisabled surviving spouses at age 60, and at age 55 if disabled. If the survivor is caring for a child of the deceased worker under age 16, a survivor's benefit will also be paid. Survivor's benefits are offset by any retired-worker benefit for which the survivor is eligible.

The age distinction in Social Security matters greatly to the change in economic status when husbands die (Holden et al. 1988). Wives younger than 60 when widowed are more likely to enter poverty after widowhood, which is evidence of the protection from age-conditioned insurance and, perhaps, of the short-term difficulties faced by younger women in adjusting their employment to the loss of a husband's income.

While Social Security allows no choice in the receipt or amount of survivor benefits, increasing labor force participation of women may reduce the protection against the loss of their husbands' earnings from this program. A widow is eligible for a benefit equal to 100% of her deceased spouse's benefit. A widow who is ineligible for her own retired-worker benefit and who had received a spouse benefit when married (equal to 50% of his) will receive a Social Security benefit equal to two-thirds of the combined benefit received when both were alive. For a couple with two equal earners, each spouse will be eligible for an identical retired-worker benefit. But a beneficiary may receive an amount equal only to the highest benefit for which she or he is eligible. Thus, the death of one spouse in an equal-earner couple will leave the survivor with only his or her benefit—an amount equal to only one-half of the combined social security benefit received when both were alive.

For low-income two-earner couples, who are likely to be more dependent on Social Security in retirement, the loss of one-half the couple's combined income may cause financial hardship. A decline in income by 50%, when the decline in consumption needs implied by the poverty threshold is only 20%, will alone cause some widows who were not poor when married to enter poverty upon widowhood. Burkhauser and Smeeding (1994) have proposed changes to the survivor benefit to equal a higher percentage of the combined couple's benefits; this would both raise incomes of widows and reduce the implicit cost to widows of greater sharing of earnings efforts between spouses.

Insuring against the Costs of Widowhood

The evidence indicates that widowhood entails an economic cost to women when their husbands die. Even when one takes account of the lower economic status of eventual widows prior to the husband's death, an estimated 12–17% of women who were widowed during the 1970s and 1980s and who were not poor prior to widowhood entered poverty upon the death of their husbands. An even larger proportion of widows experienced large changes in income relative to needs, with the drop in income increasing with the income level prior to widowhood. This contrasts with the experience of men when wives die; while loss of wives' Social Security benefits is observed, the needs-adjusted income of husbands remains stable for widowers.

The chances of widows entering poverty will diminish as wives' ownership of assets and eligibility for employer-provided pensions and Social Security retired-worker benefits provides a protective floor. However, as equality of earnings between spouses increases, the share of the couple's combined Social Security benefits continuing to the widow will decline from two-thirds for single earner couples to 50%. As wives become eligible for their own employer pensions, husbands may be less likely to provide for a survivor benefit, thereby offsetting the protective effects of the wife's own greater retirement income. For some couples, lower levels of protection from pensions may be offset by other forms of insurance. But evidence suggests severe underinsurance by couples against widowhood (Auerbach and Kotlikoff 1987).

The existing body of literature does not satisfactorily explain what factors couples consider when choosing how to allocate resources over their remaining lifetimes, including the period when only one survives. The changes in income observed among widows are large and clearly compound the emotional difficulties associated with a husband's death. In contrast to divorce, where reluctance of a husband to protect his ex-wife against the loss of his own income is expected, the decline in economic well-being upon widowhood is more difficult to explain. Until we know more about the decisions couples make about protecting the wife as a widow, it will be difficult to predict the future well-being of widows. (See also ASSETS ALLOCATION AFTER RETIREMENT, ECONOMIC STATUS OF ELDERLY WOMEN, EMPLOYEE RETIREMENT INCOME SECURITY ACT, LIFE INSURANCE, MARRIAGE AND THE ELDERLY, PENSIONS, SOCIAL SECURITY, and WILLS.)

Organization
Older Women's League

References

Auerbach, Alan J., and Laurence J. Kotlikoff. 1987. "Life Insurance of the Elderly: Its Adequacy and Determinants." In *Work, Health and Income among the Elderly,* ed. G. Burtless. Washington, DC: Brookings.

Burkhauser, Richard V., J. S. Butler, and Karen C. Holden. 1991. "How the Death of a Spouse Affects Economic Well-Being after Retirement: A Hazard Model Approach." *Social Science Quarterly* 72: 504–19.

Burkhauser, Richard V., and Timothy M. Smeeding. 1994. "Social Security Reform: A Budget Neutral Approach to Reducing Older Women's Disproportionate Risk of Poverty." Policy Brief No. 2. Syracuse, NY: Syracuse University Center for Policy Research.

Holden, Karen C., Richard V. Burkhauser, and Daniel Feaster. 1988. "The Timing of Falls into Poverty after Retirement and Widowhood." *Demography* 25: 405–14.

Holden, Karen C., and Pamela J. Smock. 1991. "The Economic Costs of Marital Dissolution: Why Do Women Bear a Disproportionate Cost? *Annual Review of Sociology* 17: 51–78.

Morgan, Leslie A. 1991. *After Marriage Ends: Economic Consequences for Midlife Women.* Newbury Park, CA: Sage.

Zick, Cathleen D., and Ken R. Smith. 1991. "Patterns of Economic Change Surrounding the Death of a Spouse." *Journal of Gerontology* 46: 310–20.

Karen C. Holden

WILLS, legal documents by which persons may direct the disposition of property upon death. The right to a will has not been common to all societies throughout history. In countries and legal systems that recognize and accord the right, it is not absolute. Strict technical formalities must be observed to create a valid will, and certain property rights cannot be altered or defeated by will. Many of the technical requirements that surround the preparation, execution, and administration of a will are because the testator (the person executing the will) is no longer available to interpret the document or supervise its administration. Thus, in the United States, the law requires that formalities be observed in the execution of a will to ensure the authenticity of documents that are admitted to probate*. In most states, the will must be executed in the presence of at least two witnesses who in turn must subscribe their names to the document. In many states, a self-proving affidavit may also be attached as part of the will. The latter is a sworn (notarized) statement of the testator and the witnesses in which they confirm that the required formalities were observed. Typically, those formalities include the testator declaring to the witnesses that he or she intends the document to become a will, the testator signing the document in the presence of the witnesses, requesting the witnesses to sign the document, and the witnesses signing the document in the presence of the testator.

In order to make a valid will, the testator must be competent and not under undue influence from any source. The competency required to make a will is generally defined as follows: the testator must be aware of the "natural objects of his or her bounty'' (i.e., the members of his family); the testator must be aware of the property that he or she owns; and the testator must understand the nature of the will and its legal effect when he or she signs it.

In most states, the surviving spouse of the decedent is entitled to a minimum portion of the estate. If less than that amount is left to the spouse by will, he or she may have the right to ''renounce'' the will in favor of the larger statutory entitlement. Marital property rights may be modified by contract between the parties. A contract executed prior to the marriage (a premarital agreement) is generally more easily enforced than a contract entered into after the marriage.

A further restriction on the right to dispose of property by will is the federal estate tax (and in most states, a state inheritance or estate tax). The federal government is often one of the largest beneficiaries of an estate.

Probate

A will does not acquire legal force or effect until it is ''probated.'' In its narrowest sense, probate is a process by which a purported will is offered to and accepted by a court and declared to be the true last will and testament of a decedent. If no one contests the validity of the offered document, probate, in its narrow sense, can be accomplished informally and quickly. If the offered will is contested, a trial may be required to determine its validity.

Naming an Executor

A necessary component of a will is the nomination of a person or institution as executor or personal representative. The executor is the person responsible for probating the will and carrying out the testator's instructions. It is a position that should be filled carefully. Generally, the choice is between one or more individuals or a bank or trust company, or a combination of the two. For example, a family member and a bank could be named to serve together as coexecutors. Banks and trust companies may offer certain advantages over individuals, but the relative expenses in connection with estate administration should be explored and weighed carefully. First, bank trust departments and trust companies are in the business of administering estates and trusts, but bank charges for these services can be sizeable. An individual, on the other hand, may not have previously administered an estate and require the services of professionals which can also be costly.

A bank trust department may also have the advantage of neutrality and objectivity. Choosing an executor from among family members could leave those not chosen feeling slighted and prone to believe that the chosen executor will be biased. In many instances, the executor is required to make decisions in the administration of the estate that are likely to upset one or more beneficiaries. Normally, one would prefer that the anger be directed outside the family (at a bank executor) rather than at a family member. As an institution, a bank or trust company also enjoys a longevity and permanence that an individual does not. An individual who is named as executor may predecease the testator, or become ill, incapacitated, or move out of the state or country and be unavailable to administer the estate. That is unlikely to happen with a sound bank. The principal disadvantage in naming an institution is that the testator does not know with certainty who in the bank will be making the critical decisions. If an individual is named, and assuming that individual survives the testator and is available to serve, the testator knows exactly who the decisionmaker will be.

Bequests and Trusts

There are several types of bequests that may be made in a will. A specific bequest is a gift of a specific item to a specific person. For example, "I give my engagement ring to my daughter, Sally." A general or pecuniary gift is a gift of a specific sum of money. For example, "I give Sally the sum of $1,000." A residuary bequest is a gift of the estate that remains after payment of debts and costs of administration and all specific or pecuniary gifts in the will.

The different types of bequests have unique advantages and disadvantages. Specific bequests may be appropriate for certain important and unique assets where it is important that they be distributed in a precise fashion. The disadvantage of specific bequests is that circumstances may frequently change, which will require the revision of the will. For example, the particular item might be given during lifetime to the intended recipient, the testator may sell or otherwise dispose of the property before his or her death, or the intended recipient may decide that he or she does not want that particular item.

A pecuniary gift is appropriate when the testator wants to recognize a friend or a charity with a fixed amount that will not fluctuate with changes in value of the overall estate. A pecuniary gift should normally be small in relation to the total value of the estate. Residuary gifts are appropriate for the principal beneficiaries. For example, if a testator wants to leave his or her entire estate to his or her two children, the statement: "After payment of my debts and the expenses of administering my estate, I give my remaining estate in equal shares to my children" may suffice. The will need not allocate assets between the two children; that can be left for the executor in consultation with the children after the testator's death.

Because a will speaks only at death and because circumstances constantly change, the testator should always direct alternate gifts if certain contingencies arise. For example, the testator may want to leave his or her estate equally to children, but an alternate disposition of each child's share should be addressed in the event that one or more of the children dies before she or he does. The gift may, for example, be left to the children of the deceased child (grandchildren of the testator) or to the other surviving children of the testator.

Trusts* may be created by will. A trust is appropriate for bequests to minors and young adults who have not matured sufficiently to prudently hold and manage the intended bequest. Similarly, a trust would be appropriate for a disabled beneficiary. However, care must be taken in the case of an individual who is receiving financial assistance through a government program that is based on need, e.g., the Supplemental Security Income (SSI)* program.

Charitable gifts may also be made by will. For example, a specific sum of money may be left to a church, school, or other charity, or a portion of the residuary estate may be given to charity. Outright charitable gifts are fully deductible for federal estate tax purposes.

Additional Contents of a Will

While the essential components of a will are: (1) directions regarding the distribution of property, and (2) naming an executor, many other provisions may also be properly included, such as funeral* instructions, anatomical gifts, and tax planning provisions.

It is generally preferable to communicate preferences or instructions regarding funeral and burial outside the will, since the will may not be found or read until after burial. However, if it is anticipated that one or more members of the family may resist the requested funeral arrangements, it is helpful to have them established in the will. Because a will is a formal legal document, inclusion of funeral instructions in the document tends to lend additional weight to those instructions and gives greater assurance that they will be followed.

If one wishes to make gifts of body organs for research, education, or transplantation (i.e., going beyond organ donation noted on a driver's license) his or her wish should be included in the will. As in the case of funeral instructions, anatomical gifts should also be recorded in a separate document since the will may not be immediately accessible and speed is necessary to effect gifts of organs. Family physicians and hospitals should be able to provide preprinted forms for making anatomical gifts.

Additionally, effective planning to reduce estate taxes may be incorporated into a will. A will is as effective as a revocable living trust for that purpose. (Irrevocable living trusts, on the other hand, offer tax planning options that cannot be duplicated by a will.) Proper tax planning is especially advisable for married couples whose combined estate exceeds the prevailing federal estate tax exemption equivalent, currently $600,000. A couple with a combined estate of $1.2 million can reduce estate taxes by $240,000 or more through proper tax planning.

Contest

Unlike the protection given to surviving spouses, there are virtually no similar inheritance protections for children or other descendants. A child or other descendant who is disinherited by his or her parent has no recourse except to contest the probate of the will. In order to bring such a suit, the contestant must have "standing," for example, the contestant must stand to benefit if he prevails in the suit. If an offered will is set aside, one of two results ensues. If there is a previously executed will still in existence, it will "move up" in line and may then be offered for probate as the last will and testament of the decedent. If there is no previous will, the decedent will be deemed to have died intestate, that is, without a will, in which case the estate will pass to those individuals designated by state law as the intestate heirs. Standing to contest a will may be established by demonstrating that the contestant is a beneficiary under a previous will that will move up in line, or by establishing that the contestant is one of the intestate heirs who would inherit in the absence of a will.

A will contest may be based on any of several grounds. The contestant may allege that the signing of the will was technically deficient in some respect. For example, wills have been denied probate when the required witnesses were not present throughout the execution of the document. The contestant may allege that the testator, who is the person executing the will, lacked "testamentary capacity," (i.e., the minimum level of competence necessary to execute a valid will). The contestant may allege that a third party brought undue influence to bear on the testator with the result that the offered will does not represent the true volitional intent of the testator but rather represents the wishes of the third party.

Will contests may be discouraged in some cases by including a "no-contest" clause in the will. A no-contest clause typically provides that if a beneficiary under the will takes any action to contest the validity of the will, the beneficiary will automatically forfeit his gift under the will. A no-contest clause is only effective if the would-be contestant receives some benefit under the will. If no benefit is received under the will, he or she risks nothing by pursuing the contest.

Will Preparation and Review

A will should be prepared by a competent attorney who has expertise specific to the task. The process of selecting an attorney should include consulting with friends and neighbors to obtain word-of-mouth references. Published references are also generally available in public libraries. Word-of-mouth references might also be obtained through the trust departments of local banks. Finally, the attorney tentatively chosen should be asked directly to confirm that he or she has particular experience in the trust and estate area.

The attorney will need information about the client's family and assets. Before the first meeting, the client should compile a list of all significant assets, the approximate fair market value of the assets, and the exact form of titling. The list should include life insurance, pension plans, and joint property, all of which will be part of the estate for federal estate tax purposes.

A list of the members of the family and others whom the client may wish to provide for under the will is also needed. The will should address a reasonable number of alternate contingencies. For example, the client may wish to leave the estate equally to his or her two children but must make an alternative plan should one or both of those children die before the client. The client should be prepared to answer those questions as early as possible in the engagement to expedite the preparation of the will. Since estate planning engagements are frequently accepted on an hourly billing basis, less time means lower cost.

Periodic review of one's will is as important as creating it. Although a will should anticipate and address a reasonable number of foreseeable contingencies, it is impossible to anticipate and address every possible event. To attempt to do so would yield a document of unmanageable length and complexity. The only alternative is to address a more modest range of possibilities and then periodically review and revise the will as circumstances change and as contingencies unfold. A will should be reviewed annually by the client, and reviewed professionally at least every five years. Circumstances that might require a revision of the will include maturing of children, births, deaths, marriages, divorces, significant changes in net worth, and changes in the law. Changes in the federal estate tax law in 1976 and 1981, for example, required broad changes in many wills.

Minor changes in a will may be made by codicil (amendment or modification of a will) rather than completely rewriting the will. However, unless the change is minor (e.g., changing the executor) it is often no less expensive to re-do the entire will, especially if the lawyer preparing the codicil is not the lawyer who prepared the will. (See also ATTORNEYS, CHARITABLE CONTRIBUTIONS, ELDER LAW PRACTICE, ESTATE PLANNING, FUNERALS, KING LEAR SYNDROME, PROBATE, and SUPPLEMENTAL SECURITY INCOME.)

References

Belin, David W. 1992. *Leaving Money Wisely: Creative Estate Planning for Middle and Upper Income Americans for the 1990s.* New York: Collier Books.

Berg, Adriane G. 1992. *Warning. Dying May Be Hazardous to Your Wealth: How to Protect Your Life Savings for Yourself and Those You Love.* Hawthorne, NJ: Career Press.

Daly, Eugene J. 1990. *Thy Will Be Done: A Guide to Wills, Taxation, and Estate Planning for Older Persons.* Buffalo, NY: Prometheus Books.

Manning, Jerome A. 1992. *Estate Planning: How to Preserve Your Wealth for Your Loved Ones.* New York: Practicing Law Institute.

Runde, Robert H., and J. Barry Zischang. 1994. *The Commonsense Guide to Estate Planning.* Burr Ridge, IL: Business One Irwin.

C. L. (Tim) Dimos

WORKING RETIREES, older full- or part-time workers who have retired from a primary job or career. Recently in the U.S. private sector, evolving demographic, economic, attitudinal, and legal changes have affected organizations' employment-related decisions regarding older workers, particularly retired workers. While experts continue to predict relatively slow growth rates in the labor force and a significant aging of the work force during the rest of the twentieth century, some industries have already experienced a dearth of young people to fill entry-level positions. From anecdotal literature, and at least one recent study, it is clear that some firms are responding to these changes by developing formal and informal methods for recruiting and utilizing retirees.

Retirement presents a range of options to older workers: a complete transition to non-work status; retirement from a primary job to begin a second career; part-time or full-time work; or a job similar to, although occasionally different from, one's primary career. Retirees wishing to return to the work force usually can find information regarding the practice of hiring retirees and information about the needs of firms that hire retirees. They may target firms that have a specific need for their skills or other characteristics. Conversely, organizations that have begun to experience specific labor shortages may find it useful to target retirees.

Case Studies of Workers Over 50, released by the Commonwealth Fund (1991), found that there were many unemployed older persons, including those who had retired from a career position, who wanted to work. Myths regarding declining work capacity and performance due to age often prevent the hiring of retirees. Paul and Townsend (1993) debunk these myths. McNaught and Barth (1992) found that older workers stayed on the job longer than younger workers, and although they were slightly more expensive to employ, they attained an increased level of productivity.

The results of a large survey of U.S. firms with 20 or more employees showed that over 46% of private-sector firms hired retirees (Hirshorn and Hoyer 1992). Few firms, however, had a written policy or formalized program directed at hiring retirees. Forty percent of the firms actively sought retirees as part of their staffing process. A number of these firms stated that either the reliability of retirees or a specific skill needed by the firm was the primary reason for hiring. Nearly one-half of the firms interviewed responded that they hired retirees simply because they applied for the job.

Companies reported that they generally hired retirees for full-year schedules rather than part-year or seasonal employment. Almost all firms hiring retirees used them mostly for regularly performed jobs, although some firms involved retirees in training or in consulting positions. The study showed that companies utilized working retirees across all occupational categories, in managerial as well as clerical and skilled positions.

Employment counselors, human resource specialists, and other practitioners who deal with the employment of older individuals must try to match specific company needs with the needs of retirees who desire employment. Organizations will benefit by studying their human resource needs and explicitly examining whether retirees may be available to fill them, particularly where occupational labor shortages exist. Finally, retirees should know that firms in most industries, and of all sizes, hire retirees for a diverse set of jobs in a broad range of occupational categories. They must make an attempt to stay abreast of which industries and firms have labor needs that they might fulfill. (See also EMPLOYMENT OF OLDER AMERICANS, RETIREMENT PLANNING, and RETIREMENT, HISTORY OF.)

Suggested Reading

American Association of Retired Persons. 1994. *How to Stay Employable: A Guide for the Mid-Life and Older Worker.* Washington, DC: AARP.

References

Commonwealth Fund. 1991. *Case Studies of Workers Over 50.* New York: Author.

Hirshorn, B., and D. T. Hoyer. 1992. *Private Sector Employment of Retirees: The Organizational Experience.* Unpublished final report to the AARP Andrus Foundation.

Hirshorn, B., and D. T. Hoyer. 1994. "Private Sector Hiring and Use of Retirees: The Firm's Perspective." *Gerontologist* 34: 50–58.

McNaught, W., and M. C. Barth. 1992. "Are Older Workers 'Good Buys'?—A Case Study of Days Inns of America." *Sloan Management Review* 33: 53–64.

Paul, R. J., and J. B. Townsend. 1993. "Managing the Older Worker—Don't Just Rinse Away the Gray." *The Academy of Management Executives* 7: 67–74.

Denise T. Hoyer and Barbara A. Hirshorn

zoning laws do not conflict with the minimum standards established in constitutional state zoning law.

How Land Use Allocation Is Implemented

When a city implements its policies of land use allocation, there is a certain framework within which the legislature must abide. A number of groups, commissions, and consultants have been created for the specific purpose of aiding the legislature in its land use decisions. For example, the planning commission and the port commission exist to aid in the allocation of land and coastline, respectively. A number of broadly interpreted laws also exist to provide guidelines for the legislature and the groups created to aid in the allocation process. The specific purposes of these groups and laws are contained in the state government code.

Of the advisory committees and laws created to aid the city council in its land use decisions, the planning commission, the city attorney's office, and the public works department play the most significant role. These groups assist with the city council's decisions on newly created or challenged land use policies and help ensure that the proposal review procedure is correct. These departments are the experts in land use policy and are cognizant of the likely effects of a proposed addition or change in policy. When a land use policy, zoning ordinance, or proposal for the redevelopment of land is submitted to the city council, the proposal is given to the planning commission for a recommendation. After the planning commission, the city attorney and/or public works department review the proposal. The planning commission then makes a recommendation to the council for accepting, rejecting, or revising the proposal. The council then considers the recommendation of the planning commission and has several options. The council can follow the recommendations of the planning commission by approving or denying the proposal, or disregard the planning commission and resubmit the proposal for further consideration. However, before any recommendations are made by the planning commission, a thorough review of the city's general plan must be made.

When a city approves a land use change, compliance with certain established legal guidelines is required. These guidelines, which are based in state planning law, are established in the area's general plan. The plan consists of a statement of development policies that include a diagram or diagrams and a text setting forth objectives, principles, standards, and plan proposals. According to state planning, the general plan is required to examine a land-use element, a circulation element, a housing element, a conservation element, an open space element, a noise element, a safety element, and any other optional elements that are specific to a proposal. According to the required elements of the general plan, the policies of zoning (e.g., public good, health, and safety) closely resemble the objectives of the general plan. In addition to the general plan, a specific plan is adopted to outline zoning, subdivisions, and public works projects. Development agreements are also a part of a city's implementation of the general

Z

ZONING, a tool for land use allocation, to reshape areas that need redevelopment. Zoning is used to change a region's land use when such use is no longer feasible or to preserve an existing land use. Its use as a tool for land allocation increases as a region's population, wants and needs grow. Zoning allocates the types of land uses that comply with state planning and more specific plans of local communities. Zoning ordinances dictate consistent, appropriate, and planned land use patterns for a particular area. A familiarity with zoning issues is helpful when planning to develop retirement communities, nursing homes*, or adult day centers.

As a tool for land use allocation, zoning significantly impacts the expansion, shrinkage, and status quo of land use patterns in states, large cities, small communities, and rural areas. As the land allocation of regions evolves into specific land use patterns, the public (i.e., local governments), continues to create and enforce land use guidelines through the police powers of zoning. However, before realizing the role, impact, and limitations of zoning as an allocative tool, an examination of land planning and land use controls related to zoning is necessary.

What Is Zoning?

Zoning is a legal vehicle for a city council or county board of supervisors, or alternatively, the legislature, to implement land use and planning regulations. Zoning can be differentiated from other rules and regulations as a "police power." Police power is a state legislature's authority to enforce conditions of land use and planning regulations that are created to promote the public good, and to protect the public health, safety, and welfare. The power of a legislature to pass zoning laws in most states is only available to the extent that those plan, except that they may be amended to reflect changing land uses. As the focus of land use narrows, our attention is directed to zoning. Zoning divides a city into districts and assigns different regulations to each according to the general and specific plans.

Limitations of and Exceptions to Zoning Regulations

Exceptions exist to the general plan, the specific plan, and zoning ordinances. These are categorized as: (1) nonconforming uses, (2) conditional uses, and (3) variances. A nonconforming use is a land use that existed before a conflicting zoning ordinance was implemented. A conditional use is a land use that is allowed to exist even though it is inconsistent with current zoning and plan policies in order to provide flexibility to the community district. A variance is a land use that is in direct conflict with the zoning and planning of a district, but the legislature allows the use since compliance with the current zoning would cause undue hardship on the owner. Compliance under a variance usually deals with aspects of parcel's size, topography, shape, or location. These exceptions are not automatic; each case is reviewed by the legislature on an individual basis, and permits are required.

Other Land Use Allocation Tools

In addition to the aforementioned exceptions, other significant allocative aspects of land use allocation include the subdivision and environmental quality regulations. Subdivision regulations are a statewide legislative tool that give control to local government agencies over the types of subdivisions to be planned in each community. They also dictate the physical improvements to the land and require that final maps of the proposed projects be filed and approved before development begins. Before approving the final map, a tentative map of the project undergoes a rigid legislative approval process. After the final map has been approved, it is then recorded and construction may begin. State environmental regulations allow local governments to require an environmental impact report on any potential project they feel may strongly affect the area surrounding the project. These subdivision and environmental quality regulations attempt to accomplish land use allocation on more of a macro level, while zoning ordinances tend to be site specific.

What Zoning Attempts to Accomplish

Most if not all zoning goals can be found in the form of municipal code ordinances. In addition to the purpose of general police power goals of zoning— to promote the public good and protect the public health, safety, and welfare— in recent years, this definition has been expanded to include the promotion and advancement of order, convenience, prosperity, and general welfare. The specific guidelines of zoning regulations encompass most of a region's land uses. The specific land uses that have been traditionally regulated by zoning ordinances include: (1) the use of buildings, structures, land, and businesses; (2) the size, shape, and color of signs and billboards; (3) the location, size, and height of structures in the path of airport approach runways; (4) the size and use of lots; (5) the percentage of a lot occupied by a structure; (6) the intensity of land use; (7) set-back requirements for buildings; (8) requirements for off-street parking; and (9) the creation of civic districts around parks, public buildings, and other public grounds.

Residential zoning is based in the theory of zoning itself by providing land uses conducive to the overall public health, safety, morale, and welfare of land users. Residential zoning can include provisions for single family dwellings, multiple family dwellings, and housing operations for income purposes such as hotels, apartments, private clubs, and boarding houses, while excluding more or less intensive land uses. When a zoning ordinance excludes a certain use designation such as a commercial use in a residentially zoned district, it must bear some reasonable relation to the overall public interest; adaptability and suitability are not valid reasons for allocating a particular type of land use. Commercial and industrial zoned areas, due to their potential for hazardous conditions, may be subjected to special regulations and are delineated as such. Commercial and industrial zoned districts, depending on the nature of operation, are subdivided into their respective uses, including general commercial districts, light commercial districts permitting retail, general industrial districts, light industrial districts, and heavy industrial districts. The creation of set-back requirements, off-street parking, and civic districts around parks, public buildings, and other public grounds can all be traced back to the original theories of zoning and why they exist.

Zoning and Elderly Housing Needs

Zoning regulations have often prevented or restricted the locations of four principal types of residential options specifically relevant to elderly Americans: (1) accessory apartments (in-law suites) or ECHO housing (elder cottage housing opportunities, also called granny flats); (2) shared living residences (unrelated occupants in the same dwelling); (3) board and care*, assisted living*, and related group housing facilities designed for the occupancy of more functionally dependent elderly persons; and (4) manufactured (mobile) housing offering an affordable shelter option (Pollak and Gorman 1989).

Opposition to these alternatives has most often occurred in neighborhoods zoned for single family use. Three types of zoning provisions have most frequently been used to protect the ''single family'' status of the neighborhood. One type restricts dwelling uses to the land use category designated for a district or locality. This effectively restricts accessory apartments, ECHO units, and group homes from many neighborhoods that allow only one dwelling unit per lot. A second type restricts household arrangements to family occupancy. Many communities have restrictive definitions of what constitutes a ''family'' for zoning purposes, with the result that various categories of household or group shelter arrangements comprised of unrelated persons would be in violation. This has effectively prohibited older persons in some communities from renting their house to a boarder or from sharing their accommodations with other unrelated older persons. A third type of zoning provision imposes excessive construction and site development standards on their residential districts. These zoning ordinances have successfully been used to exclude manufactured housing from many residential districts and to keep them confined to mobile home parks. Attempts to appeal local rulings to the state courts have had mixed success. State courts have differed, for example, in their appraisals of whether a certain group of people would constitute a family under the terms of the zoning ordinance and their willingness to view particular groups of unrelated persons as functional equivalents of families. As Pollack (1994, pp. 524–25) emphasizes, however:

To date, there has been no wholesale trend for communities to change family definitions that have not been legally challenged, to make them conform to the standards in [other] court decisions; as legislation, zoning is legal until successfully challenged.

Municipalities and their residents have not consistently opposed housing options. Some communities allow accessory apartments in single-family neighborhoods, for example, if they meet certain quality and appearance standards. Other states and communities have created a zoning class of ''senior citizens,'' whereupon a residential district can restrict occupancy to persons of an older age. Some states and courts have allowed the creation of special zoning provisions specifically for the elderly. Many state courts are viewing highly restrictive family definitions as discriminatory and violations of an individual's right to privacy that are contrary to their own state constitutions. Some states have revoked or curtailed the exclusionary zoning controls exercised by municipalities. Some municipalities have used zoning devices (e.g., conditional use permits) to encourage the development of specialized housing options.

The Fair Housing Amendments Act of 1988 (FHAA) has resulted in yet another judicial influence on zoning decisions relevant to older Americans. Among its various provisions, FHAA prohibits zoning and land use regulations from discriminating against persons with disabilities. The broad definition of *disability* would include most older persons usually defined as physically or mentally disabled or frail. Recent case law suggests that some municipal zoning laws that prevent the siting of group homes in certain residential districts are in conflict with the protections given by FHAA to disabled persons, namely, their right to live in neighborhoods of their choice.

Conclusion

As a tool for land use allocation, zoning ordinances empower a community's exercise of land use control through its police power. The guidelines that zoning ordinances create for such uses must be followed in order to preserve the safety and comfort of its inhabitants and to protect them from conditions that arise from land uses that may be reasonably anticipated from a particular activity or business. Through zoning, a pattern is developed that meets the goals of what the inhabitants expect from their land and the planned goals of state and local governments. (See also ASSISTED LIVING, BOARD AND CARE HOMES, DAY PROGRAMS FOR ADULTS, HOMEOWNERSHIP, HOUSING, NURSING HOMES, and SENIORS HOUSING FINANCE).

References

Curtin, Daniel J. 1990. *California Land-Use and Planning Law*, Tenth Edition. Solano, CA: Solano Press Books.

Pollak, Patricia B. 1994. "Rethinking Zoning to Accommodate the Elderly in Single Family Housing." *Journal of the American Planning Association* 60: 521–31.

Pollak, Patricia B., and Alice N. Gorman. 1989. *Community-Based Housing for the Elderly.* Planning Advisory Service Report Number 420. Washington, DC: American Planning Association.

Andrew Quang Do

Appendix A:
Post-ERISA Benefit Legislation,
1975–1993

CHRONOLOGY OF MAJOR POST-ERISA BENEFIT LEGISLATION

1975	Tax Reduction Act
1976	Tax Reform Act
1977	Social Security Amendments
1978	Age Discrimination Act
1980	Omnibus Reconciliation Act
1981	Economic Recovery Tax Act (ERTA)
1982	Tax Equity and Fiscal Responsibility Act (TEFRA)
1983	Social Security Amendments
1984	Deficit Reduction Act (DEFRA)
1984	Retirement Equity Act (REA)
1986	Consolidated Omnibus Reconciliation Act (COBRA)
1986	(ADEA) Amendments
1987	Pension Protection Act (PPA)
1988	Technical and Miscellaneous Revenue Act (TAMRA)
1988	HMO Act Amendments
1988	Medicare Catastrophic Coverage Act
1988	Family Support Act
1989	Section 89 repeal
1989	Omnibus Budget Reconciliation Act of 1989 (OBRA 89)
1990	Americans with Disabilities Act
1990	Older Workers Benefit Protection Act

1990   Omnibus Budget Reconciliation Act of 1990 (OBRA 90)

1991   Civil Rights Act

1992   Unemployment Compensation Amendments (UCA)

1992   Comprehensive National Energy Policy Act of 1992

1993   Family and Medical Leave Act (FMLA)

1993   Omnibus Budget Reconciliation Act of 1993 (OBRA 93)

Source: Adapted from various issues of "A Special Report," Hewitt Associates LLC, Washington, DC. Revenue laws also regularly affect the scope, types, and levels of retirement income. A useful review of deficit-reduction measures (several Omnibus Budget Reconciliation Acts, Deficit Reduction Acts, etc.) is contained in David Koitz. 1994. "Major Deficit-Reduction Measures Enacted in Recent Years." *CRS Report for Congress.* Washington, DC: Congressional Research Service. Report 94-719 EPW.

SUMMARY OF POST-ERISA BENEFIT LEGISLATION PROVISIONS

Tax Reduction Act—1975

• Increases allowable investment tax credit if contributions are made to an ESOP.

Tax Reform Act—1976

• Removes favorable tax treatment for qualified stock options.

• Allows entire lump sum distribution to be taxed at ordinary rates using 10-year forward averaging.

• Prepaid legal plans approved as a tax-free benefit.

Social Security Amendments—1977

• Provides significant increases in social security tax rates and taxable wage base.

• Adjusts social security benefit formula to produce a decline in the percentage of pay replaced by social security. Repeals "double indexing."

Age Discrimination Act—1978

• Extends protection against discriminatory treatment based on age to individuals younger than age 70.

• Permits employers to reduce benefits (within limits) for employees age 65–69, provided the reduction can be cost-justified.

Revenue Act—1978

• Reinstates favorable tax treatment for cash or deferred profit sharing arrangements and sets nondiscrimination requirements for such plans.

• Reduces taxes on long-term capital gains for individual taxpayers.

• Reemphasizes that deferred compensation is eligible for taxation only when paid or otherwise made available.

• Requires uninsured health plans to meet nondiscrimination rules.

- Excludes nontaxable cafeteria plan benefits from employee income. Sets coverage, eligibility, and benefit tests for cafeteria plans.
- Section 127 education assistance approved as a tax-free benefit.

Multiemployer Pension Plan Amendments—1980

- Restructures PBGC coverage of multi-employer pension plans.
- Requires all employers withdrawing from a multi-employer pension plan to continue funding their share of the plan's unfunded vested benefits through payment of a withdrawal liability.
- Establishes guidelines for identifying plans experiencing financial difficulties and requires these plans to enter reorganization status for corrective action.

Revenue Act—1980

- Allows employers to add a deferred compensation choice to a cafeteria program.

Economic Recovery Tax Act (ERTA)—1981

- Permits employees covered by qualified employer-provided retirement plans to make tax-deductible IRA contributions.
- Establishes incentive stock options.
- Reemphasizes that distributions from qualified retirement plans are taxed only when actually received.
- Dependent care assistance programs approved as a tax-free benefit.

Tax Equity and Fiscal Responsibility Act (TEFRA)—1982

- Reduces the Section 415 limits for defined benefit and defined contribution retirement plans.
- Subjects "top-heavy" plans to stricter qualification rules.
- Sets limits and repayment rules for loans from qualified retirement plans.
- Reduces the allowable amount of social security integration in a defined contribution plan.
- Removes exclusion for first $50,000 of life insurance for "key employees" in a discriminatory plan.
- Rules that employers must offer active employees and their dependents aged 65–69 the same health plan benefits offered younger employees. Establishes the employer's health care plan as primary to Medicare for active employees aged 65–69.

Social Security Amendments—1983

- Extends social security coverage to new federal, state, and local government employees, as well as employees of nonprofit organizations.
- Accelerates FICA payroll tax and social security tax for self-employed.
- Reduces dependent and survivor social security benefits for public pension recipients.
- Subjects Section 401(k) deferrals and non-qualified deferred taxation to FICA and FUTA taxation.

- Extends the social security normal retirement age to 67 while reducing early retirement benefits.
- Increases social security late retirement benefit.

Deficit Reduction Act of 1984 (DEFRA)

- Freezes the Section 415 limits for defined benefit and defined contribution plans until 1988.
- Permits tax-free rollovers to IRAs if the distribution is at least 50% of the employee's plan value.
- Limits tax-deductible benefits and reserve accumulation in funded welfare benefit plans.
- Rules that dividends paid on stock held by PAYSOPs/ESOPs are deductible only if distributed directly to plan participants.
- Limits the types of benefits available under cafeteria plans and restricts the percentage of cafeteria plan benefits that can be paid to key employees.
- Establishes rules for income tax exclusions for miscellaneous fringe benefits.
- Limits depreciation on company cars and adds more restrictive record-keeping requirements.
- Sets limits on "golden parachute" payments.

Retirement Equity Act (REA)—1984

- Reduces the minimum age for qualified retirement plan participation to age 21.
- Sets new break-in-service rules for crediting service in qualified retirement plans for vesting and benefit purposes.
- Rules that qualified retirement plans must provide automatic survivor benefits in the form of qualified preretirement survivor annuities to the spouse of a vested participant who has died prior to annuity start date.
- Recognizes the assignment of participant benefits to alternate payees under qualified domestic relations orders (divorce proceedings).

Consolidated Omnibus Reconciliation Act (COBRA)—1986

- Rules that employers must offer continuation of group health plan coverage to beneficiaries who no longer qualify for coverage, to terminated employees, and to employees with reduced hours.
- Increases PBGC premiums for single-employers defined pension plans.
- Increases employer liability when a single-employer defined benefit pension plan is terminated due to insufficient assets.

Tax Reform Act—1986

- Requires that all qualified retirement plans must satisfy new nondiscrimination standards, minimum vesting standards, integration rules.
- Reduces maximum early retirement benefits for defined benefit pension plans.
- Requires after-tax employee contributions to be included in calculating limits for defined contribution plans.

- Limits employee 401(k) deferrals to $7,000 per calendar year.

- Repeals 10-year averaging tax treatment for lump sum retirement plan distributions. Replaces with one-time choice of five-year forward averaging.

- Imposes additional taxes on retirement distributions taken before age 59½, and annual benefits exceeding $150,000.

- Establishes new requirements that health, group life, and dependent care plans must meet to avoid resulting in imputed income for high-paid employees.

- Reduces maximum corporate and individual tax rates.

- Repeals preferential tax treatment for long-term capital gains.

- Phases out interest deductions on consumer loans.

Omnibus Budget Reconciliation Act—1986

- Prohibits qualified retirement plans from reducing or freezing the rate of benefit accruals or contributions because of age.

- Prohibits qualified retirement plans from excluding employees hired within five years of plan's normal retirement age.

- Establishes employer's health plan as primary to Medicare for disabled employees and their family members eligible for Medicare.

Age Discrimination in Employment Amendments—1986

- Prohibits mandatory retirement because of age.

Pension Protection Act (PPA)—1987

- Increases PBGC premium from $8.50 to $16.00 per participant, plus variable-rate premium for underfunded plans.

- Increases minimum funding requirements.

- Prohibits deductions for plan contributions in excess of 150% of current liability.

- Requires FICA withholding for key employees for imputed income on group term life insurance above $50,000.

- Excludes overnight camp expenses as an eligible dependent care expense.

Medicare Catastrophic Coverage Act—1988 (Repealed in 1989)

- Expands Medicare Part A and Part B. Expansion paid for by increased Part B premiums and a supplemental premium based on income.

- Requires employers that offer coverage duplicative of expanded benefits to either refund one year's actuarial value of duplicated benefits or increase benefits by a like amount.

Health Maintenance Organization Amendments—1988

- Requires that contributions to a federally-qualified HMO may not financially discriminate against an employee enrolled in the HMO. Additional rate-setting method allowed for HMOs.
- Repeals dual-choice requirement as of October 24, 1995.

Technical and Miscellaneous Revenue Act (TAMRA)—1988

* Changes penalty for COBRA violations to an employer excise tax.
* Makes numerous technical changes to Tax Reform Act of 1986 including allowing the minimum participation test to be passed on a separate line of business basis and providing an alternative definition of highly compensated employee.
* Makes changes to Section 89 welfare plan nondiscrimination rules. (Repealed 1989.)
* Restricts favorable tax treatment of life insurance products that are primarily for investment purposes.

Omnibus Budget Reconciliation Act—1989

* Increases Social Security wage base for 1990.
* Revises physician reimbursement under Medicare using the RBRVS system.
* Lengthens COBRA period for certain disabled employees.
* Makes technical corrections to pension plan rules.
* Restricts exclusion of 50% of interest on ESOP loans to ESOPs that own at least 50% of the corporation. Deductibility of dividends limited to dividends from securities acquired by the same ESOP loan.

Repeal of Medicare Catastrophic Act—1988

* Repeals Medicare Catastrophic Act. Employers still required to make "maintenance of effort" payment for 1989.

Americans with Disabilities Act—1990

* Mandates that employers not discriminate against disabled individuals in any aspect of employment, and must make "reasonable accommodations" to enable the disabled to work.

Older Workers Benefit Protection Act—1990

* Restores the "equal benefit or equal cost" requirement for age-based differences in employee benefits.
* Allows a retirement plan to continue to have minimum age for eligibility for normal or early retirement benefits, and have subsidized early retirement benefits.
* Requires that early retirement incentives must be voluntary and "consistent with the relevant purpose or purposes of the Act."
* Requires that waivers of rights under ADEA must be made on a "knowing and voluntary" basis.

Omnibus Budget Reconciliation Act—1990

* Increases both the flat and variable rate PBGC premiums, to $19 flat and maximum $53.
* Allows employers to transfer a certain portion of excess plan assets to a retiree medical account.
* Increases tax for pension reversions from 15% to 20% or 50%.

- Prohibits a health care spending account from reimbursing for cosmetic surgery.
- Increases the Medicare wage base to $125,000.
- No longer requires employers to withhold FICA on imputed income for retiree group term life insurance.

Civil Rights Act—1991

- Overturns several recent Supreme Court cases that had made it more difficult for employees to prevail in employment discrimination cases.
- Adds punitive and compensatory damages in the case of intentional discrimination and adds the opportunity for jury trials.

Unemployment Compensation Amendments (UCA)—1992

- Extends emergency unemployment benefits.
- Expands types of distributions eligible for rollover.
- Allows employees to elect direct transfer into IRA or another qualified plan.
- Mandates 20% withholding for nonperiodic distributions not directly transferred to another qualified plan or IRA.

Family and Medical Leave Act (FMLA)—1993

- Requires employers to grant up to 12 weeks of unpaid leave to care for newborn or newly adopted children, to care for a seriously ill family member, or for the employee's own serious illness.
- Requires continuation of health coverage to employees on FMLA leave on same basis as coverage for active employees.

Omnibus Budget Reconciliation Act—1993

- Adds 36% and 39.6% income tax brackets.
- Reduces recognizable pay cap to $150,000.
- Eliminates corporate deduction for CEO and top executive pay over $1 million.
- Retroactively extends Section 127 income tax exclusion for employer-provided education reimbursement.
- Mandates various provisions and reporting requirements for group health plans, including recognition of "qualified medical child support orders."

Appendix B: Resources and Organizations

Many entries of this *Encyclopedia* refer the reader to national organizations that can be contacted for further information. These organizations provide a link between the individual and the larger structures and networks in the domain of aging and financial issues. The following listing includes the organizational resources mentioned in the articles of this volume; thus it is not exhaustive. There are many state and local organizations that can be reached through national headquarters.

There are several comprehensive directories of organizations on aging. The following two are of special interest to anyone seeking more information about elder resources and financial gerontology.

RESOURCE DIRECTORIES

Directory of Aging Resources, 1994, edited by Nancy Aldrich, Silver Spring, MD: Business Publishers.

Financial Resources for Older Americans: Funding and Support Services for Caregivers, 1994, Laurie Blum, Gaithersburg, MD: Aspen Publishers.

ELECTRONIC INFORMATION RESOURCES

Increasingly, older Americans and aging specialists use computer links with one another and to gain access to large bodies of information relevant to aging, health, finances, and activities.

SeniorNet is an independent nonprofit organization that has developed 70 computer learning centers for older persons and operates SeniorNet Online on the America Online computerized information service (1–800–716–0023).

The Retirement Living Forum is a combination bulletin board, library, and "conference center" on-line on the CompuServe computer-based information service (1–800–524–3388).

GERINET is a general professional discussion group in gerontology accessible via e-mail (send a message to LISTSERV@UBVM.CC.BUFFALO.EDU; leave the subject line blank; send a one-line message: subscribe GERINET (firstname lastname)).

All developments on the Internet that relate to aging issues and research are expertly monitored by Joyce A. Post, Librarian, Philadelphia Geriatric Center, 5301 Old York Road, Philadelphia, PA 19141, post @ hslc.org, Tel. (215) 456–2971, Fax (215) 456–2017.

ORGANIZATIONS

Aging and Developmental Disabilities Information Exchange
Center on Aging
University of Maryland
College Park, MD 20742
(301) 454–5856

Alzheimer's Association
919 N. Michigan Avenue, Suite 1000
Chicago, IL 60611–1676
(312) 335–8700/1 (800) 272–3900

American Academy of Nurse Practitioners
P.O. Box 12846
Capitol Station, LBJ Building
Austin, TX 78711
(512) 442–4262

American Association of Homes and Services for the Aging
1050 17th Street, N.W.
Washington, DC 20036
(202) 296–5960

American Association of Retired Persons
601 E Street, N.W.
Washington, DC 20049
(202) 434–2277

American Bar Association
Commission on Legal Problems of the Elderly
1800 M Street, N.W., Second Floor
Washington, DC 20036
(202) 331–2297

American Council of Life Insurance
1001 Pennsylvania Avenue, N.W.
Washington, DC 20004
(202) 624–2000

American Health Care Association
1201 L Street, N.W.

Washington, DC 20005
(202) 842–8444

American Institute of CPAs
Harborside Financial Center
201 Plaza III
Jersey City, NJ 07311
(201) 938–3000

American Pharmaceutical Association
2215 Constitution Avenue, N.W.
Washington, DC 20037
(202) 628–4410

American Rehabilitation Association
1910 Association Drive
Reston, VA 22091
(703) 648–9300

Armed Forces Discharge Review Boards:
Army:
Army Discharge Review Board
Attn: SFMR-RBB, Room 200A
1941 Jefferson Davis Highway
Arlington, VA 22202–4504

Navy and USMC:
Navy Discharge Review Board
801 N. Randolph Street, Suite 905
Arlington, VA 22203

Air Force:
Air Force Military Personnel Center
Attn: DMPDOA1
Randolph AFB, TX 78150–6001

Coast Guard:
Coast Guard
Attn: GPE1
Washington, DC 20593

Assisted Living Facilities Association of America (ALFAA)
Circle Towers Plaza
9411 Lee Highway, Suite J

Fairfax, VA 22031
(703) 691–8100

Association of Community Travel Clubs
2330 South Brentwood Boulevard
St. Louis, MO 63144
(314) 961–2300

Brookdale National Group Respite Program
Technical Assistance Office
2330 Durant Avenue
Berkeley, CA 94704
(510) 540–6734

Bureau of National Affairs
1231 25th Street, N.W.
Washington, DC 20037
(202) 452–4200

Center for Social Gerontology (legal program development and guardianship)
2307 Shelby Avenue
Ann Arbor, MI 48103
(313) 665–1126

CHAMPVA Center
4500 Cherry Creek Drive South
Denver, CO 80222
1 (800) 733–8387

Children of Aging Parents
Woodbourne Campus, Suite 302A
1609 Woodbourne Road
Levittown, PA 19057
(215) 945–6900

Community Services Block Grant
State Assistance Division
Community Services Office
Administration for Children and Families
370 L'Enfant Promenade, S.W.
Washington, DC 20447
(202) 401–9342

Conference Board
845 Third Avenue
New York, NY 10022
(212) 759–0900

Connecticut Department on Aging
175 Main Street

Hartford, CT 06106
(203) 566–7772

Consumer Credit Card Rating Service
P.O. Box 5219, Ocean Park Station
Santa Monica, CA 90405
(310) 392–7720

Consumer Credit Counseling Services
1 (800) 399–2227

Continuing Care Accreditation Commission
1129 20th Street, N.W.
Washington, DC 20036–3489
(202) 783–7286

Corporation for Independent Living
30 Jordan Lane
Wethersfield, CT 06109
(203) 563–6011

Debtors' Anonymous Association
P.O. Box 20322
New York, NY 10025–9992
(212) 642–8220

Department of Veterans Affairs
Office of Public Affairs (80D)
810 Vermont Avenue, N.W.
Washington, DC 20420
1 (800) 827–1000

Elder Care Locator
Administration on Aging
1112 16th Street, N.W., Suite 100
Washington, DC 20036
1 (800) 677–1116

Elderhostel
75 Federal Street
Boston, MA 02110
(617) 426–7788

Escapees, Inc.
Rt. 5, Box 310
Livingston, TX 77351
(409) 327–2247

Farmers Home Administration
Single Family Home Division
14th Street and Independence Avenue,
    S.W.

Washington, DC 20250–0700
(202) 720–2232

Federal Emergency Management Agency
  (FEMA)
500 C Street, S.W.
Washington, DC 20472
1 (800) 480–2520

Foster Grandparents Program
1100 Vermont Avenue, N.W., 6th Floor
Washington, DC 20525
(202) 606–4849

Golden Age Passport
c/o Information Office
U.S. Department of Interior
18th and C Streets, N.W.
Washington, DC 20240
(202) 208–3100

Grandtravel
6900 Wisconsin Avenue
Chevy Chase, MD 20815
(301) 986–0790

Group Health Association of America
1129 20th Street, N.W.
Washington, DC 20036
(202) 778–3200

Health Care Financing Administration
East High Rise Building
6325 Security Boulevard
Baltimore, MD 21207
(410) 966–3000

Hospice Association of America
519 C Street, N.E.
Washington, DC 20002
(202) 546–4759

Hospice Education Institute
"Hospice Link" 1 (800) 331–1620
(Information and advice on care, pro-
  gram, referrals, and support)

Housing and Urban Development Department (HUD)
451 7th Street, S.W.
Washington, DC 20410
(202) 708–0417

HUD Community Development Block
  Grant
(202) 708–1577

HUD Housing Counseling Assistance
  Program
(202) 708–3664

HUD Supportive Housing for the Elderly
  Program
(202) 708–2730

Independent Living Research Utilization
2323 South Shepard Street, Suite 1000
Houston, TX 77019
(713) 520–5136

Kaiser Commission on the Future of
  Medicaid
1450 G Street, N.W., Suite 250
Washington, DC 20005
(202) 347–5270

Legal Counsel for the Elderly
AARP
601 E Street, N.W., Suite 4A
Washington, DC 20049
(202) 434–2151

Lifease
2550 University Avenue West
Suite 225 North Court International
Saint Paul, MN 55114
(612) 636–6869

Medical Beneficiaries Defense Fund
1460 Broadway, 8th Floor
New York, NY 10036–7393
(212) 869–3850

Mental Health Policy Resource Center
1730 Rhode Island Avenue, N.W., Suite
  308
Washington, DC 20036
(202) 775–8826

National Academy of Elder Law Attorneys
1604 North Country Club Road
Tucson, AZ 85716
(602) 881–4005

National Asian/Pacific Center on Aging
Melbourne Tower, Suite 914
1511 Third Avenue
Seattle, WA 98101
(206) 624–1221

National Association of Area Agencies on
  Aging
1112 16th Street, N.W., Suite 100
Washington, DC 20036
(202) 296–8134

National Association of Geriatric Care
  Managers
1604 N. Country Club Road
Tucson, AZ 85716
(602) 881–8008

National Association of Home Care
519 C Street, N.E.
Washington, DC 20024–5809
(202) 547–7424

National Association of Insurance Commissioners (NAIC)
120 West 12th Street, Suite 1100
Kansas City, MO 64105–1925
(816) 842–3600

National Association of Senior Living Industries
125 Cathedral Street
Annapolis, MD 21401
(301) 263–0991

National Association of State Long-Term
  Care Ombudsman Programs
Texas Department of Aging
P.O. Box 12786
Austin, TX 78711
(512) 444–2727

National Association of State Units on
  Aging
2033 K Street, N.W., Suite 304
Washington, DC 20006
(202) 785–0707

National Caucus and Center on the Black
  Aged, Inc.
1424 K Street, N.W., Suite 500

Washington, DC 20005
(202) 637–8400

National Center for Financial Education
605 C Street
P.O. Box 34070
San Diego, CA 92103–0780
(619) 232–8811

National Center for Home Equity Conversion
7373 147th Street, Suite 115
Apple Valley, MN 55124
(612) 953–4474

National Citizens' Coalition for Nursing
  Home Reform
1224 M Street, N.W., Suite 301
Washington, DC 20005–5183
(202) 393–2018

National Citizens' Coalition for Nursing
  Home Reform
Ombudsman Program
1424 16th Street, N.W.
Washington, DC 20005
(202) 393–2018

National Committee to Preserve Social
  Security and Medicare
2000 K Street, N.W., Suite 800
Washington, DC 20006
(202) 822–9459

National Conference of Gerontological
  Nurse Practitioners
P.O. Box 270101
Fort Collins, CO 80527–0101
(303) 493–7793

National Consumer Law Center
11 Beacon Street
Boston, MA 02108
(617) 523–8010

National Consumers League
815 15th Street, N.W., #928–N
Washington, DC 20005
(202) 639–8140

National Council of Senior Citizens
1331 F Street, N.W.

Washington, DC 20004
(202) 347–8800

National Council on Independent Living
Troy Atrium
Fourth Street and Broadway
Troy, NY 12180
(518) 274–1979

National Council on the Aging
409 Third Street, S.W.
Washington, DC 20024
(202) 479–1200

National Eldercare Institute on Elder
  Abuse and State Long-Term Care Om-
  budsman Services
National Association of State Units on
  Aging
1225 Eye Street, N.W., Suite 728
Washington, DC 20005
(202) 898–2578

National Eldercare Institute on Housing
  and Supportive Services
University of Southern California
Andrus Gerontology Center
Los Angeles, CA 90089–0191
(213) 740–6060

National Executive Service Corps
257 Park Avenue South
New York, NY 10010–7304
(212) 529–6660

National Family Caregivers Association
9621 East Bexhill Drive
Kensington, MD 20898
(301) 942–6430

National Foundation for Consumer Credit
8611 Second Avenue
Silver Spring, MD 20910
(301) 589–5600

National Hispanic Council on Aging
2713 Ontario Road, N.W.
Washington, DC 20009
(202) 745–2521

National Hospice Organization
1901 North Moore Street, Suite 901

Arlington, VA 22209
Hospice Hotline: 1 (800) 658–8898

National Indian Council on Aging
6400 Uptown Boulevard, N.E., Suite
  510W
Albuquerque, NM 87110
(505) 888–3302

National Institutes of Mental Health
Mental Disorders of the Aging Research
  Branch
5600 Fishers Lane, Room 18–105
Rockville, MD 20857
(301) 443–1185

National Institutes of Mental Health
Public Inquiries Office
5600 Fishers Lane, Room 7C-02
Rockville, MD 20857
(301) 443–4513

National Institute of Senior Citizens
National Council on the Aging
409 3rd Street, S.W.
Washington, DC 20024
(202) 479–1200

National Institute on Adult Daycare
National Council on the Aging
409 3rd Street, S.W.
Washington, DC 20024
(202) 479–1200

National Institute on Aging
NIA Information
1 (800) 222–2225

National Institute on Aging
Alzheimer's Disease Education and Re-
  ferral Center
P.O. Box 8250
Silver Spring, MD 20907–8250
(301) 496–4000

National Insurance Consumer Organization
P.O. Box 15492
Alexandria, VA 22309
(703) 549–8050

National Personnel Records Center
Military Personnel Records

9700 Page Boulevard
St. Louis, MO 63132–5100
(In case of medical emergency, information from veterans' records may be obtained by phoning the National Personnel Records Center: Air Force (314) 538–4243; Army (314) 538–4261; Navy, Marine Corps or Coast Guard (314) 538–4141.)

National Recreation and Park Association
2775 South Quincy Street, Suite 300
Arlington, VA 22206
(703) 820–4940

National Rehabilitation Information Center
8455 Colesville Road, Suite 935
Silver Spring, MD 20910
1 (800) 346–2742/(301) 588–9284

National Senior Citizens Law Center
1915 H Street, N.W., Suite 700
Washington, DC 20006
(202) 887–5280

National Society for Patient Representation and Consumer Affairs
American Hospital Association
840 N. Lake Shore Drive
Chicago, IL 60611
(312) 280–6424

National Society of Public Accountants
1010 North Fairfax Street
Alexandria, VA 22314
(703) 549–6400

National Tour Association
546 East Main Street
P.O. Box 3071
Lexington, KY 40596
(606) 253–1036

Older Adult Education Network
American Society on Aging
833 Market Street, Suite 511
San Francisco, CA 94103
(415) 974–9600

Older Women's League
666 Eleventh Street, N.W., Suite 700

Washington, DC 20001–4512
(202) 783–6686

Paralyzed Veterans of America
801 18th Street, N.W.
Washington, DC 20006
1 (800) 424–8200

Partners in Caregiving: The Dementia Services Program
Bowman Gray School of Medicine
Department of Psychiatry
Medical Center Boulevard
Winston-Salem, NC 27157–1087
(910) 716–4941

Pension Rights Center
918 16th Street, N.W., Suite 704
Washington, DC 20006
(202) 296–3776

Resources for Rehabilitation
33 Bedford Street, Suite 19A
Lexington, MA 02173
(617) 862–6455

Retired Senior Volunteer Program (RSVP)
1100 Vermont Avenue, N.W.
Washington, DC 20525
(202) 606–4851

Senior Companion Program
Washington Urban League
2900 Newton Street, N.E.
Washington, DC 20018
(202) 529–8701

SeniorNet
399 Arguello Boulevard
San Francisco, CA 94118
(415) 750–5030

September Days Club
2751 Buford Highway, N.E.
Atlanta, GA 30324
(404) 728–4405

Service Corps of Retired Executives Association
409 3rd Street, S.W., Suite 5900
Washington, DC 20024
(202) 205–6759

Service Credit Program on Aging
HP Building, Room 1240
University of Maryland
College Park, MD 20742–2611
(301) 405–2469

Social Security Administration
Office of Public Inquiries
6401 Security Boulevard
Baltimore, MD 21238
1 (800) 772–1213

United Seniors Health Cooperative
1331 H Street, N.W., Suite 500
Washington, DC 20005–4706
(202) 393–6222

U.S. Department of Education
Federal Student Aid Information
   Center
P.O. Box 84

Washington, DC 20044
(202) 708–4766

U.S. Naval Home
1800 Beach Drive
Gulfport, MS 39507
1 (800) 332–3527

U.S. Soldiers' and Airmen's Home
3700 N. Capitol St. NW
Washington, DC 20317
1 (800) 422–9988

Veterans Affairs Insurance Center
P. O. Box 8079
Philadelphia, PA 19101
1 (800) 669–8477

Visiting Nurse Association of America
3801 E. Florida, Suite 900
Denver, CO 80210–2545
(303) 753–0218

Index